MOON

NEW ENGLAND

JEN ROSE SMITH

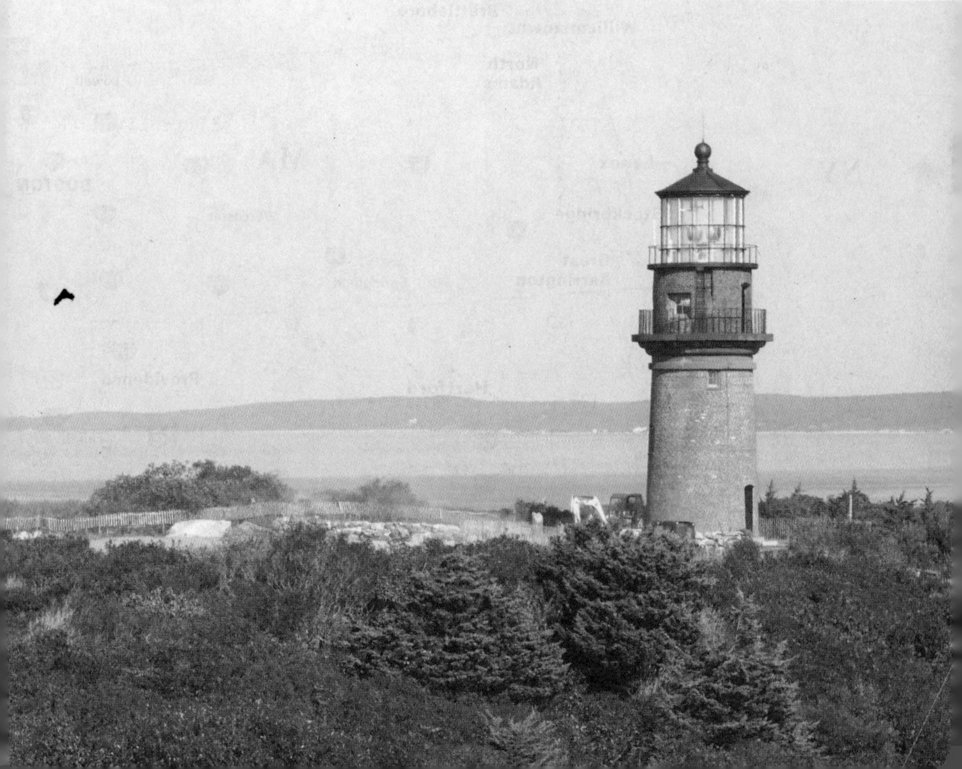

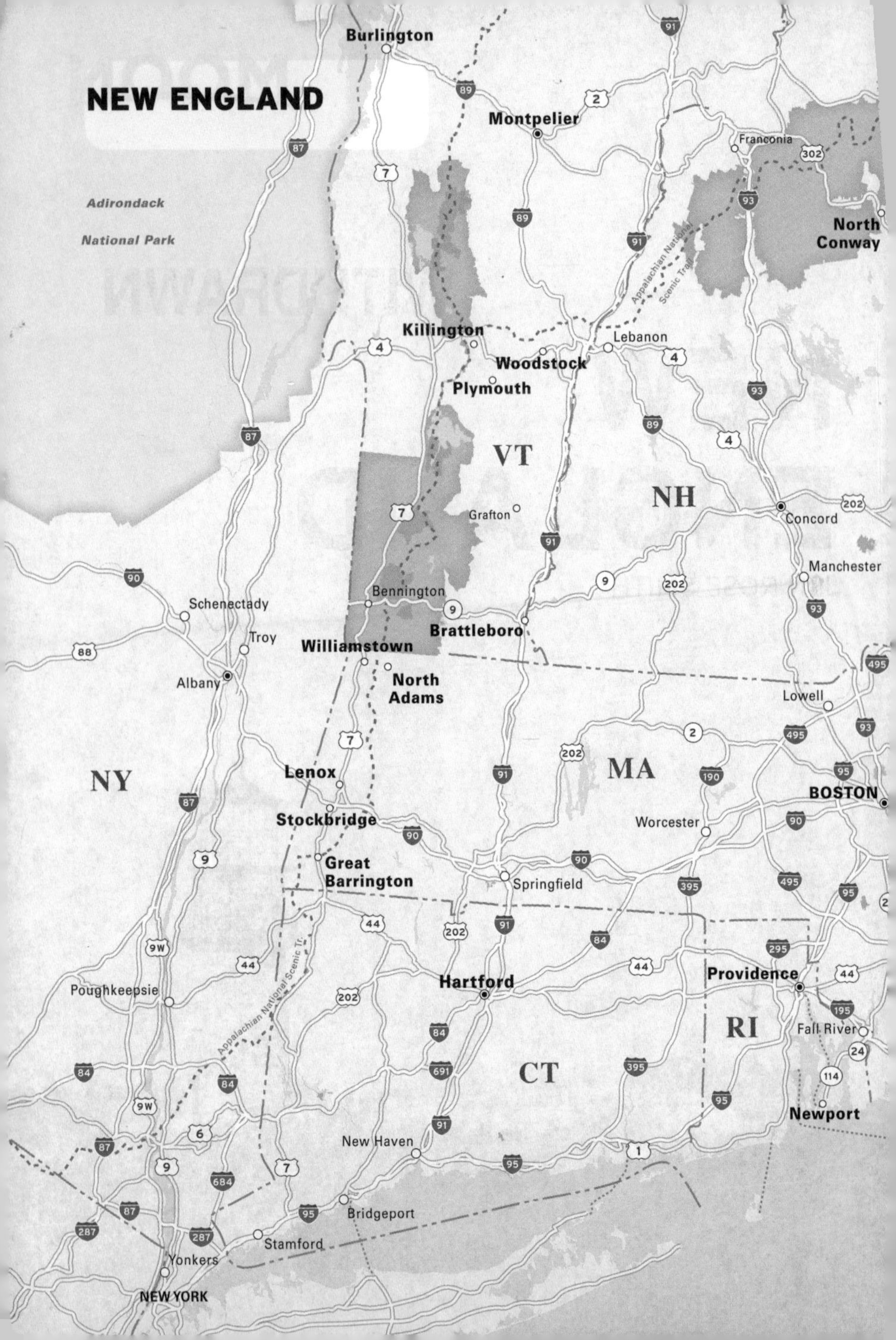
NEW ENGLAND
Burlington
Montpelier
Franconia
North Conway
Adirondack National Park
Killington
Woodstock
Lebanon
Plymouth
VT
NH
Grafton
Concord
Manchester
Bennington
Brattleboro
Schenectady
Troy
Albany
Williamstown
North Adams
Lowell
NY
Lenox
MA
BOSTON
Stockbridge
Worcester
Great Barrington
Springfield
Hartford
Providence
Poughkeepsie
RI
Fall River
CT
Newport
New Haven
Bridgeport
Stamford
Yonkers
NEW YORK
Appalachian National Scenic Trail
Appalachian National Scenic Tr.

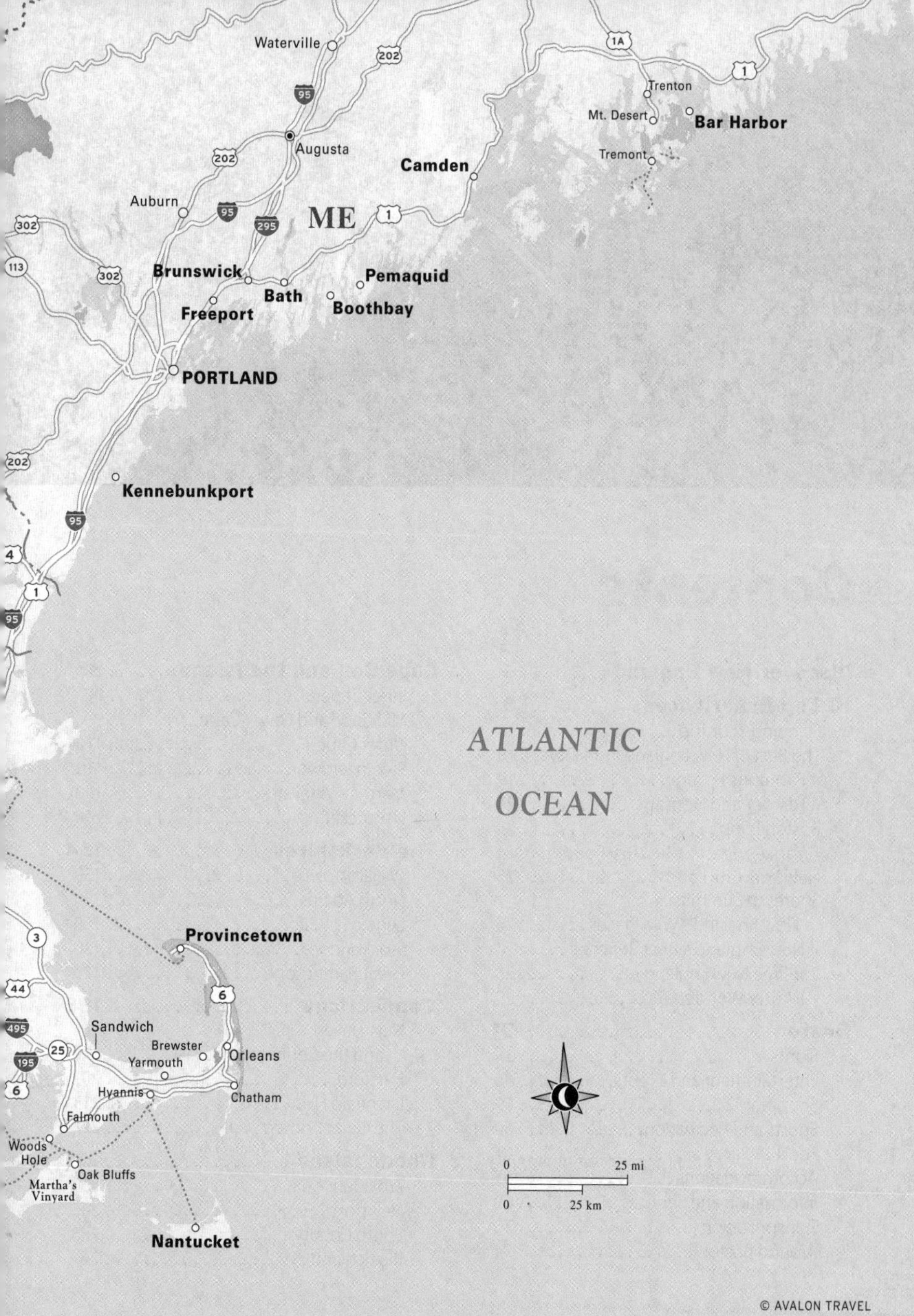
Waterville
Augusta
Camden
Trenton
Mt. Desert
Bar Harbor
Tremont
Auburn
ME
Brunswick
Bath
Pemaquid
Boothbay
Freeport
PORTLAND
Kennebunkport
ATLANTIC
OCEAN
Provincetown
Sandwich
Brewster
Orleans
Yarmouth
Hyannis
Chatham
Falmouth
Woods
Hole
Oak Bluffs
Martha's
Vineyard
Nantucket
0
25 mi
0
25 km
© AVALON TRAVEL

Contents

MOHAWK
SINCE 1938
E.M. LOEW'S
E.M. LOEW'S

DISCOVER

New England

With a landscape steeped in history, New England's geography is a map of American nostalgia.

The six northeastern states have shaped generations of artists and philosophers, whose work took on the contours of its rolling farmland, pebbled beaches, and ancient mountains. This is where Thoreau and Dickinson rambled and wrote, and scenes glimpsed from a car window resemble the canvases of Winslow Homer or Edward Hopper.

Their New England is still alive—and remains startlingly wild. Each winter, New Hampshire's high peaks are buffeted by some of the most powerful weather on earth, while nor'easters sweep along the rugged coast with its deep coves and rocky peninsulas. For visitors, that wildness can be an enticing surprise. Imagine yourself ticking off summits in the Green Mountains, paddling into the surf breaks that line Rhode Island's southern coast, or watching for moose in Maine's vast backwoods.

The people are equally inviting. In the maple groves of Vermont and the oyster farms of Massachusetts, locals still harvest the bounty of forests and fisheries. And in New England's towns and cities, a new generation of creatives is bringing youthful energy to unexpected places. Artists, musicians, chefs, and brewers are reinventing New England traditions for the 21st century. This thrilling blend of fresh takes and old ways is a standing invitation to explore.

Clockwise from top left: lupine blossoms; the Mayflower Society House and Library in Plymouth; spirits from Mad River Distillers; the Wadsworth Atheneum in Hartford; tugboats in Portsmouth; Lincoln Woods State Park in Blackstone Valley.

10 TOP EXPERIENCES

1 **Acadia National Park:** Catch America's first sunrise from Cadillac Mountain, then find a million tide pools in this historic national park (page 458).

2 Massachusetts Art Museums: From Boston's **Museum of Fine Arts** (page 48) to the contemporary art at **MASS MoCA** (page 164), Massachusetts features some of the country's best collections.

3 Fall Foliage: The changing colors spread from north to south; chase them from Vermont's extravagant maple forests to the muted hues of Cape Cod's sand dunes (page 19).

4 Cape Cod National Seashore: World-class beaches are just the beginning at this stunning preserve, where pine barrens, rolling dunes, and miles of sand are surrounded by water on all sides (page 110).

5 Newport's Mansions: Late 19th-century architecture in Newport recalls the days of robber barons, railroads, and over-the-top style (page 248).

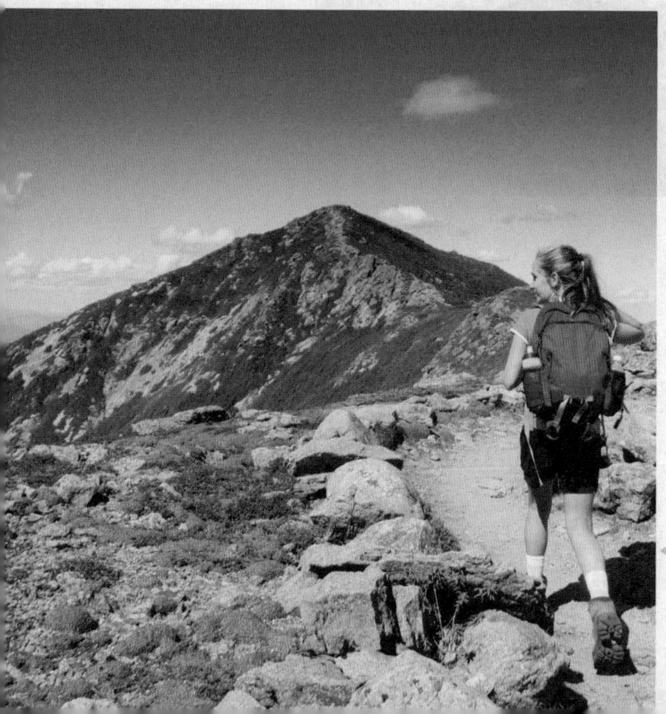

6 Hiking New Hampshire's White Mountains: Hike through a rocky landscape of summits, valleys, and plants found nowhere else (page 373).

7 The Freedom Trail: Follow in the footsteps of rebels, redcoats, and America's founders on this historical trail in Boston (page 35).

8 Maine Lobster Feasts: Whether you're dining on reinvented lobster rolls or sitting down to a traditional feast, these crustaceans are quintessential New England (page 434).

9 Cycling Block Island: Just seven miles long from tip to tail, this Rhode Island escape is easy to explore on two wheels, and the island's conserved land makes it a bird-watcher's delight (page 270).

10 Skiing and Snowboarding in Vermont's Green Mountains: Choose your mountain—Vermont's peaks offer some of the finest skiing and riding in the region, complete with great food and beer for après snow (page 300).

Planning Your Trip

Where to Go

Boston

You might contest the claim that this is the "Hub of the Solar System," but Boston is certainly the hub of New England, and the region's leading city is fascinating to explore. Even as narrow brick lanes gave way to glassy towers, Boston grew up around its history—**Revolutionary-era graveyards** line busy streets, actors in 18th-century costume walk the Freedom Trail, and immigrant communities erupt with civic pride at festivals and parades. Even if you're making a beeline for New England's beaches and mountains, Boston offers tempting diversions: catch **the Red Sox** at **Fenway Park,** spend a day in the city's **world-class museums,** or weigh in on the North End's epic **cannoli** rivalry.

Cape Cod and the Islands

Just an hour from Boston's hectic downtown, Cape Cod is a world of **sand dunes, beach roses,** and **cranberry bogs,** a changeable landscape that's shaped by every passing tide. There's room to unwind on the vast beaches of **Cape Cod National Seashore,** a beach broken up by clam shacks and lighthouses. Just offshore, **Nantucket and Martha's Vineyard** are worlds apart, island charmers that tempt travelers to linger. Not that the Cape's allure is entirely serene—among America's most vibrant LGBT vacation spots, Provincetown lights up all summer, with campy drag shows, tipsy pool parties, and a thriving community of artists.

The Berkshires

Don't be fooled by the idyllic landscape of rolling hills and farmhouses—the Berkshires are a **cultural powerhouse.** The vast collection of

Cape Cod Dunes

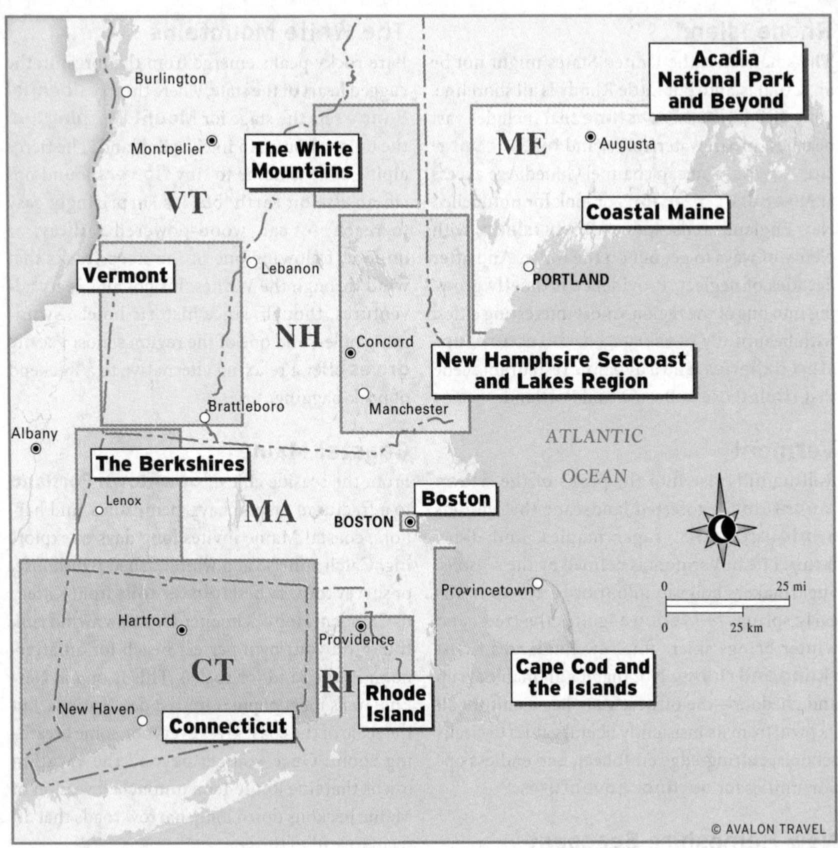

modern art at **MASS MoCA** is among the best in the country, **Jacob's Pillow Dance Festival** stages performances throughout the summer, and the **Boston Symphony Orchestra** decamps to Lenox for a season-long residency. The blend of country and creativity are an intoxicating blend, perfect for summer days that begin with a hike up **Mount Greylock** and end with a sunset performance at **Tanglewood,** where elegant picnics are elevated to high art.

Connecticut

Emerging from the suburban sprawl of New York City, Connecticut's pretty coast and rolling interior are often overlooked, but there's a lot to see and do in "the land of steady habits." The Litchfield Hills have **city elegance** at a **small-town pace,** while the northeastern "Quiet Corner" is the real deal—tiny communities linked by winding back roads and farm fields. In between stretches of overdevelopment, the southern coast offers **broad beaches** and **historic fishing villages,** including **Mystic Seaport,** a living museum that keeps 19th-century **seafaring culture** alive. Holding down the heart of the coast, **New Haven** has some city grit, academic starch, and its very own pizza recipe, while **historic Hartford** outshines its own down-at-the-heels reputation with **destination-worthy museums** and local spirit.

Rhode Island

The smallest of the United States might not be an actual island, but Little Rhody is all shoreline, with **400 miles of coastline** that includes vast beaches, urban waterfronts, and **historic vacation towns.** You can channel Gilded Age excess at **Newport's mansions** or look for untouched New England landscapes on **Block Island,** with plenty of ways to get out on the water. And after decades of neglect, Providence is quietly growing into one of the region's most interesting cities, with beautifully **preserved architecture, upstart galleries,** and a dynamic restaurant scene that rivals those in Boston and Portland.

Vermont

Rolling hills rise into the peaks of the **Green Mountains,** a forested landscape that enfolds **apple orchards,** sugar maples, and dairy farms. Life in Vermont is defined by the seasons: Sugarmakers boil sap into **maple syrup** in the early spring, **fall foliage** ignites the trees, and winter brings skiers for New England's finest **skiing and riding.** Not that it's all maple syrup and cheddar—the offbeat state has a culture all its own, from its insistently liberal values to circus schools, cutting-edge craft beer, and endless opportunities for **outdoor adventures.**

New Hampshire Seacoast and Lakes Region

Despite a fierce culture of independence, the Granite State's not entirely insulated from the outside world—New Hampshire extends a slender arm of land to the ocean that shouldn't be overlooked. Easily **walkable** and fun to explore, Portsmouth is among the finest destinations in New England for an immersion in **colonial and maritime history,** while **Hampton Beach** is a whirlwind of tanning oil, fried dough, and cruising crowds. Just inland, the forested landscape is webbed with a vast network of lakes, from the hyped-up vacation towns on **Lake Winnepesaukee** to quiet **Squam Lakes,** where silent mornings are broken only by the sound of calling loons.

The White Mountains

Bare rocky peaks emerge from the forest in the rugged heart of the state, where the **Presidential Range** sets the stage for **Mount Washington,** the tallest mountain in New England. The fierce alpine zone is home to tiny **flowers** found nowhere else on earth, but it's surprisingly easy to reach: by car, wood-powered railway, or on foot, following one of the steep tracks that wind through the Whites. It's not all sweaty adventures, though, since historic hotels, swimming holes, and one of the region's most **scenic drives** offer a relaxing alternative to a weekend of peak-bagging.

Coastal Maine

From the seaside chic of **downtown Portland** to a fractured map of bays, peninsulas, and harbors, coastal Maine invites long days of exploring. Catch sunrise at a whitewashed lighthouse, or survey the very best **lobster rolls** from Kittery to Camden. Hop a schooner for a downwind run, then find your own perfect beach for an afternoon in the sand (or rocks). This is one of New England's most popular tourist destinations, but the scale of the coast gives everyone some breathing room: Once you get beyond the vacation towns that line Route 1, an untouched version of Maine beckons down long, narrow roads that all seem to lead to the sea.

Acadia and Beyond

Sprawling from **Mount Desert Island** to the facing mainland, Acadia National Park is unlike any other. Bare **pink granite peaks** dip into alpine lakes, all with views across the Atlantic coast. The top of **Cadillac Mountain** catches some of America's first light, and a network of carriage trails means the whole thing can be reached by bicycle, or on foot. Continue past Acadia and you're in the thick of Downeast Maine: a long, quiet coast that ends in the fishing outpost of Lubec, whose candy-striped **West Quoddy Head Light** is the **easternmost point** in the continental United States.

When to Go

Dramatic seasonal changes transform New England—but there's no bad time to visit. When schools let out in late June, the region's high season begins. Everyone heads to the beach—or the mountains—and prices spike around the region. Some of New England's sweetest experiences are pure summertime: finding swimming holes to beat the heat, visiting the seasonal seafood shacks at the edge of the water, and catching Red Sox games with the crowd at Fenway Park. For the best of both worlds, plan a trip that overlaps with summer temperatures but bucks the crowds. Students disappear by late August and early September, the ocean is as warm as it's gonna get, and prices dip until the arrival of leaf peepers.

Autumn brings cooler temperatures and one of New England's starring attractions: fall color. The displays of bright leaves start to pick up at the end of September, with northernmost destinations reaching "peak foliage" in the middle of October. This season is a favorite for many, with warm, sunny days that alternate with crisp nights, and fall brings a host of fleeting pleasures: picking apples at local orchards, evenings cool enough for a crackling campfire, and outings fueled by cinnamon-scented cider donuts.

Winter weather begins in earnest at the end of December. The southern states of Connecticut, Rhode Island, and Massachusetts might get a few big snowstorms, but temperatures usually hover in the thirties and forties. Up north, however, the region can enter a deep freeze for weeks at a time—there's usually one or two weeks in northern New England when the mercury shivers in the single digits (or below). But for lovers of skiing, skating, and gorgeously frozen scenery, those winter months are a bonanza. Bring plenty of clothes and you'll be warm and cozy while skating on Boston Common, riding the snowy peaks of the Green Mountains, or rolling through the hills on a horse-drawn sleigh.

Starting in the south, then moving north, March brings **spring** in fits and starts. Blooming lilacs scent the air, and in the forest, a profusion of wildflowers appears. While the weather stays fitful until well into May, there's plenty to recommend the season. Throughout northern New England, but especially in Vermont, spring means maple syrup, and visiting between late February and early April is the chance to taste the region's sweetest harvest straight from the pan. And maple syrup's not the only seasonal treat: A recent wave of interest in foraged foods mean springtime restaurant menus feature woodsy ingredients like ramps, a kind of wild onion, and fiddleheads, the bright green tendrils of ostrich ferns.

The easiest place to fly into for launching a trip in New England is **Boston,** though **Portland, Maine,** is another major hub for the area. International visitors will need valid **passports** or **visas** to fly into the United States. If you are renting a car in any city, plan to pick it up after spending time there, as **paid parking** and **crowded streets** makes it easier to explore by public transport.

The Best of New England in 14 Days

Blending history, culture, and New England's most gorgeous scenery, this two-week trip is a whirlwind introduction to the best of the region, from the lighthouses of Penobscot Bay to Green Mountain valleys. Starting in the maritime city of Portland means an instant immersion in Maine culture before diving into the charms of the Mid-Coast, then rising into the Appalachian Mountain Range. While much of this itinerary can be accessed by public transit, you'll need a car to squeeze the hits into two weeks.

Day 1

Plan to arrive in **Portland** in time for a sunset sail across **Casco Bay,** hopping one of the city's historic schooners, then wrap up the evening with a steaming bowl of clam chowder on the waterfront. If you're itching to hit the town, visit a few of Portland's great craft breweries, or dress up for drinks at the **Portland Hunt & Alpine Club.**

Day 2

Take a morning walk through the **Old Port,** and if you're up for more time on the water, take the mail boat route to the **Casco Bay Islands** for a glimpse of offshore life within sight of the city skyline. A seafood lunch at Eventide Oyster Co. is a must, followed by an afternoon of browsing the wonderful Portland Museum of Art.

Day 3

Wake up early for a sweet breakfast from the **Holy Donut,** then plot a course along the shore—make your first destination the **Maine Maritime Museum,** in the shipbuilding city of Bath. When you've got your fill of salty history, duck down onto **Georgetown Island** for a classic lobster roll at **Five Islands Lobster Co.** From there, continue to the picturesque harbor town of Camden, stopping to stretch your legs on the short walk to **Owl's Head Light.**

the schooner *Lewis R. French* by Owl's Head

TOP EXPERIENCE

Fabulous Foliage

As the first cold days arrive in the beginning of **autumn,** the weather frosts the tips of trees with a wash of pale yellow and orange. It's an early sign of the changing season. Weeks later, the forests will be alight in brilliant hues, a display that can be shocking in its vividness.

Experiencing the changing colors is truly a highlight of exploring New England, but what's really happening in the trees? Leaves get their verdant hue from a healthy dose of chlorophyll, a key ingredient in plants' transformation of sunlight into sugars. As the season changes, chlorophyll dwindles, draining off the green color as it goes.

The yellow and gold that begins to appear are from **carotenoids,** plant pigments that have been in the leaves all along, but masked by the lush greens of midsummer. But what about the brilliant reds? Those are due to anthocyanins, the same brilliant pigments that lend cranberries, red apples, and cherries their **vibrant hues.** Anthocyanins are mostly produced in the autumn, and depending on conditions, trees might have just a little—or enough for a gaudy leaf show.

It's hard to plan for the perfect fall trip, as varied weather conditions mean the leaves change at different times each year. In the northern states of Vermont, New Hampshire, and Maine, colors begin to change in mid-September, continuing through mid-October. The first color appears at northern latitudes and high altitudes, working south and toward sea level as the season progresses.

- **Kancamagus Highway, New Hampshire:** The twists and turns of this 34-mile road through the White Mountains passes through gorgeous forests that are brilliant in autumn.
- **Mad River Valley, Vermont:** A broad valley flanked with peaks on each side, this gorgeous spot offers wide-open views and easy access to higher-elevation terrain.
- **Acadia National Park, Maine:** Offset by the island's many evergreen trees, fall colors are especially dramatic here, with kettle ponds and harbors to reflect the leaves.
- **Cape Cod, Massachusetts:** With subtler displays than in the northern forests, Cape Cod doesn't attract crowds of leaf peepers, but autumn turns its oaks a beautiful rusty hue, plants in the dunes are frosted with gold, and the area's cranberry harvest ripens in Technicolor.
- **Mount Greylock, Massachusetts:** Climb or drive to the highest point in Massachusetts for panoramic views across the Berkshires, where gently rolling farmland is flocked with deciduous forests.
- **Litchfield, Connecticut:** All white-tipped steeples and historic houses, this town offers the perfect frame for changing leaves, while local apple farms open for pick-your-own.

Days 4-5

Make a beeline for **Mount Desert Island,** where Acadia National Park encompasses some of the finest coastal scenery in Maine. On day one, choose a hike: Walk across the gentle sandbar to Bar Island, hop across the boulders on the **Ship Harbor Trail,** or try the vertiginous route up the Beehive, a mound of bare rock with views across the Penobscot Bay.

Ambitious travelers can rise early to catch sunrise from the summit of Mount Desert Island, which catches mainland America's first rays for much of the year. Bring a bike or rent some wheels for a day on the carriage trails, then pause for a Mount Desert Island tradition: fresh **popovers** with sweet strawberry jam. If you're hankering for a lobster dinner, there's no better place than **Thurston's Lobster Pound,** where you choose your bug from a tank of crawling critters, then eat with the waves beneath your feet.

Day 6

Get a taste of backwoods Maine as you drive across the state to New Hampshire's **White**

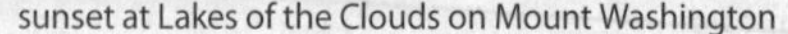

sunset at Lakes of the Clouds on Mount Washington

hiking the White Mountains

Mountains, heading from the seaside all the way to the top of **Mount Washington**—by car, cog railway, or on foot. Whatever option you choose, make your way to the historic Omni Mount Washington Resort for sunset drinks on the broad balcony, with views back toward the mountains.

Day 7

Dust off your hiking boots for another day in the White Mountains: There are all-day epics like the Presidential Traverse, or you can meander the gentle trail to **Diana's Baths,** a series of pools that are perfect for cooling off. For a more easygoing tour through the mountains, book a ticket on the **Conway Scenic Railway,** whose **Notch Train** catches some of the region's most dramatic scenery.

Day 8

Duck into the southern **Green Mountains,** where you'll trade rocky summits for lush valleys. Adorable **Woodstock** is the perfect village home for a night, with bright **covered bridges,** art galleries for browsing, and even an old-fashioned town crier message board. After getting your bearings, head to the nearby **Calvin Coolidge State Historic Site** to visit the presidential family home and cheese factory, then pause for beers at **Long Trail Brewing Company,** a local craft beer pioneer.

Days 9-10

Leave the mountains behind as you return to southern New England, taking the slow road along the **Connecticut River Valley** on your way to Providence. Settle back into city life with a walk through downtown, then visit the remarkable museum at the **Rhode Island School of Design,** which goes from ancient artifacts to cutting-edge work by modern artists. Providence has a great food scene, so make some time for a special dinner here, whether that's a tasting menu at Oberlin or an ironic pile of tater tots at **Ogie's Trailer Park.**

With Providence as a home base, you can catch the boat to Newport, arriving for a day of historic houses at the edge of the sea. If you've got a low tolerance for gilding and flounces, just pop into a single mansion, then spend the rest of the

History and Heritage

From the rich cultures of Native American peoples to the Pilgrims' first steps in the New World, New England is a dream destination for history buffs.

- **Freedom Trail, Boston:** You can cover a lot of Revolutionary sites on a 2.5-hour walk, and joining a costumed guide makes this a total immersion in colonial history.
- **Black Heritage Trail, Boston:** Start at a monument to the Civil War-era Black 54th Regiment Massachusetts Volunteer Infantry, and make your way to the oldest surviving black church in the United States, learning about Boston history along the way.
- **Plimoth Plantation and Wampanoag Homesite, Massachusetts:** A re-created 17th-century settlement is a vivid introduction to 17th-century life in a European community, while the Wampanoag Homesite shares Native traditions and practices.
- **Strawbery Banke Museum, Portsmouth, New Hampshire:** Thirty-two historic homes are the centerpiece for this living-history museum, which preserves the past of a proud merchant town.
- **Mystic Seaport, Connecticut:** Learn to hoist a sail and sing a sea shanty at this pretty village on the Mystic River, which is also America's largest maritime museum.
- **Concord, Massachusetts:** Whether you're following the trail of Revolutionaries at Minuteman National Historic Park, or you prefer the Transcendentalist paths of Thoreau and Emerson, exploring Concord is a transporting experience.
- **Newport Mansions, Rhode Island:** The Gilded Age reached a fever pitch in these over-the-top mansions, where the 19th-century American elite played out dreams of European grandeur.
- **President Calvin Coolidge State Historic Site, Vermont:** Silent Cal was sworn in on this country farm, where his family's cheese-making operation still produces wheels of artisan cheese using historic techniques.

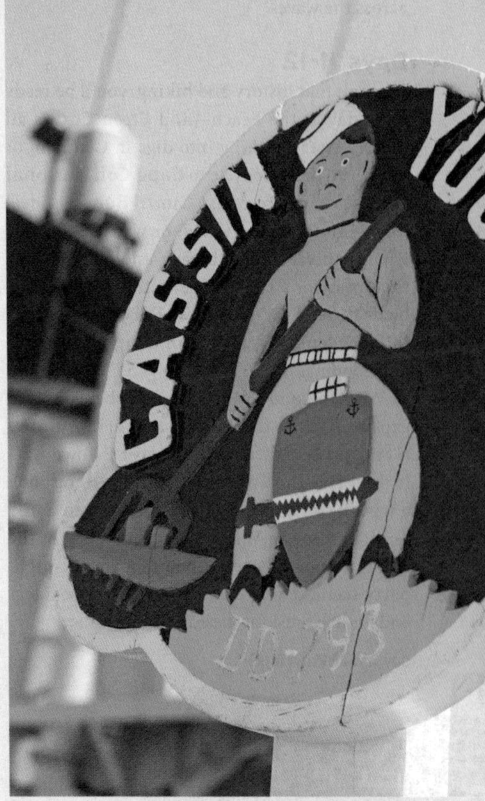

historic submarine on Boston's Freedom Trail

- **Maine's Historic Schooners:** The oldest working passenger schooner in the United States still plies the waters of Penobscot Bay, and gorgeously maintained historic vessels can be found up and down the coast.
- **Omni Mount Washington Resort, White Mountains:** Toast the American dollar at the former Bretton Arms, one of New Hampshire's remaining grand dame hotels, where the Bretton Woods Conference reshaped the global economy as World War II raged on.

afternoon aboard one of Newport's **America's Cup** yachts, sleek boats designed for speeding across the waves.

Days 11-12

After all that history and hiking, you'll be ready for a day at the beach—and **Cape Cod** is all beach. After checking into digs in Chatham or Wellfleet, drive or cycle to **Cape Cod National Seashore,** where **Coast Guard Beach** is ideal for swimming, long walks, or watching for the whales and seals that breach and blow just off the sand. For a laid-back evening, catch a double feature at the **Wellfleet Drive-In,** or head to Providence for a night of **drag shows** and bar-hopping.

With a second day in Cape Cod, there's time to explore: **Paddle** the shifting sands at **Monomoy National Wildlife Refuge,** visit P-Town **galleries,** ride the **Cape Cod Rail Trail,** or book a **whale-watching** cruise to Stellwagen Bank. Tonight, dine in Wellfleet to get a taste of the town's famous oysters, then join the all-night party scene at **The Beachcomber,** a local legend for live music at the edge of the water.

Day 13

Now that you've seen the region, it's time to walk through New England's Revolutionary-era history, following the **Freedom Trail** from **Boston Common to Bunker Hill,** stopping for an Italian ice, cannoli, or submarine sandwich in the city's Italian American **North End** neighborhood. Choose a few sites to see along the way, walking between the gravestones at the **Granary Burying Ground,** or remembering Paul Revere's ride at the **Old North Church.** In the afternoon, head to the **Boston Public Library** to browse gorgeous murals amid the stacks, or visit one of the city's wonderful art museums.

Day 14

Make the most of a final morning in Boston by crossing the Charles River to **Cambridge,** home to two of America's academic heavyweights. Stroll through the campuses of **Harvard** and **MIT,** heading inside to see one of the school's remarkable museums: Science and tech lovers shouldn't miss the **MIT Museum,** while **Harvard's Peabody Museum of Archaeology** is the spot for human history and fierce-looking dinos.

downtown Providence

Modern Pastry in Boston

Boston Loop

Landing in Boston means you're perfectly placed for trips to northern New England and the southern coast, but sticking to a compact area means more time for relaxing and exploring.

Day 1

Find a centrally located hotel for exploring the city, then set out on the **Freedom Trail,** walking through the city's history on the 2.5-mile route from downtown to **Bunker Hill.** If you're up for a full day of strolling, compare and contrast Revolutionary history with the experience of black Americans on the Black Heritage Trail, which winds through the narrow, brick-lined streets of charming Beacon Hill.

Days 2-3

Make like a local and escape the city for the beach: **Cape Cod** is just an hour away from downtown Boston. If you'd like an energetic base for your time on the Cape, book a campsite or hotel room in Provincetown, one of the most beloved destinations for LGBT travelers in New England—for a quieter experience, opt for tiny **Wellfleet** or **Chatham.**

With two days on the Cape, make the first one a trip through the classic **beaches** and **lighthouses** of **Cape Cod National Seashore,** where salt marshes and coastal forests roll right to the edge of the water. Next, rent a bike for a day of cycling, or make a day trip to one of Cape Cod's favorite islands: **Nantucket** and **Martha's Vineyard** are just a quick boat ride away, but they've got loads of history and cultures all their own.

Days 4-5

Keep it coastal on the road to **Rhode Island,** where you can choose between two ideal bases: Providence has historic architecture, art, and urban grit, while **Newport** is pure, elegant prep, with gorgeous beaches and lots of **mansions** to explore.

Whatever you decide, make the other destination a day trip, hopping the seasonal ferry that

Yankee Feasts: Must-Try Foods

From farm-to-table restaurants to classic seafood and cutting-edge craft breweries, you could spend a lifetime eating and drinking your way across New England.

- **Maine Lobster:** Maine's most famous crustacean is also its favorite meal: Try a lobster roll at the **Two Lights Lobster Shack** (page 417), then get the full, lobster dinner experience in **Thurston's Lobster Pound** (page 467).
- **Craft Brews:** From Portland's postage-stamp tasting rooms (page 410) to a hoppy stretch of cideries and breweries in Burlington (page 325), New England's beer scene is better than ever.
- **New Haven Slices:** Order "apizza with mootz" and you'll get a coal-fired meal with Neapolitan roots and a strong dose of local pride (page 199).
- **Straight from the Farm:** In Lenox, **Nudel** (page 174) celebrates the twists and turns of the season with ultra-fresh, ingredient-focused fare. For a farm of a different kind entirely, head to Portsmouth's **Row 34** (page 344), which maintains its very own oyster beds.
- **Clambake:** Bivalves get the traditional treatment—a long steam between layers of moist seaweed—at **Cabbage Island Clambakes** (page 433), where fixings include corn on the cob, Maine potatoes, and freshly baked blueberry cake.

classic lobster tail dinner in Coastal Maine

- **Boston's North End Italian:** Discover the city's Italian heritage in its tastiest form: cannolis (page 64), Regina's wood-fired pizza, and hearty submarine sandwiches from Monica's Mercato (page 63).

links Providence and Newport, getting in some views of the deep **Narragansett Bay** along the way.

Day 6

It's a quick trip from Providence back to Boston, so consider adding a morning detour to one of the sites along the Massachusetts coast. Follow in the footsteps of the **Pilgrims at Plymouth,** where the **Wampanoag Homesite** introduces visitors to some of New England's native culture, or visit witchy Salem for a weird blend of somber history, kitschy magic shops, and real-deal maritime history.

New York City Loop

The Big Apple is a region all its own, but get beyond the urban sprawl and you'll reach coastal villages, sandy beaches, and the rolling hills of the New England countryside.

Day 1

Follow the **Long Island Sound** into Connecticut, making the first stop of the day for a slice of **New Haven pizza,** a coal-fired tradition that holds its own in regional flatbread rivalries. Fortified for an afternoon of exploring, take a stroll through the **Yale campus,** where staid, brick architecture and destination-worthy museums are a quick dip into Ivy League life.

Get out of the city as you continue up the coast, watching as overdevelopment gives way to cute fishing towns and beaches. Spend the night in tiny **Mystic,** which is a world away from New York City, catching a quiet sunset from a waterfront restaurant.

Day 2

Go for the full immersion in 19th-century coastal life at **Mystic Seaport,** whose costumed actors make the historic ships and homes even more vivid, or add a trip to the nearby **Mystic Aquarium,** a family-friendly favorite for creatures from the deep.

Day 3

Trade coast for country as you drive to pretty little **Litchfield**—literature buffs should stop along the way to see Hartford's **Mark Twain** and **Harriet Beecher Stowe sites**—then arrive for a stroll on the compact **Litchfield Green.** Spend the afternoon browsing galleries and shops stocked with antiques from the surrounding farmland.

Day 4

Continue into the tumbled **Berkshire Hills,** where a pure-country landscape holds creative secrets: Sing a few lines of "Alice's Restaurant" at the **Arlo Guthrie Center,** explore the **Norman Rockwell Museum,** and catch a basement show at the Red Lion Inn before spending a quiet night in Lenox—if it's **Tanglewood** season, all bets are off, and your plans should revolve around a perfect picnic and an outdoor concert.

Day 5

Among the **Berkshires's** most glorious homes—and there are many—is **The Mount,** a mansion designed and built by author Edith Wharton, who thought her landscaping skills outstripped her writing. Start there, then head to North Adams for an afternoon at **MASS MoCA,** a staggering modern art museum set in a rusty little factory town that's gone high culture.

Day 6

Since it's a straight shot from the northern Berkshires to New York City, rise early for a **hike** up **Mount Greylock** before heading back to civilization, earning **sweeping views** of the countryside that are especially dramatic in fall.

Shores to Summits: New England's Wild Places

Make a swooping descent through the finest of the region's scenery, stopping to spy on moose, wander endless beaches, and trace perfect back roads on two wheels. There's a lifetime of exploring to do in New England's wild places, but this trip includes the undisputed highlights.

Days 1-2

Start where the **Appalachian Trail** ends—in the mountain landscape of **Baxter State Park. Mount Katahdin** isn't New England's highest mountain, but it's certainly the toughest, especially if you take on the iconic **Knife Edge,** a vertiginous trail that teeters along a narrow ridge of boulders.

Days 3-4

Rest your mountain legs on the drive to **Mount Desert Island,** where the hiking is a tad less punishing. You could push for a sunrise trek to the peak of **Cadillac Mountain,** or just take it easy on the shore, poking around the tide pools and beaches in **Acadia National Park.**

Choose your sport for day two: There's stunning rock climbing that rises straight from the waves at **Otter Cliffs,** and on-island guiding companies can get you fully kitted out. Otherwise, take to the seas for a kayak trip along the edge of Mount Desert Island, watching for whales and seals along the way.

Days 5-6

It's back to wild peaks and footpaths when you head to the **White Mountains,** where the **Presidential Range** rises above all comers. The fittest travelers could take on the whole series of mountains—an enormous hike often called the **"Death March"**—but there are trails for all

hiking Mount Katahdin's Knife Edge

New England's Best Beaches

Block Island's Crescent Beach

Spot whales off the Cape Cod sand, paddle into the surf break in Rhode Island and go tide pooling on the Maine coast—New England's got beaches for days.

- **Coast Guard Beach, Cape Cod, Massachusetts:** Endless sand lined with wild roses, dramatic cliffs, and windswept lighthouses make this one of the best beaches in the East.
- **Silver Sands State Park Beach, Connecticut:** Dunes, salt marsh, and coastal forest lead to the edge of this sprawling beach, a family-friendly escape with plenty of room to spread out.
- **Crescent Beach, Block Island, Rhode Island:** You can walk from the ferry dock to this great, curving shoreline, where day-trippers set up encampments of beach towels and umbrellas.
- **Sachuest Beach, Newport, Rhode Island:** Catch an easygoing summer swell at Sachuest Beach, a favorite surf spot just outside downtown Newport.
- **Popham Beach, Maine:** This stretch of shoreline offers the best of Maine: a sandy beach at the end of a scenic peninsula, and a little rocky island to explore at low tide.
- **Bar Island, Mount Desert Island, Maine:** The path from Bar Harbor to this forested islet only becomes a beach at low tide, which makes it the perfect place to find stranded sea creatures and tide pools.

abilities, and plenty of rivers for post-walk soaks. Watch for moose as you hop from rock to rock, or join one of the **moose-spotting tours** that stalk the enormous animals in their favorite hangouts.

Days 7-8

From there, descend back to sea level on your way to **Block Island,** a tiny gem that's been saved from development by the work of The Nature Conservancy. This is a bird-watcher's paradise, and since the whole island is just seven miles long, you can bike the entire thing in an afternoon, arriving back in town in time for **cocktails** by the water.

Car-Free New England

American cities were built for cars, but by planning your trip around the limited network of Amtrak trains, you can travel light (and without a single thought for parking).

New York City to the Green Mountains

Amtrak's Vermonter line links New York City with northern Vermont, with stops in Connecticut and Massachusetts along the way. The **Vermonter** has a special spot for bicycles, so this is the perfect way to bring your own ride along.

DAY 1

All aboard at New York City's Penn Station, then just enjoy the ride on your way along the Long Island Sound to **New Haven,** where you can kick off the trip with a cruise through the city's **"apizza" joints.** There are world-class museums on the **Yale** campus, and New Haven makes a great base for a cruise to the tiny **Thimble Islands,** or a beach day at **Silver Sands State Park.**

DAYS 2-3

Unless you're planning at day in Hartford, settle in for the trip all the way across Massachusetts, and make your next destination the quirky town of **Brattleboro,** Vermont. Linger here for two full days, and you can get in some **river swimming, apple picking, hiking,** and **cycling**—the pretty roads of southern Vermont are ideal for bikes.

DAYS 4-5

Back on the train for the trip to Burlington, Vermont's Queen City, hopping a taxi from the station in Essex Junction. Downtown's shops, craft beer bars, and live music venues are easy to navigate on foot, but with a bicycle you can ride the **Burlington Bike Path** to the **Lake Champlain Islands,** crossing a short section of lake by bicycle ferry.

Yale campus

biking in Vermont

Winter Wonderland

EXPLORING FROZEN NEW ENGLAND ON SKIS, SLEIGHS, AND SKATES

Bundle up for some time in the snow, and you'll be amply rewarded—New England sparkles through the winter, and hours out of doors just make it sweeter to pass a long winter night by the fire.

- **Get some turns in the Green Mountains:** Vermont's rolling terrain offers some of the best skiing and riding around, from the mammoth slopes of **Killington Resort** (page 297) to the old school charms of the skier-only **Mad River Glen** (page 303). And if you prefer to earn your turns, there's endless cross country in the state, starting with the **Stowe Mountain Resort,** still owned by the Austrian singers of *Sound of Music* fame (page 314).

- **Skate Boston's Frog Pond:** Lace up your ice skates for some turns in the middle of New England's most buzzing city, then head to **Union Oyster House** to warm up with some chowder (page 61).

- **Have the run of Acadia:** There's not always enough snow on Mount Desert Island for cross-country skiing, but when the temperatures drop, you'll have miles of carriage roads—and can lay tracks all the way to the top of **Cadillac Mountain** (page 461).

skiing at Mad River Glen

- **O'er the hills you go:** Head to Vermont's **Shelburne Farms** for an old-fashioned sleigh ride, complete with Percheron draft horses and jingling bells (page 330).

Boston, Maine Coast, and Providence

The **Downeaster** train has service from Boston to Brunswick, with strategic stops for beaches and city exploring along the way. There are limited places for bikes on the Downeaster, so it's worth reserving your spot ahead of time. Providence is accessible by regional service from Boston, and once you're there, a series of **ferries** links you to Newport and the coast.

DAY 1

Board a train from Boston to **Wells,** and you'll be on the beach before you finish your book—the Amtrak station is just outside of town, so you can hop a cab (or ride a bike) to **Wells Beach,** settling in for a day of sun and swimming.

DAYS 2-3

Now that you've entered vacation mode, continue up the coast to **Portland,** where you can take to Casco Bay onboard one of the city's historic **sailing schooners.** A super-active city culture means lots of ways to move around, whether you're riding bikes along the waterfront promenade, paddling a kayak with views of the city

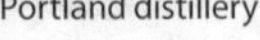
Portland distillery

surfing at Narragansett Town Beach

skyline, or just strolling the streets of the **Old Port.**

On your second day, make some time for culture at the **Portland Art Museum,** and climb to the top of the **Portland Observatory** for a panorama of the entire downtown peninsula. After sunset on the waterfront, visit a series of **Portland breweries,** from local legends to ultra-micro spots with a postage-stamp footprint.

DAYS 4-5

Head back south, but blow right through Boston on your way to Providence, whose compact downtown is perfect for exploring on foot. If you're ready for more art, make your first stop the museum at the **Rhode Island School of Design,** or just visit some of the historic landmarks that have survived from the city's earliest years.

Since Rhode Island's all about the ocean, use your second day to get out on the water, cruising from Providence to Newport on the Narragansett Bay **fast ferry.** Once you're there, a series of shuttle buses links up the **Newport mansions** and the town's charming beaches, and the **Cliff Walk** winds past the city's very best views.

Boston

Look for ★ to find recommended sights, activities, dining, and lodging.

Highlights

★ **Freedom Trail:** Trace the thin red line from Boston Common to Bunker Hill (page 35).

★ **Boston Common and Boston Public Garden:** Catch a ride on a swan boat or watch some summertime Shakespeare in the oldest park in the United States (page 40).

★ **Museum of Fine Arts:** Discover impressionist treasures and artifacts from around the world (page 48).

★ **Boston Public Library:** With masterpiece paintings and exquisite architecture, this landmark library is far more than books—but it's got millions and millions of those, too (page 50).

★ **Fenway Park:** From the Green Monster to the bleachers, this ball field is a pilgrimage destination for baseball lovers (page 52).

★ **North End Cuisine:** Pick up a cannolo, slurp an Italian ice, then watch the neighborhood drift by over a perfect cappuccino (page 62).

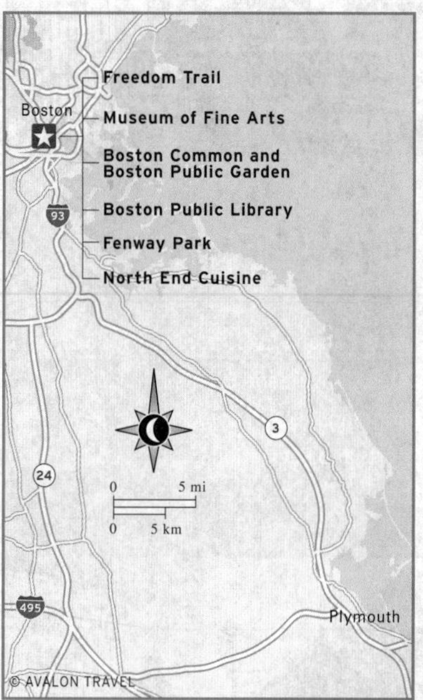

Follow the Freedom Trail through Boston to find a city that's grown up alongside its history.

Skyscrapers and modern architecture tower over—yet don't overshadow—Victorian brownstones, colonial graveyards, crooked streets, and gracious squares.

Downtown is bustling and busy, but it wraps around a park that's older than the United States, where swan boats, pavilions, and quiet pathways provide an oasis of green grass and calm. And while Greater Boston sprawls across four New England states—in addition to Massachusetts, the metro area crosses into Rhode Island, New Hampshire, and Connecticut—its principal sights are concentrated on the "Hub" of the tiny Shawmut Peninsula, making it easy to explore on foot or by public transport.

Crossing from one side to the other is a quick trip through the collective history and culture of the United States: See the Boston Red Sox's roaring fans in Fenway Park, visit the hushed reading room at the Boston Public Library, make way for ducklings in the Boston Public Garden, then walk the cobblestones where Patriots preached, fought, bled, and rebelled during the dawning days of the American Revolution.

Boston's history is anything but simple, and those Revolutionary battles are entwined with a legacy of slavery, the massacres and abuse of Native Americans, and immigration-related racial strife. Today's city, though, is thrillingly diverse: Those ethnic enclaves are celebrated as Boston's collective heritage, the African American Heritage Trail highlights the legacies of black Bostonians, and locals with roots from around the world blend with Boston's characteristic brass and bluster.

PLANNING YOUR TIME

You could spend a week exploring all that Boston has to offer. The city's small size, however, makes it easy to see different parts on the same trip, no matter how much time you have. The only mandatory sightseeing destination is a walk along the Freedom Trail, which connects all of downtown's Revolutionary War sites. The city's cultural attractions, for the most part, are grouped on the outskirts of downtown in the Back Bay, South End, South Boston, and Fenway districts. Art buffs can choose between several

Previous: Boston's Back Bay; Boston Public Garden. **Above:** Boston Light.

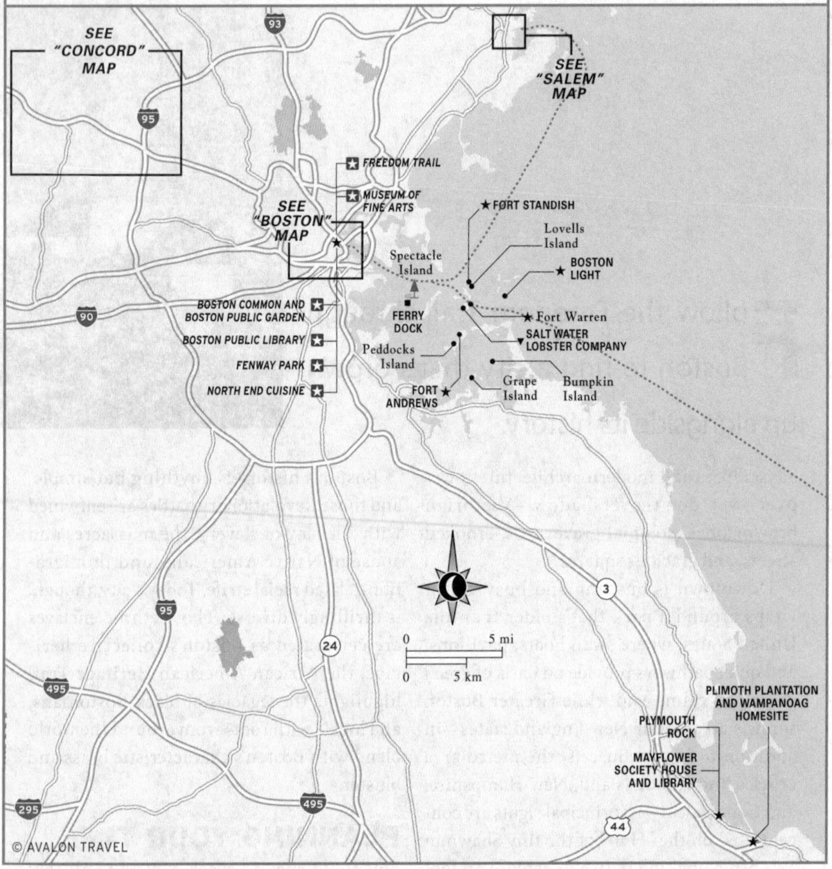

very different museums—the world-class Museum of Fine Arts, the charming Isabella Stewart Gardner Museum, or the cutting-edge Institute of Contemporary Art, while sports fans won't want to miss a guided tour of Fenway Park.

Even on a short trip, it's worth getting across the river to Cambridge, Boston's more bohemian "left bank." In addition to a more laid-back vibe, this sister city is home to Boston's most elite cultural institutions—Harvard University and the Massachusetts Institute of Technology.

ORIENTATION

The bulk of Boston's downtown still takes up the Shawmut Peninsula, with Boston Common at the center. The downtown neighborhoods are organized around the Common, with Beacon Hill and the North End to the north, the Financial District and downtown to the east, and Back Bay and the South End to the west and south. East Boston, along with Logan International Airport, is across Boston Harbor to the northeast, while South Boston and the new Seaport District form a peninsula to the southeast. Across the river to the north are intellectual Cambridge and hip Somerville.

Sights

TOP EXPERIENCE

★ FREEDOM TRAIL

John Hancock, Sam Adams, Paul Revere—history has given the names of America's Revolutionaries a nobility and purpose that might have surprised those early Bostonians. In fact, the months leading up to the War for Independence must have seemed more haphazard insurrection than organized battle for freedom to those who lived through them. Even in today's Boston, the passionate men and women who agitated for independence are vivid and accessible. It's easy to get drawn into the stories—both those that have become legendary and those that are less known.

A red line on the sidewalk connects 16 historic sites on a 2.5-mile walking trail ideal for getting your bearings in the city. Make your way from **Boston Common** to a series of churches, graveyards, and other early landmarks in downtown, then continue through the Italian American neighborhood of the **North End** to visit **Paul Revere's House** and the church where he hung signal lights for Revolutionary commanders.

The trail then crosses the Charles River via the stunning Leonard P. Zakim Bunker Hill Bridge to the **Charlestown Navy Yard** and the **Bunker Hill Monument,** where climbing 294 steep steps earns you panoramic views of the city from the top of a 221-foot obelisk that has commemorated the first major battle of the Revolution since 1843.

Visitors can walk the line themselves or take a 90-minute guided tour offered by the **Freedom Trail Foundation** (Boston Common Visitor Information Center, 148 Tremont St., 617/357-8300, www.thefreedomtrail.org, $12 adults, $10 students and seniors, $6.50 children) that covers the first 11 sites along the route; guides are costumed actors playing one of the lesser-known patriots. This is a good place to meet William Dawes, the "other" midnight rider; Abigail Adams, the intellectual letter writer and future first lady; or James Otis, who gave fiery, pro bono legal representation to colonists challenging British laws in court. The **National**

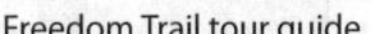

Freedom Trail tour guide

Boston

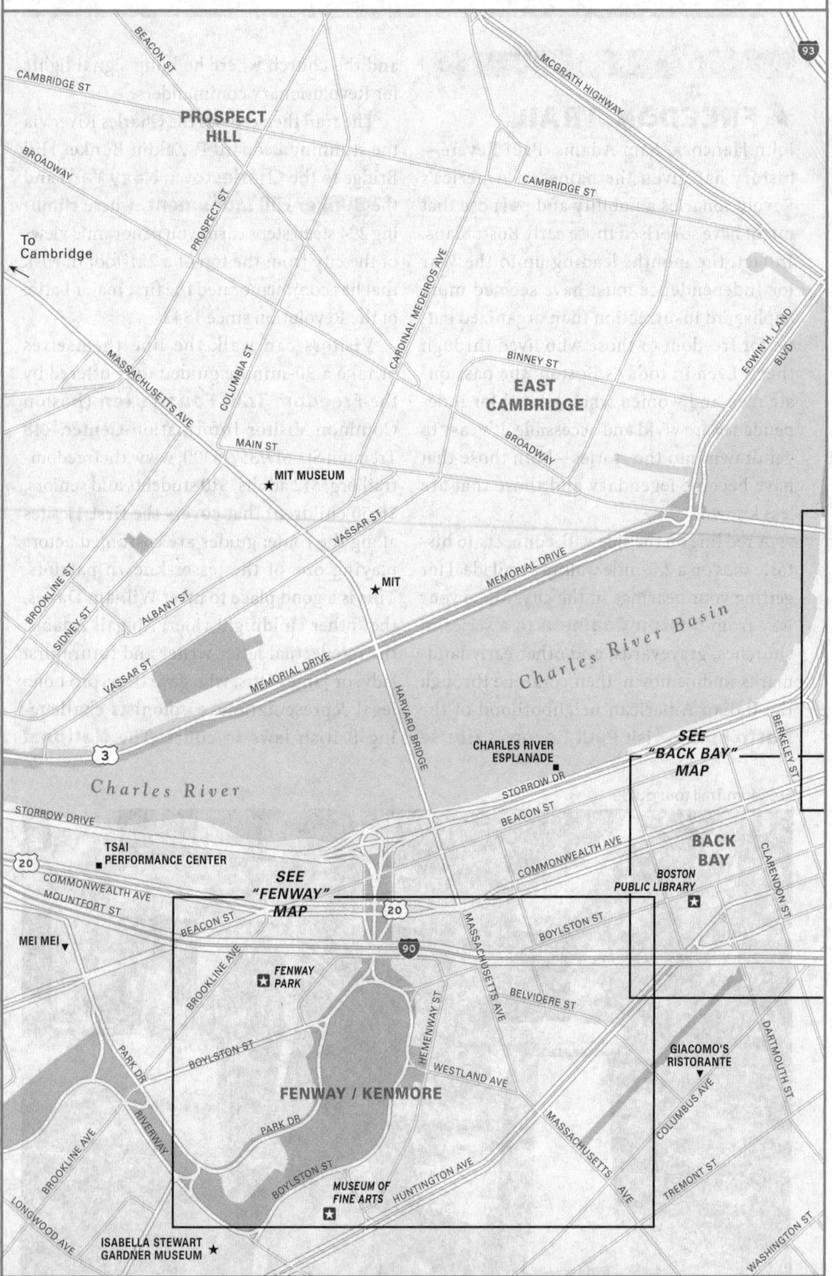

BEACON ST
CAMBRIDGE ST
PROSPECT HILL
BROADWAY
PROSPECT ST
To Cambridge
MCGRATH HIGHWAY
93
CAMBRIDGE ST
CARDINAL MEDEIROS AVE
COLUMBIA ST
MASSACHUSETTS AVE
EDWIN H. LAND BLVD
BINNEY ST
EAST CAMBRIDGE
BROADWAY
MAIN ST
MIT MUSEUM
VASSAR ST
MEMORIAL DRIVE
MIT
BROOKLINE ST
SIDNEY ST
ALBANY ST
VASSAR ST
MEMORIAL DRIVE
Charles River Basin
HARVARD BRIDGE
3
Charles River
CHARLES RIVER ESPLANADE
SEE "BACK BAY" MAP
BERKELEY ST
STORROW DR
STORROW DRIVE
BEACON ST
TSAI PERFORMANCE CENTER
20
COMMONWEALTH AVE
BACK BAY
CLARENDON ST
SEE "FENWAY" MAP
COMMONWEALTH AVE
MOUNTFORT ST
BOSTON PUBLIC LIBRARY
BEACON ST
20
MASSACHUSETTS AVE
BOYLSTON ST
MEI MEI
90
BROOKLINE AVE
FENWAY PARK
HEMENWAY ST
BELVIDERE ST
DARTMOUTH ST
PARK DR
BOYLSTON ST
GIACOMO'S RISTORANTE
WESTLAND AVE
FENWAY / KENMORE
RIVERWAY
PARK DR
COLUMBUS AVE
BROOKLINE AVE
MASSACHUSETTS AVE
BOYLSTON ST
HUNTINGTON AVE
TREMONT ST
MUSEUM OF FINE ARTS
LONGWOOD AVE
ISABELLA STEWART GARDNER MUSEUM
WASHINGTON ST

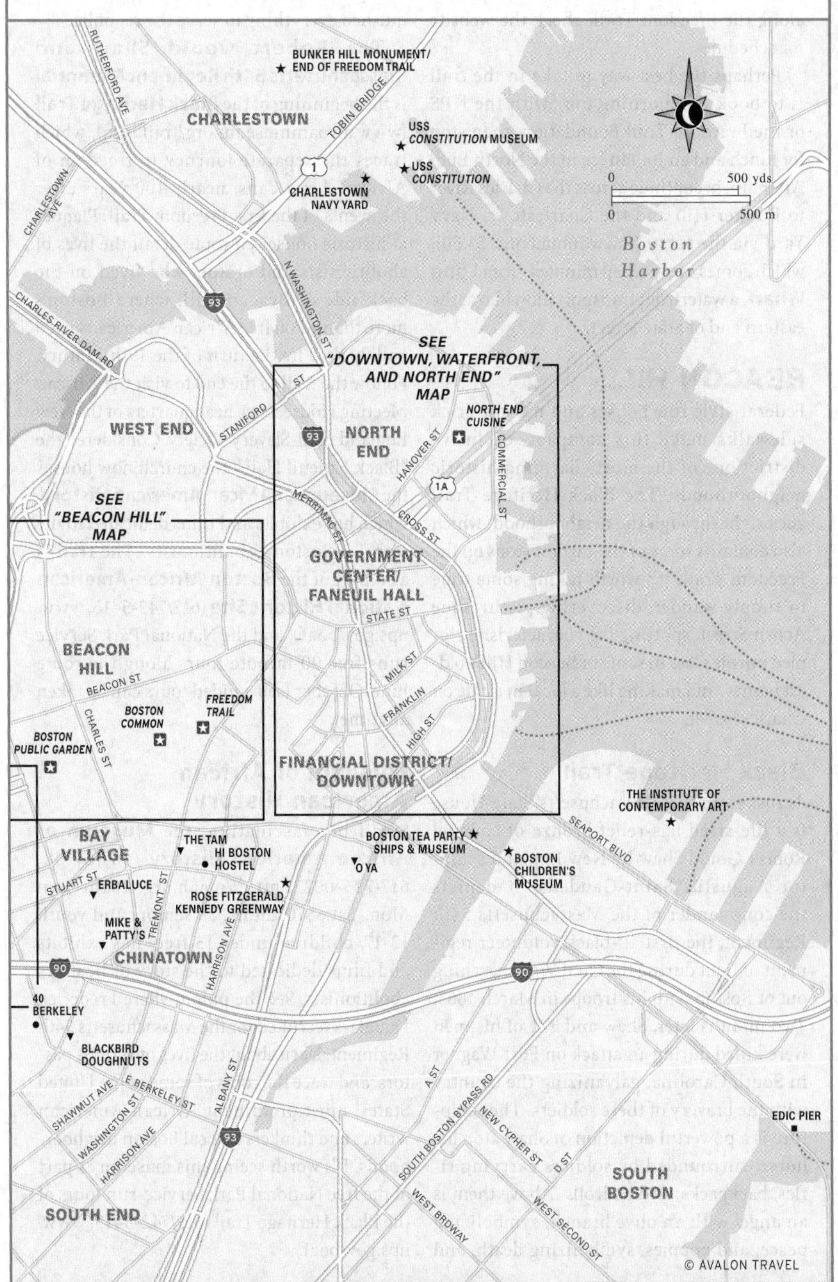

BUNKER HILL MONUMENT/ END OF FREEDOM TRAIL
CHARLESTOWN
TOBIN BRIDGE
RUTHERFORD AVE
USS CONSTITUTION MUSEUM
USS CONSTITUTION
CHARLESTOWN NAVY YARD
CHARLESTOWN AVE
0 500 yds
0 500 m
Boston Harbor
N WASHINGTON ST
CHARLES RIVER DAM RD
SEE "DOWNTOWN, WATERFRONT, AND NORTH END" MAP
ST
STANIFORD
WEST END
NORTH END
NORTH END CUISINE
HANOVER ST
COMMERCIAL ST
MERRIMAC ST
CROSS ST
SEE "BEACON HILL" MAP
GOVERNMENT CENTER/ FANEUIL HALL
STATE ST
BEACON HILL
BEACON ST
MILK ST
FRANKLIN
HIGH ST
BOSTON COMMON
FREEDOM TRAIL
CHARLES ST
BOSTON PUBLIC GARDEN
FINANCIAL DISTRICT/ DOWNTOWN
THE INSTITUTE OF CONTEMPORARY ART
SEAPORT BLVD
BAY VILLAGE
THE TAM
HI BOSTON HOSTEL
BOSTON TEA PARTY SHIPS & MUSEUM
O YA
BOSTON CHILDREN'S MUSEUM
STUART ST
ERBALUCE
ROSE FITZGERALD KENNEDY GREENWAY
TREMONT ST
MIKE & PATTY'S
HARRISON AVE
CHINATOWN
40 BERKELEY
BLACKBIRD DOUGHNUTS
SHAWMUT AVE
E BERKELEY ST
WASHINGTON ST
HARRISON AVE
ALBANY ST
A ST
SOUTH BOSTON BYPASS RD
NEW CYPHER ST
D ST
EDIC PIER
SOUTH BOSTON
WEST BROWAY
WEST SECOND ST
SOUTH END
© AVALON TRAVEL

Park Service (NPS, www.nps.gov/bost) also leads free tours and offers talks at sites along the Freedom Trail; check the website for schedules.

Perhaps the best way to take in the trail is to book the morning tour with the NPS or the Freedom Trail Foundation, then stop for lunch and an Italian ice in the North End. After lunch, continue across the Charles River to Bunker Hill and the Charlestown Navy Yard via the **ferry** (www.mbta.com, $3.50), which comes every 15-30 minutes, from **Long Wharf,** a waterfront transportation hub at the eastern end of State Street.

BEACON HILL

Federal-style row houses and narrow brick sidewalks make this compact, exclusive district one of the most charming historic neighborhoods. The Black Heritage Trail goes right through the neighborhood, which also contains some of the earliest stops on the Freedom Trail. It's worth taking some time to simply wander, discovering picturesque Acorn Street, spotting the characteristic rippled purple glass in some of Beacon Hill's oldest homes, and making like a local in a café on Charles Street.

Black Heritage Trail

Across from the Massachusetts State House is a life-sized bas-relief bronze of Colonel Robert Gould Shaw by New England sculptor Augustus Saint-Gaudens. It depicts the commander of the Massachusetts 54th Regiment, the first all-black volunteer regiment to fight during the Civil War, marching out of Boston with his troops in March 1863. Two months later, Shaw and 271 of his men were killed during an attack on Fort Wagner in South Carolina, galvanizing the country with the bravery of these soldiers. The sculpture is a powerful depiction of Shaw atop his horse, surrounded by soldiers carrying rifles, backpacks, and bedrolls. Above them is an angel with an olive branch, symbolizing peace, and poppies, symbolizing death, and the inscription "Omnia Relinquit Servare Rempublicam," which means "He relinquished everything to serve the republic."

The **Robert Gould Shaw and Massachusetts 54th Regiment Memorial** is the beginning of the **Black Heritage Trail** (www.afroammuseum.org/trail.htm), which traces the separate journey to freedom of African Americans, nearly 100 years after the events of the first Freedom Trail. Plaques at historic houses en route detail the lives of abolitionists and orators who lived on the back side of Beacon Hill, where Boston's more than 1,000 free African Americans lived and worked by the turn of the 19th century. Follow the trail to the end to visit the African Meeting House, once headquarters of the New England Anti-Slavery Society. Considered the "Black Faneuil Hall," the church now houses the **Museum of African American History,** which has exhibits and films dedicated to the story of Boston's abolitionists. The trail is also part of the **Boston African-American National Historic Site** (617/742-5415, www.nps.gov/boaf), and the National Park Service runs free 90-minute tours along the route June-October (self-guided tours can be taken anytime).

Museum of African American History

Small but fascinating, the **Museum of African American History** (46 Joy St., 617/725-0022, http://maah.org, 10am-4pm Mon.-Sat., $10 adults, $8 seniors and youth 13-17, children under 13 free) has exhibits and films dedicated to the story of Boston's abolitionists. See the pulpit where Frederick Douglass recruited for the Massachusetts 54th Regiment, learn about the lives of activist pastors, and trace the roots of some of the United States' most prominent African American writers and thinkers to local Boston neighborhoods. It's worth seeing this museum as part of the free National Park Service-run tours of the Black Heritage Trail (617/742-5415, www.nps.gov/boaf).

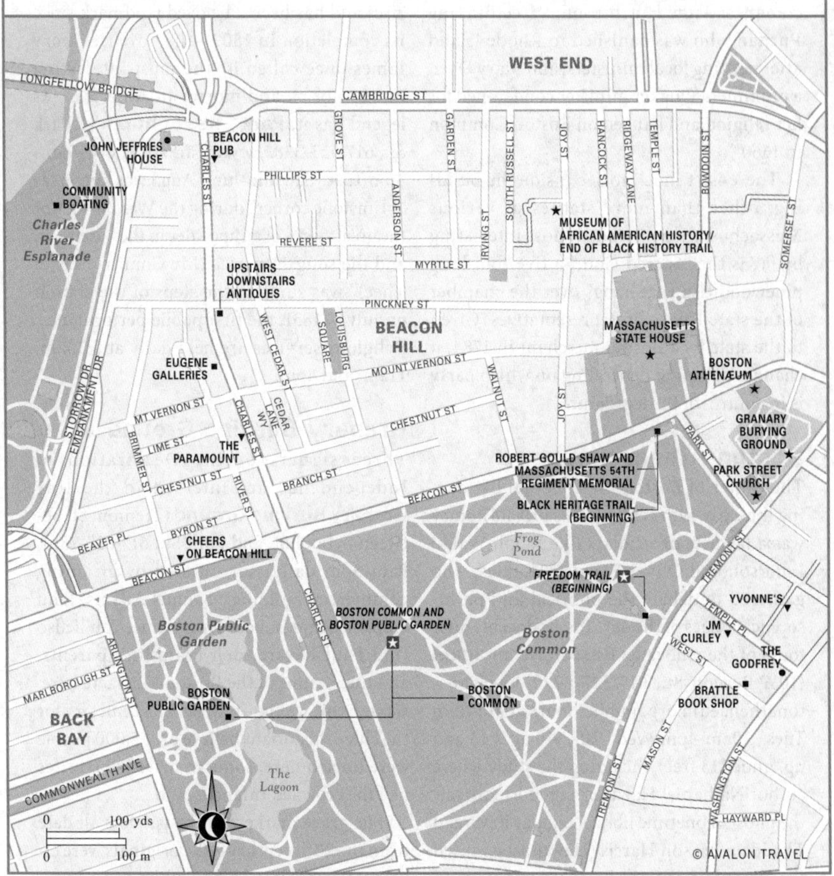

Massachusetts State House

On a sunny day, the shimmering gold dome of the state's capitol building can be seen from miles around. The brick building beneath it is the tidy federal-style structure of the **Massachusetts State House** (24 Beacon St., 617/727-3676, www.sec.state.ma.us/trs, tours 10am-3:30pm Mon.-Fri., free) designed by prominent Boston architect Charles Bullfinch and built in 1798. At the time, 15 white columns were pulled up Beacon Street in a procession of 15 white horses, one for each state. The wooden dome on top was sheathed in copper by Revolutionary renaissance man Paul Revere in 1802, then re-covered with 23-karat gold leaf in 1948. Two marble wings were added at the turn of the 20th century.

An impressive selection of statues graces the park side of the building. The equestrian statue in front of the main entrance depicts Joseph "Fighting Joe" Hooker, a Civil War general from Massachusetts who led the Army of the Potomac for all of six months. (There is no basis, however, to the myth that "hookers" are named after his troops, rumored to be frequent brothel patrons while on leave.) Other statues in front of the building are dedicated to 19th-century orator Daniel Webster and educator Horace Mann. In front of the wings are statues of two prominent women colonists: Anne Hutchinson, a freethinking Puritan who was banished to Rhode Island after nettling local ministers, and Mary Dyer, a prominent Quaker minister condemned for her religion and hanged on Boston Common in 1660.

There isn't much to see inside the building, other than more statues of various Massachusetts politicians. Most interesting by far is the "Sacred Cod," a five-foot-long pinewood fish that hangs over the chamber of the state House of Representatives. Given to the state by a Boston merchant in 1784, it changes direction depending on which party is in control of the legislature.

Boston Athenaeum

The center of Boston's intellectual life during the early 19th century, this private library was a favorite of scholars like Ralph Waldo Emerson and Oliver Wendell Holmes, who gathered to debate the political and philosophical issues of the day. Today, docents offer tours of the renovated **Boston Athenaeum** (10½ Beacon St., 617/227-0270, www.bostonathenaeum.org, public hours 10am-8pm Tues., 10am-4pm Wed.-Sat., $10 ages 13 and up, under 13 free), including the study where author Nathaniel Hawthorne reportedly saw the ghost of onetime library regular Reverend Thaddeus Mason Harris (Hawthorne mused that the good reverend might have stopped by to read his own obituary). Among the library's more unusual holdings are the private library of President George Washington and one of the world's largest collections of books about the Romany people. One-hour Art & Architecture tours of the library are offered at 5:30pm Tuesday, 3pm Thursday, and 11am Saturday. Tours are $2 in addition to regular admission charges. Free 30-minute "Up Close" tours of the Athenaeum's 1st floor are offered at 11am on Wednesday.

Park Street Church

The white-steepled church at the corner of Park and Tremont Streets looks particularly dramatic with a backdrop of downtown high-rises and has been a beloved landmark since its completion in 1809—the novelist Henry James once called it "the most interesting mass of brick and mortar in America." As legend has it, **Park Street Church** (1 Park St., 617/523-3383, www.parkstreet.org, 9am-4pm Tues.-Sat. mid-June-Aug.) was known as "brimstone corner" during the War of 1812 for the great stores of gunpowder in the basement, and the song "America (My Country 'Tis of Thee)" was sung on the steps of the church on July 4, 1831, the first public performance. Religious services are held daily at 8:30am, 11am, and 4pm.

Granary Burying Ground

Three signers of the Declaration of Independence are interred in the tiny **Granary Burying Ground** (Tremont St. between School St. and Park St., 617/635-7361, 9am-5pm daily) surrounded by gleaming commercial buildings: Samuel Adams, John Hancock, and Robert Treat Paine. You'll also find Paul Revere, Ben Franklin's parents, and the victims of the Boston Massacre here, though this was far from being a cemetery for the elite—historians believe over 5,000 people were buried here, some in mass burial sites like the crowded Infants Tomb.

The grave markers of the patriots all date from the 20th century—the originals were either stolen or "lost." Many of the gravestones date from the 17th century, weather-beaten stone slabs inscribed with moving (and sometimes flippant) epitaphs and winged death skulls.

★ Boston Common and Boston Public Garden

BOSTON COMMON

Boston Common (139 Tremont St.) began its life as a sheep and cow pasture in 1634, just a few years after the city itself was founded. By Puritan law, it was legal for any resident of the city to graze their livestock on the common land (that law was repealed in 1833, so you now need to provide your own forage for your cows and sheep). These days, the Common feels like the city's collective backyard, with space for throwing Frisbees, spreading out picnics, and playing in the grass.

Several monuments within the park are attractions in and of themselves. The stunning fountain located just a few steps down from Park Street toward Boylston is named **Brewer Fountain,** a bronze replica of a fountain exhibited at the Paris World's Fair of 1855. The objects on its base depict the sea gods and goddesses Neptune, Amphitrite, Acis, and Galatea. Opposite the gold-domed statehouse is the **Robert Gould Shaw and Massachusetts 54th Regiment Memorial,** a bas-relief by Augustus Saint-Gaudens that depicts the first all-black volunteer regiment in the Union army. Near the intersection of Park and Beacon Streets, the **Frog Pond** is an ice-skating rink in winter and a shallow fountain in summer, when it fills with kids cooling off. On the Tremont Street side, at the intersection with Boylston, the **Francis Parkman Bandstand** is used as the site for summer concerts, political rallies, and **Shakespeare on the Common** (www.commshakes.org).

BOSTON PUBLIC GARDEN

In contrast to Boston Common's open, park-like feel, the **Boston Public Garden** (4 Charles St.), right next door, is an intimate outdoor space, full of leafy trees and flower beds. Built on landfill in the 19th century, the garden was the country's first public botanical garden, envisioned by its creators as a respite from urban life. It's especially romantic at sunset, when the trees cast mysterious shadows over the walkways. The centerpiece is a lagoon, which is crossed by a fairy-tale bridge and surrounded by willow trees trailing their branch tips in the water—note the tiny island in the center of the lagoon, which is used by ducks that pad up out of the water on an adorable ducks-only ramp. Tracing lazy circles in the lagoon are Boston's famous **swan boats** (617/522-1966, www.swanboats.com, 10am-4pm daily Apr.-mid-June, 10am-5pm daily mid-June-early Sept., noon-4pm Mon.-Fri., 10am-4pm Sat.-Sun. early Sept.-mid-Sept., \$3.50 adults, \$3 seniors, \$2 children 2-15, children under 2 free), a flotilla of six large paddleboats with the graceful white birds at the stern. The boats are a mandatory attraction if you are in Boston with children, as are the nearby bronze statues of Mrs. Mallard and her eight little ducklings: Jack, Kack, Lack, Mack,

Boston Common

Nack, Ouack, Pack, and Quack. The statues pay homage to Robert McCloskey's children's book *Make Way for Ducklings*, which was partially set in the Boston Public Garden.

DOWNTOWN AND THE WATERFRONT

Downtown is where Boston's history and cutting edge coexist, an easily walkable district where colonial sites are densely packed amid skyscrapers. While not as picture-perfect as Beacon Hill, it's the heart of the action. The waterfront is pedestrian friendly, lined with parks, restaurants, and attractions. Just east of Boston Common, the Downtown Crossing area has mega stores, boutiques, and landmark theaters.

King's Chapel

Boston's original Anglican church, **King's Chapel** (Tremont St. and School St., 617/523-1749, www.kings-chapel.org, 10am-5pm Mon.-Sat., 1:30pm-5pm Sun., $3 suggested donation), was founded in 1686, but the current stone church building dates to 1749 and holds a bell cast by Paul Revere that is still rung before services. The adjoining graveyard is the oldest in Boston; as such, it contains the graves of some of the original colonists of Massachusetts, including Governor John "City on A Hill" Winthrop and Anne Prine, said to be the real Hester Prynne on whom Hawthorne based his book *The Scarlet Letter*. Along with them are several lesser-known patriots like William Dawes, the "other rider" who raised the alarm on the eve of the battles of Concord and Lexington. There's a fascinating **"Bells and Bones" tour** (617/523-1749, tours at 11am, noon, 2pm, 3pm, and 4pm Mon. and Wed.-Sat., 2pm, 3pm, and 4pm Tues. and Sun., $10 adults, $7 seniors, students, and military, $5 children under 13) of the church's bell tower and 200-year-old crypt.

Old South Meeting House

The Boston Tea Party may have ended in the harbor, but it started at the brick church building with a gray-shingled tower known as the **Old South Meeting House** (310 Washington St., 617/482-6439, www.oldsouthmeetinghouse.org, 9:30am-5pm daily Apr. 1-Oct. 31, 10am-4pm daily Nov. 1-March 31, $6 adults, $5 seniors and students, $1 children 5-17), dating from 1729. Led by Samuel Adams, over 5,000 patriots gathered here, overflowing into the streets, on the night of December 16, 1773. After fiery speeches, Adams spoke the code words: "This meeting can do no more to save our country." Those words were a prearranged signal to some members in the audience to don face paint and feathers and head down to Griffin's Wharf, where three ships stood loaded down with bins of loose tea. In all, about $1.7 million worth of tea (in today's money) was thrown into the harbor, setting the stage for the battles that followed. (As a postscript, when Queen Elizabeth II visited Boston for the Bicentennial in 1976, the mayor of the city presented her with a check to cover the cost of the tea—not counting inflation.)

The Old South Meeting House still serves as a meeting place of sorts, offering (somewhat less rabble-rousing) lectures and classical music. The meeting house museum traces the events surrounding the tea party through an audio exhibit, with actors reading the words of Sam Adams and the other patriots along with sound effects to re-create the time period. A separate multimedia exhibit dubbed *Voices of Protests* focuses on Adams, statesman Ben Franklin, and abolitionist Phyllis Wheatley, who were all members of the Old South Meeting House congregation.

Old State House

Before construction of the new state house on Beacon Hill, both British and American governors ruled from the small brick **Old State House** (206 Washington St., 617/720-1713, www.bostonhistory.org, 9am-6pm daily mid-May-early Sept., 9am-5pm daily early Sept.-mid-May, $10 adults, $8.50 seniors and students, youth under 18 free) that's now surrounded by towering offices. On one side of the building are replicas of the standing

Downtown and Waterfront

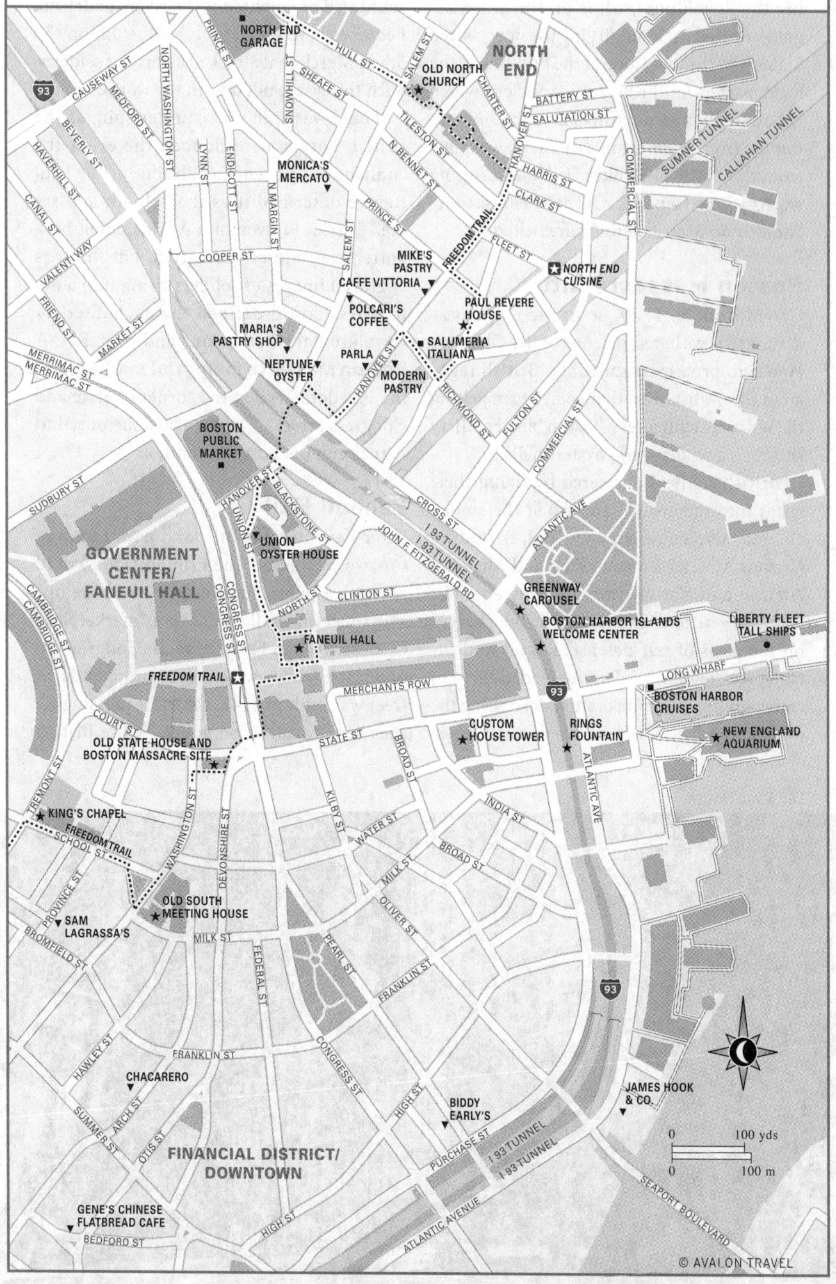
NORTH END GARAGE
NORTH END
OLD NORTH CHURCH
MONICA'S MERCATO
MIKE'S PASTRY
CAFFE VITTORIA
NORTH END CUISINE
POLCARI'S COFFEE
PAUL REVERE HOUSE
MARIA'S PASTRY SHOP
SALUMERIA ITALIANA
PARLA
NEPTUNE OYSTER
MODERN PASTRY
BOSTON PUBLIC MARKET
UNION OYSTER HOUSE
GOVERNMENT CENTER/ FANEUIL HALL
GREENWAY CAROUSEL
BOSTON HARBOR ISLANDS WELCOME CENTER
LIBERTY FLEET TALL SHIPS
FANEUIL HALL
FREEDOM TRAIL
BOSTON HARBOR CRUISES
CUSTOM HOUSE TOWER
RINGS FOUNTAIN
NEW ENGLAND AQUARIUM
OLD STATE HOUSE AND BOSTON MASSACRE SITE
KING'S CHAPEL
OLD SOUTH MEETING HOUSE
SAM LAGRASSA'S
CHACARERO
JAMES HOOK & CO.
BIDDY EARLY'S
FINANCIAL DISTRICT/ DOWNTOWN
GENE'S CHINESE FLATBREAD CAFE
0 100 yds
0 100 m
© AVALON TRAVEL

lion and unicorn that signified the crown of England (the originals were torn down during the Revolution), while on the other is a gold-covered eagle signifying the new United States. On the 2nd floor of the building is the headquarters for the Bostonian Society, which runs a small museum full of artifacts, including tea from the Boston Tea Party, weapons from the Battle of Bunker Hill, and clothing worn by John Hancock. Old State House tours and Boston Massacre tours are held daily.

Boston Massacre Site

On March 5, 1770, a group of angry Bostonians gathered in front of the Old State House to protest treatment by British regulars and royalists, and they soon began pelting the redcoats with a very Boston blend of dirty snowballs, cinders, and oyster shells.

British soldiers answered by firing their rifles into the crowd, and when the smoke cleared, five colonists lay dead, including Crispus Attucks, a former slave and whaler of African and Native American descent. The soldiers were later exonerated of the charges on the basis of self-defense; lawyer and future president John Adams defended them in court, giving a rousing oratory describing the protesters as "a motley rabble of saucy boys, Negroes and mulattos, Irish teagues and outlandish jack tars . . . the sun is not about to stand still or go out, nor the rivers to dry up, because there was a mob in Boston, on the 5th of March that attacked a party of soldiers. Such things are not new in the world."

There was spin and counter-spin, as the British government dubbed the event the "unhappy occurrence at Boston," while Paul Revere described it as the "bloody massacre." Patriot PR won out: Adams might have gotten the soldiers acquitted, but Revere's engraved images of soldiers firing into a defenseless crowd defined the encounter for Revolutionary Bostonians and posterity. A **Boston Massacre memorial marker** is on the Freedom Trail at the corner of State and Congress Streets. There's also a memorial to Attucks on the Boston Common.

Faneuil Hall

Peter Faneuil built this landmark building for two purposes: The ground floor would serve as a public food market, and the upstairs meeting hall would be a "marketplace of ideas." When **Faneuil Hall** (Congress St, 617/523-1300, www.nps.gov, 9am-5pm daily, free) was built in 1742, the most pressing issues were taxation on goods by the British

Old State House

government, and it became the main meeting space for protests and discussions by the Sons of Liberty—earning it the nickname the "Cradle of Liberty." After it was expanded in size by architect Charles Bullfinch, the hall was also the main venue for talks by William Lloyd Garrison, Frederick Douglass, and other antislavery activists. Public talks and citywide meetings are still held in the upstairs hall, lent more gravitas by the huge mural of Daniel Webster arguing against slavery that overlooks the stage. During the day, historic talks are given by national park rangers every half hour.

Downstairs, the stalls still exist, even though they have long since stopped selling food products; most are now the venue for souvenirs and other made-in-Boston goods. The adjacent Faneuil Hall Marketplace (www.faneuilhallmarketplace.com) adds far more indoor and outdoor shopping and dining opportunities.

Just behind Faneuil Hall is **Quincy Market** (367 S. Market St., 617/523-1300, www.quincy-market.com, 10am-9pm Mon.-Sat., noon-6pm Sun.), where farmers and butchers began selling their wares in 1826. Produce vendors have given way to food stalls, restaurants, and shops, making this a convenient place to grab a snack along the Freedom Trail.

Custom House Tower

Close to the waterfront is Boston's oldest "skyscraper," the 500-foot-tall **Custom House Tower** (3 McKinley Sq., 617/310-6300, www.marriott.com, lobby open 7am-11pm daily), which now houses a Marriott hotel. Built in 1915, the distinctive Beaux-Arts tower features a 22-foot-wide clock and a pair of peregrine falcons that nest atop it during summer. You can try to catch a glimpse of them, along with knockout views of the harbor, on the **26th-floor observation deck** (2pm and 6pm Mon.-Thurs. and Sat.-Sun., $7-17). The deck on the 26th floor opens twice daily: Tickets are sold 2pm-2:15pm, which is $7, or come between 4:30pm and 7pm for the evening tour, which is $10 for admission with a non-alcoholic drink included, or $17 with an alcoholic beverage. Inside the tower is also a small museum with a few paintings and American historical artifacts on loan from the Peabody Essex Museum in Salem.

New England Aquarium

The centerpiece of the massive waterfront **New England Aquarium** (Central Wharf, 617/973-5200, www.neaq.org, 9am-6pm Sun.-Thurs., 9am-7pm Fri.-Sat. July-Aug., 9am-5pm Mon.-Fri., 9am-6pm Sat.-Sun. Sept.-June, $27.95 adults, $25.95 seniors, $18.95 children 3-11, children under 3 free; IMAX: $9.95 adults, $7.95 seniors and children 3-11; whale watch: $53 adults, $45 seniors, $33 children 3-11, $16 children under 3) is a 200,000-gallon tank full of sharks, sea turtles, and giant ocean fish that rises like a watery spinal column through the center of the building. A long walkway spirals around the tank, giving viewers a chance to see sealife on all levels of the ocean, from the toothy pikes that float on the surface to the 550-pound, 80-year-old sea turtle, Myrtle, often spotted snoozing on the floor. Other crowd-pleasers are the harbor seals in the courtyard and enormous open-air penguin pool, containing three dozen rockhopper, little blue, and African penguins who fill the building with their raucous cries.

The aquarium is not just a museum, but also a research-and-rescue organization that finds stranded seals, dolphins, and other animals and nurses them back to health. You can see the aquarium's latest convalescents in a hospital ward on the 2nd floor. The aquarium also ventures out into the harbor itself for whale-watching trips, seeking out the humpbacks and right whales that make their way into Massachusetts Bay.

NORTH END

Everyone from tour guides to locals will tell you the same thing about this historic neighborhood: "It's just like being in Italy!" The truth is, though, there's something essentially

Bostonian about the Italian American North End—the home of the Celtics basketball team as well as numerous pastry shops, old-fashioned grocers, and classic red-sauce joints.

The area is the oldest part of the city, and its history overflows with Puritans and Revolutionaries, including Paul Revere, whose house still stands. But by the mid-19th-century, it was rundown and crime ridden. Poor Irish immigrants settled here after fleeing famines at home and were joined by a wave of Jewish immigrants and, finally, the Italians, who reshaped the neighborhood in the image of Genoa, Palermo, Milan, and Naples.

Even as it has gentrified over the years, the North End has retained its cultural identity, with third- and fourth-generation Italians returning on Italian feast days, when churches and community clubs try to outdo each other with lavish parades full of floats, bunting, and sizzling Italian sausage. It's a fascinating place to eat, drink, and explore: With a cannoli in hand, taking in colonial architecture and dodging Boston traffic, you wouldn't mistake it for anywhere else in the world.

Paul Revere House

Every town in New England claims to have a Paul Revere bell in its belfry or a dusty bit of Revere silver in its historical museum. The patriot who made the famous midnight ride to warn the suburbs of the British march, however, was virtually unknown until before the Civil War, when Massachusetts poet Henry Wadsworth Longfellow made him the subject of a poem to stir up passion for the Union cause. Contrary to the poem's dramatic narrative, Revere never made it to Concord to warn the minutemen of the British approach; he was arrested by the British after warning John Hancock and Sam Adams in Lexington. And he wasn't the only rider out that night. At least two other riders, William Dawes and Dr. Samuel Prescott, were also out warning the colonists.

Whatever the details of Revere's famous night, he was a riveting one-man band of the colonial world who earned his living as a silversmith, coppersmith, bell ringer, and dentist. He raised many of his 16 children in the house that still bears his name. The **Paul Revere House** (19 North Sq., 617/523-2338, www.paulreverehouse.org, 9:30am-5:15pm daily mid-Apr.-Oct., 9:30am-4:15pm daily Nov.-mid-Apr., $5 adults, $4.50 seniors and students, $1 children 5-17, children under 5 free) is a typical example of 17th-century architecture and the oldest house still standing in downtown Boston.

The house doesn't have many artifacts—the Museum of Fine Arts is the best place to go to see Revere silver—but it's an interesting window into the living quarters and implements of a typical family in colonial urban North America. Interpretive guides are on hand to lead guests up creaking narrow staircases into the snug quarters where Revere and his wife slept and entertained guests. On Saturday afternoons, artisans demonstrate colonial arts like silversmithing and gilding in the outdoor courtyards. The Education and Visitor Center has exhibits on Revere's professional and personal life as well as his famous Midnight Ride. Tours of the neighboring, brick-faced Pierce/Hitchborn House, built in 1711 in Georgian style, are by appointment only ($4 adults, $3.50 seniors and students, $1 children 5-17).

Old North Church

Paul Revere was a bell ringer in the landmark **Old North Church** (193 Salem St., 617/858-8231, www.oldnorth.com, 10am-4pm daily Jan.-Feb., 9am-5pm daily Mar.-May and Nov.-Dec., 9am-6pm daily June-Oct., $3 donation) when he was a child, so he knew just where to hang his signal lights to warn the rebels that the British were moving by sea to Charlestown, then on to Concord and Lexington. The church sexton, Robert Newman, was the unsung hero in the story—he was arrested by the British the following morning. Inside the church, reproductions of colonial flags hang from the ceiling, and every half hour a guide tells Revere's story from the pulpit.

Between Old North and Hanover Street is

the **Paul Revere Mall,** with a huge bronze statue of Revere on his horse, keeping watch over pigeons and wizened Italian ladies. Look for the plaques along the wall that honor other patriots who grew up in the North End or tell the stories of some of the original Puritan settlers of the neighborhood, including theologians Cotton and Increase Mather, governor John Winthrop, and Ann Pollard, the first woman settler to arrive in Boston.

CHARLESTOWN

The original settlement of the Puritans was named after the king they left behind. A swampy mess of a place without much access to fresh water, Charlestown was eventually abandoned when John Winthrop and company were invited over to the Shawmut Peninsula to found Boston. Charlestown, which is incorporated as a neighborhood of Boston, grew to be an important port in the 18th century. Then tragedy struck during the Revolutionary War, when the British fired cannonballs filled with incendiary oil across the channel and burned the city to the ground in retaliation for their losses at the Battle of Bunker Hill.

The city was rebuilt in the early 19th century, about the same time as the brick mansions and brownstones were going up on Beacon Hill, and it shares that neighborhood's historical, cozy feel. Gas lamps, black shutters, and window boxes abound in the neighborhood that winds up toward the Bunker Hill Monument.

Bunker Hill Monument

High on the top of Breed's Hill stands the 221-foot granite obelisk of the **Bunker Hill Monument** (Monument Sq., 617/242-5641, www.nps.gov/bost/historyculture/bhm.htm, 9am-5pm daily (last climb 4:30pm) mid-Mar.-Nov., 1pm-5pm (last climb 4:30pm) daily Dec.-mid-Mar., free) to mark the misnamed first major battle of the Revolutionary War. In it, the patriots—while defeated—inflicted such high casualties upon the British army that thousands rushed to the colonial cause to begin a protracted siege of Boston. Climb the 294 steep, winding steps to the top of the monument for fine views of Boston Harbor and the city skyline.

Across the street, the impressive **Bunker Hill Museum** (43 Monument Sq., 9am-5pm daily mid-Mar.-Nov., 1pm-5pm daily Dec.-mid-Mar., free) opened in 2007 with two floors of exhibits about the battle. In addition to artifacts such as a British cannonball, the museum features two dioramas with miniature figurines that perpetually fight the battle over again with the help of a sound and light display. The highlight, however, is the beautifully painted "cyclorama" on the 2nd floor, depicting the battle in breathtaking 360 degrees.

USS *Constitution*

The oldest commissioned ship in the U.S. Navy, the **USS *Constitution*** (10am-6pm Tues.-Sun. mid-Apr.-Oct., 2:30pm-4pm Thurs.-Fri. 10am-4pm Sat.-Sun. Nov.-Apr.)—also known as Old Ironsides—was named by President Washington and launched in 1798. In 17 years of active duty, it racked up a battle record as celebrated as any ship of its time, defeating the heavier British ships *Guerrière* and *Java* during the War of 1812, and leading a blockade of Tripoli during the War of the Barbary Coast.

She's now docked at Charlestown Navy Yard, where sailors give tours every half hour; it's thrilling to stand behind a long cannon on the gun deck or sit at the gambrel table in the captain's quarters. Some of the stones in the bilge are the originals placed there for ballast more than 200 years ago. The last time the *Constitution* detached from a tugboat to sail freely under its own power was in 1997, during its 200th anniversary; the ship, however, is towed out into Boston Harbor and turned around with a 21-gun salute every year on July 4. (Members of the public can sign up on the ship's website for a lottery to board the ship for these cruises.)

Another warship living out her days in Charlestown is the **USS *Cassin Young,*** a Fletcher-class destroyer that was active in the

Battle of Leyte Gulf and the Battle of Okinawa during World War II, then stayed in service until 1960. The *Cassin Young* is one of just four Fletcher-class vessels still afloat, and it offers a glimpse of the cramped, tidy life aboard a naval vessel.

Get the background on the ships and the naval yard at the **Charlestown Naval Yard Visitors Center** (Charlestown Navy Yard, Bldg. 5, 617/242-5601, www.nps.gov/bost/historyculture/cny.htm, 9am-5pm Tues.-Sun. late Apr.-Oct., 9am-5pm Thurs.-Sun. Nov.-late Apr.), which features a 10-minute video on the history of the yard, along with ropes, chains, uniforms, and other artifacts. Near the ship is the much larger **USS *Constitution* Museum** (Charlestown Navy Yard, 617/426-1812, www.ussconstitutionmuseum.org, 9am-6pm daily Apr.-Oct., 10am-5pm daily Nov.-Mar., suggested donation $5-10 adults, $3-5 children, $20-25 families), which displays swords, pistols, and cannonballs captured from the *Constitution*'s various engagements, along with a giant model of the ship under full sail. Several short films give more information about the ship and its history. Kids love the upper floor of the museum, which features a cannon they can swab, wad, and "fire" against an enemy ship and a rudimentary video game in which they can engage the HMS *Java* while learning the basic principles of battle under sail.

FENWAY AND BACK BAY

TOP EXPERIENCE

★ Museum of Fine Arts

This grand, neoclassical museum's art collection is one of the best and most beloved in the country. The MFA, as it's known, is particularly noted for its French Impressionist works, but it also has outstanding Asian and Egyptian collections, as well as many celebrated early American paintings and artifacts. The **Museum of Fine Arts** (465 Huntington Ave., 617/267-9300, www.mfa.org, 10am-5pm Sat.-Tues., 10am-10pm Wed.-Fri., $25 adults, $23 seniors and students, $10 youth 7-17, free for youth 7-17 after 3pm Mon.-Fri. and on weekends, children under 7 free, free for active-duty military Memorial Day-Labor Day) began its life as the painting collection of the Boston Athenaeum, the private library on Beacon Hill. Under its current leadership, the museum has taken some gambles to bring a new generation of viewers into the galleries, staging artistic exhibitions of guitars, race cars, and the World Series rings of Red Sox slugger David Ortiz alongside showstopping special exhibits featuring masterpieces by Monet, Van Gogh, and Gauguin.

At present, most visitors to the MFA make a beeline for the 2nd floor, which is home to several jaw-dropping rooms dedicated to works by French Impressionists Monet, Manet, Renoir, Van Gogh, and others. Less trafficked but equally rewarding are the American galleries, where you'll find what's arguably the most famous American painting ever: Gilbert Stuart's original unfinished painting of George Washington. The collection includes several paintings by John Singer Sargent, including the arresting *Daughters of Edward Darley Bolt*, as well as those by Boston's own adopted artist, John Singleton Copley, including his portrait of Paul Revere. Several examples of the patriot silversmith's work are on display in adjoining galleries of colonial artifacts and furniture. Tours of various collections within the museum are offered free with admission throughout the day.

Back Bay

In the most fashionable neighborhood in Boston, Back Bay's grand boulevards are lined with brownstones and large Victorian-style apartment buildings, linked by short side streets that are ordered alphabetically (Arlington, Berkeley, Clarendon, etc.). Ironically, given how swanky the neighborhood has become, the area used to be one big disease-spreading swamp—it's no accident that the neighborhood's main drag, Boylston Street, is named after a doctor. In the days when Boston used to be a peninsula, Back

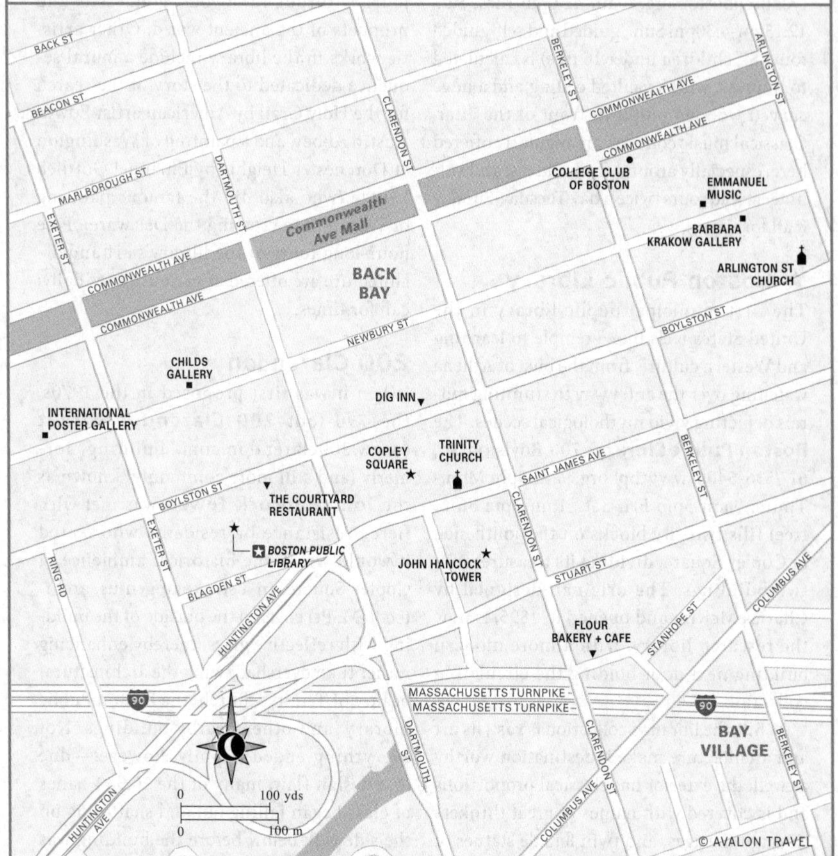

Bay was literally a bay in the Charles River, where refuse would wash up with the tides, and men and boys—including a young Ben Franklin—would fish from shore. As the city expanded in the 1800s, the earth from Beacon Hill and other high ground was used for landfill to close up the bay, and a new neighborhood was born, quickly populated with larger and more impressive houses.

Arlington Street Church

Striking Tiffany windows depict Jesus's beatitudes—a series of blessings praising the meek, merciful, and peaceful—in the Unitarian Universalist **Arlington Street Church** (351 Boylston St., 617/536-7050, www.ascboston.org, open most mornings, free), where ministers like Theodore Parker and William Ellery Channing preached about abolition and social justice in the early 19th century.

Trinity Church

This Presbyterian landmark is the undisputed masterpiece of architect H. H. Richardson, whose bold style sparked a trend called Richardson Romanesque, featuring massive blocks of stone, often worked in a contrasting checkerboard pattern, with sweeping arches and towers. The inside of the **Trinity Church** (206 Clarendon St., 617/536-0944, www.trinitychurchboston.org, 10am-4:30pm Tues.-Sat., 12:15pm-4:30pm Sun., guided and self-guided tours $7, children under 16 free) is calculated to impress, with a vaulted ceiling and a huge carved wooden pulpit in front of the altar. Classical music concerts are regularly offered here, especially around the holidays, and volunteers lead tours twice a day Tuesday-Sunday (call for times).

★ Boston Public Library

The first municipal public library in the United States feels like a temple to learning and Western culture, from the bust of Athena watching over the entryway to stunning murals depicting vivid mythological scenes. The **Boston Public Library** (700 Boylston St., 617/536-5400, www.bpl.org, 9am-9pm Mon.-Thurs., 9am-5pm Fri.-Sat., 1pm-5pm Sun., free) fills two city blocks on the south side of Copley Square, dividing its treasures into two buildings. The original, designed by Charles McKim and opened in 1895, is now the research library, with a more modern building next door holding the circulating collection.

While the library's collection is vast, its art and architecture make it destination worthy as well; the exterior has classical proportions and is covered with names of great thinkers through the ages, and twin female statues of Art and Science keep guard outside. One of the best-kept secrets of the city is the library's central courtyard, an Italianate plaza that wraps around a central fountain (high tea at the courtyard restaurant is a special treat); the Map Room Café, open for breakfast and lunch, is a lovely spot for having a drink and a sandwich over a good book.

The hushed, studious heart of the McKim building is the Bates Reading Room, a 200-foot-long hall with a barrel-vaulted ceiling; high, arched windows; and long tables lined with dimly lit green lamps. One artistic highlight is the 80-foot-long Sargent Gallery, which features painter John Singer Sargent's fantastical mural sequence *Triumph of Religion*, a sensual, often tempestuous journey through the gods, goddesses, and prophets of the ancient world. Other artistic works in the library include a mural sequence dedicated to the story of the search for the Holy Grail by American artist Edwin Austin Abbey, and a painting of Washington at Dorchester Heights by Emanuel Gottlieb Leutze (who also did the famous painting of Washington crossing the Delaware). Free hour-long tours of the library's art and architecture are offered at various times daily; call for times.

200 Clarendon

When it was first proposed in the 1970s, the 790-foot **200 Clarendon Street** (www.200clarendon.com) building, formerly (and still more commonly) known as the **John Hancock Tower,** was met with fierce resistance by residents who feared it would wreck the historical ambience of Copley Square. In a stroke of genius, architect I. M. Pei covered the outside of the building with reflective glass, thereby enhancing rather than overshadowing the architectural beauty of Trinity Church, the Boston Public Library, and other nearby buildings. Not everything ended happily, however—due to a design flaw, many of the 10,344 panes of glass began falling out and shattering on the sidewalk below before the building was completed. Pei later corrected the technique for hanging the glass (which he also used on the pyramid for the Louvre), and the building is now one of the most striking in the city skyline.

Nearby, the much smaller "old" John Hancock building features a beacon on top that changes color depending on the weather forecast. Many older Bostonians can still recite the rhyme that cracks the code: "Steady blue, clear view / Flashing blue, clouds due / Steady red, rain ahead / Flashing red, snow instead." During summer and fall, flashing red means the Red Sox game is cancelled due to weather conditions.

Field Guide to the Boston Accent

Listen closely on any inbound flight or train to Boston, and you're likely to hear a curious phrase from one of your fellow passengers: "park the car on Harvard yard." The sentence, sometimes called the **"Harvard Accent Test,"** isn't really a set of instructions on where to leave your vehicle, and it's been in circulation since at least the 1940s.

These days, it's often used as a litmus test for the authenticity of one's Boston accent, or your ability to fake one. Pronounced properly, it comes out something like this: *pahk the cah on Hahvahd Yahd.* When the phrase first started to appear, it was intended to distinguish not Boston accents, but Harvard accents—a distinction that's since been largely erased as speech patterns have shifted.

According to historical linguists, the Boston accent has its roots in the language patterns of early British and Irish colonists. Notoriously hard to replicate, the Boston accent has diminished somewhat in recent decades, but these characteristics still be easily spotted in the wild (or any downtown bar):

Non-rhoticity: In accents with non-rhoticity, word- and coda-final "r" turns into a vowel—this is the aspect of the Boston accent responsible for turning "park" and "car" into *pahk* and *cah.*

Father-Bother: Unlike earlier Americans, or our British counterparts, speakers of what linguists call "Standard American English" pronounce these two words as a rhyming pair—the two vowels have merged. A classic Boston accent, however, preserves the split. So when you have a go at the Harvard Accent Test, remember that the "a" in "park" and "car" should sound a little like the Standard American English pronunciation of "trap."

While Bostonians lampoon many actors' attempts to imitate their distinctive accents, a few movies make the grade. Aficionados point to Michael Keaton's accent in *Spotlight* as well as Matt Damon's Southie accent in *Good Will Hunting* as prime examples. And for any visitors traveling with their own vehicle, it might be worth nothing that parking is *not* allowed on the Harvard Yard, a grassy stretch of the campus that's safely enclosed by fences.

Christian Science Center

With a towering dome and a grand organ, this "mother church" is the international center for the Church of Christ, Scientist (not, as docents are at pains to point out, the totally unrelated Church of Scientology). Founded in 1879 by Mary Baker Eddy, the religion is best known for its practice of "faith healing" that forbids its practitioners to take medicine for illnesses. Eddy, however, was once a larger-than-life figure in U.S. culture who was a leader of the early women's movement and a pioneering publisher. Visitors can learn more about Eddy's life at the eclectic **Mary Baker Eddy Library** (200 Massachusetts Ave., 617/450-7000, www.marybakereddylibrary.org, 10am-4pm Tues.-Sun., $6 adults, $4 seniors, students, and youth 6-17, children under 6 free). A series of multimedia exhibits encourages visitors to develop their own life philosophies while at the same time tracing the evolution of its matriarch's ideas with refreshingly little proselytizing. Another exhibit within the museum literally provides a window into the newsroom of the *Christian Science Monitor,* which has its headquarters in the complex.

Within the Christian Science Center, one hidden gem deserves special mention. The **Mapparium** (200 Massachusetts Ave., 617/450-7000, www.marybakereddylibrary.org, 10am-4pm Tues.-Sun., $6 adults, $4 seniors, students, and youth 6-17, children under 6 free) is a 30-foot-diameter globe with the countries of the world (circa 1935) displayed in vibrant stained glass around the walls. Standing on a clear bridge in the center offers a remarkable perspective on a world whose borders have been dramatically rewritten by over 80 years of conflict. Twenty-minute tours of the Mapparium include a seven-minute light show with inspirational sound bites from antiapartheid leader

Nelson Mandela, First Lady Eleanor Roosevelt, and other seminal thinkers.

Fenway

Upon first glance, the area of the city known as "the Fenway" doesn't seem to offer much. A gritty network of streets lined with pubs and discount stores, the neighborhood has traditionally been the stomping grounds for students of nearby Boston University. Scratch beneath the surface, however, and you'll find several of the city's premier cultural attractions, including the Museum of Fine Arts and the jewel-box Isabella Stewart Gardner Museum. The neighborhood gets its name from the Back Bay Fens, a winding, swampy greensward that serves as the drainage channel for the city. Today, The Fens is a rambling parkland, lined with ball fields and community gardens, including the hidden Kelleher Rose Garden, a dreamy garden full of vine-covered trellises and over 100 varieties of roses. The center of the neighborhood is Kenmore Square, a lively crossroads of student bars, discount stores, and burrito joints, just down the street from the historic home of the Boston Red Sox: Fenway Park.

★ Fenway Park

A new banner was flapping in the breeze here after the Red Sox's come-from-behind race to win the 2004 World Series; more titles, in 2007 and 2013, were to come, putting to rest the legendary "Curse of the Bambino" that had seemingly denied the Sox a championship since 1918. While the high of those victories has infused **Fenway Park** (4 Yawkey Way, 617/226-6666, www.redsox.com, tours 9am-5pm daily May-Oct., 10am-5pm daily Nov.-Apr., hours differ on game days, $20 adults, $16 military, $14 children 3-12) with a new energy, Fenway has long been one of the most electric places to catch the national pastime. First opened in 1912, Fenway has a soul that none of the more modern parks can match. For the uninitiated, the geography of the park—with its Green Monster, Pesky's Pole, and Ted Williams's seat—can seem a little arcane, but you can get your bearings with a tour led by one of the Fenway faithful. As good as those tours may be, however, nothing quite beats taking a seat in the bleachers, grabbing a Sam Adams, and waiting for the first crack of the bat.

Fenway Park

Fenway

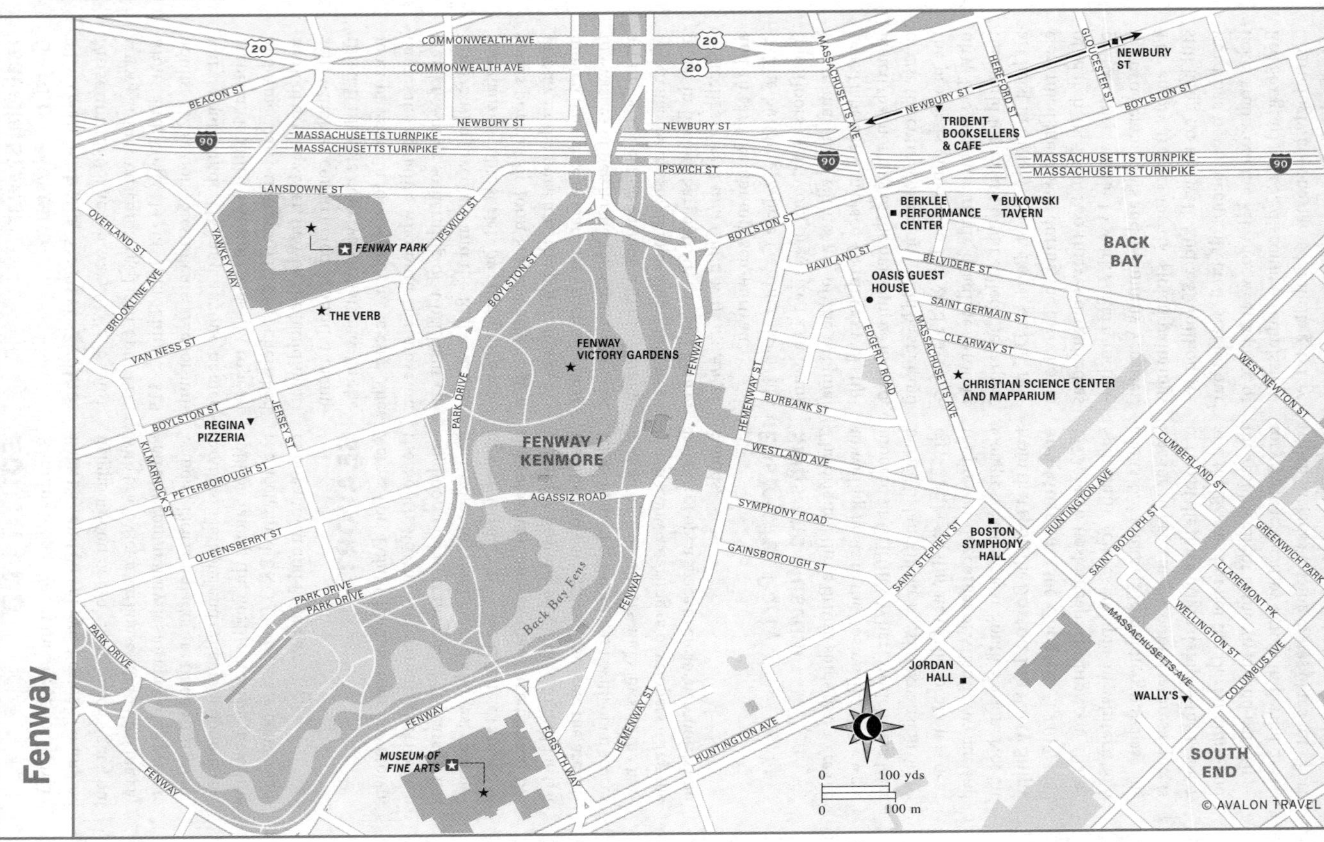
COMMONWEALTH AVE
COMMONWEALTH AVE
20
BEACON ST
NEWBURY ST
MASSACHUSETTS TURNPIKE
MASSACHUSETTS TURNPIKE
90
IPSWICH ST
LANSDOWNE ST
OVERLAND ST
YAWKEY WAY
FENWAY PARK
IPSWICH ST
BROOKLINE AVE
THE VERB
BOYLSTON ST
VAN NESS ST
FENWAY VICTORY GARDENS
PARK DRIVE
BOYLSTON ST
REGINA PIZZERIA
JERSEY ST
KILMARNOCK ST
PETERBOROUGH ST
FENWAY / KENMORE
AGASSIZ ROAD
QUEENSBERRY ST
PARK DRIVE
PARK DRIVE
Back Bay Fens
FENWAY
PARK DRIVE
FENWAY
MUSEUM OF FINE ARTS
FORSYTH WAY
HEMENWAY ST
HUNTINGTON AVE
MASSACHUSETTS AVE
HEREFORD ST
GLOUCESTER ST
NEWBURY ST
NEWBURY ST
BOYLSTON ST
TRIDENT BOOKSELLERS & CAFE
BERKLEE PERFORMANCE CENTER
BUKOWSKI TAVERN
BACK BAY
BOYLSTON ST
HAVILAND ST
BELVIDERE ST
OASIS GUEST HOUSE
SAINT GERMAIN ST
CLEARWAY ST
EDGERLY ROAD
MASSACHUSETTS AVE
CHRISTIAN SCIENCE CENTER AND MAPPARIUM
FENWAY
HEMENWAY ST
BURBANK ST
WESTLAND AVE
SYMPHONY ROAD
GAINSBOROUGH ST
SAINT STEPHEN ST
BOSTON SYMPHONY HALL
HUNTINGTON AVE
WEST NEWTON ST
CUMBERLAND ST
SAINT BOTOLPH ST
GREENWICH PARK
CLAREMONT PK
WELLINGTON ST
MASSACHUSETTS AVE
COLUMBUS AVE
JORDAN HALL
WALLY'S
SOUTH END
0 100 yds
0 100 m
© AVALON TRAVEL

Isabella Stewart Gardner Museum

The small **Isabella Stewart Gardner Museum** (280 The Fenway, 617/566-1401, www.gardnermuseum.org, 11am-5pm Fri.-Mon. and Wed., 11am-9pm Thurs., $15 adults, $12 seniors, $5 students, free for military, youth under 18, and anyone named Isabella) is filled with priceless European and American paintings. The most cherished work of art, however, may be the building itself, which is constructed around a plant-filled Italianate courtyard that may be the most pleasing indoor space in the city. The namesake socialite who built the museum was known as something of a brilliant eccentric who loved art and the Red Sox, and scandalized polite society by posing for a sensuous portrait by John Singer Sargent. (On display in the museum, the portrait was exhibited only once in Gardner's lifetime due to the wishes of her husband.) Other works of art in the collection include Titian's *Europa*, which may be the single most important work of art in Boston; Sargent's dynamic *El Jaleo*; Boticelli's *Virgin and Child with an Angel*; and an early Rembrandt self-portrait.

The building, where Gardner lived, has four floors of artwork organized as a living house museum, with some of the original typed labels still in place. Gardner's will stipulated that nothing in the museum be moved, or else the entire collection would be sold and the proceeds donated to Harvard's art faculty. The museum made headlines around the world for what's often called the largest art heist in history: As St. Patrick's Day revelers filled the streets during the early hours of March 18, 1990, two thieves disguised as police officers stole 13 works of art, including two Rembrandts and a stunning Vermeer. The empty frames for the stolen paintings still hang on the wall, and a $5 million reward has never been collected. Keep your ticket stub from the MFA (or wear a piece of Red Sox gear) for a $2 discount on admission. Charmingly, anyone named Isabella gets free entry for life.

SOUTH END

Running along the southern edge of Fenway, Back Bay, and downtown, Boston's South End neighborhood doesn't have major sights, but with brick Victorian houses and a thriving gay and arts community, it's an appealing place to wander. Pleasant parks are filled with young families. The hotel and restaurant options that spill out along the northern edge, including the acclaimed B&G Oysters, are convenient to downtown and Back Bay.

SEAPORT

Across Fort Point Channel from downtown, the South Boston waterfront district is a neighborhood in transition. For years, it has been home to New England's largest community of artists, who have taken advantage of the solid warehouses that once housed the stores for Boston's wool trade to build artist studios and performance spaces; the area itself is a visual artist's dream, with open spaces broken by iron girders and views of the harbor. It's now a darling of developers using the last bits of open space to create new hotels and condos.

Boston Tea Party Ships and Museum

The original three British ships that were the unwilling hosts to the Boston Tea Party were moored at Griffin's Wharf, which was later buried in landfill during the expansion of the city. The best estimate of the location is near the present-day corner of Atlantic Avenue and Congress Street, near South Station. Not far from that spot, the **Boston Tea Party Ships and Museum** (306 Congress St., 617/338-1773, www.bostonteapartyship.com, 10am-5pm daily (closes at 4pm in winter), $28 adults, $25 seniors, $18 children, purchase online for 10 percent discount) features replicas of two of the three original ships—the *Eleanor* and the *Beaver*, but not the *Dartmouth*—and the real highlight is the vivid, and participatory, reenactment by actors in period dress, which includes tossing crates of tea into Fort Point Channel. Among the items on display is the so-called Robinson Tea Chest, which was recovered by a participant the day after the event, and one of only two original tea chests known to survive. Early American patriots drank coffee to signal their rejection of British traditions and sovereignty, but you can still find a nice cup of tea at the on-site **Abigail's Tearoom & Terrace** (9am-6pm daily, closes an hour earlier in off-season).

Institute of Contemporary Art

The **Institute of Contemporary Art** (ICA, 25 Harbor Shore Dr., 617/478-3100, www.icaboston.org, 10am-5pm Tues.-Wed. and Sat.-Sun., 10am-9pm Thurs.-Fri., $15 adults, $13 seniors, $10 students, children under 17 free, free to all Thurs. after 5pm) was once viewed as being on par with New York's Museum of Modern Art (MoMA), on the vanguard of experimental modern art. While MoMA decided to collect the artists it exhibited and now boasts the likes of Jackson Pollock and Jasper Johns, the ICA felt that it could better remain on the cutting-edge by continually exhibiting new work. Making up for lost time, the ICA opened a new home on the waterfront in 2006, a space-age landmark that triples the size of the museum's old home in Back Bay, and more importantly added a permanent collection for the first time. In its old location, the museum garnered a reputation for staging explosive exhibitions such as the first U.S. display of the photos of Robert Mapplethorpe in the 1980s; in recent years, however, its exhibits of contemporary multimedia installations and photography have had a more uneven reception. The South Boston building, designed by edgy architectural firm Diller Scofidio + Renfro, reinvigorated the museum, providing dramatic views of the waterfront from flexible gallery spaces, and a 325-seat performing arts theater overlooking the harbor.

Boston Children's Museum

Kids can get their hands into giant bubbles, colorful art projects, and science exhibits at the fun **Boston Children's Museum** (308 Congress St., 617/426-6500, www.bostonchildrensmuseum.org, 10am-5pm Sun.-Thurs., 10am-9pm Fri., $17, children under 1 free and $1 for all admissions 5pm-9pm Fri.), which is best suited for children under the age of 11. Budding construction workers can build skyscrapers and jackhammer them down in the Construction Zone; little monkeys can tackle a brightly colored maze of tunnels, towers, and walkways called the Climb; and families can explore an authentic Japanese tea merchant's shop imported from Kyoto, a gift from Boston's sister city.

CAMBRIDGE

Two of the country's most iconic universities—Harvard and the Massachusetts Institute of Technology (MIT)—are just across the Charles River from downtown Boston in historic, quirky Cambridge. These are just a couple of the over 100 colleges and universities in the Greater Boston area, and a regular influx of students is part of what keeps Boston eternally young and energetic. Head across the river to get a taste of the intellectual scene; Cambridge is about three miles from downtown Boston and easily reached on the Massachusetts Bay Transportation Authority (MBTA) Red Line (Harvard station).

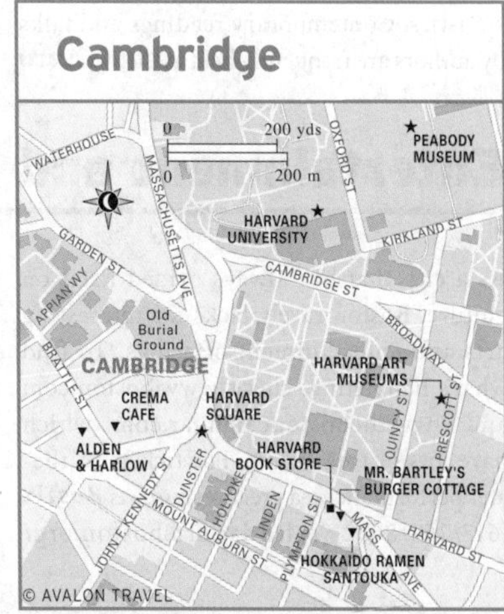

Harvard University

Download an audio tour and map to take a self-guided trip around the Harvard campus, or start the trip like a prospective undergrad on a student-led **Harvard Campus Tour** (1350 Massachusetts Ave., 617/495-1573, www.harvard.edu, free tours Mon.-Sat. 9am-5pm) that takes in the best of the university's green quads, landmark libraries, and that famous Harvard Yard.

Three separate facilities make up the **Harvard Art Museums** (32 Quincy St., 617/495-9400, www.harvardartmuseums.org, 10am-5pm daily, $15 adults, $13 seniors, $10 non-Harvard students, children under 18 free) and Harvard's **Peabody Museum** (11 Divinity Ave., Cambridge, 617/496-1027, www.peabody.harvard.edu, 9am-5pm daily, $12 adults, $10 seniors and students, $8 children 3-18, children under 3 free) is one of the oldest anthropological museums in the world.

Many of Boston and Cambridge's schools open their doors to the public for lectures by speakers from around the world. The **Harvard University *Gazette*** (www.news.harvard.edu/gazette) publishes a full schedule of talks. At Harvard you can even **attend a class** (www.college.harvard.edu/visitors-guide-larger-lectures) on anything from East Asian cinema to post-Hamlet literature and statistics. Contemporary readings and talks by authors are frequently held at the **Harvard Book Store** (1256 Massachusetts Ave., 800/542-7323, www.harvard.com).

Campus life spills into the streets at **Harvard Square** (Massachusetts Ave. and Brattle St., www.harvardsquare.com), a bustling plaza lined with shops and restaurants. Chain outlets have dimmed some of the spot's independent charm, but there are still enough buskers, artists, and studious undergraduates to make it an inviting destination.

Massachusetts Institute of Technology (MIT)

Head to **MIT** (77 Massachusetts Ave., www.web.mit.edu, 617/253-1000, free tours, call for times) for a tour of the striking campus, whose blend of old-fashioned architecture and modernist, cutting-edge buildings offers a wonderful study in contrasts. No surprise: MIT's whiz engineers also designed a **mobile app campus tour** that you can download from iTunes and Google Play. Tours are primarily for prospective students and their families; check in with the Office of Admissions on the day of your visit to see if you can join a tour.

The **MIT Museum** (265 Massachusetts Ave., 617/253-5927, www.web.mit.edu/museum, 10am-5pm daily, until 6pm July-Aug., $10 adults, $5 seniors, students, and children, children under 5 free) traces the history of science, engineering, and research. The school also publishes a full schedule of talks (www.events.mit.edu).

Entertainment and Events

As a city that has always prided itself on culture, Boston rarely lacks for interesting arts and entertainment offerings. To find what's happening, check www.boston.com and www.thebostoncalendar.com, which have lots of free events. For tickets to theater performances, a great resource is **BosTix** (617/262-8632, calendar.artsboston.org/booth-hours-locations), which offers half-price tickets the day of the show. Booths are located in the **Faneuil Hall Marketplace** (1 Faneuil Hall Sq., 617/262-8632, 10am-4pm Tues.-Sun.) and **Copley Square** (650 Boylston St., 11am-5pm Thurs.-Fri., 10am-4pm Sat.-Sun.). Hours can vary, so call or check the website before stopping by.

NIGHTLIFE

Bars

BEACON HILL

Last call for the sitcom *Cheers* was in 1993, but the Beacon Hill bar where the exterior shots were filmed is still a serious destination. Life imitates art at **Cheers on Beacon Hill** (84 Beacon St., 617/227-9605, www.cheersboston.com, 11am-1am daily), formerly the Bull & Finch Pub, where the upstairs has been reinvented as the fictitious television bar, complete with brass nameplates for the "regulars." There is a second location at Faneuil Hall, but it's worth heading to the original, which has a bit more charm to go with the cheese.

An oasis of blue-collar culture (or at least off-duty lawyers) with a tony address, **Beacon Hill Pub** (149 Charles St., 617/625-7100, 10am-2am daily, cash only) is a great spot to pull up a stool and catch a game.

The menu at chef Barbara Lynch's **No. 9 Park** (9 Park St., 617/742-9991, www.no9park.com, 5:30pm-9pm Sun.-Mon., 5:30pm-10pm Tues.-Sat., bar stays open later) includes hard-to-find bottles and old-world varietals that earned the wine program a James Beard Award. Though it's primarily a restaurant, the quiet bar is an elegant place to enjoy a glass and a snack from the à la carte menu.

DOWNTOWN AND THE WATERFRONT

The most iconic bars in Boston fall firmly into "dive bar" territory—the kind of sticky, beer-soaked neighborhood joints where St. Patrick's Day memories are forged (or erased). One classic of the genre is **The Tam** (222 Tremont St., 617/482-9182, 8am-1am Sun.-Thurs., 8am-2am Fri.-Sat., cash only), a morning-to-night destination for cheap beer, loud music, and a gruff crowd of locals. Another downtown favorite is **Biddy Early's** (141 Pearl St., 617/654-9944, 10am-2am daily), where Irish-themed decor and PBR Sriracha chicken wings pair beautifully with dartboards and arcade games.

All dark wood and scuffed signboards, the **Green Dragon Tavern** (11 Marshall St., 617/367-0055, 11am-2am daily) evokes the 1654 bar by the same name that Daniel Webster called the "Headquarters of the Revolution." The original was knocked down in 1854, but the new version is atmospheric and cozy, with an old-world feel and live music most nights.

There's an excellent selection of beers from around New England at **jm Curley** (21 Temple Pl., 617/228-5333, 11:30am-2am daily), along with very credible cocktails and fresh bar food. Bacon popcorn is a favorite here.

Some of the finest cocktails in town are at the ultra-stylish, nostalgic **Yvonne's** (2 Winter Pl., 617/267-0047, www.yvonnesboston.com, 4pm-2am daily), a Downtown Crossing supper club with two great places to drink (and take selfies): Settle in at the grand mahogany bar or grab a spot in the "library," which is lined with designer-selected vintage titles.

Quirky Victorian-era ephemera—black-and-white images of shirtless boxers, framed corsets—give **Stoddards Fine Food & Ale** (48 Temple Pl., 617/426-0048, www.stoddardsfoodandale.com, 11:30am-1am Tues.-Wed., 11:30am-2am Thurs.-Sat., 11:30am-midnight Sun.) a time-warp feel. Classic cocktails are listed by year, stretching back to the 1850s-era Sazerac, but the solid beer list is strictly 21st century.

Many of Boston's finest Irish bars are buried in hard-to-reach neighborhoods, but despite its downtown location, **Mr. Dooley's** (77 Broad St., 617/338-5656, www.mrdooleys.com, 11:30am-2am Mon.-Fri., 9am-2am Sat.-Sun.) is the real deal. Pints of Guinness and Jameson shots go well with live Irish music most weekend nights. Come ready to sing along to all the classics.

NORTH END

Somewhere between chic Italian bistro and fantasy Prohibition-era speakeasy, **Parla** (230 Hanover St., 617/367-2824, www.parlaboston.com, 4:30pm-10:45pm Mon.-Tues., 4:30pm-11:15pm Wed., 4:30pm-midnight Thurs.-Fri., 11am-midnight Sat., 11am-11:15pm Sun.)

infuses its cocktail list with seasonal ingredients and offbeat flavors, but the gorgeous space alone is worth the visit.

The North End take on the Boston dive bar is **Corner Cafe** (87 Prince St., 617/523-8997, 9am-2am Mon.-Sat., noon-2am Sun.), where locals scratch lottery tickets, drink cheap draft beer, and slurp up pudding shots (which are better than they sound). The real secret, however, is that Corner Cafe invites patrons to order food from outside, so you can grab a beer and call for a Regina's pizza.

FENWAY AND BACK BAY

In the spirit of the raunchy, beer-loving poet, the **Bukowski Tavern** (50 Dalton St., 617/437-9999, 11:30am-2am Mon.-Sat., noon-2am Sun.) has a gleefully unreconstructed feeling, but with a good draft list that transcends the usual dive bar pours.

Generic, somewhat corporate decor almost seems like a smoke screen for the incredible draft list at **The Lower Depths** (476 Commonwealth Ave., 617/266-6662, www.thelowerdepths.com, 11:30am-1am daily), which often includes cask beers and unusual brews from around the East.

Think outside the margarita at the gothic-themed **Lolita Cocina & Tequila Bar** (271 Dartmouth St., 617/369-5609, www.lolitatequilabars.com, 4pm-2am daily), where tufted black leather and red lights meet a menu of sophisticated cocktails. Mixed drinks are both fresh and fierce, but there's also an appealing menu of house-made nonalcoholic drinks. The dessert menu is legendary.

Live Music

The South End's **Wally's** (427 Massachusetts Ave., 617/424-1408, www.wallyscafe.com) hosts jazz the way it was meant to be played, in a closet-sized room that heats up both on and off stage. Meanwhile, the nearby "Harvard of jazz," the Berklee School of Music, sponsors performances of both modern legends and up-and-coming prodigies at its **Berklee Performance Center** (136 Massachusetts Ave., 617/747-2261, www.berklee.edu/BPC), which also occasionally has folk and pop acts.

In addition to **Boston Symphony Hall** (301 Massachusetts Ave., 617/266-1492 or 888/266-1200, www.bso.org), Boston has many excellent smaller halls that regularly offer classical concerts. These include New England Conservatory's acoustically refined **Jordan Hall** (30 Gainsborough St., 617/585-1260, www.necmusic.edu/jordan-hall) and Boston University's **Tsai Performance Center** (685 Commonwealth Ave., 617/353-8725, www.bu.edu/tsai).

A little-known choral gem, **Emmanuel Music** (15 Newbury St., 617/536-3356, www.emmanuelmusic.org) performs entire Bach masses on Sunday at Emmanuel Church. **Trinity Boston** (206 Clarendon St., 617/536-0944, www.trinitychurchboston.org) performs half-hour organ recitals on Friday at 12:15pm, as well as occasional choral concerts in one of the most beautiful settings in Boston—Copley Square's Trinity Church.

FESTIVALS AND EVENTS

Everyone gets a little Irish for **St. Patrick's Day** in Boston, which is celebrated with a parade through South Boston streets decked in shamrock green. In April, runners come from around the world to compete in the **Boston Marathon,** the oldest (and some say toughest) marathon in the United States. Spectators start lining the route to cheer along Beacon and Boylston Streets, all the way to Copley Square, where the finish line is painted in the street. Americans from around the country tune in to the Boston Pops performance on the **Fourth of July,** when the esplanade becomes a gallery for a fabulous fireworks show.

Numerous (often free) events take place throughout the summer months, from open-air **Shakespeare on Boston Common** (www.commshakes.org) to **outdoor concerts.** A good resource for finding current event listings is www.bostonusa.com.

Shopping

FANEUIL HALL MARKETPLACE

Touristy? Yes. Pricey? Also. But the **Faneuil Hall Marketplace** (4 S. Market St., 617/523-1300, www.faneuilhallmarketplace.com, 10am-9pm Mon.-Sat., 11am-7pm Sun.) is an outdoor mall where you can pick up all your Boston-themed souvenirs. **Best of Boston** (54 N. Market Bldg., Faneuil Hall Marketplace, 617/227-3962, 10am-9pm Mon.-Sat., noon-6pm Sun.) has a colorful selection of lobster shot glasses, Red Sox gear, saltwater taffy, and "Boston Tea Party"-brand tea for drinking or throwing in the harbor.

CHARLES STREET

Charles Street in Beacon Hill has some 40 antiques stores crammed into 0.33 mile; one of the best is **Upstairs Downstairs Antiques** (93 Charles St., 617/367-1950, 11am-6pm Sun.-Fri., 10am-6pm Sat.), a warren of rooms stuffed with tableware, glassware, and other knickknacks from a dozen decades. Armchair historians and explorers alike thrill at the selection of antique maps and charts at **Eugene Galleries** (76 Charles St., 617/227-3062, 11am-6pm Mon.-Sat., 11am-5pm Sun.), which cover Boston, New England, and the rest of the world.

NEWBURY STREET

The place to shop for high-end, stylish clothes is Back Bay's stylish **Newbury Street,** which carries outposts of international designers from Armani to Zegna, alongside local boutiques.

Newbury Street also hosts the most prestigious art galleries in the city. The biggest name on the street is the **Krakow Witkin Gallery** (10 Newbury St., 617/262-4490, www.krakowwitkingallery.com, 10am-5:30pm Tues.-Sat.), which draws nationally known contemporary artists. More traditional paintings and prints are on display at the venerable **Childs Gallery** (169 Newbury St., 617/266-1108, www.childsgallery.com, 9am-6pm Tues.-Fri., 11am-5pm Sat.-Sun.), which focuses on pre-World War II American and European work.

The kind of shop where you can settle in with a coffee and a good read, **Trident Booksellers & Cafe** (338 Newbury St., 617/267-8688, www.tridentbookscafe.com, 8am-midnight daily) has a wonderful selection of titles and hosts frequent author events and reading.

DOWNTOWN CROSSING

Most of the shopping in this bustling district is of the big-name, big-store variety, with names like H&M and Primark lining Washington Street, Summer Street, and Winter Street. One long-standing exception to downtown's plate glass window displays is **Brattle Book Shop** (9 West St., 617/542-0210, www.brattlebookshop.com, 9am-5:30pm Mon.-Sat.), where three stories cannot contain a collection of books that spills beyond the bookstore and into the adjoining alley, whose brick walls are painted with the images of iconic authors.

HARVARD SQUARE

There are still some locally owned gems among the chain stores that have crept into this triangular plaza. The thoughtfully curated **Black Ink** (5 Brattle St., Cambridge, 617/497-1221, www.blackinkboston.squarespace.com, 10am-8pm Mon.-Sat., 11am-7pm Sun.) is ideal for gifts, pretty stationery, and what the shop accurately calls "unexpected necessities." With time-warp charm and all sorts of quirk, **Leavitt & Peirce** (1316 Massachusetts Ave., Cambridge, 617/547-0576, www.leavittandpeirce.com, 9am-6pm Mon.-Wed. and Fri.-Sat., 9am-8pm Thurs., noon-5:30pm Sun.) has been Harvard's tobacconist since 1884, but also stocks a trove of games and gentlemanly gifts like cufflinks and shaving brushes. Another fun place to browse is **Goorin Bros. Hat Shop** (43 Brattle St., Cambridge, 617/868-4287, www.goorin.com, 10am-8pm Mon.-Sat., 11am-7pm Sun.), which has everything from ball caps to fedoras to Kentucky Derby wear.

Sports and Recreation

HIKING AND BIKING

Watch pink- and white-sailed dinghies tack and jibe along the shore from the **Charles River Esplanade** (www.esplanadeassociation.org), which comprises three miles of waterfront stretching from the Museum of Science to the Boston University Bridge and crisscrossed with running and biking trails. The trails are especially charming in the springtime, when blossom-laden cherry trees arch over portions of the path.

Landscape architect Frederick Law Olmsted designed a series of parks known as the **Emerald Necklace** (www.emeraldnecklace.org) that stretches from the Back Bay Fens to Forest Hills and the Arnold Arboretum, with walking and biking trails throughout. One highlight of the Back Bay Fens park is the **Fenway Victory Gardens** (www.fenwayvictorygardens.org)—while it's indistinguishable from the many community gardens that have been appearing in cities across the United States, this 7.5-acre plot was planted during World War II to supplement strained food supplies. It's the oldest continually operating garden of its kind in the country, and the 500 garden plots are now waitlist-only growing spaces for Boston residents.

When the "Big Dig" construction project put I-93 underground, it created 15 acres of surface-level space that's been transformed into the **Rose Kennedy Greenway** (www.rosekennedygreenway.org), a slender line of parks that runs 1.5 miles from the Chinatown Gate to North End Park. One highlight of the parks is the **Greenway Carousel** (Atlantic Ave. and Cross St., 888/239-7616, $3), whose colorful animals are all Massachusetts natives—don't miss the chance to ride a codfish, peregrine falcon, whale, or lobster. You'll also find some wonderful art along the way; exhibits change seasonally, but past installments have featured Chinese artist Ai Weiwei and abstract pieces with a focus on local history and nature. Many of the seven water fountains along the greenway are strategically designed for cooling off in the Boston summer. Favorites with the wading toddler crowd include the **Rings Fountain** (Central St. and Cross St.), **North & South Canal Fountains** (Cross St. and Hanover St.), and interactive **Harbor Fog Fountain** (High St. and Cross St.), where movement sensors trigger great billows of cooling mist.

BOATING

Boston Harbor remains a transportation hub for the region, and **Boston Harbor Cruises** (www.bostonharborcruises.com) runs convenient boat service to **Salem** (1 hr., round-trip ticket $45 adults, $41 seniors, $35 children 3-11) and **Provincetown** (1.5 hrs., round-trip ticket $59 adults, $55 seniors, $39 children 3-11, $23 children under 3) that are good alternatives to driving. To simply get views of the city from the water, though, take a turn on its **Historic Sightseeing Cruise** (1.5 hrs., tickets $28.95 adults, $26.95 seniors, $24.95 children 3-11), which loops along the shoreline of the inner and outer harbor to the historic Boston Light and the Harbor Islands.

Take in the harbor under sail with the **Liberty Fleet** (617/742-0333, www.libertyfleet.com, cruises $30-45 adults, $24 children under 12), which offers day sails, sunset sails, and a "Rum and Revelry" sail with costumed actors and drinks. The schooner *Liberty Clipper* is the flagship, a 125-foot gaff-rigged replica of the Baltimore Clipper-style ships prized by fast-moving privateers during the American Revolution and War of 1812. Her little sister is the 67-foot *Liberty Star*, whose classic lines are modeled on 19th-century coastal schooners—crews onboard both ships are friendly and experienced, and the sails can be as hands-on (or off) as desired.

All those postcard-ready sailboats on the Charles River belong to **Community Boating** (21 Mugar Way, 617/523-1038, www.community-boating.org, 3pm-sunset Mon.-Fri., 9am-sunset Sat.-Sun. Apr.-Oct.), an institution on the Charles River Esplanade since the 1940s. Nonmembers can rent a stand-up paddleboard or kayak for $45—a single and a double kayak cost the same, so paddling with a friend is half the price.

SPECTATOR SPORTS

With baseball, hockey, and basketball, Boston has an almost year-round sports season, with fervor to match. Most iconic are the **Red Sox** (877/733-7699, www.mlb.com/redsox) baseball team, and after suffering through the 86-year-long "Curse of the Bambino," it can finally bring home pennants again (the Red Sox sold legendary player Babe Ruth to the New York Yankees after winning the 1918 championship, and didn't catch a break until the 2004 World Series). The hockey-playing **Bruins** (617/624-2327, www.nhl.com/bruins) are another passion-inspiring team and the oldest National Hockey League team in the United States. And while the 1980s heyday of Larry Bird, Kevin McHale, and Robert Parrish has not returned, the **Celtics** (866/423-5849, www.nba.com/celtics) still pack the TD Garden to the gills. Gillette Stadium, located about halfway between Boston and Providence in Foxborough, Massachusetts, is home to the perennial Super Bowl champion **New England Patriots** (800/543-1776, www.patriots.com).

Food

BEACON HILL

The open kitchen at **The Paramount** (44 Charles St., 617/720-1152, www.paramountboston.com, 7am-10pm Mon.-Fri., 8am-10pm Sat.-Sun., $8-24) slings fresh, flavorful diner fare at breakfast and lunch: Try the caramel banana French toast, huevos rancheros, hefty salads, and sandwiches. Dinner gets a bit more grown-up with pasta dishes and entrées like citrus-brined chicken statler and steak frites. Lines can get long at this neighborhood favorite, so it's a good option to call ahead for sandwiches and have a picnic in Boston Public Garden, which is just a couple of blocks away. If you do dine in, you'll order and pay for your food at the counter, then sit down when your meal arrives.

Tucked down a brick-lined side street, **75 Chestnut** (75 Chestnut St., 617/227-2175, www.75chestnut.com, dinner 5pm-11pm Sun.-Thurs., 5pm-midnight Fri.-Sat., brunch 10:30am Sat., $11-30) is a cozy neighborhood bistro that's refined enough for a romantic evening out. The dinner menu includes classic seafood dishes and pasta, salads, steaks, and a few burgers. Brunch is especially popular here, with a short but appealing menu and a Bloody Mary bar.

Bright and stylish, **Tatte Bakery & Café** (70 Charles St., 617/723-5555, www.tattebakery.com, 7am-8pm Mon.-Fri., 8am-8pm Sat., 8am-7pm Sun., $5.50-13.50) is a good spot to nibble something sweet and watch locals drift in and out of the cozy space. Pastries are the star of the show, but there's also an appealing lineup of sandwiches and lunch items.

DOWNTOWN AND THE WATERFRONT

Orator Daniel Webster downed brandy and oysters here, and John F. Kennedy loved to sip lobster bisque in booth 18; **Union Oyster**

House (41 Union St., 617/227-2750, www.unionoysterhouse.com, 11am-9:30pm Sun.-Thurs., 11am-10pm Fri.-Sat., bar open until midnight, $13-34) is the oldest operating restaurant in the United States, and if it's acquired a few overpriced dishes, a cheesy gift shop, and a pile of Olde New Englande tat over the years, it's easy to forgive over a bowl of super-creamy clam chowder. Find all the classics here, from Boston baked beans to baked scrod, but if you just want to soak up the historic atmosphere, grab a drink and a half-dozen oysters at the downstairs raw bar or the darkly colonial-looking Union Bar.

One might never suspect this laid-back, counter-service lunch place of having the "World's No. 1 Sandwiches," but ★ **Sam LaGrassa's** (44 Province St., 617/357-6861, www.samlagrassas.com, 11am-3:30pm Mon.-Fri., $9-13) has a passionate following that lines up for enormous deli sandwiches and chowder. Roast beef and Reubens are served in classic style here, piled high with deli meat, but it's the pastrami that made this place famous. Most sandwiches can easily serve two people.

Find Chilean sandwiches piled with freshly grilled meat, veggies, and Muenster cheese at **Chacarero** (101 Arch St., 617/542-0392, www.chacarero.com, 8am-6pm Mon.-Fri., $7-10), a pocket-sized sandwich shop beloved by locals. The secret ingredient: green beans.

A little, family-run "shack" on the waterfront, **James Hook & Co.** (15-17 Northern Ave., 617/423-5501, www.jameshooklobster.com, 10am-5pm Mon.-Thurs. and Sat., 10am-6pm Fri., 10am-4pm Sun., $19-24) sells live lobsters and seafood, but it's worth stopping by for the truly satisfying (though quite pricey) lobster rolls—just mayonnaise, hot dog bun, fresh meat, and no fuss. A few tables for sitting are located outside, or you can bring your roll down to the waterfront harborwalk.

It is possible to order the namesake sandwiches at ★ **Gene's Chinese Flatbread Cafe** (86 Bedford St., 617/482-1888, 11am-6:30pm Mon.-Fri., 11:30am-7pm Sat., $5-11), but the real draw is the hand-pulled noodles that come doused in garlicky oil, mild chili powder, fresh herbs, and green onions. The noodles are a chewy delight, and Gene's is one of the only places in New England where you can find the traditional food.

The sushi and Japanese small plates at ★ **O Ya** (9 East St., 617/654-9900, www.o-ya.restaurant, 5pm-9:30pm Tues.-Thurs., 5pm-10pm Fri.-Sat., $50-70) are both creative and exquisite, and meals here are consistently ranked among the best in the city. For an all-out feast, try the 21-course tasting menu that includes one of the chef's signature dishes: Kumamoto oyster nigiri is a warm, fried oyster atop a tiny bed of rice and seaweed, topped with a froth of ethereal squid ink. In keeping with the culinary artistry, the decor is modern, simple, and elegant.

North End trattorias have the low lights and Chianti candles on lock, but **Erbaluce** (69 Church St., 617/426-6969, www.erbaluce-boston.com, 5pm-10pm Tues.-Thurs. and Sun., 5pm-11pm Fri.-Sat., $30-50) offers a more contemporary, sophisticated experience. Minimalist decor pairs well with the chef's use of simple, full-flavored northern Italian recipes and super-fresh ingredients.

Boston Public Market (100 Hanover St., 617/973-4909, www.bostonpublicmarket.org, 8am-8pm Mon.-Sat., 10am-8pm Sun.) is a covered, year-round market space with dozens of local vendors selling prepared foods, products, and groceries.

★ NORTH END

There's always a line out the door of ★ **Regina Pizzeria** (11½ Thatcher St., 617/227-0765, www.reginapizzeria.com, 11am-11:30pm Sun.-Thurs., 11am-12:30am Fri.-Sat., $8-16), but joining the line is part of the fun at this landmark destination. The kitchen turns out blistered, lightly blackened pies topped with traditional Neapolitan ingredients, but it's the crust that really shines: The pizzaoli in the open kitchen throw disks of dough that are chewy, thin, and just slightly uneven, truly some of the best in town. Walls are decked with streamers and signs from

Italian coffee shop in Boston's North End

neighborhood saints' days, tables are closely packed, and service is brusque—with a bit of a North End swagger (either native or adopted). When waits are long, large groups might do well to go elsewhere, but someone regularly goes down the line plucking out pairs and singles for seats at the bar.

Stop by **Monica's Mercato** (130 Salem St., 617/742-4101, www.monicasboston.com, 9:30am-11pm daily, $6-12) at lunchtime, and you'll order your sub or pizza alongside a line of North End cops, construction workers, and longtime locals—it's a good omen that doesn't disappoint. Sandwiches are layered with freshly sliced prosciutto, salami, and Italian cheeses, bathed in extra-virgin olive oil and balsamic vinegar and wrapped to go. There's no seating in this shoebox-sized deli, but it's a five-minute walk to the North End Park, where you'll find shaded tables, park benches, and a series of fountains that keep things cool on the steamiest Boston afternoons.

It would be easy to miss little **Polcari's Coffee** (105 Salem St., 617/227-0786, www.polcariscoffee.com, 10am-6pm Mon.-Fri., 9am-6pm Sat., Italian ice $2-3), a shop that's weighed out the neighborhood's espresso beans and spices on a pair of great brass scales since 1932. In the warm months, though, Polcari's scoops cups full of fine-grained, lemony Italian ice that's unbelievably refreshing on a hot day.

Whether you're sipping a morning cappuccino or an amaro nightcap, the marble-topped tables at **Caffé Vittoria** (290-296 Hanover St., 617/227-7606, www.caffevittoria.com, 7am-midnight Sun.-Thurs., 7am-12:30am Fri.-Sat., $3-9, cash only) are perfect for watching North End life drift by. Every surface of this old-world café is covered in antique espresso machines, vintage Italian posters, and other memorabilia. Cappuccinos come under a melting layer of powdered chocolate, and the late-night menu of cordials—these include herbal amari and sweet sips like crema di limoncello—are perfect with traditional Italian desserts.

An island of contemporary style in the thoroughly old-school North End, ★ **Neptune Oyster** (63 Salem St., 617/742-3474, www.neptuneoyster.com, 11:30am-10pm Sun.-Thurs., 11:30am-11pm Fri.-Sat., $22-39) gets a lot of hype and deserves every bit of it. The big, buttery lobster rolls are the best in Boston, but the creative seafood menu skims through the world's great coastal cuisines: Try Acadian-style redfish and chips, Veracruz-style mackerel, or North End cioppino. Raw bar offerings include East and West Coast oysters along with a rotating lineup of what's fresh. The line starts well before the doors open for lunch, and the tiny space can be cramped and loud.

Another neighborhood favorite with a constant line, **Giacomo's Ristorante** (355 Hanover St., 617/523-9026, 4:30pm-10pm Mon.-Thurs., 4:30pm-11pm Fri.-Sat., 4:30pm-9:30pm Sun., $16-26) serves huge portions of Italian American favorites like baked ziti, eggplant parmesan, and veal marsala in a simple brick dining room. Cash only.

Don't leave the North End without a

string-wrapped box filled with traditional Italian sweets. The classic cannoli rivalry is between a pair of legendary shops geographically close enough for a head-to-head comparison. The versions at **Mike's Pastry** (300 Hanover St., 617/742-3050, www.mikespastry.com, 8am-10pm Sun.-Thurs., 8am-11:30pm Fri.-Sat., $2-8) are hefty and sweet, overflowing with ricotta filling. ★ **Modern Pastry** (257 Hanover St., 617/523-3783, www.modernpastry.com, 8am-10pm Sun.-Thurs., 8am-11pm Fri., 8am-midnight Sat., $2-8) has a slight edge, serving smaller, more delicate cannolo that are filled on the spot.

Far less flashy and famous, **Maria's Pastry** (46 Cross St., 617/523-1196, www.mariaspastry.com, 7am-7pm Mon.-Sat., 7am-5pm Sun., $2-8) has a passionate cadre of supporters who swear by the *sfogliatelle* that overflow with luscious vanilla cream.

In the North End, little Italian markets are the ideal place to stock up for a picnic of cured meats and imported cheeses; one favorite is **Salumeria Italiana** (151 Richmond St., 617/523-8743, www.salumeriaitaliana.com, 8am-7pm Mon.-Sat., 10am-4pm Sun.), which also has fabulous deli sandwiches.

FENWAY AND BACK BAY

In a convenient spot by Copley Square, **Dig Inn** (557 Boylston St., www.diginn.com, 10am-10pm daily, $11-30) has a fresh menu of mix-and-match dishes that emphasize sustainable values and ingredients sourced directly from producers. Choose from a list of proteins including wild-caught fish, tofu, and farm-raised meats and add whole grains and sides, or snack on lighter options like avocado toast or a roasted kale salad. This restaurant is part of a small chain based in New York City.

Another fabulous place for something sweet is **Flour + Bakery Cafe** (131 Clarendon St., 617/437-7700, www.flourbakery.com, 6:30am-8pm Mon.-Fri., 8am-6pm Sat., 8am-5pm Sun., $3-9), one of four locations in the Boston area run by master pastry chef Joanne Chang. You'll find sandwiches and salads enough for a fine, upstanding lunch, but it's the lusciously sugary tarts, rolls, buns, and pies that bring in the crowds—a particular favorite is Chang's sticky bun, a mammoth treat that's surprisingly light beneath a coating of caramel and pecans.

Somewhat out of the way on the western side of Fenway, ★ **Mei Mei** (506 Park Dr., 857/250-4959, www.meimeiboston.com, 11am-9pm Sun. and Tues.-Wed., 11am-10pm Thurs.-Sat., $7-19) is worth the trek and an easy, five-minute walk from the Fenway T station. It's a fun, welcoming place run by the Li siblings—one brother and two sisters—who bring a lighthearted approach to a menu that leans Chinese American but doesn't shy away from eclectic dishes like pierogi or mac and cheese (which gets a whiff of Chinese heat from a spicy *gochujang* cheese sauce). Mei Mei's most famous creation, though, is its oozy, savory sandwich the Double Awesome: pesto, cheese, eggs, and meat layered between two flaky scallion pancakes.

The Boston Public Library's Italianate courtyard is a glorious place to linger in the summer—the fountain and deep, shady arcades keep it cool on even the hottest days—but many visitors never discover the restaurant overlooking the elegant spot. Stop by ★ **The Courtyard Restaurant** (700 Boylston St., 617/859-2282, www.thecatereredaffair.com, 11:30am-3:30pm Mon.-Sat., afternoon tea $49 adults with champagne, $39 without, $19 children with hot chocolate, $15 without) for the elegant high tea, and nibble on tiered platters of savory sandwiches, sweet petit fours, and scones with cream . . . and a freshly brewed pot of tea.

Small markets abound in the city, but the most convenient is the **Copley Square Boston Farmers Market** (11am-6pm Tues. and Fri. early May-late Nov.), where farmers, bakers, and chefs set up right across the street from the Boston Public Library.

SOUTH END

The treats at ★ **Blackbird Doughnuts** (492 Tremont St., 617/482-9000, www.blackbirddoughnuts.com, 7am-6pm Mon.-Fri.,

8am-6pm Sat.-Sun., $3-5) are displayed individually on cake pedestals, speared with little flags that make them look like tiny, recently discovered islands. Pillowy raised doughnuts come in flavors like salted toffee, passion fruit, and the oozing PB&J Bismarck, but the namesake sweet is a cake doughnut. The Blackbird signature flavor is a vanilla bean old-fashioned with vanilla bean glaze. Pick up treats to go, as this tiny shop has no seating.

A strong competitor for Boston's best breakfasts, ★ **Mike & Patty's** (12 Church St., 617/423-3447, www.mikeandpattys.com, 8am-2pm Mon.-Tues., 7:30am-2pm Wed.-Fri., 7:30am-2:30pm Sat.-Sun., $5-11) is a hole-in-the-wall corner café with just a handful of stools—which is why the sidewalk is filled with patrons on sunny days, enjoying egg sandwiches fresh from the griddle. Order it "classic" with American cheese and egg on an English muffin, or go "fancy" to get the works. Orders for pickup can be placed on the website.

An "indie diner" with a colorful, irreverent attitude, **Myers + Chang** (1145 Washington St., 617/542-5200, www.myersandchang.com, 11:30am-10pm Sun.-Thurs., 11:30am-11pm Fri.-Sat., $15-20) has a generous menu that ranges from dim sum brunch (on weekends) to noodle soup, Asian-influenced mains, home-style Indonesian food, and anything else that appeals to the talented kitchen. This is an especially good choice on Monday and Tuesday's "cheap date nights," with $45 prix fixe menus for two.

CAMBRIDGE

Harvard Square is jam-packed with places to recover from hard-core learning (and sightseeing). For something that transcends the budget student joints, **Alden & Harlow** (40 Brattle St., 617/864-2100, www.aldenharlow.com, 5pm-1am Mon.-Wed., 5pm-2am Thurs.-Fri., 10:30am-2pm and 5pm-2am Sat., 10:30am-2:30pm and 5pm-1am Sun., $25-35) serves exquisite, ingredient-focused small plates like fried quail, bass crudo, and chicken liver pâté.

Nostalgic alumni are sure to stop by **Mr. Bartley's Burger Cottage** (1246 Massachusetts Ave., 617/354-6559, www.mrbartley.com, 11am-9pm Tues.-Sat., $13-19) for burgers with jokey names and wonderfully crispy onion rings.

Sunny **Crema Café** (27 Brattle St., 617/876-2700, www.cremacambridge.com, 7am-9pm Mon.-Fri., 8am-9pm Sat.-Sun., $3-6) has big communal tables that give the independent coffee shop a friendly, social feel; you'll also find breakfast sandwiches and sweet treats.

Fill up on great bowls of ramen and snacks like *takoyaki* (octopus-filled battered balls) and *gyoza* (dumplings) at **Hokkaido Ramen Santouka** (1 Bow St., 617/945-1460, www.santouka-usa.com, 11am-9:30pm Mon.-Thurs., 11am-10:30pm Fri.-Sat., 11am-9pm Sun., $12-20), a chic, modern outpost of a Japanese chain that's popular with just about everybody.

Accommodations

Because Boston is so compact, all the following listings are good choices for accessing the city's main sights and attractions. They won't come cheap—Boston is among the most expensive cities in the United States for hotels and Airbnb. There are some wonderful options, however, and it's worth booking well in advance to secure a spot.

BEACON HILL

$150-250

A quaint bed-and-breakfast on the back of Beacon Hill, the ★ **John Jeffries House** (14 Mugar Way, 617/367-1866, www.johnjeffrieshouse.com, $200-335) has spartan but comfortable rooms that were originally quarters for nurses at the nearby Massachusetts Eye and Ear Infirmary. There are small kitchenettes in each room, a continental breakfast is served in the common space, and guests get a discounted rate at the Charles Street garage ($40 for 24 hrs.). Try for a room with a view of the Charles River.

$250-350

The **Beacon Hill Hotel and Bistro** (25 Charles St., 617/723-7575, www.beaconhillhotel.com, $249-449) is right in the heart of the action in this fashionable, historic neighborhood. The rooms are smallish, but charming and sweetly decorated. A full breakfast is served in the downstairs bistro, or can be brought to your room. The real star of this boutique hotel is the rooftop terrace, which offers perfect people-watching down toward Charles Street. It's an ideal spot to bring a bottle of wine at the end of the day.

DOWNTOWN AND THE WATERFRONT

$50-150

On the edge of downtown, with a great location between the theater district and Chinatown, ★ **HI Boston Hostel** (19 Stuart St., 617/536-9455, www.bostonhostel.org, dorms $55-80, private rooms $230) sets the standard for large, urban hostels, and it's easily the best budget option in the city. Dormitory rooms range from eight-bed economy options to four-bed premium rooms, both gender-specific and coed, and the thoughtful design makes them comfortable spaces to sleep for all kinds of travelers. Beds have assigned lockers, small reading lights, and charging stations, and the shared hallway bathrooms are always immaculate; private rooms have en suite bathrooms and a spare, modern style. Self-serve breakfasts of toast, cereal, and fruit are offered in the large common dining room, where there are hot drinks all day and a big kitchen for guest use. Employees organize guided walks or group activities, from brewery tours to bar hops and movie nights, which makes this a great place to meet other visitors. There's no parking on-site, but hostel staff directs guests to the **Boston Common Parking Garage** (0 Charles St., overnight $18-32), which is a 0.4-mile walk from the hostel.

One of the most unusual places to sleep on the waterfront is aboard one of the ★ **Liberty Fleet tall ships** (67 Long Wharf, 617/742-0333, www.libertyfleet.com, 2-person shared bunk room $60 pp, private $90 s, $120 d), which moor at a centrally located dock by the New England Aquarium. Accommodations are somewhat rustic, with shared bathrooms and showers and no wireless Internet—the experience is somewhere between floating hostel and tour of duty, but it's completely charming to wake up to the sounds of the Boston waterfront and lapping waves. Guests spending their first night aboard must meet a crew member for a short evening orientation but on subsequent nights may come and go freely after the last sail of the day and first morning outing (typically between 8pm and 10am); guests also receive a 30 percent discount on a sailing trip. The closest parking is at the **Harbor Garage** (70 E. India Row, $38 for 24 hrs.).

$250-350

Old-world elegance is faded but still enchanting at the **Omni Parker House** (60 School St., 617/227-8600, www.omnihotels.com/hotels/boston-parker-house, $182-717), one of downtown Boston's most storied hotels. The waitstaff have included civil rights leader Malcom X and communist Vietnam's ruler Ho Chi Minh, both of whom presumably ferried countless baskets of the Parker House Rolls that were invented here. The hotel regularly lands on the list of Boston's most haunted places (paranormal activity is said to be particularly high on the 3rd floor). If you book Table 40 in the Parker Restaurant, you'll dine where JFK proposed to the future Jackie Kennedy. In keeping with the historic building, rooms are rather small, and while they're pleasantly furnished, they're neither as historic nor as luxurious as the public spaces. Valet parking is available for $48 per person.

Over $350

One of Boston's top boutique hotels, **The Godfrey** (505 Washington St., 617/804-2000, www.godfreyhotelboston.com, $215-614) is chic and modern, and right in the thick of the Downtown Crossing shopping area. You'll find all the luxe amenities—valet parking, spa services, fitness center—along with rooted-in-Boston flourishes such as local art and designs. Splash out for a corner room for wraparound views of the city below.

NORTH END

$250-350

Just across the bridge in Charlestown, ★ **Green Turtle Floating Bed and Breakfast** (1 13th St., Pier 8, 617/340-2608, www.greenturtlebb.com, $255-375) offers a novel solution to Boston's perennial lack of space. Accommodations are in a two-bedroom houseboat or one of two motor yachts, pulling off an unusual blend of luxury and quirk. Rooms are very comfortable and well appointed, a full breakfast is delivered each morning by the friendly hosts, and the boats' kitchenettes are stocked with snacks and drinks. The bed-and-breakfast is a 1-mile walk from North End sights and close to the public ferry dock on Pier 4. A taxi from Logan Airport costs approximately $32, and a water taxi is $12 per person (inquire at the airport).

Over $350

Striking a pleasant balance between boutique style and corporate suave, **The Boxer Boston** (107 Merrimack St., 617/624-0202, www.theboxerboston.com, $184-574) is an appealing choice within easy walking distance of North End sights. In addition to more traditional king rooms, doubles, and suites, The Boxer has bunk rooms with a double bed on the bottom, and a twin-size bed on top—a good option for couples traveling with one child. The compact, comfortable, and modern rooms have flat-screen televisions and coffeemakers. Valet parking with in-and-out privileges is $47 per night.

FENWAY AND BACK BAY

$50-150

The bare-bones **Boston Fenway Inn** (12 Hemenway St., 857/250-2785, www.bostonfenwayinn.com, dorms $28-50, private rooms $49-125) is a decent option for budget travelers if the more appealing HI Boston is fully booked. All rooms have shared baths, and a basic continental breakfast is provided. Some travelers have found that rooms aren't cleaned as frequently as they'd like, and the inn tends to sell out months in advance.

$150-250

With a quiet location, **Oasis Guest House** (22 Edgerly Rd., 617/267-2262, www.oasisguesthouse.com, shared bath $89-189, private bath $119-259, 3-person suite $139-279 with breakfast and 2-night minimum on weekends) is walking distance to Fenway Park and public transportation. The somewhat faded decor leans old-fashioned, but it's a perfectly tidy, friendly place to land, whether you're in the Oasis property itself or Adams Bed and Breakfast, a neighboring outpost with similar facilities and the same management. A small continental breakfast is served, limited parking is available on-site on a first-come, first-served basis for $25, and there's a public garage nearby with 24-hour parking for $33.

Though technically in Kenmore Square, **Abigayle's Bed and Breakfast** (72 Bay State Rd., 617/720-0522, $105-175) is easy walking distance to destinations in Fenway and Back Bay. Friendly hosts and a simple continental breakfast make this a comfortable place to stay. All rooms have private baths (though the single room, which starts at $105 nightly, has a detached private bath in the hallway). The four-story house does not have an elevator. One parking space is available for $20 per night.

$250-350

Part of the charm of a Boston neighborhood is imagining the elegant homes behind the brownstones, but there aren't many ways to get past the doorstep. With elegant furnishings and a wonderfully historical feel, the ★ **College Club of Boston** (44 Commonwealth Ave., 617/536-9510, www.thecollegeclubofboston.com, shared bath $129-209 s, private bath $199-329 d) is like an invitation into one of those houses. The 11 guest rooms are named for colleges and universities, and each is furnished with unique style and charm—you'll find high ceilings and windows throughout the house, pretty secretary desks, and thoughtful touches. Shared bathrooms are pristine, and a generous continental breakfast is served in a downstairs dining room.

A trio of Back Bay town houses are linked up to make the **Newbury Guest House** (261 Newbury St., 617/670-6000, www.newburyguesthouse.com, $202-422). This bed-and-breakfast is walking distance from an appealing array of shops and cafés. Breakfast includes hot options like eggs and bacon along with croissants, fruit and yogurt, and hot drinks. Rooms are clean, light, and airy, and some have in-room fireplaces—welcome on blustery fall evenings. A few parking spaces are available on-site for $20 per night; call when booking to reserve.

The Gryphon House (9 Bay State Rd., 877/375-9003, www.innboston.com, $285-325) is a turn-of-the-20th-century Victorian brownstone that has been painstakingly preserved, with historical wallpaper and atmospheric paintings. The eight suites are spacious and well appointed, with gas fireplaces, flat-screen televisions with DVD players, wet bars, and refrigerators. The "extended continental" breakfast is an ample spread of yogurt, fruit, toast, hot and cold cereal, juice, and hot drinks, and parking is available on-site for $15 per night. Show your Red Sox ticket stub for $20 off and one day of free parking.

Over $350

Achingly cool and Instagram-ready, ★ **The Verb** (1271 Boylston St., 617/566-4500, www.theverbhotel.com, $151-567) combines a colorful rock-and-roll aesthetic with high-end service and style. The poolside scene is fun and occasionally boisterous; the bar serves strong, creative cocktails; and you can browse the lobby's vinyl library for something to spin on your in-room Crosley record player. Before a stem-to-stern overhaul, this was a Howard Johnson hotel, and The Verb raises a glass to that history at **Hojoko** (www.hojokoboston.com), its on-site Japanese tavern. Valet parking is $48 per night, and you're a baseball-throw's distance away from Fenway Park.

SOUTH END

$150-250

There's still a roller-skating rink beneath the armchairs and coffee tables at **40 Berkeley** (40 Berkeley St., 617/375-2524, www.40berkeley.com, $117-168), an enormous YWCA-turned hotel. Rooms are somewhat institutional, and shared baths are basic but recently renovated, but management has addressed one long-standing complaint by installing air-conditioning units in every room. While all rooms are private, the overall effect is hostel-like, with a room for movie nights, games, and convivial common spaces. This is a good choice for families, as triples and quads are available, with no additional charge for extra guests.

$250-350

The bright units at **Chandler Studios** (54 Berkeley St., 617/482-3450, www.chandlerstudioboston.com, $195-524) are enlivened by grainy scenes from historic Boston, giving the modern decor a bit more personality. Studios have fully equipped kitchenettes, and the one-bedroom suite has a one-bedroom sitting room with a pullout couch. Hot drinks are available 24 hours a day in the lobby. Guests get a reduced rate at a nearby parking garage ($30 for 24 hrs.), and the location is within easy walking distance from public transport and Back Bay sights.

LOGAN AIRPORT

The hotels around Boston's Logan Airport are corporate bland, but for early morning flights or avoiding city traffic, these can be a convenient option.

$150-250

Eight miles north of the airport, **Red Roof Plus Boston Logan** (920 Broadway, Saugus, 937/328-1612, www.bostonlogan.redroof.com, $116-222) is a clean, easy-to-reach budget option, convenient for anyone who is flying into Boston and leaving the next morning. Taxi service from the airport is $25 and takes 15-30 minutes, while the MBTA station is an $18 taxi ride away. Free parking is available. While the neighborhood is not much of a destination, there are stores and restaurants within walking distance of the hotel.

$250-350

The **Hilton Boston Logan Airport** (1 Hotel Dr., Logan International Airport, 617/568-6700, www.hilton.com, $175-469) is connected to the A and E terminals by a sky bridge and has 24-hour shuttle service to the airport, the MBTA Blue Line, and to water taxis, which makes it straightforward to get into downtown Boston. Hot breakfast is available, though not included with rates, and the hotel also has a fitness room and indoor pool. Parking is available for $42 (self) and $47 (valet).

Information and Services

INFORMATION

A good place to get oriented is the **Boston Common Visitor Information Center** (139 Tremont St., 888/733-2678, www.bostonusa.com, 8:30am-5pm Mon.-Fri., 9am-5pm Sat.-Sun.), located in the park halfway between the Park Street and Boylston Street T stops. There you can pick up maps and guides, along with museum discount coupons and brochures for major attractions. It's also the starting place for the Freedom Trail and several trolley tours around the city. The National Park Service (NPS) runs its own **Faneuil Hall Visitor Center** (1 Faneuil Hall, 617/242-5642, www.nps.gov/bost, 9am-6pm daily), which includes a good collection of books on Boston and Massachusetts. If you are planning ahead, you can contact the **Greater Boston Convention & Visitors Bureau** (800/733-2678, www.bostonusa.com) for additional publications with the latest tourist information. The NPS also has a Boston-specific **app** with tours, maps, and info.

Attraction Passes

While many of Boston's most appealing experiences are free (or just the cost of a cannoli), seeing the city's museums and attractions can add up quickly. A couple of cards and passes bundle attractions under a single price, often with a dizzying array of variations: The **All-Inclusive Go Boston Card** (www.smartdestinations.com, $57-175 adults, $39-119 children) has passes in increments ranging from a single day to a week and includes admission to many of the city's best sites, with no limits on the number you can visit each day. The three-, five- and seven-day options include one "premium attraction"—the aquarium's whale-watching boat tour, tickets to a Red Sox game, or the "surf and turf-style" Boston Duck Tour. Verdict: If you're a fast-moving sightseer and plan to see these sites anyway, this is a great deal. For those who like to take more time at museums and historic sites, though, it's hard to get enough value for the cost.

If just a couple of specific places are on your list, it's definitely worth purchasing tickets to them via the same company's **Build Your Own Go Boston Card,** where you select your destinations and save 15-20 percent by purchasing in advance. Another option is the **Boston City Pass** (www.citypass.com/boston, $56 adults, $44 children), which includes the New England Aquarium, Museum of Science, Skywalk Observatory, and either the Museum of Fine Arts or a harbor cruise over a nine-day period. Who it works for: anyone already planning to visit two of the higher-dollar attractions on a more relaxed schedule.

SERVICES

Emergencies

For medical emergencies, call 911. Boston has many hospitals with 24-hour emergency rooms, including **Massachusetts General Hospital** (55 Fruit St., off Cambridge St., 617/726-2000, www.massgeneral.org) and **Beth Israel Deaconess Medical Center** (330 Brookline Ave. at Longwood Ave., 617/667-7000, www.bidmc.org).

Transportation

GETTING THERE

Car

All New England highways seem to lead to Boston, which is at the intersection of I-90, I-95, and I-93. The traffic is notoriously hairy moving through the city, and when possible, it's worth planning to avoid the busy morning and afternoon commute hours. Given the possibility for traffic, all driving times are approximate and optimistic, including **New York City** (215 mi, 3 hrs., 30 min.), **Newport** (75 mi, 1 hr., 15 min.), **Cape Cod** (60 mi, 1 hr.), **Portland** (110 mi, 1 hr., 45 min.), and **Stockbridge** (135 mi, 2 hrs.).

Air

Flights to Boston's **Logan International Airport** (www.massport.com/logan-airport/) are available from almost all major cities. From Logan, ground transportation can be arranged from the information desk at baggage claim. The most efficient way to get into the city is via taxi, though expect to pay a minimum of $25 for downtown locations, or shared van service to downtown and Back Bay for $20-25 per person.

Far cheaper (and almost as quick) is the MBTA Silver Line bus (www.mbta.com); inbound rides on SL1 from Logan Airport to Boston's South Station are free, and leave from stops directly in front of each terminal. Buses leave several times an hour 5am-1am, and reach South Station (Summer St. and Atlantic Ave.) in 15-25 minutes. If you're continuing to downtown stops or Cambridge, request a free transfer for the MBTA Red Line subway route.

Train

From most destinations, **Amtrak** (South Station, Summer St. and Atlantic Ave., 800/872-7245, www.amtrak.com) runs service to both the South Station and Back Bay Station. (Amtrak trains from all destinations in Maine run to the North Station.) The **Massachusetts Bay Transportation Authority** (617/222-5000, www.mbta.com) also runs commuter rail service from locations in Greater Boston for fares of up to $6.

Bus

Bus service arrives at the South Station. Most U.S. destinations are served by **Greyhound** (800/231-2222, www.greyhound.com). However, smaller bus companies also run from various locations around the region, such as the **BoltBus** (877/265-8287, www.boltbus.com), **Megabus** (www.megabus.com), and **Peter Pan Bus** (800/343-9999, www.peterpanbus.com).

GETTING AROUND

Car

Ask local drivers about Boston's behind-the-wheel style, and they'll describe their competitive, fast-moving traffic as part of the city's Hobbesian soul and panache. Ask anyone else in New England, and they'll explain how Bostonians earned their regional nickname: Massholes.

If you can get around without it, it's far easier and cheaper to leave your car in a garage while in Boston. Check with your accommodations first, as many often have a deal with a nearby location.

PARKING

It's possible to find street parking in Boston, but regulations can be byzantine, with varied time limits and many resident-only zones. If you do find on-street parking, meters are active 8am-8pm Monday-Saturday, and most take both coins and credit cards, as well as payment through the **Park Boston app.**

In downtown, **Boston Common Garage** (0 Charles St., 617/954-2098, weekdays $28 for 3-10 hrs., $32 for 10-24 hrs.; weekends $14 for 1-3 hrs., $18 overnight) is large, convenient, and affordable. The **North End Garage** (600 Commercial St., 617/723-1488, $24 for 2-10 hrs., $34 for 10-24 hrs.) is close to TD Garden and North End sights. Prices fluctuate and some small lots offer good discounts: Parking app **SpotHero** (www.spothero.com) is an excellent way to search for nearby spots using custom time parameters, often at discounted prices—though some garages require you to print your pass. Most garages do not include in-and-out privileges.

One other option is to leave your car outside of the city entirely. Some MBTA stations have enclosed garages that are much cheaper than city parking: **Alewife station** (11 Cambridgepark W., Cambridge, www.lazparking.com, overnight parking $8) is convenient and big, with 2,733 spaces in an enclosed garage. Alewife is at the end of the Red Line, and frequent trains make the 20-minute trip to downtown Boston.

Public Transit

For peace of mind (and to save on parking costs), use public transport. The "T," which is short for **MBTA** (617/222-5000, www.mbta.com) is cheap, safe, and easy to use. Subway fares are $2.75 with a ticket—or $2.25 with a reloadable Charlie Card you can pick up at major stations. More out-of-the-way locations require taking one of the MBTA buses, which are often slow but give good coverage across the city. Fares are currently $2, or $1.70 with a Charlie Card. Often overlooked as a means of transportation are the ferries that ply Boston Harbor. A trip from Charlestown Navy Yard to Long Wharf (perfect after completing the Freedom Trail) costs $3.50.

Taxi

Keep in mind that the MBTA doesn't run 12:30am-5:30am. The only option at that time is ride-sharing or a taxi, which isn't cheap. Fares start at $2.60 for the first one-seventh mile and add $2.60 for each additional mile, with $28 for each hour of waiting time. Also note that trips to Logan are saddled with an additional $2.75 for tolls, while trips from Logan cost an extra $6.

Call a cab from the hybrid fleet of **Boston Cab Dispatch** (617/536-5010, www.bostoncab.us), which also has wheelchair-equipped cars, or try **Boston Logan Taxi Service** (617/499-7770, www.bostonairportexpresscar.com), whose website allows pre-booking for airport pickups. **Uber** (www.uber.com) and **Lyft** (www.lyft.com) services are also available in Boston.

BOSTON HARBOR ISLANDS

Boston's Harbor Islands have played an important role in the city's history that, until recently, was largely forgotten. The gateway to a city that itself was once practically an island, the 34 islands that now comprise Boston Harbor Islands State and National Park were home to important military installations, resorts, lighthouses, Native American camps, fishing communities, and—less memorably—a garbage dump.

Today, the dump on Spectacle Island has been turned into a park that has fantastic views of the city from the top of the heap, and ferries carry more than a million people each year to eight islands for exploring historic forts, tanning on the beach, hiking and boating, or enjoying a traditional seaside New England clambake.

Sights

Eight of the Harbor Islands can be reached via public ferry, and an additional 19 are accessible by private boat. Three of the islands are closed to the public, and one—Thompson Island—is only publicly accessible on the weekends. The park is open year-round; however, ferries only operate seasonally, late spring-October.

Located on distant, surf-pounded Little Brewster Island, **Boston Harbor Light** (Little Brewster Island, 617/223-8666, www.bostonharborislands.org) is the oldest light station in the United States, first established in 1716. The current, 89-foot-tall lighthouse dates to 1783, is still maintained by the U.S. Coast Guard, and is open for ranger-led tours—including climbing the 76 stairs and two ladders to get to the top. The two-acre island is one of the most distant of the Harbor Islands from downtown Boston, and tours via ferry take about 3.5 hours.

On George's Island, **Fort Warren** (www.bostonharborislands.org) was built to protect Boston from attack by sea and housed Confederate prisoners during the U.S. Civil War. Constructed between 1833 and 1860, the star-shaped fortification was an active military base through World War II, and visitors can see examples of weapons spanning the fort's 87 years of service. Take a docent-led tour or explore on your own; the views from the upper ramparts are extraordinary. A summer music festival called Rock the Fort brings live bands out to the island on Saturday afternoons.

Visitors to **Lovell's Island** can wander among the overgrown fortifications that once comprised **Fort Standish,** a coastal defense installation built in 1907, as well as the foundations of some of the 60 buildings that once stood here. There's more left of **Fort Andrews** on **Peddocks Island,** including brick barracks, former officers' quarters, and a restored chapel.

Sports and Recreation

WALKING

The Harbor Islands are mostly small, flat, and deserted, making them perfect for a quiet nature walk. **Spectacle Island** is the only one of the islands with any significant elevation, and that's only because it features a former garbage dump that rises 157 feet above sea level. A five-mile hike that departs from the visitors center includes a walk up and over the mound, which offers unobstructed 360-degree views from a gazebo at the top.

A highlight of the 5 miles of trails on **Peddocks Island** is walking the paved paths among the shuttered buildings of Fort Andrews. A 1-mile loop hike of **Grape Island** is blessed with shade, and the 2.5 miles of trails on Thompson Island include forested stretches as well as marshes, meadows, and beaches. Only open to the public on weekends, **Thompson Island** is home to an Outward Bound program and has two marked hiking trails—the 1-mile Northwest Trail and the 1.5-mile Southwest Trail.

BEACHES

The sandy beach on **Spectacle Island** is just 20 minutes from downtown Boston; it has a million-dollar view of the city skyline, calm waters, lifeguards (the only ones in the park), and easy access to the restrooms and snack bar at the island's visitors center. What it lacks is shade, so be sure to bring a beach umbrella along if you don't want to bake in the sun. The beach is just steps away from the ferry dock.

Spectacle Island's trash has become treasure in the form of sea glass, which washes up regularly on the beaches of the onetime garbage dump. Some of the glass and pottery, milled smooth by waves and sand, is more than a century old. Visitors can gather and admire the glass, but taking it home is prohibited.

To escape the crowds on Spectacle Island, the ocean-facing beach on **Lovell's Island** has soft and good swimming, though no lifeguards are on duty here. Even more remote are the slate and shell beaches at **Bumpkin Island.**

Food

There are simple cafés on George's Island and Spectacle Island, both run by Boston celebrity chef Barbara Lynch, but the menu of snacks, hot dogs, and fried fish comes with inflated prices and long waits. If you're not bringing food from the mainland, stop by **Salt Water Lobster Company** (George's Island, noon-4pm Mon.-Fri., 11am-5pm Sat.-Sun., $7-25) or **Seaglass Café** (Spectacle Island, noon-4pm Mon.-Fri., 11am-5pm Sat.-Sun., $7-25).

Harpoon Brewery also hosts a weekly **Beer Garden** on Spectacle Island, where you can snare one of the Adirondack chairs on the visitors center porch and soak in the gemütlichkeit with a lunch or dinner of German potato salad, pierogis, and bierwurst slid into a pretzel bun and topped with mustard and sauerkraut. Tickets are via **Boston Harbor Cruises** (www.bostonharborcruises.com, $55 adults, $50 children 3-12).

Another favorite event on these islands is the **Thursday night clambake** (www.bostonharborcruises.com, clambakes $99 adults, $70 children 3-12, includes ferry ticket, food, and drinks). The clambake now includes Lynch's signature clam chowder along with a sugar snap pea salad, lobster, mussels, littleneck clams, Portuguese-style linguica sausage, potatoes, corn, corn bread, and chocolate mousse for dessert. After dinner, guests can enjoy a beach fire and lawn games as the sun sets over the harbor.

Camping

There are 33 campsites scattered across **Bumpkin, Lovell's, Grape,** and **Peddocks Islands** (www.bostonharborislands.org, sites for residents $8, nonresidents $10). Campers need to bring all their own food, water, and gear, and pack out their rubbish when leaving, but the campgrounds are furnished with composting toilets, making for a remarkably rustic experience within view of the Boston skyline. Sites can be reserved online up to six months in advance and fill up quickly.

If you prefer sleeping off the ground, Peddocks Island also has six canvas-sided yurts (6-person yurts for residents $55, nonresidents $60) that, while not exactly luxurious, are spacious and clean and have electricity and access to drinking water. Each yurt sleeps six on bunk beds and has an indoor dining table.

Campsites can only be reached via boat, then campers must tote their gear by hand—Peddocks provides wheelbarrows to cart your gear from the dock to the campsites. The camping season runs late June-early September.

Information and Services

The park is open sunrise-sunset daily year-round, plus overnight for camping. Ferry service, however, is more limited, so "open" may mean using your own boat if you want to visit certain islands at certain times of the year. Visitors centers are located on Spectacle and George's Islands; both islands have cafés, and the George's Island Visitor Center also has a gift shop.

Getting There and Around

Daily ferry service is available from **Boston Harbor Cruises** (617/227-4321, www.bostonharborcruises.com, round-trip $17 adults, $12 seniors/military, $10 children 3-11, children under 3 free) from Long Wharf in downtown Boston to three of the harbor islands: **George's, Spectacle,** and **Peddocks.** Direct service to George's and Spectacle is available year-round; a separate ferry operates on a loop between all three islands during the summer only.

The closest parking for Long Wharf is at the **Boston Harbor Garage** on the corner of Atlantic Avenue and Milk Street, and the nearest MBTA stop is Aquarium on the Blue Line.

A ferry operated by Outward Bound provides public service to **Thompson Island** on Saturday and Sunday during the summer from the EDIC pier in South Boston (617/328/3900, $17 adults, $10 children 3-12, children under 3 free, cash only). Take the SL2 bus on the MBTA's Silver Line to the corner of Harbor Street and Drydock Avenue; there's also a parking garage at 16 Drydock Avenue.

From Hingham and Hull, Massachusetts, you can take a ferry to some of the less visited Harbor Islands. The MBTA operates daily direct service between Hewitt's Cove in Hingham and **George's Island** spring-fall, departing from the Hingham Shipyard (30 Shipyard Dr., Hingham, 781/749-8009, round-trip $18.50 adults, $9.25 students and seniors). There's free parking on-site, or take the MBTA Red Line to Quincey Center and connect to the #220 bus, which offers direct service to the shipyard.

In the summer, Boston Harbor Cruises operates loop service out of Hingham with stops at Grape, Hull, Peddocks, George's, Lovell's, and Bumpkin Islands before returning to Hingham (round-trip $17 adults, $12 seniors/military, $10 children 3-11, children under 3 free). The stops at Grape and Bumpkin Islands are made Wednesday-Sunday only. Passengers can board at Pembroke Point in Hull (180 Main St.) as well as in Hingham; there's free public parking on-site, but overnight parking is not permitted.

Boat tours to **Boston Harbor Light on Little Brewster Island** are offered on Friday, Saturday, and Sunday in the summer, departing from the **Boston Harbor Islands Welcome Center** (191 W. Atlantic Ave., Boston, 617/223-8666, $41 for adults wishing to climb the light, $37 seniors and military, $32 children 8-12; non-climbers are $30 adults, $25 children).

Around Boston

LEXINGTON AND CONCORD

Historians may debate where the famous "shot heard 'round the world" was actually fired, but there can be no doubt that the first armed combat of the Revolutionary War took place in the town of Lexington, 11 miles west of Boston. By all accounts, it was a tentative and slapdash affair, in stark contrast to the American victory at Concord Bridge that would take place a few hours later. Even so, it marks the first time that the rebellious colonists fired on their own country's troops, outnumbered and outgunned though they were. For that reason, the town now stands as a monument to the patriots' courage.

"I think I could write a poem to be called Concord," wrote writer and philosopher Henry David Thoreau. "For argument I should have the River, the Woods, the Ponds, the Hills, the Fields, the Swamps and Meadows, the Streets and Buildings, and the Villagers."

In addition to its role in the Revolution, Concord played another significant part in history some 60 years later, when it became the home base for a 19th-century literary and religious movement known as transcendentalism. Its proponents, among them Thoreau, Emerson, and Bronson Alcott, believed in a new philosophy inspired by nature, replacing the formalistic theology they'd inherited from Europe. Their writings helped inspire the flowering of a truly American form of literature, as well as the modern environmental movement.

Sights

WALDEN POND STATE RESERVATION

"I went to the woods because I wished to live deliberately . . ." As his famous words explain, Henry David Thoreau retired for two years to the shores of Walden Pond to seek a simpler mode of living, closer to nature. The book he wrote about the experience, *Walden*, has since inspired generations of philosophers, environmentalists, and other readers, who now come regularly to pay homage to the site of **Thoreau's cabin** (915 Walden St., 978/369-3254, www.mass.gov). While the home itself is no longer there, the hearthstone from his

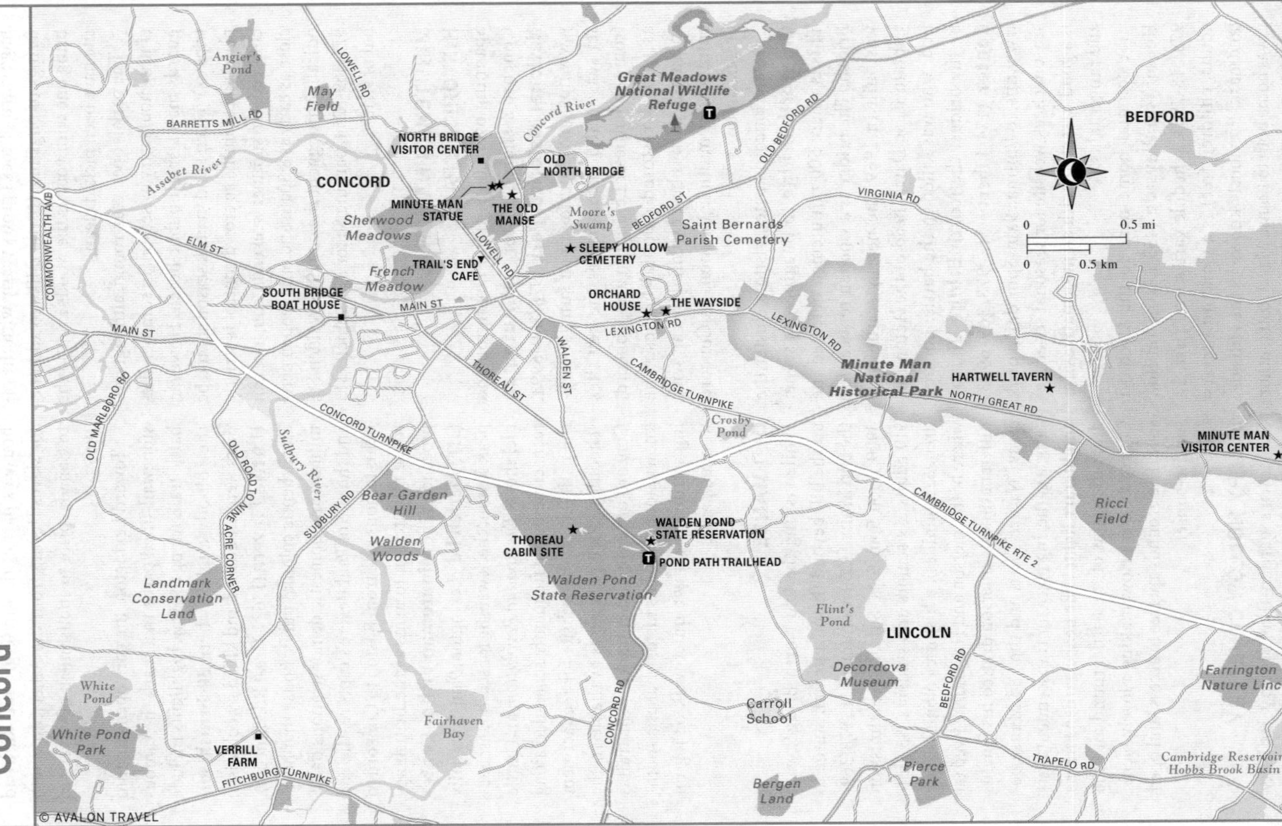
Concord
Angier's Pond
May Field
LOWELL RD
BARRETTS MILL RD
Concord River
Great Meadows National Wildlife Refuge
OLD BEDFORD RD
BEDFORD
NORTH BRIDGE VISITOR CENTER
OLD NORTH BRIDGE
Assabet River
CONCORD
MINUTE MAN STATUE
THE OLD MANSE
Moore's Swamp
BEDFORD ST
VIRGINIA RD
Saint Bernards Parish Cemetery
0
0.5 mi
0.5 km
COMMONWEALTH AVE
ELM ST
Sherwood Meadows
SLEEPY HOLLOW CEMETERY
TRAIL'S END CAFE
French Meadow
SOUTH BRIDGE BOAT HOUSE
MAIN ST
ORCHARD HOUSE
THE WAYSIDE
LEXINGTON RD
WALDEN ST
THOREAU ST
CAMBRIDGE TURNPIKE
Minute Man National Historical Park
HARTWELL TAVERN
NORTH GREAT RD
OLD MARLBORO RD
CONCORD TURNPIKE
Crosby Pond
MINUTE MAN VISITOR CENTER
OLD ROAD TO NINE ACRE CORNER
Sudbury River
SUDBURY RD
Bear Garden Hill
CAMBRIDGE TURNPIKE RTE 2
Ricci Field
WALDEN POND STATE RESERVATION
THOREAU CABIN SITE
POND PATH TRAILHEAD
Walden Woods
Landmark Conservation Land
Walden Pond State Reservation
Flint's Pond
LINCOLN
Decordova Museum
BEDFORD RD
Farrington Nature Linc
White Pond
White Pond Park
Fairhaven Bay
CONCORD RD
Carroll School
VERRILL FARM
FITCHBURG TURNPIKE
TRAPELO RD
Cambridge Reservoir/ Hobbs Brook Basin
Pierce Park
Bergen Land
© AVALON TRAVEL

chimney was uncovered years later. Nearby, a huge cairn of rocks grows yearly with the offerings of pilgrims. (If you'd like to add one, bring one with you, as the woods around the site have been picked clean.)

The park is open year-round, although operating hours vary by season. In summer, lifeguards man a small public beach. However, trips to Walden Pond in peak season should be planned carefully, as crowd control is strictly enforced. On summer weekends, entrance can close as early as 8:30am and only reopen periodically throughout the day (915 Walden St., 978/369-3254, parking $8 for MA vehicle, $15 out of state).

MINUTEMAN NATIONAL HISTORICAL PARK

Spanning over 200 years of Lexington and Concord's shared history, **Minuteman National Historical Park** (978/369-6993, www.nps.gov, grounds open sunrise-sunset seasonally) encompasses the key sites from the Battle of Lexington and Concord, as well as restored colonial homes. The sprawling park is best explored by car, with entrances at multiple locations in Concord or Lexington.

Near Concord center, visitors cluster the **Old North Bridge** to imagine the scene: This is where 500 minutemen defeated the British. The bridge is a wooden replica that was built in 1969, the nearby statue is of Captain Isaac Davis, head of the Acton militia, who was killed in the battle. Located by the bridge, the **North Bridge Visitor Center** (174 Liberty St., 978/369-6993, www.nps.gov/mima, 9am-5pm daily peak season, check website for seasonal schedule) is a good first stop, with an informative film and ranger talks.

A colonial home near to the Orchard House, **The Wayside** (455 Lexington Rd., 978/318-7863, schedule varies, call first, $7 adults, children free) is a Concord literary landmark. Previously known as the Hillside, it was home both to Louisa May Alcott (author of *Little Women*) and Nathaniel Hawthorne (*The Scarlet Letter*). It also served as a safe house as part of the Underground Railroad for slaves fleeing from the American South to Canada, prior to abolishment of slavery in 1865.

Toward Lexington, the park opens up into stonewall-lined paths that mark the famous battle trail. Along the way, highlights include the "bloody angle," where 30 British soldiers were ambushed and killed by colonists; **Hartwell Tavern** (136 N. Great Rd., Lincoln), an authentic colonial public house that hosts military and domestic demonstrations daily; and the site of Paul Revere's capture, the end of his famous ride from Boston to Concord to rouse minutemen to arms as the British approached. The **Minuteman Visitor Center** (3113 Marrett Rd., Lexington, 9am-5pm daily peak season, check website for seasonal schedule) shows *The Road to Revolution*, and battle reenactments are frequently scheduled along the path (check the website for reenactment schedules). Free parking is available in the Concord or Lexington entrances. The trail is known not only for its history but as a soothing setting to enjoy a quiet walk or jog on wooded paths.

OLD MANSE

While visiting the Old North Bridge, walk up the hill beyond the minuteman statue to the **Old Manse** (269 Monument St., 978/369-3909, noon-5pm Tues.-Sun., house admission $10 adults, $9 seniors and students, $5 children, $25 families), a historic colonial estate where both Emerson and Hawthorne lived (at different times). Emerson drafted his famous essay "Nature" here, and the Old Manse became a gathering place for transcendentalists and literary lights. The hedge gardens frame dramatic vistas of the battleground and the Concord River below, making a lovely picnic spot. The grounds are free to access, and open sunrise-sunset.

SLEEPY HOLLOW CEMETERY

The town's garden-like **Sleepy Hollow Cemetery** (34 Bedford St., 7am-7pm daily) was designed according to transcendentalist philosophies of harmony with nature, and in 1855, Ralph Waldo Emerson spoke at its dedication. The cemetery's **Melvin Memorial,** commissioned to commemorate three brothers who died in the Civil War, was sculpted by Daniel Chester French, who created the North Bridge minuteman and President Abraham Lincoln's statue at the Washington DC Lincoln Memorial. Nearby **Authors' Ridge** marks the final resting spots of Thoreau, Emerson, Bronson and Louisa May Alcott, and Hawthorne. The Friends of Sleepy Hollow Cemetery (www.friendsofsleepyhollow.org/index.html) produces a map that's available for purchase in local stores.

ORCHARD HOUSE

In 1868, Louisa May Alcott wrote the classic American novel *Little Women* while living in the last of her family's many Concord homes, the **Orchard House** (399 Lexington Rd., 978/369-4118, www.louisamayalcott.org, 10am-5pm Mon.-Sat., 11am-5pm Sun., admission and guided tour $10 adults, $8 seniors and students, $5 children 6-17, children under 6 free). Now a museum, the house retains the same structure and the majority of furnishings of the Alcott family.

Sports and Recreation

Ride from Cambridge to Lexington on the **Minuteman Bikeway** (www.minuteman-bikeway.com), a 10-mile paved and rail-trail bike route that begins at Alewife station, ending in Bedford. A series of off-shoots connects the bikeway to historic sites around Concord.

Rent a canoe or kayak at **Southbridge Boat House** (496 Main St., 978-369-9438, www.southbridgeboathouse.com, 10am-1 hour before dusk Mon.-Fri., 9am-1 hour before dusk weekends and holidays Apr. 1-Nov 1) to paddle the winding Sudbury River—it's just 1.5 miles to the Old North Bridge, or you can follow Thoreau's favorite route to enjoy a serene view of colonial houses, birds, and turtles. Parking is available in a small lot in front of the boathouse and across the street.

A prime destination for bird-watching, **Great Meadows National Wildlife Refuge** (183 Monsen Rd., www.fws.gov/refuge/great_meadows, sunrise-sunset daily, parking $4) comprises 3,800 acres of wetlands that have been conserved to protect migratory birds, spanning 12 miles across seven towns. The best way to explore is on the 2.7-mile **Dike Trail,** which can be accessed in Concord on Monsen Road, off Route 62 toward Bedford. Bring your binoculars.

Hartwell Tavern

Food

LEXINGTON

A local establishment for decades, hearty (but not heavy) Italian takes center stage at **Mario's** (1733 Massachusetts Ave., 781/861-1182, www.marioslexington.com, 11am-9:30pm Sun.-Thurs., 11am-10pm Fri.-Sat., $17-24), known most for its pastas, pizza, and casual, jovial atmosphere. Arrive early for lunch, as the dining room fills quickly.

Made-to-order fresh sandwiches, wraps, panini, salads, soups, and to-go meals are quick and satisfying at **Neillio's Gourmet Kitchen & Catering** (53 Bedford St., 781/861-8466, www.neillioscatering.com, 8am-6:30pm Mon.-Fri., 8am-4pm Sat., $5-13). A short drive from Lexington Green, this is the perfect place to get picnic supplies or a packed lunch for the trail. No seating is available.

Leave room for dessert and head to **Rancatore's Ice Cream and Yogurt** (1752 Massachusetts Ave., 781/862-5090, www.rancs.com, school year 10am-10pm Sun.-Thurs., 10am-11pm Fri.-Sat., summer 10am-11pm daily) for homemade ice cream, sorbet, and frozen yogurt. Expand your palate with flavors like ginger or green tea ice cream, or cool off with mango sorbet. Traditional flavors won't disappoint either—especially for chocolate lovers.

CONCORD

A short walk from Monument Square, **Trails End Café** (97 Lowell Rd., 978/610-6633, www.thetrailsendcafe.com, 7am-3pm Mon., 7am-3pm and 5pm-10pm Tues.-Sat., 8am-3pm and 5pm-9pm Sun., $8-26) is a welcoming eatery that serves wholesome meals using ingredients from local farms. With ample seating and a convivial atmosphere, the café is known for coffee, healthy salads, and sandwiches.

For local produce and homemade pies, stop into **Verrill Farm** (11 Wheeler Rd., 978/369-4494, www.verrillfarm.com, 9am-7pm Mon.-Sat., 9am-5pm Sun. Jan.-Feb., $3-11), across from Walden Pond. Century-old and family-owned, Verrill Farm has strawberry picking, hayrides, and a corn festival, as well as weekend breakfasts throughout the year. The deli makes fresh sandwiches and salads that are perfect to pack for a walk around Walden, but if you want a pie, better call ahead to reserve one.

Drive to the outskirts of "West Concord," to enjoy homemade breads, quiche, deli sandwiches, and freshly baked desserts at **Nashoba Brook Bakery** (152 Commonwealth Ave., 978/318-1999, http://slowrise.com, 7am-8pm Mon.-Sat., 8am-8pm Sun., sandwiches start at $7.50). Crowded at lunchtime, it's worth the wait to sit outside by the brook, or relax on a couch with a cup of coffee.

Getting There

Concord and Lexington are accessible from Boston via Route 95 to 2A (Lexington) or Route 2 (Concord). Driving from Boston, stop first in Lexington Center to visit the Green and historic houses, and then drive to Concord, stopping at the **Minuteman Visitor Center** (3113 Marrett Rd., Lexington) and Minuteman National Historical Park along the way.

Bus service from Cambridge is available from **MBTA** (www.mbta.com, Routes 76, 62, or 67 from Alewife station) to Lexington Center. There is currently no public transportation between Lexington and Concord. The MBTA commuter rail Fitchburg train line runs directly to Concord, easily picked up at North Station or Porter Square in Cambridge.

SALEM

With a grim history of deadly witch trials, Salem's tragedy has lingered through the centuries—a story of mass hysteria that's only underscored by the city's prim facade. Gothic Victorian homes stand watch at the edge of the Naumkeag River, and historic wharves still see bustling boat traffic.

Salem might still be "Witch City," but there's far more to explore here than creepy sites and modern-day magic shops. This is where Hawthorne depicted the confines of the Puritan world in his book *The House of*

Salem Witch Museum

the Seven Gables, and Salem was long an important trading port, sending ships laden with salted codfish across the globe.

These days, Salem is a bedroom community of Boston, and clusters of shops, cafés, and historic streets make the city an appealing place to explore.

Sights

WITCH TRIAL SITES

Convicted for practicing witchcraft and sorcery, 20 people were executed between February 1692 and spring of the following year, with more than 200 people accused. It was not an isolated incident—Salem's witch problems came at the tail end of a centuries-long "witch craze" that had swept Europe. Just prior to the witch trials, King William's War—a conflict between France and England that played out in the Colonies—displaced people from New York to Quebec and Nova Scotia, with many settling on the Massachusetts coast, straining resources and community bonds.

When two local girls started having "fits" in January 1692, accusations flew, with fingers pointing first toward some of the town's most vulnerable people: The first three people to go on trial included Tituba, an enslaved woman; Sarah Good, a beggar; and the impoverished, elderly Sarah Osborne.

The paroxysm of witch trials has a complex historic context, but in 1976 a new theory was introduced. Now, some believe that the mass hysteria was the result of ergotism, the effect of eating a fungus that can contaminate rye and other grains, and is known to cause spasms and hallucinations.

Many sites around Salem explore the town's dramatic history. The most affecting is the simple **Salem Witch Trials Memorial** (Liberty St., www.salemweb.com/memorial), which displays the names of the victims on stone benches next to the central burying ground. Nearby, the **Witch House** (310 Essex St., 978/744-8815, www.salemweb.com/witchhouse, 10am-5pm daily Mar. 15-Nov. 15, $10.25 adults, $8.25 seniors, $6.25 children 6-14, children under 6 free) is the former home of magistrate Jonathan Corwin, who sentenced the guilty to death. Tours detail the restored interior.

A trio of somewhat weird museums also explore this history: The most popular museum is the **Salem Witch Museum** (Washington Sq. N., 978/744-1692, www.salemwitchmuseum.com, 10am-5pm daily Sept.-June, 10am-7pm daily July-Aug., extended hours in Oct., $12 adults, $10.50 seniors, $9 children 6-14, free children under 6), whose basic displays lay the groundwork for the events of 1692-1693. Somewhat hokier, the **Salem Wax Museum of Witches and Seafarers** (288 Derby St., 978/298-2929, www.salemwaxmuseum.com, 10am-4pm daily Jan.-Mar., 10am-6pm daily Apr.-June, 10am-9pm daily July-Aug., 10am-6pm daily Sept., "extended hours" in Oct., 10am-5pm daily Nov.-Dec., $9 seniors, $7 children and students, children under 5 free) has extremely creepy wax statues posed in a series of dioramas. Strangest of all is the **Witch Dungeon Museum** (16 Lynde

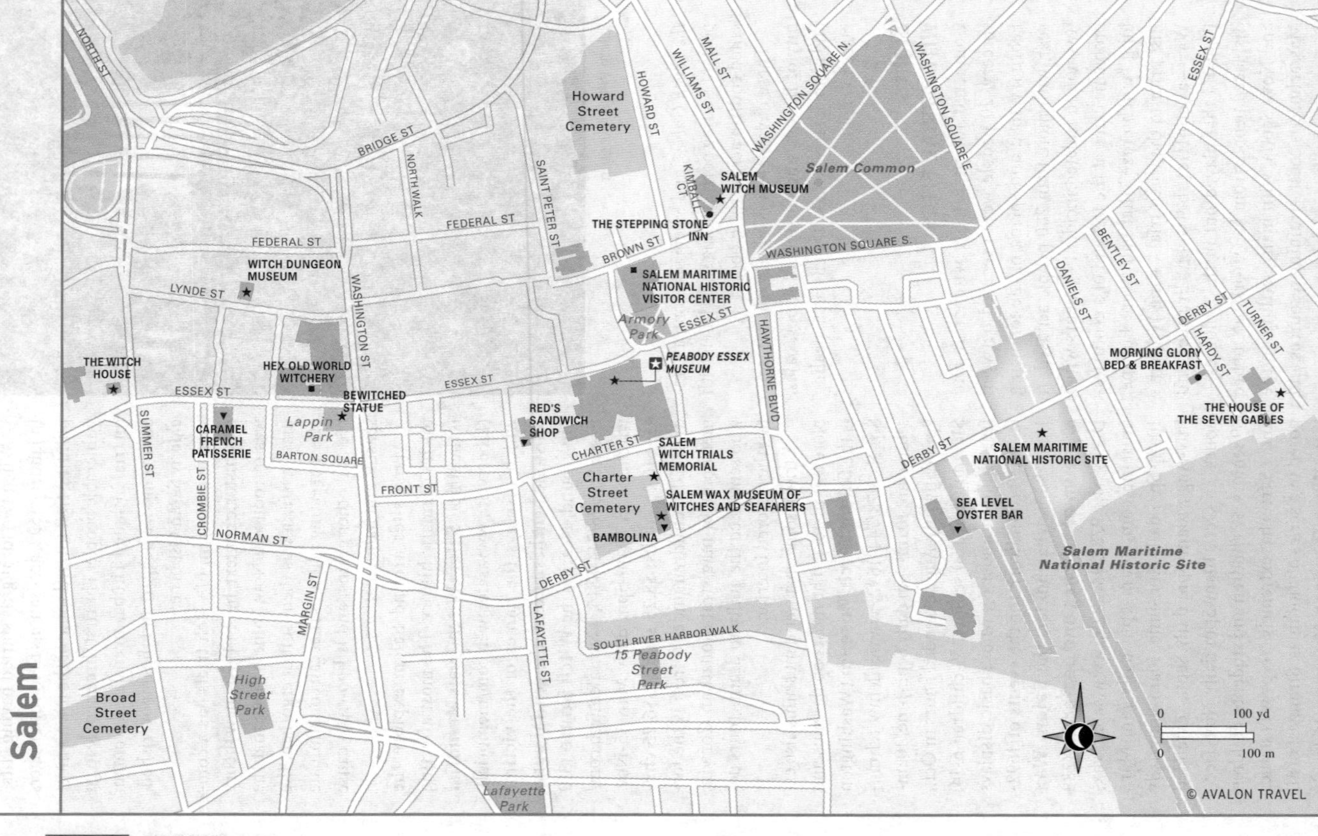
Salem
THE WITCH HOUSE
Broad Street Cemetery
SUMMER ST
NORTH ST
LYNDE ST
ESSEX ST
CROMBIE ST
CARAMEL FRENCH PATISSERIE
NORMAN ST
High Street Park
WITCH DUNGEON MUSEUM
FEDERAL ST
HEX OLD WORLD WITCHERY
BARTON SQUARE
Lappin Park
MARGIN ST
BEWITCHED STATUE
WASHINGTON ST
BRIDGE ST
FRONT ST
NORTH WALK
Lafayette Park
LAFAYETTE ST
DERBY ST
RED'S SANDWICH SHOP
SAINT PETER ST
Howard Street Cemetery
CHARTER ST
Charter Street Cemetery
BAMBOLINA
SOUTH RIVER HARBOR WALK
15 Peabody Street Park
SALEM WITCH TRIALS MEMORIAL
PEABODY ESSEX MUSEUM
Armory Park
SALEM MARITIME NATIONAL HISTORIC VISITOR CENTER
BROWN ST
THE STEPPING STONE INN
HOWARD ST
KIMBALL CT
WILLIAMS ST
MALL ST
SALEM WITCH MUSEUM
SALEM WAX MUSEUM OF WITCHES AND SEAFARERS
HAWTHORNE BLVD
WASHINGTON SQUARE W.
WASHINGTON SQUARE N.
Salem Common
WASHINGTON SQUARE S.
WASHINGTON SQUARE E.
SEA LEVEL OYSTER BAR
SALEM MARITIME NATIONAL HISTORIC SITE
Salem Maritime National Historic Site
DANIELS ST
BENTLEY ST
MORNING GLORY BED & BREAKFAST
HARDY ST
DERBY ST
TURNER ST
THE HOUSE OF THE SEVEN GABLES
ESSEX ST
0
100 yd
100 m
© AVALON TRAVEL

St., 978/741-3570, www.witchdungeon.com, 10am-5pm Apr.-Nov., extended hours in Oct., $10 adults, $9 seniors, $8 children 4-13), which stages dramatic reenactments in a downtown dungeon.

OTHER WITCHY SITES

These days, witches are largely stripped of their power to terrify, and the tragic sites of the witch trials jostle side-by-side with more upbeat supernatural landmarks. These fall into two categories, broadly speaking: Cutesy cartoon witches astride brooms decorate everything from souvenirs to the local high school, while a series of magic shops and psychics serves New England's latter-day witches, Pagans, and the curious.

Of the cute variety is the **Bewitched Statue** (235 Essex St.), an image of the nose-wiggling witch from the vintage television show. Warlocks and witches can pick up the necessary candles, crystals, and poppets at **Hex Old World Witchery** (246 Essex St., 978/666-0765, www.hexwitch.com, 11am-7pm daily), which also offers psychic readings that range from tarot cards to spirit mediumship. A variety of witch-related classes are available throughout the city.

SALEM MARITIME NATIONAL HISTORIC PARK

Comprising some of the most important historic landmarks along the waterfront, the **Salem Maritime National Historical Park** (160 Derby St., 978/740-1650, www.nps.gov, 10am-5pm daily, prices for tours vary) includes several authentic old sea captains' homes, historic wharves, and the Custom House featured in Hawthorne's *The Scarlet Letter*. The park offers a series of downloadable self-guided walking tours with topics ranging from Nathaniel Hawthorne to the city's African American heritage.

PEABODY ESSEX MUSEUM

With a fabulous collection of Asian art, some of it from the homes of Salem's historic sea captains, the **Peabody Essex Museum** (East India Sq., 978/745-9500 or 866/745-1876, www.pem.org, 10am-5pm Tues.-Sun., $20 adults, $18 seniors, $12 students, children 16 and under free) is among the top art museums in New England. Exhibits include priceless antiques from Asia and Polynesia, antique American furniture, and works by early American artists, as well as a 19th-century post-and-beam house that was disassembled and brought from China.

HOUSE OF THE SEVEN GABLES

Count the roofs at the **House of the Seven Gables** (115 Derby St., 978/744-0991, www.7gables.org, 10am-5pm Fri.-Tues. mid-Jan.-mid-Feb., 10am-5pm daily mid-Feb.-May, 10am-5pm Sun.-Thurs., 10am-7pm Fri.-Sat. June, 10am-7pm daily July-Oct., 10am-5pm daily Nov.-Dec., $14 adults, $13 seniors and students, $11 youth $13-18, $9 children 5-12, free children under 5)—they're all there. The 17th-century mansion is the stage set for Hawthorne's Puritan novel, and costumed interpreters take guests through three centuries of Salem history.

Entertainment and Events

Every October, **Haunted Happenings** (877/725-3662, www.hauntedhappenings.org) takes over the whole city, with a month of spooktastic events. All the historic sites get into the act with extended hours and special programs (such as the "Spirit of the Gables," when the Hawthorne house is open for tours by candlelight). The event culminates in a huge costume party on the Common that draws some 50,000 revelers from around the region to dance the monster mash until the wee hours.

With witch-trail landmarks spread across the city, a tour is a good way to get the whole story. Among the best are those from **The Salem Witch Walk** (798/666-0884, www.witchwalk.com, tours most days, $16), which blends historic facts from Salem's witch trials with bits and pieces about modern-day witches.

A 10-minute walk from downtown Salem, **Deacon Giles Distillery** (75 Canal St., 978/306-6675, www.deacongiles.com, 5pm-9pm Thurs., noon-10pm Fri.-Sat., noon-7pm Sun.) is worth a stop for craft cocktails made using locally distilled gin, rum, and vodka. The "Speakeasy Lab," which is open to children, also has a solid collection of board games for visitors to use.

Food

With an expansive menu and the friendly feel of a local diner, **Red's Sandwich Shop** (15 Central St., 978/745-3527, www.redssandwichshop.com, 5am-3pm Mon.-Sat., 6am-1pm Sun., $7-12) is an unpretentious place for lunch that's close to the main sites downtown. Big egg breakfasts are the staple here, as well as lots of sandwiches and pasta, but the seafood chowder gets raves from regulars.

The Neapolitan pizzas from **Bambolina** (288 Derby St., 978/594-8709, www.bambolinarestaurant.com, 11:30am-9pm Sun.-Thurs., 11:30am-10pm Fri.-Sat., $11-17) emerge from the wood-fired oven blackened and bubbling, decked out with super-fresh toppings that are (mostly) true to the old country. These are the best pies in town, in a bright, brick-lined space that can accommodate larger groups.

Top-notch classic French pastries, macarons, and lusciously flaky croissants are piled high at ★ **Caramel French Patisserie** (281 Essex St., 978/594-0244, www.caramelpatisserie.com, 8am-7pm Tues.-Fri., 9am-7pm Sat., 9am-6pm Sun., $3-7), a bright and beautiful spot that's ideal for a sightseeing break.

With a perch above Salem Harbor, **Sea Level Oyster Bar** (94 Wharf St., 978/741-0444, www.sealeveloysterbar.com, 11:30am-midnight daily, $12-25) strikes a perfect balance between the kid-friendly fryer joints and more upscale seafood—and the meals are great. The baked seafood pie is a perennial favorite, with a luscious sherry cream to offset the lobster, scallops, and shrimp, while clam chowder is an excellent standby. If you haven't tried chowder fries, a sloppy dish of french fries and chowder that's like New England's answer to Quebecois poutine, this is a good place to start.

Accommodations

Sweetly old-fashioned decor makes ★ **Morning Glory Bed and Breakfast** (22 Hardy St., 978/741-1703, www.morninggloryybb.com, $190-230) right at home in historic Salem, and you can watch ships come and go from the rooftop deck. The friendly innkeepers serve a hearty hot breakfast in the morning, and offer complimentary pickup and drop-off at the Salem ferry and train station.

Pet-friendly and laid-back, the **Stepping Stone Inn** (19 Washington St. N., 978/741-8900, www.thesteppingstoneinn.com, $145-250, Oct. rates to $350) is a great choice for travelers with kids (above 5 years old). Brightly painted rooms have simple decor, parking spots are available on-site, and the location is excellent, walking distance from everything. A continental breakfast of cereal, yogurt, fruits, and breads is served in a cheerful dining room.

Information

The **Salem Visitor Center** (2 New Liberty St., 978/740-1650, www.nps.gov/sama, 9am-5pm daily) is a great resource for maps, tour information, and brochures.

Getting There

Salem is located roughly 15 miles up the coast from Boston, though traffic can make this an hour-long drive. For those staying in Boston, public transit is a great option: **Trains** on the **Newbury/Rockport** line leave for Salem from North Station (www.mbta.com, 35 min., $7.50), while the **ferry** from **Boston Harbor Cruises** (617/227-4321, www.bostonharborcruises.com, 1 hr., 30 min., round-trip/one-way $45/25 adults, $41/23 seniors, $35/20 children) doubles as a tour of Boston Harbor, with narration pointing out key landmarks along the way.

PLYMOUTH

Even as the Pilgrims landed in the "New World" they looked back toward the old one, naming their first settlement for the English port they left behind. A rock inscribed with the year 1620 stakes a claim as the first landing point of the Pilgrims, but that's a story that didn't arrive until the mid-18th-century (just as the word "Pilgrims" was rarely used before the 19th century).

Accuracy aside, Plymouth Rock has become a symbol: For some, it represents the dreams of the independent Puritans who risked everything for a new life, while others see a memorial to an era that brought tragedy to Native Americans and enslaved Africans. As Malcolm X said in 1964, "We didn't land on Plymouth Rock. The rock was landed on us."

These days, the rock itself rests out of the weather under a stone canopy that resembles the Parthenon, set near Cole's Hill, the first cemetery used by the Mayflower Pilgrims. For a more vivid glimpse of the Pilgrims' daily lives, and at the lives of the Wampanoag people who helped them survive the harsh coastal winter, head to **Plimoth Plantation,** a working replica of a Wampanoag village and their settlement.

Sights

PLIMOTH PLANTATION AND THE WAMPANOAG HOMESITE

A living history museum, the **Plimoth Plantation** (137 Warren Ave., 508/746-1622, www.plimoth.org, 9am-5pm daily, $28 adults, $26 seniors, $16 children 5-12, children under 5 free) offers a full immersion in 17th-century life, of both Wampanoag people and Pilgrims. It's a hands-on experience, with real gardens, livestock, and craftspeople in period costumes.

The centerpiece of the site is the **1627 Village,** where actors use the names of real Pilgrims, playing out their stories amid thatched houses and weathered wood. To really take advantage of the experience, waylay an actor with questions—they can wax eloquent on everything from child-rearing to religion and cooking.

While the "Pilgrims" in the 1627 Village are playing a role, the people you'll meet at the **Wampanoag Homesite** are authentic Native Americans, whether Wampanoag or from another tribe. The structures here range from a Wampanoag *wetu*, or house, covered in mats, to a longhouse and a cooking shelter. The interpreters are deeply knowledgeable and share stories, traditions, and insight

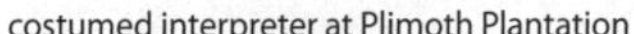

costumed interpreter at Plimoth Plantation

into what life was like in a 17th-century Native American settlement (ask for a lesson in playing *hubbub*, a game that was popular across early America).

The Plimoth Plantation also owns a wonderful replica of the *Mayflower*—it's dubbed ***Mayflower II***—which began a multiyear restoration in 2016 at Mystic Seaport in Connecticut, and is expected back in 2020 for the 400th anniversary of the Pilgrims' arrival.

PLYMOUTH ROCK

A glacial erratic boulder that's inscribed simply "1620," **Plymouth Rock** (79 Water St.) was only nominated as the Pilgrims' landing point in 1741, when the 94-year-old Thomas Faunce recalled his deceased father's assertion that the rock marked the spot. It's shrunken in size as souvenir hunters have chipped off mementos, but the rock is still enormous, with four tons visible and six tons buried beneath the sand.

MAYFLOWER SOCIETY HOUSE

Home to the General Society of *Mayflower* Descendants, the **Mayflower Society House and Library** (4 Winslow St., 508/746-3188, www.themayflowersociety.org, tours 11am-4pm daily mid-May-Oct., $7 adults, $5 youth 13-18, children under 13 free) is a gorgeous mansion built by Edward Winslow, himself a *Mayflower* passenger. The society's small museum is filled with fascinating artifacts from the time, but the house alone is worth a stop, complete with period furnishings and artwork.

Getting There

Plymouth is located just off Highway 3, making it a straight hour-long shot from Boston, and a convenient stop on the way to Cape Cod. Buses from Boston's Logan Airport and South Station are available from the **Plymouth-Brockton Bus Line** (508/746-0378, www.p-b.com, 70 mins., $22 adults, $11 children). To travel to Plymouth by bus, take the **Kingston/Plymouth Line** from Boston's South Station (www.mbta.com, 1.5 hrs., $11.50) to Plymouth Station, which is a 10-minute drive from Plimoth Plantation. Taxi service is available from **South Shore Taxi** (508/406-8908) and **Mayflower Taxi** (508/746-8294).

Cape Cod and the Islands

Look for ★ to find recommended sights, activities, dining, and lodging.

Highlights

★ **Cape Cod Rail Trail:** The going's always easy on this 22-mile, mostly flat bicycle path, even when traffic is hopelessly snarled on the Cape's one highway (page 104).

★ **Cape Cod National Seashore:** Stroll miles of sandy beaches with hypnotizing waves (page 110).

★ **Provincetown's Drag Shows:** People come to P-town to let it all hang out—and so do the wisecracking performers in the community's legendary drag shows (page 122).

★ **Whale-Watching Tours:** Whales, dolphins, and sharks flock to the nutrient-rich waters of Stellwagen Bank National Marine Sanctuary, an 842-square-mile reserve with New England's best whale-watching (page 124).

★ **Aquinnah Cliffs:** Crayon box-colored cliffs, a historic lighthouse, and excellent beaches—the perfect place to play in the waves or explore Martha Vineyard's Wampanoag heritage (page 142).

★ **Nantucket Whaling Museum:** Scrimshaw, harpoons, and a giant skeleton bring Moby-Dick to life on the island that inspired Herman Melville's epic novel (page 148).

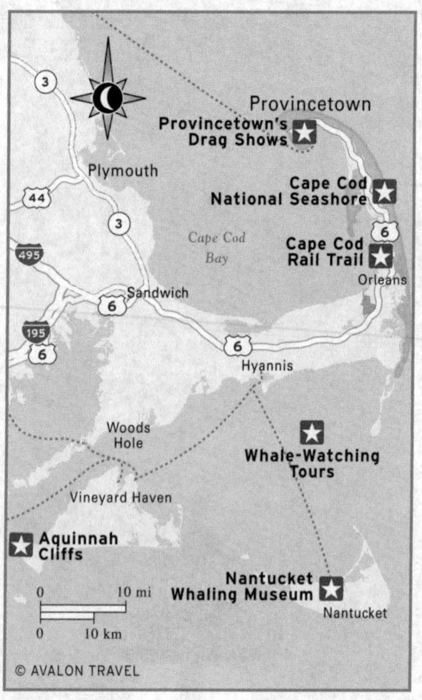

Cape Cod unfurls into the ocean from the southeastern edge of New England, a ragged hook of sand, bogs, and crashing waves just over an hour from downtown Boston.

Endless beaches and sandy cliffs line the Cape Cod National Seashore, while the interior is a maze of rustling cranberries and rolling dunes.

Cape Cod is the traditional home of the Nauset tribe, and the leading edge of colonial America—it was the first land sighted by the Mayflower Pilgrims in 1620. In the 18th century, it attracted a rugged population of Portuguese fishers and whalers, followed by generations of travelers, artists, and renegades who flocked to the Cape for its isolation and beauty.

Humpback whales patrol the coast April-October, and Provincetown's historic lighthouses command dramatic views of sunrise and sunset above the sea. The sandy coastline shifts with every storm, but the scenery feels timeless, from Chatham's tony saltbox cottages to the artist shacks scattered in the Provincetown dunes.

Cape Cod's blend of old, new, and wild offers the opportunity to weave between worlds. You can spend the morning wandering world-class galleries in an artists' colony, trace the Cape Cod Rail Trail on two wheels, then catch an evening performance at one of Provincetown's raucous drag shows. Spot wildlife from a kayak, sample clam chowder at a seaside shack, and dance the night away at a beachfront bar. Whatever your thread—whether it's nature, wildlife, history, or culture—you can follow it from Sagamore Bridge to Land's End, where the sand finally gives way to the sea.

PLANNING YOUR TIME

It's best to find a single region as a home base for your time in the Cape, as moving around the peninsula can be time-consuming when summer traffic hits. For quick chowder-and-cottage overnight stopovers, the Inner Cape is easy to reach and convenient to the mainland—this is also a good base for visiting Nantucket and Martha's Vineyard, a pair of scenic islands that have personalities all their own. The diverse Mid Cape region bundles all the Cape's charms into a single, compact

Previous: Provincetown port; Brant Point lighthouse. **Above:** Fresnel lens at Martha's Vineyard Museum in Edgartown.

Cape Cod and the Islands

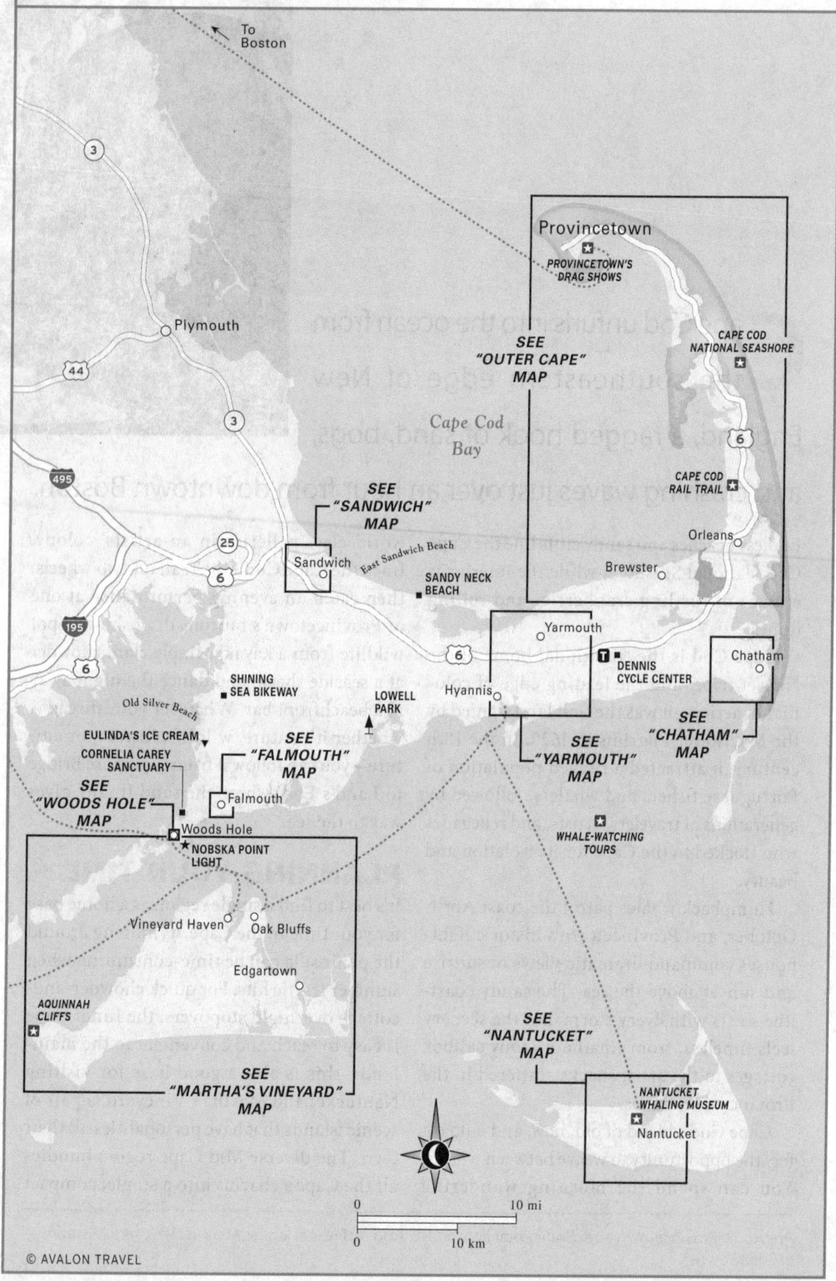

To Boston
Provincetown
PROVINCETOWN'S DRAG SHOWS
SEE "OUTER CAPE" MAP
CAPE COD NATIONAL SEASHORE
Plymouth
Cape Cod Bay
CAPE COD RAIL TRAIL
SEE "SANDWICH" MAP
Orleans
Sandwich
East Sandwich Beach
Brewster
SANDY NECK BEACH
Yarmouth
Chatham
DENNIS CYCLE CENTER
SHINING SEA BIKEWAY
Hyannis
LOWELL PARK
Old Silver Beach
SEE "CHATHAM" MAP
EULINDA'S ICE CREAM
SEE "FALMOUTH" MAP
SEE "YARMOUTH" MAP
CORNELIA CAREY SANCTUARY
SEE "WOODS HOLE" MAP
Falmouth
Woods Hole
WHALE-WATCHING TOURS
NOBSKA POINT LIGHT
Vineyard Haven
Oak Bluffs
Edgartown
AQUINNAH CLIFFS
SEE "NANTUCKET" MAP
SEE "MARTHA'S VINEYARD" MAP
NANTUCKET WHALING MUSEUM
Nantucket
0
10 mi
0
10 km

corridor of kitsch and charm, from family-friendly Yarmouth to romantic Chatham.

When you turn the 90-degree corner at Chatham to the Lower Cape, though, things begin to get wilder (in every sense). Come here to explore the lonely dunes and sprawling beaches of the Cape Cod National Seashore, or sip planter's punch with a crowd of shirtless tea dancers in Provincetown, known locally as "the end of the world." P-town's bustling center is all the more thrilling for being so isolated; it's easy to get away from the hustle and walk to rustic artists' shacks, discover thriving wildlife, and catch stunning sunsets from Pilgrim Point.

ORIENTATION

The writer Henry David Thoreau called Cape Cod the "bared and bended arm of Massachusetts: the shoulder is at Buzzard's Bay . . . and the sandy fist at Provincetown." It's a good description of the Cape's distinctive shape. Severed from the mainland by the Cape Cod Canal, the historic towns of Cape Cod's "shoulder" are part of the Inner Cape, and if you keep driving east, you'll be traveling through the Lower Cape.

Make a 90-degree turn at Chatham, and you'll arrive at the oak forests of the Mid Cape. Thoreau's "sandy fist" is what Codders call the Outer Cape, the slender passage that extends from Truro to Provincetown.

For driving purposes, the Cape is simple; it's accessed by the Sagamore Bridge if approaching from the north, and the Bourne Bridge when driving from the west. Route 6 runs from the Sagamore Bridge to Land's End and is paralleled by two smaller highways on the Mid Cape, Route 6A and Route 28.

Inner Cape

If the Cape is a place apart, then the Cape Cod Canal is what protects the lifelong residents and weekend trippers from the rest of the world. As soon as you cross the Bourne or Sagamore Bridge, interstate highways sliver into smaller roads that wind past historic towns and fishing villages. From historic **Sandwich** to the bustling villages of **Falmouth** and **Woods Hole,** the Inner Cape is an easy place to get a quick taste of Cape Cod without driving all the way to Provincetown. These towns also make good stops for travelers heading for the Martha's Vineyard or Nantucket ferries. Route 6 is the main route between towns along the northern edge of the Inner Cape, but with extra time to explore, Route 6A is especially scenic, lined with cranberry bogs and antiques stores.

SANDWICH

Refugees from Boston's chaotic traffic are relieved to find this quiet town just a few miles past the Sagamore Bridge. Founded 17 years after the Pilgrims touched down, Cape Cod's oldest town remains quaintly old-fashioned, with saltbox houses, tree-lined streets, and a gray-shingled gristmill at the edge of a swan pond. Sandwich is the place to exhale, slow down, and adapt to the pace of life on the Cape. Spend an afternoon exploring small historic sites and browsing antiques, or pedaling along the seven-mile canal that divides Cape Cod from the rest of the world.

Sights

CAPE COD CANAL VISITORS CENTER

Before the Cape Cod Canal let captains bypass the route, sailing around Cape Cod's shifting sands was slow and shockingly dangerous. The early 17th-century colonists were the first to dream of a canal that would provide a shortcut, and there were repeated surveys through the years, but the real digging didn't start until 1909. The mammoth undertaking was slowed by the enormous, ice age

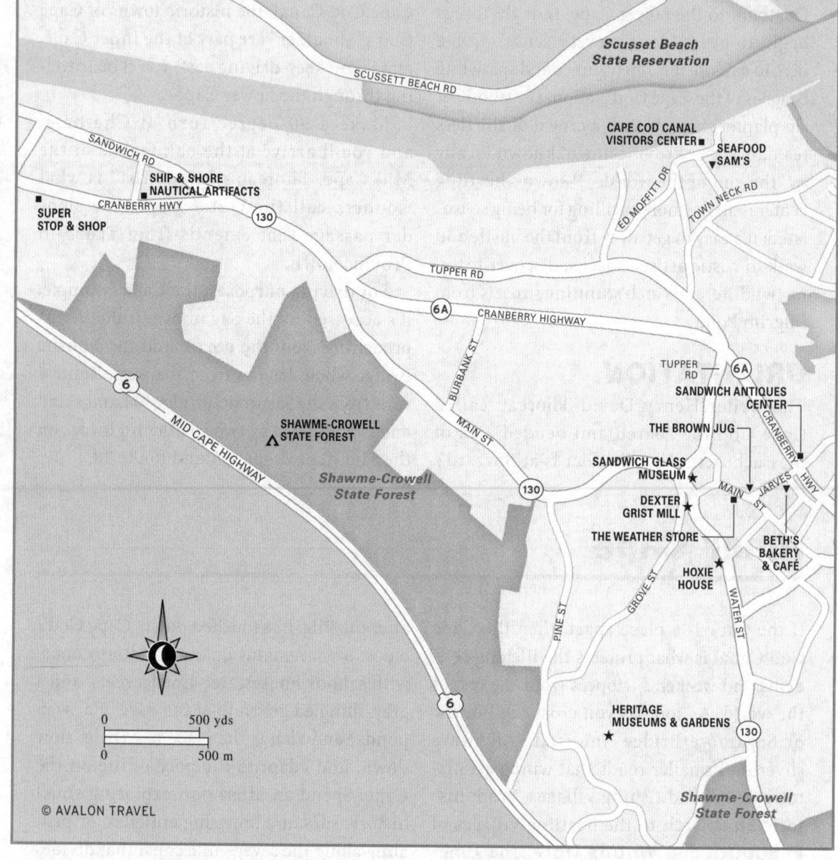

boulders that had to be blown apart by hand-placed, underwater dynamite charges. The toll scheme intended to finance the canal never became profitable, and the canal was eventually turned over to the U.S. Army Corps of Engineers. Learn the whole story at the fascinating **Cape Cod Canal Visitors Center** (60 Ed Moffit Dr., 508/833-9678, www.capecodcanal.us, 10am-5pm daily early May-late Oct., free), where kid-friendly interactive displays bring the canal's construction, shipping, and ecology to life. Take the helm of a 40-foot patrol boat, learn to signal using marine flags, and pick up maps of the **bike trail** (www.capecodbikeguide.com/canal.asp) that links the Bourne and Sagamore Bridges and offers unparalleled views of boat traffic.

HERITAGE MUSEUMS & GARDENS

Explore pharmaceutical mogul J. K. Lilly's obsessive collections of classic cars, art, and Americana at **Heritage Museums & Gardens** (67 Grove St., 508/888-3300, www.heritagemuseumsandgardens.org, 10am-5pm daily mid-Apr.-mid-Oct., $18 adults, $8 children 3-11, children under 3 free) on his superbly maintained former estate. One hundred acres of display gardens wrap around

At Home on the Cape

Cape Cod lent its name to one of America's most ubiquitous architectural styles, but the region's real signature is the wood-framed, asymmetrical home known as the **"saltbox,"** a reference to the wooden boxes once used to store salt under sloping lids. It's easy to spot the distinctive houses around New England; when seen head-on, they look just like the simple, English style of houses that the first colonists built, with two rooms on the first floor, two on the second, and a squat brick chimney in the center of the roof. From the side, however, one can see that the rooflines extend almost to the ground. When a blustery gale is blowing off the ocean, the houses look like they've hunched their backs against the chilly wind.

Legend has it that the style of house became popular when settlers sought to avoid Queen Anne's tax on homes greater than one story (the thinking goes that the roofline would exempt the house from the extra levy), but growing colonial families were likely a bigger factor. Adding an extended roofline is a relatively simple way of expanding the living space on the first floor of a boxy home, and the additional area generally included a central kitchen, a bedroom, and a dairy, which was sometimes sunk into the ground for natural cooling. Cape Cod's most historic saltbox is the **Hoxie House** (18 Water St., 508/888-4361, 11am-4:30pm Mon.-Sat., 1pm-4:30pm Sun. late May-mid-Oct., $4 adults, $3 children 9-17) in Sandwich.

What most Americans call **"Cape Cod"** houses didn't earn the name until the early 19th century, but they were also adapted from English building styles, evoking cottages in Cornwall and Devon. They're generally 1.5 stories high, with four rooms on the lower floor, a central chimney and staircase, and a pair of 2nd-floor bedrooms with sloping roofs and windows on the gable ends. Cape Cod houses are endlessly adaptable and can take on a patchwork appearance as years go by. Henry David Thoreau said that it looked like each inhabitant "had punched a hole where his necessities required it . . . without regard to outside effect. There were windows for the grown folks, and windows for the children—three or four apiece." To see a historic example of a Cape Cod house (albeit one with a gambrel roof), visit the **Atwood House Museum** (347 Stage Harbor Rd., Chatham, 508/945-2493, www.chathamhistoricalsociety.org, 1pm-4pm Tues.-Sat. June and Sept.-Oct., 10am-4pm Tues.-Fri., 1pm-4pm Sat. July-Aug., $10 adults, $8 students 8-18, children under 8 free).

living mazes and labyrinths that bloom with wisteria, honeysuckle, and hyacinth. Inside the museum, browse three sprawling galleries that house a vintage carousel, automobiles, art, and traveling exhibitions, along with a noteworthy collection of Nantucket baskets and other New England folk art. The grounds are especially breathtaking in late May, during the **rhododendron festival,** which draws flower lovers from around the world.

OTHER SIGHTS

Get a taste of life in 17th-century Sandwich at a historic saltbox house—the oldest house on Cape Cod. Named for a 19th-century whaling captain, the **Hoxie House** (18 Water St., 508/888-4361, 11am-4:30pm Mon.-Sat., 1pm-4:30pm Sun. late May-mid-Oct., $4 adults, $3 children 9-17) is carefully maintained with period antiques, and the enthusiastic docents are full of information about how early Cape Codders worked, played, ate and—occasionally—bathed.

Just down the road from the Hoxie House is the 1654 **Dexter Grist Mill** (2 Water St., 508/888-4361, 11am-4pm Mon.-Fri., 1pm-4:30pm Sun. late June-mid-Oct., $4 adults, $3 children 6-12). With a working waterwheel and shingles faded to silver gray, it's a pretty spot for taking photos of the swans that bob around in the adjacent pond. Take a picnic to enjoy by the water's edge, and bring some bread to feed the swans, but don't think about abandoning your personal geese and ducks there—a very specific sign warns of a steep fine if you're apprehended.

The Boston Sandwich & Glass Company supplied 19th-century Americans with mold-blown glassware that imitated the cut glass from England and Ireland at much lower prices. See historic pieces and glassblowing demonstrations at the **Sandwich Glass Museum** (129 Main St., 508/888-0251, www.sandwichglassmuseum.org, 9:30am-4pm Wed.-Sun. Feb.-Mar., 9:30am-5pm daily Apr.-Dec., $9 adults, $2 children 6-14, children under 6 free), which also has an excellent on-site shop full of traditional and contemporary glass pieces.

Food

Stock up for an elegant picnic at **The Brown Jug** (155 Main St., 508/888-4669, www.thebrownjug.com, 8am-8pm Tues.-Thurs., 8am-11pm Fri.-Sat., noon-8pm Sun., pizzas $11-22), which has an excellent selection of wines, cheeses, and other goodies. The real treat, though, is the wood-fired pizza, which is among the best on the Cape. Pies emerge from the oven blistered and bubbling, with thin crusts topped by traditional ingredients. The menu also includes sandwiches, salads, and house-baked pastries, and while seating inside the shop is limited, the outdoor patio is a sunny place to enjoy a slice in fine weather.

The cavernous dining room and counter service at **Seafood Sam's** (6 Coast Guard Rd., 508/888-4629, www.seafoodsams.com, 11am-8:30pm Sun.-Thurs., 11am-9pm Fri.-Sat., $5-21) might not win awards for ambience, but that can be just the ticket when your party is caked with sand and looking for lunch. Fried whole belly clams, lobster bisque, and clam chowder are favorites among regulars, and midday specials (11am-4pm) include well-priced plates of seafood with coleslaw and sides.

Hefty scoops of hard-packed ice cream draw a steady crowd to **Twin Acres Ice Cream** (21 Route 6A, 508/888-0566, www.twinacresicecreamshoppe.com, 11am-10pm daily late May-early Sept., 11am-9pm daily early Sept.-early Oct., $3-8), which serves a laundry list of flavors in a pretty garden location. There's also a short menu of fast food from the grill, but the ice cream is the headliner—especially when stuffed into a chocolate chip cookie ice cream sandwich.

The busy ovens at **Beth's Bakery and Café** (16 Jarves St., 508/888-7716, www.bethsbakery.net, 8am-3pm Mon.-Thurs., 8am-4pm Fri.-Sat., 9am-3pm Sun., $4-10) turn out a tempting array of scones, cinnamon rolls, and cookies. Homey decor and comfortable seats make this a pleasant place to linger over tea and a treat, and a simple lunch menu of salads, soups, and sandwiches is freshly prepared and appealing.

Pick up basics at **Super Stop & Shop** (65 Rte. 6A, 508/833-1302, 6am-midnight Mon.-Sat., 6am-10pm Sun.).

Entertainment and Events

Sandwich quiets down after dark, but the **Tavern at the Daniel Webster Inn** (149 Main St., 508/888-3622, www.danlwebsterinn.com, 4:30pm-9pm Sun.-Thurs., 4:30pm-10pm Fri.-Sat.) is a great place for a beer in a bar that feels like the interior of a ship, with live music on Friday nights.

The **Sandwich Arts Alliance** (www.sandwichartsalliance.org) organizes occasional concerts, art walks, and book readings in the village.

Shopping

Boutiques and souvenir shops cluster around Main Street and Jarves Street in downtown Sandwich. It's easy to while away an afternoon browsing art, antiques, and cottagey home furnishings.

The bits and bobs of Cape Cod life sift into the **Sandwich Antiques Center** (131 Rte. 6A, 508/833-3600, www.sandwichantiquescenter.com, 10am-5pm daily) along with some unique finds and a good selection of Sandwich glass. If antique barometers and state-of-the-art weather systems are more your style, however, don't miss **The Weather Store** (146 Main St., 800/646-1203, www.theweatherstore.com, open "by chance" or appointment), where you'll find everything you need to know which way the wind blows. It's a fascinating place stocked with beautiful tide charts, compasses, hygrometers, brass telescopes, and other esoterica, as well as practical tools for modern-day sailors. Call ahead.

Visitors in search of maritime antiques, signal flags, and ship wheels will find their hearts' desire at **Ship & Shore Nautical Artifacts** (165 Cranberry Hwy., Sagamore, 508/888-9545, www.nauticalartifacts.com, 10am-6pm Mon.-Sat. noon-5pm Sun.), a museum-like shop that's two miles from the center of Sandwich.

Sports and Recreation

If you can find a place to park or leave your car in town, **East Sandwich Beach** (parking at western end of N. Shore Blvd., $15) offers grass-covered dunes and soft sand with serene views to the north. To get a closer look at the area's fragile dunes and salt marshes, walk the 1,350-foot **boardwalk to Town Neck Beach** (parking at end of Boardwalk Rd., $10). The walk down the rocky beach is especially scenic at sunset, when the dune grass glows a dusky pink, and is a favorite among bird-watchers.

There's more parking (and people) farther east at **Sandy Neck Beach** (425 Sandy Neck Rd., Barnstable, 508/362-8300, Memorial Day-Labor Day $20 weekend parking, $15 weekday parking, off-season parking free), six miles of pebbly sand rimmed by rolling dunes that extend all the way to Barnstable, where the beach's main access points are located. A network of walking trails threads between the dunes, from a 0.5-mile loop to a 13-mile round-trip hike that goes within sight distance of the Sandy Neck lighthouse. Campfires are allowed on Sandy Neck Beach after 7pm.

Accommodations and Camping

With oodles of vacation-home owners, Airbnb is a good option for trips to Sandwich, though summer weekends are booked solid for months in advance.

$100-150

Basic rooms at the **Earl of Sandwich Motel** (378 Rte. 6A, East Sandwich, 508/888-1415, www.earlofsandwich.com, $85-150) are spruced up, with a few old-fashioned frills. The appealing, garden-like grounds are an extra perk of this affordable, family- and pet-friendly location, with hammocks, a swimming pool, and a duck pond. Rates include a continental breakfast during the summer months, and all rooms have air-conditioning, refrigerators, and televisions.

$150-250

Airy, updated decor makes the ★ **Sandwich Inn and Suites** (14 Rte. 6A, 508/888-0409, www.sandwichinnandsuites.com, $125-200) one of the best options in the area. Regular rooms and studios are spread across four acres dotted with towering oaks that offer privacy and shade, and the studios are equipped with galley kitchens—a great choice for families. The continental breakfast goes above and beyond, with sweet and savory options, strong-brewed coffee, and fresh fruit served in a sunny dining room.

Charming without being fussy, the **1750 Inn at Sandwich Center** (118 Tupper Rd., 508/888-6958, www.innatsandwich.com, $185-225) is wonderfully hospitable. Breakfast is hearty and home-cooked, and the innkeepers keep the living room stocked with fresh cookies and hot drinks. There's an early evening wine tasting during the summer months, followed by after-dinner drinks and chocolates, and plenty of vacation perks like loaner beach chairs and a book exchange.

CAMPING

The pine-shaded campsites at **Shawme-Crowell State Forest** (42 Main St., 508/888-0351, tent sites $20, yurts $55-60) are just outside of Sandwich, three miles past the Sagamore Bridge. It's the perfect base for visiting the Inner Cape, and with 285 sites, it tends to have more vacancies than the popular campgrounds near Provincetown. For groups, the yurts are a particularly good deal, though the simple wall tents don't come with linens—bring your own sleeping bag.

Information

Information about Sandwich and surrounding towns is available at the **Sandwich Visitor Center** (Rte. 130, 774/338-5605, www.capecodcanalchamber.org, 10am-5pm daily mid-May-early Oct.), though the volunteer-run spot does occasionally close for lack of staff.

Getting There and Around

Plymouth and Brockton (508/746-0378, www.p-b.com) offers daily bus service from Boston to the **Sagamore Park and Ride,** (Rte. 3, Bourne, $24 adults, $12 children), which is four miles from downtown Sandwich. At the Sagamore Park and Ride, transfer to the **Cape Cod Regional Transit Authority**'s (800/352-7155, www.capecodtransit.org, $2) Sandwich Line, with several buses to downtown Sandwich each day.

Parking in downtown Sandwich can be a challenge during the busy summer months, but free parking is available at the now-closed **Wing School** (33 Water St.), which is walking distance from downtown Sandwich. The Wing School is also a stop on the free, seasonal **Sandwich Park & Ride Trolley** (www.sandwichchamber.com. 10am-4:30pm Fri.-Sun., July-Sept.); trolleys depart every hour for a handful of stops in the center of town as well as at the Cape Cod Canal Visitors Center.

FALMOUTH AND WOODS HOLE

Many travelers pass through Falmouth and Woods Hole on their way to the Martha's Vineyard ferry, but a scenic harbor, summery beaches, and a world-renowned oceanographic center make this a fine Cape Cod destination of its own. Falmouth loves to boast that it was the childhood home of Katherine Lee Bates, a professor and poet who wrote "America the Beautiful," but visitors may be more impressed with the town's beloved clam shack, a Cape Cod classic at the water's edge that's a pilgrimage spot for great piles of fried seafood. Anyone interested in marine science should be sure to catch a tour of the Woods Hole Oceanographic Institution, which keeps tabs on everything below the waves.

Sights

WOODS HOLE OCEANOGRAPHIC INSTITUTION

The scientists from the **Woods Hole Oceanographic Institution,** or **WHOI** (pronounced "hooey"), spend their time exploring sunken ships, tracking the global climate, and keeping an eye on the critters that live beneath the ocean surface, from whelks to whales. Learn about their work at the small **Ocean Science Exhibit Center** (15 School St., Woods Hole, 508/548-1400, www.whoi.edu/main/ocean-science-exhibit-center, 10am-4:30pm Mon.-Fri. late Apr.-May, 10am-4:30pm Mon.-Sat. June-Oct., 10am-4:30pm Tues.-Fri. Nov.-Dec., $3 suggested donation), which has a replica of the Alvin submersible that first explored the wreck of *Titanic*, as well as exhibits and videos on some of the ocean's weirdest, wonderful life-forms.

Get an insider's look at WHOI's latest work by joining one of the institute's free, volunteer-led **walking tours** of the dock area and research facilities that aren't regularly open to the public (93 Water St., 508/289-2252, 1.25 hrs., 10:30am and 1:30pm Mon.-Fri. July-Aug., reservations required).

WOODS HOLE SCIENCE AQUARIUM

Do your own research on the adorable—and adorably ugly—things of the deep at the small, kid-friendly **Woods Hole Science Aquarium** (166 Water St., Woods Hole, 508/495-2001, http://aquarium.nefsc.noaa.gov, 11am-4pm Tues.-Sat., donations accepted) that's just down the street from WHOI. The aquarium is home to around 140 species of native New England fish and invertebrates, and kid-friendly touch tanks are a fun, hands-on break from all the learning. Time your visit to see the fascinating seal feedings at 11am and 4pm most days; the seals are rescues that can't survive in the

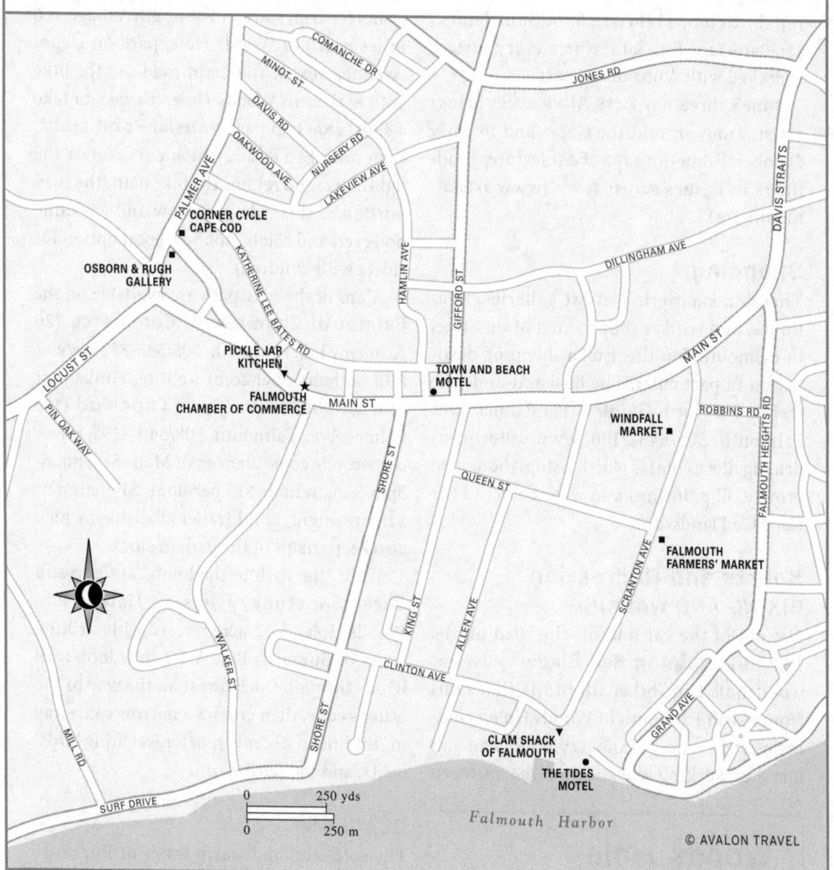

wild, including a blind seal named Bumper that survived a shark attack and is living the good life on a hand-fed diet of fresh fish.

NOBSKA POINT LIGHT

Sailors shooting the narrow channel between Woods Hole and Nonamesset Island don't have much leeway, and the 1828 **Nobska Point Light** (233 Nobska Rd., Woods Hole, www.friendsofnobska.org) is an essential waypoint. Even in the days of sophisticated satellite navigation, the light and foghorn are reassuring presences to passing mariners, and Nobska is a sublime place to watch the sun set over Buzzards Bay, with views that stretch clear to Martha's Vineyard. There's limited parking on-site, so during busy periods it's worth walking the one mile from downtown Woods Hole (though the narrow road can be dangerously busy).

Entertainment and Events

There are frequent live acts and a (mostly) sedate, older crowd at **Jack's Restaurant and Bar** (327 Gifford St., Falmouth, 508/540-5225, www.jacksrestaurantfalmouth.com, 4pm-11pm Mon.-Thurs., 4pm-midnight Fri.-Sat., 4pm-10pm Sun.), in contrast to the raucous

Quahog Republic Dive Bar (97 Spring Bars Rd., Falmouth, 508/540-4111, www.quahog-republic.com, 11am-11:30pm Sun.-Thurs., 11:30am-1am Fri.-Sat.), where every surface is decked with scuba diving kits.

June's three-day **Arts Alive** event brings artists from around the Cape, and in early October, Falmouth's **JazzFest** features headliners in venues across town (www.artsfalmouth.org).

Shopping

There's a smattering of art galleries, boutiques, and trinket shops along Main Street in Falmouth, but this isn't a shopping destination in particular. The husband-and-wife **Osborn & Rugh Gallery** (114 Palmer Ave., Falmouth, 508/548-2100, www.osborneandrughgallery.com) is worth a stop, though, to browse oil paintings and watercolors of the Cape Cod landscape.

Sports and Recreation

BIKING AND WALKING

Get out of the car and off the road on the 10.7-mile **Shining Sea Bikeway** (www.woodshole.com/bikepath.html) that runs from North Falmouth to Woods Hole, winding past beaches, cranberry bogs, and salt marshes. Parking is available at the northern terminus, on the north side of Route 151 in North Falmouth, just west of Route 28A. For a shorter trip, start in Falmouth Village, 3.6 miles north of Woods Hole; park on Depot Avenue, west of the main road. As the bike path arrives in Woods Hole, it's easy to take a short side trip past **Nobska Point Light;** turn onto Fay Road, which curves past the lighthouse and rejoins the bike path (the road portion of this ride is narrow and winding, however, and might not be a good option for riders with children).

Maps of the bike path are available on the **Falmouth Chamber of Commerce** (20 Academy Ln., Falmouth, 508/548-8500, www.falmouthchamber.com) website. Find a pair of wheels at **Corner Cycle Cape Cod** (115 Palmer Ave., Falmouth, 508/540-4195, www.cornercycle.com, 10am-6pm Mon.-Sat., noon-5pm Sun., rentals $12 per hour, $17 half day, $25 overnight, child trailer available), which also keeps maps of the path in stock.

Walk "the path to the knob" at **Cornelia Carey Sanctuary** (Quissett Harbor Rd., Woods Hole), a 12-acre reserve with striking views of Buzzards Bay. A 1.2-mile loop trail winds through thick forest on the way to the water's edge, then crosses a narrow causeway to "the knob," a scenic spot for watching birds, boats, and the setting sun.

Woods Hole

BEACHES

The soft sand and warm water of Buzzards Bay make **Old Silver Beach** (Quaker Rd., Falmouth, May-Sept., parking $20) a favorite among locals and visitors alike, and it's among the best places to throw out your beach blanket on the entire Inner Cape. There are restrooms, showers, and a snack bar on-site, but parking can be an issue during high season.

Food

FALMOUTH

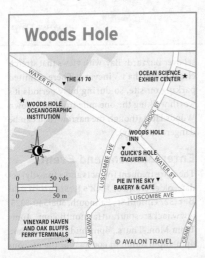

The harborside ★ **Clam Shack of Falmouth** (227 Clinton Ave., Falmouth, 508/540-7758, 11:30am-7:30pm daily late May-early Sept., $6-21, cash only) is a pilgrimage place for fried fare. Fried clams and scallops are lightly battered and succulent, and the Clam Shack is especially nice on sunny days, when you can watch passing boats from an outdoor picnic table.

Super-fresh ingredients and bright flavors make the **Pickle Jar Kitchen** (170 Main St., Falmouth, 508/540-6760, www.picklejarkitchen.com, 7am-3pm Thurs.-Mon., $6-15) an inviting spot for breakfast and lunch in downtown Falmouth. Regulars love the vegetarian-friendly options and house-made hash, as well as substantial salads, hearty sandwiches, and absurdly delicious deep-fried pickle appetizers. The brightly painted casual dining room fills up quickly on weekend mornings, so come early to snag a table. If you haven't guessed, many of the menu items come with delicious house pickles, which are also available by the pound.

Joining the crowd at **Eulinda's Ice Cream** (634 W. Falmouth Hwy., West Falmouth, 508/457-1060, noon-10pm daily late Apr.-Oct., $2-6) is a summertime tradition in Falmouth, with a location that's right off the bike path. The tiny shack serves a long list of ice cream flavors; sundaes are piled with hot fudge and whipped cream; and frappes are thick and creamy.

Pick up organic produce and gourmet food at the small **Windfall Market** (77 Scranton Ave., Falmouth, 508/548-0099, www.windfallmarket.com, 8am-8pm Mon.-Sat., 8am-7pm Sun.) and more standard fare at Falmouth's **Super Stop & Shop** (20 Teaticket Hwy., Falmouth, 508/540-7481, 6am-midnight Mon.-Sat., 7am-10pm Sun.). Find local pastries, handmade souvenirs, and produce at the **Falmouth Farmers' Market** (180 Scranton Ave., Falmouth, www.falmouthfarmersmarket.org, noon-6pm Thurs. late May-early Oct.).

WOODS HOLE

A perennial favorite for whiling away the time before the ferry is the sweet-as-can-be ★ **Pie in the Sky Bakery & Cafe** (10 Water St., Woods Hole, 508/540-5475, www.pieintheskywoodshole.com, 5am-10pm daily, $3-9). The freshly baked pastries are the stars here, from fruit pies to bread pudding and brioche, but a lunch menu of salads, soups, and sandwiches (at distinctly un-Cape prices) is satisfying and simple. Grab a cup of organic, house-roasted coffee inside the colorful café, or settle into a seat on the sunny deck.

The refined cuisine at the ★ **Water Street Kitchen** (56 Water St., Woods Hole, 508/540-5656, www.waterstreetkitchen.com, 5pm-close Tues.-Sat., $17-32) blends ingredients from Cape Cod farms and fisheries with global flavor. Menus of small plates and entrées change with the season, but the lobster steamed bun is a perennial favorite, as is the lighthearted cocktail list. With views of the sea, the dining room strikes a compelling balance between rustic and elegant.

Get your seafood in taco form and "wicked fresh" at **Quick's Hole Taqueria** (6 Luscombe Ave., Woods Hole, 508/495-0792, www.quicksholewickedfresh.com, 11am-8:30pm Sun.-Thurs., 11am-9:30pm Fri.-Sat. mid-May-Sept., $9-25), an offbeat spot with counter-service Mexican food, local beer, and a sunny deck. The lobster tacos win raves, but there are plenty of options for landlubbers and vegans, like pulled-pork burritos or tacos piled with fire-roasted veggies.

Accommodations and Camping

$100-150

Good budget options are scanty in this part of the Cape, which makes **Town and Beach Motel** (382 Main St., Falmouth, 508/548-1380, www.townandbeachmotel.com, $75-195) an excellent find. The rooms in the low-rise building are somewhere between outdated and vintage, but the motel is walking distance from the village, and nautical bedspreads and wood-paneled walls feel like an unpretentious taste of a different time.

$150-250

Another pleasantly retro place to land is **The Tides Motel** (267 Clinton Ave., Falmouth, 508/548-3126, www.tidesmotelcapecod.com,

$120-200 d, $195-260 6-person suite). The Tides has basic, sunny rooms that are spotlessly clean, but what keeps this place a perennial favorite is the motel's private beach; 1st-floor rooms can open a door to the sand, with a pair of beach chairs for watching boats go in and out of Falmouth's narrow harbor.

OVER $250

Charmingly decorated rooms, complimentary bikes, and thoughtful amenities make the ★ **Woods Hole Inn** (28 Water St., Woods Hole, 508/495-0248, www.woodsholeinn.com, $260-449) feel like a place to escape to, as do the sumptuous breakfasts. In keeping with the town's science and conservation bent, the inn makes an effort to keep it green with local products, biodegradable cleaners, and employees that bike to work. The inn is located across the street from the Martha's Vineyard ferry.

CAMPING

Set on 53 acres with playgrounds, three swimming pools, a lake, and indoor common spaces, **Cape Cod Campresort and Cabins** (176 Thomas B. Landers Rd., East Falmouth, 508/548-1458, www.capecampresort.com, tent sites $34-65, RV sites $39-117) has a family-friendly, vacationland feel. The sites range from basic spots to pitch a tent to more elaborate setups with grills, patios, and Wi-Fi (Wi-Fi is also available at the campground's clubhouse and café.)

Information

Info for Falmouth and Woods Hole is available from the **Falmouth Chamber of Commerce** (20 Academy Ln., Falmouth, 508/548-8500, www.falmouthchamber.com, 8:30am-4:30pm Mon.-Fri., 10am-2pm Sat. Memorial Day-Labor Day).

Getting There and Around

Peter Pan bus line (800/343-9999, www.peterpanbus.com) has service from Boston's Logan International Airport and South Station to the **Falmouth Bus Depot** and the **Woods Hole Steamship Pier** (many buses daily, 2 hrs./2.25 hrs., $32-45).

The **Cape Cod Regional Transit Authority** (800/352-7155, www.capecodtransit.org, hourly $2 adults, $1 children) runs the **SeaLine** on a route from Woods Hole to the Falmouth Bus Depot, then along the coast to Hyannis and Barnstable.

There's free, on-street parking in Falmouth that's limited to three hours, and a few public lots that are good options when the town is crowded: **Peg Noonan Municipal Parking Lot** (300 Main St.), **Mullen-Hall School** (130 Katherine Lee Bates Rd., July-Aug. only), and **Lawrence School** (113 Lakeview Ave., July-Aug. only).

Mid Cape and Lower Cape

This stretch of the Cape is where vacationland hits a fever pitch, with a healthy (and sometimes hilarious) mix of olde New England meets Moby-Dick-themed mini golf. It's one of the easiest places to settle in with a family, because it's driving distance from Cape Cod National Seashore, the old-fashioned town of Chatham, and Monomoy National Wildlife Refuge. The Nantucket ferry departs from the Mid Cape's biggest town, Hyannis, which is not as quaint as other Cape towns, but has a few excellent budget accommodations.

HYANNIS

Bustling Hyannis is the transportation hub for Cape Cod, where ferries, trains, and buses converge. It's also a party town, with college bars in place of Provincetown's drag joints, and it kicks into high gear for summer. But don't be fooled by the strip malls, happy hours, and souvenir shops. The longtime retreat of the Kennedy clan, Hyannis has deep New England roots, and it's the home base for the Cape Cod Baseball League, with a Hall of Fame museum and its very own baseball team—the Hyannis Harbor Hawks.

Sights

Follow the footsteps of generations of Kennedys on the **Hyannis Kennedy Legacy Trail** (508/244-4840, www.kennedylegacytrail.com), a 1.6-mile route through downtown Hyannis, with stops at the Kennedys' longtime church, the Peace Corps memorial, and the Hyannis Armory, where the future president John F. Kennedy accepted the Democratic party nomination. There are plaques at each of the 10 stops, and maps are available online and at the John F. Kennedy Museum. To get more information about any given site, call the trail phone number, or use a smartphone to scan the plaque's QR code.

Get a more personal look at the family at the small **John F. Kennedy Hyannis Museum** (397 Main St., 508/790-3077, jfkhyannismuseum.org, 10am-4pm Mon.-Sat., noon-4pm Sun. mid-Apr.-May and Nov., 9am-5pm Mon.-Sat., noon-5pm Sun. June-Oct., $10 adults, $7 seniors, $5 students and children 8-17, children under 8 free), where you'll find photographs of the Kennedys sailing and relaxing at their summer home. Short films, interviews with the Kennedys, and historic TV footage are a fascinating glimpse of their lives, and rotating exhibits explore more in-depth themes.

The bottom floor of the museum was devoted to the **Cape Cod Baseball League Hall of Fame** (www.capecodbaseball.org, currently free with admission to the JFK museum), but plans were under way to relocate the museum's fun exhibits of baseball memorabilia to another location. Long closed to the public, the **Kennedy Compound** has been acquired by the **Edward M. Kennedy Institute for the United States Senate** (617/740-7000, www.emkinstitute.org), with plans to open the family home for tours.

Entertainment and Events

If you catch one event in Hyannis, make it a Harbor Hawks baseball game, but there's also lively nightlife and frequent concert series.

A good spot for afternoon drinks is **Cape Cod Beer** (1336 Phinney's Ln., 508/790-4200, www.capecodbeer.com, 10am-6pm Mon.-Fri., 11am-4pm Sat.), a microbrewery with a huge range of beers of draft. With board games and a foosball table, it's a nice place to while away a rainy afternoon, and there are free tours of the brewery each day at 1pm. Right across from the JFK Museum, the **British Beer Company** (412 Main St., 508/771-1776, Sun.-Thu. 11am-11pm, Fri.-Sat., 11am-1am, www.britishbeer.com) is a cozy hangout with Guinness on tap, dart boards, and a family-friendly vibe. Firmly planted on the Las Vegas circuit, the **Cape Cod Melody Tent** (21 W.

Main St., 508/775-5630, www.melodytent.com) draws deathless crooners such as Tony Bennett and Engelbert Humperdinck during the summer months on a revolving stage. Calling chowder soup is like calling filet mignon steak. Lovers of New England's favorite appetizer flock to the **WCOD Chowder Festival** (Cape Cod Melody Tent, W. Main St., June) to sample the best offerings from local restaurants.

Sports and Recreation

BEACHES

With steady winds for much of the year, **Kalmus Beach** (670 Ocean St., parking $20) is popular with windsurfers, and the beach is divided into swimming and windsurfing sections. There's a large parking lot, a snack bar, and restrooms, and a lifeguard is on duty during the summer months. Closer to downtown, **Veterans Beach** (480 Ocean St., parking $20) is a bit more sheltered, and is a good spot to watch boats sail in and out of the harbor. There's also a playground on-site.

Food

A favorite for hearty breakfasts and lunch, **The Daily Paper** (644 W. Main St., 508/790-8800, www.dailypapercapecod.com, 6am-2pm Mon.-Sat., 7am-1pm Sun., $7-10) is justifiably busy, with a bustling diner atmosphere. Breakfasts range from eggs over easy to fig-stuffed brioche French toast, while a lunch menu of soups, sandwiches, and salads is perfect if you're ready for a break from seafood. Budget-friendly early-bird specials are available until 8am Monday-Friday.

In a compact, aquamarine cottage outside of town, **Bangkok Kitchen** (339 Barnstable Rd., 508/771-2333, www.bkkitchen339.com, 11am-10pm Mon.-Sat., 4pm-9pm Sun., $8-16) is a homey spot for great Thai food. The red curry is a popular option, and the menu is a blend of classic Thai dishes, a few Lao-influenced plates, and Asian American options like crab Rangoon. Tables fill up quickly, making this a good option for picking up food to eat by the harbor.

Hyannis has more than its fair share of fried seafood joints, but with ocean views and outdoor seating, **Spanky's Clam Shack and Seaside Saloon** (138 Ocean St., 508/771-2770, www.spankysclamshack.com, 11am-9pm Mon.-Thurs., 11am-9:30pm Fri.-Sun., $8-27) edges out the competition. Bowls of clam chowder are a favorite, and plates of fried shrimp and scallops come in enormous, shareable portions. It's walking distance to both of Hyannis's ferry terminals.

Find a more upscale take on local seafood at the **Naked Oyster Bistro and Raw Bar** (410 Main St., 508/778-6500, www.nakedoyster.com, noon-9:30pm Mon.-Thurs., noon-10pm Fri.-Sat., lunch $12-19, dinner $16-36), a romantic spot in the center of town with exposed brick walls and colorful art. Oysters, littlenecks, and quahogs are from the Barnstable harbor, where the restaurant has its own oyster beds.

While the house-made gelato at **Caffe Gelato Bertini** (20 Pearl St., 508/778-0244, www.capecodgelato.com, 11:30am-7:30pm Thurs.-Tues. May-Oct., $3-8) is based on an old, Italian family recipe, the flavors have Cape Cod flair. Try versions made with native beach roses and beach plums, cranberries, or blueberries—they're a far cry from Florence. This sweet spot is tucked into a sunny cottage, and also makes a full menu of espresso drinks . . . the affogato with espresso, gelato, and whipped cream is divine.

Accommodations

UNDER $100

In a well-maintained home in downtown Hyannis, the **Hyannis Hostel** (111 Ocean St., 508/775-7990, late May-Oct. $35-40 dorms, $79-149 private rooms) is the best option for budget travelers in the Mid Cape, with tidy dorms and private rooms for up to six people. Comfortable common spaces and an outdoor fire pit make this a good spot to meet other travelers, and the kitchen, continental breakfast, and free parking are good perks. Bring earplugs.

Cape Cod Baseball

summer game in the Cape Cod Baseball League

As the beaches fill and clam shacks open their doors, some of the most talented college baseball players descend on the Cape for a season in the **Cape Cod Baseball League** (www.capecod-baseball.org), one of 11 summer leagues across the country. Teams like the Brewster Whitecaps, Chatham Anglers, and Hyannis Harbor Hawks have sent over 1,000 players to the major leagues, and Cape Cod regulars have seen some big names in their small-town venues, including Hall of Famers Harold "Pie" Traynor, Carlton Fisk, Frank Thomas, and Craig Biggio. The league is volunteer run, charges no admission, and many of the young players are hosted in local homes. Attending a game is a fun way to take part in a Cape Cod tradition, and there are games most days of the week from mid-June to early August. Check the website for an updated schedule, but here are some favorite places to catch a game:

Lowell Park, Cotuit: Home field of the Cotuit Kettleers, Lowell Park is the most picturesque baseball diamond on Cape Cod: an old-fashioned field and bleachers surrounded by dense forest that looks like the backdrop for a Norman Rockwell painting (www.kettleers.org).

McKeon Park, Hyannis: You can smell the ocean (along with the peanuts and Cracker Jack) when you watch the Hyannis Harbor Hawks go to bat in the heart of the Mid Cape. Head to the "Osprey's Nest" on the third-base line for the best views of the action (www.harborhawks.org).

Eldredge Park, Orleans: Bring a blanket or lawn chair to this laid-back park, which has terraced hills along both baselines, but come early—the Orleans Firebirds have a devoted fan base that arrives hours before the first at-bat to stake their claim on prized pieces of grass (www.orleansfirebirds.com).

To get the whole story behind the Cape Cod Baseball League, visit the **Cape Cod Baseball League Hall of Fame** (397 Main St., Hyannis, 508/790-3077, www.capecodbaseball.org, 10am-4pm Mon.-Sat., noon-4pm Sun. mid-Apr.-May and Nov., 9am-5pm Mon.-Sat., noon-5pm Sun. June-Oct., $10 adults, $7 seniors, $5 children 8-17, children under 8 free), part of the John F. Kennedy Museum.

$100-150

Walking distance from Hyannis beaches and the ferry terminals, **Cape Cod Harbor House Inn** (119 Ocean St., 508/771-1880, www.harborhouseinn.net, $95-224) has views of the water and simple, motel-style suites. All the rooms have stoves, refrigerators, microwaves, and coffeemakers, and dogs are welcome on the ground floor.

Centrally located but quiet, the **Green Mountain Inn B & B** (328 Sea St., 508/778-4278, www.capecod-greenmtn-bb.com, $140-150, 4-person efficiency $230) is close to the pretty Sea Street Beach, and has a gracious, shady porch that encourages lounging. Rooms are homey and a bit old-fashioned, and the innkeepers serve a generous, home-cooked breakfast.

Information and Services

The **Cape Cod Chamber of Commerce** (Rte. 6 and Rte. 132, 508/362-3225, May-Sep. 9am-5pm daily; Oct.-Nov. 9am-4pm Mon.-Sat.; Dec. 9am-4pm Mon.-Fri.; Jan.-Apr. 10am-3pm Mon.-Fri., www.capecodchamber.org) runs a comprehensive center for the region. The **Hyannis Area Chamber of Commerce** (388 Main St., Wed.-Sat. 10am-4pm, 508/775-2201, www.hyannis.com) focuses on the city.

The area's largest full-service hospital is **Cape Cod Hospital** (27 Park St., Hyannis, 508/771-1800, www.capecodhealth.org). Fill prescription needs at the 24-hour branches of **CVS Pharmacy** (176 North St., Hyannis, 508/775-8462 or 105 Davis Straights, Rte. 28, Falmouth, 508/540-4307, www.cvs.com).

Getting There and Around

For travelers arriving in Cape Cod by public transit, Hyannis is by far the easiest place to reach. Impervious to Cape Cod traffic jams, the **CapeFlyer** (508/775-8504, www.capeflyer.com, 2.5 hrs., $22/40 one-way/round-trip) train has weekend service from Boston's South Station to Hyannis, timed so you can leave Boston after working hours and return on Sunday evening.

The **Peter Pan** bus company (800/343-9999, www.peterpanbus.com) has service to Hyannis from **Boston** (1.5 hrs., $5), Providence (3 hrs., $28), and **New York City** (7 hrs., $55). For destinations within Cape Cod, transfer in Hyannis to a local bus run by the **Cape Cod Regional Transit Authority** (800/352-7155, www.capecodtransit.org), with lines to Woods Hole and Orleans.

This is also the place to catch a ferry to Nantucket or Martha's Vineyard. **Steamship Authority** (508/477-8600, www.steamshipauthority.com) has several high-speed passenger ferries each day to **Nantucket** (1 hr., round-trip tickets $69 adults, $35 children 5-12, children under 5 free, $14 bicycles) and a slower traditional ferry (2.25 hrs., round-trip tickets $37 adults, $19 children 5-12, children under 5 free, $14 bicycles). Reduced rates may be available on weekdays.

The competition is **Hy-Line Cruises** (800/492-8082, www.hylinecruises.com), with high-speed service to **Nantucket** (year-round, 1 hr., round-trip tickets $38.50 adults, $25.50 children 5-12, children under 5 free, $7 bicycles) and the Martha's Vineyard town of **Oak Bluffs** (May-Oct., 1 hr., round-trip tickets $59 adults, $39 children 5-12, children under 5 free, $14 bicycles).

YARMOUTH

A cluster of Yarmouths—West Yarmouth, South Yarmouth, and Yarmouth Port—straddle the Mid Cape. The communities have a proud history of shipbuilding, and workers at the sheltered harbor on the Royal River crafted sloops, schooners, barks, and brigantines that would sail the New England coast and the globe. On the northern edge of the Cape, Yarmouth Port is all white-steepled churches and old-fashioned homes, but the south is packed with family-friendly vacation kitsch that visitors tend to love or hate, so choose your Yarmouth accordingly.

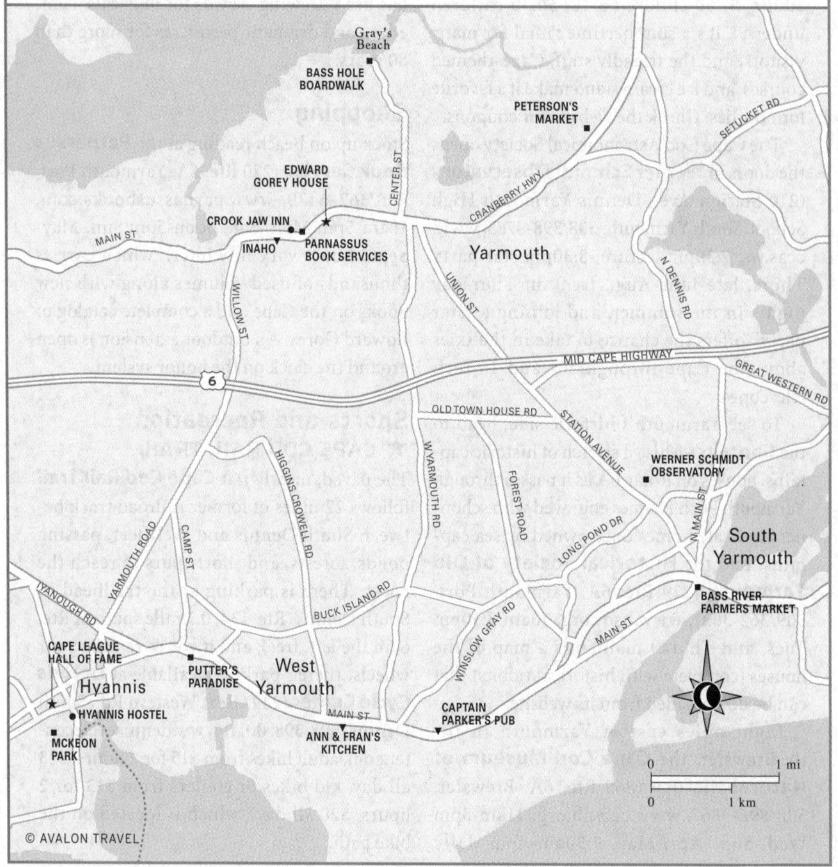

Sights

EDWARD GOREY HOUSE

Fans of cheerfully macabre art won't want to miss the **Edward Gorey House** (8 Strawberry Ln., Yarmouth Port, 508/362-3909, www.edwardgoreyhouse.org, 11am-4pm Thurs.-Sat., noon-4pm Sun mid-Apr.-early July, 11am-4pm Wed.-Sat., noon-4pm Sun. early July-early Oct., 11am-4pm Fri.-Sat., noon-4pm Sun. mid-Oct-Dec., $8 adults, $5 students and seniors, $2 children 6-12, children under 6 free), now an intimate museum that celebrates his work and devotion to animal welfare. The author, illustrator, and costume designer might be best known for the introduction to *Masterpiece Mystery*. His drawings and rhymes in the *Gashlycrumb Tinies*—"A is for Amy, who fell down the stairs; B is for Basil, assaulted by bears"—are as delightful today as they were in 1963. In addition to guided tours, the museum also has a scavenger hunt that's great for kids.

OTHER SIGHTS

Take aim at Captain Ahab, lighthouses, and an eye-catching pink octopus at **Putter's Paradise miniature golf** (119 Rte. 28, West Yarmouth, 508/771-7394, www.

puttersparadise.net, 9am-10pm daily Apr.-Oct., hours may vary in spring and fall, $8.50 adults, $7.50 children 5-12, $6.50 children under 5). It's a summertime ritual for many visitors, and the friendly staff, Cape-themed courses, and ice cream stand make it a favorite for families. Check the website for coupons.

The Cape Cod Astronomical Society opens the doors to **Werner Schmidt Observatory** (210 Station Ave., Dennis-Yarmouth High School, South Yarmouth, 508/398-4765, www.ccas.ws, 7:30pm lecture, 8:30pm star party Thurs. late-June-Aug., free) on Thursday nights in the summer, and joining a "star party" offers the chance to take in the skies above the Cape through 16- and 18-inch telescopes.

To see Yarmouth's historic side, head to the **Captain's Mile,** a stretch of historic captains' houses on Route 6A as it passes through Yarmouth Port. Plaques engraved with schooners indicate homes once owned by sea captains, and the **Historical Society of Old Yarmouth** (229 Rte. 6A, Yarmouth Port, 509/362-3021, www.hsoy.org, 10am-3:30pm Tues. and Thurs.) maintains a map of the houses (complete with historical tidbits) that can be downloaded from its website.

Eight miles east of Yarmouth in little Brewster, the **Cape Cod Museum of Natural History** (869 Rte. 6A, Brewster, 508/896-3867, www.ccmnh.org, 11am-3pm Wed.-Sun. Apr.-May, 9:30am-4pm daily June-Aug., 11am-3pm daily Sept., 11am-3pm Wed.-Sun. Oct.-Dec., $15 adults, $10 seniors, $6 children 3-12, children under 3 and active military free) brings the Cape's geology and natural history to life with wave tanks, interactive exhibits, and art. During the summer months, visitors can meet the vivid butterflies in the Pollinator House, and a trail behind the museum leads to salt marshes and a beach that attracts flocks of migratory birds.

Entertainment and Events

Bette Davis, Humphrey Bogart, and Jane Fonda have all graced the stage at the **Cape Playhouse** (820 Rte. 6A, Dennis Village, 508/385-3911, www.capeplayhouse.com), the nation's oldest summer theater, which has been drawing crowds for musicals, comedies, and dramatic premieres for more than 80 years.

Shopping

Stock up on beach reading at the **Parnassus Book Service** (220 Rte. 6A, Yarmouth Port, 508/362-6420, www.parnassusbooks.com, 10am-5pm Mon.-Sat., noon-5pm Sun. May-Sept., hours vary in winter), which carries thousands of used volumes along with new books on the Cape and a complete catalog of Edward Gorey. An outdoor extension is open around the clock on the honor system.

Sports and Recreation

★ CAPE COD RAIL TRAIL

The paved, mostly flat **Cape Cod Rail Trail** follows 22 miles of former railroad track between South Dennis and Wellfleet, passing ponds, forests, and short spurs to reach the coast. There is parking at the trailhead in South Dennis (Rte. 134, 0.5 mile south of Rte. 6 on the left, free), and if you're renting your wheels, there's parking available at **Dennis Cycle Center** (249 Great Western Rd., South Dennis, 508/398-0011, www.denniscyclecenter.com, adult bikes from $15 for 2 hours, $23 all day, kid bikes or trailers from $13 for 2 hours, $20 all day), which is located on the bike path.

BEACHES

The **Bass Hole Boardwalk** crosses 900 feet of tidal marshes beside **Gray's Beach** (Center St., Yarmouth Port, parking $15), the perfect vantage point for watching scurrying crabs, shorebirds, and tidal sloughs, though the bugs can be daunting on calm days. The beach itself is small, sandy, and sheltered from waves, and the roped-in swimming area is a popular choice for families with small children.

Food

Seafood lovers weary of fried food can get their fish fix at **Inaho** (157 Rte. 6A, Yarmouth

Port, 508/362-5522, www.inahocapecod.com, 5pm-close Tues.-Sat., $20-35), a sushi restaurant in a perky converted Cape Cod house. The intimate dining room is comfortable and casual. Regulars rave about the raw scallops in an avocado shell and ultra-fresh sashimi.

Tucked into an adorable cottage with a striped awning, **Ann & Fran's Kitchen** (471 Main St., West Yarmouth, 508/775-7771, 7am-2pm daily, $8-12) serves classic diner-style breakfast and lunch. Pancakes and waffles of all stripes and hearty savory breakfasts bring in summertime crowds, but this is a local favorite year-round. Arrive early or plan to wait for a table.

Thick, creamy chowder is the star of the show at **Captain Parker's Pub** (668 Rte. 28, West Yarmouth, 508/771-4266, www.captainparkers.com, 11am-9pm Sun.-Thurs., 11am-10pm Fri.-Sat., $10-29), a family-friendly pub that also serves hearty American steak house classics in the laid-back dining room.

A few miles northeast of downtown Yarmouth, **Captain Frosty's Fish & Chips** (219 Rte. 6A, Dennis, 508/385-8548, www.captainfrosty.com, 8am-11pm Wed.-Mon. Apr.-Sept., $5-22) is a classic family seafood stop, with thick ice cream frappes that go perfectly with big piles of onion rings and soft crab rolls. The clam chowder is another favorite, packed with a generous helping of clams and creamy as can be. Stand in line to order at the counter, then wait for your food at outdoor picnic tables.

Stock up on locally grown berries, fresh bread, and all things artisanal at **Bass River Farmers Market** (311 Old Main St., Yarmouth, www.bassriverfarmersmarket.org, 9am-1:30pm Thurs. and Sat. mid-June-mid-Sept.).

You can find picnic supplies—and just about anything else you need—at locally owned **Peterson's Market** (918 Rte. 6A, Yarmouth Port, 508/362-2147, www.smithfieldmarkets.com, 7am-9pm daily).

Accommodations

For families looking for a home base to explore the Mid Cape, **The Escape Inn** (1237 Rte. 28, South Yarmouth, 508/694-7153, www.theescapeinn.com, $85-175) is a sunny, comfortable, and distinctly un-fussy option. Air-conditioned rooms come with one or two beds, there's a lounge chair-lined pool that's perfect for sunny days, and the continental breakfast is a cut above the competition.

With great access to a private beach and a laid-back, family resort atmosphere,

Cape Cod Rail Trail

Surfcomber by the Ocean (107 South Shore Dr., South Yarmouth, 508/398-9229, www.surfcombermotel.com, $95-265) is welcoming and easy. Prices drop dramatically apart from school vacation months, making this property a great oceanside bargain in May and September. A swimming pool, shuffleboard court, and beach chairs round out the property, and rooms are equipped with coffeemakers, microwaves, and refrigerators.

The elegant ★ **Liberty Hill Inn** (77 Main St., Yarmouth Port, 508/306-4536, www.libertyhillinn.com, $175-275) is a wonderfully romantic retreat. Gas fireplaces, four-poster beds, and luxurious linens make the rooms a haven, but it's worth venturing out to lounge in the common spaces (including a living room with a grand piano!). Big, home-cooked breakfasts are served each morning, and a jar full of fresh cookies appears in time for afternoon snacks.

Information and Services

Yarmouth has an **information center** (424 Rte. 28, West Yarmouth, 9am-5pm Mon.-Sat., 508/778-1008, www.yarmouthcapecod.com). There's free **wireless Internet access** at the **South Yarmouth Library** (312 Old Main St., 508/760-4820, www.yarmouthlibraries.com, 10am-8pm Mon. and Wed., 10am-5pm Tues. and Thurs.-Fri., 10am-4pm Sat., noon-4pm Sun.).

Getting There

The **Cape Cod Regional Transit Authority** (800/352-7155, www.capecodtransit.org) links Hyannis to Dennisport, Chatham, and Orleans on the H20 line.

CHATHAM

Perfectly placed on the outer edge of Cape Cod's "elbow," Chatham is an elegant spot with sweet boutiques, a compact downtown, and many year-round residents, which is perhaps why it's quieter than other towns on the Mid Cape. There are plenty of family-friendly beaches for sand castles and sunbathing here, and it's the access point to the extraordinary Monomoy National Wildlife Refuge. The refuge's barrier islands provide habitat for a constantly changing population of seabirds, including protected piping plover and the roseate tern, and they're perfect for exploring on a boat tour or kayak trip.

Sights

CHATHAM LIGHT

It's easy to see why sailing off the Chatham coast would be treacherous work even on the clearest day. "Nowhere on the Cape's shorelines has the sea kept busier than among these storm-bitten sands," wrote Provincetown author Josef Berger in 1937. "Monomoy lies beckoning like the bony finger of death which it has been to countless ships." When the twin beams at **Chatham Lighthouse** (37 Main St., tours 1pm-3:30pm Wed. July-Aug., free) were illuminated in 1808, they must have seemed like a godsend to mariners in a storm; the lighthouse still serves sailors to this day. With a red-roofed Coast Guard station and a snapping flag, it's picture-postcard smart. You may spot seals, whales, and flocks of migratory birds just off the nearby beach. There are sporadic tours available in the spring and fall; for more information, contact the **Chatham Chamber of Commerce** (508/945-5100, www.chathaminfo.com).

OTHER SIGHTS

Learn about life in historic Cape Cod at the small but well-curated **Atwood House Museum** (347 Stage Harbor Rd., 508/945-2493, www.chathamhistoricalsociety.org, 1pm-4pm Fri.-Sat. late May-June, 10am-4pm Tues.-Sat. July-Aug., 1pm-4pm Tues.-Sat. Sept.-early Oct., 1pm-4pm Fri.-Sat. early Oct.-Oct. 31, $10 adults, $5 students 8-18, children under 8 free), located in an old Cape Cod house with a gambrel roof. Knowledgeable docents decked in period attire help animate the museum's stories of sea captains, shipwrecks, and day-to-day life.

Brightly painted, "railroad Gothic" detailing makes Chatham's 1887 railway depot an eye-catching home for the **Chatham**

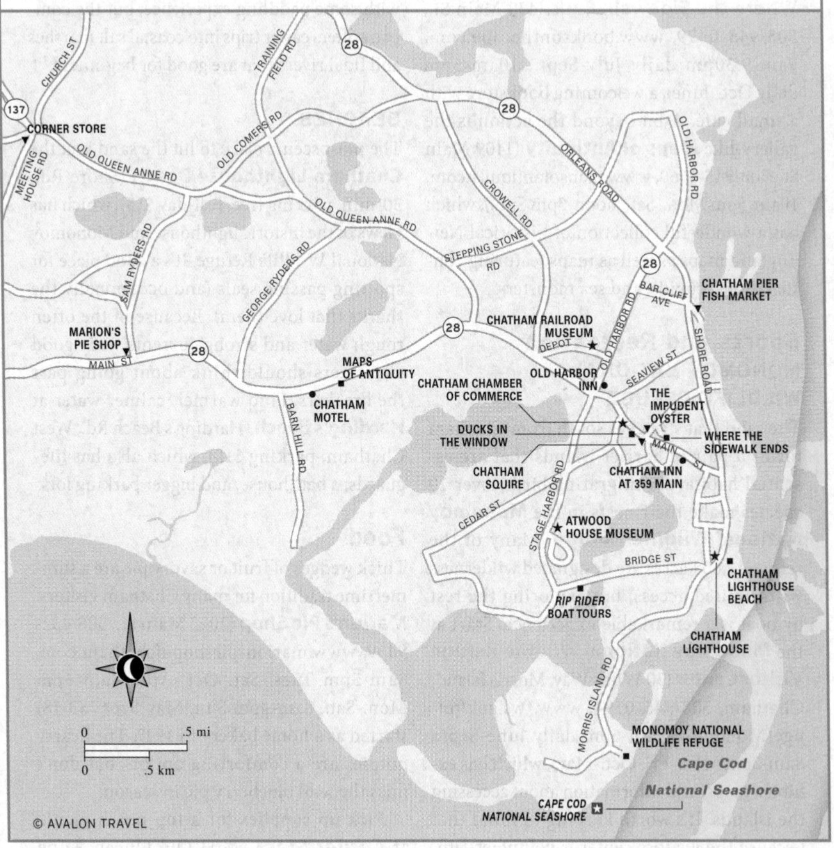

Railroad Museum (153 Depot Rd., 508/945-5100, www.chathamrailroadmuseum.com, 10am-4pm Tues.-Sat. mid-June-mid-Sept., free). It doesn't take long to browse the small collection of model trains, railroad history exhibits, and the fully restored wooden caboose, but it's an interesting glimpse of the golden age of rail.

Wireless buffs will enjoy the techy displays at the **Chatham Marconi Maritime Center** (847 Orleans Rd., North Chatham, 508/945-8889, www.chathammarconi.org, 10:30am-4:30pm Tues.-Sat., 1pm-4pm Sun. mid-June-early Oct., $7.50 adults and children 11-18, children under 11 free), where you can brush up on Morse code and the Enigma Machine, which German spies used to write secret codes during World War II.

Shopping

Most of the action in Chatham (shopping and otherwise) is clustered on Main Street. You'll find sweet boutiques, upscale design shops, and souvenir joints on the walkable stretch between Old Harbor Road and Willow Bend. Pick up disco ducks, mad scientist ducks, and "celebriducks" at **Ducks in the Window** (507 Main St., 508/945-0334, www.ducksinthewindow.com, 11am-5pm daily, extended hours during peak times), the undisputed claimant to the Cape's largest rubber duck collection. Find beach reads and local authors at **Where the Sidewalk Ends** (432 Main St., 508/945-0499, www.booksonthecape.com, 9am-9:30pm daily July-Sept., 10am-5pm daily Oct.-June), a welcoming bookstore with a small café. A bit beyond the action is the gallery-like **Maps of Antiquity** (1409 Main St., 508/945-1660, www.mapsofantiquity.com, 10am-5pm Mon.-Sat., noon-5pm Sun.), which has a wonderful collection of historical New England maps as well as maps featuring constellations, cupids, and sea monsters.

Sports and Recreation

MONOMOY NATIONAL WILDLIFE REFUGE

The sand that stretches south from Chatham forms a pair of barrier islands that are essential habitat for migrating birds; over 10 species make their nests in the **Monomoy National Wildlife Refuge.** Many of the refuge's 7,604 acres are designated wilderness with limited access, but exploring the rest by boat is a remarkable experience. Start at the **Monomoy National Wildlife Refuge Visitor Center** (30 Wikis Way, Morris Island, Chatham, 508/945-0594, www.fws.gov/refuge/Monomoy, 9am-5pm daily June-Sept., 8am-5pm Mon.-Fri. Oct.-May), which has exhibits, maps, and information about accessing the islands. It's worth keeping in mind that because the visitors center is volunteer-run, the off-season hours are aspirational—if there are no volunteers, the doors stay closed, so call ahead. The 40-acre Morris Island is the only part of the refuge that's accessible by car. A 0.78-mile **hiking trail** leaves from the visitors center along the shore and coastal forests.

Among the best tours are those run by Captain Keith Lincoln aboard the ***Rip Rider*** (80 Bridge St., 508/237-0420, www.monomoyislandferry.com, 1.5-hour cruises $35 adults, $30 children under 10), a 32-foot motorized tour boat that visits colonies of grey and harbor seals.

To see the islands under your own power, join a guided paddling tour by **Cape Kayaks** (508/247-7402, www.capekayaking.com, 3-hour tours $70); wind and open water mean that tours of the refuge are best suited to those with some paddling experience, but the company offers easier trips into coastal salt marshes and tidal rivers that are good for beginners.

BEACHES

The most scenic place to hit the sand is at the **Chatham Lighthouse Beach** (Shore Rd., 30-min. parking free, full-day $15), which has views of the historic lighthouse and Monomoy National Wildlife Refuge. It's a good place for spotting passing seals (and occasionally the sharks that love them). Because of the often rough water and strong currents, only good swimmers should think about going past the breakers. Find warmer, calmer water at **Harding's Beach** (Harding's Beach Rd., West Chatham, parking $15), which also has lifeguards, a bathhouse, and bigger parking lots.

Food

Thick wedges of fruit or savory pie are a summertime tradition for many Chatham visitors. **Marion's Pie Shop** (2022 Main St., 508/432-9439, www.marionspieshopofchatham.com, 8am-5pm Tues.-Sat. Oct.-Apr., 8am-6pm Mon.-Sat., 8am-4pm Sun. May-Sept., $3-18) started as a home bakery in 1947. The hearty potpies are a comforting option, but don't miss the wild blueberry pie in season.

Pick up supplies for a top-notch picnic at **Corner Store** (1403 Old Queen Anne Rd., 508/432-1077, www.freshfastfun.com, 6:30am-6:30pm daily, $6-10), whose burrito bar, sandwiches, and homey whoopie pies are super fresh and simple. Breakfast burritos stuffed with scrambled eggs, home fries, and tomato salsa are a highlight.

Watch the fishing boats come and go as you eat at ★ **Chatham Pier Fish Market** (45 Barcliff Ave., 508/945-3474, www.chathampierfishmarket.com, 10am-6pm Sun.-Thurs., 10am-7pm Fri.-Sat. May-Sept., $7-27), a simple takeout shack that's right by the docks. Big portions of fish-and-chips, fried clams, and creamy chowder make this spot a perennial favorite; eat at the picnic tables in the parking lot, or head to the 2nd-story observation deck for views of the harbor.

The seafood menu at **The Impudent Oyster** (15 Chatham Bars Ave., 508/945-3545, 11:30am-9pm daily, $14-35) leans more toward international classics like *pesce fra diavolo* and shrimp scampi, mixed in with substantial salads and sandwiches. In a small, shingled building just off Main Street, dark wood paneling and a cozy dining room make for a warm, welcoming feel—reservations are essential on busy weekends.

In a building that rambles along Main Street, the **Chatham Squire** (487 Main St., 508/945-0945, www.thesquire.com, 11:30am-1am Mon.-Sat., noon-1am Sun., $9-25) is the kind of bar where people bring their kids. Choose a spot in the homey dining room for salads, pastas, and hearty mains alongside fried bar food classics, or head to the pub side to drink local drafts in a room lined with antique license plates and Cape Cod bric-a-brac. A seat at the bar is a friendly place to meet locals and other visitors.

Accommodations

$150-250

Just outside of town, the **Chatham Motel** (1487 Main St., 800/770-5545, $130-225) is perfectly tidy, bright and updated, and an excellent deal for the area. Refrigerators, coffeemakers, and a swimming pool make this a relaxed place to stay.

In a cheery, yellow house with a pretty garden, ★ **Chatham Guest Rooms** (1409 Main St., 508/945-1660, www.chathamguestrooms.com, $95-195), is upstairs from and managed by the owner of Maps of Antiquity. Each of the three rooms has a private entrance, two are suites, and one has its own kitchen. Everything is beautifully taken care of, and it's located 1.5 miles outside of downtown on the main road.

OVER $250

Old-fashioned and romantic, the **Old Harbor Inn** (22 Old Harbor Rd., 800/942-4434, www.chathamoldharborinn.com, $299-449) is a sweet bed-and-breakfast filled with thoughtful extras. Elegant common spaces are furnished in English Country style, and the inn is walking distance to Chatham's lighthouse and beach.

With beautiful design and luxurious touches, ★ **Chatham Inn at 359 Main** (359 Main St., 508/945-9232, www.359main.com, $319-499) feels perfectly beachy and refined. Guests get all the usual amenities plus a full breakfast, afternoon cookies, and common spaces that include an outdoor terrace and a cozy room for games and drinks.

Information

The Chatham Chamber of Commerce operates a **seasonal visitors booth** (533 Main St., 508/945-5199, www.chathaminfo.com, 10am-5pm daily mid-May-mid-Oct.), with information on parking in the area, hotels with current vacancies, and beaches and boat landings. Information is also available year-round at the **main chamber office** (2377 Main St., 508/945-5199, www.chathaminfo.com, 10am-5pm Mon.-Sat. mid-May-mid-Oct., 10am-2pm Thurs.-Sat. mid-Oct.-mid-May).

Getting There and Around

The **Cape Cod Regional Transit Authority** (800/352-7155, www.capecodtransit.org) links Chatham with Hyannis and Orleans on the H20 line. Chatham taxi service is available from **Cape Cab Taxi** (508/240-1500, www.capecabtaxi.com). There are several **public parking lots** in downtown Chatham, the largest being the Stage Harbor Road Municipal Lot, on the east side of Stage Harbor Road just south of the intersection with Main Street.

Outer Cape

When Cape Cod makes a sharp, left-hand turn at Orleans, the peninsula narrows to a sandy slip of land, sometimes just under a mile across. It's far enough from the mainland to feel like a real escape from solid ground, and the Outer Cape is stunning, from the lovely beaches of the Cape Cod National Seashore to the rolling dunes and historic lighthouses. It's not all nature, but a great deal of the Outer Cape is preserved from development, and it's ideal for long days on windblown beaches followed by drinks at waterfront bars, or a double feature at the Wellfleet Drive-In.

EASTHAM

It would be easy to miss Eastham, an indeterminate little town whose most compelling places are tucked behind a strip of generic storefronts on Route 6A. Get off the main road, though, and you'll find the main gateway to Cape Cod National Seashore, whose beaches and dunes are an undisputed highlight of the Cape Cod shoreline. Excellent hiking and biking trails, and several budget-friendly hotels that are great for families, make this a good home base for active trips to the Cape.

Sights

TOP EXPERIENCE

★ CAPE COD NATIONAL SEASHORE

The **Cape Cod National Seashore** is an utterly beautiful swath of coastline, with the longest unbroken beaches in New England. Coastal dunes are speckled with blushing wild roses, and historic lighthouses stand proudly at the edge of the sea. Shores and salt marshes are an important destination for migratory birds traveling the Atlantic coast, and the water teems with harbor seals, grey seals, whales, sea turtles, and even the occasional great white shark (contrary to Hollywood films, shark attacks are vanishingly rare).

The biodiversity in the national seashore is partly due to the extraordinary variety of ecosystems found here. In addition to the

Cape Cod National Seashore

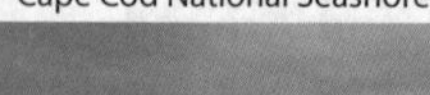

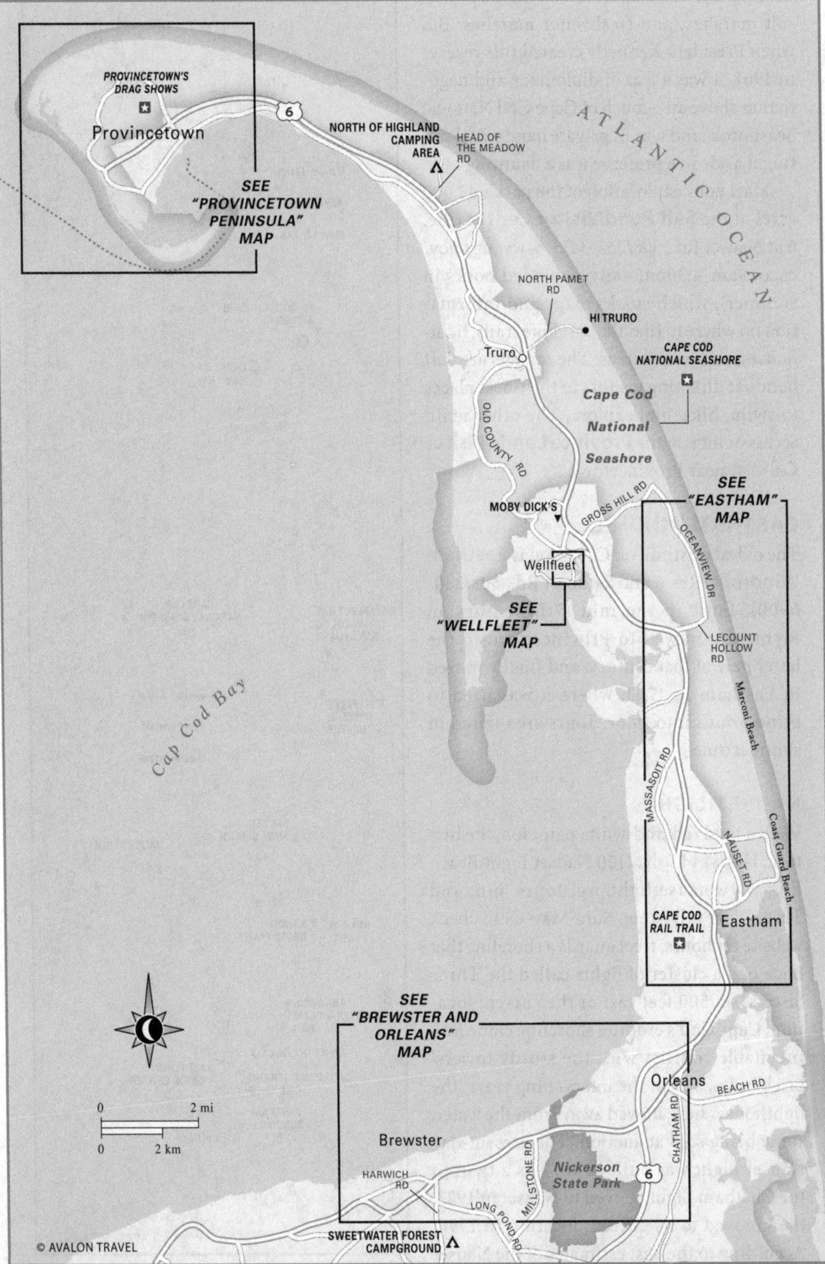
Outer Cape
PROVINCETOWN'S DRAG SHOWS
Provincetown
6
NORTH OF HIGHLAND CAMPING AREA
HEAD OF THE MEADOW RD
ATLANTIC OCEAN
SEE "PROVINCETOWN PENINSULA" MAP
NORTH PAMET RD
HI TRURO
Truro
CAPE COD NATIONAL SEASHORE
Cape Cod National Seashore
OLD COUNTY RD
MOBY DICK'S
GROSS HILL RD
SEE "EASTHAM" MAP
OCEANVIEW DR
Wellfleet
SEE "WELLFLEET" MAP
LECOUNT HOLLOW RD
Marconi Beach
Cap Cod Bay
MASSASOIT RD
NAUSET RD
Coast Guard Beach
CAPE COD RAIL TRAIL
Eastham
SEE "BREWSTER AND ORLEANS" MAP
Orleans
BEACH RD
0
2 mi
0
2 km
Brewster
CHATHAM RD
MILLSTONE RD
Nickerson State Park
HARWICH RD
LONG POND RD
SWEETWATER FOREST CAMPGROUND
© AVALON TRAVEL

intertidal zones, dunes, and seagrass beds that most visitors see, there are also grasslands, heathlands, woodlands, forests, kettle ponds, salt marshes, and freshwater marshes. But when President Kennedy created this reserve in 1961, it was a feat of diplomacy and negotiation above all—much of Cape Cod National Seashore's land was in private hands, and setting it aside in a preserve was a daunting task.

Start your exploration of the park's 43,000 acres at the **Salt Pond Visitor Center** (Rte. 6 at Nauset Rd., 508/255-3421, www.nps.gov/caco, 9am-4:30pm daily, extended hours in summer), which stocks maps and information on where to find the best bike trails, lighthouses, and picnic areas. The rangers are deft hands at directing visitors to the finest places to swim, hike, and explore. The other main access point is at the **Province Lands Visitor Center,** near Provincetown.

EASTHAM WINDMILL

The oldest gristmill on Cape Cod is **Eastham Windmill** (Rte. 6 and Samoset Rd., 508/240-5900), built in the mid-17th century in Plymouth, moved to Provincetown in the latter part of that century, and finally moved to Eastham in 1793, where it was used to grind grains into flour. Tours are offered in summertime.

NAUSET LIGHT

With a bold red-and-white paint job, the historic **Nauset Light** (120 Nauset Light Beach Rd., www.nausetlight.org, tours Sun. and Tues.-Wed. July-Aug., Sun. May-Oct., check website for hours, free) guards a shoreline that once had a cluster of lights called the Three Sisters, set 500 feet east of the current location. Cape Cod's eroding shoreline came into inevitable conflict with the sturdy towers' brick bases, and in the intervening years, the lighthouses have moved away from the water, some being sold at auction. The present-day Nauset Light was built in 1877 as a twin to the Chatham Light, moved to Nauset in 1923, then moved to its current location in 1996. According to the best estimates of the Nauset

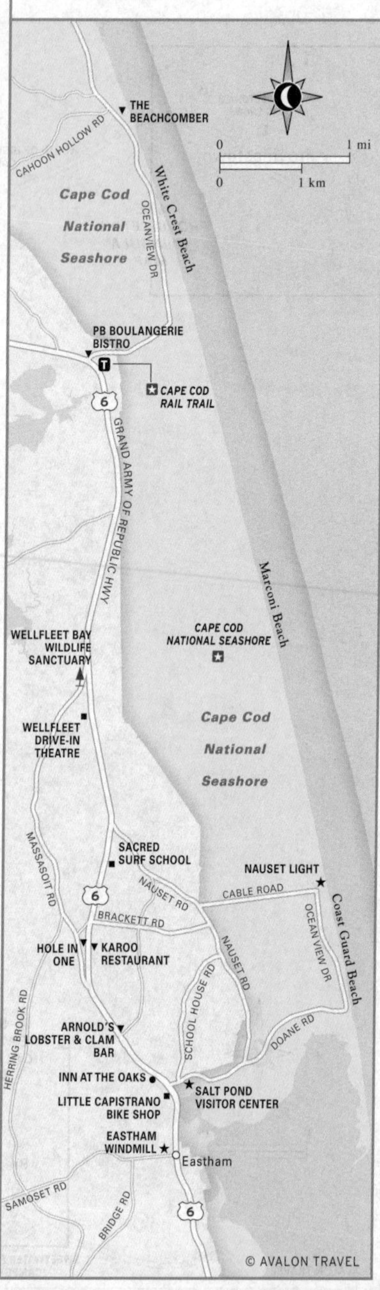

Light Preservation Society, it should be safe until 2050, when the sea will once again approach its base.

Sports and Recreation

BEACHES

With a broad swath of sand backed by eroding cliffs, **Coast Guard Beach** is a strong contender for the best beach in New England. It's eternally popular with everyone from beachcombers to sand castle-building families, but so huge that there's always a place to stretch out by the shore. There is excellent swimming, restrooms, and a wheelchair ramp that extends all the way to the sand. The parking area for Coast Guard Beach is closed to visitors mid-June-Labor Day (disabled visitors may use it), but there's free parking in a lot off Doane Road, and a free shuttle bus to the beach that runs every 5-10 minutes.

If you're looking for a long walk on the beach, there's a lovely stretch of sand between the Coast Guard Beach parking lot and **Nauset Light,** a roughly mile-long walk.

HIKING AND BIKING

The **Cape Cod Rail Trail** travels the length of Eastham, with several spots to hop on. If you're renting a bike, **The Little Capistrano Bike Shop** (30 Salt Pond Rd., 508/255-6515, www.littlecapistranobikeshop.com, 9am-5pm daily May-Oct., bikes $15 for 2 hours, $30 for 24 hours) is a quick jaunt from the trail, and allows customers to leave their cars while out riding. Free parking is also available at the nearby Salt Pond Visitor Center, the starting point for the excellent **Nauset Bike Trail,** a winding, 3.2-mile out-and-back that rolls through the forest on the way to Coast Guard Beach, passing Doane Rock Picnic Area along the way.

There are also several appealing walking trails winding through Eastham's pine forests and marshes. Departing from the Salt Pond Visitor Center, the **Nauset Marsh Trail** is a gentle 1.3-mile loop that passes Salt Pond and Nauset Marsh, with a 1.5-mile spur trail that leads to **Coast Guard Beach.** Another good, short option is the **Fort Hill Trail,** a 1-mile loop that weaves past a patchwork of salt marshes and is known for excellent birdwatching. To reach the trailhead, turn east onto Fort Hill Road, 1.3 miles south of Salt Pond Road, then park in the small lot across from the **Captain Penniman House** (70 Fort Hill Rd.).

Food

Arnold's Lobster & Clam Bar (3580 Rte. 6, 508/255-2575, www.arnoldsrestaurant.com, 11:30am-9pm daily late May-Oct., $5-20) is a Cape Cod clam shack that's spit-shined and streamlined, and it's about as kid friendly as it gets. Children's meals come on Frisbees, and the "shack" is in a shiny indoor cafeteria. In addition to well-made standards like fried seafood, lobster rolls, and chowder, Arnold's has a raw bar with ultra-fresh seafood and oysters.

Even oyster farmers need a break from chowder sometimes, and the unexpected, vibrant **Karoo Restaurant** (3 Main St., 508/255-8288, www.karoorestaurants.com, 4:30pm-8:30pm Wed.-Sun., $12-19) delivers with hearty South African foods like curried lamb stew and peri-peri chicken. Bright South African flourishes and friendly service make this a lively place to dine, and Karoo has a good selection of vegetarian options as well.

Hand-cut cake donuts are the starring attraction at **Hole in One** (4295 Rte. 6, 508/255-9446, www.theholecapecod.com, 5am-2pm daily, $2-9); the sweet treats are worth the wait even when the line stretches out the door. Arrive early to enjoy yours with coffee at a long counter lined with classic diner stools.

A few miles south of Eastham, **The Knack** (5 Rte. 6A, Orleans, 714/316-4595, www.theknackcapecod.com, 11am-8pm daily, $6-17) serves unusually fresh and flavorful versions of snack bar favorites. Burgers, hand-cut fries, fish sandwiches, and homemade ice cream sandwiches are served at outdoor picnic tables that fill up with families fresh from the beach.

Accommodations and Camping

UNDER $100

With an old-fashioned, summer-camp feel, **HI Eastham** (75 Goody Hallet Dr., 508/255-2785, mid-June-mid-Sept., $37 dorms, $155 4- to 5-person private cabins) has mess hall picnic tables, bunk beds, and a quiet, wooded location. The facilities are dated but tidy, and include board games and volleyball courts.

$100-150

Quiet and comfortable, **Midway Motel & Cottages** (5460 Rte. 6, 800/755-3117, www.midwaymotel.com, $82-178, 2-bedroom suite and efficiency $152-212) is a great choice for families, with a convenient location that's midway between Eastham and Wellfleet, and a stone's-throw from the Cape Cod Rail Trail. Rooms are simple but very well kept, with fridges, microwaves, and small sitting areas, and a common room is stocked with board games that are ideal for whiling away a rainy evening.

$250 AND ABOVE

In a cheerfully painted Victorian home, ★ **Inn at the Oaks** (3085 Rte. 6, 508/255-1886, www.innattheoaks.com, $195-395) retains a historical feel that's fresh, bright, and accommodating. The inn is full of nautical flourishes and tempting spots to curl up with a book; the generous continental breakfast includes fresh fruit and baked goods; and warm homemade cookies appear like clockwork in the afternoon. Henry Beston stayed at the inn while visiting the Cape and writing his classic book *The Outermost House*, which helped inspire the creation of Cape Cod National Seashore.

CAMPING

Six miles from Eastham, the 400 tent sites and yurts at **Nickerson State Park** (3488 Main St., Brewster, 508/896-3491, tent sites from $27, yurts from $50) have enviable beach access and are set in a shady forest threaded with walking trails. Bring a sleeping bag to sleep in the yurts, and beware the poison ivy that creeps around many of the campsites.

Information

The **Eastham Tourist Information Booth** (1700 Rte. 6 at Governor Prence Rd., 508/255-3444, www.easthamchamber.com, 9am-7pm daily May-Oct.) doles out information on local businesses, maps, and tides.

Getting There and Around

Plymouth and Brockton (508/746-0378, www.p-b.com) offers daily bus service from Boston to Hyannis (1 hr., 40 min, $20), where you can connect to Eastham (45 min., $8). Taxi service is available from **Cape Cab Taxi** (508/240-1500, www.capecabtaxi.com). There is a large **public parking lot** at the Salt Pond Visitor Center.

WELLFLEET

Tiny Wellfleet is a wonderful destination, with a small, walkable village center filled with galleries and restaurants. Even though it fills up with tourists during the summer months, it retains an off-the-beaten-path feel that continues to attract a year-round population of writers and artists. Wellfleet's oysters are known as some of the best in the East—their rich flavor is said to be the result of the town's cold, relatively salty water, big tides, and idiosyncratic phytoplankton—and the town goes all in for the yearly Wellfleet Oyster Fest.

Entertainment and Events

Catch a double feature beneath the stars at the **Wellfleet Drive-In Theatre** (51 Rte. 6, 508/349-7176, www.wellfleetcinemas.com, daily May-Sept., $11 adults, $8 seniors and children 4-11, children under 4 free, cash only), which is also the site of a sprawling flea market on Saturday and Sunday (call 508/349-0541 for updated flea market information).

If life in Wellfleet seems suspiciously quiet for a beach town, it's just because the party's at ★ **The Beachcomber** (1120 Cahoon Hollow Rd., 508/318-4877, www.thebeachcomber.

com, 11:30am-1am daily), an insanely popular beach bar and restaurant that's mostly known just as "da coma." Live music, powerful drinks, and an excellent location keep this place packed all summer; a laid-back daytime crowd of families is replaced by a raging crew of 20-somethings as the moon pops out of the ocean.

Learn the basics of opening oysters, or test your skills against the pros in the annual shucking contest at the **Wellfleet Oyster Fest** (www.wellfleetoysterfest.org, mid-Oct.), when the whole town turns out to celebrate its fabulous shellfish.

Shopping

There are art shops and boutiques in between Wellfleet's pretty galleries, and one fabulous bookstore-cum-seafood joint: **The Bookstore and Restaurant** (50 Kendrick Ave., 508/349-3154, www.wellfleetoyster.com, 11:30am-8pm daily) carries rare and antique books (perhaps infused with a light, briny scent from the neighboring oyster beds).

Sports and Recreation

BEACHES

Fishing boats and seals aren't the only things you'll spot from the Cape's beaches—the Atlantic coast is a destination for surfers. Hard-core riders hit the beaches when hurricanes stir up enormous swells, but relatively gentle waves and sandy bottoms mean that Cape Cod's surf breaks are very beginner friendly.

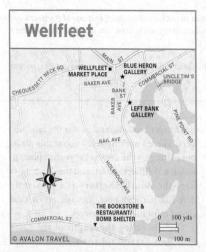

Wellfleet's **Marconi Beach** (Marconi Beach Rd., parking $20) and **Whitecrest Beach** (Ocean View Dr., parking $20) are good places to start; pick up a rental board (or book a lesson) at **Sickday** (361 Main St., 508/214-4158, www.sickday.cc, 9am-9pm Mon.-Sat., $30 board, $18 wetsuit). If that sounds like way too much exertion for a beach vacation, both places make for excellent lounging.

HIKING AND BIKING

Spot migratory birds in the salt marshes, barrier beaches, and pine forests of **Wellfleet Bay Wildlife Sanctuary** (291 Rte. 6, 508/349-2615, www.massaudubon.org, 8:30am-5:30pm daily late May-mid-Oct., 8:30am-5pm Tues.-Sun. mid-Oct.-late May, $5 adults, $3 seniors and children). Five miles of walking trails wind through the property, and it's common to see fiddler crabs, herons, and kingfishers along the way. Inside the sanctuary's small nature center are aquariums and art focused on Cape Cod's coastal ecosystems.

The 22-mile **Cape Cod Rail Trail** ends in Wellfleet at LeCount Hollow Road (parking $5). If you're renting wheels in town, you can leave your vehicle at **The Little Capistrano Bike Shop** (1446 Rte. 6, 508/349-2363, www.littlecapistranobikeshop.com, 9am-5pm daily May-Oct., bikes $15 for 2 hours, $30 for 24 hours); this is also a good stop for maps and advice.

Food

Wellfleet's got its very own spiffed-up clam shack, and **Moby Dick's** (3225 Rte. 6, 508/349-9795, www.mobydicksrestaurant.com, 11:30am-9pm daily late May-Oct., $7-21) is a favorite for relaxed, family-friendly seafood. Locals are divided about whose chowder and clams win out, but the BYO drinks policy at this spot might just tip the balance.

Working Waterfront: Farming Oysters on Cape Cod

Wellfleet's famously flavorful oysters are grown in a limited number of waterfront plots called "grants," so when Katie Murphy and Michael DeVasto were offered the chance to work a family member's grant in 2011, they jumped at the rare opportunity. That first year, they seeded 250,000 oysters, and since then they've worked up to a million, clustered near a freshwater channel between two wildlife reservations. They purchase baby oyster "seeds" from a local hatchery, then tend to the growing shellfish in woven bags affixed to stainless steel racks in the intertidal zone—a stand-in for the natural reefs where oysters grow in the wild. On a break from tending to the oysters, Katie shared a bit about life as an oyster farmer.

WHAT'S A TYPICAL DAY LIKE FOR YOU?

The tide changes every day by about 40 minutes, so we're always on the tide. You need to harvest on the tide, within two hours of exposure—that's when your oysters came out of the water. And there's also a lot of work to do off the tide. Oysters grow at different rates, and in order to grow nice oysters you need to separate the oysters by size, so the larger ones aren't crowding out the smaller ones.

WHAT DO YOU LIKE ABOUT BEING AN OYSTER FARMER?

I like being outside, and I like the physicality of it. It's a job that has tangible results. It's growing food. Oysters filter the water, which is great. The harbor wouldn't be nearly as pristine if it weren't for how many oysters were in there. So many people have jobs where there's a disconnect between what they do and the impact they have—but I know where my oysters are going, I know all the people I sell them to, and I'm really close to the other farmers. It's just real.

WHAT CHALLENGES FACE OYSTER FARMERS IN THE COMING YEARS?

The thing that worries us the most is the climate and ocean acidification, but that hasn't affected the East Coast yet. Right now, water quality is great, but that is the most immediate issue. There's a big project here to open up the Herring River, an estuary and salt marsh that was really vital to town. They're reopening it over the next 10 years, so all the tides will flush up the river and help maintain the water quality in the years to come.

HOW DO YOU LIKE TO EAT OYSTERS?

Mostly raw, just while we're working. I do prefer to put lemon on them, and one of the best ways to eat oysters is just to put them on the grill, where they cook in their own juices. And then there's oysters Rockefeller . . . .

Check out more pictures of Katie and Michael working their grant on Instagram @fieldpointoysterfarm.

Surely the first (and only) of its kind, **The Bookstore and Restaurant** (50 Kendrick Ave., 508/349-3154, www.wellfleetoyster.com, 11:30am-8pm daily, $15-29) is just what the name suggests—plus an oyster farm. Order a dozen on the half shell here, and you can be assured they came from just across the street at the family's oyster beds; shellfish and fish stews are the stars of the menu, which also has burgers, salads, and pastas for landlubbers. There's nothing fancy about this place, but seating on the deck is the perfect place to watch a Wellfleet sunset, and the downstairs bar—the **Bomb Shelter**—is a pleasantly dive-like bar with pool, foosball, and a local crowd most nights of the week.

Cyclists riding the length of the Cape Cod Rail Trail train their sights on the

Paris-perfect tarts and éclairs at ★ **PB Boulangerie Bistro** (15 Lecount Hollow Rd., 508/349-1600, www.pbboulangeriebistro.com, bakery 7am-7pm daily, $3-8, bistro 5pm-10pm Fri.-Sat., 10am-2:30pm Sun., $9-35), along with beautiful croissants and oozy croque monsieur sandwiches. The weekend bistro menu features old-school French classics like *canard à l'orange* and house-made *pâté de campagne*, as well as American-style brunch with continental flair. You won't miss the bright-pink building by the side of the road.

Get beach snacks and drinks at the little **Wellfleet Marketplace** (295 Main St., 508/349-3156, 7am-7pm daily) in the center of town, which also has a deli—if you're looking for a bottle to go with your bivalves, grab The Oyster, a California sauvignon blanc that funds a Wellfleet wild oyster restoration project: one bottle equals 100 seed oysters.

Accommodations and Camping

UNDER $100

Midway between Wellfleet and Provincetown, **HI Truro** (111 N. Pamet Rd., Truro, 508/349-3889, late June-early Sept., dorms $42) is a hostel with beautiful sea views—the building was originally constructed as a Coast Guard station—and you can reach the beach by a sandy trail through the dunes. Breakfast is included in the rate, and there's a communal kitchen available for guests.

$100-150

Set right at the edge of the Cape Cod Rail Trail, **Even'tide Resort Motel and Cottages** (650 Rte. 6, 508/349-3410, www.eventidemotel.com, rooms $79-195, cottages $125-370) has Ping-Pong, a playground, and an indoor pool that make it a comfortable place to land with kids. Motel rooms are plain and simple, so it's the setting that shines, with plenty of space to lounge in the shade.

$150-250

The 18th-century **Gull Cottage Bed and Breakfast** (50 Steele Rd., 508/905-5021, www.gullcottagewellfleet.com, $225-250) is set in a pretty forest between two ponds, an idyllic setting that includes a walking trail to a private beach. There's just one room, a charming detached studio decorated with old-fashioned simplicity, so snap it up as soon as you can. Rates include a hearty breakfast.

CAMPING

With a great location on the Cape Cod Rail Trail and near the Wellfleet Bay Wildlife Sanctuary, **Maurice's Campground** (80 Rte. 6, 508/349-2029, www.mauricescampground.com, late May-mid-Oct., tent sites $42-60, cabins from $110) has simple facilities in a shady pine forest that's biking distance from the beach. The compact cabins are simple and rustic, but equipped with air conditioners, picnic tables, and small televisions.

Information

The **Wellfleet Chamber of Commerce Information Center** (1410 Rte. 6, 508/349-2510, www.wellfleetchamber.com, 9am-6pm daily late May-mid-Oct.) stocks maps and the usual brochures.

Getting There and Around

Plymouth and Brockton (508/746-0378, www.p-b.com) offers daily bus service from Boston to Hyannis (1 hr., 40 min, $20), where you can connect to Wellfleet (1 hr., $10). Taxi service is available from **Cape Cab Taxi** (508/240-1500, www.capecabtaxi.com). There is a large **public parking lot** at the Salt Pond Visitor Center.

Provincetown

Provincetown's eclectic population of artists, writers, and creative types like to call it "the end of the world." And this curling, shifting plot of sand does feel like a place apart. With a spare landscape of shore and water, it's easy to imagine how barren it looked when the Mayflower Pilgrims stopped in November 1620. But as the Native American Nauset tribe knew, there was a bounty beneath the waves, and Provincetown eventually grew into a thriving fishing and whaling village.

By the late 19th century, the village had become a destination for painters, playwrights, and novelists drawn to the spot's scenic isolation. Rustic shacks began to appear amid the rolling sand and wild roses, creating what became the oldest artist colony in the United States. Over the years, luminaries from Eugene O'Neill to Jack Kerouac, Norman Mailer, and Jackson Pollock came to the end of the Cape to work amid the dunes.

Even as the town has acquired a measure of wealth and commercialism, the undeveloped dunes and shacks remain a refuge. Full of creative spirit and spontaneity, P-town is also one of America's most popular LGBT vacation spots, and has been for decades. On any summer Saturday evening, Commercial Street is a bustling mix of vacationing families, drag show touts, wedding processions, and revelers kicking off parties that will still be going strong at sunrise.

SIGHTS

Lighthouses

Provincetown's three lighthouses are among the prettiest on the Cape. The most easily accessible is the 45-foot cast-iron **Race Point Light** (Race Point Beach, Rte. 6, 508/487-9930, www.racepointlighthouse.org), built in 1876 to replace an existing stone structure. It can be reached by a 30-minute walk over marsh grass and sand to the far edge of the cape from the parking lot at **Province Lands Visitor Center** (171 Race Point Rd., 508/487-1256, 9am-5pm daily May-Oct.). It's open for tours 10am-2pm on the first and third Saturday June-October. You can also stay in the adjoining keeper's house during the summer, when it becomes a bed-and-breakfast.

The other two beacons stand sentinel on the bay side of Provincetown's curving claw. You can hike 1.25 miles across the breakwater at the west end of town to reach **Wood End Light.** From there, continue another 1.5 miles to **Long Point Light.** Most of the walk is along soft sand, so it can take *much* longer than you expect. Another way to reach Long Point Light is on a boat shuttle from **Flyer's Boatyard** (MacMillan Pier, Slip 8, 508/487-0898, www.flyersrentals.com, hourly departures 10am-5pm daily during summer months, $10 one-way, $15 round-trip).

Pilgrim Monument & Provincetown Museum

Before the Pilgrims touched down at Plymouth Rock, they spent five weeks in Provincetown, where they wrote the Mayflower Compact and met the Nauset Indians for the first time. The **Pilgrim Monument** (High Pole Hill Rd., 508/487-1310, www.pilgrim-monument.org, 9am-5pm daily Apr.-May and mid-Sept.-Nov., 9am-7pm daily June-mid-Sept., $12 adults, $10 seniors and students, $4 children 4-12, children under 4 free, free parking with admission) that memorializes their landfall is an Italianate tower dominating the skyline and offering unmatched views. After you make it up (and down) the tower's 60 ramps and 116 steps, visit the small **Provincetown Museum,** whose classically kitschy dioramas depict the story of the Pilgrims in living color. The museum also has an interesting collection of Wampanoag artifacts, Cape Cod furniture, household items, and ephemera.

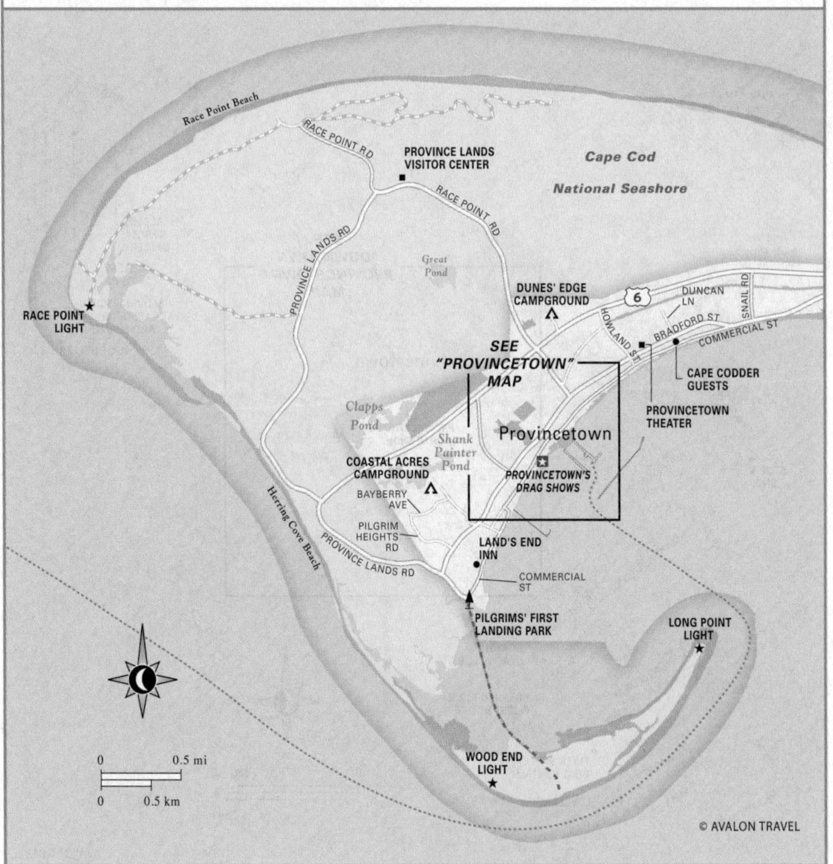

Provincetown Art

Decades of artists that fell for the life and lines of Cape Cod mean a downtown that's packed with galleries, right between the T-shirt shops and drag bars. The majority are on Commercial Street between Montello Street to the west, and Howland Street, at the eastern edge of the strip. From east to west, some not-to-be-missed galleries include **Julie Heller East** (465 Commercial St., 508/487-2166, www.juliehellergallery.com, 11am-5pm Thurs.-Mon.), where the art historian owner curates a collection of historic and modern Provincetown artists that's a fascinating look at the Cape's evolving art, and **Gallery Voyeur** (444 Commercial St., 508/487-3678, www.voy-art.com, 11am-4pm daily late May-June, 11am-4pm and 6pm-10pm daily July-late Sept.) to see Johniene Papandreas's large-format portraits. The **Albert Merola Gallery** (424 Commercial St., 508/487-4424, www.albertmerolagallery.com) also has a good collection of contemporary and historic work from the Cape. Opening hours are typically 11am-4pm daily in season (June-Sept.), though can be variable, especially in the off-season, so call ahead for information or to make an appointment. If you were only to

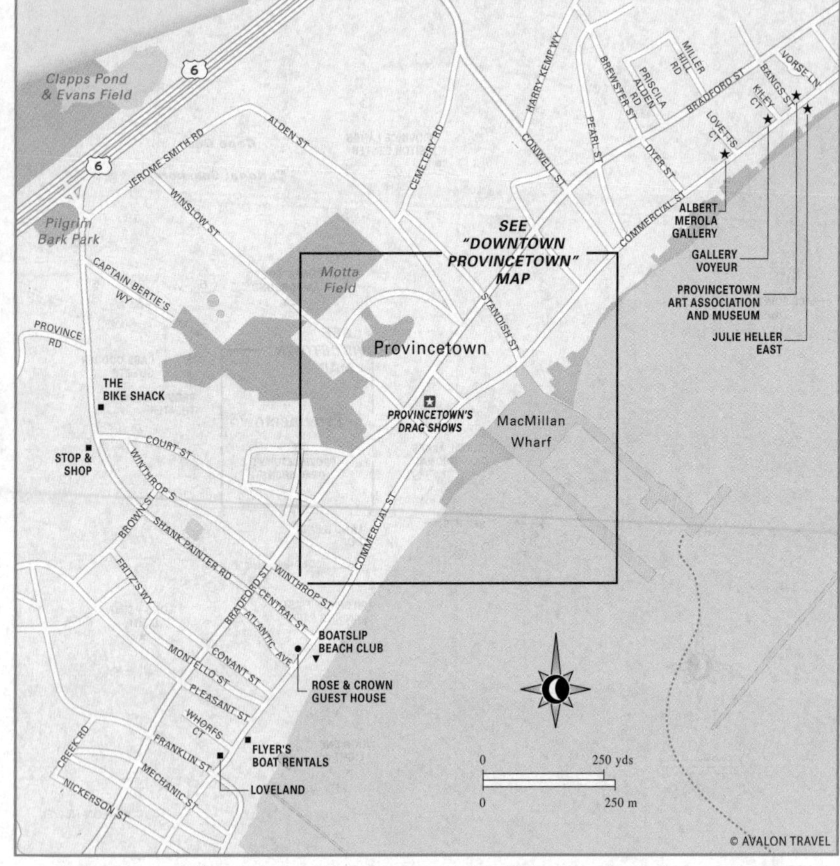

make one stop for art in Provincetown, however, the **Provincetown Art Association and Museum** (460 Commercial St., 508/487-1750, www.paam.org, 11am-8pm Tues.-Thurs., 11am-10pm Fri., 11am-5pm Sat.-Mon. June-Sept., noon-5pm Thurs.-Sun. Oct.-May, $10 adults, children under 13 free, free after 5pm Fri.) is a treasure trove of Cape Cod and Provincetown art.

Other Sights

Step on the same ground that the Pilgrims did at **Pilgrim's First Landing Park** at the west end of Commercial Street. A plaque there memorializes the Pilgrims' touchdown on November 21, 1620.

It would be easy to read away a rainy day on the coast at the **Provincetown Public Library** (356 Commercial St., 508/487-7094, www.provincetownlibrary.org, 10am-8pm Mon.-Thurs., 10am-5pm Fri., 1pm-5pm Sat.-Sun.), which has a great collection of books on the area. Stop in anyway to look at the half-sized replica of the *Rose Dorothea* fishing schooner, which sails the stacks on the library's 2nd floor.

To learn more about **Stellwagen Bank National Marine Sanctuary,** visit the free

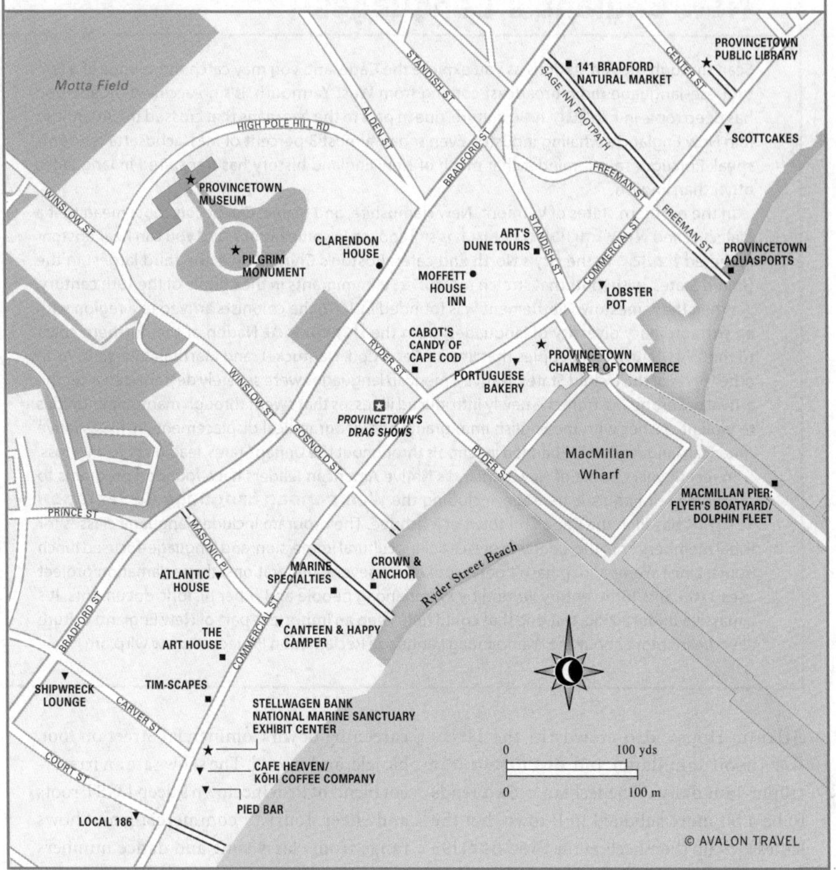

exhibit center (205-209 Commercial St., 781/545-8026, www.stellwagen.noaa.gov, 11am-6pm daily July-Aug., 11am-6pm Fri.-Sat. June and Sept., free), which explains the unique habitat with touch-screen computer exhibits and other displays.

ENTERTAINMENT AND EVENTS

Nightlife

The nightclub scene is as LGBT friendly as any in New England. Some venues are scene-specific, while others have open-door policies. Festivities kick off early at the late afternoon **Tea Dance** at the **Boatslip Beach Club** (161 Commercial St., 508/487-1669, www.boatslipresort.com, 4pm-7pm daily summer, 4pm-7pm weekends spring and fall), where revelers sip dangerously powerful planter's punch, which sloughs off both inhibitions and clothing.

Predominantly for men, the **Atlantic House** (4-6 Masonic Pl., 508/487-3821, www.ahouse.com) is a classic gay nightclub with underwear-clad bartenders, smoke machines, and an upstairs **Macho Bar** (10pm-1am daily) that features lots of leather, Levi's, and sexy videos on continuous loop. The

Rádio Português: Listening for New England's Languages

Scan through the AM stations as you explore the Cape, and you may catch the sounds of a Portuguese-language radio broadcast coming from West Yarmouth. It's no accident—Cape Cod has deep roots in **Portuguese** culture, due in part to the Azoreans that crossed the Atlantic to join New England's whaling industry. Even today, almost 3 percent of Massachusetts residents speak Portuguese, a reminder that much of New England history has transpired in languages other than English.

In the northern states of Vermont, New Hampshire, and Maine, Québecois roots mean that a dialect called **New England French** is still spoken in some homes, and you can hear Boston-inflected **Italian** in the city's North End cafés. Boston's Chinatown is the third largest in the United States, with roots that stretch to **Chinese** immigrants in the middle of the 19th century.

When the Jamestown Settlement was founded in 1607, the colonists arrived to a region with an extraordinary diversity of languages, from the **Penobscot** Nation of the northern coast to the **Wampanoag** peoples that live on Cape Cod, Nantucket, and Martha's Vineyard. As in other parts of the United States, Native American languages were severely destabilized after the arrival of Europeans, from the newly introduced illnesses that swept through many communities to violent clashes with the English immigrants and geographical displacement. In 1887, Native American languages were banned in schools throughout the United States, leading to further loss.

In recent years, some of New England's Native American leaders have founded programs to preserve their linguistic heritage, including the **Wampanoag Language Reclamation Project** based in the Cape Cod town of Mashpee. The program includes language classes for tribal members from the elderly to preschoolers, cultural immersion, and language-focused lunch hours. Since Wampanoag hasn't been spoken for several generations, the reclamation project uses 17th- and 18th-century writing by Wampanoag people and other historic documents. It's a massive undertaking, but one that could help keep an important part of New England culture alive. Learn more about the Wampanoag Language Reclamation Project at www.wlrp.org.

Atlantic House also crowds in the **Little Bar** (noon-1am daily) and **Big Room bar** (10pm-1am daily). The lesbian crowd tends to be a bit more subdued in P-town, but the ladies kick up their heels at the **Pied Bar** (193 Commercial St., 508/487-1527, www.piedbar.net, noon-midnight Sat.-Sun. May-June and Oct.-Nov., noon-midnight daily July-Aug.), which is open to all comers. Most of the patrons stay fully clothed at the **Shipwreck Lounge** (10 Carver St., 508/487-1472, www.ptownlounge.com, 5pm-1am daily), which feels like a cozy beach house living room with excellent cocktails.

★ DRAG SHOWS

The drag scene is a classic P-town experience. You don't need to look for a drag show in Provincetown, as one is likely to find you—watch for flamboyantly dressed performers careening down Commercial Street on foot, bicycle, and moped. The shows are an irreverent blend of Provincetown's deep LGBT roots and sheer, touristy commercialism. Shows range from classy song and dance numbers to raunchy humor with big hair, big smiles, and outsized personalities.

The surreal **Dina Martina** is a fixture of the scene, with regular appearances at the **Crown & Anchor** (247 Commercial St., 508/487-1430, www.onlyatthecrown.com, $28). Dina's offbeat monologues and comically bad singing make her a P-town favorite. With vampy, pinup charm, **Jinkx Monsoon** brings a fun theatricality to her routine, and she makes frequent appearances at **The Art House** (214 Commercial St., 508/487-9222, www.ptownarthouse.com, $32), another popular venue for drag shows. Drag queen residencies come and go; if there are performers you'd like to see, it's worth looking up where their show is now. To find out what's happening, pick up a copy of the free *Provincetown Magazine*, which is available in many downtown shops and at the visitors bureau. The magazine is updated each Wednesday.

Theater

Local thespians date the beginning of American drama to 1916, when the first Eugene O'Neill play was performed on P-Town's Lewis Wharf. The theater community was reborn in 2001 with the construction of the beautiful 200-seat **Provincetown Theater** (238 Bradford St., 508/487-7487, www.provincetowntheater.org, $20-75), which stages everything from campy musicals to heart-wrenching original dramas.

Festivals and Events

Filmmaker John Waters is a regular at the **Provincetown International Film Festival** (508/487-3456, www.p-townfilmfest.org, mid-June), which showcases truly independent films. The town's thriving fishing community celebrates its heritage during the weekend-long **Provincetown Portuguese Festival** (508/487-0086, www.provincetownportuguesefestival.com, late June, free) that culminates with the annual Blessing of the Fleet. The **Fourth of July Celebration** (508/487-7000, www.p-townchamber.com, July 4, free) has the best beachside fireworks on the Cape. Last but not least, **Carnival Week** (508/487-2313, www.p-town.org, late Aug.) is a seven-day Mardi Gras that features a parade, elaborate dance parties, and performances by internationally renowned drag queens.

But during the summer months in Provincetown, it seems like every week is a "week," with a different slice of the scene seizing a piece of the calendar, from **Bear Week** (stop by in early July to fête large, hairy men with leather vests take on masculinity) to **Whale Week** (come the last week in July to celebrate the marine mammal).

SHOPPING

Art galleries, penny-candy stores, and sex shops line Commercial Street, which is the best place in Cape Cod to browse for souvenirs and unique gifts. A few boutiques stock wonderfully curated collections of clothes and accessories. Browse for "bohemian marine" treasures at **Loveland** (120 Commercial St., 508/413-9500, www.lovelandprovincetown.com, noon-6pm Thurs.-Sun. May-June, 11am-11pm daily July-Aug., noon-6pm daily Sept.). At **Tim-Scapes** (208 Commercial St., 917/626-4052, www.timscapes.com, 11am-8pm daily late May-early Sept., 11am-5pm Sat.-Sun. Sept.-May), artist Tim Convery uses duct tape to create bold graphic designs. Find diving bells, antique lifesaving rings, and other intriguing flotsam at **Marine Specialties** (235 Commercial St., 508/487-1730, noon-5pm Sun.-Fri., 11am-6pm Sat.), and stock up on penny candy or saltwater taffy at **Cabot's Candy of Cape Cod** (276 Commercial St., 508/487-3550, www.cabotscandy.com, 11am-7pm daily).

SPORTS AND RECREATION

Beaches

Stunning **Race Point Beach** is an eight-mile stretch of crashing waves and soft sand edged with dune grass. To access the beach, park at the **Province Lands Visitor Center** (171 Race Point Rd., 508/487-1256, 9am-5pm daily May-Oct.), which has observation decks, interpretive displays, and a knowledgeable staff. For sunsets over the surf, it's hard to beat a spot at **Herring Cove Beach,** a peaceful swath that's just a few miles from the center of Provincetown. Turn right at the parking lot to set up at the family-oriented part of the beach, or turn left to reach the more swinging real estate, where visitors tend to self-sort by gender and orientation.

Like other beaches in the Cape Cod National Seashore, parking fees and entrance fees are collected in season ($20 cars, $10 motorcycles, $3 pedestrians). Parking lots get crowded, so it's worthwhile to access the beaches by public transport or bicycle. Shuttles leave MacMillan Wharf for Race Point every 15-30 minutes 7am-8pm and for Herring Cove every 20 minutes 9am-half hour before sunset. To get to Race Point by bike, head down Conwell Street to Race Point Road, where a bike path parallels the roadway. For Herring Cove, cyclists have two options: They can ride right on Route 6, or take the longer but nicer ride along the bike path through the Province Lands. Pick up the trail at the Beech Forest Parking Area off Race Point Road.

Boating and Fishing

Rent anything from a kayak to a 19-foot sloop at **Flyer's Boat Rentals** (131A Commercial St., 508/487-0898, www.flyersrentals.com, starting at $30), which also offers two-hour sailing lessons ($130 one person, $30 each additional person). Find a stand-up paddleboard at **Provincetown Aquasports** (333R Commercial St., 508/413-9563, www.ptownaquasports.com, $20 per hour, $50 full day). The 73-foot gaff-rigged schooner ***Bay Lady II*** (20 Berry Ln., 508/487-9308, www.sailcapecod.com, $28-33 adults, $15 children) sails several times daily for the Corn Hill bluffs and Long Point Light. Sportfishing boats lining MacMillan Wharf include the ***Ginny G*** (508/246-3656, www.ginnygcapecodcharters.com), which goes in search of bluefish, bass, cod, and tuna.

Hiking and Biking

Just across from Provincetown's vibrant downtown are the **Province Lands,** a rugged, shifting stretch of dunes that can feel wild and otherworldly, a transporting reminder of why generations of artists came to the Cape to escape the world. The sand is held together with webs of wild, five-petal roses and grass, sagging fences, and a few spiny scrub pines, and is especially stunning in the fall, when the plants take on a subtle rusty hue. The artists' shacks are the only rustic structures in the dunes have no electricity or running water.

A good place to orient yourself to the dunes' natural history, plants, and trails is the **Province Lands Visitor Center** (171 Race Point Rd., 508/487-1256, 9am-5pm daily May-Oct.), which offers ranger-guided hikes and outings.

To see the dunes' historical and scenic highlights, though, you can't beat local knowledge, and **Art's Dune Tours** (4 Standish St., 508/487-1950, www.artsdunetours.com, Apr.-Nov., $29 adults, $18 children 6-11, children under 6 free) has operated tours of the sand in 4x4 vehicles since 1946. Art's offers every possible variation on the dune tour—add a sunset, clambake, lighthouse, lake, or kayak trip—and has several departures daily.

One of the best **walking trails** into the dunes starts at **Snail Road** off Route 6. Limited parking is available. A sandy road leads to a path that winds past dunes, shacks, and hollows to the shore. It's just a mile or so to the beach, but wandering up and over soft dunes takes much longer than hiking on firm ground. The trail braids and splits at times, so take note of your route throughout the walk, and bring shoes and plenty of water—the sand gets surprisingly hot.

Or do as P-town locals do: Park your car and explore on two wheels. An excellent network of bike paths and bike-friendly roads makes it easy. The 5.45-mile **Province Lands Bike Trail** is a dreamy route through dunes, with spurs to Race Point Beach and Herring Cove Beach. Pick up a map of the trail at **Province Lands Visitor Center** (Race Point Rd., 508/487-1256, 9am-5pm daily May-Oct.) or at a bike shop in town. To rent a bike, stop by **The Bike Shack** (63 Shank Painter Rd., 918/660-7183, www.provincetownbikeshack.com, bikes start at $10 per hour, $17 per day), whose fleet includes beach cruisers, road and mountain bikes, and baby trailers.

★ Whale-Watching Tours

Just north of Land's End is a shallow, sandy rise in the ocean floor called Stellwagen Bank, where a nutrient-rich upwelling and a U.S. National Marine Sanctuary attract a diverse population of dolphins, sea turtles, and whales. April-October, whales migrate to this coast to feed on schooling fish, and a dozen tour operators offer trips into the sanctuary to spot humpback, finback, minke, sei, and pilot whales. In the winter of 2016, a cluster of endangered right whales appeared off the Cape Cod coast, a sign that the struggling population has found a safe, nourishing place to feed; a whale-watching tour is a rare chance to spot one of the known 500-some surviving right whales.

The **Dolphin Fleet** (MacMillan Pier, 800/826-9300, www.whalewatch.com, mid-Apr.-Oct., $47 adults, $31 children 5-12, children under 5 free) departs many times a day during the season from downtown Providence, with open decks, enclosed cabins, and free tickets if no whales are sighted. Onboard naturalists help identify any fins and flukes you spot, and, though they're not always operated, some of the boats are equipped with hydrophones for listening for whale vocalizations. Tours last 3-4 hours.

FOOD

Provincetown is lined with excellent places to eat, mostly clustered around Commercial Street. Business hours can vary with season and demand; restaurants sometimes close early on slow nights or keep serving as long as the tables are full. It's always worth calling ahead.

It's hard not to love ★ **Canteen** (225 Commercial St., 508/487-3800, www.thecanteenptown.com, 8am-8pm daily, off-season hours and days vary, $7-19), a tourist joint that's also a local favorite. The nautical theme of this casual lunch spot is bright and hip. The lack of elbow room at large communal tables means it's easy to make friends over plates of excellent fish-and-chips, crispy Brussels sprouts, house-made Portuguese sausage, and a good selection of local beers on draft. Its little sibling next door, **Happy Camper** (227 Commercial St., 508/487-3800, www.happycamper.cool, 7:30am-11pm daily, off-season hours and days vary, $2-8) takes a summery-cool approach to doughnuts and ice cream.

The distinctive neon sign at the **Lobster Pot** (321 Commercial St., 508/487-0842, www.ptownlobsterpot.com, 11:30am-9pm daily late Apr. or early May-Nov., $16-27) has been signaling chowder-hungry crowds for years. Among the dozens of places that claim "best chowder" on the Cape, the Lobster Pot is a strong contender. The Portuguese soup is another favorite dish that's steeped in Cape Cod history, and the long menu meanders on to lobster, steaks, tacos, and sushi. The

whale-watching tour

cavernous restaurant has table seating on two levels and a bar upstairs—the 2nd floor has better views. The raw bar is a good alternative when the wait for a table gets long.

Decked with bright, big art and handwritten menu boards, **Cafe Heaven** (199 Commercial St., 508/487-9639, 8am-2pm and 6pm-10pm daily Apr.-Nov., $7-16) is a cheerful spot for breakfasting on piles of French toast, home fries, pancakes, and fruit. The compact café stays busy throughout the day, serving sandwiches on homemade bread, hearty soups, and salads.

Enjoy a chewy, sugary taste of Cape Cod's heritage at ★ **Portuguese Bakery** (299 Commercial St., 508/487-1803, 8am-5pm daily Apr.-Nov., $2-8), which piles its shelves with fried-dough *malasadas*, lightly caramelized egg tarts, and cream-filled *bolas de berlim*.

Burgers made with pasture-raised beef and topped with everything from fried avocado to lobster are the stars of the menu at **Local 186** (186 Commercial St., 508/487-7555, www.local186.com, 11am-1am Mon.-Thurs., May-Oct., $13-22), a stylish restaurant with butcher charts painted on the walls and a sunny porch for prime people-watching. A solid draft list and creative cocktails round out the menu of clams, oysters, and salads.

When pink-frosted cupcakes are all that will do, head to **ScottCakes** (353 Commercial St., 508/487-7465, www.scottcakes.com, 11am-midnight daily, $3), where pink-frosted cupcakes are all that's on the menu. The simple yellow cakes are a P-town icon, and the pink hole-in-the-wall bakeshop is just as sweet. Where else can you find a "legalize gay cupcakes" T-shirt?

Find the best coffee in Provincetown at the stylish, diminutive **Kōhi Coffee Company** (199 Commercial St., 774/538-6467, www.kohicoffee.com, 7:30am-5pm daily, $3-7), which brews organic, single-origin beans into espresso and pour-over drinks. On hot days, the lightly sweet chicory and coffee blend in the New Orleans Iced is sublime. The tiny shop has a prime spot between the beach and Commercial Street.

Shop for natural, organic food and healthy ready-to-eat options at **141 Bradford Natural Market** (141 Bradford St., 508/487-9784, www.the141market.com, 8am-7pm Mon.-Wed., 8am-8pm Thurs.-Sat., 9am-6pm Sun.), or pick up supplies at **Stop & Shop** (56 Shank Painter Rd., 508/487-4903, 6am-9pm Mon.-Sat., 7am-9pm Sun.).

ACCOMMODATIONS AND CAMPING

Under $100

The simple rooms at **Cape Codder Guests** (570 Commercial St., 508/487-0131, www.capecodderguests.com, May-Nov., rooms $65-90, apartment $185) don't have televisions or private baths, but they're perfectly clean and comfortably furnished in an old-fashioned home with a blooming garden. The guesthouse also has a private beach with a sundeck and a nearby parking lot.

$100-150

A painted figurehead greets guests arriving at the **Rose & Crown Guest House** (158 Commercial St., 508/487-3332, www.roseandcrownptown.com, rooms $115-195, apartments $150-180, parking $15), a unique place to stay in the center of town. Rooms are small but imaginatively designed; one is decked out with purple fabrics and Victorian antiques, another features exposed beams and a stately brass bed. Three less expensive rooms upstairs share a bath.

Cozy and relaxed, **Moffett House Inn** (296A Commercial St., 508/487-6615, www.moffetthouse.com, continental breakfast included July-Aug., $60-184) feels like a family vacation house that just happens to be walking distance from the action on Commercial Street. Limited parking is available on-site for $5-18 per night, or guests can get discounted access to a nearby parking lot ($20). For guests that take advantage of the two bicycles provided with each room, the Moffett House Inn is one of the best deals in town.

$150-250

There are just six rooms in the **Clarendon House** (118 Bradford St., 508/680-4444, www.theclarendonhouse.com, June-Jan., $175-235, free parking), which was updated in 2016 with furniture that's old-fashioned but thoroughly unstuffy. The friendly owners are a highlight, as are full breakfasts and around-the-clock snacks, coffee, and tea.

If you've been dreaming of the lighthouse keeper's life, the house that adjoins **Race Point Light** (Race Point Beach, Rte. 6, 508/487-9930, www.racepointlighthouse.org, $115-205) is a bed-and-breakfast May-November, whose three simple rooms boast the most dramatic location on the Cape.

Over $250

The elegant, secluded ★ **Land's End Inn** (22 Commercial St., 508/487-0706, www.landsendinn.com, $405-680, free parking) commands sweeping views of the ocean, so guests can watch the sun rise—and set—from a glassed-in tower. The owner's exceptional collection of art nouveau antiques fills every conceivable nook of the common areas, while guest rooms feature skylights, interior balconies, and domed ceilings. A breakfast buffet, afternoon wine bar, and 24-hour tea and coffee make this a soothing place to watch the tide come in.

Camping

Just a 10-minute walk from Provincetown, **Dunes' Edge Campground** (386 Rte. 6, 508/487-9815, www.thetrustees.org, late May-early Oct., basic sites $35-49, hookups $50-61) has 85 tent sites in a wooded area that have access to coin-operated hot showers and laundry. The sites are small and relatively densely packed, so the campground can get pretty noisy on busy weekends. Sites often fill up weeks in advance, but a handful are released each morning, so it's worth calling on the same day. Slightly seedy but very friendly, **Coastal Acres Campground** (76R Bayberry Ave., 508/487-1700, www.coastalacresprovincetown.com, Apr.-Nov., basic sites $39-49, hookups $49-59) is a mile from downtown, with grassy sites and serviceable facilities.

INFORMATION

The **Provincetown Chamber of Commerce** (307 Commercial St. at Lopes Sq., 508/487-3424, www.p-townchamber.com, 9am-5pm daily May-Oct., 10am-3pm Mon.-Tues. and Thurs.-Sat. Nov.-Dec. and Mar.-Apr., 10am-3pm Mon. and Fri. Jan.-Feb.) runs a visitors center just off the ferry landing.

GETTING THERE AND AROUND

The most pleasant way to reach P-Town from Boston is by ferry. **Bay State Cruise Company** (World Trade Center, 200 Seaport Blvd., Boston, 877/783-3779, www.baystatecruises.com, mid-May-mid-Oct.) runs both a 90-minute fast ferry (one-way/round-trip $59/$88 adults, $55/$78 seniors, $39/$65 children 3-12, $23/33 children under 3, $8/16 bicycles) and a three-hour slow boat ($30/$60 adults, children under 12 free). **Cape Air** (800/352-0714, www.flycapeair.com) runs daily flights from Boston.

Buses by **Plymouth & Brockton** (508/746-0378, www.p-b.com) stop at the chamber of commerce building. This is the end of the line from Hyannis (1.5 hrs., $11), where it's possible to change buses and continue to Boston (2 hrs., $31).

The Cape Cod Transit Authority runs the **Breeze shuttle** (800/352-7155, www.thebreeze.info), which provides transport to the airport, beaches, and town center, and taxi service is available from **Cape Cod Taxi** (506/487-2222, www.capcabtaxi.com).

Martha's Vineyard

Celebrity vacation spot, family retreat, rural getaway . . . after more than 200 years of summer people, Martha's Vineyard's diversity still comes as a surprise. It's easy to find your own slice of this wonderfully scenic island, whose quaint villages and tourist traps are interspersed with coastal dunes, pale beaches, and farmland. The Wampanoag tribe has a stronger presence here than elsewhere in the Cape and islands, and families of Vineyard sailors, farmers, and fishers still maintain deep roots.

It's a fun place to explore on a day trip to Oak Bluffs or Edgartown, but really experiencing the Vineyard means taking the time to discover back roads and up-island fishing communities. While the island has a reputation as an expensive retreat, prices aren't far off from those on Cape Cod, and a wonderful hostel and campground offer a taste of Vineyard life on a budget.

Residents divide the island into **down-island** (east) and **up-island** (west). The former is home to the island's three main population centers: touristy Vineyard Haven, posh Edgartown, and charming Oak Bluffs. Up-island is more rural, with the cow pastures of West Tisbury and Chilmark sharing space with the scenic fishing village of Menemsha and the cliffs of Aquinnah.

VINEYARD HAVEN

Ferries arriving in this compact harbor town thread past world-class sailing yachts, tall ships, and fishing boats guarded by an attractive pair of lighthouses. With tourist shops, historic homes, and a pair of public beaches right in town, Vineyard Haven is the first stop for most visitors to the island. Even at its most crowded, it's remarkably charming.

Sights

The finest examples of mid-19th-century captains' houses are clustered in the **William Street Historic District** that runs south from Woodlawn Avenue to just past Camp Street. The best way to see the homes is following a self-guided walking tour available at the **Martha's Vineyard Chamber of Commerce** (24 Beach St., 508/693-0085, www.mvy.com, 9am-5pm Mon.-Fri.).

It's an easy, two-mile jaunt from downtown Vineyard Haven to **West Chop Light** (W. Chop Rd.). While the historic lighthouse isn't open to the public, the low picket fence allows for great views from the road.

Entertainment and Events

The small, nonprofit **Martha's Vineyard Playhouse** (24 Church St., 508/696-6300, www.mvplayhouse.org) stages readings, live music, and plays at a small theater in town, as well as outdoor Shakespeare productions at Tisbury Amphitheater.

Shopping

The walkable center of Vineyard Haven is crowded with beachy boutiques and souvenir shops, but the mother of all tourist traps is the **Black Dog Bakery and General Store** (3 Water St., 508/338-4440, www.theblackdog.com, 8am-6pm daily), which sells everything imaginable emblazoned with the company's distinctive canine logo. Find beautiful images of the island by local photographer Jeff Serusa at **Seaworthy Gallery** (34 Beach Rd., 508/693-0153, www.seaworthygallerymv.info, 10am-5pm daily). The best selection of books by local authors is at **Bunch of Grapes Bookstore** (35 Main St., 508/693-2291, www.bunchofgrapes.com, 9am-6pm Mon.-Sat., 11am-5pm Sun.).

Sports and Recreation

BIKING

Plenty of bike paths and fellow cyclists mean that riding on Martha's Vineyard is easier (and safer) than anywhere in New England.

One Day in Martha's Vineyard

MORNING

Pack your bathing suit and walking shoes, and catch the first boat of the day to Oak Bluffs, a bustling community whose star attractions are walking distance from the ferry landing. After picking up pastries-to-go at the **Martha's Vineyard Gourmet Café and Bakery,** take a stroll through the winding streets of **The Campground,** a onetime Methodist revival camp lined with sweet Carpenter Gothic cottages in vibrant colors.

AFTERNOON

Get a taste of the Vineyard's rural up-island scenery by hopping the island bus to **Aquinnah Cliffs** and the **Gay Head Light,** where members of the Vineyard's Wampanoag maintain a cluster of shops and an exhibit on Wampanoag culture.

Save room for pie after a seafood lunch at **Aquinnah Shop Restaurant,** then walk down to the nearby beach to watch for celebrities and soak up the sun before catching a bus back to Oak Bluffs, where a tempting array of souvenir shops, fudge stores, and boutiques stay bustling all summer.

EVENING

Watching the stars from the open deck of the ferry is the perfect end to a day on the island, but before you leave for the mainland, try to snag the brass ring at the **Flying Horses Carousel,** the oldest in the United States.

Bring your own, or rent from **Martha's Bike Rentals** (4 Lagoon Pond Rd., 800/559-0312, www.marthasbikerentals.com, Apr.-Nov., 1-day rental from $27), where you can also pick up biking maps of the island. Popular rides from Vineyard Haven include the four-mile loop ride to **West Chop Light** on quiet roads, or the seven-mile bike path to **Edgartown.** Biking maps are also available at the town's visitors center.

BOATING

All eyes are on the soaring canvas and proud bowsprits of the schooners *Alabama* and *Shenandoah* as they cruise the Vineyard Haven harbor. Both are part of **The Black Dog Tall Ships** (Black Dog Wharf, 20 Beach St., 508/693-1699, www.theblackdogtallships.com, late May-early Oct., 3-hour sail $75 adults, $50 children 4-11). Its fleet makes several daily outings during the summer season. Aspiring sailors can take a turn raising sails or manning the helm, and the sailing outings are BYOB.

PADDLING

Explore the coast at your own pace with a rental from **Wind's Up** (199 Beach Rd., 508/693-4252, www.windsupmv.com, 10am-5pm daily June-Sept., rentals from $16 per hour, $50 per day). Find anything with a paddle from kayaks to canoes and stand-up paddleboards (SUPs), or rent a Sunfish or 15-foot sloop. The shop also offers lessons from $50 per person.

BEACHES

Just a thin strip of sand off Main Street, **Owen Park Beach** might not be the island's most scenic, but its location not far from the ferry terminal is a good stop for a quick picnic or one last swim before vacation ends. There are lifeguards on duty during the summer months, making it a popular option for families.

A bit farther afield, **Lake Tashmoo Town Beach** is at the outlet between a shallow lake and the sea, so swimmers can choose between the warm, brackish inland water or cooler

Martha's Vineyard

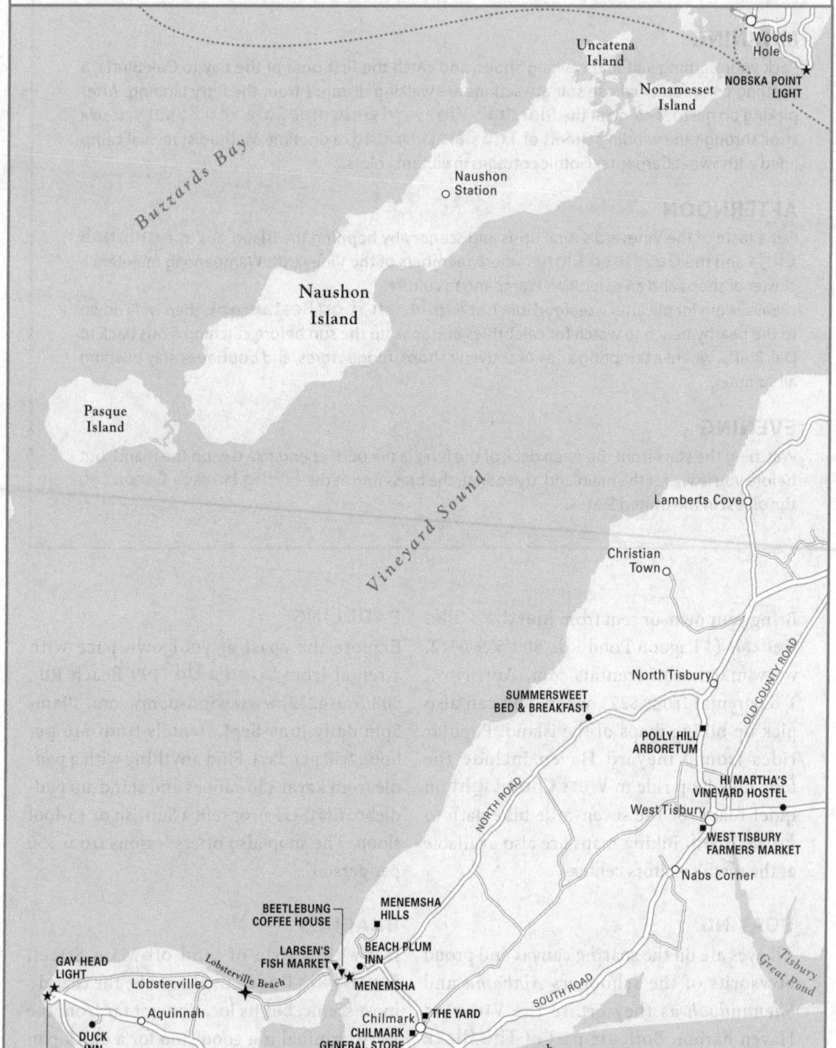

Woods Hole
Uncatena Island
Nonamesset Island
NOBSKA POINT LIGHT
Buzzards Bay
Naushon Station
Naushon Island
Pasque Island
Vineyard Sound
Lamberts Cove
Christian Town
OLD COUNTY ROAD
North Tisbury
SUMMERSWEET BED & BREAKFAST
POLLY HILL ARBORETUM
HI MARTHA'S VINEYARD HOSTEL
West Tisbury
WEST TISBURY FARMERS MARKET
NORTH ROAD
Nabs Corner
Tisbury Great Pond
BEETLEBUNG COFFEE HOUSE
MENEMSHA HILLS
LARSEN'S FISH MARKET
BEACH PLUM INN
MENEMSHA
GAY HEAD LIGHT
Lobsterville
Lobsterville Beach
Aquinnah
DUCK INN
Chilmark
THE YARD
CHILMARK GENERAL STORE
SOUTH ROAD
Lucy Vincent Beach
Indian Lands
STATE ROAD
AQUINNAH CLIFFS
AQUINNAH SHOP RESTAURANT
Nashaquitsa
Squibnocket

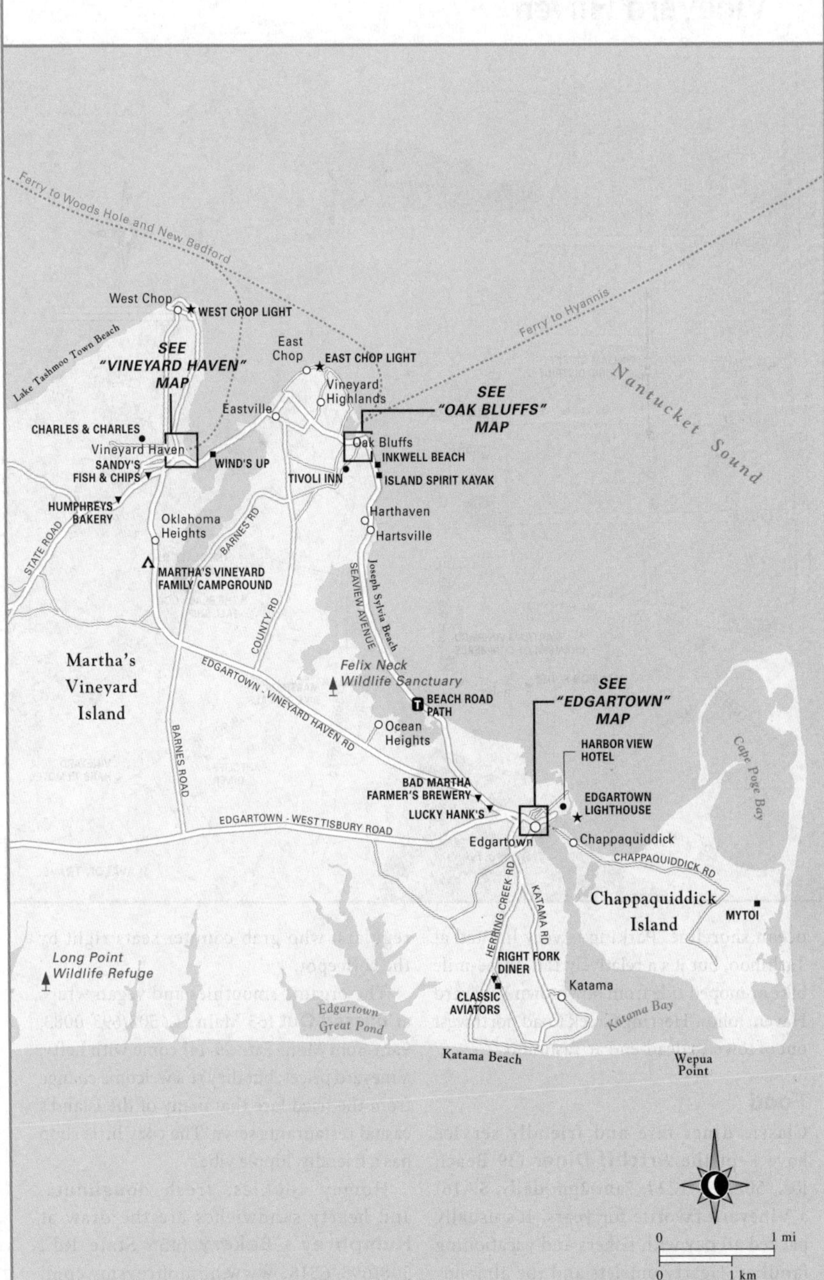
Ferry to Woods Hole and New Bedford
Ferry to Hyannis
Nantucket Sound
West Chop
WEST CHOP LIGHT
Lake Tashmoo Town Beach
SEE "VINEYARD HAVEN" MAP
East Chop
EAST CHOP LIGHT
Vineyard Highlands
SEE "OAK BLUFFS" MAP
Eastville
CHARLES & CHARLES
Vineyard Haven
WIND'S UP
SANDY'S FISH & CHIPS
Oak Bluffs
INKWELL BEACH
TIVOLI INN
ISLAND SPIRIT KAYAK
HUMPHREYS BAKERY
Oklahoma Heights
BARNES RD
Harthaven
Hartsville
STATE ROAD
MARTHA'S VINEYARD FAMILY CAMPGROUND
SEAVIEW AVENUE
Joseph Sylvia Beach
COUNTY RD
Martha's Vineyard Island
EDGARTOWN - VINEYARD HAVEN RD
Felix Neck Wildlife Sanctuary
BEACH ROAD PATH
SEE "EDGARTOWN" MAP
Ocean Heights
BARNES ROAD
HARBOR VIEW HOTEL
Cape Poge Bay
BAD MARTHA FARMER'S BREWERY
LUCKY HANK'S
EDGARTOWN LIGHTHOUSE
EDGARTOWN - WEST TISBURY ROAD
Edgartown
Chappaquiddick
CHAPPAQUIDDICK RD
HERRING CREEK RD
KATAMA RD
Chappaquiddick Island
MYTOI
Long Point Wildlife Refuge
RIGHT FORK DINER
Katama
CLASSIC AVIATORS
Katama Bay
Edgartown Great Pond
Katama Beach
Wepua Point
0 1 mi
0 1 km

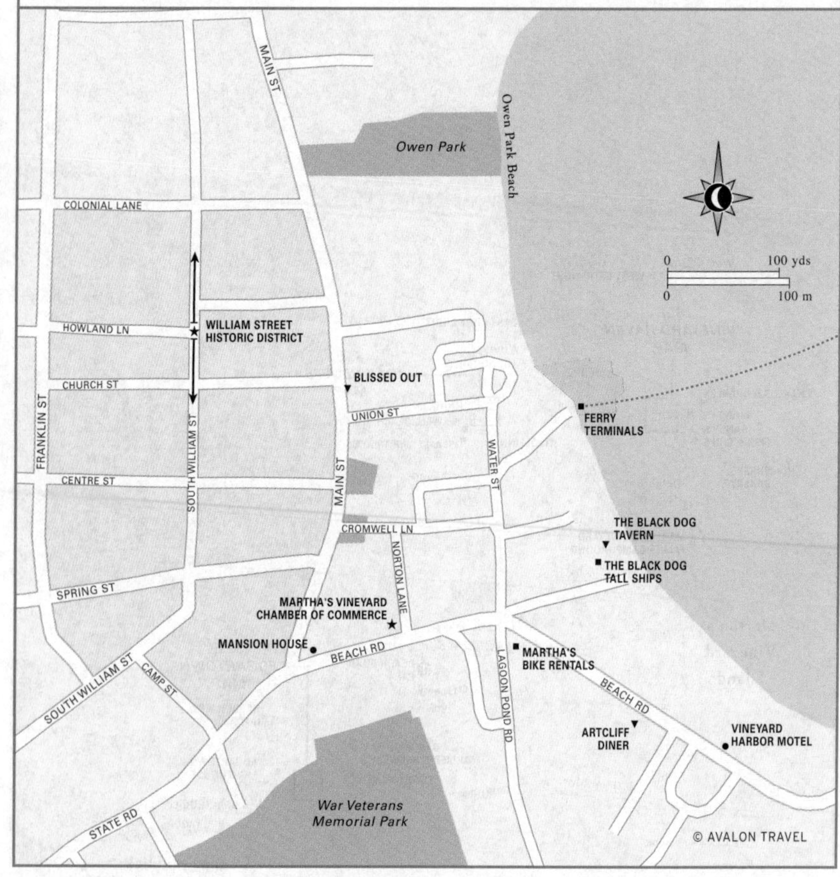

ocean shoreline. Parking is very limited at Tashmoo, but it's a relatively flat, three-mile bike or moped ride from downtown Vineyard Haven; follow Herring Creek Road northwest out of town to dead-end at Tashmoo.

Food

Classic diner fare and friendly service have kept the **Artcliff Diner** (39 Beach Rd., 508/693-1224, 7am-2pm daily, $7-16) a Vineyard favorite for years. It's usually packed all day with fishers and vacationing families. Hearty omelets and the almond-crusted French toast are favorites among regulars, who grab counter seats right by the coffeepot.

The organic smoothies and vegan wraps at **Blissed Out** (65 Main St., 508/693-0083, 9am-4pm Mon.-Sat., $9-14) come with hefty, Vineyard prices, but they're a welcome change from the fried fare that many of the island's casual restaurants serve. The cozy little shop has a friendly, hippie vibe.

Homey cookies, fresh doughnuts, and hearty sandwiches are the draw at **Humphrey's Bakery** (455 State Rd., 508/693-6518, www.humphreysmv.com, 5am-4pm Mon.-Sat., 9am-2pm Sun., $3-12), a comfy place with brightly painted chairs and a devoted following. The most beloved sandwich is the Turkey Gobbler, a Thanksgiving-inspired behemoth filled with roasted turkey, stuffing, and house-made cranberry sauce.

Tuck into fried clams, fish cakes, and chowder at **Sandy's Fish and Chips,** inside **John's Fish Market** (5 Martin Rd., 508/693-1220, 11am-7pm daily, call for off-season hours, $7-24), one of the best places on the island for clam shack fare. There's nowhere to sit inside the basic market, but in fine weather you can eat at the parking lot tables or order seafood to go.

If you've been rolling your eyes at the sea of Black Dog T-shirts, caps, and bumper stickers, **The Black Dog Tavern** (21 Beach St. Extension, 508/693-9223, www.theblackdog.com, 7am-4pm and 5pm-9pm daily, $14-31) may come as a pleasant surprise. It's real and rustic, decked with grainy images of old-fashioned schooners and excellent views of the harbor. Island specialties like quahog or codfish chowder are good, as are the hearty breakfasts. The tavern is mobbed from the beginning of summer until the leaves change.

Every Friday during the summer months, a kitchen crew of local seniors turns **Grace Episcopal Church** (36 Woodlawn Ave., 508/693-0332, 4pm-7:30pm Fri. late May-mid-Oct., lobster roll meals $22, pie $5) into a lobster roll factory, piling the buns high with lobster meat touched with mayo and freshly ground pepper. The lobster rolls come with chips and a drink, and the parish members also serve hot dogs and slices of truly delightful homemade pie. Show up early to avoid the wait, then order yours to go—to rolls are perfect for a sunset picnic by the water.

Accommodations and Camping

$150-250

The rooms at **Vineyard Harbor Motel** (60 Beach Rd., 508/693-3334, www.vineyardharbormotel.com, $185-300, suites $179-355) are somewhat dated and worn, but the waterfront location includes a private beach, and there are pleasant decks for watching the sun set over the water. Some rooms have full kitchens with cooking supplies.

Tchotchke-leery travelers will appreciate the ★ **Charles & Charles** (85 Summer St., 508/338-2351, www.charlesandcharlesmv.com, $200-300) guarantee of "no decorative plates on the walls!" The intimate, six-room inn delivers a charming blend of modern design and New England style. On sunny days, it's hard to beat their poolside breakfast. Perks like free bicycles, luxurious linens and soaps, and comfy beds make it a wonderful spot to land. The inn is a 10-minute walk from the ferry.

OVER $250

The historic **Mansion House** (9 Main St., 508/693-2200, $309-400) has an unbeatable location a few minutes' walk from the ferry dock. Bright, comfortable rooms and an on-site health club make it a great getaway. Don't miss the rooftop lounge, which is stocked with cold lemonade in the afternoons and has panoramic views.

CAMPING

Oak-shaded sites, playgrounds, and a spot right on the bicycle path make **Martha's Vineyard Family Campground** (569 Edgartown Rd., 508/693-3772, www.campmv.com, mid-May-mid-Oct., tent sites with 2 adults $60, additional adult $15, additional child 3 and over $5, cabins $150-170) an excellent choice for families. Cabins are clean and comfortable with access to an outside gas grill and picnic tables (no cooking equipment), and the larger, two-room cabins sleep six people in double beds and bunks.

Information

The **Martha's Vineyard Chamber of Commerce** (24 Beach St., 508/693-0085, www.mvy.com, 9am-5pm Mon.-Fri.) is stocked with maps and brochures. Its website has a helpful listing of last-minute rooms on the island.

Getting There and Around

The **Martha's Vineyard Transit Authority** (508/693-9440, www.vineyardtransit.com, fares $1.25-5) bus service links Vineyard Haven to all other major destinations on the island, departing from the Vineyard Haven Steamship Authority Terminal on the waterfront end of Union Street. All buses are wheelchair accessible. Several taxi services are also available, including **Stagecoach Taxi Co.** (508/627-4566, www.mvstagecoachtaxi.com).

Unless you are going to be spending a lot of time up-island, having a car can be more trouble than it's worth, but **Sun'n'Fun** (508/693-5457, www.sunfunrentals.com) offers free pickup when renting its Jeeps and Mini Coopers. (For ferry information, see *Getting to Martha's Vineyard.*)

OAK BLUFFS

Walking through Oak Bluffs's gingerbread cottages and brightly painted homes feels like a glimpse of an almost-forgotten period of New England history, when charismatic preachers packed enthusiastic crowds into summertime revivals. The town's most distinctive neighborhood is Wesleyan Grove, a cluster of Carpenter Gothic homes surrounding an open-air Tabernacle, the site of popular 19th-century Methodist camp meetings. The elaborate, whimsical style of those cottages spreads throughout the town: The grassy common is lined with hundreds of miniature homes that face an old-fashioned gazebo where bands play weekly concerts.

The historical heart of Martha's Vineyard's African American community, Oak Bluffs was a longtime favorite of intellectuals and luminaries like novelist Dorothy West and Edward Brooke, America's first popularly elected African American senator. It's still a popular vacation spot for Black Americans (and photos of locals with former President Barack Obama take pride of place in many Vineyard businesses). With great access to beaches, atmospheric neighborhoods, and wonderful parks, Oak Bluffs is far and away the best family destination on Martha's Vineyard.

Sights

Don't miss strolling through the adorable cottages in **Wesleyan Grove,** which center around the open-air **Trinity Park Tabernacle** (80 Trinity Park, 508/693-0525, www.mvcma.org), an area known as **The Campground.** It's easy enough to explore on your own, but for a bit of perspective on the neighborhood's history, time your visit to join one of the Martha's Vineyard Campground Meeting Association's **walking tours** (www.mvcma.org, 10am Tues. and Thurs. July-Aug., 1.5-hour tours $12 walk-ups, $10 online registration), which start at the Tabernacle.

A perennial favorite is the **Flying Horses Carousel** (15 Oak Bluffs Ave., 508/693-9481, 11am-4:30pm daily, call for off-season hours, $2.50), a national landmark and the oldest continually operating platform carousel in the United States. During the summer months, throngs of children wait to ride one of 20 carved wooden horses and take turns grabbing for the brass ring, accompanied by a 1923 Wurlitzer Band Organ that plays the original paper rolls. Past generations of islanders skipped rope to a sweet rhyme about the carousel: *There's a carousel in Oak Bluffs town, the horses don't go up and down, the horses just go round and round, on the carousel in Oak Bluffs town.*

With commanding views of the sea, the **East Chop Light** (229 E. Chop Dr., www.mvmuseum.org) is a fine place for a picnic. The 1.5-mile walk or ride from downtown passes through an exclusive neighborhood lined with beautiful homes. The **Martha's Vineyard Museum** (59 School St., Edgartown, 508/627-4441, www.mvmuseum.org) offers tours of the lighthouse on Sunday evenings in the summer.

Entertainment and Events

Summer on the Vineyard officially kicks off with the **Oak Bluffs Harbor Festival** (www.oakbluffsmv.com, mid-June), when

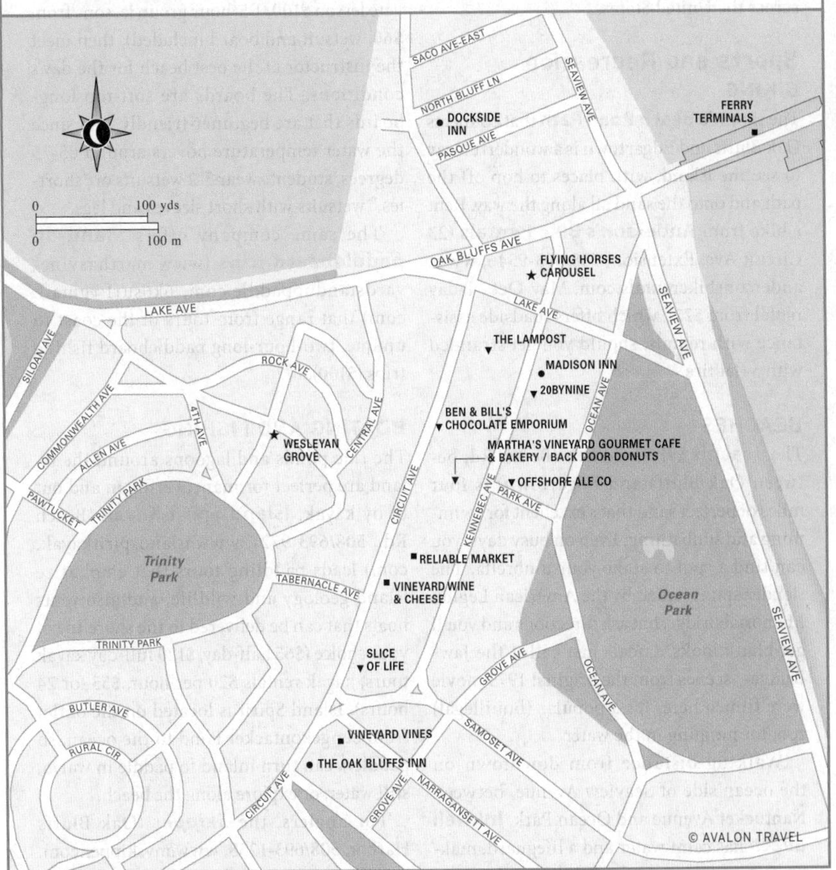

the waterfront fills with live music, craft vendors, and food booths, and the annual chalk-art contest sees fierce competition. One of the most anticipated nights of the summer is the **Grand Illumination** (The Campground, 508/693-0525, mid-Aug.), when the gingerbread cottages of the Oak Bluffs revival camp are lit up with thousands of paper lanterns. Depending on your frame of mind, the effect can be romantic or intensely spiritual.

Several bars in Oak Bluffs feature live music at night, including **Offshore Brewing Company** (Kennebec Ave., 508/693-2626, www.offshoreale.com, 11:30am-9pm Sun.-Thurs., 9:30am-10pm Fri.-Sat.) and **The Lampost** (6 Circuit Ave., 508/693-4032, www.lampostmv.com, 4pm-1am daily), which also offers a sweaty dance floor catering to the under-30 set.

Shopping

Most of Oak Bluffs's shops line **Circuit Avenue,** which runs through the heart of downtown and is easy to explore on foot. The most iconic shop in town might be **Vineyard Vines** (56 Narragansett Ave., 508/687-9841, www.vineyardvines.com, 10am-6pm Mon. and Thurs.-Sat., 11am-5pm Sun.), a nautical-themed boutique that's spread Vineyard-prep and spouting whale logos across the United States.

Sports and Recreation

BIKING

The six-mile **Beach Road Path** that connects Oak Bluffs and Edgartown is a wonderful way to see the island, with places to hop off the path and onto the sand all along the way. Rent a bike from **Anderson's Bike Rentals** (23 Circuit Ave. Extension, 508/693-9346, www.andersonsbikerentals.com, May-Oct., 1-day rental from $22), which offers roadside assistance with rentals, should you get stranded with a flat tire.

BEACHES

The **Joseph Sylvia Beach** (Beach Rd. between Oak Bluffs and Edgartown) is four miles of perfect sand that's excellent for swimming and sunbathing. Even on busy days, you can find a spot to stake your umbrella. The slender spit is joined by the American Legion Memorial Bridge, but ask directions and you'll get blank looks. Locals just call it the Jaws Bridge—scenes from the original 1975 movie were filmed here. It's a popular (but illegal) spot for jumping in the water.

Walking distance from downtown on the ocean side of Seaview Avenue, between Nantucket Avenue and Ocean Park, **Inkwell Beach** has calm water and a lifeguard, making it a popular spot for families with young children. Historically this was a gathering place for the town's African American community; the name was originally a sneering racial reference, but it's since been adopted by Martha's Vineyard's black residents as a point of pride.

SURFING AND STAND-UP PADDLEBOARDING

With coastlines pointing every which way, there's usually somewhere to surf on Martha's Vineyard, and the relatively gentle summer swell means it's a good place to catch your first wave. Book private or group lessons with **6k6 Surf School** (www.marthasvineyardsurflessons.com, 6k6surf@gmail.com, 1.5-hour private lesson $100, 1.5-hour group lessons from $60, wetsuit and board included), then meet the instructor at the best beach for the day's conditions. The boards are soft-top longboards that are beginner-friendly, and since the water temperature hovers around 65-75 degrees, students wear 3-2 wetsuits or "shorties," wetsuits with short sleeves and legs.

The same company offers **stand-up paddleboard trips** (www.marthasvineyardstanduppaddle.com, 6k6surf@gmail.com) that range from tours of the coast to unique, two-hour-long paddleboard fishing trips ($100).

BOATING AND FISHING

The tide ponds and lagoons around the island are perfect for maneuvering in and out of by kayak. **Island Spirit Kayak** (Beach Rd., 508/693-9727, www.islandspiritkayak.com) leads paddling tours that emphasize island geology and wildlife, and also rents boats that can be delivered to the shoreline of your choice ($65 half-day, $120 full-day kayak tours, kayak rentals $20 per hour, $55 for 24 hours). Island Spirit is located on the outlet from Sengekontacket Pond to the ocean, so paddlers can turn inland to paddle in warm, still water, or explore along the beach.

For anglers, the ***Skipper*** (Oak Bluffs Harbor, 508/693-1238, www.mvskipper.com, half-day trips $65 adults, $55 children 12 and under) bills itself as a "party fishing boat," which takes family-friendly trips in search of fluke, flounder, and striped bass.

Food

Crushed peanut shells litter the floor at ★ **Offshore Ale Co.** (30 Kennebec Ave., 508/693-2626, www.offshoreale.com, 11:30am-4pm and 5pm-8:30pm Sun.-Tues., 11:30am-4pm and 5pm-9pm Thurs.-Sat., $11-32), a warehouse turned brewpub in Oak Bluffs with nautical decor and a friendly atmosphere. Brick-oven pizzas and hamburgers join traditional Vineyard fare like fisherman's stew and thick, creamy chowder. Offshore Ale Co. keeps nine beers on tap and has live music most weeks.

Tiny and tucked off the main street, **Red Cat Kitchen** (14 Kennebec Ave., 508/696-6040, www.redcatkitchen.com, 6pm-close Mon.-Sat., $25-40) is an excellent choice for a special dinner. Many of the ingredients are sourced locally and sustainably, the decor is homey, and the cooking is on point. The menu changes constantly, but fried chicken wins raves, as do creative preparations of seafood. Reservations are essential, and as the restaurant has no air-conditioning, it can be sweltering on hot nights.

If the fried green tomato BLT sandwich were the only thing on the menu, it would still be worth a trip to **Slice of Life** (50 Circuit Ave., 508/693-3838, www.sliceoflifemv.com, 11am-8pm Tues.-Sat., 8am-2pm Sun., $10-22), a sunny café furnished with intimate tables and folding chairs. Thin-crust pizzas, goodie-loaded salads, and addictive truffle fries round out the menu. Sunday brunch is very popular—arrive early to get a seat on the enclosed porch.

Upscale food on the Vineyard can be a little lackluster, which makes ★ **20byNine** (16 Kennebec Ave., 508/338-2065, www.20bynine.com, 5:30pm-midnight Wed.-Mon., summer brunch 10am-2pm Sun., $24-30) a gem. Small plates of charcuterie, cheeses, and seafood are packed with flavor. The entire menu is designed to share, which might be the secret to this tiny gastropub's intimate, convivial feel. Chef Scott Cummings sources many ingredients locally, and the house cocktail menu is a highlight (no "sharkaritas" here).

Show up at **Martha's Vineyard Gourmet Café and Bakery** (5 Post Office Sq., 508/693-3688, www.mvbakery.com, 7am-5pm Mon.-Sat., 7am-2pm Sun.Apr.-Oct., $3-9) during normal business hours to pick up sweet and savory baked goods that make prime picnic fare. This place really starts hopping at night, though, when doughnut lovers line up around back. Noshing on a fresh apple fritter in the alleyway **Back Door Donuts** (7pm-1am Thurs.-Sat.) might be a well-known tradition, but it still feels like you're in on a sweet, gooey secret.

Martha's Vineyard has more fudge and ice cream shops than you could shake a waffle cone at, but **Ben & Bill's Chocolate Emporium** (20 Circuit Ave., 508/696-0008, www.benandbills.com, 11am-8pm Mon.-Fri., 11am-9pm Sat.-Sun. Apr.-Oct., extended hours midsummer, $2-10) is one of the best. Drop into the dark-walled interior for a handful of candy from old-fashioned bins of saltwater taffy and brittle, or get a cone of the absurdly rich butter pecan crunch ice cream.

Pick up supplies and snacks at the town's small grocery store, **Reliable Market** (36 Circuit Ave., 508/693-1102, www.thereliablemarket.com, 8:30am-6pm Mon.-Sat., 9am-1pm Sun.). Gourmet treats, spirits, and wine are available just up the street at **Vineyard Wine & Cheese** (38 Circuit Ave., 508/693-0943, 9am-6pm daily Apr.-Dec.).

Accommodations

The inns in Oak Bluffs are welcoming and comfortable, with prices that plummet in the off-season. Some of the privately owned historic cottages in **The Campground** (www.mvcma.org, starting at $2,000 per week) are available to rent for visits of a week or more.

$150-250

Country charm and a friendly innkeeper make the **Tivoli Inn** (125 Circuit Ave., 508/693-7928, www.tivoliinn.com, shared bath $95-175, private bath $125-255) a good, relatively low budget option. It's a leisurely walk from downtown. Continental breakfast is a full spread of breads, pastries, and cereal served on the gracious porch in fine weather. Less expensive rooms have a tidy shared bathroom.

Brightly painted rooms and pleasant common spaces are the draw at the **Madison Inn** (18 Kennebec Ave., 508/644-8226, www.madisoninnmv.com, $199-269), which also has unexpected amenities for the price. Start the day with coffee and teas; snack on cookies, ice cream, and fruit at will; and use beach towels, toys, chairs, and umbrellas. Rooms also come with white-noise machines, which is good, as the walls are a bit thin.

OVER $250

With a prime spot on the waterfront, the **Dockside Inn** (9 Circuit Ave. Extension, 508/693-2966, www.vineyardinns.com, $259-409) is simple and immaculate. A comfortable seat on the deep, wraparound porch is a dreamy place to watch sails float by, and bits of modern flair keep the hotel feeling fresh. Perks include a garden hot tub and the stylish, 1956 Rolls Royce that's used for courtesy pickups—the car service is included with your stay, but there's a set tip for the driver ($20 from the Vineyard Haven ferry, for example). Higher-priced rooms accommodate four or five people, an excellent deal for the location.

A pink wedding cake of a house at the top of the main drag, **The Oak Bluffs Inn** (64 Circuit Ave., 800/955-6235, www.oakbluffsinn.com, Apr.-Oct., $225-695) is appointed with a tasteful mix of modern country furniture and English antiques. The informal, lived-in air and afternoon cookies and lemonade on the porch make it a sweetly hospitable place to stay.

Getting There and Around

The **Martha's Vineyard Transit Authority** (508/693-9440, www.vineyardtransit.com, fares $1.25-5) bus service links Oak Bluffs to all other major destinations on the island. The town's main bus stop is on the northern edge of Ocean Park. All buses are wheelchair accessible. Several taxi services are also available, including **Stagecoach Taxi Co.** (508/627-4566, www.mvstagecoachtaxi.com).

Unless you are going to be spending a lot of time up-island, having a car can be more trouble than it's worth, but **Sun'n'Fun** (508/693-5457, www.sunfunrentals.com) offers free pickup when renting its Jeeps and Mini Coopers. (For ferry information, see *Getting to Martha's Vineyard*).

EDGARTOWN

Through the 1800s, this compact port was a thriving whaling town, and a walk along the harbor would have revealed a surprisingly global culture, with ships, sailors, and languages from around the world. And where there was whaling there was money—at least for the luckiest captains, who built the gorgeous homes that line Edgartown's narrow lanes.

With whaling far in the past, Edgartown is Martha's Vineyard's most elegant destination. Those sea captains' homes are now transformed into summer cottages and inns, and there's fine dining and tony boutiques. It's a fine day trip on the ferry from Falmouth, but for the full Edgartown experience, stay the night and catch a sunset over the Edgartown lighthouse.

Sights

Get a glimpse of Vineyard life before the fudge shops and celebrities at the **Martha's Vineyard Museum** (59 School St., 508/627-4441, www.mvmuseum.org, 10am-5pm Mon.-Sat., noon-5pm Sun. late May-mid-Oct., 10am-4pm Mon.-Sat. mid-Oct.-late May, $10 adults, $9 seniors, $5 children 6-12, children under 6 free, $2 discount for adults and seniors in spring and autumn). Kid-focused history exhibits make it a pleasant break from the beach. Artifacts from Martha's Vineyard's Wampanoag people, whalers, and early colonists offer a broad perspective on the island's past. The gorgeous Fresnel lens in the center of the compound used to shine from the Gay Head Light.

On an island that offers every possible angle of ocean views, the finest place to watch the sunrise may be **Edgartown Lighthouse** (121 N. Water St.). Located on a slow strip of sand surrounded by calm bay water, it looks like it was placed by a landscape architect (as opposed to the U.S. Coast Guard). The lighthouse is a 10-minute walk from the ferry landing in downtown Edgartown; follow North Water Street northeast, and when the Harbor View Hotel is on your left, take

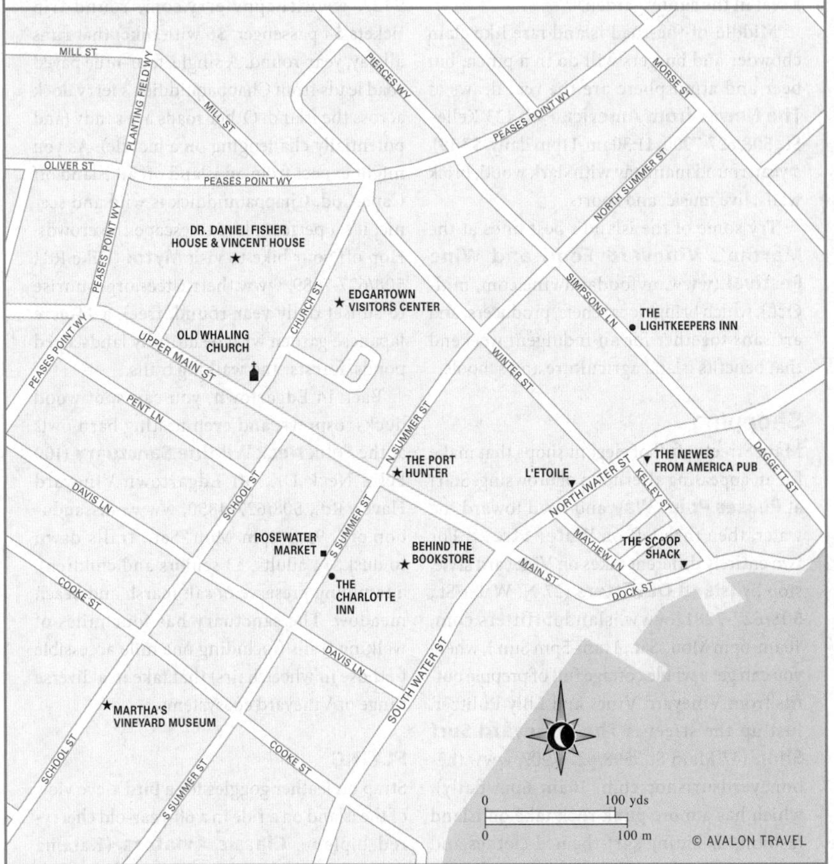

the short, sandy path to the right that leads toward shore.

Perhaps the best way to soak in Edgartown's historical charm is on foot, and it's easy to see the town's highlights in an hour of walking. A good place to start is the **Edgartown Visitors Center** (29 Church St. 9am-6pm daily mid May-mid Oct., no phone), where you can pick up maps of the town; highlights include the nearby **Old Whaling Church** (89 Main St.), an impressive Greek Revival building whose clock tower is visible far out at sea, and the **Dr. Daniel Fisher House** and **Vincent House** (both 99 Main St.), the oldest unaltered house on Martha's Vineyard. Late May-mid-October, the **Martha's Vineyard Preservation Trust** opens these three properties for 45-minute guided tours (508/627-4440, www.mvpreservation.org, Mon.-Fri., $10).

Entertainment and Events

Edgartown is pretty sedate by Vineyard standards, but you can catch live shows (and try your hand at the lawn games) at **Bad Martha Farmer's Brewery** (270 Upper Main St., 508/939-4415, www.badmarthabeer.com, noon-7pm Sun.-Fri., noon-9pm Sat. May-Oct.,

$4-10). A mason jar full of the flagship Martha's Vineyard Ale pairs beautifully with a seat in the sunny garden.

Middle-of-the-road island fare like clam chowder and burgers will do in a pinch, but beer and atmosphere are the real draws at **The Newes from America Pub** (23 Kelley St., 508/627-7900, 11:30am-11pm daily, $7-19), a year-round mainstay with dark wood, brick walls, live music, and sports.

Try some of the island's best bites at the **Martha's Vineyard Food and Wine Festival** (www.mvfoodandwine.com, mid-Oct.), which brings local chefs, producers, and artisans together for an indulgent weekend that benefits island agriculture and schools.

Shopping

Main Street is full of elegant shops that make for an appealing afternoon of browsing. Start at **Peases Point Way** and head toward the water, then turn left on **Water Street.** For two entirely different takes on Vineyard style, stop by **Island Outfitters** (27 N. Water St., 508/627-7281, www.islandoutfitters.com, 10am-6pm Mon.-Sat., 11am-5pm Sun.), where you can get a whole cottage full of preppie outfits from Vineyard Vines and Lilly Pulitzer. Just up the street is **The Boneyard Surf Shop** (47 Main St., 508/627-7907, www.theboneyardsurfshop.com, 10am-6pm daily), which has a more punk rock take on island fashion, including surf-themed clothes and swimwear.

Sports and Recreation

HIKING AND BIKING

Pick up a cycling map at Edgartown's visitors center and hop on one of the paths that connect to island beaches and forest. There are countless places to hit the beach along the **six-mile trail** that connects Edgartown and Oak Bluffs, and a relatively flat, **three-mile bike path** leads to Katama Beach on the south shore.

To really get away from it all, take your bike to the less developed **Chappaquiddick Island,** which is connected to Edgartown by a small **passenger ferry** (53 Dock St., vehicle waiting line forms on Daggett St., 508/627-9427, www.chappyferry.com, round-trip tickets $4 passenger, $6 with bike) that runs all day, year-round. A single, four-mile paved road leads from Chappaquiddick's ferry dock across the island. Other roads are sandy (and potentially challenging on a bicycle). As you might expect from an island off an island off Cape Cod, Chappaquiddick is wild and scenic; it's a perfect place to escape the crowds. Hop off your bike to visit **Mytoi** (Dike Rd., 508/627-7689, www.thetrustees.org, sunrise to sunset daily year-round, free), a 14-acre Japanese garden with beautifully landscaped ponds, forests, and walking trails.

Back in Edgartown, you can spot wood ducks, ospreys, and even nesting barn owls at the **Felix Neck Wildlife Sanctuary** (100 Felix Neck Dr., off Edgartown-Vineyard Haven Rd., 508/627-4850, www.massaudubon.org, 9am-4pm Mon.-Sat., trails dawn to dusk, $4 adults, $3 seniors and children), a rambling preserve of salt marsh and beach meadow. The sanctuary has four miles of walking trails (including one mile accessible to those in wheelchairs) that take in a diverse range of Vineyard ecosystems.

FLYING

Strap on leather goggles for a bird's-eye view of the island on a ride in a 60-year-old cherry-red biplane. **Classic Aviators** (Katama Airfield, 508/627-7677, www.biplanemv.com, 2-person tours from $229) runs sightseeing trips that range 15-60 minutes, buzzing over the island's beaches and towns in the company of an experienced guide.

BEACHES

To access the slender **Joseph Sylvia State Beach** from Edgartown, just hop on the scenic bike path that fronts Beach Road. Don't let the fact that scenes from *Jaws* were filmed here dissuade you; this beach is a good choice for less confident swimmers, as it's fairly sheltered from ocean swells.

A more dramatic landscape is **Katama**

Beach, a narrow barrier beach three miles south of Edgartown, with surf crashing on one side and a warm saltwater lagoon on the other. Follow South Water Street southeast from downtown, then turn left on Katama Road to find the beach parking area.

BOATING

Set sail from Edgartown's harbor on the ***Magic Carpet*** (508/627-5889, www.sail-magiccarpet.com, June-Oct., 2-hour sails $65), a beautiful 56-foot yawl—a two-masted sailboat that's rigged fore and aft. The friendly and experienced owners, Todd and Lee, plot a course with views of the most elegant homes along the coast.

PADDLING

Rent a kayak at **Joseph Sylvia State Beach** from **Island Spirit Kayak** (Beach Rd., Oak Bluffs, 508/693-9727, www.islandspiritkayak.com, kayak tours $65 half day, $120 full day, kayak rentals $20 per hour, $55 for 24 hours), which also delivers around the island.

Food

It's easy to miss the tiny café that's tucked behind Edgartown Books, but ★ **Behind the Bookstore** (46 Main St., 774/549-9278, www.btbmv.com, 7am-5pm daily mid-Apr.-Dec., later hours and dinner during peak season, $5-15) is among the most appealing places to eat in town. Seats are available on an enclosed, sunny patio; the espresso is from Intelligentsia Coffee; and the menu's full of fresh, flavorful gems like farro and black rice grain bowls and gem lettuce and fennel salad. The dinner menu is only served in the middle of the summer and includes more elaborate (and expensive) seafood plates and mains.

If you can get yourself out to the Katama Airfield, the **Right Fork Diner** (12 Mattakesett Way, 508/627-5522, 7am-2pm daily May-Oct., $5-14) is a strong contender for the best diner on the Vineyard. Watch small planes touch down as you dig into hearty omelets and scrambles, soups, salads, and sandwiches.

Comfort food made with plenty of local ingredients is the draw at ★ **Lucky Hank's** (218 Upper Main St., 508/939-4082, www.luckyhanksmv.com, 8am-2:30pm and 5pm-9pm Thurs.-Tues., $7-27), a small restaurant in a cozy converted home. Dinner plates like duck cassoulet and cod amandine are hearty and full-flavored. Brunch is very popular (the pancakes get rave reviews).

Romantic and softly lit, **L'Etoile** (22 N. Water St., 508/627-5187, www.letoile.net, 5:30pm-close Thurs.-Sun. May-Nov., $30-55) is Edgartown's last word on date night. The French-inspired menu changes frequently, but foie gras, Katama Bay oysters, and beautifully filleted trout are perennial favorites. The dinner menu is also available in the more relaxed bar, which is a fine place for cocktails and snacks.

A little bit hipper than the Edgartown average, ★ **The Port Hunter** (55 Main St., 508/627-7747, www.theporthunter.com, 5:30pm-1am Tues.-Sun. late May-Oct., $17-40) feels like a lively telegram from the next generation of Vineyard chefs. An emphasis on local fish and produce is welcome, and the smoked bluefish, oysters, and fish served whole are highlights. As dinnertime winds down, this becomes a happening spot downtown, with live music, shuffleboard, and powerful drinks.

Old-fashioned candy and offbeat ice cream flavors keep **The Scoop Shack** (22 Dock St., 508/627-7829, 11am-11pm daily, $4-8) bustling all summer. The house-made s'mores ice cream is summer vacation in a cone.

Find prepared foods, gourmet treats, and baked goods at **Rosewater Market** (20 S. Summer St., 508/627-1270, www.rosewatermv.com, 6:30am-6pm Mon.-Sat.), which stocks many products made on-island. It also has a simple, thoughtful take-away menu. More basic provisions are available at the town's **Stop & Shop** (225 Upper Main St., 508/627-9522, 7am-10pm Mon.-Sat., 7am-9pm Sun.).

Accommodations

UNDER $100

Plan ahead if you'd like to stay at ★ **HI Martha's Vineyard Hostel** (525 Edgartown-West Tisbury Rd., 508/693-2665, mid-May-mid-Oct., dorms $37-39, private rooms $99-150), the island's only hostel—it's a fabulous deal. Enjoy a generous breakfast, volleyball courts, kitchen, and relaxed common spaces. While it's located in the rural center of the island, it's easy to reach by bike and bus; the #6 bus from Edgartown stops just in front.

$250 AND ABOVE

The quaint, airy suites at **The Lightkeepers Inn** (25 Simpsons Rd., 508/627-4600, www.thelightkeepersinn.com, 4-person suites $215-350) are just a short walk from the ferry dock. Kitchenettes, coffeemakers, and sitting areas make these comfortable places for a family. The inn's bright-blue shutters and shingled exteriors exemplify classic Vineyard style.

Sunrise is best viewed with a cup of coffee from the porch of the **Harborview Hotel** (131 N. Water St., 508/627-7000, www.harborview.com, $499-800). The sprawling historic building looks out over the town's scenic lighthouse—the gracious front porch is a treat for sunset rocking chair time. Rooms in the main building have wonderful sea views, while the Captain's Cottage suites are a good choice for families, with kitchens, living rooms, and dining areas stocked with luxe amenities.

The Charlotte Inn (27 S. Summer St., 508/627-4151, www.relaischateaux.com, $395-795) is a romantic old-world retreat. The elegant house is furnished with English antiques; the perfectly tended gardens overflow with blooming flowers and hidden sitting areas; and an à la carte menu is available in a glass-walled dining room.

Getting There and Around

The **Martha's Vineyard Transit Authority** (508/693-9440, www.vineyardtransit.com, fares $1.25-5) bus service links Edgartown to all other major destinations on the island. The town's main bus stop is on Church Street. All buses are wheelchair accessible. Several taxi services are also available, including **Stagecoach Taxi Co.** (508/627-4566, www.mvstagecoachtaxi.com).

Unless you are going to be spending a lot of time up-island, having a car can be more trouble than it's worth, but **Sun'n'Fun** (508/693-5457, www.sunfunrentals.com) offers free pickup when renting their Jeeps and Mini Coopers. (For ferry information, see Getting to Martha's Vineyard.

UP-ISLAND

Despite the celebrity sightings and souvenir shops, much of Martha's Vineyard's remains fundamentally rural—even if it's a retirement-friendly, spiffed-up version of rural life. Up-island roads wind past cattle barns, sleepy corner stores, and fishing villages. While it's nice to have a car to really do justice to the area, frequent buses pass by all the major sites. Although up-island roads are quite narrow and often have no shoulder, experienced cyclists can certainly make the trip. The Vineyard buses have racks that accommodate three or four bikes, so it's possible to bike out to Gay Head and return on the bus, but you may find that others had the same idea, and end up waiting some time for a bus with an open rack.

Addresses on Martha's Vineyard can be confusing, and some destinations listed in Vineyard Haven turn out to be right in the center of the island, but Aquinnah and Chilmark stake out the slightly bulbous, left-hand corner of the island, and are the gateway to the teeny Menemsha fishing community.

Sights

★ AQUINNAH CLIFFS

Striped with wild layers of ochre clay, green sand, and glittering quartz, the **Aquinnah Cliffs** are a stunning and dramatic sight that have drawn mainland tourists for centuries. The cliffs also feature in Wampanoag stories about the island's formation: The legendary, supernatural giant Moshup resided in a den beside the cliffs, where he lived off a hearty diet of roasted whales—one per meal. When he saw a whale approach the shore, he'd kill it by heaving it against the cliffs, then cook it over the enormous fire that he tended all day and all night. Streaming red whale blood, black coals, and pale bones stained the cliffs, lodging in each layer, still visible to this day. The walkway to the cliff overlook is lined by shops and information booths maintained by the Wampanoag, and is a great place to learn more about their history and culture.

GAY HEAD LIGHT

In rusty brick that echoes the nearby cliffs, the **Gay Head Light** (9 Aquinnah Cir., Aquinnah, www.gayheadlight.org, 11am-4pm daily late May-mid-Oct., sunset tours 6pm-8pm Thurs., $5, children under 12 free) is among the most picturesque in New England. A lighthouse was built on this spot in 1799, just on the edge of the cliff—a little too close, as it turned out. The lighthouse was moved back from the erosion-prone cliff in 1844, and a second time in 2015.

MENEMSHA HARBOR

Fishing villages don't get any prettier than old-fashioned **Menemsha Harbor,** where weathered, gray-shingled shacks stand watch over an active fleet of trawlers and lobster boats. Watch the Vineyard's fishers bring in the day's catch while nibbling on clam shack fare. If you're exploring by bike, Menemsha is connected by a convenient but somewhat unpredictable bike ferry, so you don't have to climb back up the big hill that leads into town. Does the town look familiar? It's the site of the fictional Amity Island in the movie *Jaws.*

Entertainment and Events

The dancing at **The Yard** (1 The Yard, off Middle Rd. near Beetlebung Corner, Chilmark, 508/645-9662, www.dancetheyard.org) ranges from top-notch contemporary and tap performances to joyful, themed public dance hall events (registration required).

Every Sunday during the warmer months, local artists and crafters display their wares at the **Vineyard Artisans Fair** (Grange Hall, West Tisbury, www.vineyardartisans.com, mid June-early July Sun. 10am-2pm; early July-Aug. Sun. & Thu.10am-2pm; Sep. 1-Sep. 24 Sun.10am-2pm). There is always a good selection of watercolors and photography of island scenes.

The week following the Grand Illumination is the annual Martha's Vineyard Agricultural Society **Livestock Show and Fair** (West Tisbury, 508/693-4343, www.

Aquinnah Cliffs

marthasvineyardagriculturalsociety.org), which for almost 150 years has celebrated the farming history of the island. Displays include sheep and cow pens, wood-chopping competitions, country bands, fireworks, and, of course, a Ferris wheel.

Shopping

At first glance, the shops that line the path to the Aquinnah Cliffs lookout seem like run-of-the-mill kitsch, but they're worth exploring further. Located on traditional Wampanoag land, many of the shops are operated by tribe members selling handmade gifts among the T-shirts. Wampum jewelry made from shells, hand-thrown pottery, and silver make exquisite souvenirs.

Sports and Recreation

HIKING AND BIKING

The Vineyard's off-road bike paths don't reach up-island, but experienced cyclists can make the trip from Edgartown (18 miles) or Vineyard Haven (16.5 miles). A bike ferry crosses the short channel at Menemsha starting in late May, but hours are a bit sporadic.

Three miles of hiking trails thread through the **Menemsha Hills** (North Rd., Chilmark), passing wetland, woodland, and coastal plain on the way up **Prospect Hill**—at a towering 308 feet above sea level, it's just shy of the tallest point on the Vineyard, Peaked Hill, which has an extra 3 feet of height. In August, the highbush blueberries along the path make for blissful grazing.

Island naturalist Polly Hill gathered nearly 1,000 different species of plants at the **Polly Hill Arboretum** (809 State Rd., West Tisbury, 508/693-9426, www.pollyhillarboretum.org, sunrise-sunset daily, $5, children under 12 free), which has miles of walking paths through wildflower meadows and woodland of dogwood and magnolia.

The 600-acre **Long Point Wildlife Refuge** (Long Point Rd., West Tisbury, fees June-Sept. $10 car, $5 cyclist or pedestrian, children under 15 free) wraps around the long, narrow Long Cove Pond and ends in a wildly scenic barrier beach. Two miles of hiking trails pass through coastal dunes and dry forest, and paddleboards and kayaks are available to rent on-site (from $30 per hour).

BEACHES

One of the finest up-island beaches is **Lucy Vincent Beach,** which is only open to Chilmark residents and renters in the summer (and is reason enough to make friends with a local). For the rest of us, Aquinnah's **Lobsterville Beach** is a favorite for beachcombing, with plenty of shells and sea glass washing up on the shore. Bring your bike, however, as there is no parking along the road.

The beach at the base of the Aquinnah Cliffs is no longer accessible, but the **Aquinnah Public Beach** is a beautiful, family-friendly spot to spend the afternoon; the beach is a 10-minute walk from the parking lot (summer parking $15).

BOATING

Cruise around the sweet Menemsha Harbor with a kayak, stand-up paddleboard, powerboat, or sailboat from **Book-A-Boat** (Menemsha waterfront, 508/645-2400, www.bookaboatmv.com, rentals from $40 half day, $60 full day). Fish with Captain Buddy Vanderhoop of **Tomahawk Charters** (508/645-3201, www.tomahawkcharters.com, half-day charters from $700), a local fishing celebrity and Wampanoag tribal member.

Food

A meal at the **Aquinnah Shop Restaurant** (27 Aquinnah Cir., Aquinnah, 508/645-3867, www.theaquinnahshop.com, 10:30am-3pm Tues.-Fri., 8:30am-11am and 11:30-3pm Sat.-Sun. May-Oct., reduced hours in shoulder season, $12-30) feels like eating at the end of the world, with stunning views of ocean and cliffs. Seafood basics like fish-and-chips or lobster rolls are solid bets, but save room for pie—the owner bakes it daily with fresh peaches, blueberries, and seasonal fruits.

Dig into Katama Bay oysters, lobster bisque, and steamers at ★ **Larsen's Fish Market**

(29 Basin Rd., Menemsha, 508/645-2680, www.larsensfishmarket.com, 9am-7pm daily May-Oct., $5-18), where you can watch the fishing fleet unload from a seat at the outdoor tables—lobster traps topped with unfinished plywood.

The hip little **Beetlebung Coffee House** (24 Basin Rd., Menemsha, 508/645-9956, 9am-7pm daily late June-Sept., $4-14) has good alternatives to Menemsha's seafood shack fare. Hearty sandwiches, smoothies, and bagels are fresh and appealing, and the coffee is the best in town.

The **Beach Plum Inn** (50 Beach Plum Ln., Menemsha, 508/645-9454, www.beachpluminn.com, 5:30pm-10pm Mon.-Sat. May-Oct., call for off-season hours, $30-42) has one of the island's finest restaurants, with a rustic, romantic garden aesthetic and beautifully cooked food. The menu changes with the season, but always includes seafood, meat, and vegetarian options.

Meet the Vineyard's farmers at the **West Tisbury Farmers Market** (Grange Hall, West Tisbury, 508/693-4359, www.thewesttisburyfarmersmarket.com, 9am-noon Sat. June-Oct., also 9am-noon Wed. mid-June-late Aug.), where you can also find prepared foods and handicrafts.

Part old-fashioned general store, part overpriced tourist trap, the **Chilmark General Store** (7 State Rd., Chilmark, 508/645-3739, www.chilmarkgeneralstore.com, 7am-3pm Sun.-Fri., 7am-5pm Sat., mid-May-June and Sept.-early Oct., 7am-7pm daily June-Sept.) has picnic supplies, souvenirs, and a decent menu of pizza and sandwiches.

Accommodations

$150-250

Visiting **Summersweet Bed & Breakfast** (9 Shaler's Way, Chilmark, 508/645-8017, www.summersweet.org, $215-225), with just two guest rooms, feels like staying with friends. The owners, Gail and Don, are nice as can be, and the rural location, hearty breakfasts, and decor are a taste of the old Vineyard. A comfortable deck, hammock, and yard are appealing places to relax, and guests have access to beautiful Lucy Vincent Beach.

OVER $250

The secluded **Duck Inn** (10 Duck Pond Way, Aquinnah, 508/645-9018, www.duckinnonmv.com, $135-315) is located in an 18th-century home with bohemian furnishings and a knockout ocean view. One room has a bathtub in the middle, and another is swept at night with the beam from Gay Head Light. The personable owner is a 30-year island resident who gives therapeutic massages and makes killer organic breakfasts.

On the other side of the island, the **Beach Plum Inn** (50 Beach Plum Ln., Menemsha, 508/645-9454, www.beachpluminn.com, $320-535) is a secluded retreat, with six acres of hilltop property overlooking Vineyard Sound and the Elizabeth Islands. Rates include a full breakfast and a coveted pass to the residents-only Lucy Vincent Beach, one of the most beautiful on the island.

Getting There and Around

The **Martha's Vineyard Transit Authority** (508/693-9440, www.vineyardtransit.com, fares $1.25-5) bus service links Up-Island locations to all other major destinations on the island. Main Up-Island bus stops include the Gay Head Light and Menemsha Harbor. Several taxi services are also available, including **Stagecoach Taxi Co.** (508/627-4566, www.mvstagecoachtaxi.com).

Up-Island is the only spot on the Vineyard where having a car can be a real advantage. **Sun'n'Fun** (508/693-5457, www.sunfunrentals.com) offers free pickup when renting its Jeeps and Mini Coopers. (For ferry information, see *Getting to Martha's Vineyard.*)

MARTHA'S VINEYARD INFORMATION AND SERVICES

Find all the maps and information you need to get around the island—plus advice on accommodations and dining—at **Martha's Vineyard Chamber of Commerce** (24

Beach Rd., Vineyard Haven, 508/693-0085, www.mvy.com, 9am-5pm Mon.-Fri.).

The island's full-service hospital is **Martha's Vineyard Hospital** (One Hospital Rd., Oak Bluffs, 508/693-0410, www.mvhospital.com), with emergency services offered 24 hours a day. Fill prescription needs at **Leslie's Pharmacy** (65 Main St., Vineyard Haven, 508/693-1010, 8:30am-5:30pm Mon.-Sat., 9am-2pm Sun.). The commercial centers of Edgartown and Vineyard Haven are home to several **banks.** Each has an **ATM**—which are also scattered around the streets of those towns, as well as in Oak Bluffs.

Major cell phone networks function within the main towns, but can be undependable in the island's less crowded areas. Free **Internet access** and terminals are offered at the **Vineyard Haven Public Library** (200 Main St., Vineyard Haven, 508/696-4211, www.vhlibrary.org, 10am-5:30pm Mon., Wed., and Sat., 10am-8pm Tues. and Thurs., 1pm-5:30pm Fri., noon-4pm Sun.) and **Edgartown Free Public Library** (58 N. Water St., Edgartown, 508/627-4221, www.edgartownlibrary.org, 10am-5pm Mon. and Thurs.-Sat., 10am-8pm Tues.-Wed.).

GETTING TO MARTHA'S VINEYARD

Ferries to Martha's Vineyard depart from Cape Cod, Nantucket, New Bedford, New York City, Boston, and New Jersey.

On **Cape Cod,** frequent, year-round ferries from **Woods Hole** connect to **Vineyard Haven** and **Oak Bluffs,** run by the **Steamship Authority** (508/477-8600, www.steamshipauthority.com, 0.75 hr., one-way tickets $8.50 adults, $4.50 children, $4 bicycles, $43-78 cars).

Passenger-only ferries from **Falmouth** to **Oak Bluffs** are operated by **Island Queen** (508/457-0598, www.islandqueen.com, late May-mid-Oct, 0.5 hr., one-way tickets $14 adults, $8 children 5-12 and active military, $4 bicycles).

To reach **Vineyard Haven** from **Hyannis** or **Nantucket,** book passage on **Hy-Line Cruises** (800/492-8082, www.hylinecruises.com, May-Oct., 1 hr., one-way from Hyannis $29.50 adults, $19.50 children, $7 bicycles or from Nantucket $36 adults, $24 children, $7 bicycles).

From New Bedford, New York City, and New Jersey, take the **Seastreak** (800/262-8743, www.seastreak.com, May-Oct., one-way tickets from $40 adults, children under 12 free except first and last trip of the day $22, $7 bicycles) to Oak Bluffs. Seastreak also operates a bus from Boston to the ferry terminal in New Bedford.

During the summer, many flights a day are offered by **Cape Air** (508/771-6944, www.flycapeair.com) from Boston, New Bedford, Hyannis, New York City, and Nantucket.

Nantucket

With cobblestone streets and misty beaches, pretty Nantucket is a dreamy world unto itself, a tiny curve of sand that points out toward the sea. It's among the most exclusive (and expensive) destinations in New England, but before the blue bloods and boutiques arrived, the island had a salty history of Native Americans, colonial refugees, and whalers. Then, as now, Nantucket seemed like the last place on earth: Early colonists arrived fleeing restrictive mainland towns and found Wampanoag residents who'd fled the European encroachments on Cape Cod—the island's name means "the faraway place" in their language.

That faraway place took an outsized role on the world stage when Nantucketers began pursuing whales, first right off the coast, then into deeper and deeper waters. For a century and a half, Nantucket men left the island to hunt whales for years at a time, producing a vast

Nantucket

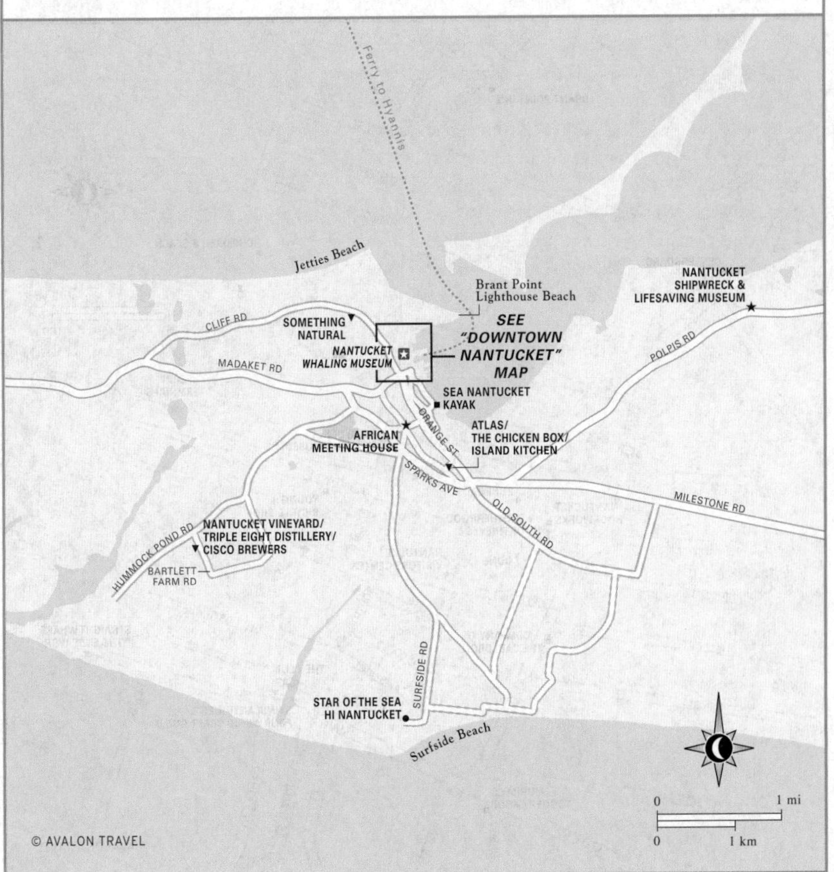

flood of oil that helped ease the screaming machinery of the Industrial Revolution and light 18th-century homes. It was a harsh, addictive trade to depend on. Whaling was incredibly dangerous work: It's the world of Herman Melville's *Moby-Dick*, and of the doomed whale ship *Essex*. And when the world's whale population plummeted in the mid-19th century, it collapsed as quickly as it began.

These days, Nantucket is the finest place to see the historic architecture of maritime New England; picture-perfect saltbox houses are crowned with widow's walks and five-petal roses, and residents still "go laning," strolling the narrow streets that wind through the center. It's impossibly charming on foggy summer mornings when the harbor is smooth as glass, or when the whole island takes cover as nor'easter storms rage across the coast. It's taken deep pockets and vigilant zoning laws to maintain the island's character, though, and at times, Nantucket seems overly sanitized. In Melville's words, though, "These extravaganzas only show that Nantucket is no Illinois." And it's all part of the island experience.

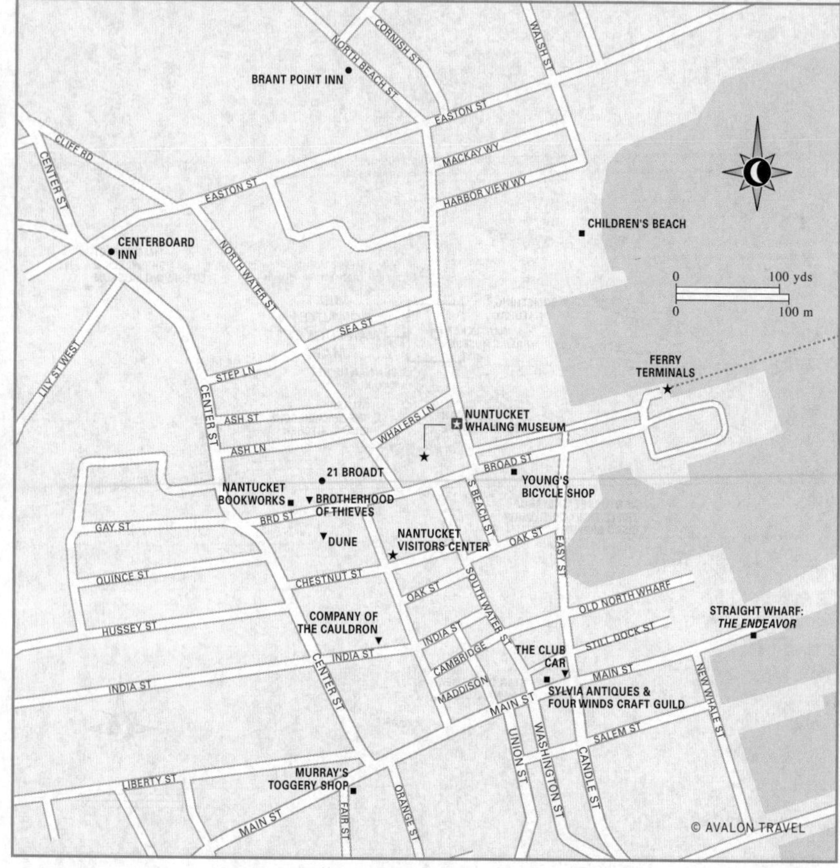

SIGHTS

★ Nantucket Whaling Museum

The world's whaling industries have a lasting legacy of destruction that obliterated some species of whale and left others teetering at the brink of extinction. Now that the oil in our cars, machines, and furnaces comes from below the ground, it's easy to forget that it used to roll off whaling ships in great wooden vats, the fruit of dangerous hunting trips that could last for years. Standing between a fragile, open whaleboat and the 46-foot skeleton of a sperm whale puts it all in perspective at the wonderful **Nantucket Whaling Museum** (15 Broad St., 508/228-1894, www.nha.org, 10am-5pm daily late May-late Oct., call or check online for off-season hours, $20 adults, $18 seniors and students, $5 children 6-17, free children under 6). Explore a fully restored candle-making factory and see the souvenirs that Nantucket whalers brought home from around the world, and the scrimshaw and carvings they made to pass long hours belowdecks.

Other Sights

The shoals around Nantucket have wrecked

hundreds of ships throughout the years, and many more lives would have been lost without the islanders that plunged into the breakers to look for survivors. Hear their stories at the **Nantucket Shipwreck & Lifesaving Museum** (158 Polpis Rd., 508/228-2505, www.nantucketshipwreck.org, 10am-5pm daily late May-mid-Oct., $10 adults, $7 seniors and students, $5 children 6-17), which is 3.5 miles from town by the Polpis bicycle path. The small **African Meeting House** (29 York St., 508/228-9833, www.afroammuseum.org/afmnantucket.htm, 10am-4pm Mon.-Fri., 10am-2pm Sat., noon-4pm Sun. June-Sept., $5 adults, $3 seniors and youth 13-17, children under 13 free) dates to 1827, when it was used as a meeting place and schoolhouse for escaped slaves, Cape Verdeans, and Native Americans.

ENTERTAINMENT AND EVENTS

With long, dark winters and party-fueled summers, it's no surprise that Nantucket has an on-island source of alcohol. Locally owned **Nantucket Vineyard, Cisco Brewers, and Triple Eight Distillery** (5 Bartlett Farm Rd., 508/325-5929, www.ciscobrewers.com, 11am-7pm Mon.-Sat., noon-6pm Sun., tours $20) produce everything from aged rum to pinot noir in a facility just outside of town, with a free shuttle service from the downtown visitors center that runs every 20-30 minutes during high season. Guided tours include tastes of spirits, wine, and beer, and this is the place to be in the late afternoon, when outdoor shows by regional and local bands attract a laid-back crowd of locals and visitors.

Later on in the evening, things can get pretty raucous at **The Chicken Box** (16 Dave St., 508/228-9717, www.thechickenbox.com, noon-1am daily)—a fried-chicken stand turned roadhouse—with reggae and rock bands several nights a week; it's a hike from downtown, so plan to return in a cab. Tucked into a former train car, **The Club Car** (1 Main St., 508/228-1101, www.theclubcar.com, dining 11am-3pm and 5:30pm-10pm daily, bar 11am-1am daily May-Oct.) is an atmospheric place to get a drink downtown, with a nightly sing-along piano show, elegant snacks, and a good selection of wine. Music starts at 8:30pm.

Nantucket lights up the first weekend in December for **Christmas Stroll Weekend** (www.christmasstroll.com), when the town goes all out with period carolers, nautical Santas, and lighthouses dressed for the holidays. Once the weather warms up, there's the **Daffodil Festival** (508/228-1700, www.nantucketchamber.org) in April, which takes over with parades of blossom-festooned antique cars and a tailgating picnic.

SHOPPING

There are a few classic Nantucket souvenirs that are truly distinct, starting with the fine selection of **Nantucket lightship baskets** at **Four Winds Craft Guild** inside **Sylvia Antiques** (15 Main St., 508/228-9623, www.fourwindscraftguild.com, 10am-5pm Mon. and Wed.-Sat., 11am-3pm Sun.), and you can pick up all sorts of clothes in distinctive "Nantucket red"—actually a faded pink—at **Murray's Toggery Shop** (62 Main St., 508/228-0437, www.nantucketreds.com, 10am-5pm Mon.-Sat.), a longtime preppy pilgrimage spot.

Legend has it that every inn on the island used to stock guest rooms with a copy of *Moby-Dick*, which is full of Nantucket references and over 700 pages long. Unsurprisingly, most visitors didn't finish the book before leaving, so more and more disappeared with every departing ferry. Buy your own copy at **Nantucket Bookworks** (25 Broad St., 508/228-4000, www.nantucketbookworks.com, 10am-8pm Mon.-Thurs., 10am-9pm Fri.-Sat., 10am-6pm Sun.), which also has an excellent collection of works by local authors.

SPORTS AND RECREATION

Beaches

Nantucket's beaches are soft and sandy, and they're the center of life on the island, when

The Rise and Fall of American Whaling

When colonists first hunted whales in New England, the marine mammals were plentiful, and by 1644 whalers worked the coast by scanning the waters near the shore and launching small boats when whales were sighted. In those early days, whales were killed with harpoons secured to wooden floats—when the whales tired from dragging the floats, the whalers would use lances to finish the job, then drag the carcasses to shore. The whales they caught helped fuel a changing world, from the whale-oil lamps that illuminated London streets to lubrication for the machines of the Industrial Revolution.

An early American example of environmental depletion, whales became rare along the coast in just a few generations. By the 1720s, whalers faced a stark alternative: take on longer, more dangerous journeys, or see the end of New England whaling. It proved too profitable to give up, and as the industry changed, Nantucket played a central role. Islanders pioneered trips to pursue whales into deeper water in schooners and brigs, then launching nimble, fragile whaleboats when their quarry was sighted.

Life aboard whaling ships was incredibly grueling and dangerous. In his *Etchings of a Whaling Cruise*, J. Ross Browne described his ship's fo'c'sle, or living quarters, as "black and slimy with filth, very small and hot as an oven. It was filled with a compound of foul air, smoke, sea-chests, soap-kegs, greasy pans, [and] tainted meat." Ships left for voyages that lasted for six months to four years, and income was entirely dependent on the catch. Each member of the crew had a "lay," a predetermined percentage of the profits. An inexperienced crewman might make a first trip on a whaling ship to earn a 1/350th share, and the average worker might have earned $25 for a years-long voyage. After purchases from a ship's store, a crewmember could return to shore in debt to the captain, with little choice other than to sign up for another stint aboard.

But despite the harsh realities of whaling life, the industry brought an unexpected globalism to the New England coast. Captains and crew brought back goods from ports of call around the world. The whaleboats themselves were filled with white and Native American crewmembers from New England, African Americans, Cape Verdeans, and Pacific Islanders, and though racism prevented some sailors from advancing, their coexistence and cooperation was remarkable for the time.

Deepwater whaling was an enormously profitable industry, and America dominated the market. By the mid-19th century, the United States had three times more whaling vessels than the rest of the world combined. But just decades later, American whaling had all but collapsed. Why? The reasons seem almost contemporary.

Excessive hunting meant that whale populations declined around the world, and at the same time, the United States shifted its thirst from whale oil to petroleum—the combination of those two factors is the classic explanation for the fall of American whaling. According to recent scholarship, however, the true killer was a changing workforce. In the late 19th century, American wages were rising, driven by new industries back on shore, making whaleboats a less attractive career choice. So when the American whaling industry ground to a halt, it didn't disappear—it just moved to countries, like Norway, where the ugly work of killing whales on the water could happen for less.

fine weather turns all eyes to the sea. The first one you'll spot as you approach the coast on the ferry is **Brant Point Lighthouse Beach** (on Brant Point, at the tip of Easton St.), at the mouth of Nantucket's sheltered harbor. It's a quiet and very small beach, about a 15-minute walk from town. As it has no facilities or lifeguard, it's frequented mostly by those looking for a brief stroll or a view of the lighthouse or town. A quick 5-minute walk from town, just around the bend in the harbor toward Brant Point, is **Children's Beach.** With very few waves, a small park, a lifeguard on duty, and restrooms, it's a perfect spot to take the tykes. On the outskirts of town, equipped with lifeguards and restrooms, is **Jetties**

(508/228-5358, www.nantucketchamber.org). There's also a playground; a concession stand selling burgers, ice cream, and such; and boat rentals. Take a shuttle or ride a bike to the island's south side to reach **Surfside** (www.nantucketchamber.org), a big, wide stretch of sand that catches a heavy swell and has an excellent snack bar.

Biking

With off-road paths, mellow traffic, and gentle terrain, a bicycle is one of the best ways to explore the island. You can pick up wheels just off the ferry at **Young's Bicycle Shop** (6 Broad St., 508/228-1151, www.youngsbicycleshop.com, 9am-5pm daily, rentals $20 per hour, $35 for 24 hours). It stocks helpful maps of popular bike rides, and its website has links to a number of the best, with step-by-step instructions and maps. The 4.2-mile self-guided tour of downtown takes in the lighthouse and Nantucket's most historic neighborhoods. Other good choices are the flat, 3.5-mile ride to **Surfside Beach,** or the scenic, 19-mile ride that heads out to **Sconset** via Milestone and comes back on the Polpis bike path.

Boating

One of the most peaceful ways to see the island is from the water, and **Sea Nantucket Kayak** (76 Washington St., 508/228-7499, www.seanantucketkayak.com, 9am-5pm daily, boats $25 per hour, $55 all day, SUPs $30 per hour, $100 all day) rents kayaks and stand-up paddleboards from a waterfront location that's walking distance from downtown. The friendly staff is full of tips on where to paddle.

To explore the harbor under sail, book a place on ***The Endeavor*** (Straight Wharf, Slip 1015, 508/228-5585, www.endeavorsailing.com, 1.5-hour daytime sails $45, sunset sails $60), a 31-foot Friendship sloop that makes four trips a day. Captain Jim Genthner is at the helm, and an experienced "shantyman" sings sea ballads as the boat gets under way.

FOOD

Slipping into the basement door at **Brotherhood of Thieves** (23 Broad St., 508/228-2551, www.brotherhoodofthieves.com, 11:30am-late daily, $13-26) feels like discovering a shined-up sailors' pub, with brick walls, thick wooden beams, and long, dark wooden tables. Burgers, sturdy mains, and bar food are well prepared (if unremarkable), and a seat at the bar is an excellent place for striking up conversations. When the basement is crowded, more seating is available upstairs, but the dining room seems a bit too brightly lit after the atmospheric gloom on the lower level.

Pick up a sandwich on the way to the beach, or just eat at the sunny picnic tables outside **Something Natural** (50 Cliff Rd., 508/228-0504, www.somethingnatural.com, 8am-3pm daily Apr.-Oct., $5-13.50). House-made bread and super-fresh ingredients make the menu of simple sandwiches an appealing option, especially when combined with a thin, crispy chocolate chip cookie. Skip the wait by calling in your order.

Simple breakfasts and affordable lunch and dinner plates make ★ **Island Kitchen** (1 Chins Way, 508/228-2639, www.nantucketislandkitchen.com, 7am-2pm Sun.-Mon., 7am-2pm and 5:30pm-close Tues.-Sat., $6-18) a year-round favorite, and the meal-sized salads are a refreshing break if you've been living off chowder and clam shack fare. Diner-like counter seating looks into the small, open kitchen, and the tables at this casual joint fill up quickly, so arrive early on weekends or come prepared to wait.

The roaring fire and comfortable chairs at **Atlas** (130 Pleasant St., 508/825-5495, www.atlasnantucket.com, 5pm-12:30am daily, $16-32) may leave you wishing for a cold, foggy evening to enjoy the hearty, creative menu of barbecue and seafood. Slabs of ribs and tender pulled pork are highlights of the menu, and this is an excellent place to stop by for a drink and snacks; classic cocktails are prepared with thoughtful ingredients, and the beer list is gathered from craft breweries around the country.

A pale, minimalist dining room is a serene backdrop for the showstopping food at **Dune** (20 Broad St., 508/228-5550, www.dunenantucket.com, lunch 11:30am-2:30pm daily mid-May-Oct., dinner 5:30pm-9:30pm Tues.-Sat. year-round, $45-65); the menu changes seasonally, but always features elegant seafood presentations with brightly flavored sides that lean French. The rich corn chowder is a perennial favorite, and the soft shell crab is a crispy, crunchy bite of heaven.

Another destination-worthy restaurant is ★ **Company of the Cauldron** (5 India St., 508/228-4016, www.companyofthecauldron.com, 7pm-close Mon.-Sat., $75-100), an intimate, romantic spot with prix fixe dinners that are among the best on the island. Fresh flowers and candles encourage a leisurely feel, and the restaurant has just one seating each evening, so reservations are essential.

ACCOMMODATIONS

With the exception of an excellent hostel, it is very challenging to find a place to sleep for under $350 during Nantucket's peak season, though prices drop dramatically in the shoulder season. Simple rooms are available on Airbnb for less than the commercial options, but still start at $150 in the summer.

Under $100

One of New England's most memorable hostels, the ★ **Star of the Sea HI Nantucket** (31 Western Ave., 508/228-0433, www.hiusa.org, late May-late Sept., $42) was built as a lifesaving station in 1873 and is included on the National Register of Historic Places. It's just across the street from Surfside Beach, so it can be easily reached by bike or an island shuttle, and has a fire pit, grill, communal kitchen, and a good-sized breakfast.

Over $250

Walking distance from the lighthouse, **Brant Point Inn** (6 N. Beach St., 508/228-5442, www.brantpointinn.com, $225-295) is one of the better values in town, and the hospitable owner makes this a particularly welcoming place to stay. Homemade muffins for breakfast and a gracious front porch with comfy rocking chairs are nice touches, as are the beach chairs and umbrellas that are available to guests.

Friendly and old-fashioned, the **Centerboard Inn** (8 Chester St., 508/283-7156, www.centerboardinn.com, $399-550) is a romantic option in the former home of a whaling captain. The owners have meticulously restored the building's Victorian details and added luxurious, comfortable common spaces that feel like a retreat. Board games, beach chairs, an appealing breakfast, and an afternoon wine-and-cheese hour are fun touches, and the inn's three-bed studio is a good option for families, especially during the shoulder season.

The airy decor at ★ **21 Broad** (21 Broad St., 508/228-4749, www.21broadhotel.com, $450-689) is a vibrant blend of modern lines and Nantucket style, both urban and beachy. Elegant extras are less stuffy than at other high-end hotels on the island: A mix-your-own cocktail bar, small-plate breakfasts, in-room iPads, and an on-site steam room are more fun than formal. During the summer, a deck with an outdoor fireplace is a haven in the heart of downtown Nantucket.

INFORMATION AND SERVICES

Get the lowdown on where to stay, where to eat, and how to get there from the centrally located **Nantucket Visitors Center** (25 Federal St., 508/228-0925, www.nantucket-ma.gov, 9am-5pm daily Apr.-Nov., 9am-5pm Mon.-Sat. Dec.-May), which maintains a list of the rooms that are available each day.

The island's only emergency medical facility is **Nantucket Cottage Hospital** (57 Prospect St., 508/825-8100, www.nantuckethospital.org), which offers 24-hour care. Fill prescription needs at **Island Pharmacy** (122 Pleasant St., 508/228-6400, www.islandrx.com, 8am-7pm Mon.-Fri., 8am-6pm Sat.-Sun.).

$10, cars from $87). Reduced rates vailable on weekdays.

ne Cruises (800/492-8082, www.hy- es.com) also offers high-speed service **ucket** from **Hyannis** (year-round, 1 d-trip tickets $77 adults, $51 chil- , children under 5 free, $14 bicycles), **Bluffs** (late May-early Oct., 1 hr. 10 nd-trip tickets $65 adults, $45 chil- , children under 5 free, $14 bicycles).

ost of traveling to Nantucket with car is high, and while several agen- vehicles from Nantucket Airport, a eally necessary given the size of the bicycle is a fun choice, as is a scooter: gle- or double-seater at **Nantucket Shop** (4 Broad St., 508/228- vw.nantucketbikeshop.com). The **ket Regional Transit Authority** -7025, www.nrtawave.com) does us loops between Straight Wharf cket Town and Madaket, Surfside, t, and the airport.

The Berkshires

All rolling hills and twisting rivers, the Berkshires' gentle landscape shelters quaint villages, grand mansions, and one of New England's most vibrant arts communities.

It's an unexpected mix, but one that's thrived since the days of authors Edith Wharton and Nathaniel Hawthorne, and the region's artists, farmers, and well-heeled Yankees seem to get along just fine. Berkshire County stretches all along the western edge of Massachusetts, defined by the silhouette of the Taconic Range, where the occasional rocky peak breaks the forest canopy for views of the Catskills and Green Mountains.

In the north, pretty Williamstown and industrial North Adams are just a few miles apart, a town-and-gown matched set with museums that draw art lovers from around New England. Follow the Hoosic River down-county to discover the extravagant mansions where 19th-century socialites escaped the heat and noise of the city, establishing a creative connection to Boston and New York that thrives to this day. In the summer season here, the hills are filled to the brim with music and dance, when the Boston Symphony Orchestra (BSO) plays for a sea of picnickers on the lawn at the Tanglewood music venue, and the Jacob's Pillow Dance Festival brings world-class performers onto a forest stage.

With all those highbrow cultural attractions, it would be easy to while away a trip focusing on art alone, so for culture-savvy visitors, the real surprise is that the headlining acts are set in one of New England's truly bucolic settings. In between the museums and shows, find a back road to follow at a country pace, leaving plenty of time to take in the views.

PLANNING YOUR TIME

Compact and simple to navigate, the Berkshires are easy to see from a single home base: Choose one of the towns in the northern part for access to fabulous art museums and the trails of Mount Greylock, or stay in the more southerly section for a taste of Gilded Age glamour and village life.

As with other summer destinations in New England, July and August are peak season in the Berkshires, but the whirlwind schedule of concerts and performances

Previous: gardens designed by Edith Wharton at The Mount; fall in the Berkshires. **Above:** the gardens at Naumkeag.

The Berkshires

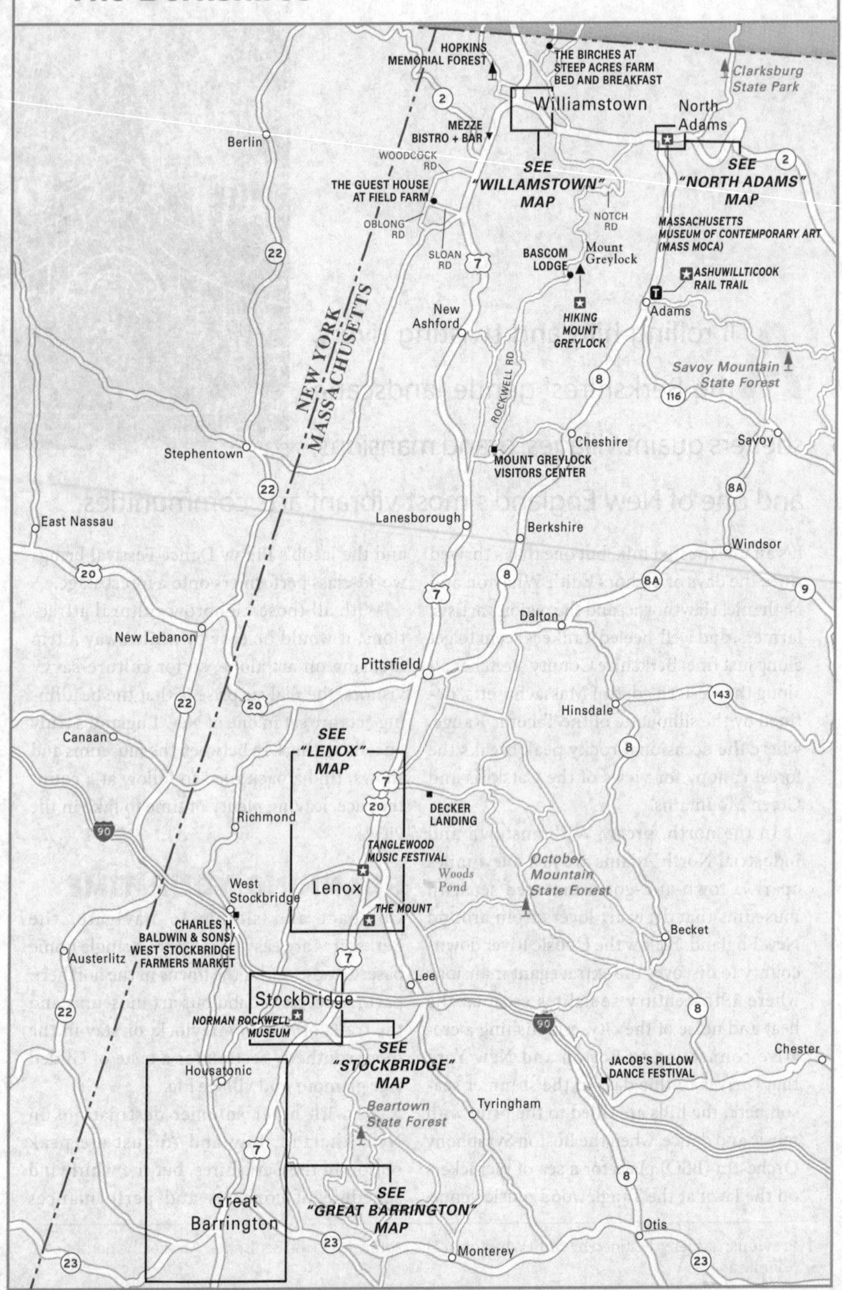
HOPKINS MEMORIAL FOREST
THE BIRCHES AT STEEP ACRES FARM BED AND BREAKFAST
Clarksburg State Park
Williamstown
North Adams
MEZZE BISTRO + BAR
Berlin
WOODCOCK RD
SEE "WILLAMSTOWN" MAP
SEE "NORTH ADAMS" MAP
THE GUEST HOUSE AT FIELD FARM
OBLONG RD
SLOAN RD
NOTCH RD
MASSACHUSETTS MUSEUM OF CONTEMPORARY ART (MASS MOCA)
BASCOM LODGE
Mount Greylock
ASHUWILLTICOOK RAIL TRAIL
Adams
New Ashford
HIKING MOUNT GREYLOCK
NEW YORK
MASSACHUSETTS
ROCKWELL RD
Savoy Mountain State Forest
Cheshire
Savoy
Stephentown
MOUNT GREYLOCK VISITORS CENTER
East Nassau
Lanesborough
Berkshire
Windsor
Dalton
New Lebanon
Pittsfield
Hinsdale
Canaan
SEE "LENOX" MAP
DECKER LANDING
Richmond
TANGLEWOOD MUSIC FESTIVAL
October Mountain State Forest
Woods Pond
West Stockbridge
Lenox
THE MOUNT
CHARLES H. BALDWIN & SONS/ WEST STOCKBRIDGE FARMERS MARKET
Becket
Austerlitz
Lee
Stockbridge
NORMAN ROCKWELL MUSEUM
SEE "STOCKBRIDGE" MAP
Chester
Housatonic
JACOB'S PILLOW DANCE FESTIVAL
Beartown State Forest
Tyringham
Great Barrington
SEE "GREAT BARRINGTON" MAP
Otis
Monterey

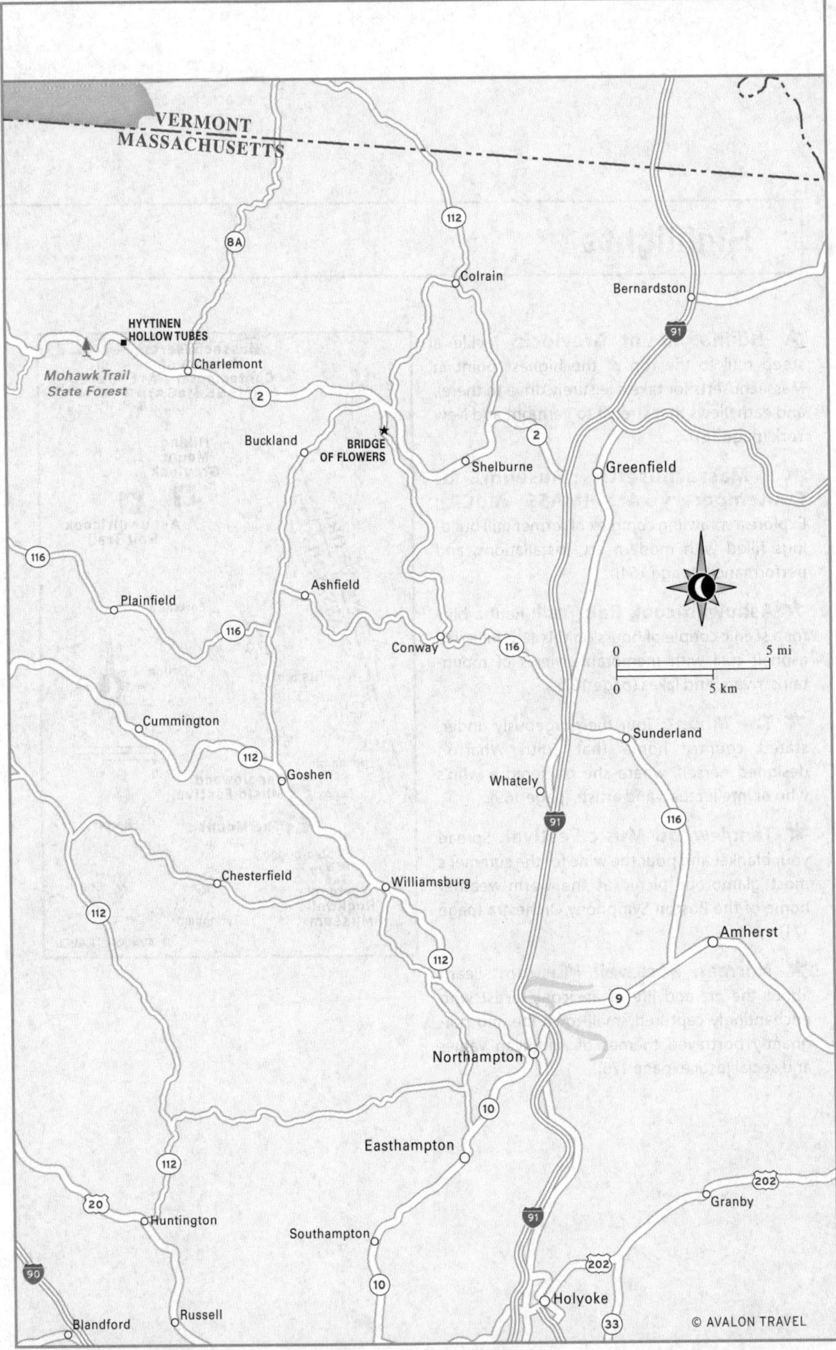
VERMONT
MASSACHUSETTS
HYYTINEN HOLLOW TUBES
Mohawk Trail State Forest
Charlemont
Colrain
Bernardston
Buckland
BRIDGE OF FLOWERS
Shelburne
Greenfield
Plainfield
Ashfield
Conway
Cummington
Goshen
Sunderland
Whately
Chesterfield
Williamsburg
Amherst
Northampton
Easthampton
Granby
Huntington
Southampton
Holyoke
Blandford
Russell
0 5 mi
0 5 km
© AVALON TRAVEL

Look for ★ to find recommended sights, activities, dining, and lodging.

Highlights

★ **Hiking Mount Greylock:** Tackle a steep trail to the top of the highest point in Massachusetts (or take a leisurely drive to there), and earn views that stretch to Vermont and New York (page 161).

★ **Massachusetts Museum of Contemporary Art (MASS MoCA):** Explore a sprawling complex of former mill buildings filled with modern art, installations, and performances (page 164).

★ **Ashuwillticook Rail Trail:** Rent a bike for a scenic couple of hours on this 11.2-mile flat, asphalt trail with memorable views of mountains, rivers, and lakes (page 167).

★ **The Mount:** Tour the gorgeously understated country home that Edith Wharton designed herself, where she gathered a who's who of intellectuals and artists (page 169).

★ **Tanglewood Music Festival:** Spread your blanket and pour the wine for the summer's most glamorous picnic at the warm-weather home of the Boston Symphony Orchestra (page 171).

★ **Norman Rockwell Museum:** Learn about the art and life of an iconic artist who enchantingly captured small-town life and poignantly portrayed themes of American values and social justice (page 176).

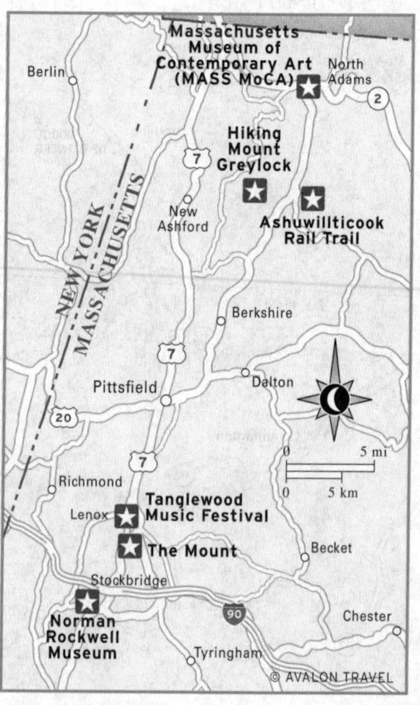

at Tanglewood—which lasts eight weeks from the end of June to the beginning of September—makes everything a little more intense, from hotel prices to traffic. Attending a Tanglewood concert is an unforgettable experience, worth planning far ahead to get tickets and a place to stay. But if you're not coming for a show, consider visiting outside of that frenetic time, when lines dwindle and prices return to earth. Lilacs and tulips burst into bloom in late May, and autumn is an enchanting time to visit, with bright foliage and roaring fires in many bed-and-breakfasts. In the true off-season of late fall and winter, there are plenty of options for winter sports, and many museums and stores remain open, but some places do close or have reduced hours (sometimes unpredictably), so it's a good idea to call ahead before visiting.

ORIENTATION

Berkshire County stretches from the northern to southern edges of Massachusetts on the state's west side, but the key destinations are a series of villages mostly accessible along Route 7. In the north, Williamstown and North Adams are side by side; about an hour south, Lenox and Stockbridge are on opposite sides of I-90, with Great Barrington an additional 20-minute drive down Route 7.

Williamstown

A sign at the crossroads of Williamstown's center designates the town "the village beautiful," and few would dispute the claim. Completely ringed by mountains, it's dominated by Williams College, and the green lawns, old-fashioned architecture, and student-filled cafés are straight from central casting. The school is one of the oldest in the country, founded in 1791 through the will of Colonel Ephraim Williams, who was killed during the French and Indian Wars but left his money for the establishment of a "free school" in the town of West Hoosac—provided it changed its name to Williamstown. Just 30 years after its founding, the president and half the student body left to found Amherst College in the southeast, thus ensuring a rivalry that continues to the present day.

SIGHTS

Clark Art Institute

The extensive collection of high-quality art at the **Clark Art Institute** (225 South St., 413/458-2303, www.clarkart.edu, 10am-5pm daily July-Aug, 10am-5pm Tues.-Sun. Sept.-June, $20 adults, students and children under 18 free) is remarkable, as is the institute's parklike setting. The Clark is one of the best small museums in the country, with a collection full of gems by Renoir, Monet, Degas, Copley, Remington, and other well-known artists that seem handpicked for their individual beauty or interest. Beyond the gallery walls are 140 acres of walking trails, meadows, and forest, free to access at any time; one of the most romantic ways to enjoy the campus is to make a late-night trip to the Clark's reflecting ponds, where comfortable Adirondack chairs invite all for an evening of stargazing.

Williams College

Historic buildings and a picture-perfect backdrop make the **Williams College campus** (880 Main St., 413/597-3131, www.williams.edu) an excellent place to explore on your own, with a few highlights not to be missed. Rounding out the town's reputation as a showstopping arts destination is the **Williams College Museum of Art** (15 Lawrence Hall Dr., 413/597-2429, wcma.williams.edu, 10am-8pm Thurs., 10am-5pm Fri.-Wed. June-Aug., 10am-8pm Thurs., 10am-5pm Fri.-Tues. Sept.-May, free). The museum has a focus on modern and contemporary art, American art, and the art of world cultures, and houses a noteworthy collection of works by Edward

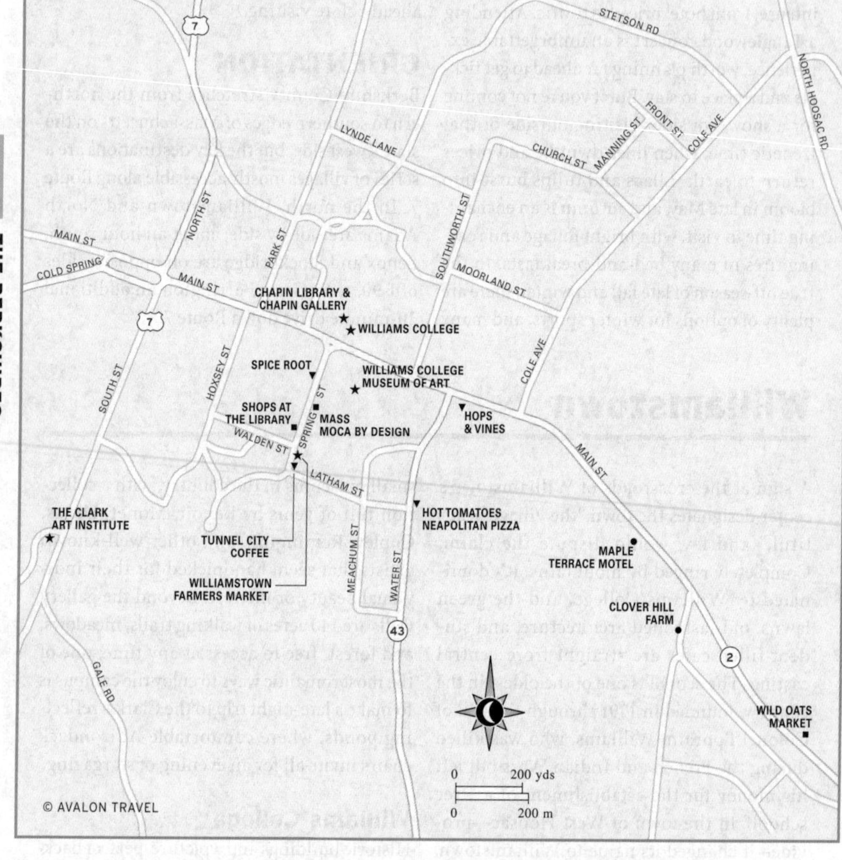

Hopper and Maurice Prendergast. Housed in the thoroughly modern-looking Sawyer Library, Williams's **Chapin Library** is the only institution outside the National Archives to have an original copy of each of the four founding documents of the United States: The Declaration of Independence, Constitution, Bill of Rights, and Articles of Confederation are on permanent display in the **Chapin Gallery** (Sawyer Library, Rm. 406, Williams College campus, 10am-5pm Mon.-Fri., free).

ENTERTAINMENT AND EVENTS

For more than 60 years, some of the biggest Hollywood names have descended upon the **Williamstown Theatre Festival** (413/458-3200, www.wtfestival.org, June-Aug.) to try out their acting chops on the stage. The festival runs a range of productions, from gala premieres to intimate play readings, allowing theatergoers a chance to see a different side of well-known and up-and-coming stars.

Music in the Berkshires

Long a destination for bohemians and cultured Bostonians, the Berkshires fill with music throughout the year, from symphony orchestras to back-road pubs. These are some favorite ways to catch a show:

- Pack a deluxe picnic and a bottle of wine and head to the **Tanglewood Music Festival** (297 West St., Lenox, 413/637-1600, www.bso.org). The Boston Symphony Orchestra is the headliner here, but the summerlong festival draws big-name performers late June-early September.
- Each Tuesday in July, the **Clark Art Institute** (225 South St., Williamstown, 413/458-2303, www.clarkart.edu) hosts free, outdoor concerts on the gorgeous museum grounds, where reflecting pools and art installations are fascinating to explore after hours.
- Join a hootenanny at **The Guthrie Center** (2 Van Deusenville Rd., Great Barrington, 413/528-1955, www.guthriecenter.org), the legacy of Arlo Guthrie, who attended school in the Berkshires. The church-turned-music sanctuary and museum was once the home of Alice and Ray Brock, immortalized in the song "Alice's Restaurant," and hosts weekly jam sessions that are open to all.
- Let loose in a museum at a show presented by **MASS MoCA** (1040 MASS MoCA Way, North Adams, 413/662-2111, www.massmoca.org/performances), which hosts outdoor concerts and more intimate performances in the indoor theater.
- Though it doesn't pull in the big names, the **Lion's Den** (30 Main St., Stockbridge, 413/298-5545, www.redlion.com) is a laid-back place to catch a show, with music every night of the week in a cozy below-ground pub that's especially welcoming on chilly nights.
- Step into a folk music time machine at the ramshackle **Dream Away Lodge** (1342 Country Rd., Becket, 413/623-8725, www.thedreamawaylodge.com), where Bob Dylan, Joan Baez, Arlo Guthrie, and Sam Shepard filmed the four-hour Renaldo and Clara while on their Rolling Thunder Revue tour. Black-and-white photos document the events, and there's live music most weekends.

SHOPPING

The main drag of **Spring Street** is full of college-themed shops geared to alumni and stocked with gear in Williams College's single color: purple. Awkwardly, the school's traditional rivals at Amherst College opted for purple and white, so the "Ephs" (that's short for Ephraim Williams, the college's founder) tend to spruce up their gear with some yellow to underscore the difference. For gifts in other hues, **MASS MoCA by Design** (50 Spring St., 413/652-2143, 10am-6pm Mon.-Sat., noon-5pm Sun.) carries a carefully curated selection of art books, decor, and doodads, while the **Shops at the Library** (70 Spring St., 413/458-3436, www.shopsatthelibrary.com, 10am-5:30pm Wed.-Sat., 11am-5pm Sun.) combines an antiques store and a pair of clothing retailers into a single, eclectic location.

SPORTS AND RECREATION

Hiking

★ MOUNT GREYLOCK

The 3,491-foot summit of **Mount Greylock** (Rockwell Rd., Lanesborough, 413/499-4262, www.mass.gov, access free, summit parking $6), the highest peak in Massachusetts, is both accessible and wild, and it and the surrounding peaks are favorites for overnight hikes or leisurely afternoon drives. Several trails lead up into the mountains from both North Adams and Williamstown: Trace some of Henry David Thoreau's 1844 hike to the peak on a challenging 9.6-mile loop, which takes about 6-8 hours, from Notch Road in North Adams—follow **Bellows Pipe Trail** to the **Appalachian Trail** (A.T.), and return via the A.T. and **Bernard Farm Trail.**

Or try the slightly easier, 6.2-mile round-trip summit hike that takes 4-5 hours from the Mount Greylock Campground. This route starts off signed as the **Campground Trail,** then follows **Hopper Trail** for 1.4 miles and links up with the Appalachian Trail for the final 1.1 miles.

As there are many trails in the area, it's essential to have a detailed map, available at the **Mount Greylock Visitor Center** (30 Rockwell Rd., 413/499-4262, 9am-4:30pm daily late May-Columbus Day, 9am-4pm Sat.-Sun. Columbus Day-May).

If all that sounds a bit strained, you can take a scenic, winding road straight to the top of Mount Greylock, where there's a snack bar and visitors center with information on short hikes and nature activities.

Mount Greylock dominates the landscape here, but there are many ways to get into the woods from Williamstown. One favorite outing is the trail up **Pine Cobble,** a quartzite outcropping with views of the Hoosic River Valley. To reach the trailhead, take Cole Avenue from Route 7 and turn right onto North Hoosic Road. Turn left on Pine Cobble Road and park 0.2 mile up on the left, opposite the trailhead. The 1.6-mile trail to Pine Cobble is moderately steep and takes at least an hour; the trail is maintained by the **Williams Outing Club** (www.woc.williams.edu), which has detailed trail descriptions on its website.

Find a more extensive trail system in **Hopkins Memorial Forest** (entrance on Northwest Hill Rd., 109 yards north of Bulkley St., www.hmf.williams.edu), where 15 miles of paths wind through forests and fields. A good place to start is the 1.5-mile **Lower Loop,** which takes roughly one hour, and the hike can be extended by connecting to the 2.6-mile **Upper Loop,** which takes an additional two hours; together, the two loop trails form a figure-eight shape.

summit marker at Mount Greylock

Winter Sports

While just a molehill compared to the big mountains in New Hampshire and Vermont, the best small-mountain skiing in the area can be found at **Jiminy Peak** (11 Corey Rd., Hancock, 413/738-5500, www.jiminypeak.com, $74-81 adults, $65-71 seniors and teens 13-18, $55-61 children 6-12), which has a good set of steep summit trails and a half pipe for snowboarders.

See New England athletes compete in the **Bay State Games** (www.baystategames.org/winter-games), an annual winter sports festival held January-March. Alpine and cross-country skiing, figure skating, ice hockey, and snowshoe racing events are held at Berkshire County venues, including Williams College and Canterbury Farms in Becket.

FOOD

The floor-to-ceiling windows at **Tunnel City Coffee** (100 Spring St., 413/458-5010, www.tunnelcitycoffee.com, 6am-6pm daily, $2-7) are flung wide open on warm days, and students kick back in comfortable couches and armchairs. Aside from the people-watching, locally roasted coffee is the draw, along with pastries and snacks.

Chewy crusts and freshly prepared sauces make **Hot Tomatoes Neapolitan Pizza** (100 Water St., 413/458-2722, www.hottomatoespizza.com, 11am-2pm and 4pm-9pm Mon.-Fri., noon-10pm Sat.-Sun., $10-14) a perennial favorite. This is primarily a takeout place, but outdoor picnic tables offer fine river views, and the adjoining park is a nice place for a picnic and a stroll.

The village's culinary jewel is ★ **Mezze Bistro + Bar** (777 Rte. 7, 413/458-0123, www.mezzerestaurant.com, 5pm-9pm Sun.-Thurs., 5pm-10pm Fri.-Sat., $16-28), a sophisticated restaurant in a beautifully renovated 19th-century home just south of town. Local ingredients are transformed on an international menu with an Italian emphasis; small plates, mains, and pasta dishes star alongside an extensive (and very reasonable) wine list.

In the persistently quaint Berkshires, the colorful decor and bold Indian flavors at **Spice Root** (23 Spring St., 413/458-5200, www.spiceroot.com, 11:30am-2:30pm and 5pm-10pm Tues.-Sat., noon-3pm and 5pm-10pm Sun., $12-19) are a tonic. The ample vegetarian and vegan choices are popular here, and the weekday lunch buffet is a fabulous deal.

The classed-up bar food at **Hops & Vines** (16 Water St., 413/884-1372, www.hopsandvinesma.com, 4pm-9pm Tues.-Sat., $11-31) is served in a relaxed, modern dining room and on a garden-like patio. The menu is brief—favorites include a lamb burger, smoked bacon macaroni, and Brussels sprouts—but the wine and beer lists are long and thoughtful.

Grab provisions at **Wild Oats Market** (320 Main St., 413/458-8060, www.wildoats.coop, 7am-8pm Mon.-Sat., 9am-8pm Sun.), where some produce, prepared foods, and other groceries are sourced locally. Shop for bread, crafts, honey, produce, and local arts and crafts at the **Williamstown Farmers Market** (125 Spring St., 9am-1pm Sat., late May-Oct.), which also has prepared foods.

ACCOMMODATIONS AND CAMPING

Under $100

Simple rooms are clean and well appointed at **Maple Terrace Motel** (555 Main St., 413/458-9677, www.mapleterrace.com, $89-149), whose convenient Main Street location is walking distance to the Williams College campus. The continental breakfast of good coffee and fresh bread is an unexpected treat, but the real treasure is behind the motel, where a swimming pool and lawn abut a rolling horse pasture that feels like a bit of country in the middle of town.

$100-150

Just a mile outside of town, **Steep Acres Farm** (520 White Oaks Rd., 413/281-8510, www.steepacres.com, $125-195) includes a pond with rowboats for rent, trails, and apple trees—and fabulous homemade breakfasts. At press time it was transitioning to a cannabis-friendly property.

$150-250

While scores of "farms" to stay at abound in the Berkshires, you'll find the real thing at ★ **Clover Hill Farm** (249 Adams Rd., 413/458-3637, www.cloverhillfarm.net, $135-215), home to horses, chickens, ducks, and an adorably grouchy goat named Susie (after she took on a few too many cars, her horns were wrapped in soft cloth—bottles labeled "Goat H2O" are stashed all over the farm to rebuff her mostly harmless butts). The wonderful owners have two single rooms, a five-person suite, and a guesthouse that are casual, comfortable, and dog-friendly. This is a great choice for families, and riding lessons can be arranged in advance.

A tiered, cubist exterior, painted in hues of teal and mauve, is your first sign that **The Guest House at Field Farm** (554 Sloan Rd., 413/458-3135, www.thetrustees.org/field-farm, $200-350) is not your ordinary bed-and-breakfast. A Bauhaus-inspired modernist masterpiece, the home is full of modern art and design-conscious period furniture. A heated outdoor pool, private decks, and terrycloth robes create a sense of peaceful refuge, combined with the natural setting—300 protected acres surround the house.

Camping

Shady and quiet, the campground at **Clarksburg State Park** (1199 Middle Rd., Clarksburg, 413/664-8345, www.mass.gov, late May-early Sept., $20) has 44 sites, five miles northeast of Williamstown's center. The park also has extensive hiking trails and a tempting pond (where swimming is not allowed).

GETTING THERE AND AROUND

The closest airport to the region is **Albany International Airport** (737 Albany Shaker Rd., Albany NY, 518/242-2200, www.albanyairport.com). Taxi service from the airport is available from a variety of car services including **Capitaland Taxi Services** (518/242-4222, www.capitalandtaxi.com), which charges $116 to Williamstown.

Williamstown is just across the border from **Bennington, Vermont** (15 mi, 0.5 hr.), a short drive south on **Route 7. Peter Pan Bonanza** (800/343-9999, www.peterpanbus.com) connects Boston's South Station with Williamstown (4 hrs., $46) in a route that includes a transfer in Albany. Peter Pan also has service from New York City's Port Authority Bus Terminal to Williamstown (5 hrs., $56). Buses throughout the region are run by the **Berkshire Regional Transit Authority** (413/449-2782 or 800/292-2782, www.berkshirerta.com). Williamstown itself is easily walkable, and metered parking is available on Spring Street.

North Adams

With hulking factory buildings and a gritty, rustbelt mood, North Adams isn't a place you'd expect to find an enormous collection of modern art, and the Massachusetts Museum of Contemporary Art can seem like a colonial outpost of some hip, faraway community. But if you take the time to explore the town, you'll find art entwined with the old brick structures, vibrant murals brightening up highway bridges, and studios tucked above Main Street shops. MASS MoCA brought energy, visitors, and an infusion of much-needed cash after the town's leading employer, Sprague Electric, shut its doors in the 1980s, ending North Adams's long history as a mill and manufacturing town. Faded Victorian homes and an elegant public library are legacies of those prosperous years, when whirring woolen mills, shoe factories, sawmills, and ironworks were powered by the twin branches of the Hoosic River.

SIGHTS

TOP EXPERIENCE

★ Massachusetts Museum of Contemporary Art (MASS MoCA)

Built on the sprawling campus of Sprague Electric, the size of the **Massachusetts Museum of Contemporary Art** (1040 MASS MoCA Way, 413/662-2111, www.massmoca.org, 10am-6pm Sun.-Wed., 10am-7pm Thurs.-Sat. late June-Sept., 10am-5pm Wed.-Mon. Sept.-late June, $20 adults, $18 seniors, $12 students, $8 children 6-16, children under 6 free) is stunning. Composed of 27 redbrick former factory buildings and connected by an interlocking network of bridges, walkways, and courtyards, it has vast gallery spaces that allow for artwork of an unusually epic scale—from enormous installations to expansive performance art. The

North Adams

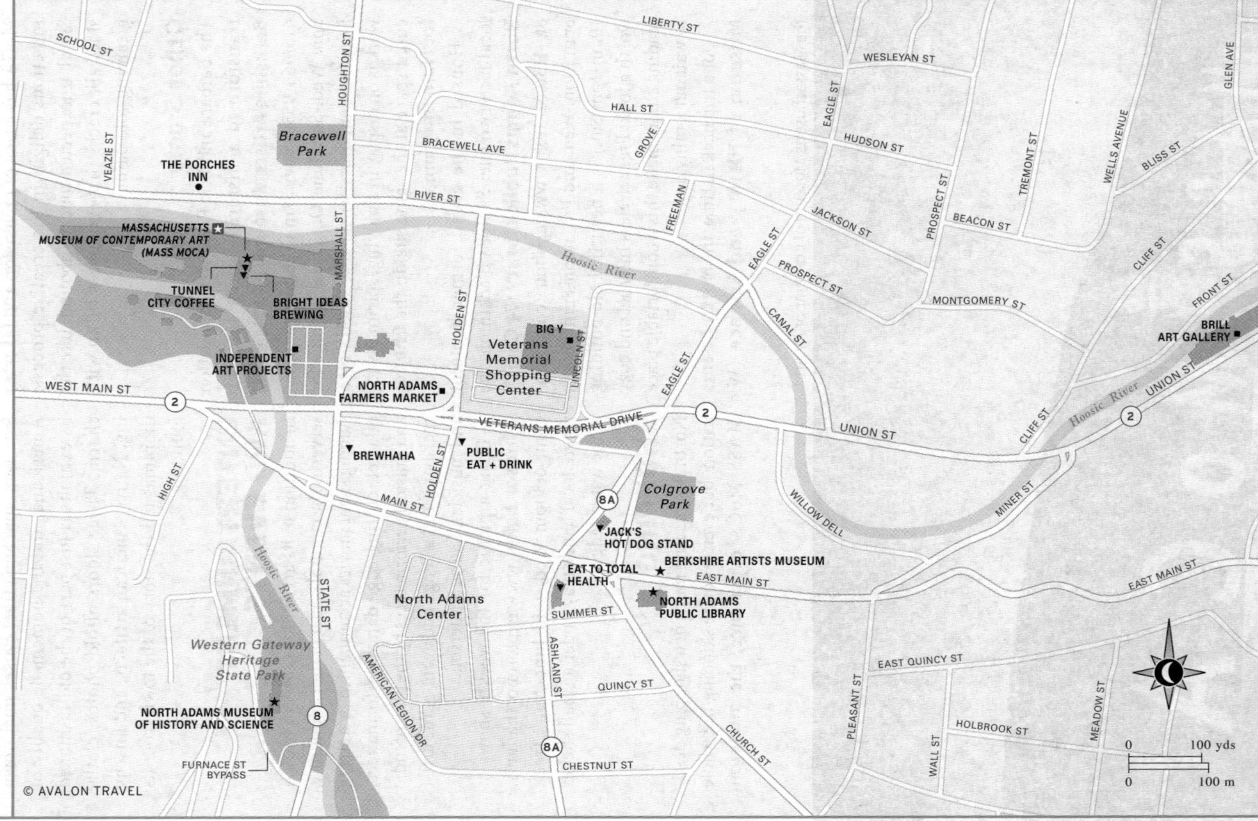
MASSACHUSETTS MUSEUM OF CONTEMPORARY ART (MASS MOCA)
THE PORCHES INN
TUNNEL CITY COFFEE
BRIGHT IDEAS BREWING
INDEPENDENT ART PROJECTS
NORTH ADAMS FARMERS MARKET
BREWHAHA
PUBLIC EAT + DRINK
BIG Y
Veterans Memorial Shopping Center
Bracewell Park
Colgrove Park
JACK'S HOT DOG STAND
BERKSHIRE ARTISTS MUSEUM
EAT TO TOTAL HEALTH
NORTH ADAMS PUBLIC LIBRARY
North Adams Center
Western Gateway Heritage State Park
NORTH ADAMS MUSEUM OF HISTORY AND SCIENCE
BRILL ART GALLERY
Hoosic River
SCHOOL ST
VEAZIE ST
HOUGHTON ST
LIBERTY ST
WESLEYAN ST
HALL ST
BRACEWELL AVE
GROVE
HUDSON ST
EAGLE ST
TREMONT ST
WELLS AVENUE
BLISS ST
GLEN AVE
RIVER ST
FREEMAN
JACKSON ST
PROSPECT ST
BEACON ST
CLIFF ST
MARSHALL ST
PROSPECT ST
MONTGOMERY ST
FRONT ST
CANAL ST
HOLDEN ST
LINCOLN ST
WEST MAIN ST
VETERANS MEMORIAL DRIVE
UNION ST
HIGH ST
MAIN ST
WILLOW DELL
MINER ST
STATE ST
EAST MAIN ST
SUMMER ST
AMERICAN LEGION DR
ASHLAND ST
QUINCY ST
CHESTNUT ST
CHURCH ST
EAST QUINCY ST
PLEASANT ST
HOLBROOK ST
WALL ST
MEADOW ST
FURNACE ST BYPASS
2
8
8A
0
100 yds
0
100 m

scale of the museum also affords more inclusiveness than many institutions, and MASS MoCA has a lack of pretension and takes an infectious delight in the creative process: Small, unexpected touches abound, like the sidewalk cracks that employees fill in with gleaming gold paint.

Other Sights

The Barbara and Eric Rudd Art Foundation transformed a historic church into the **Berkshire Artists Museum** (159 E. Main St., 413/664-9550, www.bamuseum.org, 10am-5pm Wed.-Sun. June-Oct., free), a home for local contemporary work. Eric Rudd's own work is on display in a moving, spiritually focused space at the same site, in the **Chapel for Humanity** annex.

Housed in the grand former home of local factory owner Sanford Blackinton, the **North Adams Public Library** (74 Church St., 413/662-3133, www.naplibrary.com, 9am-5pm Mon.-Wed. and Fri., noon-8pm Thurs., 10am-1pm Sat.) is a beautiful old building worth a look. Free wireless Internet and cozy reading chairs make this a comfortable place to wait out a rainy day.

For a trip back in time, the **North Adams Museum of History and Science** (W. Gateway State Park, 413/664-4700, www.northadamshistory.org, 10am-4pm Thurs.-Sat., 1pm-4pm Sun., free) evokes small-town Americana, and the homemade quality of its exhibits is just part of the old-fashioned charm. Three floors of old photos, clothing, Native American artifacts, and kitschy dioramas tell the story of the town from its founding.

ENTERTAINMENT AND EVENTS

In addition to its art exhibits, **MASS MoCA** serves as the cultural center of the community, staging silent movies accompanied by a string quartet, cutting-edge dance performances, and musical performances by the likes of indie rock band Yo La Tengo and avant-garde artist and musician Laurie Anderson.

Bring a picnic for the weekly shows at **Windsor Lake** (www.explorenorthadams.com, 6:30pm Wed. mid-June-Aug., free), where local bands play under a small shelter at the water's edge.

SHOPPING

North Adams isn't much of a shopping destination, but even if you're skipping the whole MASS MoCA experience, the **museum**

the Massachusetts Museum of Contemporary Art

store could supply a year's worth of creative Christmas presents. Take home a piece of the North Adams art scene from **Independent Art Projects** (1315 MASS MoCA Way, 413/346-4004, www.independentartprojects.com, 11am-5pm daily July-Aug., 11am-5pm Wed.-Sun. Sept.-June), a gallery with beautifully curated works in a museum-like space. Another good spot for contemporary work is the **Brill Art Gallery** (243 Union St., 413/664-4353, www.brillgallery109.com, 10am-5pm daily), which often has standout photography shows.

SPORTS AND RECREATION

★ Ashuwillticook Rail Trail

The 11.2-mile **Ashuwillticook Rail Trail** runs from just behind the **Adams Visitor Center** (3 Hoosac St., Adams, 413/743-8358), about a 15-minute drive south of North Adams, to the small town of Lanesborough, with views of mountains, rivers, and lakes. It's a pleasant, easy trail, and you can rent a bike just off it at **Village Bike Rental** (31 Park St., Adams, 413/743-2453, www.villagebikerental.com, 10am-6pm Mon., 9am-6pm Tues.-Sun. late May-Oct., hybrid bikes $23 for 2 hours, $33 for 4 hours, $42 full day).

Winter Sports

Rent cross-country skis and snowshoes at **Berkshire Outfitters** (Rt. 8, Grove St., Adams, 413/743-5900, www.berkshireoutfitters.com, 10am-6pm Mon.-Fri., 10am-5pm Sat., 11am-4pm Sun., touring skis $29, skate skis $39), then head to **Windsor Lake** (Bradley St. and Kemp Ave., 413/662-3000 ext. 3047, www.explorenorthadams.com/item/windsor-lake), where a network of ungroomed trails circles the lakeshore, or to **Notchview** (83 Rte. 9, Windsor, www.notchview.org, 8am-4:30pm daily, $8-15 adults, $3-6 children), where there are 10 miles of trails groomed for classic skiing and 7 for skate skiing.

There are some steep, challenging runs at **Berkshire East** (66 Thunder Mountain Rd, Charlemont, 413/339-6618, http://berkshireeast.com; $65 adults, $55 students, $45 seniors 65 and over and children 6-12), which is about a half hour east of North Adams. There's also a snow tubing park (2 hours $20 adults, $15 children 12 and under) on-site.

Peter W. Foote Vietnam Veterans Memorial Skating Rink (1267 S. Church St., 413/664-8185, http://northadams-ma.gov) is a small indoor rink.

The third weekend in February, North Adams puts on **WinterFest** (www.explorenorthadams.com), when the community comes out for ice sculpting, horse-drawn wagon rides, a craft market, and a chowder competition.

FOOD

Locals have been sidling up to the counter at **Jack's Hot Dog Stand** (12 Eagle St., 413/664-9006, www.jackshotdogstand.com, 10am-7pm Mon.-Sat., $1-4) since 1917 for a simple menu of hot dogs, burgers, and fries. If the microwave figures more visibly into kitchen prep than is conducive to misty-eyed nostalgia, Jack's is right at home in gritty North Adams, and the friendly service and vintage pricing are unbeatable.

Just down the street (and in a different world entirely) is the vegan, "allergy-free" **Eat to Total Health** (14 Ashland St., 413/346-4357, www.eattototalhealth.com, 11am-7pm Mon.-Fri., 11am-4pm Sat., $5-11), which sells fresh smoothies, prepared foods, and assorted healthy groceries in a small shop with a friendly staff.

Like its sister café in Williamstown, North Adams's **Tunnel City Coffee** (87 Marshall St., 413/398-5304, 7:30am-5pm Mon.-Fri., 9am-5pm Sat.-Sun., $2-7) serves pastries, snacks, and locally roasted coffee. This one, however, is inside the MASS MoCA complex (though the café can be accessed without buying a museum ticket), which means your cappuccino comes with a side of world-class people-watching, as the museum employees and visitors come and go.

Also in the MASS MoCA complex,

★ **Bright Ideas Brewing** (111 MASS MoCA Way, 413/346-4460, www.brightideasbrewing.com, check website for hours, $3-7) is full of references to North Adams's industrial past, with gorgeous brick walls and a 40-foot bar made by local workers. Its diverse lineup of beers manages to bridge the divide between the town's art lovers and townies.

Modern, industrial decor and a gastropub menu make ★ **Public Eat + Drink** (34 Holden St., 413/664-4444, www.publiceatanddrink.com, $10-20) the most stylish place to eat in town, and regulars love the fish-and-chips, burgers, and great drink menu, which includes beers from around New England.

Popular with the locals, the casual **Brewhaha** (20 Marshall St., 413/664-2020, www.facebook.com/brewhahacafe, 7am-5pm daily, $3-10) serves coffee, sandwiches, salads, and excellent soups in a small café. Music, friendly staff, and bright posters on the wall make this a welcoming spot.

Pick up the essentials at **Big Y** (45 Veterans Memorial Dr., 413/663-6549, 7am-9pm daily), a basic grocery store in the center of town. Or if you're in town on a Saturday in season, head to the **North Adams Farmers Market** (intersection of Rte. 8 and St. Anthony Drive, 413/664-6180, 9am-1pm Sat. early June-late Oct.), a producers-only market, which also has live music 10am-noon.

Dine on top of Mount Greylock at **Bascom Lodge** (30 Rockwell Rd., Lanesborough, 413/743-1591, www.bascomlodge.net, Tues.-Sun June and daily July-Oct., breakfast 8am-10:30am, lunch 11am-4:30pm, sunset drinks Wed.-Sun. 5pm-7pm, dinner seating 7pm, breakfast/lunch $4-10, prix fixe dinner $35-45), an Arts and Crafts-style mountain hut with an unbeatable location. The simple breakfast and lunch menus include basic sandwiches, egg dishes, hot dogs, and hamburgers, and the fixed price dinner comes with salad and dessert. While the food gets mixed reviews, dining at heavy communal tables in a mountaintop dining room is the real experience, and the "sunset beverage hour" commands some of the finest views in the Berkshires.

ACCOMMODATIONS

There aren't many places to stay in North Adams, so unless you're splashing out at The Porches Inn, it's worth booking a room in Williamstown. Alternatively, there are quite a few places listed on Airbnb and other private rental sites for significantly less than the local hotels, and if you're prepared to drive to the summit of Mount Greylock, you'll find a historic Arts and Crafts-style lodge with unforgettable views.

If you've come prepared with backpacking gear, the remote tent sites at **Mount Greylock Campground** (park 413/499-4262, reservations 877/422-6762, www.mass.gov, mid-May-Oct. $8, free off-season) are blissfully backcountry, and a series of five **lean-to shelters** within the park are open year-round (register at 413/499-4262, free).

One remarkable way to experience the Mount Greylock State Reservation is by spending the night at ★ **Bascom Lodge** (30 Rockwell Rd., Lanesborough, 413/743-1591, www.bascomlodge.net, May-Nov., bunks $40, private rooms $125), on the mountain's summit, which also serves meals in the on-site dining room. The Arts and Crafts-style lodge has shared bathrooms, and staying in it provides a hostel-like experience, a chance to rub shoulders with ropy Appalachian Trail thru-hikers, and the best views in the county. The lodge is a 25-minute drive from downtown North Adams.

With a focus on design and impeccable comfort, ★ **The Porches Inn** (231 River St., 413/664-0400, www.porches.com, $299-485) stands out for channeling the spirit of North Adams—both old and new. Workers' row houses from the 1890s have been transformed into luxury guest rooms with ultrasoft sheets and lighthearted touches. Each room is different, with vintage decor and thoughtfully chosen color schemes (and just about everything that's not bolted to the floor is for sale). Rates include a fresh, appealing continental breakfast, and coffee and baked goods are available in-room by request.

INFORMATION

The **Adams Visitors Bureau** (3 Hoosac St., Adams, 413/743-8358, 413/743-8300 x 100) runs a mammoth visitors center providing information on the entire Berkshires region, open seasonally 9am-5pm daily late June-mid-October.

GETTING THERE AND AROUND

From **Brattleboro, Vermont,** drive about **23 miles** west on **Route 9** to Searsburg, then turn left on **Route 8.** After about 5 miles, turn right to remain on Route 8. After 8.5 miles and crossing the state line, turn right onto Middle Road, which becomes Franklin Street, then Eagle Street, and leads into downtown **North Adams** (45 mi., 1.25 hrs.).

Peter Pan Bonanza (800/343-9999, www.peterpanbus.com) has service from New York City's Port Authority Bus Terminal to North Adams (6.75 hrs., $52). Bus services for the region are provided by **Berkshire Regional Transit Authority** (413/449-2782 or 800/292-2782, www.berkshirerta.com).

Lenox

In the midst of the glamorous Gilded Age excess of the late 19th century, Boston's barons of industry erected palatial homes in the Berkshires, which became their carefully sculpted haven from city life. For that very small, exclusive society, it was one of a few summertime escapes along with places like Newport, Rhode Island, and Bar Harbor, Maine—where the wealthy made extended visits surrounded by small armies of servants. More than any other town in the area, Lenox retains that sheen of upscale country living, and when the Boston Symphony Orchestra takes up its annual summertime residence at Tanglewood, the town is packed to the gills. Lenox also has the greatest concentration of places to stay in the area, along with a thriving arts scene, dance festival, and celebrated yoga retreat.

SIGHTS

★ The Mount

Edith Wharton's incisive, prolific writing is among the best in American literature, but she once contended that she was "a better landscape gardener than novelist." Judge for yourself at **The Mount** (2 Plunkett St., 413/551-5100, www.edithwharton.org, 10am-5pm daily mid-May-Oct., 10:30am-3pm Sat.-Sun. Nov.-Feb., $18 adults, $17 seniors, $13 students, $10 military, youth under 18 free), the gorgeously restored estate she designed from the ground up. With the exception of the library, most of the author's personal belongings and furniture are long gone, but Wharton's taste for symmetry, balance, and allusion are everywhere. And while visiting the house takes just an hour or so, the expansive grounds are an inviting place to linger—in the cool sunken garden, by a blossom-fringed fountain, or on the trails that wrap through the woods and past neat lines of tilia trees. On weekends in July and August, there are informal jazz sessions on the outdoor terrace, and professional actors perform readings of Wharton's writing on Wednesday in the summer ($5, check website for events calendar). The grounds are open sunrise-sunset all year and free to access outside visiting hours, which makes this a perfect place for a quiet, early morning or evening walk.

Other Sights

Part of the movie *The Cider House Rules* was filmed at the **Ventfort Hall Mansion and Gilded Age Museum** (104 Walker St., 413/637-3206, www.gildedage.org, 10am-5pm Mon.-Sat., 10am-3pm Sun. late May-Oct. 31, 10am-4pm Mon.-Sat., 10am-3pm Sun. Nov. 1-late May, tours hourly, $18

Lenox

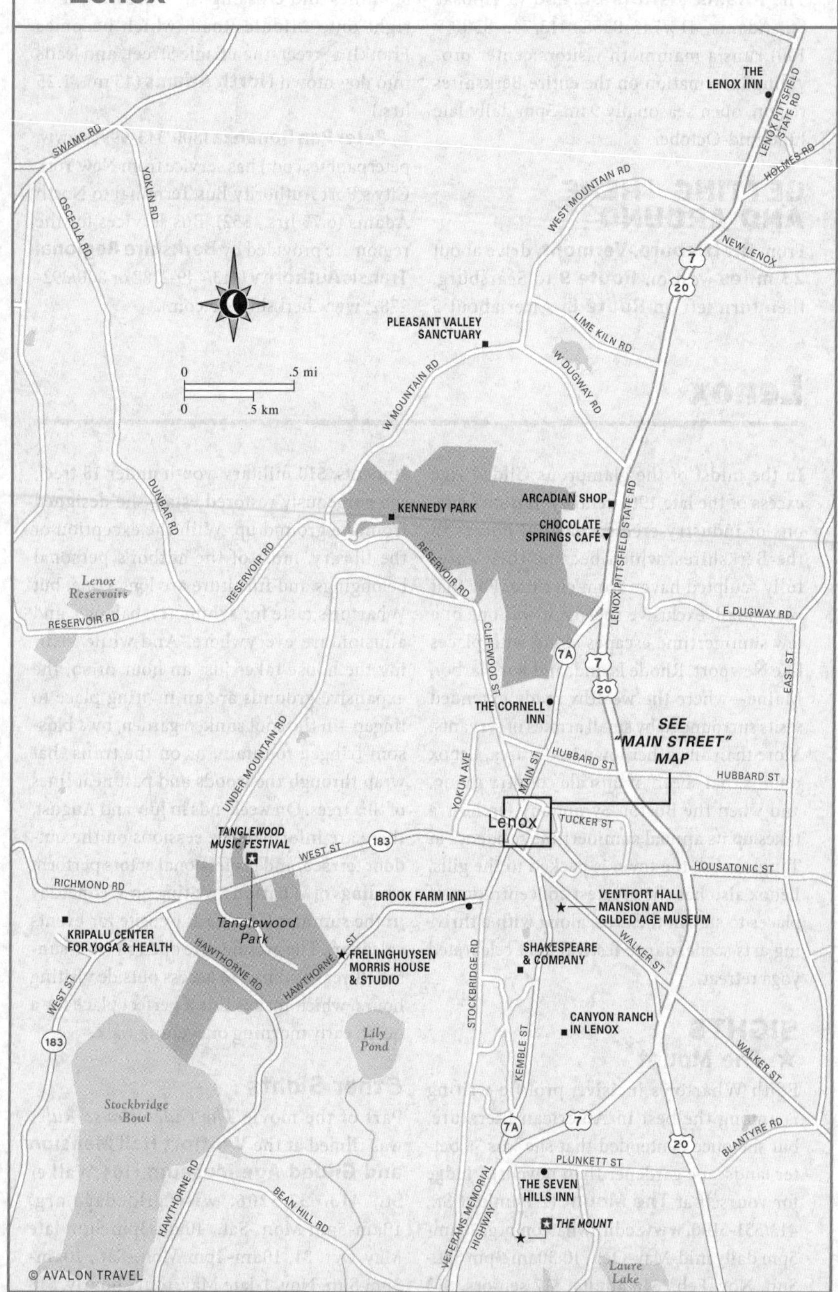
THE LENOX INN
LENOX PITTSFIELD STATE RD
HOLMES RD
WEST MOUNTAIN RD
NEW LENOX
SWAMP RD
YOKUN RD
OSCEOLA RD
7
20
PLEASANT VALLEY SANCTUARY
LIME KILN RD
W DUGWAY RD
0
.5 mi
0
.5 km
W MOUNTAIN RD
DUNBAR RD
KENNEDY PARK
ARCADIAN SHOP
CHOCOLATE SPRINGS CAFÉ
LENOX PITTSFIELD STATE RD
Lenox Reservoirs
RESERVOIR RD
RESERVOIR RD
E DUGWAY RD
CLIFFWOOD ST
7A
7
20
EAST ST
THE CORNELL INN
SEE "MAIN STREET" MAP
UNDER MOUNTAIN RD
YOKUN AVE
MAIN ST
HUBBARD ST
HUBBARD ST
Lenox
TUCKER ST
TANGLEWOOD MUSIC FESTIVAL
WEST ST
183
HOUSATONIC ST
RICHMOND RD
BROOK FARM INN
VENTFORT HALL MANSION AND GILDED AGE MUSEUM
Tanglewood Park
KRIPALU CENTER FOR YOGA & HEALTH
HAWTHORNE RD
HAWTHORNE ST
FRELINGHUYSEN MORRIS HOUSE & STUDIO
SHAKESPEARE & COMPANY
WALKER ST
STOCKBRIDGE RD
WEST ST
183
Lily Pond
CANYON RANCH IN LENOX
KEMBLE ST
WALKER ST
Stockbridge Bowl
7A
7
BLANTYRE RD
20
PLUNKETT ST
BEAN HILL RD
HAWTHORNE RD
THE SEVEN HILLS INN
VETERANS MEMORIAL HIGHWAY
THE MOUNT
Laure Lake
© AVALON TRAVEL

adults, $17 seniors and students, $7 youth 5-17, children under 4 free), a celebration of all things Victorian. The restored mansion was once owned by J. P. Morgan's sister, and tours bring alive the 1890s, when the Berkshires were the playground of the superrich.

Explore the gorgeous Bauhaus-style home that artists George L. K. Morris and Suzy Frelinghuysen built to live and work in at **Freylinghuysen Morris House & Studio** (92 Hawthorne St., 413/637-0166, www.frelinghuysen.org, 10am-3pm Thurs.-Sun. June 22-Labor Day, $15 adults, $14 seniors, $7.50 students, children under 12 free). In addition to the couple's own abstract art, the house has a noteworthy collection of works that include Picasso, Braque, and Gris as well as beautiful period furniture.

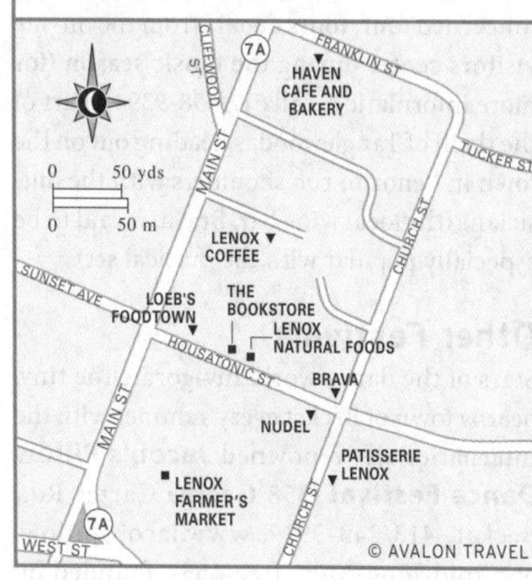

ENTERTAINMENT AND EVENTS

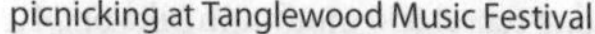

★ Tanglewood Music Festival

During summer, the Boston Symphony Orchestra (BSO)—along with a suite of other performers—brings world-class music to **Tanglewood** (297 West St., 413/637-1600, www.bso.org), a sprawling venue named for a collection of stories by Nathaniel Hawthorne, who spent a summer writing on the property. The Tanglewood season runs late June-early September, and popular shows often sell out within days of their first availability in January, as do rooms in town.

Music, however sublime, is only part of the experience. Elegant picnics at Tanglewood have been a tradition since the BSO performed here in the late 1930s, and afternoons on the lawn have a nostalgia-tinged, languid charm. Show up several hours early to stretch the

picnicking at Tanglewood Music Festival

picnic into an all-afternoon affair, or explore the Tanglewood campus on a 1.5-hour, volunteer-led tour; tours depart from the on-site visitors center during the music season (for more information, call 617/638-9394). Part of the thrill of Tanglewood is heading out on the town in Lenox to rub shoulders with the musicians (the local wine bar, Brava, is said to be especially popular with the musical set).

Other Festivals

Stars of the dance world invigorate the tiny, nearby town of Becket every summer with the internationally renowned **Jacob's Pillow Dance Festival** (358 George Carter Rd., Becket, 413/243-9919, www.jacobspillow.org, mid-June-Aug., free-$55), founded by modern-dance pioneer Ted Shawn. Every style from hip-hop to ballet gets its time in the spotlight during the two-month celebration, which includes dozens of free performances and gallery talks. The main draw, however, is the showcases of artists from around the world, featuring both established companies such as Mark Morris and Alvin Ailey alongside emerging choreographers. Some of the best summer Shakespeare in the country is performed by **Shakespeare & Company** (70 Kemble St., 413/637-3353, www.shakespeare.org, free-$79) in a mix of indoor and outdoor theaters. Year-round the company stages performances both by the Bard and others, plus presents special public events and runs workshops for theater professionals.

SHOPPING

The main street of Lenox is packed with little boutiques that invite browsing, mostly clustered along **Church Street** and **Housatonic Street.** Only at **The Bookstore** (11 Housatonic St., 413/637-3390, www.bookstoreinlenox.com, 10am-6pm Mon.- Sat., 10am-4pm Sun., open late on busy summer evenings), though, can you browse the shelves with a glass of wine in your hand from the house wine bar.

SPORTS AND RECREATION

Hiking and Biking

Just a few miles north of town, Massachusetts Audubon's **Pleasant Valley Sanctuary** (472 W. Mountain Rd., 413/637-0320, www.massaudubon.org, visitors center: 9am-4pm Mon.-Fri., 10am-4pm Sat.-Sun. May-Oct., 10am-4pm Tues.-Sun. Nov.-Apr., $5 adults, $3 seniors and youth 2-12, trails: sunrise-sunset) has over 1,000 acres of wetlands, forests, and meadows with seven miles of trails for exploring the eastern slope of Lenox Mountain. The strenuous, three-mile **Ledges-Overbrook Loop** goes to the 2,126-foot summit for views of Mount Greylock, the Taconic Range, and the Catskills, while the gentler 1.5-mile **Yokun-Beaver Lodge Trails Loop** is popular for birding.

Right in the center of town, **Kennedy Park** (275 Main St., www.townoflenox.org) has over 10 miles of old carriage roads, multiuse trails, and single-track popular for mountain biking. The trails, which connect to more extensive single-track outside the park's boundaries, aren't particularly well marked, but it's hard to get lost for too long without crossing a road. For rental bikes, maps, and friendly advice about where to ride, the **Arcadian Shop** (91 Pittsfield Rd., 413/637-3010, www.arcadian.com, full-day rental $50 mountain bike or $40 hybrid bike) is a great resource and is located right next to Kennedy Park.

Boating

The gentle Housatonic River is scenic and approachable for boaters of all skill levels, and one of the prettiest stretches is the meandering section between **Decker Landing,** between Lenox and Pittsfield, and **Wood's Pond** in Lenox, a 4.6-mile trip that takes 2-3 hours and has great views of the mountains. **Arcadian Shop** (91 Pittsfield Rd., 413/637-3010, www.arcadian.com, $35 single or $60 tandem kayak) rents boats, and will drop your boat at Decker Landing and pick it up at Wood's Pond for $20. Another good option is

Travels with New England's Writers

Looking for the perfect book to bring along for a New England adventure? The region has a long literary tradition, from the woodsy ramblings of Henry David Thoreau to Edith Wharton's high society intrigue. Listing them all would be a book unto itself, but some writers' lives and prose are so tightly woven into New England's landscape and culture that they've helped to define them.

- The first woman to win a Pulitzer Prize, **Edith Wharton** left an indelible mark on American literature with nuanced novels about the wealthy Gilded Age society she was born into. While her home at **The Mount** (2 Plunkett St., Lenox, MA, 413/551-5100, www.edithwharton.org) offers a fascinating glimpse of her life, visiting Newport's mansions feels like stepping into the pages of *The Age of Innocence*.
- Another Berkshires habitué was **Herman Melville,** who wrote much of *Moby-Dick* from his desk at **Arrowhead** (780 Holmes Rd., Pittsfield, MA, 413/442-1793, www.mobydick.org). He hadn't yet set foot on **Nantucket** when he penned the iconic (and hefty) novel, but his spirit lives on there, with whaling history and Melville-era maritime architecture around every corner.
- Descendent of a Salem witch trial judge, it's only fitting that **Nathaniel Hawthorne** filled his novels with the darkest side of New England's Puritan culture. The **House of the Seven Gables** (115 Derby St., Salem, MA, 978/744-0991, www.7gables.org) still stands near Salem harbor, and the **Nathaniel Hawthorne Birthplace** (27 Hardy St., Salem, MA) has been conveniently plunked down next door.
- In between long walks in the woods, **Henry David Thoreau** wrote a series of books, essays, and articles that have inspired the American environmental movement ever since. The most iconic Thoreau pilgrimage might be to his former cabin site beside **Walden Pond** (915 Walden St., Concord, MA, 978/369-3254), but the popular state park can be a bit noisy for communing with his contrarian spirit. For that, follow in the writer's footsteps on a hike up **Mount Greylock** or **Mount Katahdin.**
- The former poet laureate of Vermont, **Robert Frost** filled volumes with scenes from a rural New England life. His former homes in Vermont and New Hampshire are now museums: the **Robert Frost Stone House Museum** (121 Rte. 7-A, Shaftsbury, VT, 802/447-6200, www.frostfriends.org) and **The Frost Place** (158 Ridge Rd., Franconia, NH, 603/823-5510, www.frostplace.org).

to join a group from **Berkshire Canoe Tours** (413/442-2789, www.berkshirecanoetours.org, $50 adults, $30 children), which makes a 2-hour trip from Decker Landing multiple times daily during summer months in canoes and kayaks.

Spas and Yoga

East meets western Massachusetts at the **Kripalu Center for Yoga & Health** (297 West St., 413/448-3152, www.kripalu.org, day pass $125), one of the foremost yoga training centers in the country. The sprawling campus has fabulous views and lots of places to lounge on the grass between workshops on yoga, meditation, and mindfulness, and offers healthy meals in the dining room as well as dormitories and private rooms for those who want to stay over.

At the other end of the spectrum, the ultra-luxe **Canyon Ranch in Lenox** (165 Kemble St., 413/637-4100, reservations 800/743-9000, www.canyonranch.com/lenox, day pass $370) opens its elegant spa to the public for daytime access, including classes, use of spa pools and gyms, lunch in the Canyon Ranch restaurant, and treatments like massages and facials.

FOOD

In a strip mall just north of town, **Chocolate Springs Café** (55 Pittsfield Rd., 413/637-9820, www.chocolatesprings.com, 9am-9pm

Sun.-Fri., 9am-10pm Sat., $3-9) is a cozy little space devoted to all things chocolaty, from rich gelato to truffles with whisper-thin shells. A comfortable seating area makes this a nice place to read, and the café often hosts local musicians at night.

Picture-perfect French pastries are the highlights of **Patisserie Lenox** (30 Church St., 413/551-9050, www.patisserielenox.com, 8:30am-7:30pm Mon.-Sat., 8:30am-6:30pm Sun., may close early in off-season, $3-12), whose brioche, macarons, and éclairs will leave you dreaming of Paris. The shop also has prepared salads and light lunch items, though the intimate tables for two fill up quickly.

The farm-to-table superstar of the Berkshires is ★ **Nudel** (37 Church St., 413/551-7183, www.nudelrestaurant.com, 5pm-9:30pm Tues.-Sat., 5pm-9pm Sun., $19-28), whose diminutive, modern dining room displays artistic portraits of ingredients. Chef Bjorn Somlo's thoughtful, creative menu changes frequently and reads like an ode to the twists and turns of New England seasons.

Appealing small plates and a showstopping wine list make **Brava** (27 Housatonic St., 413/637-9171, www.bravalenox.com, 5pm-1am daily, $14-22) a treat for a slow dinner, and the tiny spot keeps the lights on far later than anyone in town; many Tanglewood musicians make this their hangout while summering in the Berkshires, so it's a good place to rub shoulders with the performers at the casual bar. No reservations.

For an easy, fresh breakfast or lunch, ★ **Haven Cafe and Bakery** (8 Franklin St., 413/637-8948, www.havencafebakery.com, 7:30am-3pm Mon.-Fri., 8am-3pm Sat.-Sun., $4-12) is the hands-down locals' favorite. It has laid-back counter service, plenty of seating, and a menu of burgers, salads, and sandwiches, as well as a pleasant outdoor patio for warm afternoons.

Tucked back from the main drag in a shingled house, **Lenox Coffee** (52 Main St., 413/637-1606, 7am-6pm Mon.-Thurs., 7am-7pm Fri.-Sat., 8am-6pm Sun., $2-5) has a good selection of pastries and the best espresso in town, made from locally roasted coffee, in addition to seats on a shady porch, wireless Internet, and fun local art on the walls.

Friendly and locally owned, **Loeb's Foodtown** (42 Main St., 413/637-0270, www.loebsfoodtown.com, 7am-6pm Mon.-Thurs. and Sat., 7am-7pm Fri., 7am-4pm Sun.) has all the usual groceries along with deli foods and snacks; just down the block, **Lenox Natural Foods** (11 Housatonic St., 413/637-2721, 10am-6:30pm Mon.-Sat., 10am-5pm Sun.) is diminutive but all organic. Local farmers and other artisans ply their wares each week at the **Lenox Farmer's Market** (Roche Reading Park, Main St., 1pm-5pm Fri. May-Oct.), a good place for an outdoor lunch.

ACCOMMODATIONS AND CAMPING

The region's travel department estimates the Berkshires offer 4,500 hotel rooms, and that 30,000 people descend on the area during busy summer weekends. Lenox is the heart of the action, and prices spike during Tanglewood season. Many locals list their guest bedrooms on Airbnb, which can be a convenient alternative to commercial options.

$100-150

Clean rooms and affordable prices make **The Lenox Inn** (525 Pittsfield Rd., 412/499-0324, www.thelenoxinn.com, $65-155) a decent option, and the roadside motel has an outdoor pool, welcoming after a day of exploring.

$150-200

The three carefully restored historic buildings at ★ **The Cornell Inn** (203 Main St., 413/637-4800, www.cornellbb.com, $189-209) have an ideal location that's walking distance from downtown Lenox and Kennedy Park's trails. In warm months, the fresh breakfasts are served on an outdoor deck, and the friendly, accommodating owners infuse the inn with hospitable spirit.

It's possible to spend the night at the **Kripalu Center for Yoga & Health** (297 West St., 413/448-3152, www.kripalu.org), which has somewhat charmless dormitories and more appealing private rooms. All-inclusive retreats start at $376 for two nights; if you're booking within a week of your visit, however, one-night stays may be available from $189.

$200-250

Elegant and historic, the manor house at **The Seven Hills Inn** (40 Plunkett St., 413/207-9330, www.sevenhillsinn.com, $210-320) is full of antiques and old-world charm, and surrounded by perfectly manicured grounds. When booking a room in the manor house, review the online gallery, as decor varies from charmingly restrained to somewhat lurid boudoir plush. In addition to rooms in the manor house are motel and carriage house options. The least expensive rooms are in the on-site **Terrace Country Motel,** and though they're somewhat dated and dingy, the high-rent setting makes this spot a good choice if you're not planning to linger in your room. A third option is the **Carriage House,** where prices fall in between the inn and motel, and furnishings are light, pretty, and modern (and a suite with a kitchenette is also available). The inn is closed between December 1 and April 1.

Over $250

The comfortable, welcoming rooms at ★ **Brook Farm Inn** (15 Hawthorne St., 413/637-3013, www.brookfarm.com, $329-475) are full of country charm, ruffles, and floral wallpaper. The house has a few barrier-free rooms that are fully accessible, and the appealing breakfasts incorporate food from local farms and artisans. The inn has a long literary tradition dating back to the art-loving original owners, and one highlight for many guests is the wonderful collection of poetry books; the inn hosts occasional poetry readings.

Camping

October Mountain State Forest (317 Woodland Rd., Lee, 413/243-1778, www.mass.gov, May-Oct., tent sites $20, yurts $45-55) is just seven miles west of town, with hiking trails, a scenic gorge, and a secluded campground with 47 sites, rustic yurts, and bathrooms with hot showers. Book yurts well in advance, and bring your own sleeping bags or bedding.

INFORMATION

The **Lenox Chamber of Commerce** (12 Housatonic St., 413/637-3646, www.lenox.org, 9am-5pm daily mid-May-mid-Oct., 10am-5pm Mon.-Thurs. mid-Oct.-mid-May) runs a visitors center in town.

GETTING THERE AND AROUND

Located on Route 20 a few miles north of I-90, Lenox has a compact, easily walkable town center. **Peter Pan Bonanza** (800/343-9999, www.peterpanbus.com) connects Boston's South Station with Lenox (3.25 hrs., $36), and also has service from New York City's Port Authority Bus Terminal (4 hrs., $49). **Berkshire Regional Transit Authority** (413/449-2782 or 800/292-2782, www.berkshirerta.com) provides bus services throughout the region.

Stockbridge

On summer mornings before the tour buses arrive, Stockbridge has all the quiet charm of Norman Rockwell's classic painting of the town's main street. Rockwell painted here for the last 25 years of his life in a 19th-century carriage-barn-turned-studio behind Stockbridge center, and the museum dedicated to his work is one of the region's most popular attractions. The town has gone to great lengths to preserve its Rockwellian character, with white picket fences and a general store packed with nostalgic bits and bobs. You could walk the strip in a few minutes flat, and there isn't much in the way of nightlife or events in town, but it's a nice place to linger; from the shady porch at the Red Lion to the alleyway cafés, time in Stockbridge is all about watching life drift by.

SIGHTS

★ Norman Rockwell Museum

Norman Rockwell charmingly depicted kids at soda fountains and quirky small-town characters, but images that resonate after a visit to the **Norman Rockwell Museum** (9 Rte. 183, 413/298-4100, www.nrm.org, 10am-5pm daily May-Oct., 10am-4pm Mon.-Fri., 10am-5pm Sat.-Sun. Nov.-Apr., $20 adults, children under 18 free) also include six-year-old Ruby Bridges being escorted to school in 1960 and the iconic Four Freedoms. Don't miss the lower level, which displays all of Rockwell's *Saturday Evening Post* covers and shows a short film that includes real-life photos of his models, many who were his Stockbridge neighbors. The museum's pastoral 36-acre site includes the artist's well-preserved barn studio (open May-early Nov.). High-profile changing exhibitions include works by the likes of Warhol and Wyeth.

Other Sights

Even if you've never heard of sculptor Daniel Chester French, you've likely seen images of his work, most famously the Lincoln Memorial in Washington DC to *Minute Man* in Concord, Massachusetts. His country home and "heaven" was **Chesterwood** (4 Williamsville Rd., 413/298-3579, www.chesterwood.org, 10am-5pm daily Memorial Day-Columbus Day, residence closed 12:30pm-2pm daily, $18 adults, $17 seniors, $9 youth 13-17, children under 13 free). Self-guided tours take visitors through his elegantly appointed house, intimate studio, and 122 acres of grounds designed by the artist.

Another of the Berkshire's Gilded Age "cottages," **Naumkeag** (5 Prospect Hill Rd., 413/298-8146, www.thetrustees.org, 10am-5pm daily June-mid-Oct., 10am-5pm Sat.-Sun. Apr.-May and late Oct.-Nov., $15 adults, children under 13 free), which was designed by McKim Mead & White, stands out for being preserved in its entirety, with gorgeous original furnishings that make visiting the house a transporting experience. For many visitors, though, the grounds are the real draw, with deep pools, rustling groves of birch trees, and great mounds of blooming flowers that are perfectly manicured and maintained.

The flowers at the **Berkshire Botanical Garden** (5 W. Stockbridge Rd., 413/298-3926, www.berkshirebotanical.org, 9am-5pm daily May-Oct., $15 adults, $14 seniors, $12 students, children under 12 free) are carefully chosen so there's a new crop of fresh blooms each week, and the 15-acre grounds are a pleasure for plant lovers. Tables and benches invite afternoon picnics, and many of the trails are wheelchair accessible.

Thousands flock to Easter Services at the **National Shrine of the Divine Mercy** (Eden Hill, 413/298-3931, www.thedivinemercy.org, free), an important pilgrimage place for American Roman Catholics. Non-pilgrims can also enjoy the beautiful main church and large (350 acres!), peaceful grounds.

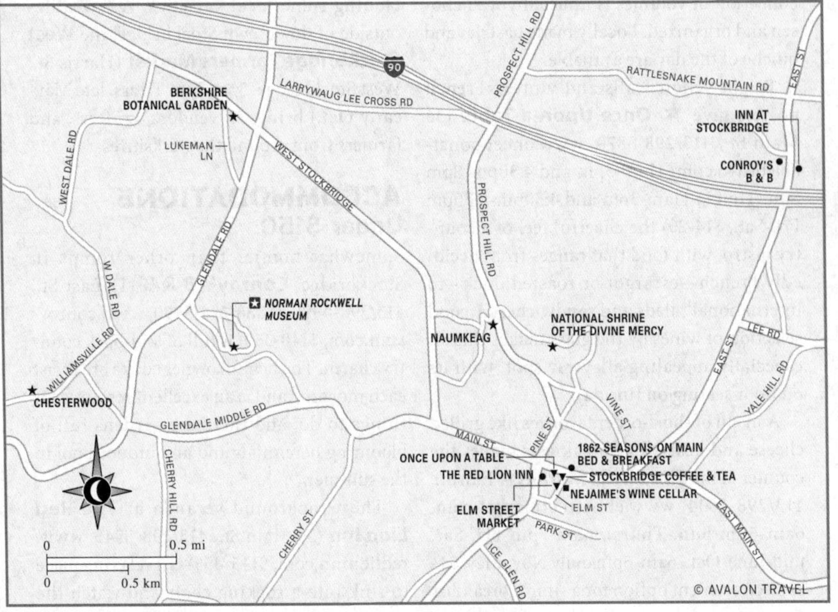

SHOPPING

Stock up on penny candy, gadgets, and old-fashioned knickknacks at **Charles H. Baldwin & Sons** (1 Center St., West Stockbridge, 413/232-7785, www.baldwinextracts.com, 9am-5pm Mon.-Sat., 11am-3pm Sun.), a family-owned country store that also dispenses homemade syrups and extracts that Berkshire bakers swear by.

SPORTS AND RECREATION

Hiking

Just outside of town, the **Ice Glen Trail** (1-mile round-trip, www.laurelhillassociation.org) wraps around giant boulders in a glacial ravine. To reach the trail, follow Park Street to the Housatonic River, crossing on the Goodrich Memorial Footbridge. Cross the railroad tracks and stay right at the fork, following the path into a shaded valley where pockets of snow and ice last well into the summer.

In center Stockbridge, follow Park Street to its dead end for a trailhead for three hikes: Laura's Tower, Ice Glen, and Mary Flynn. Find out more and hire a guide if desired through **Berkshire Hiking** (203/788-7665, http://berkshirehiking.com). **Housatonic Heritage** (860/435-9505, http://housatonicheritage.org) details a 16-mile bike trip around Stockbridge and neighboring towns that can be cut in half if you're short on time or steam. To follow a bike route that Rockwell himself frequently took, search for "bike" on the website of the Norman Rockwell Museum (www.nrm.org).

FOOD

Just off Main Street, **Stockbridge Coffee & Tea** (6 Elm St., 413/931-7044, www.stockbridgecoffeeandtea.com, 7am-5pm daily,

$2-8) serves espresso drinks and Harney & Sons tea in a cozy bookshop, where the small collection of volumes is unusually well chosen and organized. Locally made pastries and quiche of the day are available.

Bright yellow walls and vintage French posters give ★ **Once Upon a Table** (36 Main St., 413/298-3870, www.onceuponatablebistro.com, 11am-3pm and 4:30pm-8pm Sun.-Thurs., 11am-3pm and 4:30pm-8:30pm Fri.-Sat., $14-29) the cheerful feel of a country bistro, with food that ranges from decidedly French—escargot or roasted duck—to international salads and sandwiches. A good selection of wines by the glass makes this an especially appealing alleyway spot, with its outdoor seating on fine days.

A menu of short-order favorites like grilled cheese and hearty egg breakfasts makes the counter at the **Elm Street Market** (4 Elm St., 413/298-3634, www.elmstreetmarket.com, 6am-6pm Sun.-Thurs., 6am-7pm Fri.-Sat. mid-June-Oct., 6am-6pm daily Nov.-May, $4-13) a convenient option for a simple breakfast or lunch, and the stools at the counter have a charming Rockwellian feel to them. It also sells basic groceries.

It's easy to imagine any of the five American presidents that have stayed at **The Red Lion Inn** (30 Main St., 413/298-5545, www.redlion.com, 7:30am-9:30pm daily, $23-34) tucking into the dining room menu of meat and potatoes, which combines with dark wood, old china, and white tablecloths to thoroughly old-fashioned effect. If that's not your scene, you can head down the hall to the casual and atmospheric **Widow Bingham's Tavern** (5pm-8:45pm daily, $11-17) for burgers, sandwiches, and salads under a ceiling bristling with beer steins. A similar menu is available downstairs at the pleasantly cave-like **Lion's Den** (food served 5pm-8pm daily, $9-20), a pub popular with locals and visitors alike, and it hosts live music nightly (8pm-11pm Sun.-Thurs., 9pm-midnight Fri.-Sat., free).

Nejaime's Wine Cellar (3 Elm St., 413/298-3454, www.nejaimeswine.net, 9am-9pm Mon.-Sat., 11am-6pm Sun.) has a great selection of wine, spirits, and beer, including some local varieties. A few miles outside of downtown Stockbridge, the **West Stockbridge Farmers Market** (Harris St., West Stockbridge, 3pm-7pm Thurs. late May-early Oct.) brings in vendors, crafters, and farmers from around the Berkshires.

ACCOMMODATIONS

Under $150

Somewhat homier than other rooms in Stockbridge, **Conroy's B & B** (11 East St., 413/298-4990 or 888/298-5990, www.conroysinn.com, $140-350) is full of laid-back country charm. The helpful owner cooks breakfast each morning and is an excellent resource for things to do, and there are gardens full of blooming perennials and an outdoor pool in the summer.

The wraparound veranda at **The Red Lion Inn** (30 Main St., 413/298-5545, www.redlioninn.com, $115-455) is a relaxing place to sink into a rocking chair and watch the passersby, and the warren-like inn is a fascinating place to explore. Rooms in the main building are furnished with appealing antiques, and the bowed floors and crackled portraits give the hotel a deliciously "olde New England" feel. Stockbridge is something of a company town, and the Red Lion owns much of the block it occupies, with annexes, guesthouses, and a wonderful turn-of-the-20th-century firehouse that was the subject of a Rockwell painting.

$150-250

The friendly innkeepers at ★ **1862 Seasons on Main Bed & Breakfast** (47 Main St., 413/298-5419, www.seasonsonmain.com, $189-395) strike a welcoming balance of luxury and leisure at a convenient location in town; each of the seasonally themed rooms is beautifully decorated but completely livable, and the historic house is full of places to enjoy the inn's morning coffee, afternoon wine, and ice cream nightcaps. Breakfasts are cooked to order and served at the enormous dining room table, and the inn has a private theater furnished with comfy armchairs.

On the road from Stockbridge to Lenox, the **Inn at Stockbridge** (30 Rte. 7, 855/713-0473, www.stockbridgeinn.com, $200-400) is another plush find, with inviting common spaces and treasures from the owners' travels around the world. Home-cooked breakfasts, a heated pool, all-day snacks, and an exercise room are appealing perks, but the inn's location by the highway means more noise than elsewhere.

INFORMATION

The **Stockbridge Chamber of Commerce** (413/298-5200, www.stockbridgechamber.org) has a small, unstaffed visitors' booth on Main Street with information.

GETTING THERE AND AROUND

Stockbridge is located on Route 102, just south of I-90. On-street parking is usually available, but there's no parking on Main Street on Sunday before 2pm—head to South Street, West Main Street, or East Main Street.

Amtrak (800/872-7245, www.amtrak.com) offers service from New York City to Hudson, New York (2 hrs., from $38), 32 miles west of Stockbridge. **Peter Pan Bonanza** (800/343-9999, www.peterpanbus.com) has service from New York City's Port Authority Bus Terminal to Stockbridge (3.5 hrs., $49). Regional buses are run by the **Berkshire Regional Transit Authority** (413/449-2782 or 800/292-2782, www.berkshirerta.com).

Great Barrington

Trees and picket fences give way to faded mill buildings along the Housatonic River when you cross the border into Great Barrington. With restored brick buildings and a mix of old-fashioned hardware stores, boutiques, and restaurants, downtown Great Barrington is a refreshing change of scenery from the curated centers of Lenox and Stockbridge, and a good base for exploring if you need a break from all the quaintness.

Just up the road, the village of Housatonic is an unexpected gem, a tiny satellite of Great Barrington where disused railway depots and crumbling factory buildings keep watch over a tiny downtown with a celebrated bakery and a hip café. Not much remains besides a few signs and markers, but Great Barrington was the childhood home of the great African American writer and academic W. E. B. DuBois, who attended an integrated public school in the late 19th century and left for college with the support of the local church.

SIGHTS

The tiny spire and whitewashed facade of the old Trinity Lutheran Church seem an unlikely place to celebrate a raucous, rebellious folk singer—but peace sign windows offer a hint of what's inside **The Guthrie Center** (2 Van Deusenville Rd., 413/528-1955, www.guthriecenter.org, 10am-4pm Tues.-Sat., free). Arlo Guthrie's album covers and posters decorate every surface of the church's small welcome center, which hosts interfaith services 11am-noon Sunday (services are "BYOG," or "bring your own god"). Free lunch is served to all comers each Wednesday at noon, and local musicians gather for an informal hootenanny on Thursday nights (doors 7pm, show 8pm, $5, performers free). Back when Arlo Guthrie was a student at a progressive boarding school in Stockbridge, the church was home to Alice and Ray Brock, and was immortalized in the rambling, shaggy-dog, antiwar song "Alice's Restaurant."

Fill your bags with blueberries and crisp fall apples at **Windy Hill Farm** (686 Stockbridge Rd., 413/398-3217, www.windyhillfarminc.com, 9am-5pm daily Apr.-Dec.), where pretty rows of Paula Red and Gingergold apples give way to stunning views of nearby Monument Mountain and rolling berry fields. Blueberry

Great Barrington

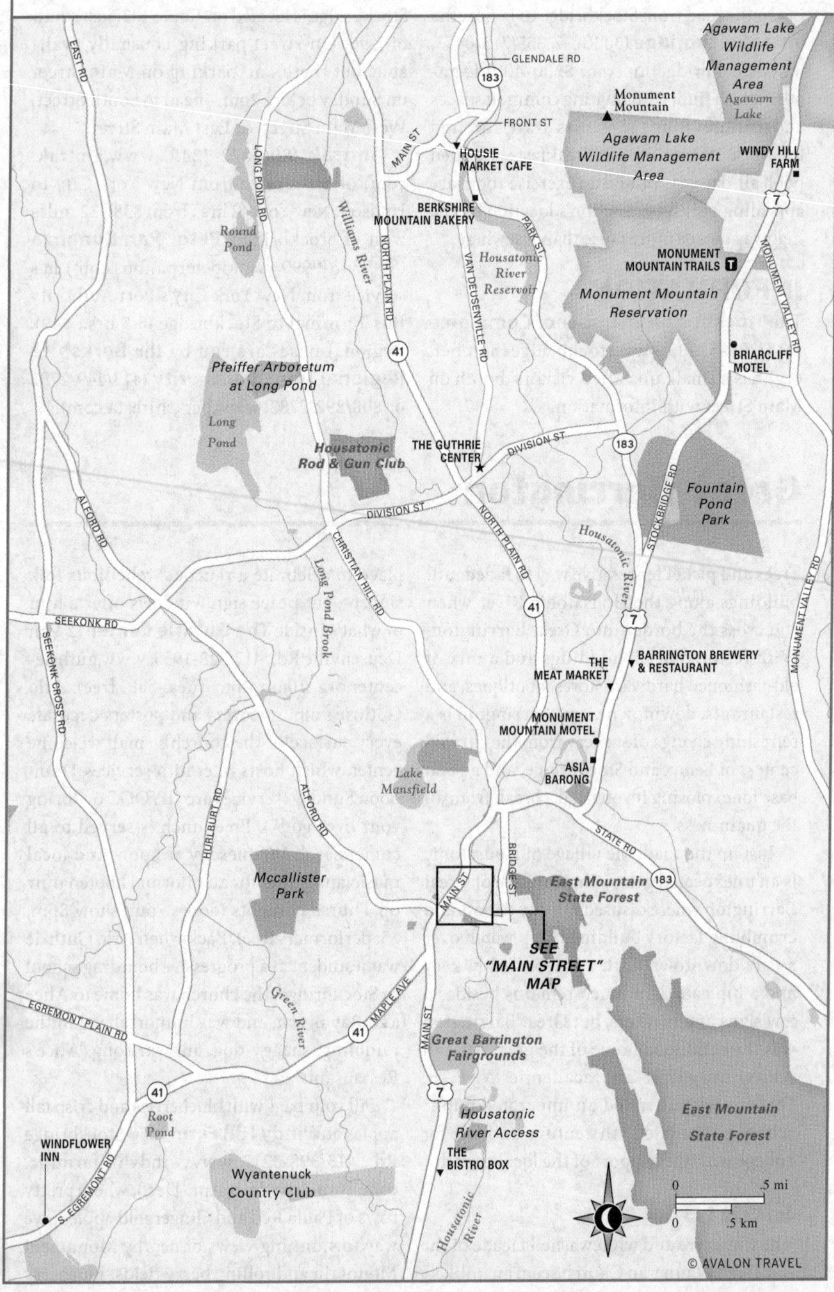

GLENDALE RD
183
FRONT ST
MAIN ST
HOUSIE MARKET CAFE
BERKSHIRE MOUNTAIN BAKERY
Agawam Lake Wildlife Management Area
Agawam Lake
Monument Mountain
Agawam Lake Wildlife Management Area
WINDY HILL FARM
7
EAST RD
LONG POND RD
Williams River
Round Pond
NORTH PLAIN RD
VAN DEUSENVILLE RD
PARK ST
Housatonic River Reservoir
MONUMENT MOUNTAIN TRAILS
MONUMENT VALLEY RD
Monument Mountain Reservation
41
BRIARCLIFF MOTEL
Pfeiffer Arboretum at Long Pond
Long Pond
Housatonic Rod & Gun Club
THE GUTHRIE CENTER
DIVISION ST
STOCKBRIDGE RD
Fountain Pond Park
ALFORD RD
CHRISTIAN HILL RD
Housatonic River
Long Pond Brook
SEEKONK RD
SEEKONK CROSS RD
THE MEAT MARKET
BARRINGTON BREWERY & RESTAURANT
MONUMENT MOUNTAIN MOTEL
ASIA BARONG
HURLBURT RD
Lake Mansfield
STATE RD
BRIDGE ST
Mccallister Park
East Mountain State Forest
SEE "MAIN STREET" MAP
EGREMONT PLAIN RD
MAPLE AVE
Green River
Great Barrington Fairgrounds
Root Pond
Housatonic River Access
WINDFLOWER INN
S EGREMONT RD
Wyantenuck Country Club
THE BISTRO BOX
Housatonic River
East Mountain State Forest
0 .5 mi
0 .5 km
© AVALON TRAVEL

season opens around the beginning of July, and apples are ripe from September until late autumn.

ENTERTAINMENT AND EVENTS

Pronounced muh-HAY-wee, **The Mahaiwe Performing Arts Center** (14 Castle St., 413/528-0100, www.mahaiwe.org) is located in a restored 100-year-old theater and presents a first-rate, if eclectic, lineup of music, spoken-word, and theater performances. What Tanglewood is to symphony music, the **Aston Magna Festival** (Daniel Arts Center, Alford Rd., 413/528-3595 or 888/492-1283 for tickets, www.astonmagna.org, $40 per concert) is to chamber music. During weekends in July and early August, both vocal and instrumental masters of the form perform at Simon's Rock College.

SHOPPING

There are plenty of places to browse for antiques in town, but one of the most intriguing is **Asia Barong** (199 Stockbridge Rd., 413/528-5091, http://asiabarong.com, 11am-5pm Wed.-Mon.), an enormous multilevel collection of art from all over Asia that encompasses everything from treasures to trinkets. For more antiques, outside of Great Barrington, the stretch of Route 7 down to Sheffield is known as **antiques alley** for its many fine such stores (maps of the antiques stores are available at most destinations). One particularly worthy stop is the **Painted Porch** (102 S. Main St., Sheffield, 413/229-2700, www.paintedporch.com, 10am-5pm Thurs.-Mon.), whose owners scour the English and French countrysides for rare furniture.

Founded by supporters of the progressive Rudolf Steiner School, Great Barrington's **Matrushka Toys & Gifts** (309 Main St., 413/528-6911, www.berkshiretoys.com, 10am-5pm Mon.-Sat., 11am-4pm Sun.) is strictly electronics free, instead filled with handcrafted toys made from natural materials, as well as children's costumes, clothes, and books.

Main Street

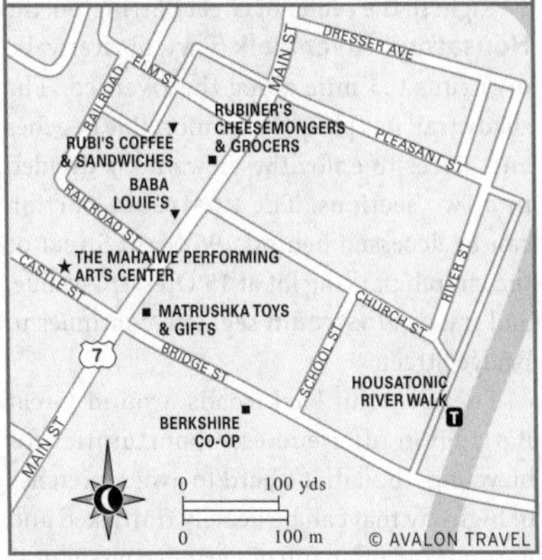

SPORTS AND RECREATION

Hiking and Biking

Find a clear day to ascend **Monument Mountain,** and you'll get views from Mount Greylock on the Vermont border to the New York Catskill Mountains, with plenty of Housatonic River Valley scenery in between. Two trails leave from a small parking lot on Route 7 (just north of Briarcliff Motel, parking $5): Turn left onto the 1.5-mile **Indian Monument Trail,** which traces a relatively gentle path past crumbling stone walls and carriage roads, or head right on the 0.8-mile **Hickey Trail** and pick a line straight up the slope. The two trails join at 0.6 mile beneath the summit, where the **Squaw Peak Trail** reaches the finest views of the hike. Regardless of the route, plan on two hours for a round-trip to the summit.

The **Appalachian Trail** passes just south of Great Barrington as it winds from Georgia to Maine, and you can get a taste of the 2,160-mile trail in **Beartown State Forest** (69 Bluehill Rd., Monterey, 413/528-0904, $10), which has miles of hiking and multiuse trails. Walking on the Appalachian is generally an out-and-back that can be as long, or short, as you like, but the forest's most popular trail is the gorgeous **Benedict Pond Loop Trail,** an easy hike that wraps 1.5 miles around a tree-fringed lake.

Right in the center of Great Barrington, the **Housatonic River Walk** (www.gbriverwalk.org) runs 0.5 mile along the riverbed. The shady trail has plenty of comfortable benches and places to enjoy the view and is divided into two sections. The **upstream** portion can be accessed behind 195 Main Street or the church parking lot at 15 Dresser Avenue, and the **downstream** segment continues to Bridge Street.

The plentiful back roads around Great Barrington offer endless opportunities for bicycling, though it's hard to avoid stretches of highway that can be heavily trafficked and narrow (and often full of meandering sightseers). An excellent resource for finding a route is **Great Barrington Trails & Greenways** (www.gbtrails.org), whose online map designates the roads best suited for cycling; among the best is the 15-mile ride down the Housatonic River Valley to Sheffield and back. Get a bike (and some helpful advice) at **Berkshire Bike and Board** (29 State Rd., 413/528-5555, www.berkshirebikeandboard.com, 10am-6pm Mon.-Fri., 10am-5pm Sat., 11am-5pm Sun., rentals $25 for 4 hours, $40 for 24 hours).

Winter Sports

Ski Butternut (380 State Rd., 413/528-2000, www.skibutternut.com, $25-65 ages 14 to 69, $20-55 youth 7 to 13, $15-30 children under 7, $20-55 seniors over 69) is known for teaching first-time skiers. Every day at 10:30am and 2pm, anyone who has never skied before gathers at the sign "Never Skied Start Here" after first paying for a $75 package that includes boot and ski rentals (helmets are $15 extra). Butternut also has eight tubing lanes ($20 for 2 hours) on the far left side of the parking lot—a "magic carpet" lift makes getting to the top again easy.

A large-for-the-area, family-run mountain, **Catamount** (17 Nicholson Rd., S. Egremont, 518/325-3200 or 413/528-1262, www.catamountski.com, $36 ages 16-69, $31 youth 7-13 and seniors 70-79, $17 children under 7) is 15 minutes west of Great Barrington, straddling the state line between Massachusetts and New York.

FOOD

Simple grilled sandwiches are transformed by beautiful cheeses and cured meats at ★ **rubi's coffee & sandwiches** (256 Main St., 413/528-0488, www.rubiners.com, 7am-6pm Mon.-Fri., 8am-6pm Sat., 8am-5pm Sun.,

hiking Monument Mountain

$5-13), the café cousin of Great Barrington's cheesemonger, Rubiner's. The tuna melt oozes with rich comté and crisp baby dill pickles, and a country-style pâté gets a vinegar bite from rustic Dijon mustard. The small café serves espresso and natural wines by the glass, and the small outdoor courtyard is an appealing place to enjoy a meal.

Great Barrington's answer to the New England snack bar is ★ **The Bistro Box** (937 S. Main St., 413/717-5958, www.thebistrobox.rocks, 11am-7pm Mon.-Tues. and Thurs.-Sat., 11am-4pm Sun., May-Nov., $4-10), run by a pair of married chefs with serious kitchen chops. Hand-cut truffle fries are luxurious alongside grass-fed burgers topped with tomato jam and garlic aioli, and the chefs incorporate fresh and foraged foods into specials like wild ramp pesto and blueberry lemonade. Lawn seating and picnic tables are available.

The thin and crusty sourdough pizza at **Baba Louie's** (286 Main St., 413/528-8100, www.babalouiepizza.com, 11:30am-3pm and 5:30pm-9:30pm Mon.-Thurs. and Sun., 11:30am-3pm and 5:30pm-10pm Fri.-Sat., $8-13) is a strong contender for the best in the Berkshires, and the cozy hole-in-the-wall restaurant is impressively laid-back for the quality of its pies. Gluten-free crusts get raves, and the fig, Gorgonzola, and prosciutto pizza is an outrageously flavorful blend of sweet and savory.

The sprawling menu of sandwiches, salads, burgers, and other classic American mains might not make any headlines in Great Barrington's food scene, but **Barrington Brewery & Restaurant** (420 Stockbridge Rd., 413/528-8282, www.barringtonbrewery.net, $5-20) is relaxed and appealing and offers a serious list of great beers. Head straight through the dining room for the bar, where regulars' potter mugs hang overhead, and coasters from breweries around the world are tacked onto every possible surface. The tap lists changes with the season, but the Black Bear Stout and Barrington Brown are local favorites.

Young, hip, and totally unexpected, **Housie Market Cafe** (226 Pleasant St., Housatonic, 413/274-0261, www.housiemarket.com, 7am-5pm Mon.-Fri., 8:30am-4pm Sat.-Sun., $3-9) is right at home in Housatonic's cheerfully ramshackle downtown. Breakfast bowls, sandwiches, and hearty lunches range from comforting to offbeat: Local workers come in for the "contractors special" of eggs, cheddar, and bacon between two slabs of bread, but some regulars swear by the peanut butter and kimchi sandwich.

Pack the picnic hamper of your dreams at **Rubiner's Cheesemongers & Grocers** (246 Main St., 413/528-0488, www.rubiners.com, 10am-6pm Mon.-Sat., 10am-5pm Sun.), which stocks cheese from farms in the Berkshires, Vermont, and beyond, along with a charcuterie case filled with rich pâtés, dried sausages, and duck confit. Then find award-winning wholesome loaves in Housatonic's **Berkshire Mountain Bakery** (367 Rte. 136, Housatonic, 413/274-1313, www.berkshiremountainbakery.com, 8am-7pm Mon.-Sat., 8:30am-6pm Sun.), where baker Richard Bourdon has been making artisanal bread since long before it was cool. Many grains are sprouted and ground on-site, and breads are naturally fermented. Cooperatively owned and stocked with piles of local food, **Berkshire Co-op** (42 Bridge St., 413/528-9697, www.berkshire.coop, 8am-8pm daily) also has a good deli with smoothies, sandwiches, and salads.

ACCOMMODATIONS AND CAMPING

The sweet country style at **Windflower Inn** (684 S. Egremont Rd., 413/528-2720, www.windflowerinn.com, $140-250) perfectly befits the Berkshires' old-fashioned charm. Fires blaze in a stone fireplace in one room, an outdoor swimming pool is ringed by perennial blooms, and the homemade breakfasts and comfortable beds are divine.

Rooms are a bit dated but neat as a pin at the **Monument Mountain Motel** (247

Stockbridge Rd., 413/551-4615, www.monumentmountainmotel.com, $105-215) on Route 7, which is lined with similar properties. The in-ground pool, play area, and basketball court make it a nice choice for families.

The standard, roadside exterior of the ★ **Briarcliff Motel** (506 Stockbridge Rd., 413/207-9420, www.thebriarcliffmotel.com, $90-250) offers few clues to the freshly renovated rooms, which are decorated with modern flair and a great sense of style. Each is unique, with artwork on the walls and small sitting areas, as well as several barrier-free, accessible bathrooms, a rarity in the Berkshires. Great coffee and homemade granola are served along with pastries, organic yogurt, and hard-boiled eggs for the continental breakfast, and DVD players, a fire pit, and a pleasant wooded location outside of town make this a nice place to relax.

Camping

Beartown State Forest (69 Bluehill Rd., Monterey, 413/528-0904, www.mass.gov, $16) has just 12 sites (and no showers), but the 10,000-acre preserve is a wonderfully quiet place to spend the night about 30 minutes outside of Great Barrington, especially if you can snag site 11, which occupies an idyllic, private spot on the edge of a lake.

INFORMATION

The **Southern Berkshires Chamber of Commerce** runs a **visitors center** (326 Main St., 413/528-1510, www.southernberkshirechamber.com, 11am-5pm Sat.-Mon.) with information on the town as well as the rest of the region. The hours at this small office can vary somewhat unpredictably, especially during off-season months, so call before visiting.

GETTING THERE AND AROUND

Route 7 runs through the middle of Great Barrington, where ample parking is available downtown. **Peter Pan Bonanza** (800/343-9999, www.peterpanbus.com) has service to Great Barrington from Boston (7 hrs., 15 min., $63) and New York City's Port Authority Bus Terminal (3 hrs., 35 min., $50). Regional buses are run by the **Berkshire Regional Transit Authority** (413/449-2782 or 800/292-2782, www.berkshirerta.com).

Connecticut

Look for ★ to find recommended sights, activities, dining, and lodging.

Highlights

★ **Yale University Campus:** Spend an Ivy League afternoon—or week—in the university's wonderful museums, which range from natural history to British art (page 194).

★ **Paddling the Thimble Islands:** Keep your eyes peeled for pirate gold as you explore the tiny islets that speckle Long Island Sound (page 197).

★ **Silver Sands State Park:** Take time to wander the expansive salt marshes and dunes, but the beach is the real draw here, with gorgeous sand that invites lazy days by the water (page 198).

★ **Mystic Seaport Museum:** Step into the life of a 19th-century seafaring community at this living museum, where you can hoist a sail, meet costumed interpreters, or belt out a sea shanty (page 202).

★ **Mashantucket Pequot Museum & Research Center:** The foremost Native American research institute in New England is also a fascinating museum (page 202).

Though often overshadowed by its showstopping neighbors, the "land of steady habits" is full of quirky surprises—don't make the mistake of dismissing Connecticut as an extended New York suburb. Drive the state's scenic coastal road and you'll find dreamy beaches, old-fashioned fishing villages, and an archipelago of tiny islands scattered across Long Island Sound. Head inland to discover a landscape of farms, fields, and forests, then explore New England's native cultures at the Mashantucket Pequot Museum & Research Center.

Of all the states in New England, Connecticut embodies the greatest contrasts, and nowhere is that more apparent than in the eastern part of the state, which is home to big cities, rural farm country, and the state's largest tourist attractions: Mystic Seaport and a pair of behemoth casinos. East of the Connecticut River, the state looks more toward New England than New York, and much of the land here is—or was—devoted to farming. The remnants of stone walls and foundations are still visible through the trees in land that has been slowly reclaimed by forest.

PLANNING YOUR TIME

If you have just one day to spend in eastern Connecticut, head straight to the historic shipbuilding center of Mystic. The reconstructed 19th-century community of **Mystic Seaport** is among New England's top historical attractions, and one of the best maritime museums anywhere. With a bit more time, spend several days along the southeast coastline, exploring the salty city of New London and the historic village of Stonington.

For a taste of Connecticut's high culture, overnight in the revitalized university city of New Haven, home to Yale's gorgeous campus and fine museums. The jewel in its crown is the highly acclaimed **Yale Center for British Art.** After a day or two in New Haven, give yourself another two or three days to drive down the coast.

And while the northeastern Quiet Corner offers few formal attractions, it would be easy to while away a few days there, relaxing with long looping bike rides through dairy farms and picking your own apples at country orchards.

Previous: aerial view of New Haven; Silver Sands State Park Beach. **Above:** Essex Riverfront.

Connecticut

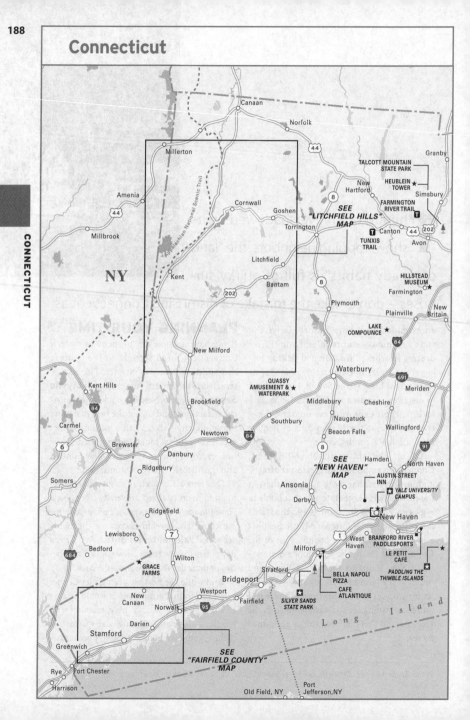

NY
Canaan
Norfolk
Millerton
Amenia
Millbrook
Cornwall
Goshen
Torrington
Appalachian National Scenic Trail
Litchfield
Kent
Bantam
Plymouth
New Milford
Granby
TALCOTT MOUNTAIN STATE PARK
HEUBLEIN TOWER
New Hartford
Simsbury
FARMINGTON RIVER TRAIL
SEE "LITCHFIELD HILLS" MAP
Canton
Avon
TUNXIS TRAIL
HILLSTEAD MUSEUM
Farmington
New Britain
Plainville
LAKE COMPOUNCE
Waterbury
QUASSY AMUSEMENT & WATERPARK
Meriden
Middlebury
Cheshire
Naugatuck
Southbury
Wallingford
Beacon Falls
Kent Hills
Brookfield
Carmel
Newtown
Brewster
Danbury
Ridgebury
Somers
SEE "NEW HAVEN" MAP
Hamden
North Haven
AUSTIN STREET INN
YALE UNIVERSITY CAMPUS
Ansonia
Derby
New Haven
Ridgefield
Lewisboro
Bedford
Wilton
GRACE FARMS
West Haven
BRANFORD RIVER PADDLESPORTS
Milford
LE PETIT CAFÉ
Stratford
BELLA NAPOLI PIZZA
PADDLING THE THIMBLE ISLANDS
Bridgeport
CAFE ATLANTIQUE
New Canaan
Westport
Fairfield
SILVER SANDS STATE PARK
Norwalk
Long Island
Darien
Stamford
Greenwich
SEE "FAIRFIELD COUNTY" MAP
Rye
Port Chester
Harrison
Old Field, NY
Port Jefferson, NY

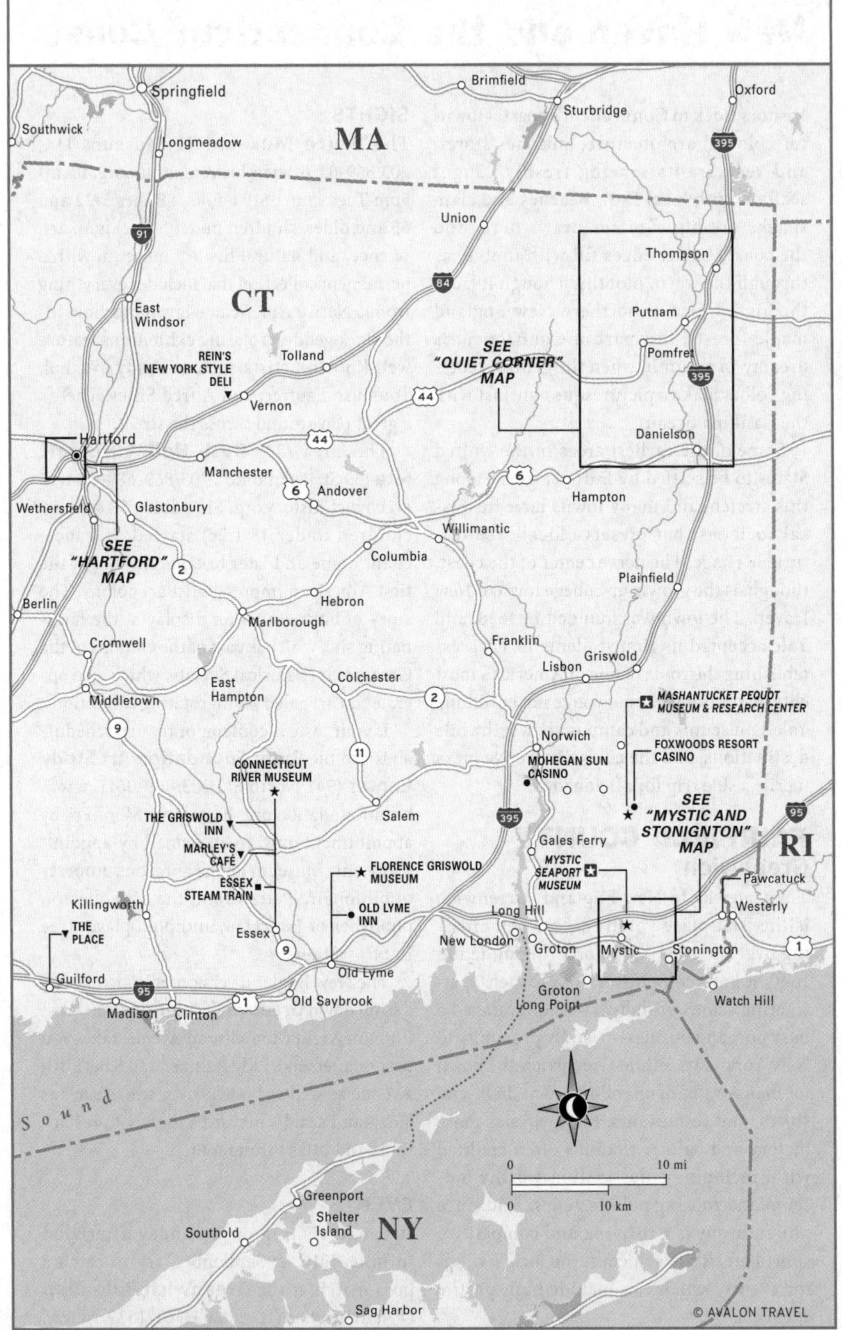

MA
CT
RI
NY
Springfield
Southwick
Longmeadow
Brimfield
Sturbridge
Oxford
Union
Thompson
Putnam
Pomfret
Danielson
East Windsor
Tolland
REIN'S NEW YORK STYLE DELI
Vernon
SEE "QUIET CORNER" MAP
Hartford
Manchester
Andover
Hampton
Wethersfield
Glastonbury
SEE "HARTFORD" MAP
Willimantic
Columbia
Plainfield
Berlin
Hebron
Marlborough
Cromwell
Franklin
Griswold
Lisbon
East Hampton
Colchester
Middletown
MASHANTUCKET PEQUOT MUSEUM & RESEARCH CENTER
Norwich
FOXWOODS RESORT CASINO
MOHEGAN SUN CASINO
CONNECTICUT RIVER MUSEUM
SEE "MYSTIC AND STONINGTON" MAP
THE GRISWOLD INN
Salem
Gales Ferry
MARLEY'S CAFÉ
MYSTIC SEAPORT MUSEUM
FLORENCE GRISWOLD MUSEUM
ESSEX STEAM TRAIN
Pawcatuck
Killingworth
OLD LYME INN
Long Hill
Westerly
THE PLACE
Essex
New London
Groton
Mystic
Stonington
Guilford
Old Lyme
Groton Long Point
Watch Hill
Madison
Clinton
Old Saybrook
Sound
0
10 mi
0
10 km
Greenport
Shelter Island
Southold
Sag Harbor
© AVALON TRAVEL

New Haven and the Connecticut Coast

Visitors flock to Connecticut's coastal towns for colonial architecture, antiques stores, and restaurants serving freshly caught seafood with local flair. Beaches and clam shacks are big summer draws here, and the coast's sandy edges fill with umbrellas through the warm months. Though it lacks the high drama of northern New England maple forests, this part of Connecticut is dreamy in autumn, when the gently changing colors make a picturesque contrast with the flanking ocean.

Some of the earliest areas in the United States to be settled by Europeans are along this stretch, and many towns have historical societies that preserve local architectural heritage. The nerve center of the coast, though, is the grown-up college town of New Haven. The town was founded in 1638, and Yale accepted its first students in 1701, establishing the roots of one of America's most elite institutions. Even if you're not enrolling, Yale's museums and campus are worthwhile destinations, and the city's distinctive pizza merits a side trip for aficionados.

FAIRFIELD COUNTY

Greenwich

The Gateway to New England, Greenwich is the first place you'll reach when crossing over the New York border. Founded in 1640, it has a long history of prosperity, attracting scions of industry who leveraged a busy port and business-friendly proximity to New York City. While Greenwich is known for mansions built on rolling lawns, high-end stores, and restaurants, the town has more history and culture than it's often credited with, including a destination-worthy museum and rousing polo matches. And since philanthropy is a thriving and competitive sport here, it's worth checking local listings for events, which can include high-profile speakers.

SIGHTS

The **Bruce Museum** (1 Museum Dr., 203/869-0376, www.brucemuseum.org, 10am-5pm Tues.-Sun., $10 adults, $8 ages 5-22 and 65 and older, children under 5 free) is an art, science, and natural history museum with a permanent collection that includes everything from a Native American wigwam to glow-in-the-dark geodes; rotating exhibitions feature well-known artists such as Andy Warhol, Toulouse-Lautrec, and Alfred Sisley. There's a great playground across the street.

The circa 1730 **Bush-Holley Historic Site** (39 Strickland Rd., 203/869-6899, www.greenwichhistory.org, $10 adults, $8 seniors, children under 18 free) started as a merchant home and later became the site of the first American impressionist art colony. The story of both eras is on display at the fascinating site, which is part of the campus of the Greenwich Historical Society, which also operates an art gallery with rotating exhibitions.

If your taste is contemporary art, schedule a visit to the **Brant Foundation Art Study Center** (941 North St., 203/869-0611, www.brantfoundation.org, 10am-4pm Mon.-Fri. by appointment only, free), a small by-appointment-only museum on the gorgeous property of billionaire Peter Brant, the art collector, publisher of *Interview*, and polo player (see *Events* section).

The New England version of Rodeo Drive, a stroll down **Greenwich Avenue** from West Putnam Avenue to Railroad Avenue takes you past retailers like Lilly Pulitzer and Saks Fifth Avenue as well as homegrown stores such as Hoagland's and Vineyard Vines, with restaurants and cafés throughout.

EVENTS

If you're visiting on a Sunday afternoon in June, July, or September, try to catch a polo match at the **Greenwich Polo Club** (1 Hurlingham Dr., 203/561-1639, www.

Fairfield County

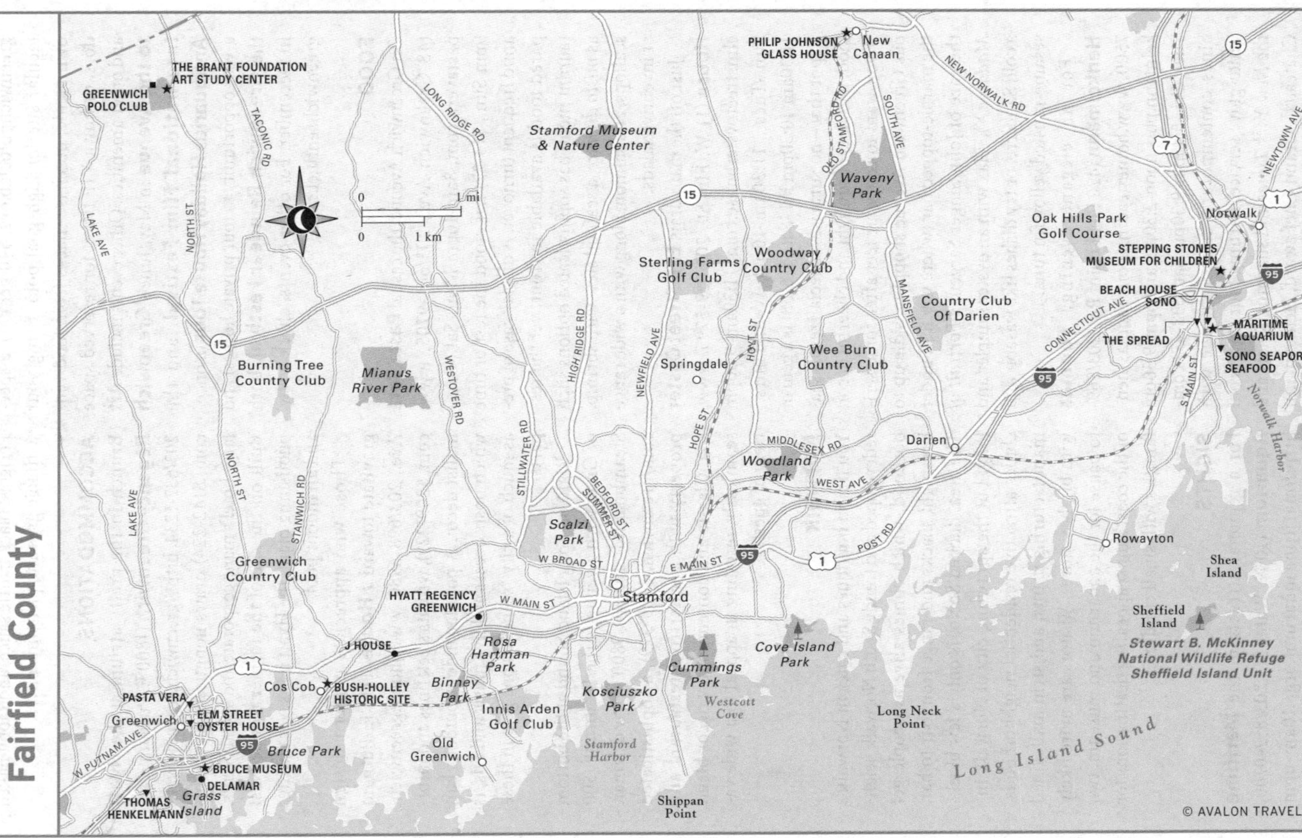

greenwichpoloclub.org, $40 per car), a spectacular site for high-goal polo. Bring your own picnic, purchase snacks from food vendors, or buy a VIP ticket for reserved space and other amenities. Other events include **Art to the Avenue** in May, June's **Greenwich International Film Festival,** and the **Antiquarius Holiday House Tour** (a once-a-year opportunity to tour private homes) and the **Greenwich Reindeer Festival,** both in December. For other events, check www.greenwichsentinel.com.

FOOD

On Greenwich Avenue, the casual **Pasta Vera** (48 Greenwich Ave., 203/661-9705, www.pastavera.com, 8am-10pm Mon.-Sat., 8am-9pm Sun., $13-27) has stood the test of time amid frequent turnover. A display case of prepared food is available in front, yet the restaurant menu has sophisticated options such as *misto di mare*, a seafood stew with shrimp, scallops, and salmon, along with a wide range of inventive salads.

Just off the main drag, **Elm Street Oyster House** (11 W. Elm St., 203/629-5795, www.elmstreetoysterhouse.com, 11:30am-9:30pm Sun.-Tues., 11:30am-10pm Wed.-Thurs., 11:30am-10:30pm Fri.-Sat., $16-38) is a gem of a spot that—no surprise—specializes in seafood, with lots of sunlight and cheerful decor. If you want to rest your feet after some serious Greenwich Avenue shopping, sidle up to the marble-topped bar (where you'll sit under the gaze of John Singer Sargent's *Portrait of Madame X*), relax with an oyster sampler and a cold Sancerre, or try dishes like wasabi- and sesame-crusted yellowfin tuna.

For an elegant evening, **Thomas Henkelmann** (420 Field Point Rd., 203/869-7500, www.homesteadinn.com/thomas-henkelmann.php, noon-2:30pm and 6pm-9:30pm Tues.-Fri., 5:45pm-9:30pm Sat., $38-47) combines contemporary French cuisine with white-glove service. Earning four stars from the *New York Times* and snagging Relais and Châteaux's Grand Chef award, Henkelmann is known for classics like sweetbreads in a Périgord black truffle sauce, and rabbit baked with foie gras and picholine olives.

ACCOMMODATIONS

Brunch in the pretty atrium at the **Hyatt Regency Greenwich** (1800 E. Putnam Ave., 203/637-1234, http://greenwich.regency.hyatt.com, $142-224) draws nonguests, as do this large hotel's many corporate and social events. Built on the site of the former Condé Nast publishing plant, the Hyatt has several wings and an indoor pool.

Those who appreciate modern design gravitate toward **J House** (1114 E. Putnam Ave., 203/698-6980, www.jhousegreenwich.com, $209-229), with its sleek lines and minimalist decor. A popular indoor/outdoor bar, which hosts occasional live music and DJs, is as much of a city "scene" as one gets in these parts.

Right on Long Island Sound at the bottom of Greenwich Avenue is the **Delamar** (500 Steamboat Rd., 203/661-9800, www.delamar.com/greenwich, $309-329), a sophisticated property with a waterfront restaurant and spa. Classic and contemporary decor blend seamlessly, resulting in appeal to a wide variety of guests.

Norwalk

You'll find boutiques and cafés in Norwalk's redeveloped and trendy South Norwalk neighborhood, which comes alive as people get late-night snacks and range from bar to bar. The area, dubbed SoNo, is only a few blocks long, but the sprawling city of Norwalk includes attractive residential neighborhoods, manufacturing plants, and strip malls lined with big-box stores. Visitors are more likely to pause for the aquarium and museum, two of the coast's most appealing destinations for families with small children.

SIGHTS

For a regional attraction, the **Maritime Aquarium** (10 N. Water St., 203/852-0700, http://maritimeaquarium.org, 10am-6pm daily July-Aug., 10am-5pm daily Sept.-June,

$22.95 adults, $20.95 children 13-17 and seniors 65 and above, $15.95 children 3-12) impresses with sharks, both a ray and jellyfish touch pool, and a few profoundly adorable meerkats. The aquarium also operates an IMAX theater and harbor cruises that focus on the natural history of the area.

A favorite with the preschool crowd, **Stepping Stones Museum for Children** (303 West Ave., 203/899-0606, www.steppingstonesmuseum.org, 10am-5pm daily June-Aug., 10am-5pm Tues.-Sun. Sept.-May, $15 adults and children, $10 seniors over 62, free active military and infants under 1 year) has an indoor water-play area, a seasonal miniature train ride, and a separate location for toddlers to explore, ride the mini school bus, and play dress up. At the back of the parking lot and not affiliated with the museum, **Devon's Place Playground** has equipment for both younger and older kids as well as a seasonal, outdoor water splash pad.

FOOD

With a patio of picnic tables overlooking Norwalk Harbor, **SoNo Seaport Seafood** (100 Water St., 203/854-9483, sonoseaportseafood.com, 11am-10pm daily summer, 11am-9pm daily winter, $8-26) is a classic go-to spot in the summer for New England-style seafood. There's indoor seating as well so people can get their fix of fried clams, soft shell crabs, shrimp, and oysters year-round. In addition to fried specialties, the menu offers blackened shrimp salad, lobster potpie, and Alaskan king crab legs.

Get your fill of shrimp and grits or chicken and waffles at **Beach House SoNo** (19 N. Water St., 203/956-7171, www.beachhousesono.com, 11:30am-3pm and 5pm-10pm Mon.-Thurs., 11:30am-3pm and 5pm-10:30pm Fri., 11:30am-2:30pm and 5pm-10:30pm Sat., 10:30am-5pm Sun., $12-29), which also serves more refined options, like crackling duck with carrot-ginger purée. Brunch draws crowds for pitchers of bacon-infused Bloody Marys and eggs Benedict with a Southern twist.

You can make a meal of the small plates at **The Spread** (70 N. Main St., 203/939-1111, www.thespreadsono.com, 5pm-10pm Mon.-Thurs., 5pm-11pm Fri.-Sat., 11am-4pm and 5pm-10pm Sun., $17-36), a lively restaurant and bar with an industrial-chic vibe. Mexican-born chef Carlos Baez trained in top Connecticut seafood restaurants and combines those influences into vibrant dishes like grilled Portuguese octopus with chorizo topped with cotija cheese.

New Caanan

A sleepy, leafy, New York City suburb, compact New Canaan is less cosmopolitan than Greenwich or Norwalk. In the tidy, walkable town center there's a selection of restaurants and coffee shops, shops, and a theater, but the quiet town has some surprising finds. Both the Philip Johnson Glass House and Grace Farms are pilgrimage places for architecture buffs, with modern design that melds with the bucolic scenery.

SIGHTS

This suburban town seems an unlikely vanguard for modernist architecture, but this is where the renowned architect Philip Johnson built his groundbreaking Glass House in 1949. Operated by the National Trust for Historic Preservation since Johnson's death in 2005, the **Philip Johnson Glass House** (Visitor Center, 199 Elm St., 203/594-9884, www.theglasshouse.org, 9:45am-2:30pm Thurs.-Mon. May-Nov., 1-hour tour $25, 3-hour tour $100 weekdays, $120 weekends) is fascinating to explore. Tours, which take in the house, landscape design, and the sculpture and art sprinkled throughout the property, depart from the visitor center in downtown New Canaan.

Also featuring sublime glass architecture, **Grace Farms** (365 Lukes Wood Rd., 203/920-1702, www.gracefarms.org, 10am-6pm Tues.-Sat., noon-6pm Sun., free) has five buildings that are connected by an undulating covered walkway that rolls down the fall line of the hillside. Set on 80 acres and used by nonprofit organizations, this relaxing space is especially beautiful in the autumn.

Getting There and Around

Greenwich, Norwalk, and New Canaan are in Fairfield County, which is served by major roads I-95 and Route 15 (Merritt Parkway).

The **Metro-North** (877/690-5116, www.mta.info) commuter rail line has stations in these towns, while the closest **Amtrak** (800/872-7245, www.amtrak.com) station is Stamford, which has rental car agencies and a taxi stand on the northbound side. You will need quarters for parking in downtown Greenwich; Norwalk meters accept change of all types as well as credit cards; New Canaan meters vary in their acceptance of change, bills, and credit. **Greenwich Taxi** (203/869-6000, www.greenwichtaxiinc.com) deploys taxis from the northbound platform of the Greenwich Metro-North train station, and Fairfield County is also served by **Uber. Norwalk Transit** (www.norwalktransit.com) operates public buses that connect the Greenwich and Norwalk train stations with popular locations in those towns.

NEW HAVEN

The sprawling city of New Haven is a blend of historic architecture, picturesque town greens, and some unpolished urban grit that's survived recent revitalization. One of the country's oldest cities, New Haven thrived for three centuries as an active port, then fell under the malaise that struck many other Connecticut cities in the mid-20th century, effectively making Yale an island in a city with a reputation for drugs and violence.

More than any other city in the state, however, New Haven has experienced a rebirth—led by an active decision by the university to invest in the city's infrastructure and improve its image. Nowadays, New Haven is known around the state as a funky and educated oasis with active arts programming and venues that attract major music and sporting events. The real surprise, however, are the rural delights just beyond the city limits, from the beautiful Thimble Islands to the small-town charmers that stretch east along the coast.

Sights

★ YALE UNIVERSITY CAMPUS

Founded in 1701, Yale was the third college in the United States, and quickly established a rivalry with its northern neighbor Harvard, founding a tradition of one-upmanship that's alive and well. In contrast with Harvard's distinctive brick buildings, many of Yale's buildings are done in a striking Gothic style, making a tour of the campus a genuine visual treat. Tours start at the **Yale University Visitor Center** (149 Elm St., 203/432-2300, www.yale.edu/visitor, 10:30am and 2pm Mon.-Fri., 1:30pm Sat.-Sun., free) and include visits to several of Yale's libraries, including the rare-book library, which holds a copy of the Gutenberg Bible.

In addition to its collection of British art, Yale also has several other outstanding museums. The **Yale University Art Gallery** (1111 Chapel St., 203/432-0600, http://artgallery.yale.edu, 10am-5pm Tues.-Fri., 11am-5pm Sat.-Sun., until 8pm Thurs. Sept.-June, free) holds works from all over the world, with a strong collection of medieval European paintings and several fine canvases by American modernist Edward Hopper.

The **Yale Collection of Musical Instruments** (15 Hillhouse Ave., 203/432-0822, http://collection.yale.edu, 1pm-4pm Tues.-Fri., 1pm-5pm Sun. Sept.-June, free) includes instruments from all over the globe, starting with a 1,000-year-old Incan conch trumpet; a "sound gallery" plays highlights from Yale concerts.

The **Peabody Museum of Natural History** (170 Whitney Ave., 203/432-5050 or 203/432-8987, www.yale.edu/peabody, 10am-5pm Tues.-Sat., noon-5pm Sun., $13 adults, $9 seniors, $6 students and children 3-18, free to all 2pm-5pm Thurs. Sept.-June) has exhibits drawn from Yale expeditions, including a fascinating study of the history of evolution. The centerpiece, however, remains the famous dinosaur skeletons—including stegosaurus,

Downtown New Haven

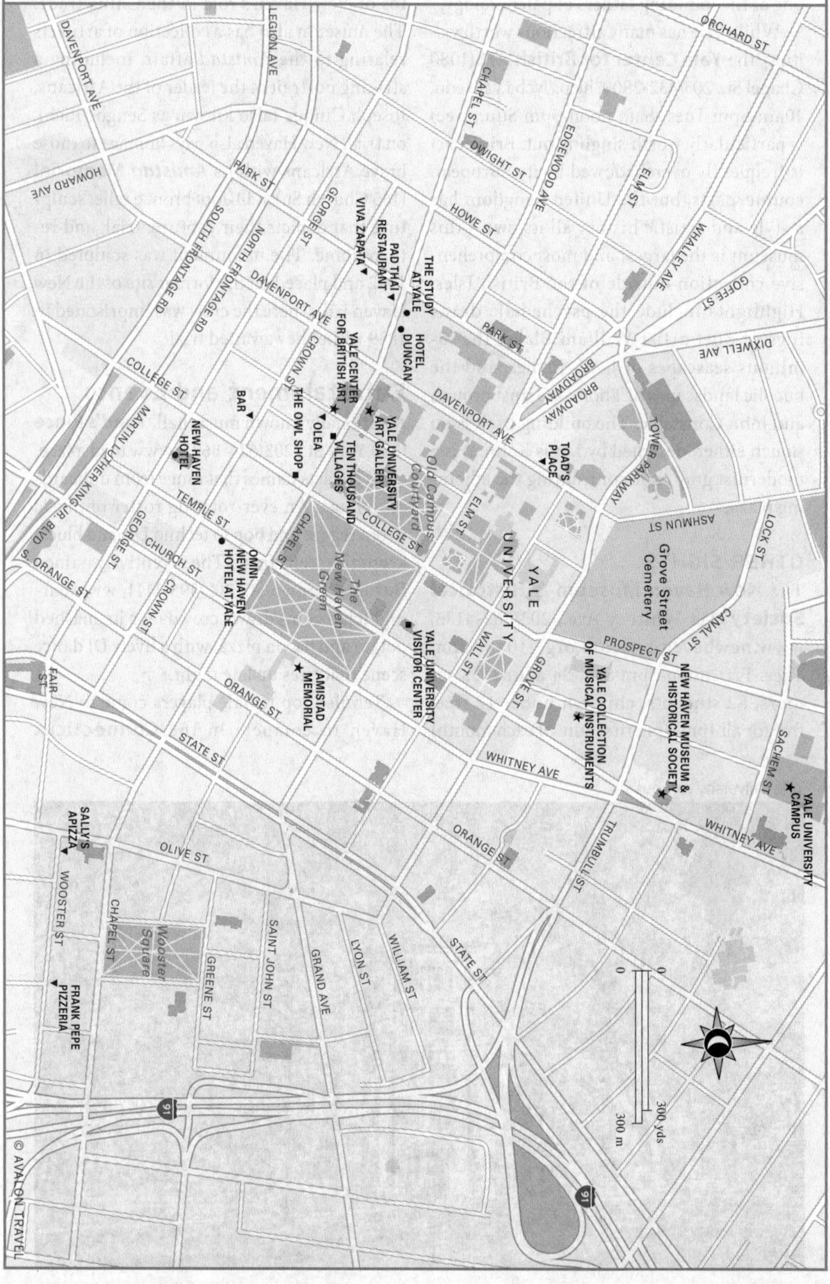

DAVENPORT AVE
LEGION AVE
CHAPEL ST
ORCHARD ST
EDGEWOOD AVE
DWIGHT ST
ELM ST
HOWARD AVE
PARK ST
GEORGE ST
SOUTH FRONTAGE RD
NORTH FRONTAGE RD
VIVA ZAPATA
PAD THAI RESTAURANT
THE STUDY AT YALE
HOWE ST
WHALLEY AVE
GOFFE ST
DAVENPORT AVE
HOTEL DUNCAN
YALE CENTER FOR BRITISH ART
PARK ST
DIXWELL AVE
BROADWAY
BROADWAY
COLLEGE ST
CROWN ST
BAR
THE OWL SHOP
OLEA
YALE UNIVERSITY ART GALLERY
DAVENPORT AVE
TOWER PARKWAY
TOAD'S PLACE
NEW HAVEN HOTEL
TEN THOUSAND VILLAGES
Old Campus Courtyard
MARTIN LUTHER KING JR BLVD
TEMPLE ST
COLLEGE ST
ELM ST
ASHMUN ST
LOCK ST
GEORGE ST
CHURCH ST
CHAPEL ST
OMNI NEW HAVEN HOTEL AT YALE
The New Haven Green
YALE UNIVERSITY
Grove Street Cemetery
S. ORANGE ST
CROWN ST
YALE UNIVERSITY VISITOR CENTER
WALL ST
PROSPECT ST
CANAL ST
FAIR ST
AMISTAD MEMORIAL
ORANGE ST
GROVE ST
YALE COLLECTION OF MUSICAL INSTRUMENTS
NEW HAVEN MUSEUM & HISTORICAL SOCIETY
STATE ST
WHITNEY AVE
SACHEM ST
YALE UNIVERSITY CAMPUS
WHITNEY AVE
SALLY'S APIZZA
OLIVE ST
ORANGE ST
TRUMBULL ST
WOOSTER ST
CHAPEL ST
Wooster Square
GREENE ST
SAINT JOHN ST
GRAND AVE
LYON ST
WILLIAM ST
STATE ST
FRANK PEPE PIZZERIA
0 300 yds
0 300 m
91
91

triceratops, and brontosaurus—collected by C. O. Marsh, the museum's first director and one of the founding fathers of paleontology.

While Yale has many attractions worth visiting, the **Yale Center for British Art** (1080 Chapel St., 203/432-2800, http://ycba.yale.edu, 10am-5pm Tues.-Sat., noon-5pm Sun., free) is particularly worth singling out. British art is frequently overshadowed by its European counterparts, but the United Kingdom has a style and artistic history all its own—this museum is the largest and most comprehensive collection outside of the British Isles. Highlights include the psychedelic drawings of poet-artist William Blake, the luminous seascapes of J. W. Turner, and the bucolic landscapes of Thomas Gainsborough and John Constable. The building itself is no slouch either; designed by Louis Kahn, it is a modernist gray cube confronting the adjoining plaza.

OTHER SIGHTS

The **New Haven Museum & Historical Society** (114 Whitney Ave., 203/562-4183, www.newhavenmuseum.org, 10am-5pm Tues.-Fri., noon-5pm Sat., $4 adults, $3 seniors, $2 students, children under 12 free, free for all 1pm-4pm first Sun. of each month) contains a mishmash of 350 years of history, ranging from Quinnipiac artifacts to mementos of New Haven's role in the China trade. The museum also has a collection of artifacts relating to the *Amistad* affair, including a striking portrait of the leader of the Africans, Joseph Cinque (also known as Sengbe Pieh), on trial. New Haven also pays homage to those brave Africans with its ***Amistad* Memorial** (165 Church St.), a 14-foot bronze relief sculpture that depicts their capture, trial, and return home. The monument was sculpted in 1992 and placed on the former site of the New Haven jail, where the crew was imprisoned in 1839 while they awaited trial.

Entertainment and Events

A nationally known music hall, **Toad's Place** (300 York St., 203/624-8623, www.toadsplace.com) attracts names that range from unheard-of to huge. An ever-rotating roster of music (from reggae and pop to techno DJs and blues) keeps the scene fresh. The inventively named **Bar** (254 Crown St., 203/495-1111, www.barnightclub.com) draws crowds for its mashed potato and bacon pizza, with a lively DJ dance scene that fires up late night.

Tennis's top female players come to New Haven to compete in the **Connecticut**

Yale University campus

Open (Connecticut Tennis Center at Yale, 45 Yale Ave., 855/464-8366 or 203/776-7331, www.ctopen.org, mid-Aug.), which benefits a range of community causes. Just in time for the holidays, New Haven launches a **Celebration of American Crafts** (203/562-4927, www.creativeartsworkshop.org, Nov.-Dec.), a juried craft show exhibition featuring jewelry, ceramics, and other items from hundreds of artisans from all over the country.

Shopping

Behind the kitschy-retro facade at **Owl Shop** (268 College St., 203/624-3250, www.owlshopcigars.com, 10am-1am Mon.-Thurs., 10am-2am Fri.-Sat., noon-1am Sun.), one of the oldest cigar and tobacco shops in the country, you'll come upon imported pipes and endless glass cases filled with smoking accessories. Take a seat in the adjoining brick-walled café, have a drink, and puff away. The New Haven outpost of **Ten Thousand Villages** (1054 Chapel St., 203/776-0854, www.tenthousandvillages.com/newhaven, 10am-6pm Mon.-Thurs., 10am-8pm Fri.-Sat., 1pm-6pm Sun.) is chock-full of fairly traded crafts from all over the planet. Pick up a hand-carved giraffe for the living room, a chunky necklace made of semiprecious beads, or handwoven table linens.

Sports and Recreation

★ PADDLING THE THIMBLE ISLANDS

The scattered archipelago off the coast of Branford is named after the thimbleberry, a cousin to the raspberry that grows wild on the islands. They could just as well be named for their diminutive size, however; in addition to 24 populated islands, literally hundreds of pink granite outcroppings poke their peaks out of the waves. The islands are home to a variety of critters, including a winter population of seals—and a summer influx of rich people from New York, who have built elaborate mansions, tiny cottages, and even little gazebos on the rocks.

In addition to being unlike anything else on the New England coast, the islands have spawned dozens of legends, such as an enduring myth that the pirate Captain Kidd buried treasure on so-called Money Island. The best way to take in the islands is at sea level, from the vantage of your very own sea kayak. **Branford River Paddle Sports** (50 Maple St., Branford, 203/980-8451, www.branfordriverpaddlesports.com) leads kayak and

Thimble Islands

paddleboard expeditions to the Thimbles. If you'd rather let someone else do the paddling, sign up for a 45-minute narrated tour with "Captain Mike" on the *Sea Mist*, operating under the name **Thimble Island Cruise** (Thimble Island Rd., Stony Creek, 203/488-8905, http://thimbleislandcruise.com, May-Oct., $13 adults, $12 seniors, $6 children under 12).

★ SILVER SANDS STATE PARK

The 297 acres of beach, dunes, restored salt marsh, open areas, and woods of **Silver Sands State Park** (1 Silver Sands Pkwy, Milford, 203/735-4311, www.ct.gov/deep/silversands, 8am-sunset daily, free) includes the 14-acre Charles Island, which is connected to the park by a sandbar that's submerged during high tide. Legend has it that Captain Kidd buried his treasure on this island, which is closed May-August to protect egrets and other bird rookeries. Construction on a concession stand, new restrooms, and increased parking is expected to be finished in late 2018. Lifeguards are on duty Wednesday-Sunday.

Food

NEW HAVEN

Pizza was reportedly introduced to America in New Haven, so it's only natural that the city's pizzerias would be its pride. Exhibit A is ★ **Frank Pepe's Pizzeria Napoletana** (157 Wooster St., 203/865-5762, www.pepespizzeria.com, 11am-10pm daily, pizzas from $7). The simple interior lets the pies take center stage, with toppings from mozzarella and bacon to mushrooms and fresh clams.

Pull up a chair at one of the wide, burnished-wood tables of **Viva Zapata** (161 Park St., 203/562-2499, http://vivazapatanewhaven.com, 11:30am-1am Sun.-Thurs., 11:30am-2am Fri.-Sat., $6-16) and brace your taste buds for some simple-but-good Mexican food. Staples like tostadas and fajitas are always available, as are seafood chimichangas and *filet con queso* (filet mignon stuffed with jack cheese and jalapeños).

Serving inventive Spanish and Mediterranean cuisine, ★ **Olea** (39 High St., 203/780-8925, www.oleanewhaven.com, 5pm-9:30pm Mon.-Thurs., 5pm-10pm Fri.-Sat., $26-35) tops many lists of best restaurants in the area. Chef Manuel Romero was born in Spain and knows how to prepare bacalao, ceviche, and rabbit, but shellfish lovers should not pass up the *fideuà* (vermicelli with squid ink, mussels, shrimp, and clams).

The name of **Pad Thai Restaurant** (1170 Chapel St., 203/562-0322, www.padthai-newhaven.com, 11:30am-10pm Sun.-Thurs., 11:30am-10:30pm Fri.-Sat., $6-17) may be a little on the pedestrian side, but the food is anything but. Authentic Thai is all over the menu here—from the spicy *chaiya* noodles with seafood and basil to the coriander-scented fried fish.

AROUND NEW HAVEN

Oozing with cheese, the pies at **Bella Napoli Pizza** (864 Boston Post Rd., Milford, 203/877-1102, www.bellanapolipizzaonline.com, 11am-10pm Sun.-Thurs., 11am-11pm Fri.-Sat., $6-19) are said to feed half of Milford on weekend nights. Specialty pizzas include creations like clams casino, an egg and cheese breakfast pie, and the Philly cheesesteak.

With wide windows and a simple interior, **Café Atlantique** (33 River St., Milford, 203/882-1602, www.cafeatlantiquedtm.com, 7am-8pm Mon.-Tues., 7am-9pm Wed.-Thurs., 8am-10pm Sat., 8am-6pm Sun., $5-9) is an ideal spot for quick-but-tasty (and inexpensive) lunches. Order up a pesto-chicken panini and smoothie, or opt for the crepes, which are the stars of the show. There are savory renditions like goat cheese, olives, and almonds, and a lovely banana Nutella crepe for dessert.

The chef-owner of **Le Petit Cafe** (225 Montowese St., Branford, 203/483-9791, www.lepetitcafe.net, 6pm-9pm Wed.-Sun., $57.50 prix fixe for 4 courses) may be originally from Hong Kong, but the restaurant itself is a perfect evocation of a French bistro. Four-course prix fixe dinners are served in a dining room that feels formal without pretension. The

Apizza with Mootz: New Haven's Best Slices

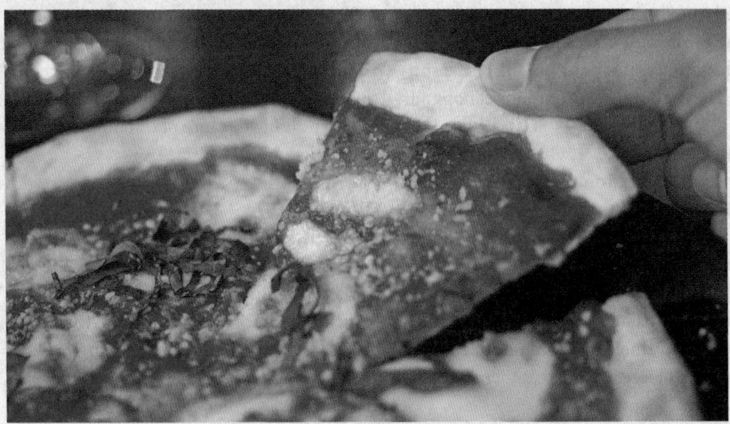

New Haven Pizza

Neopolitan, New York style, Chicago style . . . in the oozy, blistered geography of pizza, New Haven's oddball flatbreads are unique and beloved. Strictly speaking, New Haven makes **apizza,** pronounced "ah-beets," and if you could sequence the apizza genome, it would point straight back to Naples—a century ago, the New Haven neighborhood of Wooster Square was known as Little Naples for the high concentration of immigrants who traced their roots to the city that invented pizza, and that's still where you'll find the city's top slices.

What makes it apizza? A classic New Haven pie is tossed by hand, stretched thin, then baked in a searing hot coal-fired oven, whose internal temperature can rise well above 650 degrees Fahrenheit. Order it plain and it comes topped with crushed tomatoes, olive oil, a dusting of pecorino cheese, and a bit of oregano—add some **mootz** to layer the pie with bubbling mozzarella. Not that that's the only option. According to the fervent partisans of New Haven pizza, local pizza joint Frank Pepe's Pizzeria also invented **white clam pizza,** and its version comes topped with fresh clams, garlic, olive oil, and a restrained layer of grated cheese.

The granddaddy of New Haven pizza is **Frank Pepe's Pizzeria Napoletana** (157 Wooster St., 203/865-5762, www.pepespizzeria.com, 11am-10pm daily, pizzas from $7), where pies come crisp and sooty at the edges, with gorgeously toasted fillings in between. Clam pizza is delightfully simple and gets even better with the addition of chopped bacon.

Neck-and-neck with Frank Pepe's for the best in the city is **Sally's Apizza** (237 Wooster St., 203/624-5271, www.sallysapizza.com, 4pm-9pm Wed.-Thurs., 4pm-10pm Fri., 3pm-10pm Sat., 3pm-9pm Sun., pizzas from $7.50), which has been doling out pies with a side of terse service since 1938. The tomato pie wins extra acclaim here, but the differences are subtle and personal—judge for yourself.

Something to drink with that pizza? If you're going for the full immersion in New Haven flavors, opt for a **Foxon Park** soda—it's been made in East Haven since 1922, with a long list of throwback flavors, including white birch, iron brew—a Scottish cross between cream soda and root beer—and *gassosa*, an Italian-style lemon-lime soda.

menu includes French standards like escargot and duck confit, expertly prepared by Chef Roy Ip. As a nod to his homeland, however, a couple of Asian-inspired dishes have been slipped into the menu.

One of the best places in New England to sample native seafood is also one of the simplest. The red-and-white outdoor canopy sits right along Route 1 at ★ **The Place** (901 Boston Post Rd./Rte. 1, Guilford, 203/453-9276, 5pm-9pm Mon.-Thurs., 5pm-10pm Fri., 1pm-10pm Sat., noon-9pm Sun. May-Oct., $9-25), where all manner of seafood is cooked on a huge outdoor grill. "Guests" sit down on stumps along large picnic tables to dig into fire-roasted lobster, clams, and, if they are lucky, melt-in-your-mouth filets of smoky fresh bluefish. Note that there's a cash-only policy.

Accommodations

UNDER $100

Vintage couches and a marble lobby belie the low nightly price tag of **Hotel Duncan** (1151 Chapel St., 203/787-1273, www.hotelduncan.net, $65-100), located a block away from Yale. It's the oldest hotel in the city—a fact that does show through in timeworn furnishings—but the age also lends a comfortable charm to the venerable institution. Rooms on the top floor have outstanding views.

$100-150

Located smack downtown and close to just about everything, **New Haven Hotel** (229 George St., 203/498-3100, www.newhavenhotel.com, $144-199) is both convenient and quiet. The property offers good perks, including a 24-hour fitness center, restaurant, and evening wine and cheese reception.

$150-200

Built with Ivy League bigwig visitors in mind, the **Omni New Haven Hotel at Yale** (155 Temple St., 203/772-6664, www.omnihotels.com, $170-394) is the luxury choice for its health club, rooftop restaurant, function space, and scads of business services (including a business center).

An 1820 Greek Revival bed-and-breakfast, ★ **Austin Street Inn** (9 Austin St., 203/387-1699, www.austinstreetinn.net, $179-189) has four guest rooms. In the Westville Village Historic District, a former industrial center that's now an artists' community, the inn is within walking distance of restaurants, shops, and parks.

OVER $200

The Study at Yale (1157 Chapel St., 203/503-3900, http://studyatyale.com, $229-279) appeals to the guest whose idea of relaxation is picking a book from the floor-to-ceiling bookcase in the lobby and kicking back in a leather chair with a view of Yale's redbrick arts campus. A gallery exhibits works by Yale students, while a restaurant, café, and fitness center round out amenities.

Information

New Haven is served by the **Greater New Haven Convention and Visitors Bureau** (169 Orange St., 203/777-8550, www.newhavencvb.com). For maps, brochures, and reservations, stop by **Visit New Haven** (545 Long Wharf Dr., 203/777-8550, www.visitnewhaven.com), which runs an information center downtown.

Getting There and Around

New Haven is located at the intersection of I-91 and I-95: it's 1.75 hours from New York City, 2 hours from Boston, and 1.75 hours from Providence.

Both **Amtrak** (800/872-7245, www.amtrak.com) and **Metro North** (800/638-7646, www.mta.info) run trains to and from Union Station (50 Union Ave.); **Greyhound** (203/772-2470, www.greyhound.com) and **Peter Pan Bus Lines** (800/343-9999, www.peterpanbus.com) provide bus routes to the same location.

The New Haven regional service of **CT Transit** (203/624-0151, www.cttransit.com)

operates buses around the city and immediate suburbs. **Milford Transit** (203/874-4507, www.ci.milford.ct.us) runs shuttle buses around the town of Milford. The **Shore Line East** (800/255-7433, www.shorelineeast.com) commuter rail service runs trains to Guilford, Branford, and other eastern suburbs, continuing on to New London.

ESSEX

A tidy package of quintessential New England, the village of Essex has a Main Street lined with beautifully preserved historic homes and a park crowned by a pristine gazebo. It won't take more than an hour to stroll around the compact downtown, but there are a handful of historical highlights that make it worth lingering. The Connecticut River Museum explores the maritime heritage of the Connecticut River Valley, while the Essex Steam Train & Riverboat keep the golden age of travel alive.

Sights

At the end of Main Street by the town dock, the **Connecticut River Museum** (67 Main St., 860/767-8269, http://ctrivermuseum.org, 10am-5pm daily Memorial Day-Columbus Day, 10am-5pm Tues.-Sun. Columbus Day-Memorial Day, $10 adults, $8 seniors, $7 students, $6 children 6-12, children under 6 free) explains the importance of the river in the area's history. A highlight of the collection is a replica of *The Turtle*, a wooden submersible built in 1775 by Yale student David Bushnell to transport a bomb to British ships during the Revolutionary War. His efforts were unsuccessful, but his invention was the precursor to the submarine.

It's not just small children who flock to Essex to ride the old-fashioned **Essex Steam Train & Riverboat** (1 Railroad Ave., 860/767-0103, www.essexsteamtrain.com, hours and prices vary), which connects to a riverboat for a 2.5-hour excursion. There are white-tablecloth fine-dining excursions for adults as well as a sunset, cigars, and whiskey cruise. Much programming is geared toward little ones, however, with Thomas the Train and pirate-themed days, plus Santa Claus shows up in season.

Food and Accommodations

If you don't have time for a big water excursion, hop a little ferry to **Marley's Café** (11 Ferry St., 860/853-0133, hours vary widely, May-Oct., $5-30), in the Essex Island Marina. This unique, casual spot is accessible via a quick ride on a little boat—and somehow hopping a boat to the restaurant gives it the feel of a getaway.

One of the longest continually operating inns in the United States, the ★ **Griswold Inn** (36 N. Main St., 860/767-1776, www.griswoldinn.com, entrées $19-35, rooms $195-345) first opened its doors in 1776. Simple, elegant rooms and suites are appointed with antique furnishings in keeping with the inn's historic feel—some have fireplaces, while others have views to the ocean. Stop into a tavern that's decked with memorabilia, or pause for a bite in the Library or Gun Room, adorned with books and firearms that date to the 15th century. The cuisine highlights classic New England fare such as a creamy clam chowder and perfectly roasted cod; there's a kids' menu for the younger set. A museum-worthy maritime art collection is on display in the public areas. Ask for literature about the inn's history at the front desk.

Getting There and Around

Essex is easily accessible from I-95 and I-91 via Route 9. There are plenty of marinas in the area if you're traveling by boat. **9 Town Transit** (860/510-0429, http://estuarytransit.org) operates 15 buses on four flexible routes (fixed stops with deviations) throughout the region, including connections to New Haven, New London, and Middletown. Fares, which can be purchased online or on the bus (but the driver cannot make change) are $1.75 for adults, $.85 for seniors, and free for children under four.

MYSTIC AND STONINGTON

The little town of Mystic made its fortunes in shipbuilding, and the community now thrives by keeping that salty history alive. Set on the edge of the Mystic River, the Mystic Seaport Museum is a full immersion in New England's seafaring past, as a proud whaling vessel bobs at her moorings and sailor-interpreters lead visitors in rousing sea shanties.

Just across the river, the quiet village of Stonington is home to Connecticut's sole remaining fishing fleet, which sets out each morning to troll the coastal waters for bottom fish, clams, and scallops. Stonington achieved brief fame during the War of 1812, when its two 18-pound cannons repelled an attack by five British warships, but nothing so dramatic has unfolded in the ensuing years. These days, it's all nostalgia—perfect for a stroll by the sea or a day of imagining life before the mast.

Sights

★ MYSTIC SEAPORT MUSEUM

Situated a mile upriver from downtown, the **Mystic Seaport Museum** (Rte. 27, Exit 90 off I-95, 860/572-5315, www.mysticseaport.org, 9am-5pm daily Apr.-Oct., 10am-4pm daily Nov.-Mar., $28.95 adults, $26.95 seniors and students, $18.95 children 4-14, children under 4 free) has more than 500 vessels in a miniature city that is a careful reproduction of a bustling 19th-century seaport.

The most engaging attractions, however, are the village folk and old salts who regale visitors with tales of the sea, and the *Charles W. Morgan,* America's last surviving whale ship, launched in New Bedford in 1841. Interpreters detail how the tryworks rendered all that whale blubber, and also lead parties in hoisting sails, complete with authentic sea shanties. There are plenty of interactive experiences for kids, a boat-themed play area, a cooperage, and much more, with frequent demonstrations of old-fashioned sailor skills. In case you're visiting on your birthday, let the ticket office know—birthday visitors get in free.

★ MASHANTUCKET PEQUOT MUSEUM & RESEARCH CENTER

A highlight of the visitor experience at the very large, interactive **Mashantucket Pequot Museum & Research Center** (110 Pequot Tr., Mashantucket, 860/411-9671, www.pequotmuseum.org, 9am-5pm Wed.-Sat. Mar. 29-Oct. 31, 9am-5pm Tues.-Sat. Nov.,

Mystic Seaport Museum

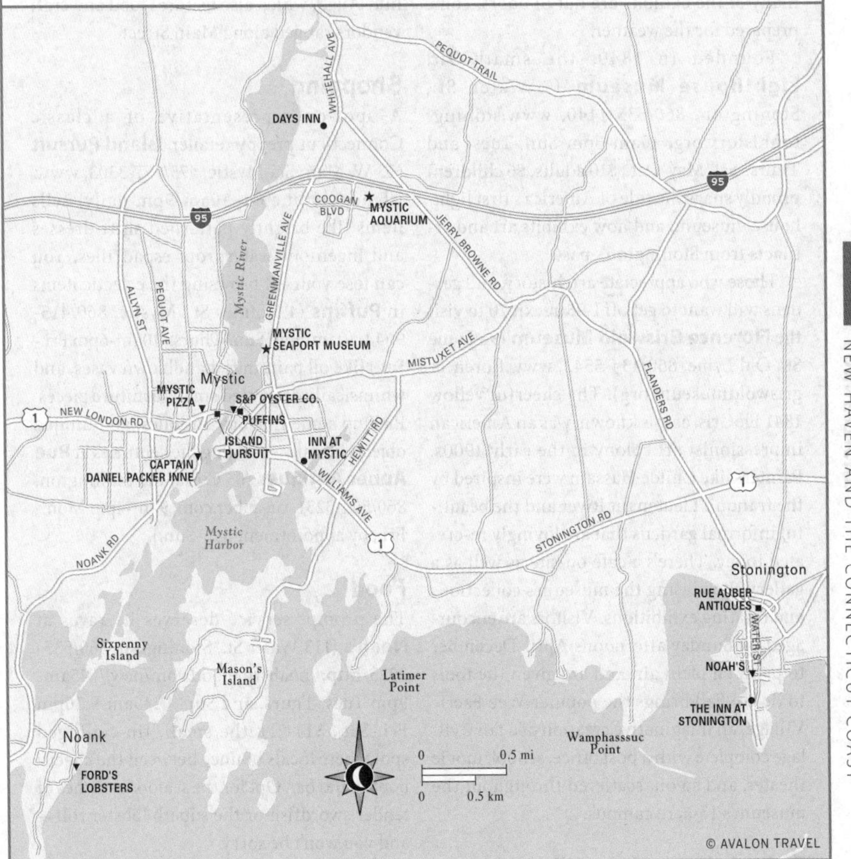

$20 adults, $15 seniors, $12 children 6-15, children under 6 free) is walking through a re-created village that brings pre-European culture to life.

Learn how people built their homes, hunted, and cared for their sick by pressing buttons on a phone-like device that has explanations for each setting. The museum, which is also a prominent research facility, doesn't mince words as it recounts the decimation of Native American tribes through warfare and disease. With a collection of some 150,000 books, the center's primary mission is researching, collecting, and preserving Native American artifacts from southern New England.

OTHER SIGHTS

Be first in line when the **Mystic Aquarium** (55 Coogan Blvd., Mystic, 860/572-5955, www.mysticaquarium.org, 10am-4:50pm daily Jan. 2-Feb. 17 and Dec. 1-24, 9am-4:50pm daily Feb. 18-Mar. 31, Sept. 5-Nov. 30, and Dec. 26-Jan. 1, 9am-5:50pm daily Apr. 1-Sept. 4, $35.99 adults, $30.99 seniors, $29.99 children 13-17, $25.99 children 3-12, children under 3 free) opens to beat the throngs of visitors at this popular attraction. Beluga whales, penguins, and a ray touch tank are crowd pleasers, as are daily seal shows in an indoor theater. Since many of the exhibits are out of doors, come prepared for the weather.

Founded in 1840, the small **Old Lighthouse Museum** (7 Water St., Stonington, 860/535-1440, www.stoningtonhistory.org, 10am-5pm Sun.-Tues. and Thurs.-Sat. May-Oct., $10 adults, $6 children) proudly snags the title of America's first lighthouse museum, and now exhibits art and artifacts from Stonington's past.

Those who appreciate art, history, and gardens will want to get off I-95 at exit 70 to visit the **Florence Griswold Museum** (96 Lyme St., Old Lyme, 860/434-5542, www.florencegriswoldmuseum.org). The cheerful yellow 1841 FloGris, as it is known, was an American impressionist art colony in the early 1900s. Painters like Childe Hassam were inspired by the tranquil Lieutenant River and the beautiful informal gardens that are lovingly re-created today. There's a café on-site as well as a gallery showcasing the museum's collections and rotating exhibitions. Visitors are encouraged on Sunday afternoons April-December to paint en plein air, and are given the tools to do so. Fall brings the popular Wee Faerie Village, an imaginative creation of a fairy village complete with a post office, school, movie theater, and so on, scattered throughout the museum's 13-acre campus.

Entertainment and Events

Marching bands, floats, and even Miss Connecticut turn out for the annual **Blessing of the Fleet** (Stonington Fishermen's Dock, 1 High St., Stonington, late July, free), which begins with a mass at St. Mary Church followed by a parade through downtown and culminates with a clambake on the waterfront and boats moored in the harbor.

A parade of antique and classic vessels set off from Mystic Seaport during the **Antique and Classic Boat Rendezvous** (888/973-2767, www.mysticseaport.org, July); the boats can be seen at the seaport that weekend. More than 250 visual artists compete each year in the juried **Mystic Outdoor Art Festival** (860/572-5098, www.mysticchamber.org, mid-Aug.), which also features food and craft vendors ranged along Main Street.

Shopping

A spot-on representative of a classic Connecticut preppy retailer, **Island Pursuit** (23 W. Main St., Mystic, 475/777-3303, www.islandpursuit.com, 10am-9pm daily) sells items like brightly patterned shift dresses and ingenious waterproof espadrilles. You can lose yourself browsing the eclectic items in **Puffins** (4 Holmes St., Mystic, 860/415-9644, 10am-5pm Sun.-Thurs., 10am-6pm Fri.-Sat.) like oil paintings, handblown vases, and whimsically decorated small furniture pieces. Pick up some fine art, antiques, and unique objects literally spanning the centuries at **Rue Auber Antiques** (65 Cutler St., Stonington, 860/504-3251, rueauber.com, 9am-4pm Mon.-Fri., by appointment Sat.-Sun.).

Food

The prompt service deserves its raves at **Noah's** (113 Water St., Stonington, 860/535-3925, http://noahsfinefood.com/new, 7:45am-9pm Tues.-Thurs. and Sun., 7:45am-9:30pm Fri.-Sat., $14-21), the small, tin-ceilinged spot where locals bounce between the cheery booths and bar. Opt for the seafood—dishes of tender swordfish or the superb lobster roll—and you won't be sorry.

★ **Mystic Pizza** (56 W. Main St., Mystic, 860/536-3700, 10am-10pm daily, $8-14), the real-life pizza restaurant that served as the inspiration for Julia Roberts's 1988 film of the same name, is still churning out pies every night. Tables can get crowded for dinner, so be prepared to wait.

A lively spot right on the water near the drawbridge, **S & P Oyster House** (1 Holmes St., Mystic, 860/536-2674, www.sp-oyster.com, 11:30am-9pm Sun.-Thurs., 11:30am-10pm Fri.-Sat., $26-49) is not surprisingly heavy on seafood, but there's a kids' menu if you're dining with picky little eaters. There's both indoor and outdoor seating; make

Connecticut for Kids

Yale's Peabody Museum

Connecticut isn't all fragile antiques and quiet inns—the state is packed with kid-friendly spots. In fact, there's loads of hands-on fun for the wee ones in these parts, starting with the **Beardsley Zoo** (1875 Noble Ave., Bridgeport, 203/394-6565, www.beardsleyzoo.com), the state's only zoo, where you can see plenty of species (some endangered) in well-kept environments. There's a tropical rainforest full of exotic birds, a carousel, a restaurant, and picnic areas.

At New Haven's **Peabody Museum of Natural History** (page 194), you'll find live animals alongside brontosaurus and stegosaurus skeletons and exhibits on evolution and ancient Egypt, plus rocks, minerals, and meteorites. For a day on the move, the **Essex Steam Train & Riverboat Ride** (page 201) lets families cruise a riverboat down the Connecticut River, then hop onboard an authentic steam locomotive. Travelers with younger kids shouldn't miss the **Stepping Stones Museum for Children** (page 193), where little visitors can climb inside an ambulance and follow floating balls in a water play area.

It's all fun and games at **Quassy Amusement Park** (page 210), the 20-acre family playground on Lake Quassapaug with interactive water attractions, swimming, boat rides, and live entertainment. Still more water fun happens at **Mystic Aquarium** (page 203), home to beluga whales, penguins, and many marine animals. Or, head straight into the state's historic relationship with the sea at the nearby **Mystic Seaport Museum** (page 202). Sure it's crowded, but for good reason: Kids love exploring the wooden whalers and historic tall ships, the planetarium, and a working shipyard.

Continuing the water theme, about a half hour inland from Mystic, **The Dinosaur Place** (1650 Hartford-New London Turnpike, Montville, 860/443-4367, http://naturesartvillage.com/the-dinosaur-place, 10am-6pm daily Apr. 1-Nov. 26; Apr. 1-May 12 and Oct. 1-Nov. 26 $16.99 ages 2-59, $14.99 over 60, May 13-June 16 and Sept. 5-30, $19.99 ages 2-59, $16.99 over 60, June 17-Sept. 4 $23.99 ages 2-59, $20.99 over 60; children under 2 always free) has a dinosaur-themed water park (spray areas, not rides), a playground, a maze, and mini golf, but the main draw are the enormous life-sized dinosaur statues that line easy, wide trails that are fine for strollers.

reservations (well, they call it "priority seating" and they don't guarantee your preferred time slot) if you are going in season.

A contender for best lobster eggs Benedict in the universe can be found at **Kitchen Little** (36 Quarry Rd., Mystic, 860/536-2122, http://kitchenlittle.org, 7:30am-2pm Mon.-Fri., 6:30am-1pm Sat.-Sun., $.99-18.99), a small, unassuming spot on the 2nd floor of the Mystic Marina. Serving hearty breakfasts since 1980, Kitchen Little has a comfortable porch with views of sleek yachts.

In the village of Noank, about 10 minutes from Mystic, **Ford's Lobster** (15 Riverview Ave., Noank, 860/536-2842, www.fordslobster.com, 11:30am-9pm Mon.-Sat., 10am-9pm Sun., $19-42) sits right on a dock and is a perfect spot to dig into dishes like the lobster bomb or grilled halibut if you are lucky enough to get a table right away (no reservations). It's BYOB, so come prepared.

Fans of traditional New England dining will enjoy a meal at **Captain Daniel Packer Inne** (32 Water St., Mystic, 860/536-3555, www.danielpacker.com, 11am-10pm daily, $20-34), a 1756 downtown establishment housing both pub and restaurant. In the latter, take a seat near the fireplace and sup on lemon-peppered chicken and baked scallops from nearby Stonington.

Accommodations

UNDER $100

Utilitarian and budget-friendly, **Days Inn Mystic** (55 Whitehall Ave., 860/572-0574, www.daysinn.com/mystic, $60-100) is convenient to all sights and right off I-95, and there's a free buffet breakfast with bagels, waffles, cereal, yogurt, and more. Oh, and there's a pool.

$100-150

Old Lyme Inn (85 Lyme St., Old Lyme, 860/434-2600, www.oldlymeinn.com, $135-175) is a perfect balance of sophistication and relaxation. Rooms all have queen or king canopy beds and pretty views, and include an excellent (and filling) continental breakfast.

$150-250

Foxwoods Resort Casino (350 Trolley Line Blvd., Mashantucket, 860/312-2000, www.foxwoods.com, $129-694) has four hotels: the upscale Grand Pequot Tower featuring 1,400-square-foot villas, restaurants, including one from Guy Fieri, an indoor pool and spa, and Tanger Outlet stores; Great Cedar Hotel, in the center of the casino action; Two Trees Inn, an off-site property designed to feel like a country inn; and the Fox Tower, with a spa and a huge outdoor pool. A golf course, bowling alley, arcade, impressive Pequot Museum, and miles of trails on the 2,000-acre property ensure even non-gamblers will be kept busy.

With three casinos to Foxwoods' seven, **Mohegan Sun** (1 Mohegan Sun Blvd., Uncasville, 888/777-7922, www.mohegansun.com, $149-499) is smaller, with only two hotels: Sky Tower, which has a 10,000-square-foot indoor pool, and the smaller (400 rooms versus Sky Tower's 1,563) and more recently built Earth Tower. There are two spas, a golf course, and an advantage over Foxwoods for parents: Kids up to age 12 can be dropped off at Kids Quest/Cyber Quest, an entertainment venue with activities like karaoke and rock climbing.

Its majestic views overlook Mystic Harbor and Long Island Sound, but that's just part of what makes ★ **The Inn at Mystic** (Rtes. 1 and 27, Mystic, 860/536-9604, www.innatmystic.com, $95-325) so darn pretty. Between the beautifully manicured flower gardens, the rooms outfitted in designer fabrics and massive beds (some with fireplaces, whirlpools, and patios), and the charming mansion itself, it's hard to decide where to look next.

OVER $250

All the major travel publications have raved about **Inn at Stonington** (60 Water St., Stonington, 860/535-2000, www.innatstonington.com, $195-490) at one point or another, and with excellent reason. The superbly run, impeccably kept spot offers personal (but never intrusive) service. The 18 rooms all look as though Martha Stewart herself decorated them; each comes with fireplaces and oversized bathrooms, and most have whirlpool tubs and modem ports, to boot. There's also a homemade continental breakfast, free bike loans, and use of the exercise room.

Information

The **Greater Mystic Chamber of Commerce** (860/572-1102, www.mysticchamber.org) and the **Connecticut Office of Tourism** (800/288-4748, www.ctvisit.com/mystic) can provide further information about this region.

Getting There and Around

Amtrak (800/872-7245, www.amtrak.com) runs trains to stations in Mystic (Rte. 1), New London (27 Water St.), and Old Saybrook (455 Boston Post Rd.). **Greyhound** (800/231-2222, www.greyhound.com) operates bus service to New London (45 Water St.). New London is also a major hub for ferries crossing Long Island Sound, including the **Cross Sound Ferry** (2 Ferry St., 860/443-5281, www.longislandferry.com) to Orient Point, the **Viking Fleet** (631/668-5700, www.vikingfleet.com) to Montauk Point and Martha's Vineyard, and the **Block Island Express** (800/444-4624, www.goblockisland.com) to Block Island.

Bus company **Southeast Area Transit** (SEAT, 860/886-2631, www.seatbus.com) operates routes through area towns including New London, Groton, East Lyme, and Stonington.

Hartford

Sitting proudly in the middle of the state, surrounded by a spider web of interstate highways, Connecticut's capital has a long history and a bad rap. The city was settled just after Boston and spent 200 years as a flourishing port city, linked to the ocean by the wandering Connecticut River.

This is where the first law school in America was founded in 1784, and the location of America's first insurance company—two claims to fame that earned the city's title of "America's Filing Cabinet." Since then, Hartford has seen a long decline, rising crime, and a layer of grime that's taken the shine off the early American glory.

But there are glimmers of energy and revitalization in the city, where all that history is shot through with the vibrancy of university life, plenty for a day of exploring. And in the communities that surround the capital, you'll find historic house museums and offbeat attractions that are seriously under the radar.

SIGHTS

Mark Twain House & Museum

Samuel Langhorne Clemens—the writer who become known to the world as Mark Twain—is more often associated with the wide, muddy flow of the Mississippi River than urban Connecticut. But many of his masterpieces, including *The Adventures of Huckleberry Finn* and *The Adventures of Tom Sawyer*, were penned in this Victorian Gothic manse, now the **Mark Twain House & Museum** (351 Farmington Ave., 860/247-0998, www.marktwainhouse.org, 9:30am-5:30pm daily, closed Tues. Jan.-Feb., $20 adults 17-64, $18 seniors, $11 children 6-16, children under 6 free), just outside of downtown Hartford. Twain lived here for 16 years, and while he was here, he formed the nucleus of a literary group that included Harriet Beecher Stowe, Booker T. Washington, and other giants of the Gilded Age.

Inside, docents give tours of the house, including the billiards room where Twain did most of his writing; the elaborate Middle Eastern-inspired decor by Louis Comfort Tiffany; and Twain's telephone, one of the first installed in a private residence. Fun options include tours led by actors playing Twain's staff including his butler and housekeeper.

Hartford

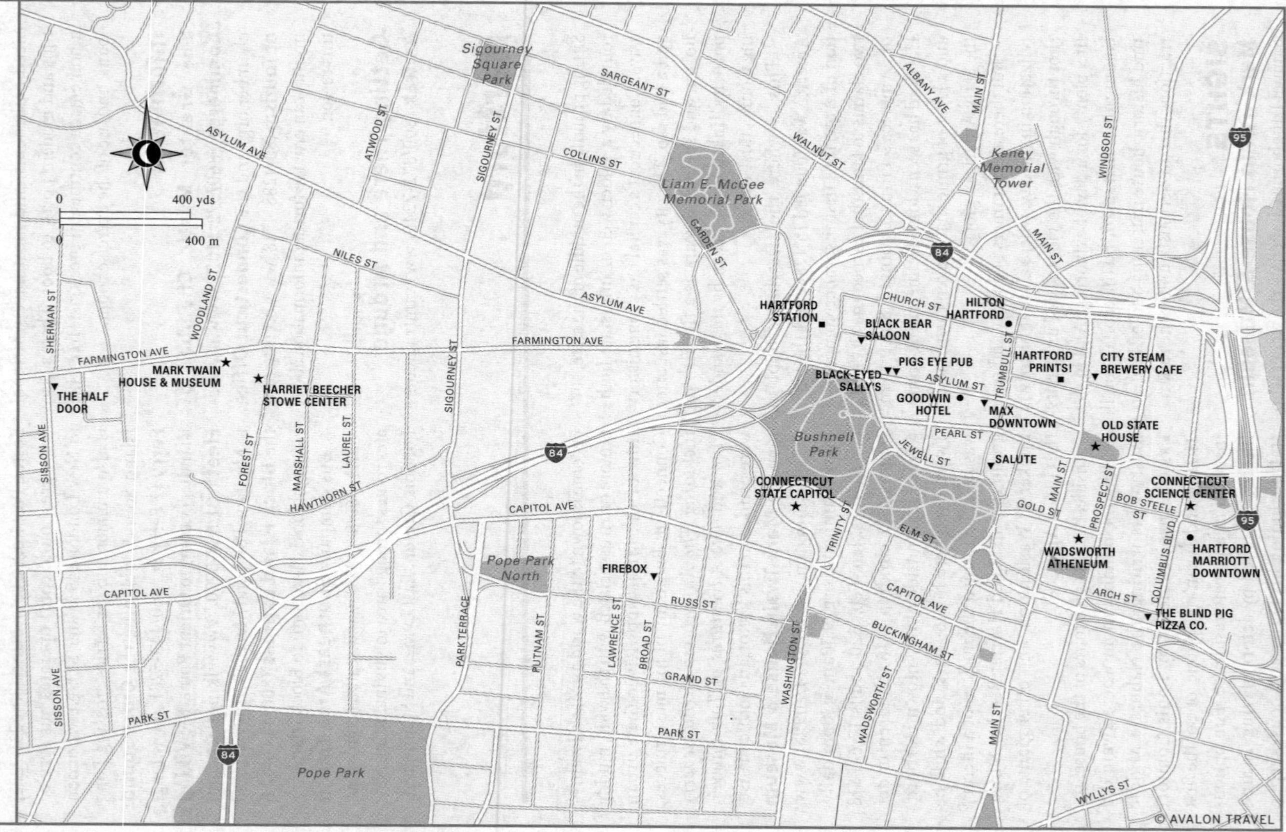
Sigourney Square Park
SARGEANT ST
ALBANY AVE
MAIN ST
ASYLUM AVE
ATWOOD ST
SIGOURNEY ST
COLLINS ST
WALNUT ST
Liam E. McGee Memorial Park
Keney Memorial Tower
WINDSOR ST
95
0
400 yds
0
400 m
NILES ST
GARDEN ST
84
MAIN ST
WOODLAND ST
SHERMAN ST
ASYLUM AVE
HARTFORD STATION
CHURCH ST
HILTON HARTFORD
BLACK BEAR SALOON
FARMINGTON AVE
FARMINGTON AVE
MARK TWAIN HOUSE & MUSEUM
HARRIET BEECHER STOWE CENTER
THE HALF DOOR
SIGOURNEY ST
PIGS EYE PUB
BLACK-EYED SALLY'S
TRUMBULL ST
HARTFORD PRINTS!
CITY STEAM BREWERY CAFE
ASYLUM ST
GOODWIN HOTEL
MAX DOWNTOWN
OLD STATE HOUSE
SISSON AVE
FOREST ST
MARSHALL ST
LAUREL ST
84
Bushnell Park
PEARL ST
JEWELL ST
SALUTE
HAWTHORN ST
CONNECTICUT STATE CAPITOL
MAIN ST
PROSPECT ST
CONNECTICUT SCIENCE CENTER
BOB STEELE ST
CAPITOL AVE
GOLD ST
TRINITY ST
ELM ST
95
COLUMBUS BLVD
HARTFORD MARRIOTT DOWNTOWN
WADSWORTH ATHENEUM
Pope Park North
FIREBOX
CAPITOL AVE
CAPITOL AVE
ARCH ST
THE BLIND PIG PIZZA CO.
RUSS ST
PARK TERRACE
PUTNAM ST
LAWRENCE ST
BROAD ST
WASHINGTON ST
BUCKINGHAM ST
GRAND ST
SISSON AVE
PARK ST
WADSWORTH ST
MAIN ST
PARK ST
84
Pope Park
WYLLYS ST

Some tours fill in advance, so it's worth booking ahead. Visitors receive a $3 discount at the Stowe Center next door.

Harriet Beecher Stowe Center

Harriet Beecher Stowe lived in this **Victorian "cottage"** (77 Forest St., 860/522-9258, www.harrietbeecherstowecenter.org, 9:30am-5pm Mon.-Sat., noon-5pm Sun., closed Tues. Jan.-Mar., $14 adults, $12 seniors, $8 children 5-12, children under 5 free) right next door to the Mark Twain House for 33 years. Through objects, photographs, and interactive media, docents tell the story of the author and the lasting impact of her novel *Uncle Tom's Cabin*. Exhibits explore the author's passion for social justice, including emancipation and women's rights, and a specially designed tour for children ages 5-12 provides a wonderful introduction to these concepts. Visitors receive a $3 discount at the neighboring Mark Twain House.

Wadsworth Atheneum

The gargantuan **Wadsworth Atheneum** (600 Main St., 860/278-2670, www.wadsworthatheneum.org, 11am-5pm Wed.-Fri., 10am-5pm Sat.-Sun., $15 adults, $12 seniors, $5 students, children 18 and under free, free for all 4pm-5pm Wed.-Sun. and 10am-1pm second Sat. of each month) is not only America's oldest art museum, it's also one of its best. Founded in 1842 by arts patron Daniel Wadsworth, the Atheneum has a broad range of genres, including works by European masters such as Monet, Picasso, and Dali; a fantastic collection of Classical bronzes; and early American portraiture, including the oldest known American portrait, *Elizabeth Eggington*. But two collections outshine the rest: the paintings of the Hudson River School, which formed the original basis of Wadsworth's collection, and the Amistad Center for Art and Culture, which documents the African American experience through fine art, photography, historical artifacts, memorabilia, and rare books.

Other Sights

Plan to spend a few hours at the **Connecticut Science Center** (250 Columbus Blvd., 860/724-3623, www.ctsciencecenter.org, 10am-5pm Tues.-Sun. Sept.-June, 10am-5pm daily July-Aug., $23.95 adults, $21.95 seniors 65 and over, $16.95 children 3-17, children under 3 free), a nine-story Cesar Pelli-designed museum featuring 165 hands-on exhibits and activities. Special events like a

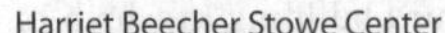
Harriet Beecher Stowe Center

Minecraft competition and attractions such as a butterfly garden and 3-D nature films keep this museum hopping.

The regal facade of the 1796 **Old State House** (800 Main St., 860/522-6766, www.cga.ct.gov/osh/, 10am-5pm Tues.-Sat. early July-early Oct., 10am-5pm Mon.-Fri mid-Oct.-early July, $6 adults, $3 children 6-17, students, and seniors, children under 5 free) dominates Hartford's downtown. The building was designed by Charles Bulfinch, the foremost architect of the federal period, who also designed the Massachusetts State House and redesigned the U.S. Capitol. Inside the state house is an amusing "museum of curiosities," drawn from the private collection of a colonial portrait artist who had his studio in the building and collected, among other things, the horn of a unicorn and a two-headed calf. A self-guided audio tour covers the building's many historic dramas, including the trials of the enslaved Africans who took over the ship *Amistad* and abolitionist educator Prudence Crandall.

The modern-day **Connecticut State Capitol** (210 Capitol Ave., 860/240-0222, www.cga.ct.gov, guided tours hourly 9:15am-1:15pm Mon.-Fri. Sep.-June; 9:15am-2:15pm Mon.-Fri. July-Aug., self-guided tours 8am-5pm Mon.-Fri. year-round, free) is a mishmash of architectural styles dominated by a soaring central tower capped by a 12-sided golden dome. Tours take in the building's ornate interior, as well as works of painting and sculpture important to the state.

Very worth the 15-minute drive to Farmington, **Hillstead Museum** (35 Mountain Rd., 860/677-4787, http://hillstead.org, 10am-4pm Tues.-Sat., $15 adults, $12 seniors, $8 children 6-12, children under 6 free) is a colonial revival house museum noteworthy for its art collection, famous guests, and builder—one of the first female American architects. The stately grounds sprawl across 152 acres and include a sunken garden and walking trails.

Half an hour beyond Hartford are two wonderful, small, family-focused amusement/water parks, each at the edge of a scenic lake. With 20 rides, waterslides, and a toddler-friendly play area, **Quassy Amusement Park and Waterpark** (2132 Middlebury Rd., Rte. 64, Middlebury, 203/758-2913, www.quassy.com, hours and days vary, May-Oct., $28 over 45 inches tall, $25 under 45 inches tall) also has paddleboats, canoes, and kayaks available to rent on the beach. Opened in 1846, **Lake Compounce** (186 Enterprise Dr., Bristol, 860/583-3300, www.lakecompounce.com, hours and days vary, May-Sept., $44 over 52 inches tall, $34 under 52 inches tall, $23 seniors) is the oldest continuously operating amusement park in the United States. With a wooden roller coaster and a triple-launch steel coaster, Lake Compounce attracts families with older kids, but little ones can try the Dino Expedition and Flying Elephants. The adjoining water park has wave pools, waterslides, and a family rafting adventure.

ENTERTAINMENT AND EVENTS

Worried you'll miss a crucial play in the big game? Not if you're at **Black Bear Saloon** (187 Allyn St., 860/524-8888, www.blackbearhartford.com), which has 30 TVs and takes its sports seriously. With more than a dozen craft beers on tap and nine levels of a historic 19th-century building in which to enjoy them, **City Steam Brewery Café** (942 Main St., 860/525-1600, http://citysteam.biz) is a popular gathering place. A festive, Irish pub atmosphere enlivens **The Half-Door** (270 Sisson Ave., 860/232-7827, www.thehalfdoorhfd.com), where regulars chow down on bangers and mash and catch frequent live music. With cheap drinks and plenty of pool tables, **Pigs Eye Pub** (356 Asylum St., 860/278-4747, www.pigseyepub.com) draws the college crowd, who hit the dance floor after a few "pigtails." Don't miss the outdoor space with a view of Bushnell Park.

Honoring the city's founder, the **Thomas Hooker Day Parade and Festival** (www.facebook.com/hookerdayparade, mid-May) in Bushnell Park resembles Mardi Gras with costumed revelers throwing beads and candy, marching bands, and giant puppets, plus food trucks, local vendors, child-friendly activities, and a classic car show. Hartford celebrates the start of summer with **Rose Weekend** (Prospect Ave. and Asylum Ave., 860/231-9443, http://elizabethparkct.org/whats_happening.html, 11:30am-4pm mid-June), an event in Elizabeth Park that features the blooming of 15,000 roses along with music, poetry, and storytelling. From Thanksgiving until after Christmas, Hartford is brightened nightly by the **Festival of Light** (860/742-2267, www.holidaylightfantasia.org, late Nov.-early Jan., $15 per car), during which a million lights transform Goodwin Park into a starry fantasia celebrating Christmas, Hanukkah, and Three Kings Day.

SHOPPING

Much of the city's shopping lies outside of the city itself, in suburbs like Farmington, West Hartford, and Avon. That said, there are some distinctive souvenirs to be found at **Hartford Prints!** (42½ Pratt St., 860/578-8447, www.hartfordprints.com, 11am-7pm Tues.-Sat.), where you can pick up a cutting board in the shape of Connecticut, a Small State Great Beer pint glass, and a CT QT onesie for any baby in your life. Also check out the **Museum Store at the Old State House** (800 Main St., 860/522-6766, www.cga.ct.gov/osh/, 10am-5pm Tues.-Sat. July-early Oct., 10am-5pm Mon.-Fri. mid-Oct.-early July), which carries a solid stash of books about Connecticut, distinctive jewelry, and games and toys.

SPORTS AND RECREATION

Hiking and Biking

Perched high up on the Metacomet Ridge west of Hartford, the 165-foot Heublein Tower makes a tantalizing goal for hikers in **Talcott Mountain State Park** (Rte. 185, Bloomfield, 860/242-1158, www.ct.gov.dep, noon-2pm Thurs.-Sun., free). Reached by a moderate 1.5-mile stretch of the Metacomet Trail, the tower is done in the Tyrolean style, and has a rich history, including a visit by President Dwight Eisenhower. The Metacomet Trail stretches for 40 miles up the ridge and is also accessible from other parks in the region, including **Peak Mountain** in Granby. Another good spot for some outdoor exercise is the **Windsor Lock Canal State Park** (Bridge St., Windsor Locks to Canal St., Suffield, www.ct.gov/dot), which has 5 miles of level trails overlooking the river and its ingenious series of locks.

The 18-mile **Farmington River Trail** (www.traillink.com/trail/farmington-river-trail) is a loop trail that mostly follows the river and passes through several towns. It connects to **Farmington Canal Heritage Trail** (http://fchtrail.org)—an 80-mile rail corridor and a canal tow path—in Farmington and Simsbury.

Traversing eight towns in north-central Connecticut, the 38.5-mile **Tunxis Trail** (www.ctwoodlands.org/blue-blazed-hiking-trails/tunxis-trail) has options for loop hikes and a variety of terrain for all experience levels. Highlights of the northern section, accessed from Barkhamsted (http://barkhamsted.us), are the Indian Cave and Soapstone Quarry dating to 800 BCE.

FOOD

Currently undergoing renovations, Hartford's standby is **Max Downtown** (185 Asylum St., 860/522-2530, maxrestaurantgroup.com/downtown, 11:30am-2:30pm and 5pm-10pm Mon.-Thurs., 11:30am-2:30pm and 5pm-11pm Fri., 5pm-11pm Sat., 4:30pm-9:30pm Sun., $21-49), a 30-year favorite with chophouse classics. At the time of writing, the restaurant planned to add lighter fare and small plates to the venerable menu.

Founded in 2007 by a charity that supports the local community, **Firebox** (539 Broad St., 860/246-1222, www.fireboxrestaurant.com, 11:30am-2:30pm and 5:30pm-10pm Tues.-Fri., 5:30pm-10pm Sat., 11am-2pm and 4:30pm-8:30pm Sun., $24-34) has a long list of farm suppliers on a New American menu. Duck with a cherry demi-glace arrives alongside goat feta polenta, and it's well worth perusing the excellent wine list.

They don't call it soul food for nothing; the comfort fixings at ★ **Black-Eyed Sally's** (350 Asylum St., 860/278-7427, www.blackeyedsallys.com, 11:30am-10pm Mon.-Thurs., 11:30am-11pm Fri.-Sat., 11:30am-8pm Sun., $10.95-19.95) are first-rate. Blackened catfish and jambalaya are house specialties, but the big don't-miss is the rib-and-sausage "Sally's Pig Out" (you'll understand the true meaning of that name after you eat the entire thing).

A relative downtown newcomer, trendy **Salute** (100 Trumbull St., 860/899-1350, www.salutehartford.com, 11:30am-9pm Mon.-Sat., 3pm-9pm Sun., $17-36) walks the line between a casual and upscale Italian restaurant. The lively space with stone walls, leather banquettes, and flattering lighting draws crowds for dishes like shrimp piccata and short ribs served with goat cheese mashed potatoes. There's always a gluten-free pasta special and vegetarian options like "spasta pesto"—julienned vegetables in a nest of spaghetti squash with pesto and tomato sauce.

For inventive pizzas including a kimchi Reuben and bacon-chicken-ranch, head to **The Blind Pig Pizza Co.** (89 Arch St., 860/744-4333, http://blindpigpizza.com, 11am-10pm Sun.-Wed., 11am-11pm Thurs.-Sat., $10-14). Opened in 2016 by the team behind Bear's Smokehouse BBQ, Blind Pig offers four barbecue pies as well as gluten-free options.

Worth the 15-minute trip east of Hartford, the New York-style ★ **Rein's New York Style Deli** (435 Hartford Turnpike, Vernon, 860/875-1344, www.reinsdeli.com, 7am-10pm Sun.-Thurs., 7am-midnight Fri.-Sat., $6-14) is always abuzz with devotees downing delicious traditional Jewish delicacies from matzo ball soup and cheese blintzes to chopped liver and whitefish salad. On your way out the door, grab a few black-and-white cookies for the road.

ACCOMMODATIONS

Right next to the XL Center and just a few blocks from the state capitol, **Hilton Hartford** (315 Trumbull St., 860/728-5151, www.hilton.com, $100-339) is a tightly run operation of about 400 rooms. Expect all the usual Hilton amenities (in-room coffeemakers and high-speed Internet access) plus an indoor pool and fully outfitted fitness center.

In the center of the action, the **Hartford Marriott Downtown** (200 Columbus Blvd., 860/249-8000, $130-189) has two restaurants, an indoor pool, a hot tub, and a fitness center. Club-level rooms allow access to a private lounge with free continental breakfast and evening appetizers.

The hippest place to stay in downtown Hartford, the **Goodwin Hotel** (1 Hayes St., 860/246-7500, www.goodwinhotel.com, $99-299) got a boutique makeover in 2017. Those hoping to channel some of J. P. Morgan's financial success can stay in the suite named for its most famous guest—Morgan was born across the street and was a cousin of the Goodwin brothers who in 1881 built this red-brick hotel, which is on the National Register of Historic Places. Don't miss the chance to stop by the hotel's bar for an "adult snow cone."

INFORMATION AND SERVICES

The **Hartford Business Improvement District** (hartford.com) and **Central Regional Tourism District** (www.centerofct.com) operate websites with area tourism information; the latter has a guide you can order or download. ***Hartford Magazine*** (www.hartfordmag.com) is a publication of the *Hartford Courant* newspaper, which is also behind www.ctnow.com.

GETTING THERE AND AROUND

Hartford is located at the intersection of I-84 and I-91, 2 hours, 20 minutes from New York City, and 1 hour, 40 minutes from Boston.

Amtrak (800/872-7245, www.amtrak.com) runs trains to Hartford's train station at One Union Place, with additional service to Windsor and Windsor Locks. **Greyhound** (800/231-2222, www.greyhound.com) offers buses to many area locations, including Enfield, Farmington, and Middletown.

CT Transit (860/522-8101, www.cttransit.com) operates bus service throughout Hartford and the greater Connecticut River Valley. The E line runs from the corner of Main and Travelers Streets to West Hartford (15 min.) and Farmington (35 min.). The N line runs from the Old State House (800 Main St.) to Windsor center (45 min.), and the U line runs from the Old State House to Middletown (1 hr.). All fares are $1.75. For taxi service, try **City Cab** (860/416-6587), or pick one up at the taxi stand in front of Union Station.

Litchfield Hills

Tucked into the state's northwestern corner, the Litchfield Hills are blissfully quiet, studded with lush hills, farms, and small villages. This is prime leaf-peeping territory in autumn, and a favorite country escape from New York City. Not that anyone goes to the Litchfield Hills to live off the land—this is rural New England gone upscale, with excellent restaurants, luxe inns, and a lifetime of high-end shopping.

LITCHFIELD

Litchfield was settled in 1721, and very much looks the part of a quaint colonial town. Restored to a high shine, 18th-century architecture clusters around a pristine town green, and wide avenues are lined with historic homes. Things are quiet enough today, but Litchfield was a hotbed of Revolutionary sentiment and played a big part during the Revolutionary War era, with hometown figures that include Vermont's militia captain Ethan Allen, future vice president Aaron Burr, and several signers of the Declaration of Independence.

Because of that tradition—not to mention its almost impregnable position deep in the hills—Litchfield served as a command center and storehouse during the war. General George Washington passed through four times during 1780 and 1781, and Litchfield and its surrounding communities have painstakingly marked his steps and noted every place he laid his head at night.

Sights

A story in the *Litchfield Monitor* in 1803 reported that the **Litchfield Green,** a wide, oval expanse in the center of town was filled with broken fences, woodpiles, and overgrown shrubbery, with hogs, not to mention truants, wandering around at will. Such an image today is all but inconceivable. Litchfield's town green stretches as much as a football field from end to end and is lined on one side by shops and restaurants, all trying to outdo each other to exude a combination of colonial forthrightness and upscale panache.

Just looking up at the white clapboard facade of the 1828 **First Congregational Church** recalls the era of tricornered hats, musketry, petticoats, and breeches. It's interesting to know, then, that the church wasn't on the green more than 50 years before it was moved to make room for a more "fashionable" Gothic church. The original meetinghouse was used as an armory, dance hall, and even a skating rink before a colonial revival effort in the 20th century restored it to its commanding location on the green.

Though all of Litchfield might be considered an open-air history museum, the peerless collection at the **Litchfield Historical Society** (7 South St., 860/567-4501, www.

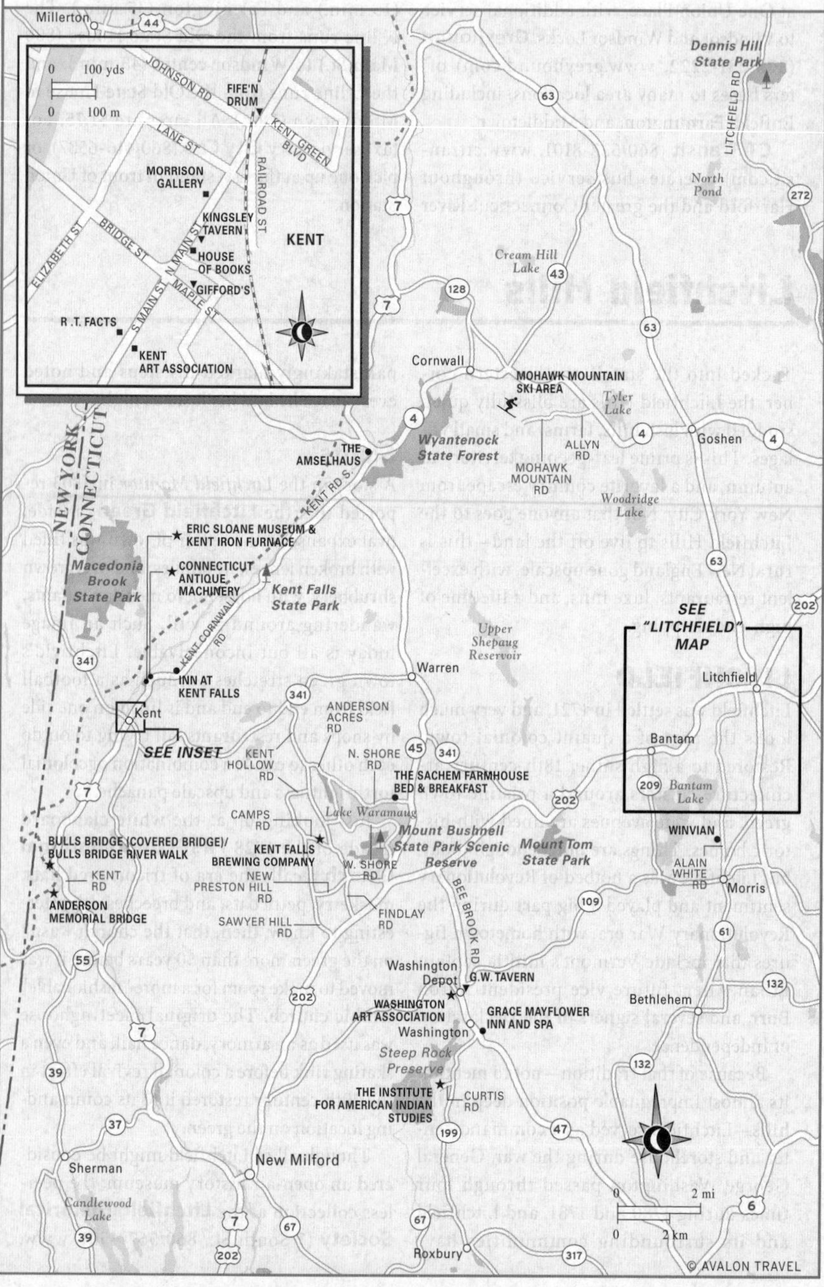
Litchfield Hills
Millerton
44
0 100 yds
0 100 m
JOHNSON RD
FIFE'N DRUM
KENT GREEN BLVD
LANE ST
RAILROAD ST
MORRISON GALLERY
KINGSLEY TAVERN
KENT
ELIZABETH ST
BRIDGE ST
N MAIN ST
HOUSE OF BOOKS
GIFFORD'S
MAPLE ST
S MAIN ST
R.T. FACTS
KENT ART ASSOCIATION
Dennis Hill State Park
LITCHFIELD RD
63
North Pond
272
7
Cream Hill Lake
43
128
63
Cornwall
MOHAWK MOUNTAIN SKI AREA
Tyler Lake
Goshen
4
Wyantenock State Forest
THE AMSELHAUS
ALLYN RD
MOHAWK MOUNTAIN RD
Woodridge Lake
NEW YORK
CONNECTICUT
KENT RD S.
ERIC SLOANE MUSEUM & KENT IRON FURNACE
CONNECTICUT ANTIQUE MACHINERY
Macedonia Brook State Park
Kent Falls State Park
KENT CORNWALL RD
SEE "LITCHFIELD" MAP
202
Upper Shepaug Reservoir
341
INN AT KENT FALLS
Warren
Litchfield
Kent
SEE INSET
ANDERSON ACRES RD
KENT HOLLOW RD
N. SHORE RD
45
Bantam
209
Bantam Lake
THE SACHEM FARMHOUSE BED & BREAKFAST
CAMPS RD
Lake Waramaug
Mount Bushnell State Park Scenic Reserve
Mount Tom State Park
WINVIAN
BULLS BRIDGE (COVERED BRIDGE)/ BULLS BRIDGE RIVER WALK
KENT FALLS BREWING COMPANY
W. SHORE RD
KENT RD
NEW PRESTON HILL RD
BEE BROOK RD
ALAIN WHITE RD
Morris
ANDERSON MEMORIAL BRIDGE
109
SAWYER HILL RD
FINDLAY RD
61
55
Washington Depot
G.W. TAVERN
WASHINGTON ART ASSOCIATION
GRACE MAYFLOWER INN AND SPA
Washington
132
Bethlehem
Steep Rock Preserve
39
THE INSTITUTE FOR AMERICAN INDIAN STUDIES
CURTIS RD
37
199
47
Sherman
New Milford
0 2 mi
0 2 km
Candlewood Lake
67
6
317
Roxbury
© AVALON TRAVEL

litchfieldhistoricalsociety.org, 11am-5pm Tues.-Sat., 1pm-5pm Sun. mid-Apr.-Nov., free) is especially worthwhile. Stop to see artifacts from colonial, federal, and Victorian times, including period furniture, clothing, accessories, pewter, tavern signs, manuscripts . . . the list goes on.

The Historical Society also gives tours of the **Tapping Reeve House** (82 South St., 11am-5pm Tues.-Sat., 1pm-5pm Sun. mid-Apr.-Nov., free), a colonial home that once housed a law school run by future Supreme Court Justice Tapping Reeve at the turn of the 19th century. More than 1,000 students were educated there, including 130 future U.S. senators and congressmen and such luminaries as Horace Man, Noah Webster, and John C. Calhoun.

The area's take on farm-to-bottle distilling, **Litchfield Distillery** (569 Bantam Rd., 860/361-6503, www.litchfielddistillery.com, tours and tastings on the hour noon-5pm Wed.-Sun., free), uses locally sourced grains for its award-winning bourbon, vodka, and gin. Tours explain the distilling process, concluding with a tasting of the distillery's spirits.

WHITE MEMORIAL CONSERVATION CENTER

One of New England's best natural-history centers, and Connecticut's largest wildlife refuge and nature center, the **White Memorial Conservation Center** (80 Whitehall Rd., off Rte. 202, 860/567-0857, www.whitememorialcc.org, 9am-5pm Mon.-Sat., noon-5pm Sun., $6 adults, $3 children 6-12) is a 4,000-acre preserve that combines an impressive museum with 35 miles of trails. The museum is full of high-quality dioramas painted by James Perry Wilson, who created the ones at the American Museum of Natural History in Manhattan, with interactive exhibits that appeal to all ages.

The trails, however, are the main draw—a mix of paths for cycling, walking, and horseback riding, plus cross-country skiing and snowshoeing in winter. Along the way, some 30 observation platforms have been set up to afford visitors a vantage point for spotting birds and other wildlife. The rare golden-ringed warbler is one of 116 species known to breed here; also of note are the 2,500 mergansers that descend on Bantam Lake in December. The most popular trail is **Little Pond Boardwalk,** a 1.5-mile wood path over the water and wetlands of the pond. There are campgrounds on-site, and educational programs, events, and guided walks are offered year-round.

Very much a Litchfield Hills take on agriculture, **Arethusa Farm** (556 S. Plains Rd., 860/567-8270, www.arethusafarm.com) was founded by a pair of executives from Manolo Blahnik—a shoe company famed for exorbitant prices. Here, cows' tails are shampooed with Pantene Pro V, and the animals live in pristine white barns. Tours of the farm are held 12:30pm-2:30pm each Saturday, or you can stop by **Arethusa Farm Dairy** (822 Bantam Rd., Bantam, 860/361-6600, 10am-8pm Sun.-Thurs., 10am-10pm Fri.-Sat.) to taste milk and ice cream from the pampered bovines.

Entertainment and Events

Litchfield's annual **Gallery on the Green** (860/567-8298, www.jwclitchfieldhills.org, June) isn't a permanent gallery, but a yearly installment of around 100 artists and artisans who set up shop to exhibit original watercolors, oil paintings, jewelry, and other crafts. The **Litchfield Jazz Festival** (Goshen County Fairgrounds, 116 Old Middle Rd./Rte. 63, Goshen, 860/567-4162, www.litchfieldjazzfest.com, Aug.) has drawn an impressive roster of jazz greats like Dave Brubeck and Diana Krall for music under the stars since 1996.

Shopping

Jeffrey Tillou Antiques (39 West St., 860/567-9693, www.tillouantiques.com, 10:30am-5pm Mon. and Wed.-Sat., 11am-4:30pm Sun.), on the Litchfield Green, specializes in fine 18th- and early 19th-century American furniture and paintings. Selling

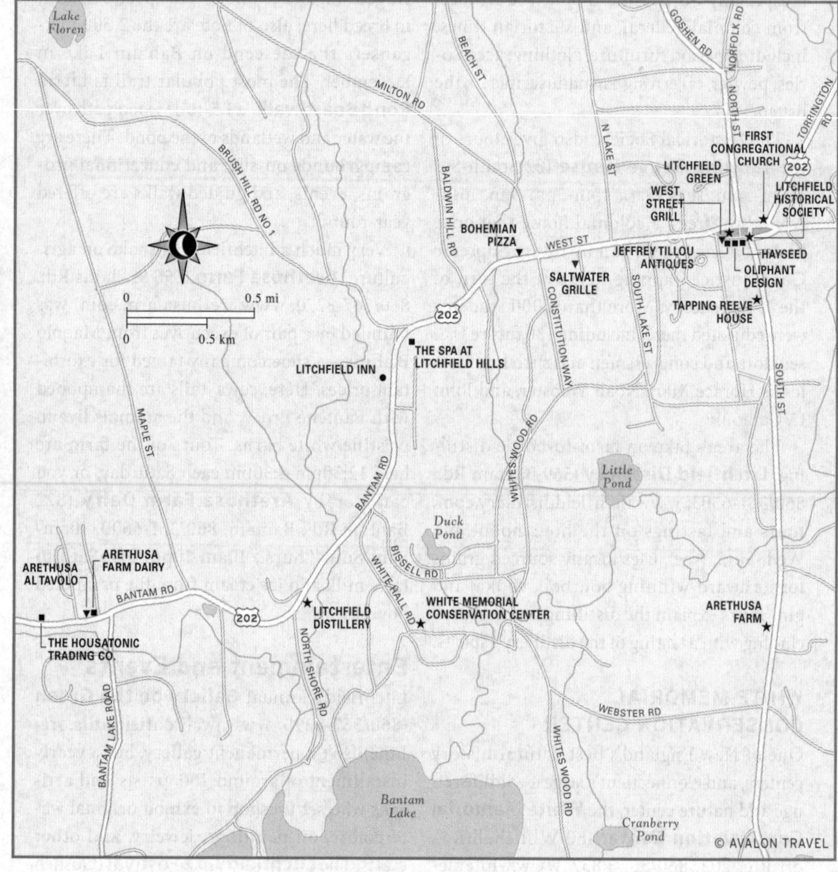

both new and antique furniture, art, and gift items, **Housatonic Trading Company** (920 Bantam Rd., Bantam, 860/361-6299, www.housatonictradingcompany.com, 8am-5pm Mon.-Tues. and Thurs.-Sun.) also operates a café offering coffee and panini.

Look for the store with large white columns on the Litchfield Green and enter the fresh and colorful world of **Oliphant Design** (29 West St., 860/567-8199, http://oliphantdesign.com, 11am-5:30pm Mon.-Fri., 10am-6pm Sat., noon-5pm Sun.), which sells women's and children's clothing, jewelry, and home decor. The name **Hayseed** (On the Green, 860/567-8775, 11am-5pm Mon.-Tues., 10am-5pm Wed.-Sat., noon-5pm Sun.) is strictly tongue-in-cheek, as this "country couture" clothing store stocks the latest high-fashion items no self-respecting woman with a second home in the Litchfield Hills would be without. Think Ralph Lauren and then some.

Sports and Recreation

HIKING

Half an hour north of town, **Dennis Hill State Park** (Norfolk, www.litchfieldhills.com) is a favorite destination for walkers. The two-mile **Romantic Ramble at**

Dennis Hill loop trail leads to a hilltop gazebo with sweeping views of the Litchfield Hills. From there, you can continue to the top of 1,627-foot Dennis Hill to look across three states—Connecticut, Massachusetts, and Vermont—from an observation platform on the roof of a once-grand bungalow.

BIKING

The Litchfield Hills area is a fantasyland for bikers, where hilly climbs and long, winding back roads lead to white-steepled churches and country stores. The **Bicycle Tour Company** (9 Bridge St., Kent, 888/711-5368, www.bicycletourcompany.com) offers guided tours of the northwestern corner of the state, including both of Connecticut's covered bridges. Rentals are $25 per day, $75 per week, with specials for families and other groups.

If you're up for a 49-mile route, **The West as It Gets Ride** (Kent, www.ctbikeroutes.org) travels through Lime Rock, Lakeville, and Sharon and also visits Duchess County, New York, traveling mainly on roads with low car traffic.

Spas

Relax after all that shopping in one of the plush treatment rooms at **The Spa at Litchfield Hills** (407 Bantam Rd., Litchfield, 860/567-8575, www.litchfield-spa.com, 9am-6pm Mon.-Thurs., 9am-7pm Fri., 9am-6pm Sat., 10am-5pm Sun.). There, the detoxifying Moor mud bath or the one-hour whirlpool pedicure will restore all your energies for the next shopping trip.

Food

Highly acclaimed and for good reason, ★ **West Street Grill** (38 West St., 860/567-3885, www.weststreetgrill.com, lunch: 11:30am-2:30pm Mon. & Wed.-Fri, 11:30am-3:30pm Sat.-Sun; dinner: 5:30pm-9pm Sun. & Wed.-Thu, 5:30pm-10pm Fri.-Sat., $23-42) is a little bit of big city in the country—a contemporary, buzzing bistro on Litchfield Green, with the requisite exposed brick and distressed wooden floors. Global flavors are the kitchen's focus, which translates to specialties such as pan-seared scallops with celery root and fire-roasted salmon with heirloom tomatoes. There are always vegan choices, and a top-notch wine list is also offered. Check ahead to find out the schedule for popular "bistro nights," with an affordable prix fixe menu and wine specials.

Arethusa Farm is behind the fine-dining restaurant **Arethusa al Tavolo** (828 Bantam Rd, Bantam, 860/567-0043, www.arethusaaltavolo.com, 5:30pm-9pm Wed.-Thurs., 5:30pm-10pm Fri., 11:30am-2pm and 5:30pm-10pm Sat., 11:30am-2pm and 5pm-8:30pm Sun., $30-39), whose chef Dan Magill trained under Daniel Boulud. Small and stellar, this gem offers dishes such as roasted local striped bass and ravioli filled with spinach and Arethusa camembert.

Calling itself the "weirdest restaurant in Litchfield County and quite possibly the world," **Bohemian Pizza** (342 Bantam Rd., 860/567-3980, 11:30am-8:30pm Mon.-Thurs., 11:30am-9:30pm Fri.-Sat., 11:30am-7:30pm Sun., $15-21) tries hard to live up to the name, with an energetic young vibe and decor ranging from a canoe to Holstein-patterned seats. The little restaurant is serious about its pizza, however, turning out awesomely good pies topped with everything from sun-dried tomatoes to andouille sausage, alongside a full menu of pastas, meal salads, and other simple-but-tasty entrées.

With a menu that changes daily, **Winvian** (155 Alain White Rd., Morris, 860/567-9600, http://winvian.com, 6:30pm-9pm Wed.-Fri., 12:30pm-2pm and 6:30pm-9pm Sat.-Sun., $98-115 prix fixe) expertly prepares creative three-course meals such as a crudo of kampachi starter, hand-rolled ravioli filled with guinea hen and chestnut as a pasta course, followed by a duo of braised short rib and New York strip steak. A series of charming dining rooms with fireplaces are decorated with antiques, oil paintings, and Oriental rugs, enveloping diners in the warmth of a 1775 farmhouse. The restaurant is part of a unique hotel that hosts guests in creatively themed cottages; guests must announce themselves at the gate.

Known for its fresh seafood and warm-weather patio dining, **Saltwater Grille** (26 Commons Dr., 860/567-4900, www.litchfield-saltwatergrille.org, 4pm-8:30pm Mon.-Thurs., 11:30am-9:30pm Fri.-Sat., 11:30am-8:30pm Sun., $18-42) is a casual, hopping spot with fun items like Oysters Saltafeller (baked with a spinach-artichoke cream and topped with bacon) and classics such as seared tuna. A jazz band is a welcome addition to Sunday dinners. Non-fish eaters and kids will find options as well.

Accommodations

The colonial-style **Litchfield Inn** (432 Bantam Rd./U.S. 202, 860/567-4503, www.litchfieldinnct.com, $161-339) is actually a recently built hotel with modern amenities operated by Best Western. There are 32 accommodations, including 12 themed rooms such as Log Cabin and Contessa. The on-site restaurant, Tavern Off the Green, serves quite good modern American fare.

The Sachem Farmhouse Bed & Breakfast (15 Hopkins Rd., Warren, 860/868-0359, www.thesachemfarmhouse.com, $200-310) overlooks Lake Waramaug and is next to Hopkins Vineyard. The elegantly decorated 1870 farmhouse has four guest rooms, two with private baths; the other two share a hall bath. Guests are invited to meet the sheep and the guard donkey named Georgia on this working sheep farm.

Among the area's most exclusive and luxurious options, **Winvian** (155 Alain White Rd., Morris, 860/567-9600, http://winvian.com, $549-1,500) has 18 themed cottages nestled on 113 acres. A real helicopter inside your cottage outfitted with a bar and TV is one option; another is a tree house perched 35 feet above the forest floor. Brainchild of a variety of designers, the cabins are all very different, but each has a deep Jacuzzi tub, shower, fireplace, and a private outdoor space such as a screened-in patio or deck, plus bicycles to explore the area.

Information

The **Northwest Connecticut Convention & Visitors Bureau** (860/567-4506, www.litchfieldhills.com) runs an information booth on the village green, open unreliably May-October.

Getting There and Around

Litchfield is located about 30 miles west of Hartford on Route 202. The closest public transit goes to Waterbury: **Metro North** (800/638-7646, www.mta.info) runs trains while **Peter Pan Bus Lines** (800/343-9999, www.peterpanbus.com) offers bus service. **CT Transit** (www.cttransit.com) has local bus service within Waterbury (203/753-2538) and Bristol (203/327-7433), but in the Litchfield Hills, having your own car is almost essential. Car service is available from **Kelly Transit** (30 Railroad Sq., Torrington, 860/489-9243, www.kellytransit.com).

WASHINGTON

Incorporated during the Revolutionary War, in 1777, the picturesque little town of Washington made the ultimate gesture of loyalty by naming itself after the Continental Army's general-in-chief. (The town was originally called Judea.) Like the towns around it, Washington has its share of restored colonial houses—however, nature here tends to outshine anything people have built. The town has garnered a reputation for putting on one of the best foliage displays every year, with sugar maple, scarlet oak, beech, and honey locust trees each contributing their unique colors to the palette. Washington Village is arranged around an attractive green with its own picturesque clapboard church, and just down the hill is Washington Depot, the town's commercial center.

Sights

A highlight of the **Institute for American Indian Studies** (38 Curtis Rd., 860/868-0518, www.iaismuseum.org, 10am-5pm Wed.-Sat., noon-5pm Sun., $10 adults, $8 seniors, $6 children 3-12) is a life-sized 16th-century

Algonquain village, complete with three wigwams, a longhouse, and a native plant garden. The dedicated, knowledgeable staff at this research and education center discuss the history of area Native Americans (ask about the tribe that has a quarter acre in Trumbull), explain customs and traditions, demonstrate how they measured the calendar year with the shell of a snapping turtle, and so much more. Fascinating rotating exhibitions about Native people from across the United States include artwork, crafts, and clothing. Several trails allow easy exploration of the 15-acre wooded property.

In nearby Washington Depot, the **Washington Art Association** (4 Bryan Memorial Plaza, Washington Depot, 860/868-2878, www.washingtonart.org, 10am-5pm Tues.-Sat., 10am-2pm Sun., free) is a top-notch exhibitor of local artwork. The association holds regular gallery openings, as well as art classes, speakers, and a popular holiday sale.

Events

Over Columbus Day weekend, Washington holds a **Design & Antiques Show** to support the local library, which also has a museum dedicated to area history. No small affair, the 2017 event featured 18 dealers, two parties, and Cornelia Guest as the honorary chair. Around Halloween, the **Gunn Memorial Library and Museum** (5 Wykeham Rd., 860/868-7756, www.gunnlibrary.org) leads a popular evening cemetery tour, with costumed actors bringing notable past residents to life.

Shopping

The quaint commercial center of Washington Depot is anchored by the **Hickory Stick Bookshop** (2 Green Hill Rd., Washington Depot, 860/868-0525, www.hickorystickbookshop.com, 9am-5:30pm Mon.-Sat., 11am-5pm Sun.), the area's cultural hub, with well-stocked shelves of contemporary fiction and nonfiction books. The shop also hosts numerous local-author readings. Authors with Litchfield Hills homes who have read here in the past include Arthur Miller, Madeleine L'Engle, and William Styron.

Food

With a blend of country charm and urban sophistication, **Marty's Café** (6 Green Hill Rd./Rte. 47, Washington Depot, 860/868-1700, http://m.mainstreethub.com/martyscafe, 7am-5pm daily, $7-16) is a stylish espresso bar with enough rustic touches to remind you that you are in the sticks. In addition to Wi-Fi and racks full of newspapers, it offers up creative sandwiches—try the trio of sliders with pulled pork, portobello and goat cheese, and turkey club with bacon.

The staid name aside, **Mayflower Dining Room** (118 Woodbury Rd./Rte. 47, 860/868-9466, www.gracehotels.com/mayflower, noon-2pm and 6pm-9pm Tues.-Thurs. and Sun., noon-2pm and 6pm-10pm Fri.-Sat., $16-54) is a white-tablecloth joint that overlooks the beautiful Shakespeare Garden at the elegant Grace Mayflower Inn. An appetizer of Japanese hamachi crudo and trout roe can be followed by rack of lamb with foraged ramps. There's also the more casual, dimly lit Tap Room, where you can get a burger if the mood strikes.

George Washington never slept at **G. W. Tavern** (20 Bee Brook Rd., Washington Depot, 860/868-6633, www.gwtavern.com, 11:30am-9pm Sun.-Tues. and Thurs., 11:30am-10pm Fri.-Sat., $13-36), but the casual pub and eatery does everything it can to honor him, with a framed picture of you-know-who over the fireplace and a bust overlooking the light and airy dining room. After a full day of leaf-peeping, a piping-hot crock of French onion soup topped with gooey gruyère cheese is just the ticket. Entrées like ground-pork meatloaf and chicken potpie are similarly comfort-food oriented. Specials are updated nightly online.

Accommodations

The **Grace Mayflower Inn and Spa** (118 Woodbury Rd./Rte. 47, 860/868-9466, www.gracehotels.com/mayflower, $565-1,765) invites superlatives. A Relais & Chateaux property, it is a sublimely elegant hotel with a stunning destination spa (for guests only), indoor and outdoor pools, sophisticated dining, and beautiful gardens (the American Poets' Garden is on one side of the Grace Mayflower and the Shakespeare Garden is on the other—get it?). There are 30 accommodations in four buildings that range 368-1,200 square feet; some have a balcony, fireplace, and/or sitting area. A putting green and tennis courts add to the amenities in the warmer weather; the hotel can provide cross-country skis and snowshoes in winter to explore its 58 acres. Children under 12 are not allowed except at the restaurants.

A sophisticated and intimate Dutch Colonial country house overlooking a nature preserve, **Hidden Valley Bed and Breakfast** (226 Bee Brook Rd., 860/868-9401, www.hiddenvalleyct.com, $260-280) has three guest rooms and a heated plunge pool. For more privacy, choose the ground-floor Red Guest Suite, which has a private entry and kitchenette. In the main house, the Blue Master Bedroom's draws are a thermal spa bath and sweeping valley views. If you are traveling with a child, there's a daybed in the Green Bedroom.

Unusual for a bed-and-breakfast with only two rooms, the **Orange Gild Bed and Breakfast and Spa** (137 Nichols Hill Rd., 860/868-9636, www.orangegild.com, $300-350) has a sauna for guests' use. And not only one sauna but a Finnish sauna, an infrared sauna, and a steam shower. These spa experiences are included in the rate as is breakfast, which usually includes Dutch *beschuit*, fruit, a smoothie, and freshly baked Dutch pastries like *puddingbroodje* (the proprietors are from the Netherlands). Rooms are large and have a king bed and private bath. There's a whirlpool in one and an additional twin bed in the other.

It looks like an unremarkable motel from the street, but most of the rooms at the **Rocky River Inn** (236 Kent Rd., New Milford, 860/355-3208, www.therockyriverinn.com, $92-202) are refreshingly contemporary in design. On 10 acres on the Housatonic River and near Candlewood Lake, this 36-room property has multiple room categories; the ones called economy are less expensive and have not received the upgrades the ones in the luxury class have.

On the town green, the **Homestead Inn** (Elm St., New Milford, 860/354-4080, www.homesteadct.com, $109-249) renovated rooms in its two buildings—the 1853 Homestead B&B (no children under 13) and the 1938 Treadwell House—in 2016. Book the Marilyn Monroe Suite if you're a fan: She actually stayed here. Rooms are individually decorated and are more sophisticated in the B&B. Treadwell accommodations are more kid-friendly, with sleeper sofas, bunk beds, and the like.

Getting There

Washington is located 1 hour west of Hartford on diminutive Route 47, and is a 70- minute drive from New Haven. There is currently no public transit to Washington.

KENT

With more of a downtown to explore than elsewhere in the Litchfield Hills, Kent's population of 3,000 swells with out-of-towners on the weekends. In the 19th century, Kent was an industrial town, producing pig iron, but that gritty past has given way to galleries and design stores supported by the thriving creative community. A few traces of the old days are on display at a pair of museums that explore the years of iron smelting and mining, and there's plenty of hiking nearby, including Connecticut's only covered bridges and the state's highest waterfall.

Sights

Once the home of artist, author, and collector Eric Sloane, **Eric Sloane Museum & Kent Iron Furnace** (31 Kent-Cornwall Road/Rte. 7, 860/927-3849, www.ericsloane.com/museum.htm, 10am-4pm Fri.-Sun. May-Oct., $8 adults, $6 seniors over 59 and college students, $5 children 6-17, children under 6 free) reconstructs Sloane's studio and displays his extensive collection of early tools that are examples of great American craftsmanship. Also on-site are a pioneer cabin built by Sloane using information in Noah Blake's 1805 *Diary of an Early American Boy*, and the remains of the Kent Iron Furnace, which operated 1826-1892.

The **Connecticut Antique Machinery** (31 Kent Cornwall Rd., 860/927-0050, www.ctamachinery.com, 10am-4pm Wed.-Sun. May-Oct., free, donations welcome) museum, which shares a driveway with the Sloane Museum, explores the history of the state's mining operations for iron, copper, garnets, marble, limestone, basalt, and brownstone, as well as local clay deposits and brickmaking operations. There's an extensive collection of Connecticut minerals and a special exhibit about how Native Americans used quartz and other materials from the earth to make tools.

Connecticut's first farm brewery, **Kent Falls Brewing Company** (33 Camps Rd., 860/398-9645, http://kentfallsbrewing.com, 2pm-7pm Thurs.-Fri., noon-5pm Sat., farm tours 2pm Sat.) was established in 2014 on the 50-acre mixed-use Camps Road Farm, land that has been in continuous agricultural use for more than 250 years. Brews range from IPAs and lagers, with a few offbeat options like the sour wheat Meyer lemon and shaved coconut-infused lemon coconut gose (whew!).

Events

The Connecticut Antique Machinery's **Fall Festival** (www.ctamachinery.com, Sept.) attracts thousands of people to see steam engines, farm equipment, and blacksmiths at work, while shops display creative gingerbread structures during the **Kent Gingerbread Festival** (www.kentctgingerbreadfest.com, Dec.).

Shopping and Galleries

A community hub with frequent readings by local authors, **House of Books** (10 N. Main St., 10am-5pm Mon.-Thurs., 10am-5:30pm Fri.-Sat., 11am-5pm Sun.) is also a trove of information about the region, from free tourist booklets to hiking guides and children's books.

For going on 100 years, the **Kent Art Association Gallery** (21 S. Main St., 860/927-3989, www.kentart.org, 1pm-5pm Thurs.-Sun. Mar.-Oct,) has showcased the works of emerging and established artists, and organizes art-related programs. Its calendar is active throughout the year, so check the website for updates.

The high-profile **Morrison Gallery** (25 N. Main St., 860/927-4501, www.morrisongallery.com, 11am-5pm Thurs.-Sat., 1pm-4pm Sun.) showcases contemporary and modern paintings and sculpture. At press time, a larger gallery with outdoor space able to exhibit large-scale sculpture and installations was under construction at 60 North Main Street.

Close your eyes and say the name **R.T. Facts** (22 S. Main St. and 8 Old Barn Rd./Kent Barns, 860/927-1700, http://rtfacts.com, 10am-5pm Mon.-Sat., noon-5pm Sun.)—the "artifacts" in question are a collection of eclectic furniture, lighting, garden and architectural details, and lots of unique objects. Some items are antiques and others are made locally. The Main Street shop has three buildings and garden spaces; the 7,000-square-foot museum-like showroom in the Kent Barns collection of businesses is two blocks away.

Whimsical handcrafted ceramics, jewelry, clothing, glass items, rugs, and sculpture have kept **Heron American Craft Gallery** (16 N. Main St., 860/927-4804, http://heroncraftgallery.com, 11am-5pm daily) a destination for shoppers for 30 years. Kids of all ages will get a kick out of a specially curated selection of "unusual playthings."

Sports and Recreation

HIKING

There are two covered bridges open to cars in Connecticut, and both are in the Litchfield Hills. For a great view of one of them plus a hike on a portion of the Appalachian Trail, do the four-mile **Bull's Bridge River Walk** (www.litchfieldhills.com) that links Bull's

Bridge with Anderson Memorial Bridge, following the Housatonic River.

The state's highest waterfall is in **Kent Falls State Park** (Rte. 7, www.ct.gov/deep/kentfalls), a 250-foot cascade reached by an easy 0.25-mile trail with a few steep sections. It passes through a covered bridge that was built in 1974 for foot traffic only.

SKIING

A small, family-friendly spot, **Mohawk Mountain Ski Area** (46 Great Hollow Rd., Cornwall, 860/672-6100, www.mohawkmtn.com, 9:30am-8pm Mon.-Wed., 9:30am-10pm Thurs.-Fri., 8:30am-10pm Sat., 8:30am-4pm Sun., $64 ages 16 and over, $56 children 5-15, $15 children under 5) is regarded as having the best skiing in the state. There's no terrain park, but the ski instruction is comprehensive for a variety of experience levels. An alternative to the cafeteria in the main lodge is the full-service ski-in, ski-out restaurant partway up the mountain on Pine Trail.

covered bridge in Kent Falls State Park

Food

A town fixture, the **Fife 'n Drum** (53 N. Main St., 860/967-3509, http://fifendrum.com, 11:30am-3pm and 5:30pm-9:30pm Mon.-Thurs., 11:30am-3pm and 5:30pm-10pm Fri.-Sat., 11am-8:30pm Sun., $23-36) is the kind of old-school place that tosses Caesar salad and flambés duck tableside. There's live music on Friday evenings and 13 rooms available in the inn upstairs.

At **Kingsley Tavern** (14 N. Main St., 860/592-0261, http://kingsleytavern.com, 5pm-9pm Wed.-Thurs., 5pm-9:30pm Fri., 11:30am-3pm and 5pm-9:30pm Sat., 11:30am-8pm Sun., $10-28), kids are happy with burgers, and adults gravitate to the jerk chicken and Saigon sandwich made with pork, shrimp, or tofu on a baguette with pickled daikon, cucumber, jalapeño, and spicy mayo. Grab a table outside in nice weather to watch the comings and goings of the town. Reservations are accepted only for parties of five or more.

Specializing in seasonal, New American cuisine from high-end local provisioners, **Gifford's** (9 Maple St., 860/592-0262, http://giffordsrestaurant.com, 5pm-9pm Fri., noon-9pm Sat., 11am-7pm Sun., $18-36) is around the corner from Kent's main drag. Surprises like chicken and waffles and pad thai enliven a menu of American standards such as pan-roasted scallops and lemon chicken. Everything is prepared in-house, from the bread to the desserts.

Accommodations

Set on two acres in the middle of downtown, **Starbuck Inn** (88 N. Main St., 860/927-1788, http://starbuckinn.com, $207-267) goes the extra mile, offering a daily afternoon tea and a thoughtful breakfast. Six guest rooms each feature a custom-built armoire, Frette linens and towels, a pillow-top mattress, and a private bath. There's a queen bed and shower in three rooms, and two rooms have king beds and a bathtub/shower; the king suite's main appeals are its private entry, comfortable living area, and large walk-in shower.

For more space and accommodations for more than two people, a good option is **The Amselhaus** (6 Rug Rd., Cornwall, 860/248-3155, www.theamselhaus.com, $175-325). The two multi-floor suites each has a kitchen, living room, dining room, porch, and private entrance. There are two bedrooms plus a sleeper sofa in the South Suite, and the North Suite has three bedrooms. An 1830 farmhouse, the inn is 13 minutes from Kent and four miles from Cornwall's famous covered bridge, near Mohawk Mountain.

Consistently voted the best B&B in the state, **The Inn at Kent Falls** (107 Kent Cornwall Rd., 860/927-3197, www.theinnatkentfalls.com, $245-385) is a sophisticated, welcoming home dating to the 1700s but renovated and updated with private baths and modern amenities. There are three smaller rooms plus four suites that have sitting areas and additions like a fireplace and daybed. Professionally designed gardens with walking paths, an outdoor pool, and a patio add to its charms; cooler temperatures find guests gathering by the fireplaces and piano in the common rooms.

Information

The **Kent Chamber of Commerce** (860/592-0061, http://kentct.com) has an informative website and produces a comprehensive pocket guide to the area, including maps, business listings, and a calendar of events. Pick one up around town—House of Books usually has it in stock.

Getting There

Kent is located at the intersection of Route 341 and Route 7, by the New York border. It's 80 minutes from Hartford, and 90 minutes from New Haven. There is currently no public transit to Kent.

The Quiet Corner

A satellite photo of the eastern seaboard at night shows the entire coast from Washington DC to Boston lit up like a Christmas tree—except one small portion, the northeastern corner of Connecticut. Tucked into a pocket between the big cities of Worcester, Hartford, and Providence, the upper-right corner of the state has been called the "last green valley" for its miles of wooded back roads and romantically decayed farmhouses and stone walls. While that may be a bit of hyperbole, the area's other nickname, the "Quiet Corner," seems just about right. The pace of life *is* quieter here, with a country-store mentality that seems more like Vermont than Connecticut.

Not that the Quiet Corner was always so quiet; back at the turn of the 19th century, the area's swift-flowing rivers and proximity to the early mill industry of Rhode Island meant that it was one of the first areas to industrialize. For decades, the Quinebaug River currents churned the wheels of textile mills of manufacturing centers like Putnam and Willimantic until they gradually fell into disuse in the 20th century.

PUTNAM

Named in honor of Revolutionary War hero General Israel Putnam, who was from nearby Brooklyn, Connecticut, Putnam was incorporated in 1855. The town flourished in the 19th century as a center for textile production, with cotton mills providing clothing to Civil War troops. Located on the Quinebaug River and with a railroad line crossing the town, Putnam was ideally placed for industry. The river hasn't always been a benevolent force, however. Two massive floods in 1955 devastated Putnam, but it bounced back with a focus on antiques dealers. Since the antiques trade dissipated in the last decade or so due to Ebay and other digital retail platforms, Putnam has diversified into arts and crafts venues, boutiques, and a variety

The Quiet Corner

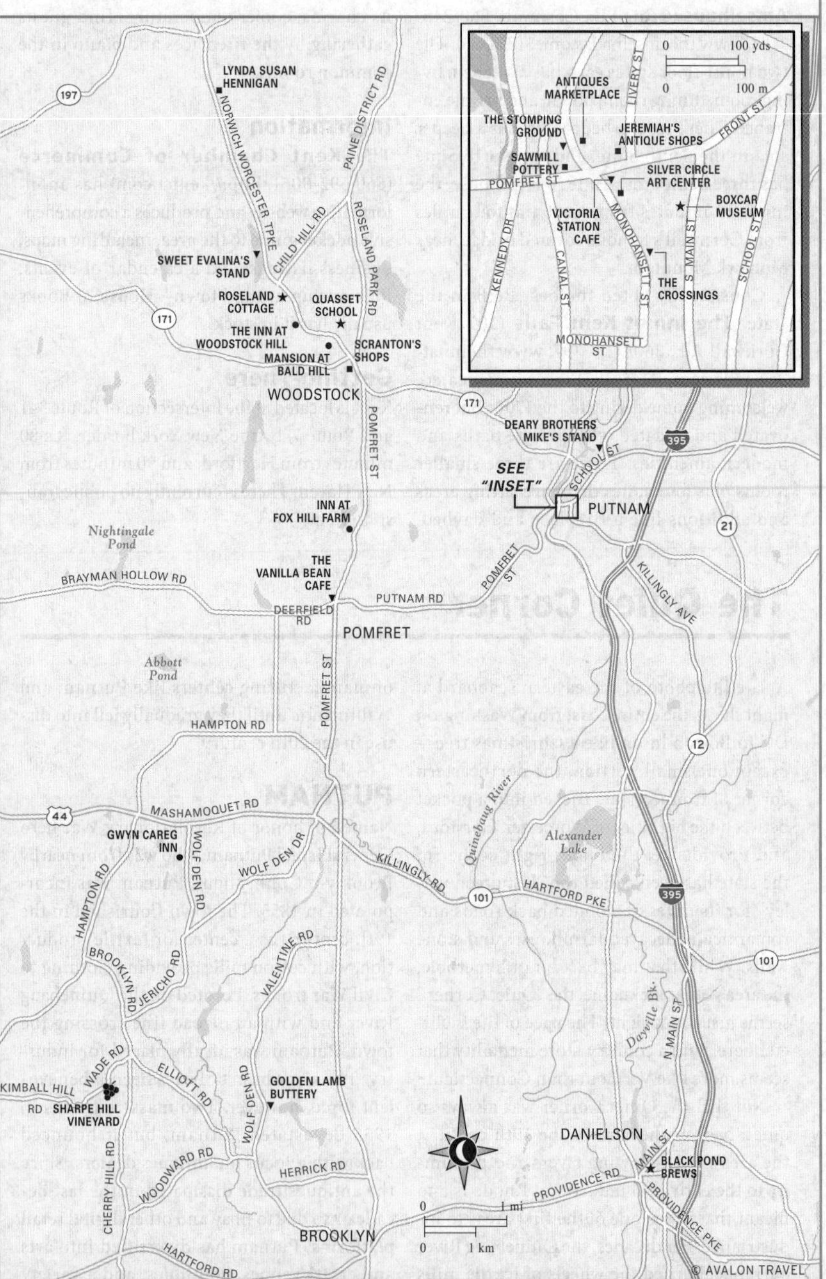
LYNDA SUSAN HENNIGAN
NORWICH WORCESTER TPKE
PAINE DISTRICT RD
197
CHILD HILL RD
ROSELAND PARK RD
SWEET EVALINA'S STAND
ROSELAND COTTAGE
QUASSET SCHOOL
171
THE INN AT WOODSTOCK HILL
SCRANTON'S SHOPS
MANSION AT BALD HILL
WOODSTOCK
POMFRET ST
INN AT FOX HILL FARM
Nightingale Pond
THE VANILLA BEAN CAFE
BRAYMAN HOLLOW RD
PUTNAM RD
DEERFIELD RD
POMFRET
Abbott Pond
HAMPTON RD
44
MASHAMOQUET RD
GWYN CAREG INN
WOLF DEN RD
WOLF DEN DR
KILLINGLY RD
HAMPTON RD
BROOKLYN RD
JERICHO RD
VALENTINE RD
WADE RD
ELLIOTT RD
KIMBALL HILL RD
SHARPE HILL VINEYARD
GOLDEN LAMB BUTTERY
CHERRY HILL RD
WOODWARD RD
HERRICK RD
HARTFORD RD
BROOKLYN
0
1 mi
1 km
0 100 yds
0 100 m
ANTIQUES MARKETPLACE
LIVERY ST
THE STOMPING GROUND
JEREMIAH'S ANTIQUE SHOPS
FRONT ST
SAWMILL POTTERY
POMFRET ST
SILVER CIRCLE ART CENTER
BOXCAR MUSEUM
VICTORIA STATION CAFE
KENNEDY DR
CANAL ST
MONOHANSETT ST
S MAIN ST
SCHOOL ST
THE CROSSINGS
MONOHANSETT ST
DEARY BROTHERS MIKE'S STAND
395
SCHOOL ST
SEE "INSET"
PUTNAM
21
POMFRET ST
KILLINGLY AVE
12
Quinebaug River
Alexander Lake
101
HARTFORD PKE
395
101
Dayville Bk.
N MAIN ST
DANIELSON
MAIN ST
BLACK POND BREWS
PROVIDENCE RD
PROVIDENCE PKE
© AVALON TRAVEL

of restaurants and bars, and also stages festivals and events that bring people downtown.

Sights

If you're a fan of Gertrude Chandler's children's book series The Boxcar Children, climbing into an actual boxcar across the street from the author's childhood home will be a thrill. At the **Boxcar Museum** (1 S. Main St., no phone, http://boxcarchildrenmuseum.com, 11am-4pm Sat.-Sun. mid-May-mid-Oct., free but donations appreciated), visitors will find a collection of original signed books, photos, and artifacts from the author's life, and a re-creation of the Boxcar Children's living space.

The largest winery in Connecticut, **Sharpe Hill Vineyard** (108 Wade Rd., 860/974-3549, www.sharpehill.com, 11am-5pm Fri.-Sun., tastings $10-15) has racked up awards for a wide range of wines, which include everything from Riesling to cabernet franc. It's a lovely spot, and worth a stop to enjoy wines with views of the rolling vineyards, which turn rusty in autumn.

Ten minutes south of Putnam, the small town of Killingly is also worth a stroll—in the borough of Danielson, Main Street is filled with shops, and you'll find one of the area's most interesting breweries: **Black Pond Brews** (21 Furnace St., Danielson, 860/207-5295, www.blackpondbrews.com, 5pm-8pm Thurs.-Fri., 3pm-8pm Sat., 1pm-5pm Sun.) mixes up small batches of everything from American IPAs to a jalapeño saison.

Entertainment and Events

A restored century-old vaudeville theater in the heart of Putnam's antiques district, **Bradley Playhouse** (30 Front St./Rte. 44, 860/928-7887, www.bradleyplayhouse.org, shows $19 adults, $15 students and seniors, musicals $23 adults, $20 students and seniors) plays host to amateur drama and musicals. You can hear live music six days a week at The Stomping Ground (132 Main St., 860/928-7900, www.the-stomping-ground.com, 11am-1am Tues.-Sun.), across the street from the Bradley. Potpies and grilled cheese with creative ingredients set the tone for the eclectic food menu.

Shopping

A mind-boggling selection awaits at **Antiques Marketplace** (109 Main St., 860/928-0442, 10am-5pm Wed.-Mon.), the largest and most diverse antiques mall around. Pore over goods in more than 325 exhibits on four floors, including furniture, art, jewelry, and collectibles from seemingly every time period and several continents. The same owners curate **Jeremiah's Antique Shops** (26 Front St., 860/928-0666, www.facebook.com/jeremiahsantiques, 10am-5pm Wed.-Mon.), which sells the wares of 70 dealers, with everything from estate jewelry to comic books.

A large arts collective selling paintings, ceramics, sculptures, notecards, scarves, and more from local artists and artisans, **Silver Circle Art Center** (75 Main St., Ste. 3, 860/928-2900, www.silvercirclegallery.com, noon-4pm Sun. and Wed.-Thurs., 11am-5pm Fri.-Sat.) is an impressive display of local talent. Locally made, vividly glazed bowls and platters line the shelves at **Sawmill Pottery** (112 Main St. #14, 860/963-7807, www.sawmillpottery.com, 10am-4pm Mon. and Sat., 10am-9pm Tues.-Thurs., 10am-8pm Fri., noon-4pm Sun.), which also offers studio sessions and classes.

Sports and Recreation

HIKING AND BIKING

Tracing a 26-mile path from Putnam to Pomfret, the **Air Line State Park Trail** (860/928-6121, www.ct.gov/deep) follows a former railroad bed through pretty farms and woodlands. Both Putnam and Killingly have paved riverfront paths for walking and cycling. The **Putnam River Mills Heritage Trail** winds for 1 mile between Pomfret and Providence streets; the town's history and historic mill buildings are explained via signs. Pick up Killingly's 3.5-mile trail at the parking lot on Water Street, off Route 12.

The roads in the region are particularly good for cycling, with sparse traffic, gentle grades, and scenery with every mile. The brochure *Northeast Connecticut's Bike Guide* details 10 self-guided loops through the region. Bikes can be rented at **Scott's Cyclery** (1171 Main St., Willimantic, 860/423-8889, www.scottscyclery.com).

Food

The **Vanilla Bean Café** (450 Deerfield Rd., Pomfret, 860/928-1562, www.thevanillabeancafe.com, 7am-3pm Mon.-Tues., 7am-8pm Wed.-Thurs., 7am-9pm Fri., 8am-9pm Sat., 8am-8pm Sun., $7-14) has been the center of life in sleepy Pomfret since 1989. At the juncture of Routes 169, 97, and 44, the 90-seat Vanilla Bean is a gathering place for a great cup of coffee (try the Nutella latte), freshly made sandwiches, and burgers; plus it hosts folk, blues, and jazz musicians on Saturday evenings.

In a former train station, **The Crossings** (45 Main St., 860/928-3663, http://crossingsbrewpub.com, 11:30am-11pm daily, $7-21) is a large, casual restaurant with high, pressed-tin ceilings. It serves several of its own beers and elevated pub grub like the standout seasonal BLT lobster roll, made with fresh Maine lobster.

Ice cream lovers will not want to walk past **Victoria Station Café** (91 Main St., 860/928-2600, www.victoriastationcafe.com, 6am-9pm Mon.-Thurs., 6am-11pm Fri., 8am-11pm Sat., 8am-9pm Sun., $6-18) without ordering a cone. About 30 homemade flavors change often but might include ginger peach, caramel apple, and limoncello. Coffee, pastries, and light lunch items like quiche and stuffed croissants invite lingering. Upstairs is a space for live music.

A family-owned seasonal food stand that's been serving cheap and tasty burgers, hot dogs, chicken, seafood, and ice cream since 1937, **Deary Bros. Mike's Stand** (12 Intervale St., 860/928-1191, www.dearybrosmikesstand.com, 11am-9:30pm Sun.-Thurs., 11am-11pm Fri.-Sat. mid-Apr.-mid-Sept., $3-23) is a local institution. Order at the window and enjoy your fried goodness—including the unusual options of grilled cheese and tuna, pepper steak, and a choice of bay or sea scallops—or handcrafted ice cream like Dinosaur Crunch and Bubble Gum, at a picnic table.

A restaurant that embodies the Quiet Corner experience, **Golden Lamb Buttery** (499 Wolf Den Rd., Brooklyn, 860/774-4423, http://thegoldenlamb.com, noon-2:30pm Thurs., noon-2:30pm and 7pm-9pm Fri.-Sat., $75 prix fixe dinner, à la carte lunch entrées range $12-17) offers a hayride through its picturesque farm, wine on the terrace overlooking the pond and a pasture with roaming horses, and a prix fixe meal in a rustic barn. The restaurant, which is roughly 15 minutes south of Putnam, is on the 1,000-acre Hillandale Farm, which supports sheep, cows, and donkeys, grows herbs and vegetables, and has trails that guests are welcome to explore.

Accommodations

It's worth planning ahead to snag the single cottage at the ★ **Inn at Fox Hill Farm** (760 Pomfret St., Pomfret Center, 860/928-5240, www.innatfoxhillfarm.weebly.com, $215), a romantic escape whose private back deck overlooks the farm's pretty lake. Rates include a hearty breakfast prepared by the friendly innkeepers, and the cottage's fridge is stocked with complimentary snacks.

The tastefully decorated colonial revival **Gwyn Careg Inn** (68 Wolf Den Rd., Pomfret Center, 860/928-5018, http://gwyncareginn.com, $150-200) sits on 14 acres that include a large pond and a Spanish garden surrounded by 10-foot stone walls. One of the six guest accommodations is furnished with two twin beds; the rest are suites with a sitting area, and two even have two separate bedrooms. All have a private bath and come with a full country breakfast.

Information

The Route 169 corridor is promoted by the nonprofit **The Last Green Valley** (107

Providence St., 860/963-7226 or 866/363-7226, www.thelastgreenvalley.org), which runs a well-stocked information center in downtown Putnam. Operating from Putnam, **WINY Radio** (860/928-1350, www.winyradio.com) is a useful source of up-to-the-minute information about Putnam and all of eastern Connecticut. Find it online or at 1350 AM. The **Putnam Business Association** runs an informative website at www.discoverputnam.com.

Getting There

Putnam is in northeastern Connecticut on Route 21, a short distance from Interstate 395. It's 1 hour from Hartford, and 1.5 hours from New Haven.

WOODSTOCK

The 8,000 residents of this rural community are spread across 62 square miles, so exploring feels like a true taste of rural life. A farming town in the 18th century, Woodstock became known for the summer parties of its most famous resident, Henry Bowen, whose oddball Victorian house is now the area's main tourist draw.

Sights

ROSELAND COTTAGE/ BOWEN HOUSE

The first thing you notice about the quirky Victorian **Roseland Cottage/Bowen House** (556 Rte. 169, 860/928-4074, www.historicnewengland.org, tours hourly 11am-4pm Wed.-Sun. June-mid-Oct., $10 adults, $9 seniors, $5 students) is the color: bright rose pink. In fact, that was the original shade that Henry Bowen painted the cottage, which he gave as a gift to his wife, a lover of roses. The building is now the country's best surviving model of the Gothic Revival architecture that was all the rage for a brief period of time in the mid-19th century. The exterior is all quatrefoils and balustrades, and the interior feels more like a cathedral, with high ceilings and stained glass in the parlors.

Today the home is owned by Historic New England, which has restored the house. Because the home was continuously in the hands of the family, all the furniture and artwork is original to the house—a rarity in house museums. As a special treat, don't miss the 19th-century bowling alley, with wooden pins and balls, in a barn on the property.

Roseland Cottage/Bowen House

OTHER SIGHTS

One of the oldest one-room schoolhouses in America, **Quasset School** (Frog Pond Rd., off Rte. 171, 860/968-0208, www.townofwoodstock.com, 1pm-4pm Sun. July-Aug.) held classes 1690-1944. As a wonderful connection to history, the town's third graders even today spend a week in the school, which is close to the Woodstock Elementary School.

Shopping

Lynda Hennigan re-creates 19th-century sailors' valentines that she sells in her eponymous **Lynda Susan Hennigan** gallery (1089 Rte. 169, 860/315-5334, www.lyndasusanhennigan.com, open Sat.-Sun., call for hours). Formerly a blacksmith shop, post office, and auto repair shop, **Scranton's Shops** (300 Rte. 169, South Woodstock, 860/928-3738, www.scrantonsshops.com, 11am-5pm Wed.-Mon.) has 85 dealers selling antiques, furniture, collectibles, art, and crafts.

Events

At the **Woodstock Fair** (281 CT-169, 860/928-3246, http://woodstockfair.com, Labor Day weekend), everything from cattle to guinea pigs and giant vegetables to quilts are entered into competition. Carnival rides, a horse show, and a barnyard babies birthing center add to the fun.

Food

A roadside favorite, with big slices of pie and an old-fashioned menu, **Sweet Evalina's Stand** (688 Rte. 169, 860/928-4029, www.sweetevalinas.com, 7am-8pm daily, $5-11) is perfect for getting a glimpse of local life. Farmers belly up to big burgers or bowls of chili, or just opt for ice cream at an outdoor picnic table. Both of the following accommodations also have on-site restaurants.

Accommodations

Built by a Bowen, as was Roseland Cottage, **The Mansion at Bald Hill** (29 Plaine Hill Rd., 860/974-3456, www.mansionatbaldhill.com, $140-230) is a Victorian home with six guest rooms and a restaurant that's open to the public. The four-story landmark sits on 90 acres, with extensive gardens and hosts many weddings and private events.

Of the 21 guest rooms at the **Inn at Woodstock Hill** (94 Plaine Hill Rd., 860/928-0528, www.woodstockhill.com, $160-260), eight rooms have working gas fireplaces and six have four-poster beds. Other accommodations in this white clapboard house built in 1816 include a separate sitting areas, cedar bathrooms, skylights, or cathedral ceilings. A beautiful patio overlooks the expansive grounds. If you're traveling with a group, the three-bedroom guest cottage next door is a great option. Continental breakfast is complimentary, and there's a fine-dining restaurant on the premises. This former home was built for the grandson of the Roseland Cottage Bowen.

Information

The **Woodstock Business Association** (www.explorewoodstock.com) produces a brochure that's downloadable from its informative website.

GETTING THERE AND AROUND

To get to the Quiet Corner by car, take I-395 south from Worcester (30 miles or 40 minutes to Putnam); U.S. 6 west from Hartford (30 miles or 40 minutes to Willimantic); or U.S. 6 east from Providence (30 miles or 50 minutes to Brooklyn).

Windham Region Transit District's (860/456-2223, www.wrtd.net) service area includes Ashford, Chaplin, Columbia, Coventry, Lebanon, Mansfield, Scotland, Willington, and Windham, none of which gets you exactly to the Quiet Corner. A car is necessary to explore this region.

Rhode Island

Look for ★ to find recommended sights, activities, dining, and lodging.

Highlights

★ **Rhode Island School of Design Museum:** Set on the campus of the design school, this museum's remarkable collection ranges from jewelry worked by ancient artists to modern installations (page 233).

★ **WaterFire:** Watch downtown Providence light up as floating braziers ignite on the city's rivers (page 238).

★ **Newport's Mansions:** Channel the 19th-century elite while visiting summer homes that combine Gilded Age glamour, exquisite art, and monumentally bad taste (page 248).

★ **Cliff Walk:** Stroll between the mansions and the sea on this seven-mile walking path (page 255).

★ **South County Beaches:** Paddle into the waves at Narragansett Town Beach or bring your binocs to Napatree Hill—the barrier beaches of the southern coast have something for everyone (page 263).

★ **Cycling Block Island:** You'll pass more bicycles than cars on your way around this tiny island, where almost half the land is in conservation (page 270).

Nothing's far from anywhere in this tiny state, but there's a lot to explore in Little Rhody, whose coastline wraps around deep bays, islands, and inlets before taking a long, straight run at the edge of the Atlantic.

Barrier beaches draw summer crowds for surfing and sun, then turn beautifully vacant in the cooler months, perfect for spotting the migratory birds that flock to the coast.

Long overlooked by travelers, the capital city of Providence has cutting-edge art galleries alongside gorgeous historic architecture, while Newport's Gilded Age mansions are fascinating temples to 19th-century gilt and gaud.

Founded by the theologian Roger Williams—who was kicked out of Massachusetts when his free thinking annoyed the Puritans—Rhode Island later became New England's most prominent trafficker in African slaves, a trade that flourished *after* the first abolition law was passed in the colonies. Those contradictions between an independent identity, religious tolerance, inequality, and the legacy of slavery have shaped the state's history and landscape, from rundown mill towns to moneyed enclaves.

At the northern end of Rhode Island, the Blackstone Valley was the birthplace of America's Industrial Revolution, with churning mills that eventually turned the Blackstone River into the country's most toxic waterway. Workers lived in appalling conditions, even as the up-and-coming barons of industry built their summertime palaces in Newport. In Providence, money from slavery helped lay the bricks of Brown University, long considered the most liberal of the Ivy League schools.

And there's a milder contrariness that runs through Rhode Island, too, a delightful weirdness that draws the visitor in, from the spine-tingling writing of Providence writer H. P. Lovecraft to the legends behind Newport's Touro Tower, and a lineup of offbeat foods that can only be found in the Ocean State.

Previous: Block Island wildflowers; Narragansett Town Beach. **Above:** Providence architecture.

Rhode Island

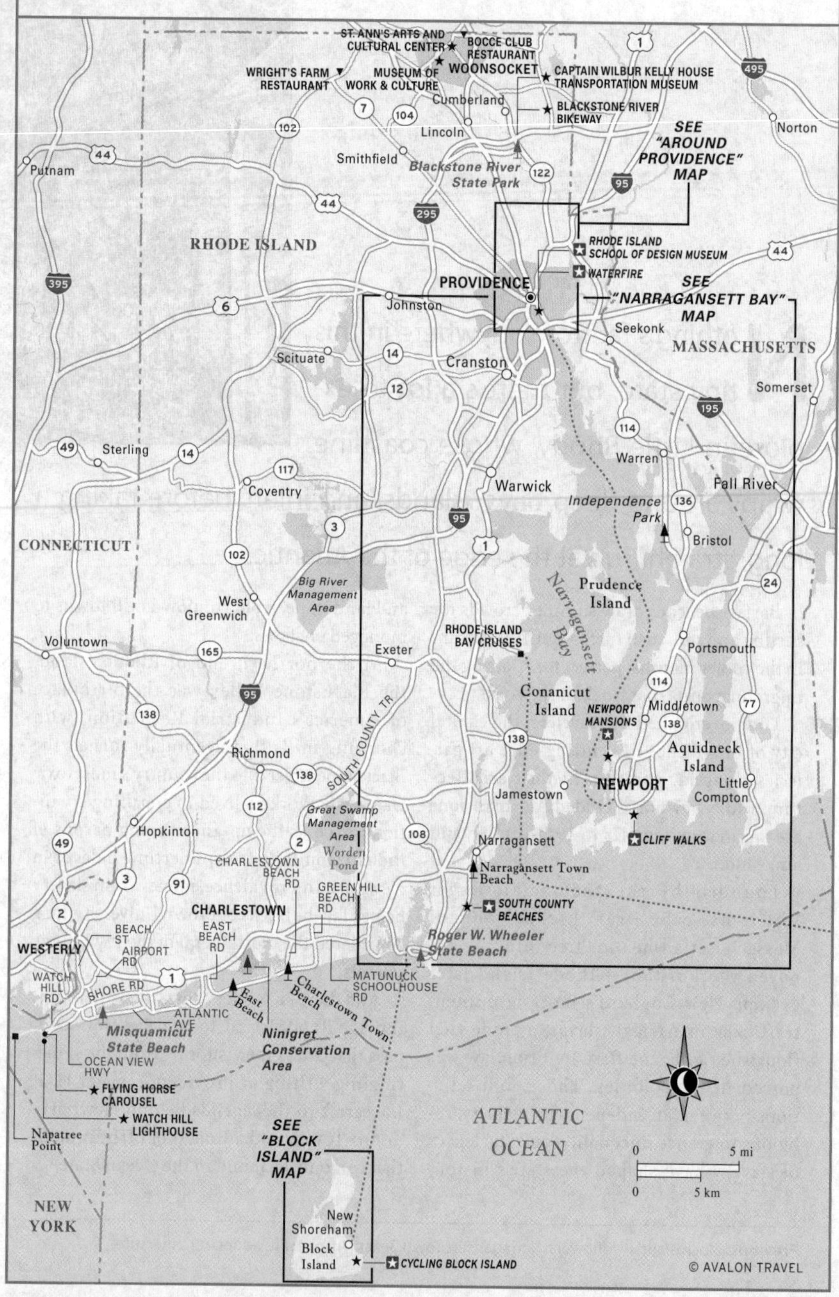
ST. ANN'S ARTS AND CULTURAL CENTER
BOCCE CLUB RESTAURANT
WRIGHT'S FARM RESTAURANT
MUSEUM OF WORK & CULTURE
WOONSOCKET
CAPTAIN WILBUR KELLY HOUSE TRANSPORTATION MUSEUM
Cumberland
BLACKSTONE RIVER BIKEWAY
Lincoln
Norton
Putnam
Smithfield
Blackstone River State Park
SEE "AROUND PROVIDENCE" MAP
RHODE ISLAND
RHODE ISLAND SCHOOL OF DESIGN MUSEUM
WATERFIRE
PROVIDENCE
SEE "NARRAGANSETT BAY" MAP
Johnston
Seekonk
MASSACHUSETTS
Scituate
Cranston
Somerset
Sterling
Warren
Coventry
Warwick
Fall River
Independence Park
Bristol
CONNECTICUT
Narragansett Bay
Prudence Island
Big River Management Area
West Greenwich
Voluntown
RHODE ISLAND BAY CRUISES
Exeter
Portsmouth
Conanicut Island
NEWPORT MANSIONS
Middletown
SOUTH COUNTY TR
Aquidneck Island
Richmond
NEWPORT
Jamestown
Little Compton
Great Swamp Management Area
Hopkinton
Narragansett
CLIFF WALKS
Worden Pond
CHARLESTOWN BEACH RD
Narragansett Town Beach
GREEN HILL BEACH RD
CHARLESTOWN
SOUTH COUNTY BEACHES
BEACH ST
EAST BEACH RD
WESTERLY
AIRPORT RD
Roger W. Wheeler State Beach
WATCH HILL RD
SHORE RD
MATUNUCK SCHOOLHOUSE RD
East Beach
Charlestown Town Beach
ATLANTIC AVE
Misquamicut State Beach
Ninigret Conservation Area
OCEAN VIEW HWY
FLYING HORSE CAROUSEL
WATCH HILL LIGHTHOUSE
Napatree Point
SEE "BLOCK ISLAND" MAP
ATLANTIC OCEAN
0 5 mi
0 5 km
NEW YORK
New Shoreham
Block Island
CYCLING BLOCK ISLAND
© AVALON TRAVEL

PLANNING YOUR TIME

With just a few days in Rhode Island, you can cover a lot of territory. Depending on whether you're interested in city culture or historic mansions, Providence and Newport are the two logical bases for exploring, with the state's beaches within easy day-tripping distance. Add a few more days to your itinerary and Block Island is in reach, ditching the day visitors on a two-night trip.

ORIENTATION

First things first—Rhode Island is not an island. Many of the state's most important destinations are at the edge of the water, however, overwhelmingly clustered around Narragansett Bay, which extends to the outlet of the Providence River. Newport is on an island, the long isle of Aquidneck, linked to the mainland by a series of bridges.

Providence

Once overlooked and grimy, Providence is now among the most interesting cities in New England. A pair of landmark colleges draws creative students from around the world, and graduates that stay on inject a vibrancy visible in the thriving art scene, cafés, and up-and-coming neighborhoods.

Keep your head up as you walk through the historic center to see architectural detailing hidden in plain view above the bustling streets. There are statues tucked high over the sidewalks, elegant rooflines, and busts that have kept watch over the city through some long, lean years.

From the start, Providence has had an independent spirit. Roger Williams founded a colonial settlement here after getting kicked out of Puritanical Massachusetts for his religious beliefs, and Providence became the very first colony to declare independence from England in 1776.

The city retains a bit of grit and smoke from the long era when no tourist would head to Providence for a weekend away, but things were largely transformed by the legendary mayor Buddy Cianci, a force of nature with mob connections, a felony conviction, and a vision for the future. It's a sign of the times that as Providence appears on lists of America's coolest cities, some locals have begun to wax nostalgic about the old days—a reminder to visit Providence now, before it gets too clean and too cool entirely.

SIGHTS

★ Rhode Island School of Design Museum

Browse art by ancient Egyptians and midcentury modern designers at the extraordinary **Rhode Island School of Design Museum of Art** (20 N. Main St., 401/454-6500, www.risdmuseum.org, 10am-5pm Tues.-Sun., $12 adults, $10 seniors, $5 college students, $3 children 5-18, children under 5 free), usually simply called the RISD Museum (that's ris-dee). The breadth of the collection is remarkable in itself, and it's especially striking to see art and design from ancient Greece and Egypt, then travel through the centuries to cutting-edge work.

Another highlight is the enormous holdings of costumes and textiles, with the earliest clothing items dating back to 1500 BCE, and articles from historic Japan, the European Renaissance, and Native American groups.

Brown University and College Hill

Set high above the city, the Ivy League **Brown University** campus (Admission Office, 45 Prospect St., 401/863-1000, www.brown.edu) is the crest of the College Hill neighborhood. It's a pleasant place to walk through clusters of brick buildings, and the university is deeply entwined with Rhode Island's history, both good and tragic. The independent spirit of early Rhode Island remains in a less

Around Providence

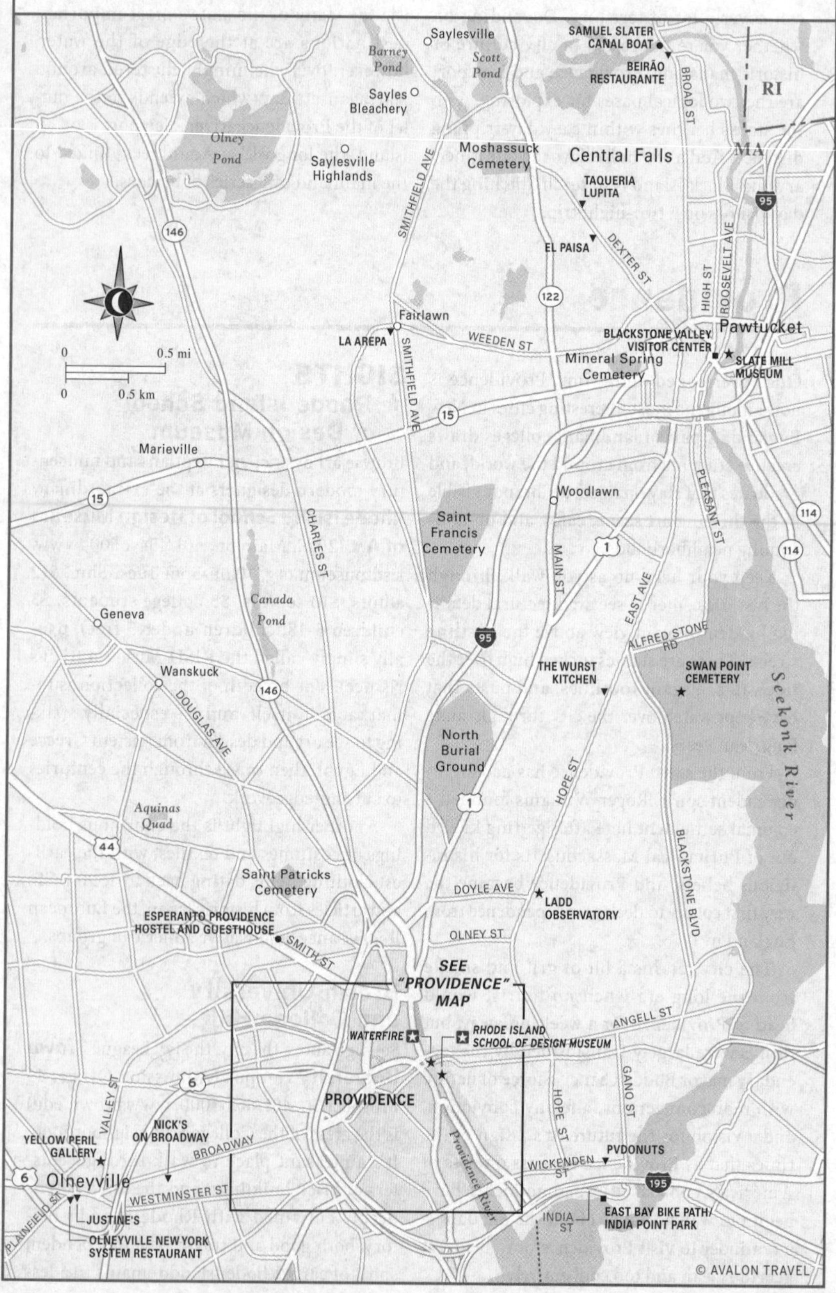
Saylesville
Barney Pond
Scott Pond
SAMUEL SLATER CANAL BOAT
BEIRÃO RESTAURANTE
BROAD ST
RI
MA
Sayles Bleachery
Olney Pond
Saylesville Highlands
Moshassuck Cemetery
Central Falls
SMITHFIELD AVE
TAQUERIA LUPITA
EL PAISA
DEXTER ST
95
146
HIGH ST
ROOSEVELT AVE
122
Fairlawn
LA AREPA
WEEDEN ST
Pawtucket
BLACKSTONE VALLEY VISITOR CENTER
SLATE MILL MUSEUM
Mineral Spring Cemetery
0
0.5 mi
0
0.5 km
15
Marieville
Woodlawn
CHARLES ST
PLEASANT ST
114
Saint Francis Cemetery
MAIN ST
1
EAST AVE
Canada Pond
Geneva
ALFRED STONE RD
Wanskuck
THE WURST KITCHEN
SWAN POINT CEMETERY
Seekonk River
DOUGLAS AVE
North Burial Ground
HOPE ST
Aquinas Quad
44
BLACKSTONE BLVD
Saint Patricks Cemetery
DOYLE AVE
LADD OBSERVATORY
ESPERANTO PROVIDENCE HOSTEL AND GUESTHOUSE
SMITH ST
OLNEY ST
SEE "PROVIDENCE" MAP
ANGELL ST
WATERFIRE
RHODE ISLAND SCHOOL OF DESIGN MUSEUM
VALLEY ST
6
PROVIDENCE
GANO ST
NICK'S ON BROADWAY
YELLOW PERIL GALLERY
BROADWAY
Providence River
PVDONUTS
WICKENDEN ST
Olneyville
WESTMINSTER ST
195
PLAINFIELD ST
JUSTINE'S
OLNEYVILLE NEW YORK SYSTEM RESTAURANT
INDIA ST
EAST BAY BIKE PATH/ INDIA POINT PARK
© AVALON TRAVEL

traditional approach to education than other Ivy League landmarks, but the university's ties to the transatlantic slave trade haunts the institution to this day—the Brown family owned and traded slaves, as did many early members of Brown's governing board. Self-guided tours of the campus are available on the university website.

For a peek into the daily life of abolitionist John Brown, who gave his name to the local university, pop into the **John Brown House** (52 Power St., 401/331-8575, www.rihs.org, 10:30am-4:30pm Tues.-Sat. Apr.-Dec., 10:30am-4:30pm Fri.-Sat. Jan.-Mar., $10 adults, $8 seniors and students, $6 children 7-17, free children under 7). Meticulously restored, the grand Georgian mansion, built in 1788, is chock-full of excellent-quality period antiques and local art.

Another highlight of the neighborhood is the **Providence Athenaeum** (251 Benefit St., 401/421-6970, www.providenceathenaeum.org, 9am-7pm Mon.-Thurs., 9am-5pm Fri.-Sat., 1pm-5pm Sun.), a historic library that was a favorite haunt of Edgar Allan Poe and H. P. Lovecraft.

Downtown

The downtown neighborhood swirls around the **Rhode Island State House** (82 Smith St., 401/222-2357), worth a look for its freestanding enormous dome—one of the largest of its kind in the world. Cross the river to another gem of Providence architecture, the **Providence City Hall** (25 Dorrance St., 401/421-7740, www.providenceri.com, 8:30am-4:30pm Mon.-Fri.), a gorgeous Beaux-Arts landmark wrought in brass and marble. The city hall appears in the writing of local horror author H. P. Lovecraft, as does the former Industrial Trust Tower at 111 Westminster Street that's often referred to as **The Superman Building,** the tallest building in Rhode Island.

Federal Hill

Colorful and a bit corny, this Italian American enclave is full of red-sauce joints, Italian bakeries, and little neighborhood markets. Beyond first impressions, though, there's a lot of fascinating history here—a good option for exploring are the gourmet walking tours of the neighborhood by **Savoring Rhode Island** (800/656-0713, www.savoringrhodeisland.com, 3-hour tours $55), which blend local stories and culinary heritage.

Roger Williams Park & Zoo

Several miles outside of the city, the historic **Roger Williams Park & Zoo** (1000 Elmwood Ave., 401/785-3510, www.rwpzoo.org, 10am-5pm daily Apr.-Sept., 10am-4pm daily Oct.-Mar., $14.95 adults, $12.95 seniors, $9.95 children 2-12) was one of the first in the United States and remains among the best in New England. Highlights include a miniature Nubian goat, red pandas, wildebeest, cotton-top tamarins, and a Linne's two-toed sloth.

Surrounding the zoo is a 427-acre park that's free to access, with a series of paths that wind around manicured gardens, ponds, and pavilions. The park is especially lovely in the fall, when the trees and Japanese Garden are brightly lit by colorful leaves.

Art Galleries

Providence hums with creative energy, which powers dozens of local art galleries and art spaces—too many to visit on a single trip to the city. You'll find an entire complex of galleries and performance spaces at **AS220** (95 Mathewson St., Unit 204, and 115 Empire St., 401/831-9327, www.as220.org, 1pm-6pm Wed.-Fri., noon-4pm Sat.), with work by more than 150 artists in a series of rotating exhibits.

Another favorite for contemporary art is **Yellow Peril Gallery** (60 Valley St. #5, 401/861-1535, www.yellowperilgallery.com, 11am-8pm Thurs.-Sun.), where you'll find works by midcareer and more-established names that explores themes from society and pop culture.

To see what creative minds at the Rhode Island School of Design are making, stop by the **Gelman Student Exhibitions Gallery at RISD** (20 N. Main St., 401/709-8660, www.

Providence

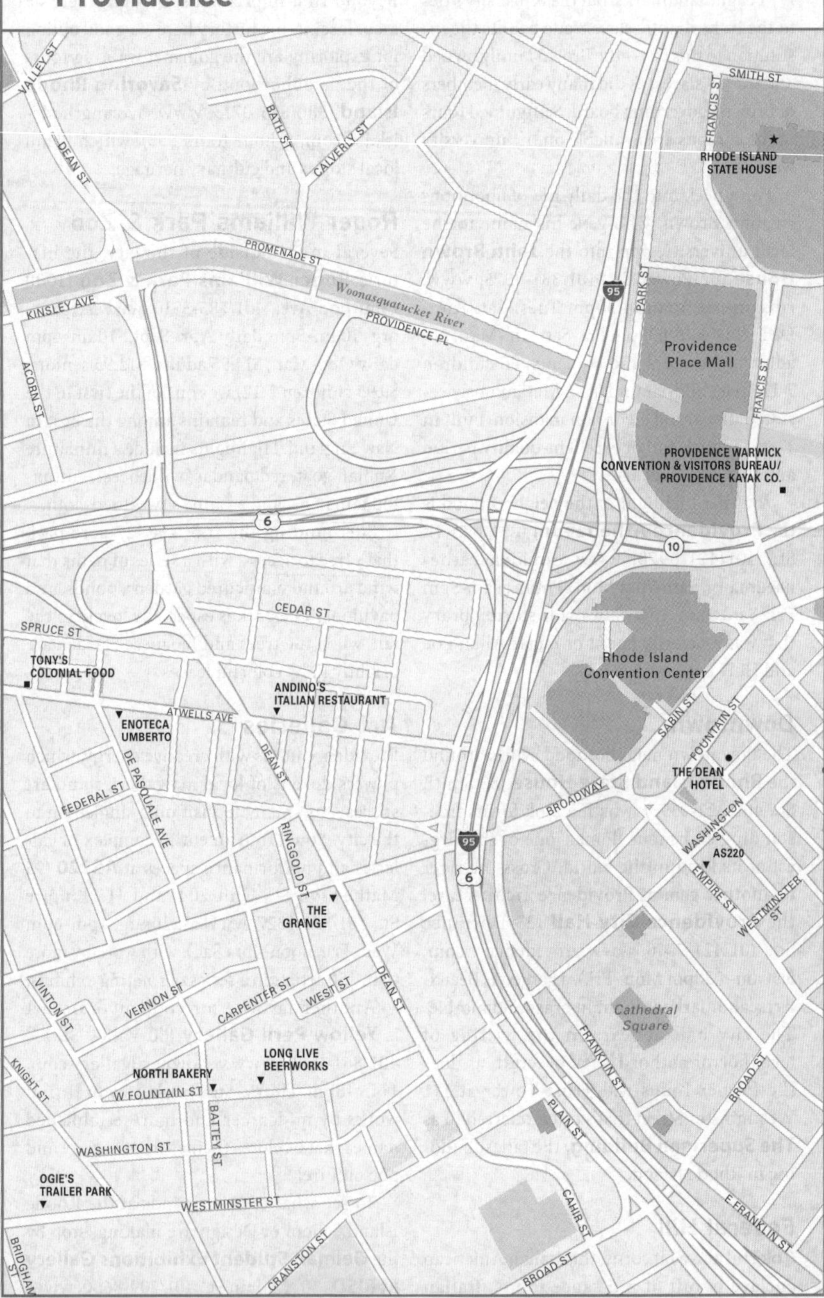
VALLEY ST
DEAN ST
BATH ST
CALVERLY ST
SMITH ST
FRANCIS ST
RHODE ISLAND
STATE HOUSE
PROMENADE ST
Woonasquatucket River
KINSLEY AVE
PROVIDENCE PL
PARK ST
95
ACORN ST
Providence
Place Mall
FRANCIS ST
PROVIDENCE WARWICK
CONVENTION & VISITORS BUREAU/
PROVIDENCE KAYAK CO.
6
10
CEDAR ST
SPRUCE ST
TONY'S
COLONIAL FOOD
ANDINO'S
ITALIAN RESTAURANT
Rhode Island
Convention Center
ATWELLS AVE
ENOTECA
UMBERTO
DEAN ST
SABIN ST
FOUNTAIN ST
DE PASQUALE AVE
THE DEAN
HOTEL
FEDERAL ST
BROADWAY
RINGGOLD ST
95
WASHINGTON
ST
AS220
6
EMPIRE ST
WESTMINSTER
ST
THE
GRANGE
VINTON ST
VERNON ST
CARPENTER ST
WEST ST
DEAN ST
Cathedral
Square
FRANKLIN ST
LONG LIVE
BEERWORKS
KNIGHT ST
NORTH BAKERY
W FOUNTAIN ST
BATTEY ST
BROAD ST
PLAIN ST
WASHINGTON ST
OGIE'S
TRAILER PARK
CAHIR ST
WESTMINSTER ST
E FRANKLIN ST
BRIDGHAM
ST
CRANSTON ST
BROAD ST

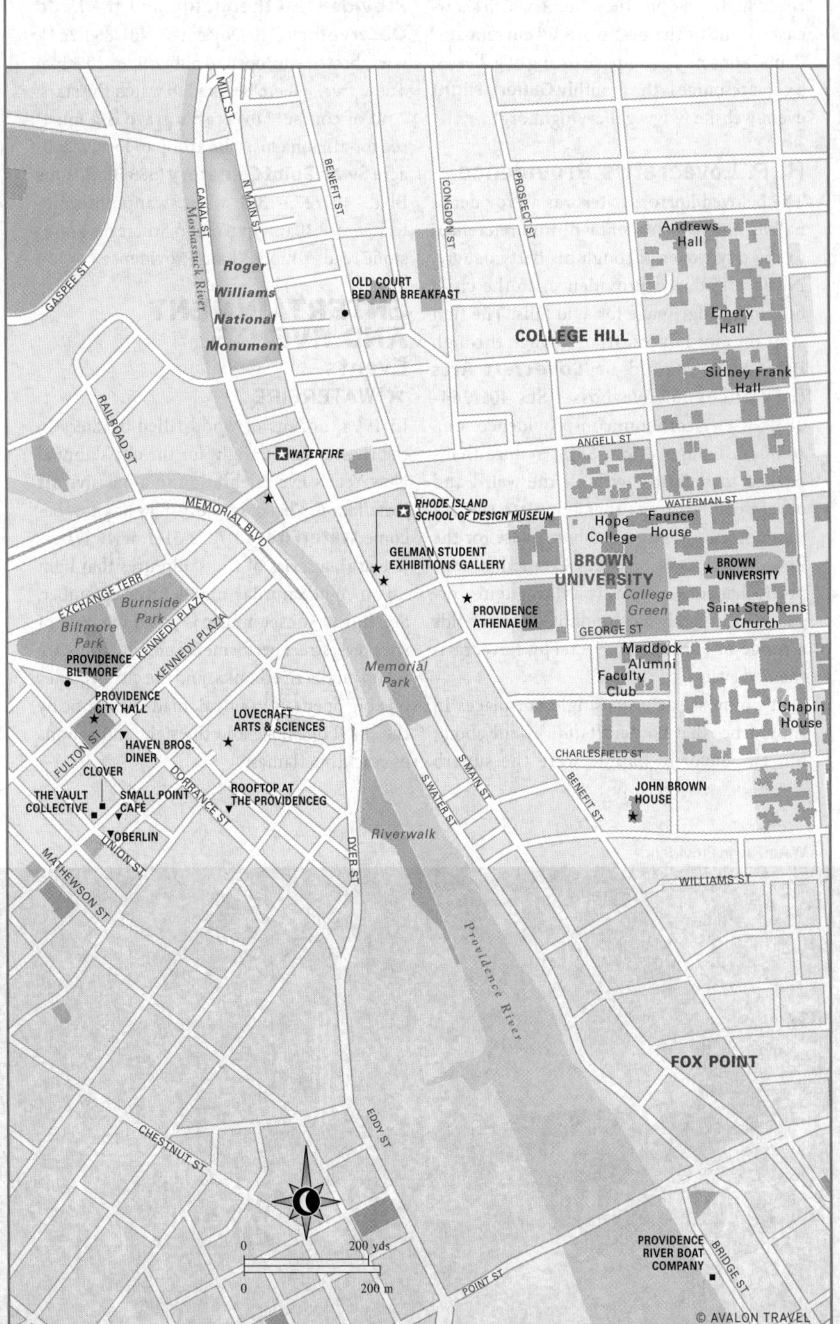
MILL ST
CANAL ST
Moshassuck River
N MAIN ST
BENEFIT ST
CONGDON ST
PROSPECT ST
GASPEE ST
Roger
Williams
National
Monument
OLD COURT
BED AND BREAKFAST
Andrews
Hall
Emery
Hall
COLLEGE HILL
Sidney Frank
Hall
RAILROAD ST
ANGELL ST
WATERFIRE
MEMORIAL BLVD
RHODE ISLAND
SCHOOL OF DESIGN MUSEUM
WATERMAN ST
Hope
College
Faunce
House
GELMAN STUDENT
EXHIBITIONS GALLERY
BROWN
UNIVERSITY
BROWN
UNIVERSITY
EXCHANGE TERR
Burnside
Park
KENNEDY PLAZA
KENNEDY PLAZA
Biltmore
Park
College
Green
PROVIDENCE
ATHENAEUM
Saint Stephens
Church
GEORGE ST
PROVIDENCE
BILTMORE
Maddock
Alumni
Memorial
Park
Faculty
Club
PROVIDENCE
CITY HALL
LOVECRAFT
ARTS & SCIENCES
Chapin
House
HAVEN BROS.
DINER
FULTON ST
CLOVER
DORRANCE ST
CHARLESFIELD ST
S MAIN ST
BENEFIT ST
JOHN BROWN
HOUSE
THE VAULT
COLLECTIVE
SMALL POINT
CAFÉ
ROOFTOP AT
THE PROVIDENCEG
S WATER ST
OBERLIN
UNION ST
Riverwalk
DYER ST
MATHEWSON ST
WILLIAMS ST
Providence River
FOX POINT
EDDY ST
CHESTNUT ST
0
200 yds
0
200 m
PROVIDENCE
RIVER BOAT
COMPANY
BRIDGE ST
POINT ST
© AVALON TRAVEL

risd.edu, 10am-5pm Tues.-Sun.), which showcases some of the best work by current students. For a more complete listing of galleries, a great resource is the monthly **Gallery Night** event website (www.gallerynight.org).

H. P. Lovecraft's Providence

The beloved horror writer was a Providence native, and avid readers will find references to the city woven through his hefty oeuvre. Lovecraft adored Providence, so the city's become a pilgrimage for avid fans. The first stop on any Lovecraftian voyage through Providence should be **Lovecraft Arts & Sciences** (65 Weybosset St., 401/264-0838, www.necronomicon-providence.com, 10:30am-6:30pm Mon.-Sat.), a store that's packed to the gills with all the weird and otherworldly things that populate the author's stories. It's also the home base for the Lovecraft Arts & Sciences Council, a non-profit that runs Lovecraft walking tours, organizes the yearly NecronomiCon, and holds a range of appropriately creepy Lovecraft-themed events.

It's almost easier to single out places in Providence that Lovecraft *didn't* write about, but two favorite haunts were the superb **Providence Athenaeum** and the **Ladd Observatory** (210 Doyle Ave., 401/862-2641, www.brown.edu, open to public 9pm-10:30pm Tues., free), where he liked to watch the stars. And of course, Lovecraft's grave is a must-see for aficionados, who troop to lovely, 200-acre **Swan Point Cemetery** (585 Blackstone Blvd., 401/272-1314, www.swanpointcemetery.com, 8:30am-4pm daily), where his gravestone reads simply: "I am Providence."

ENTERTAINMENT AND EVENTS

Events

★ WATERFIRE

In 1994, dozens of wood-filled braziers in the river were set alight for the city's annual New Year's Eve celebration in a massive art installation. That onetime display has now become **WaterFire** (401/272-3111, www.waterfire.org), a series of fire sculptures that light up on eight Saturday nights July-September. Starting at sunset, music is piped in on giant speakers, street performers and food stalls are set up on the riverbanks, and the city becomes one big open-air carnival, made romantic by the smell of smoke and the sight and sounds of crackling flames.

WaterFire in Providence

GALLERY NIGHT

On the third Thursday of every month, 21 Providence art spaces open their doors for **Gallery Night** (www.gallerynight.org, 5pm-9pm). There's a printable gallery map available on the website, or you can join a free guided tour on the Art Bus that leaves from One Regency Plaza every 20 minutes between 5:30pm and 7pm. Free parking is also available on gallery nights, with lots marked on the gallery map.

Nightlife

With a retractable glass roof and amazing views of downtown Providence, the **Rooftop at the Providence G** (100 Dorrance St., 401/632-4904, www.rooftopattheg.com, 5pm-10pm Mon.-Wed., 5pm-2am Thurs., 4pm-2am Fri.-Sat., 4pm-10pm Sun.) is stylish and trendy, and it's a glorious spot to watch the stars appear above the city. Experienced hands recommend bypassing the food for a drink by one of the outdoor fire pits.

For something completely different, **Ogie's Trailer Park** (1155 Westminster St., 401/383-8200, www.ogiestrailerpark.com, 4pm-1am Mon.-Thurs., 3pm-2am Fri., 4pm-2am Sat., noon-1am Sun.) is a mishmash of kitsch, cat-themed art, and mid-century design. Food includes bygone snacks like grilled peanut butter and jelly sandwiches, along with a menu of old-fashioned cocktails that features some tiki classics. Beer comes in cans, naturally.

The "speakeasy" experience might be a little contrived, but walking through a lingerie shop to get into **Justine's** (11 Olneyville Sq., 401/454-4440, 7pm-1am Tues.-Thurs., 7pm-2am Fri.-Sat.) makes this feel like a slightly risqué discovery. Low lighting and vintage decor keep the atmosphere romantic (excellent cocktails don't hurt, either).

With a lineup of high-quality, hop-focused beers, **Long Live Beerworks** (425 W. Fountain St., Unit 104, www.longlivebeerworks.com, 4pm-9pm Wed.-Thurs., 4pm-10pm Fri., 1pm-10pm Sat.) makes some of Rhode Island's best pours. There's indoor and outdoor seating in the stylish tasting room, and food trucks circle the wagons to provide drinking snacks.

SHOPPING

Downtown

The art-rich Providence community means hipper-than-average stores filled with everything from ultramodern fashion to vintage treasures. One favorite is the men's and women's clothing boutique **Clover** (233 Westminster St., 401/490-4626, www.cloverprovidence.com, 11am-6pm Mon.-Sat., noon-6pm Sun.), with an industrial-chic vibe and super-stylish lines. A collectively run vintage store with finds by a handful of local dealers, **The Vault Collective** (235 Westminster St., 401/250-2587, www.thevaultri.com, 11am-7pm daily) is organized by era, making it a fun place to browse looks gone by.

Federal Hill

Shopping in this Italian American neighborhood is all about snapping up old-world treats for the trip home. The classic standby is **Tony's Colonial Food Store** (311 Atwells Ave., 401/621-8675, www.tonyscolonial.mybigcommerce.com, 8:30am-6pm Mon.-Thurs., 8am-6:30pm Fri., 8am-6pm Sat., 8am-5pm Sun.), whose shelves are packed with olive oils, imported pasta, and other treats.

SPORTS AND RECREATION

Walking and Biking

Weaving through some of Providence's top sites, the 2.5-mile **Independence Trail** (401/441-6401, www.independencetrail.businesscatalyst.com) is an excellent orientation to the city, looping through downtown, up to the Rhode Island State House, and across the river to College Hill. Follow along on the downloadable map, then call the trail phone number at a series of plaques to listen to short recordings about each site.

Running 14.5 miles from Providence to Bristol, the **East Bay Bike Path** (www.dot.ri.gov) makes a great day trip out of the city, and it's almost entirely flat. Hop on at the northern terminus of the trail at **India Point Park** (India St., Providence), then ride south across a series of inlets and coves on your way along the curving shore of Narragansett Bay. If you only want to ride one way, put your bike on the #60 RIPTA bus from Providence to Newport, which stops at Roger Williams University in Bristol, a couple of easy miles from the Bristol Trail terminus at **Independence Park** (Thames St., Bristol).

Boating

Since the Providence and Woonasquatucket Rivers flow right through downtown Providence, getting out on the water offers a great perspective on the cityscape. Single and tandem kayaks are available to rent from **Providence Kayak Company** (Waterplace Park, 10 Memorial Blvd., 401/829-1769, www.providencekayak.com, rentals from $20) in downtown. There's also a range of Providence boat tours, including the informative **Providence River Boat Company** (575 S. Water St., 401/580-2628, www.provideceriverboat.com, daytime tours $22 adults, $17 children 12 and under), whose 50-minute tours cover history, architecture, and local culture. The open-air boats run after dark during **WaterFire,** which is a remarkable way to see the flaming art installations up and down the rivers.

FOOD

Downtown

Standard diner fare and a postage-stamp seating area can't keep **Haven Brothers Diner** (Fulton St. between Exchange St. and Memorial Blvd., 401/603-8124, 5pm-3am Sun.-Thurs., 5pm-4am Fri.-Sat., $4-10) from legendary status. It's been slinging meals since 1893, though the onetime horse-drawn food truck is now a shiny silver trailer with seating inside. The classic order is the super-sloppy "murder burger," topped with bacon, mushrooms, sautéed onions, and a fried egg.

Young, creative chef Benjamin Sukle started cropping up on best-in-America lists when he opened **Oberlin** (186 Union St., 401/588-8755, www.oberlinrestaurant.com, 5pm-11:30pm Thurs.-Mon., $20-30) in 2016. It's a wine bar with wonderful small plates: an innovative raw bar, delicate Italian American fare, and thoughtful recipes using sustainably caught fish. The simple interior can get loud as the evening wears on, and reservations are a good idea.

If you're looking for breakfast or lunch in downtown, **Small Point Café** (230 Westminster St., 401/228-6999, www.smallpointcafe.com, 7am-7:30pm Mon.-Fri., 7:30am-7:30pm Sat., 8am-7:30pm Sun., $5-10) is a welcome break from the bustle. A brief menu of sandwiches, salads, and simple breakfasts is served with good, strong coffee, and the student atmosphere makes for fun people-watching.

Federal Hill

Dine on farm-to-table fare at **Nick's on Broadway** (500 Broadway, 401/421-0286, www.nicksonbroadway.com, 8am-3pm and 5:30pm-10pm Wed.-Sat., 8am-3pm Sun., brunch $7-13, dinner $18-26), a New American bistro whose bar looks straight into the bustling open kitchen. The menu includes creative vegetarian options and locally sourced meat and fish, and the four-course tasting menu is created with the best of what's super fresh—$65 for a specially designed feast.

Treats like hand-sized meat pies, savory biscuits, and piles of cookies keep **North Bakery** (70 Battey St., 401/421-4062, www.northbakery.com, 7am-6pm Mon.-Thurs., 7am-11pm Fri.-Sun., $2-9) among the city's best places for an afternoon snack, and a solid cocktail menu keeps the casual spot busy well into the evening. The DanDan hand pie is the classic order: It's a full-flavored goat pastry spiced with dried chile and black pepper.

The airy dining room at the eclectic vegetarian restaurant **The Grange** (166 Broadway, 401/831-0600, www.providencegrange.com, 8am-midnight Sun.-Thurs., 8am-1am Fri.-Sat., $10-17) feels like a rustic loft, with lots of pockmarked wood and railroad spike beer taps. The roasted cauliflower is a perennial favorite on the wide-ranging menu, and there's live music on some weekend nights.

A strong contender for the best Italian meal on Federal Hill, ★ **Enoteca Umberto** (256 Atwells Ave., 401/272-8466, 5pm-1am Tues.-Thurs., 5pm-2am Fri.-Sat., $20-35) serves southern Italian cuisine from a teeny kitchen. Dishes of handmade pasta and braised meats are served in bowls that are ready to share, and the restaurant has a convivial, family-style vibe that can feel like the best kind of dinner party. Wine pairings are superb, and reservations are essential.

For more of a classic Italian American experience, **Andino's Italian Restaurant** (171 Atwells Ave., 401/453-3164, www.andinositalianrestaurant.com, 11:30am-11pm daily, $14-25) has old-style favorites like eggplant parmigiana, pasta with meatballs and red sauce, and tiramisu. If you're hoping to try snail salad—an Italian-Rhode Island mainstay—this is a great place to order one.

Other Neighborhoods

The laid-back little brother of restaurant Chez Pascal, ★ **Wurst Kitchen** (960 Hope St., 401/421-4422, www.chez-pascal.com, lunch 11:30am-2:30pm Tues.-Sun., dinner 5:30pm-9pm Tues.-Thurs., 5:30pm-10pm Fri.-Sat., $7-10) has garnered a cult following for housemade hot dogs and sausages that include brats, knackwurst, kielbasa, and chorizo, all beautifully spiced. There are small plates as well, but the simple hot dog topped with kraut is a reminder of how good a meal that can be.

Local chain **Olneyville New York System Restaurant** (18 Plainfield St., 401/621-9500, www.olneyvillenewyorksystem.com, 11am-2am Sun.-Thurs., 11am-3am Fri.-Sat., $3-8) won an America's Classic Award from the James Beard Foundation in 2014 for its distinctive take on the Rhode Island wiener, which comes topped with mustard, meat sauce, chopped onions, and a bit of celery salt.

A fried-dough joint that inspires rapturous odes, **PVDonuts** (79 Ives St., www.pvdonuts.com, 8am-4pm Wed.-Sun., $2-5) slow-raises its brioche doughnuts for a richer flavor, then dunks the little confections in everything from pop rocks to cereal milk. The old-fashioned doughnuts are a delight as well, especially when they're fresh from the fryer.

ACCOMMODATIONS

Aside from hotels and inns, there are many rental options on Airbnb—notably a handful of houseboats moored in the heart of town.

Under $100

A 15-minute walk from downtown, the bare-bones **Esperanto Providence Hostel and Guesthouse** (62 Nolan St., 401/216-8807, www.providencehostel.com, 4-bed dorms $29-50, private rooms $69-125) is easily the best deal in town. A fully equipped kitchen, luggage and bicycle storage, and common spaces make this a convenient spot for travelers, though basic amenities are seriously basic.

$100-150

The hippest spot in town is ★ **The Dean** (122 Fountain St., 401/455-3326, www.thedeanhotel.com, $99-179), where vintage furniture and artwork meet a modern aesthetic. Much of the artwork in the hotel was created by local artists, and all the design feels conspicuously boutique. Despite the almost overwhelming cool, rooms are simple and surprisingly affordable, with buddy-trip-friendly bunk beds and single rooms. If you love the style, it would be easy to spend the entire weekend inside: The Dean also has a karaoke bar, coffee shop, beer hall, and "cocktail den."

$150-250

Built in a former rectory that's stocked with antiques, **Old Court Bed & Breakfast** (144 Benefit St., 401/751-2002, www.oldcourt.com, $145-235) is convenient to Brown University and RISD. The house is full of character, and the friendly innkeeper furnishes guests with cooked-to-order breakfasts and plates of warm cookies. Off-street parking is especially welcome in the middle of town, where finding a spot can be a hassle.

Harkening back to the olden days of Rhode Island style is the Hilton-run **Providence Biltmore** (11 Dorrance St., 401/421-0700, www.providencebiltmore.com, $199-400), where plush carpets and over-the-top chandeliers strike a balance between camp and class. This hotel is full of ghost stories and lore, and was once named America's Most Haunted Hotel—among the extremely dubious claims made about the Biltmore is that one of the financial backers was a practicing Satanist, who supposedly had a chicken coop installed on the roof to provide chickens for sacrifices.

INFORMATION AND SERVICES

For maps, updates on the city's events, and any other tourist information, call or stop by the **Providence Warwick Convention and Visitors Bureau** (10 Memorial Blvd., 401/456-0200, www.goprovidence.com, 8:30am-5pm Mon.-Fri.). To learn the colorful story of former Providence mayor Buddy Cianci, the podcast miniseries **Crimetown** (www.gimletmedia.com/crimetown) is highly recommended and packed with details from Rhode Island's world of organized crime.

The city's major hospitals are **Miriam Hospital** (164 Summit Ave., 401/793-2500, www.lifespan.org/partners/tmh) and **Roger Williams Medical Center** (825 Chalkstone Ave., 401/456-2000, www.rwmc.com).

GETTING THERE

Air

The state's airport is **T. F. Green** (2000 Post Rd., Warwick, 401/737-8222, www.pvd-ri.com), an international, clean, and efficient facility with plenty of parking. About a 30-minute drive from downtown Providence, the airport is also easily accessed by buses run by **Rhode Island Public Transit Authority** (RIPTA, 401/781-9400, www.ripta.com). Many Providence hotels also offer free shuttle service.

Train

The commuter line that runs frequently every day between Boston and Providence is operated by the **Massachusetts Bay Transportation Authority** (MBTA, 617/222-3200, www.mbta.com). Also, **Amtrak** (800/872-7245, www.amtrak.com) runs regular service between Providence and Washington DC, stopping in Boston and New York, among other cities, along the way.

Bus

Peter Pan Bus Lines (401/331-7500, www.peterpanbus.com) operates several routes in and out of Providence from key cities—including Boston, New York City, Newport, Cape Cod, and others. The discount carrier **Megabus** (www.megabus.com) also offers service to New York City, New Haven, Dartmouth, and New Bedford.

GETTING AROUND

Providence is a remarkably walkable city, and anywhere you can't get on foot is served by **RIPTA** (Rhode Island Public Transit Authority, 401/781-9400, www.ripta.com). All bus routes start at Kennedy Plaza (in front of the State House) and cover the city for the usual fare of $2.

Parking can be a hassle in downtown, but the on-street meters are free 9pm-2am, as well as all day Sunday. Many meters have a time limit of two hours. The website www.parkdowntownprovidence.com has a helpful map of all the city's parking garages.

PAWTUCKET AND THE BLACKSTONE VALLEY

If Providence has been overlooked by travelers, Pawtucket—long known by the unflattering nickname "The Bucket"—remains almost invisible. For decades, the fourth-largest city in the state cropped up in national news reports with terrible headlines: The Environmental Protection Agency (EPA) named the Blackstone River the most polluted in the United States, while nearby

Central Falls was nominated the cocaine capital of the United States.

But things have changed. Life has returned to the once-toxic Blackstone River, with muskrats and egrets on banks once covered in industrial effluent. While Pawtucket remains rough around the edges, there are microbreweries and artists' collectives settling into formerly abandoned spaces. Central Falls, meanwhile, has some of the best Portuguese and Colombian food in New England, a seriously under-the-radar destination for a foodie adventure.

And the Blackstone River Valley is fascinating, a nascent National Historic Park that was established in 2014 and extends northeast to Woonsocket. Arguably the American birthplace of the Industrial Revolution, the Blackstone River powered spinning bobbins and looms, drawing a steady flow of immigrants that began in the early 1800s and continues to this day.

Sights

Built inside the mill that started everything, the interactive **Slater Mill Museum** (67 Roosevelt Ave., Pawtucket, 401/725-8638, www.slatermill.org, 10am-4pm daily July 4-Labor Day, 10am-4pm Tues.-Sun. May-June and Sept.-Oct., 11am-3pm Sat.-Sun. Mar.-Apr. and Nov., $12 adults, $10 seniors and students, $8.50 children 6-12, children under 6 free) is housed in original 18th- and 19th-century buildings. Admission includes a 90-minute tour of the mill led by costumed interpreters who demonstrate the enormous amount of work it took to produce clothing and food by hand—contrasted with the hulking Old Slater Mill, its industrial counterpart, which demonstrates how clothing and tool production became increasingly mechanized. You'll leave treating your cotton shirt with newfound respect.

The planned Blackstone River Valley National Historic Park doesn't have much infrastructure yet, so another good place to explore the river's industrial past is **Blackstone River State Park** (Lower River Rd., Lincoln, www.riparks.com, dawn-dusk daily). Long and narrow, the park is part of the **Blackstone River Bikeway** (www.cycleblackstone.com) a 10-mile, off-road bike path that extends from Woonsocket to Pawtucket, descending gradually with the Blackstone River. Within the state park itself, the small **Captain Wilbur Kelly House Transportation Museum** (1075 Lower River Rd., Lincoln, 401/333-0295, 9am-5pm daily,

Blackstone River Bikeway

free), tells the story of changing times on the Blackstone River, from Native Americans to canal boats and the Industrial Revolution. The museum parking lot is also an excellent place to start a ride on the Blackstone River Bikeway.

Sports and Recreation

A surprisingly large green space that's hemmed in by suburbia, **Lincoln Woods State Park** (park entrances on Rte. 123 and Rte. 146, 401/723-7892, www.riparks.com, sunrise-sunset daily, free) has an enormous pond with swimming beaches, picnic tables, walking trails, mountain biking, and some of the best **bouldering** in New England—walk through the woods and you'll see rock climbers hiking with big pads on their back, headed for freestanding rocks that they climb without ropes.

Food

Sit down to a meal at ★ **Beirão Restaurante** (1374 Broad St., Central Falls, 401/729-7966, 10am-9pm daily, $12-20), and tuck into a Portuguese feast, and listen for the listing accents of Portuguese and Cape Verdean locals. The menu includes classics like *caldo verde,* and it's always worth asking about specials, which can feature wonderfully traditional preparations of local seafood. Vinho Verde is plentiful, cheap, and perfect with the salty fare.

The Mexican fare at **Taqueria Lupita** (765 Dexter St., Central Falls, 401/724-2650, www.taquerialupitari.com, 11am-9pm Tues.-Thurs., 11am-10pm Fri.-Sat., 1pm-8pm Sun., $8-12) ranges from Mexican American standbys like nachos and quesadillas to rich hominy soup, sweet tamales, and chicken sauced with ground pumpkin seeds. The tortillas are made by hand and the food is consistently excellent, the atmosphere brightened up with souvenirs and textiles from south of the border.

With cuisine straight from the mountains of northwest Colombia, **El Paisa** (598 Dexter St., Central Falls, 401/726-8864, www.elpaisa.com, 7am-10pm Sun.-Thurs., 7am-11pm Fri.-Sat., $9-20) is a transporting experience. The long menu includes treats like picada, great fried piles of Colombian sausage and vegetables, as well as platters of fish and meat with all the fixings. Order *la bandeja paisa* for a traditional, over-the-top serving of meat, rice, beans, yucca, potato, ham, corn cakes, fried bananas, and salad. Cash only.

A basic eatery with counter service, **La Arepa** (574 Smithfield Ave., Pawtucket, 401/335-3711, www.laarepari.com, 11am-8:30pm Mon.-Sat., 11am-7pm Sun., $4-8) excels at making the Venezuelan treats the restaurant is named for—little corn cakes patted around fillings like stewed beef or black beans and cheese. Get a plate for a hearty meal with plantains, salad, rice, and beans.

Accommodations

Most visitors to the Blackstone Valley stay in Providence, where there are more options and a livelier atmosphere. There is one notable exception, however: the wonderful **Samuel Slater Canal Boat** (Blackstone River, Central Falls, 401/724-2200, from $149), built in the traditions of the low-lying canal boats that once plied the Blackstone River. Sleeping on the boat is a great experience, a private haven in the middle of the city. Run by the Blackstone Valley Tourism Council, the boat can be booked through Airbnb.

Information

Close to the Samuel Slater Mill in downtown Pawtucket, the **Blackstone Valley Visitor Center** (175 Main St., Pawtucket, 401/724-2200, www.tourblackstone.com, 10am-4pm daily, hours vary in winter) is a great resource for exploring the entire region, with a series of museum-like exhibits that are worth a stop in themselves.

Getting There

Pawtucket is five miles north of Providence, just off I-95. The **Rhode Island Public Transit Authority** (401/784-9500, ext. 2012, www.ripta.com) operates frequent buses to Pawtucket from downtown Providence.

WOONSOCKET

Nestled in among a handful of quieter suburbs, this well-groomed town of roughly 50,000 centers around the Blackstone River. Like Pawtucket, Woonsocket was at the heart of America's early industrialization, with more than 20 mills operating in the area by the mid-19th century. The French Canadians who flocked to the mills still make up much of the community, and the Museum of Work and Culture tells their stories.

Sights

Explore the town's past as a center for wool manufacturing at the **Museum of Work and Culture** (42 S. Main St., 401/769-9675, www.woonsocket.org, 9:30am-4pm Tues.-Fri., 10am-4pm Sat., 1pm-4pm Sun., $8 adults, $6 seniors and students, children under 10 free), a former textile mill full of interactive exhibits and French Canadian immigrant history.

Both unexpected and delightful, **St. Ann's Arts and Cultural Center** (84 Cumberland St., 401/356-0713, www.stannsartsandculturalcenter.org, 1pm-4pm Sun., $10 adults, $8 seniors and students, children 4 and under free) is a small-town church with the largest collection of frescoes in the United States. The 93-year-old church was painted in 1940 by Canadian artist Guido Nincheri, and according to local lore, the faces on the cherubs are those of young Woonsocket locals at the time the frescoes were made.

Food

The Woonsocket area lays claim to *two* of Rhode Island's most legendary destinations for "chicken family-style," a hearty spread of roast chicken, pasta with marinara sauce, rolls, french fries, and salad that is especially beloved in the Blackstone Valley. The all-you-can-eat meals have been popular since at least the 1930s, but the heavyweight contender is **Wrights Farm Restaurant** (84 Inman Rd., Harrisville, 401/769-2856, www.wrightsfarm.com, 4pm-9pm Thurs.-Fri., noon-9pm Sat., noon-8pm Sun., $12-15), a vast dining hall that attracts families and groups from around the state. While the eatery gets mixed reviews for the quality of the fare, the founders of the **Bocce Club Restaurant** (226 St. Louis Ave., Woonsocket, 401/767-2000, 5pm-10pm Tues.-Sat., noon-9pm Sun., $12-20) are said to have invented chicken family-style when they opened the first version of the Bocce Club in their basement, feeding crowds that would then play bocce on the lawn.

Getting There

Woonsocket is 30 minutes from Pawtucket off Route 146, and there's RIPTA service from Providence that passes through Lincoln (401/784-9500, ext. 2012, www.ripta.com, #54).

Newport

From its early days in the 17th century, Newport was a haven for freethinkers, heretics, and dissidents drummed out of Puritan settlements, who thrived and intermingled while the town gradually grew into a bustling port city.

When the U.S. economy turned to railroads and industry, Newport became a summertime escape for Eastern elite, whose opulent "cottages" were the toast of New York's polite society. Their surviving homes are maintained to a high gloss and filled with antiques and designs that offer a fascinating glimpse of what Mark Twain sardonically dubbed the Gilded Age, a time of runaway fortunes, dollar princesses, and raw inequality.

But beyond the flashy ballrooms and boudoirs, summer in Newport is pure New England, and it would be easy to spend a week sailing Narragansett Bay, surfing beach breaks, and taking in ball games at Cardines Field. The city has a thriving

Newport

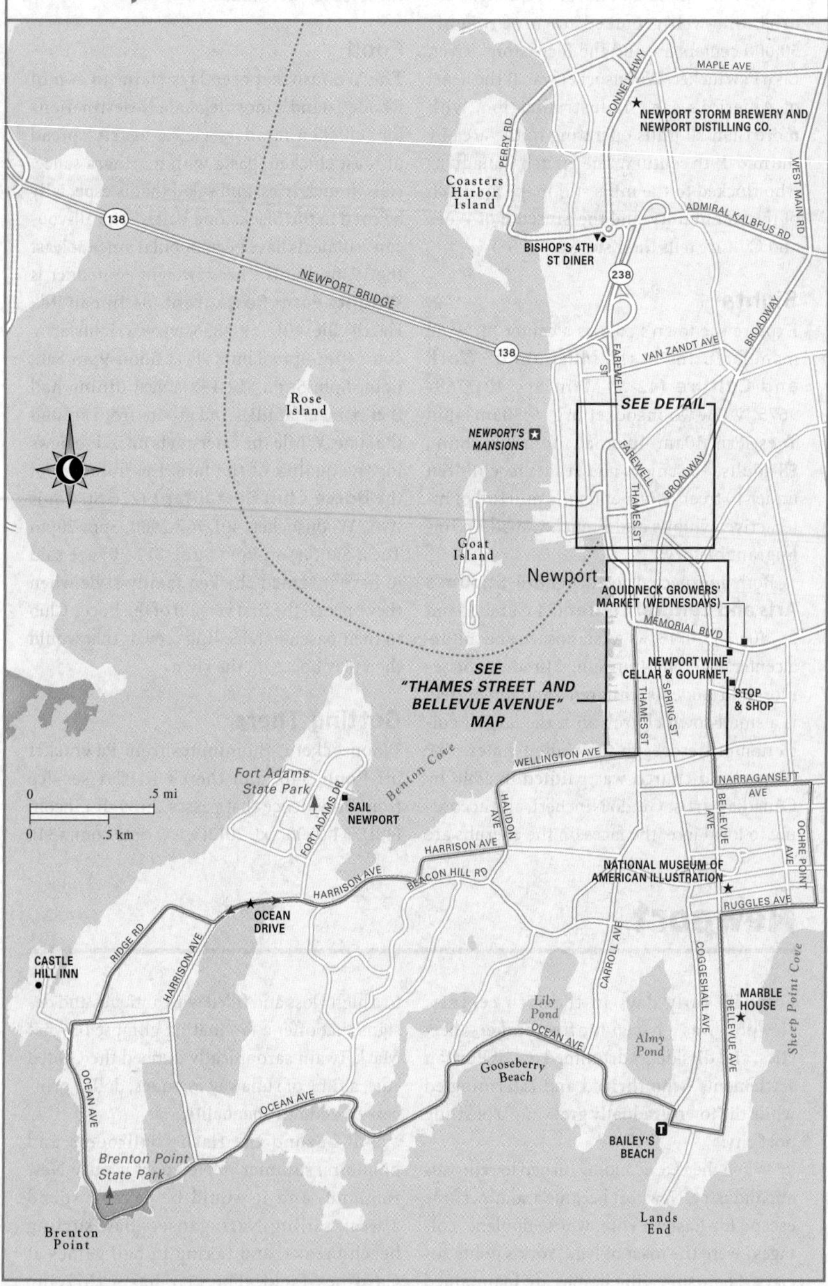
MAPLE AVE
CONNELL HWY
NEWPORT STORM BREWERY AND
NEWPORT DISTILLING CO.
PERRY RD
WEST MAIN RD
Coasters
Harbor
Island
ADMIRAL KALBFUS RD
138
BISHOP'S 4TH
ST DINER
238
NEWPORT BRIDGE
BROADWAY
VAN ZANDT AVE
FAREWELL
ST
138
SEE DETAIL
Rose
Island
NEWPORT'S
MANSIONS
FAREWELL
BROADWAY
THAMES ST
Goat
Island
Newport
AQUIDNECK GROWERS'
MARKET (WEDNESDAYS)
MEMORIAL BLVD
NEWPORT WINE
CELLAR & GOURMET
STOP
& SHOP
SEE
"THAMES STREET AND
BELLEVUE AVENUE"
MAP
THAMES ST
SPRING ST
WELLINGTON AVE
Benton Cove
Fort Adams
State Park
0
.5 mi
0
.5 km
SAIL
NEWPORT
FORT ADAMS DR
HALIDON
AVE
NARRAGANSETT
AVE
BELLEVUE
AVE
OCHRE POINT
AVE
HARRISON AVE
BEACON HILL RD
HARRISON AVE
NATIONAL MUSEUM OF
AMERICAN ILLUSTRATION
RUGGLES AVE
OCEAN
DRIVE
RIDGE RD
HARRISON AVE
CASTLE
HILL INN
CARROLL AVE
COGGESHALL AVE
Lily
Pond
OCEAN AVE
Almy
Pond
BELLEVUE AVE
MARBLE
HOUSE
Sheep Point Cove
Gooseberry
Beach
OCEAN AVE
OCEAN AVE
BAILEY'S
BEACH
Brenton Point
State Park
Brenton
Point
Lands
End

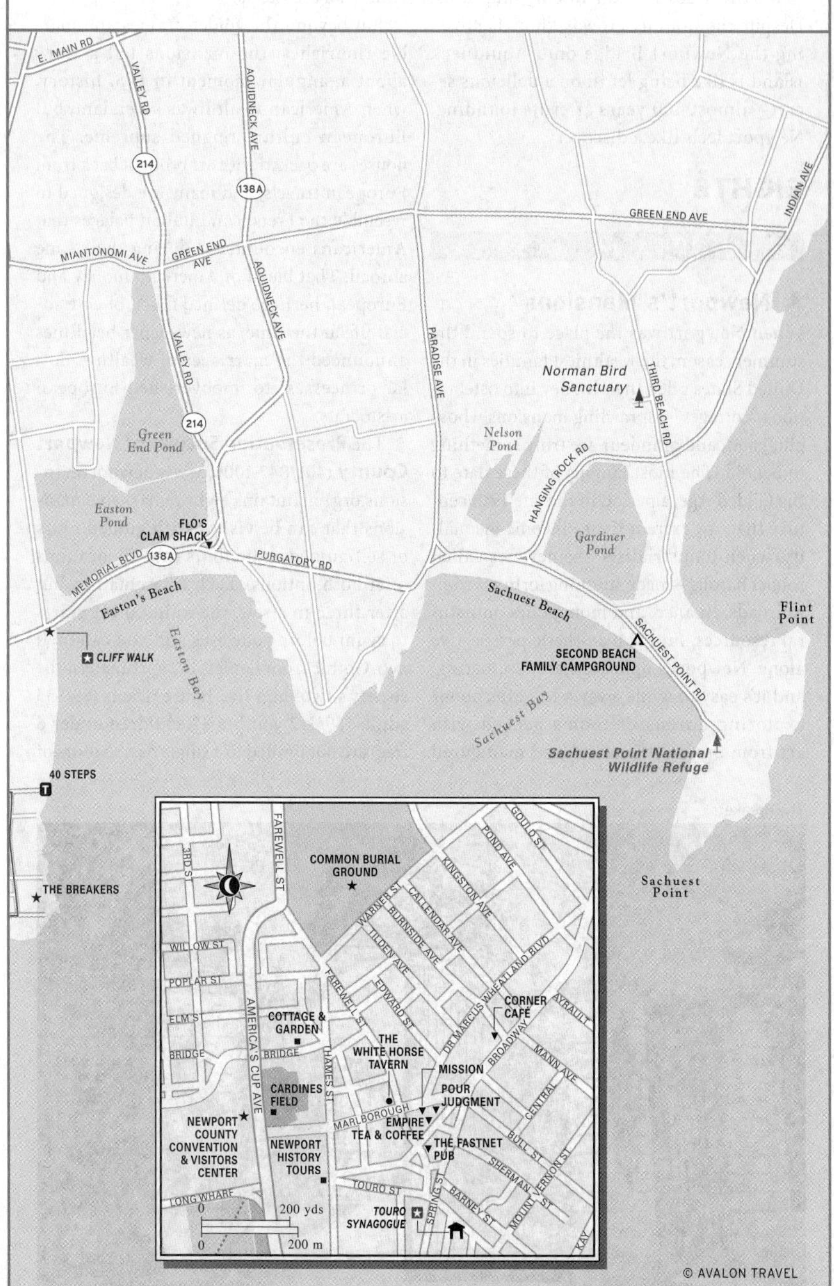
E. MAIN RD
VALLEY RD
AQUIDNECK AVE
214
138A
INDIAN AVE
GREEN END AVE
MIANTONOMI AVE
GREEN END AVE
PARADISE AVE
THIRD BEACH RD
Norman Bird Sanctuary
Nelson Pond
HANGING ROCK RD
Green End Pond
Easton Pond
Gardiner Pond
FLO'S CLAM SHACK
MEMORIAL BLVD
PURGATORY RD
Easton's Beach
Sachuest Beach
Flint Point
SACHUEST POINT RD
CLIFF WALK
Easton Bay
SECOND BEACH FAMILY CAMPGROUND
Sachuest Bay
Sachuest Point National Wildlife Refuge
40 STEPS
Sachuest Point
THE BREAKERS
FAREWELL ST
GOULD ST
POND AVE
KINGSTON AVE
COMMON BURIAL GROUND
3RD ST
WARNER ST
CALLENDAR AVE
BURNSIDE AVE
TILDEN AVE
WILLOW ST
POPLAR ST
ELM ST
BRIDGE
EDWARD ST
DR MARCUS WHEATLAND BLVD
CORNER CAFÉ
AYRAULT
AMERICA'S CUP AVE
COTTAGE & GARDEN
THE WHITE HORSE TAVERN
THAMES ST
BROADWAY
MANN AVE
MISSION
CARDINES FIELD
POUR JUDGMENT
MARLBOROUGH
CENTRAL
EMPIRE TEA & COFFEE
NEWPORT COUNTY CONVENTION & VISITORS CENTER
NEWPORT HISTORY TOURS
THE FASTNET PUB
BULL ST
SHERMAN ST
MOUNT VERNON ST
TOURO ST
LONG WHARF
SPRING ST
BARNEY ST
0
200 yds
0
200 m
TOURO SYNAGOGUE
KAY
© AVALON TRAVEL

arts scene, from a year-round film festival to a pair of destination-worthy museums. Despite the summer crowds, though, crossing the Newport Bridge onto Aquidneck Island is like being let in on a delicious secret—almost 400 years after its founding, Newport feels like a discovery.

SIGHTS

TOP EXPERIENCE

★ Newport's Mansions

When Newport was *the* place to spend the summer season, the wealthiest families in the United States piled their money into ostentatious "cottages"—sprawling mansions whose gilt, gaud, and grandeur are truly something to behold. The most famous of these date to the Gilded Age, a period in the late 19th century that saw extraordinary income inequality, when industrialists—sometimes called robber barons—made stunning fortunes from railroads, finance, and monopolies on natural resources. From an aesthetic perspective alone, Newport's mansions are fascinating, and it's easy to while away a few afternoons exploring dozens of rooms packed with art from around the world and manicured grounds designed by some of the most famous American architects.

But beyond the golden frames and marble flourishes, the mansions tell a story about a singular moment in U.S. history, when American wealth was ascendant, but European culture reigned supreme. The houses are packed with art brought back from European travels, and many are designed to resemble the French and Italian palaces that Americans encountered during their time abroad. That blend of American money and European heritage defined much of elite social life at the time, as newspaper headlines announced the marriages of wealthy "dollar princesses" to impoverished European aristocrats.

The **Preservation Society of Newport County** (401/847-1000, www.newportmansions.org) maintains eight remarkable mansions that can be visited with guided tours or self-guided audio tours (not all locations offer both options). Each is fascinating, but after three in a row, the wainscoting starts to swim before your eyes and you can't tell neo-Gothic from Louis XIV. Fortunately, the society's two- and five-house tickets ($9/$35 adults, $9/$12 youth 6-17, children under 6 free) are not limited to a single day, so tours of

The Breakers

aristocratic boudoirs can be interspersed with time at the beach. Tickets to The Breakers are sold separately, but to visit any other single house, purchase a one-house ticket at any mansion or online ($17.50 adults, $8 youth 6-17, children under 6 free). The operating schedules are complex and subject to change, so it's worth calling the Preservation Society prior to visiting.

With time for just one mansion, however, **The Breakers** (44 Ochre Point Ave., 9am-6pm daily late-June-Aug., 9am-5pm daily Sept.-late June, $24 adults, $8 children 6-17, children under 6 free) is Newport's showstopper. Commodore Cornelius Vanderbilt II built the Italianate behemoth to resemble an open-air palazzo, and downy clouds arc above the central Great Hall. The house was created by Richard Morris Hunt, founder of the first American architectural school, and he wove the story of the Vanderbilt fortune into his design, with marble railcars and dozens of stylized acorns and oak leaves.

Marble House (596 Bellevue Ave., 10am-5pm daily) can't rival the scale of The Breakers, but the sumptuous, French-inspired home is filled with extraordinary art, extravagant furniture, and an imposing amount of gold leaf and marble. The remarkable Gothic Room is a famous example of Gothic Revival in the United States.

A favorite among mansion aficionados is **The Elms** (367 Bellevue Ave., 9am-6pm daily late June-Aug., 9am-5pm daily Sept.-late June), one of the most elegant of the Newport homes. French-inspired architecture and furnishings are set amid Classic Revival gardens that feature grand old trees and some surprising statuary—don't miss the imaginative bronze of a tiger attacking an alligator. Darker and more subdued, **Kingscote** (253 Bellevue Ave., 10 am-5pm daily) is among the earliest mansions in Newport, and it's set apart by Gothic Revival architecture and older technologies. Built by plantation owner George Noble Jones, Kingscote dates to an earlier generation of Newport elite, when wealthy, antebellum Southerners came north to escape the heat.

Ocean Drive

The perfect Newport day might start with early morning light at Cliff Walk, but the scenic, 10-mile **Ocean Drive** (www.oceandrivenewport.com) has got sunset on lock. To begin, follow **Thames Street** south from downtown, turning right onto **Wellington Avenue,** continuing on as it becomes **Halidon Avenue,** then making a right onto **Harrison Avenue.** While Ocean Drive follows various roads, it's clearly **signposted** at every turn.

Keep watch for fainting goats, llamas, and sheep as you pass the **Swiss Village Foundation** (www.svffoundation.org) on Harrison Avenue; the foundation is an egg and sperm bank for endangered livestock breeds that's open to the public just one day each year.

Duck off the main road onto Fort Adams Drive for a side trip through historic **Fort Adams** (401/847-2400, www.riparks.com, free), then continue south along Harrison Avenue to Ridge Road. Turn right onto Castle Hill Avenue then right again onto Ocean Avenue to pause for a drink on **The Lawn at Castle Hill Inn** (590 Ocean Dr., 401/849-3800, www.castlehillinn.com), one of the most elegant stretches of grass in Newport. After your break at the inn, turn right on **Ocean Avenue** to stay on the Ocean Drive route to **Brenton Point State Park** (Ocean Ave., 401/849-4562, www.riparks.com, free), which wraps all the way around the point where Narragansett Bay meets the Atlantic Ocean. Brenton Point's consistent winds make it the best **kite-flying** spot around, so bring your own or pick one up at the park's small shop, then grab a **Del's Lemonade** from one of the trucks that prowl the parking lot. For an interesting glimpse of a once-grand Newport mansion, peek through the fence at **The Bells,** now crumbling into a creepy, atmospheric ruin on the park's

Thames Street and Bellevue Avenue

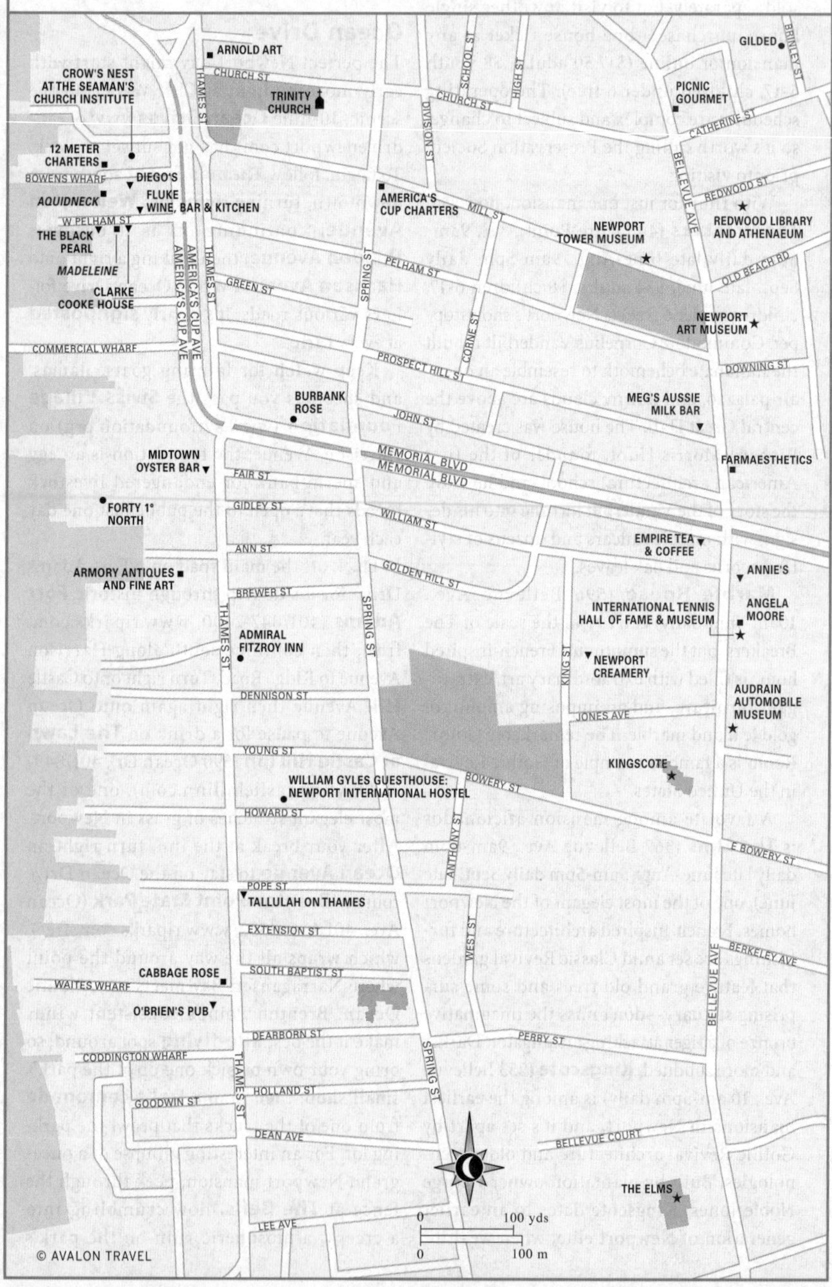
ARNOLD ART
CROW'S NEST AT THE SEAMAN'S CHURCH INSTITUTE
CHURCH ST
TRINITY CHURCH
THAMES ST
12 METER CHARTERS
BOWENS WHARF
DIEGO'S
AQUIDNECK
FLUKE WINE, BAR & KITCHEN
W PELHAM ST
THE BLACK PEARL
MADELEINE
CLARKE COOKE HOUSE
AMERICA'S CUP AVE
COMMERCIAL WHARF
AMERICA'S CUP CHARTERS
DIVISION ST
SCHOOL ST
HIGH ST
MILL ST
PELHAM ST
GREEN ST
SPRING ST
CORNE ST
PROSPECT HILL ST
BURBANK ROSE
JOHN ST
MEMORIAL BLVD
MIDTOWN OYSTER BAR
FAIR ST
GIDLEY ST
FORTY 1° NORTH
WILLIAM ST
ANN ST
ARMORY ANTIQUES AND FINE ART
GOLDEN HILL ST
BREWER ST
ADMIRAL FITZROY INN
DENNISON ST
YOUNG ST
WILLIAM GYLES GUESTHOUSE: NEWPORT INTERNATIONAL HOSTEL
HOWARD ST
POPE ST
TALLULAH ON THAMES
EXTENSION ST
CABBAGE ROSE
SOUTH BAPTIST ST
WAITES WHARF
O'BRIEN'S PUB
DEARBORN ST
CODDINGTON WHARF
HOLLAND ST
GOODWIN ST
DEAN AVE
LEE AVE
GILDED
BRINLEY ST
PICNIC GOURMET
CATHERINE ST
BELLEVUE AVE
REDWOOD ST
REDWOOD LIBRARY AND ATHENAEUM
NEWPORT TOWER MUSEUM
OLD BEACH RD
NEWPORT ART MUSEUM
DOWNING ST
MEG'S AUSSIE MILK BAR
FARMAESTHETICS
EMPIRE TEA & COFFEE
ANNIE'S
INTERNATIONAL TENNIS HALL OF FAME & MUSEUM
ANGELA MOORE
NEWPORT CREAMERY
KING ST
JONES AVE
AUDRAIN AUTOMOBILE MUSEUM
KINGSCOTE
BOWERY ST
E BOWERY ST
ANTHONY ST
WEST ST
BERKELEY AVE
PERRY ST
BELLEVUE COURT
THE ELMS
0 100 yds
0 100 m
© AVALON TRAVEL

Newport's Legacy of Slavery

Rhode Island's founders came to Aquidneck Island to find freedom from the strictures of Puritan society, but the first recorded slaves arrived less than 15 years later. The colony became a leader in the New England slave trade—between 1709 and 1807, local merchants sent 930 slave ships to Africa—and by the mid-18th century, it had the highest percentage of enslaved inhabitants in the North.

While many slaves were forced to work in Rhode Island homes and plantations, much of the area's involvement in human trafficking was a part of New England's "triangle trade." Newport rum distilleries imported molasses from Caribbean sugar plantations that depended on enslaved laborers, and shipped rum to Africa to trade for slaves who'd be brought back to the Caribbean to swap for molasses. That tragic commerce permeates Rhode Island's history: Brown University, the Touro Synagogue, and the Redwood Library and Athenaeum were built with money from slave-trading families, and Newport's Brick Market and Old Colony House was constructed in part by enslaved workers.

Many Newport slaves were buried in the **Common Burial Ground** (Warner St. and Farewell St., www.colonialcemetery.com), known by the local African American community as "God's Little Acre." **Newport History Tours** (127 Thames St., www.newporthistorytours.org, 1.25-hour tours $15 adults, $5 children 5-12) offers guided visits to the cemetery, as well as an **African American History Tour.**

grounds. To find the building, follow the grassy road behind the restrooms.

You'll eventually loop up by way of **Bellevue Avenue.** Ocean Drive can take a brisk 35 minutes or extend through a leisurely afternoon.

National Museum of American Illustration

In 1998, one of Newport's great mansions was transformed into the **National Museum of American Illustration** (492 Bellevue Ave., 401/851-8949, www.americanillustration.org, 11am-5pm Thurs.-Sun. late May-early Sept., 11am-5pm Fri. Sept.-late May, guided tours 3pm Fri. year-round, $20 adults, $18 seniors, $14 students, $10 children 5-12, children under 5 not admitted), the first museum in the country devoted to illustration art. The collection includes work by N. C. Wyeth, Maxfield Parrish, and Norman Rockwell, the most iconic names from the golden age of American illustration, which stretched from the post-Civil War era to the 1950s. It's a fascinating look at the intersection of popular culture, propaganda, and fine art, and the knowledgeable docents offer insight into U.S. art history. Don't leave the museum without exploring the grounds of Vernon Court; a romantic rose garden, terraces, and a sunken garden are beautifully maintained in the neoclassical style.

Fort Adams State Park

As the British navy set up floating blockades during the War of 1812, the militia at Fort Adams manned an impressive array of 17 cannons that would give any invading fleet a rough welcome to the Newport Harbor. Join a guided tour at **Fort Adams State Park** (90 Fort Adams Dr., 401/841-0707, www.fortadams.org, tours hourly 10am-4pm daily May-Oct., noon and 2pm Sat.-Sun. Nov.-Jan., noon and 2pm daily late Mar.-Apr., $30 families, $12 adults, $6 youth 6-17, children under 6 free; self-guided tours $15 families, $6 adults, $3 youth 6-17, children under 6 free) to explore officers' quarters, the ramparts, and fascinating tunnels to the outer defenses, or visit the fort at your own pace (though tunnels aren't accessible on self-guided tours).

The rest of the park is free to explore, and swimming beaches, picnic areas, and rolling grass make it a pleasant spot on warm afternoons. The 2.2-mile **Bay Walk** loops along the shoreline, up the western side of the park, with views of the Narragansett Bay, and back down the eastern edge, where you can see the bristling masts and white sails of Newport Harbor.

Newport Art Museum

Browse modern and historical art in (yet another) historic mansion at the **Newport Art Museum** (76 Bellevue Ave., 401/848-8200, www.newportartmuseum.org, 10am-4pm Tues.-Sat., noon-4pm Sun., $10 adults, $8 seniors, $6 students and military, children under 6 free). The John N. A. Griswold house was built by Richard Morris Hunt (of The Breakers fame), and is one of the earliest and best-known American Stick-Style buildings. It's an atmospheric place to see works by William Trost Richards, Gilbert Stuart, and other New England artists, and the rotating exhibitions are a highlight.

Touro Synagogue

Rhode Island is thought to be the first civil authority in the world to guarantee religious freedom to all citizens, and it became a haven for Quakers, Jews, and freethinkers that Puritans saw as a threat to their social fabric. Perhaps the most vivid place to hear about this part of Rhode Island's legacy is at the historic **Touro Synagogue** (85 Touro St., 401/847-4794, www.tourosynagogue.org, synagogue 10am-3:30pm, visitors center 9:30am-430pm Sun.-Fri. July-early Sept.; synagogue 10am-1:30pm, visitors center 9:30am-2:30pm Sun.-Fri. Sept.-Oct.; synagogue noon-1:30pm, visitors center 11:30am-2:30pm Sun. Nov.-Dec., $12 adults, $10 seniors, $8 students and military, children under 14 free), the only surviving colonial-era synagogue in the United States.

Construction on the building began in 1759, and the layout resembles that of synagogues in the Caribbean islands and Amsterdam; Newport's Jewish community was descended from the Sephardic people expelled from Spain by the Inquisition, who continued to more tolerant homes in the Netherlands and the New World. The synagogue itself is a stunning building, with an airy balcony for the formerly gender-divided congregation, a 500-year-old Torah, and a framework of 12 Ionic columns—one for each tribe of Israel.

Each year, community members gather to celebrate Rhode Island's spirit of religious liberty by reading a historic letter from President George Washington to the congregation, expressing his support for their freedom. "It is now no more that toleration is spoken of as if it were the indulgence of one class of people," he wrote, "the Government of the United States . . . gives to bigotry no sanction, to persecution no assistance."

Newport Storm Brewery and Newport Distilling Co.

Sample locally made beer and rum at **Newport Storm Brewery and Newport Distilling Co.** (293 J.T. Connell Hwy., 401/849-5232, www.thomastewrums.com, noon-5pm Sun.-Mon. and Wed., noon-6pm Thurs.-Sat., beer tastings $9, rum tastings $10). Guided tours are available each day at 3pm, but you can explore the brewing and distilling processes anytime with a self-guided option; the tour climbs to a balcony above the brewery floor, past a towering stack of oak barrels filled with enough rum for a lifetime of daiquiris. A couple centuries ago, Newport had 22 rum distilleries, but things got pretty dry for local spirit lovers after 1842—Newport Distilling Co. is the first legal Newport distillery since then. Its Thomas Tew rum is distilled from domestically produced blackstrap molasses and got its name from a local privateer-turned-pirate.

Trinity Church

Just down the street from the synagogue is another beautiful and historic house of worship. The airy, light-filled sanctuary of **Trinity Church** (141 Spring St., 401/846-0660, www.trinitynewport.org, 10am-4pm Mon.-Sat., 11:30am-12:30pm Sun. late May-Oct.,

Newport's Mysterious Tower

The round stone structure in Touro Park looks harmless enough, but the 28-foot tower has been the source of endless speculation, study, and a bit of intrigue. Over the years, it's been variously attributed to ancient seafaring Norsemen, pre-Columbian Chinese sailors, 17th-century English settlers, Knights Templar, Portuguese explorers, and an Elizabethan astronomer and natural philosopher. Radiocarbon dating of the tower's mortar suggests that it was constructed between the mid- and late 17th century, but those tests haven't put the controversy to rest. An important clue is a reference by Benedict Arnold—Rhode Island's first governor and great-grandfather of the famously traitorous American general—to a stone windmill on his property, which included present-day Touro Park. Elements of the tower's construction differ from other windmills of the time, however, prompting some to ask: "What did Benedict Arnold have to hide?"

Visitors ready for a deep dive into the subject are welcome at the **Newport Tower Museum** (152 Mill St., 401/447-6757, www.newporttowermuseum.com, 10am-5pm Mon.-Sat., free), where curator Jim Egan offers a passionate and detailed analysis of the possibilities. The short version is this: Egan believes that the tower is a horologium, a building that allows for detailed astronomical observations and functions as a timepiece and calendar. According to Egan, holes in the tower walls weren't built to support mill infrastructure, but are a camera obscura that projected outside images into the tower's interior. He proposes that Elizabethan scientist and occult philosopher **John Dee** designed the tower, which was then constructed as part of an abortive early effort to colonize the Americas, at a time that coincided with a broad interest in improving the calendar system. Egan has spent years researching and reading about the topic, and his explanation includes a dramatic demonstration of a camera obscura, a side trip into theoretical math, and a fascinating glimpse of John Dee's life and work. If the museum is shuttered during opening hours, it's worth calling the curator's number, as he's often nearby.

11:30am-12:30pm Sun. Nov.-May, $5 adults, children under 13 free) is occupied by fascinating architectural details and artwork that can be explored with a self-guided tour. George Washington, Queen Elizabeth, and the Anglican bishop Desmond Tutu have all attended worship here, and the public is welcome to join services at 10am on Sunday.

Redwood Library and Athenaeum

Leather-bound books and historic portraits line the walls at the **Redwood Library and Athenaeum** (50 Bellevue Ave., 401/847-0292, www.redwoodlibrary.org, 9:30am-5:30pm Mon.-Tues. and Thurs.-Sat., 9:30am-8pm Wed., 1pm-5pm Sun., $10 adults, students, youth under 18, and Rhode Island library cardholders free), the oldest surviving lending library in the United States. Though the admission fee seems high for this relatively diminutive spot, it's still an intriguing place to explore; come at 10:30am to join a guided tour (free with admission), or find the library's artistic and architectural highlights with a self-guided brochure. Don't miss the self-portrait of Gilbert Stuart, a native Rhode Islander and 18th-century portraitist who created the most famously unfinished canvas of George Washington.

International Tennis Hall of Fame and Audrain Automobile Museum

In the heart of Bellevue Avenue's shops and cafés is a pair of museums that may split the true aficionados from their less dedicated companions (who may be more interested in an "Awful Awful" shake across the road at Newport Creamery). Tennis fans won't want to miss the **International Tennis Hall of Fame Museum** (194 Bellevue Ave., 401/849-3990, www.tennisfame.com, 10am-6pm daily July-early Sept., 10am-5pm daily Sept.-Dec., 10am-5pm Wed.-Mon. Jan.-Mar., 10am-5pm daily Apr.-June, $15 adults, $12 seniors, students, and military, youth under 17 free), a shrine to the history, arcana, and heroes of the game, complete with a life-sized talking hologram of tennis great Roger Federer. Even the setting is infused with tennis history; the museum grounds once housed the Newport Casino, a social club that hosted the first U.S. National Men's Singles Championship in 1881. The museum's impeccable grass courts may be booked for games ($80 per half hour, $120 per hour).

At the other end of the block, the **Audrain Automobile Museum** (222 Bellevue Ave., 401/856-4420, www.audrainautomuseum.org, 10am-4pm daily, $14 adults, $10 seniors, military, and students, $8 youth 6-17, children under 6 free) is a celebration of the finest cars and motorcycles ever made; the museum exhibits rotate completely every few months to bring in vehicles from several private collections. Recent exhibitions have focused on American muscle cars, a rare collection of prewar vehicles, custom hot rods, and "speed machines," a show that included Michael Schumacher's Ferrari F310B and a Porsche 918 Spyder with a top speed of 214 mph.

ENTERTAINMENT AND EVENTS

Nightlife

Thames Street is the heart of the action, and some of the waterfront's restaurants double as the area's most appealing bars. **The Black Pearl, Diego's, Midtown Oyster Bar,** and **Fluke Wine, Bar & Kitchen** are all appealing places to cozy up to a pint or cocktail, and the walkable district is so compact that it's easy to wander until you find a happening place. One safe bet is **O'Brien's Pub** (501 Thames St., 401/849-6623, 11:30am-1am daily), an easygoing spot with a big bar and outdoor seating that's bustling all year. Another is **Clarke Cooke House** (26 Bannister's Wharf, 401/849-2900, www.bannistersnewport.com, 11:30am-1am daily), where you can watch the sunset from the back patio, then stay through the evening, when things get pretty lively.

When summertime crowds overwhelm Thames Street, however, locals retreat to the watering holes on Broadway, a few of which retain enough seedy charm to be a refreshing change from the waterfront. One favorite spot is **Pour Judgement** (32 Broadway, 401/619-2115, www.pourjudgementnewport.com, 11am-1am Mon.-Fri., 11:30am-1am Sat., 10am-1am Sun.), which combines a pleasantly divey feel—neon signs, bric-a-brac—with great craft beers and a surprisingly appealing menu of bar food and healthier options. Regulars love the wings, the burgers, and the sloppily delicious Gouda cheese fries.

More history-minded barflies stop by **The White Horse Tavern** (26 Marlborough St., 401/849-3600, www.whitehorsetavern.us, 11am-10pm Sun.-Thurs., 11am-11pm Fri.-Sat.) to channel colonial-era conspirators and Newport pirates—the atmospheric bar is one of a handful of claimants to "oldest tavern in America," and might just take the award. The White Horse has been serving drinks since 1673 and retains clapboard walls and huge ceiling beams typical of original 17th-century architecture. The dinner menu is more dated than historic, but it's worth a visit just to enjoy the remarkable space.

Newport's Music Festivals

For two weekends each summer, generally the last weekend of July and the first weekend in August, Newport fills to the brim with music lovers, drawn to two of the country's most important—and historic—festivals. **Newport Jazz Festival** (www.newportjazz.org) is the original, a three-day extravaganza that always includes some of the genre's biggest names. Dizzy Gillespie and Billie Holiday played the 1954 festival, and Miles Davis, Duke Ellington, and Ella Fitzgerald each released live albums of their Newport performances. Five years later, **Newport Folk Festival** (www.newportfolk.org) kicked off with a memorable show that included the debut performance of 18-year-old Joan Baez (who invited Bob Dylan to join her on stage in 1963). He came back in 1964 and 1965, when he famously played his first live electric set;

after being booed by some members of the audience, he didn't return to the festival for 37 years.

Both festivals remain vital, and artists that range from rock and roll to R&B pack the fields at Fort Adams State Park. To make the festivals a part of your road trip, start planning soon—tickets and many of the accommodations in the area sell out the previous winter, and prices skyrocket during both weekends. Visit the festival websites for more information, and be aware of the festivals while planning your trip; if you're not in town *for* the festivals, you'd likely rather be somewhere else entirely.

SHOPPING

As in all New England tourist towns, there are plenty of fudge shops and kitschy souvenir stores around Newport, but there are also some beautiful places to browse nautical knickknacks, clothing, and gifts.

Thames Street and Downtown

Tempting shops are sprinkled all along the waterfront, but a good place to start would be the cavernous **Armory Antiques and Fine Art** (365 Thames St., 401/848-2398, 10am-5pm Mon.-Wed., 10am-6pm Thurs.-Fri., 10am-7pm Sat.), where dozens of dealers pile up everything from ships in bottles to leather-bound books and fine china. A bit closer to the center, **Cabbage Rose** (493 Thames St., 401/846-7006, 11am-7pm daily) charms with pretty accessories and locally printed T-shirts.

From lithographs of J-class sloops to oil paintings of Newport beaches, **Arnold Art** (210 Thames St., 800/352-2234, www.arnold-art.com, 9:30am-5:30pm Mon.-Sat., noon-5pm Sun.) brings together marine artists like Keith Reynolds and Helena Sturtevant—some of the area's most recognizable.

Bellevue Shopping District

Tony boutiques around Bellevue Avenue sell charming bits of the Newport lifestyle, like the perfectly sweet **Cottage & Garden** (9 Bridge St., 401/848-8477, www.cottageandgardennewport.com, 10am-5pm Tues.-Sat., noon-5pm Sun. July-Aug., 10am-5pm Tues.-Sat. Sept.-Jan. and Mar.-June), where displays of vintage furnishings, antiques, and garden supplies are arranged just so. If you're getting ready for a yacht party—or just want to play dress-up as if you were—sloop-ready fashions are at **Angela Moore** (190 Bellevue Ave., 401/619-1900, www.angelamoore.com, 10am-5:30pm Mon.-Sat., noon-5pm Sun.).

SPORTS AND RECREATION

★ Cliff Walk

Get the best views in town from the narrow path that threads between Newport's most elegant homes and the rocky edge of the Atlantic Ocean. **Cliff Walk** (www.cliffwalk.com) winds 3.5 miles from **Easton's Beach** (175 Memorial Blvd., signed entrance to Cliff Walk at the western edge of the beach), also known as First Beach, to **Bailey's Beach** at Bellevue Avenue, known locally as "Reject's Beach" since it's open to, you know, the public. The finest stretch of scenery starts at the **40 Steps,** an engraved granite staircase at the end of Narragansett Avenue. Heading north, the path is smooth and well-constructed for a 0.5 mile and passes behind The Breakers, Rosecliff, and Marble House. After Ruggles Avenue, the going gets a bit harder, and a sturdy pair of walking shoes is required.

Limited street parking is available at First Beach and on Narragansett Avenue, but it can be challenging to find a parking spot in the popular Bellevue Avenue area. The #67 **RIPTA bus** (401/784-9500, ext. 2012, www.ripta.com/67, $2, full-day pass $6) is convenient for making a one-way trip from 40 Steps to Ruggles Avenue or Bailey's Beach; buses run every 20-30 minutes and pass close by the entry and exit points.

Beaches

Much of Newport's coastline is rocky and rugged, but those salty points shelter wonderful beaches that are bustling all summer—though some are livelier than others.

Watch surfers catch waves and take a ride on the vintage carousel at **Easton's Beach** (aka First Beach, 175 Memorial Blvd., 401/845-5810, parking $20 weekends, $10 weekdays), a 0.75-mile stretch of sand that fills up with a friendly crowd of families. With ice cream shops and frozen lemonade trucks, this is a sweetly nostalgic place to enjoy the sun, and the on-site **Rosie's Beach Store** rents out umbrellas, chairs, and boogie boards. It's sometimes possible to find free parking on the side streets off Memorial Boulevard.

A few miles past Easton's Beach is **Sachuest Beach** (aka Second Beach, 474 Sachuest Point Rd., 401/847-1993, parking $20 weekends, $10 weekdays), where there are better waves and sometimes a thinner crowd. This beach is also the home of **Rhody Surf** (401/206-9283, www.rhodysurf.com, private lessons $95 for 1 person, $165 for 2 people, $65 each additional person), which offers surfboard rentals and surfing lessons with certified instructors. The western edge of the beach catches the biggest swell, while the eastern end is calmer, so toss out your beach blanket accordingly.

A rocky cove shelters **Gooseberry Beach** (123 Ocean Ave., parking $20), making it a good choice for quiet swims and smaller children, and the beach is often less crowded than other places in town. Open-topped kayaks are available for rent, but the nearby beach club is not open to the public, so it's worth bringing your own supplies. Avoid the Bellevue Avenue traffic and expensive parking by hopping on public transportation; Gooseberry Beach is just under a mile from the final stop on the RIPTA #67 bus route.

Boating

Aspiring yachties and ambitious landlubbers can hit the harbor in 12-meter America's Cup sailboats—a class of racing boats designed for the prestigious America's Cup race—with a pair of local charter companies. **America's Cup Charters** (63 Mill St., 401/849-5868, www.americascupcharters.com, 2-hour sail $75 adults, $40 children under 11, $195 3-hour racing experience) has the largest fleet of winning boats in the world, while **12 Meter Charters** (12 Bowen's Wharf, 401/851-1216, www.12metercharters.com, 2-hour harbor sail $98 adults, $50 children 5-12, $139 3-hour racing experience) has a slightly smaller, but equally impressive quiver of sailing yachts.

Slower-moving and breathtakingly

Cliff Walk

beautiful, old-fashioned schooners fly some of the prettiest sails on Narragansett Bay, and they're notably more comfortable than the sleek and speedy America's Cup boats. The 80-foot, teak-trimmed ***Aquidneck*** (32 Bowen's Wharf, 401/849-3333, www.sightsailing.com, $32 1.75-hour sightseeing cruise, $41 sunset sail with drinks, $5 discount for children 6-12) has gaff-rigged sails and a broad, comfortable deck that's perfect for a glamorous turn around the coast. Two-masted, wooden ***Madeleine*** (24 Bannister's Wharf, 401/847-0298, www.cruisenewport.com, $32 1.5-hour sightseeing cruise, $41 sunset sail, $5 discount for children under 12) is 72 feet and impossibly elegant, with a pretty mermaid figurehead to lead the way across the water.

Experienced sailors can rent their own boat from **Sail Newport** (60 Fort Adams Dr., 401/846-1983, www.sailnewport.org, 3-hour keelboat rental from $126); after being checked out by a staff member, hit the harbor at the helm of a J22 or a Rhodes 19.

Parks

In addition to the seven-mile **Cliff Walk** and the trails at **Fort Adams State Park,** there are plenty of ways to escape the crowds on scenic trails near the sea. Remember: It's important to be aware of ticks while hiking in this area.

With woodland habitat, streams, and fields, **Norman Bird Sanctuary** (583 Third Beach Rd., Middletown, 401/846-2577, www.normanbirdsanctuary.org, 9am-5pm daily, $3) attracts a diverse range of birds, from bobolinks to black-crowned night herons. Seven miles of hiking trails thread through 325 acres: The 1.4-mile **Nelson Pond Trail** traces a ridge covered with cedar and oak trees stunted by the wind and salt air, while the 1.2-mile **Valley Trail** passes through one of the preserve's most diverse areas. Each of the tree species that grows within Norman Bird Sanctuary may be found along the trail, including four species of oak and eastern red cedar, the area's only native conifer.

Borrow a pair of binoculars and a wildlife identification guide from the visitors center at **Sachuest Point National Wildlife Refuge** (Sachuest Point Rd., Middletown, 401/364-9124, www.fws.gov, 10am-4pm daily, free), then watch for snowy owls, harlequin ducks, and incredibly adorable New England cottontail rabbits. The 1.5-mile **Ocean View Loop** offers lots of water access and can be linked to the 1.2-mile **Flint Point** trail for a longer walk. Don't miss the explanation of the area's fascinating geological history at the visitors center—the rock record in the refuge retains traces of Rhode Island's 356 million-year-old run-in with present-day Africa.

Spectator Sports

Grab a wiener and some popcorn, then watch the Collegiate League **Newport Gulls** go to bat at **Cardines Field** (W. Marlborough St. and America's Cup Ave., 401/845-6832, www.newportgulls.com, $5 adults, $2 seniors and youth 13-18, $1 children under 13), where there's baseball two or three times a week from early June through the August playoffs. The historic field offers an old-fashioned taste of the sport that's largely been lost in the corporatized professional leagues, and is a blissful, family-friendly way to spend a summer evening.

On Saturday afternoons June-September, Newport dons its pearls and polo shirts for the matches at **Newport Polo** (250 Linden Ln., Portsmouth, 401/846-0200, www.nptpolo.com, lawn seating $12 adults, youth under 16 free). It's the perfect place to bring an elegant picnic and enjoy the sunshine as national and international teams hook, bump, and pass their way through a series of chukkas, or periods. At halftime, spectators are invited onto the field to stomp the grass back into place after being torn up by flying hooves. Matches begin at 5pm and gates open at 1pm (noon in Sept.), so plan to arrive early for prime picnic spots.

FOOD

Bustling Thames Street is lined with fudge shops, fine dining, and everything in between, including some of Newport's best seafood restaurants. It's the heart of the tourist scene and can get jammed with visitors, but joining the summer crowds by the water is just part of the Newport experience. In recent years, however, a cluster of hip, locals-oriented places have opened on Broadway, and when Thames Street starts looking like an out-of-control yacht party, it's worth heading over there to enjoy a meal away from the din.

Thames Street

Seafood stars at the modern, romantic **Fluke Wine, Bar & Kitchen** (41 Bowen's Wharf, 401/849-7778, www.flukewinebar.com, 5pm-9:30pm Mon.-Thurs., 4pm-10pm Fri.-Sat., 5pm-9pm Sun., mains $28-36), which takes up three sunny floors on Bowen's Wharf with views of the water. Crispy oysters with mango pepper relish and chili mayo are a perennial favorite, as is the ultra-local Point Judith fluke. Grab a linen-topped table in the downstairs dining room for a leisurely meal, or head to the 3rd floor, where the casual bar is the perfect place to enjoy rounds of oysters and drinks from Fluke's menu of excellent cocktails.

Cozy up to the bar at ★ **The Black Pearl** (Bannister's Wharf, 401/846-5264, www.blackpearlnewport.com, 11:30am-10:30pm daily, $8-30) for a bowl of award-winning chowder—rumor has it that The Black Pearl won Newport's chowder cook-off so frequently it got barred from entry. The casual tavern is the place to be here, where you can rub elbows with sailors and sightseers in a room that feels like a piece of maritime history.

You can watch all of Newport come and go at **Midtown Oyster Bar** (345 Thames St., 401/619-4100, www.midtownoyster.com, 11:30am-10pm daily, lunch $10-17, dinner $10-36), a popular hangout with a raw bar, dining room, and comfortable pub. The outdoor decks are dreamy on hot summer evenings, and you can wander around until you find the perfect place to sit. Mains like caramelized sea scallops with cauliflower mash are appealing and super fresh, but the appetizers tend to be Midtown's most creative options; tuna tartare tacos are a favorite with regulars, and the charred octopus is a highlight. The bar's especially good on Tuesday, when you can get a free trio of oysters with a featured drink.

Even if it weren't for the fresh, creative Mexican food, **Diego's** (11 Bowen's Wharf, 401/619-2640, www.diegosnewport.com, 11:30am-1am Mon.-Fri., 9am-1am Sat.-Sun., $13-18) youthful rock-and-roll atmosphere would set it apart in elegant Newport. Mexican wrestlers' masks, mason jar cocktails, and punk music are tonic after a morning in the Gilded Age, and the house drinks are among the best in town. Spiced sangrias are displayed at the bar, along with an apothecary's assortment of funky drink ingredients, from rosebuds to tamarind. Crispy pork belly tacos come with a local fruit pico de gallo and chipotle *crema*, and the over-the-top crack fries have a cult following—order them "dirty Donald" style for a dollop of spicy duck gravy.

Broadway

Newport's best burgers are served with piles of fresh toppings and minimal fuss at ★ **Mission** (29 Marlborough St., 401/619-5560, www.missionnpt.com, 11am-10pm Tues.-Sat., 11am-9pm Sun., $8-10), a casual spot just off Broadway. Organic, grass-fed beef is freshly ground for burgers and hot dogs, and the restaurant uses Newport-grown potatoes for its crisp, golden, hand-cut fries. Counter service can be poky, and tables in the small dining rooms fill up quickly, but with an excellent selection of canned beers, impeccable food, and very un-Newport prices, Mission is a rare find.

Settle in with a good book and better coffee at the Broadway outpost of **Empire Tea & Coffee** (22 Broadway, 401/619-1388, ext. 1, www.empireteaandcoffee.com, 6am-6pm Sun.-Thurs., 6am-8pm Fri.-Sat., $3-6), a rambling café with plenty of spots to work and read. Wireless Internet, well-made espresso, and excellent teas make this an appealing place to while away a rainy day.

It's worth getting up early to beat the weekend breakfast crowd at the homey **Corner Café** (110 Broadway, 401/846-0606, www.cornercafenewport.com, 7am-2:30pm Mon.-Wed., 7am-9:30pm Thurs.-Sat., 7am-4pm Sun., $5-15). Hearty omelets come with herb-flecked home fries, and regulars love the Portuguese French toast, but there are pages of options that cover the entire breakfast canon. Morning's the real draw here, but a lunch menu of salads and sandwiches and the evening pizza lineup are respectable options for an unpretentious meal.

Bellevue and Beyond

Tucked into the same tony block as the International Tennis Hall of Fame and the Audrain Automobile Museum, **Annie's** (176 Bellevue Ave., 401/849-6731, www.anniesewport.com, 7:30am-4:30pm daily, $5-18) is refreshingly old-fashioned and unpretentious. Homey booths and a diminutive diner counter are pleasant places to sit down to a bowl of lobster bisque or corn and clam chowder, and hearty breakfast plates are served all day. House-made corned beef hash and home fries are a local favorite.

Another respite from Bellevue glitz is ★ **Meg's Aussie Milk Bar** (111 Bellevue Ave., 401/619-4811, www.megsmilkbar.com, 8am-3pm Mon.-Sat., $5-12), a cozy breakfast and lunch place run by a Newport local and her Australian husband. Breakfast classics are very reasonably priced, and a lunchtime lineup of soups, salads, and sandwiches are the perfect fuel for browsing the mansions and/or hitting the beach. Australian knickknacks and menu items are an enjoyable touch; hand-sized meat pies are comforting treats, and the uninitiated should try ordering a "Tim Tam Slam" with their hot drink—it's an Aussie tradition worth globalizing.

An Awful Awful from the **Newport Creamery** (Newport Mall, 181 Bellevue Ave., 401/846-6332, www.newportcreamery.com, 7am-10pm daily, $4-10) is a summertime tradition in Rhode Island; the name of the thick ice cream shake stands for "awful big, awful good." A somewhat generic selection of sandwiches and burgers rounds out the menu, and the low prices make the Newport Creamery a decent option for families, but this place is all about the ice cream.

There's another outpost of **Empire Tea & Coffee** (112 William St., 401/619-1388, ext. 4, www.empireteaandcoffee.com, 6am-6pm daily, $3-6) just off Bellevue Avenue, which is a convenient place to stop for light lunches, like salads and panini, along with a coffee, tea, and wireless Internet while exploring the sights.

Head past the sandy crescent of Easton's Beach for another Rhode Island food pilgrimage; ★ **Flo's Clam Shack** (4 Wave Ave., Middletown, 401/847-8141, www.flosclamshacks.com, 11am-9pm daily, $5-22) has been ruling the old-school seafood scene since 1936. Buoys, lobster traps, fishing nets, and Rhode Island kitsch hang from every surface, and the menu features all the seafood shack classics: Golden fried clams come piled atop french fries and coleslaw; generous lobster rolls and oyster rolls overflow from a toasted, buttered hot dog bun; and chowder arrives creamy, clear, or red. Flo's does brisk business in Rhode Island-style clam cakes, a fried, hush puppy-like dumpling speckled with bits of clam meat that can be ordered singly or by the dozen. When coming to Flo's during the summer months, be prepared to wait in line; there's a small parking lot out back, otherwise try across the street, near the park.

Head north from Bellevue Avenue and you can try another Rhode Island classic, jonnycakes, at Newport's unassuming **Bishop's 4th St. Diner** (184 Admiral Kalbfus Rd., 401/847-2069, 6am-2pm Mon.-Fri., 6:30am-2pm Sat.-Sun., $4-9).

Picnic Fare and Markets

From sandy beaches to polo matches, there are plenty of prime picnic spots in town. Pick up basic supplies at the centrally located **Stop & Shop** (250 Bellevue Ave., 401/848-7200,

Little Rhody Eats

SNAIL SALAD, COFFEE MILK, AND HOT WIENERS (ALL THE WAY)

For such a tiny state, Rhode Island claims some of New England's most distinctive menu items, and there's a long list of must-try foods if you're exploring Ocean State cuisine.

- **Chicken Family-Style:** A satisfying meal that's designed to feed bellies, chicken family-style has its roots in the working-class Blackstone Valley—each restaurant adds a personal twist, but the all-you-can-eat feast generally includes roast chicken, pasta, french fries, and salad. The classic place to try chicken family-style is the cavernous **Wrights Farm Restaurant** (84 Inman Rd., Harrisville, 401/769-2856, www.wrightsfarm.com, 4pm-9pm Thurs.-Fri., noon-9pm Sat., noon-8pm Sun., $12-15), in the northern part of the state.
- **Coffee Milk and Cabinets:** Rhode Island's state drink is the unassuming **coffee milk,** a sweet blend of cold milk and coffee syrup that's available everywhere (the two major labels are almost identical, but each claims passionate partisans). Order a milk shake here, and you'll get sweetened milk; the frosty, blended ice cream drink is called a **cabinet,** and the very last word in cabinets is the **Awful Awful** from **Newport Creamery** (Newport Mall, 181 Bellevue Ave., 401/846-6332, www.newportcreamery.com, 7am-9pm Sun.-Thurs., 7am-10pm Fri.-Sat., $4-10). It's "awful big, awful good."
- **Hot Wieners:** Muster up the gumption to ask for a "hot weiner all the way," and your sausage will arrive in a steamed bun topped with beef sauce, chopped onions, and a bump of celery salt. Try one with a side of coffee milk at the Providence location of **Olneyville New York System Restaurant** (18 Plainfield St., Providence, 401/621-9500, www.olneyvillenewyork-system.com, 11am-2am Sun.-Thurs., 11am-3am Fri.-Sat., $3-8) . . . just don't call it a hot dog.
- **Jonnycakes:** The Algonquain tribe taught early settlers to make cakes from cornmeal—and legend has it that that's the origin of these crisp, fried corn cakes that are a Rhode Island breakfast staple. There's a (hotly contested) handful of ways to prepare the simple cakes, but state law

7am-10pm daily), or pack your hamper with more elegant fare at **Picnic Gourmet** (26 Bellevue Ave., 401/619-1181, www.picnicnewport.com, 7am-7pm daily), which spreads out a tempting array of house pastries, baguette sandwiches, soups, and specialty cheeses.

Another excellent stop is **Newport Wine Cellar & Gourmet** (13 Memorial Blvd., 401/619-3882, www.newportwinecellar.com, 10am-7pm Mon.-Sat., noon-5pm Sun.), offering ready-to-eat salads, fresh bread, and cheese that pairs well with an excellent wine selection.

Find local provisions at the **Aquidneck Growers Market** (9am-1pm Sat. year-round, 909 E. Main Rd. Middletown; 2pm-6pm Wed. late-May-Oct., Memorial Blvd between Chapel and Edgar, Newport; 401/848-0099, www.aquidneckgrowersmarket.org), a good place to meet farmers, bakers, fishers, and chefs.

ACCOMMODATIONS AND CAMPING

There's an inn on every corner in Newport's compact downtown, but finding a bed that won't break the bank can be a challenge in peak season. Rooms fill up months in advance for popular festival weekends, and many places maintain a two-night minimum on the weekends. That said, there are some incredible places to stay in town, ranging from homey dorms to aristocratic suites, and off-season prices are considerably lower than those listed.

Under $100

With a central location and a homey atmosphere, **William Gyles Guesthouse: Newport International Hostel** (16 Howard St., 401/369-0243, www.newporthostel.com, May-Nov., dorm beds $29-79) is an unbeatable decrees that they may not contain sugar, flour, or an *h* (don't even try ordering "johnnycakes" until you cross state lines). Try some topped with butter and syrup at Newport's unassuming **Bishop's 4th St. Diner** (184 Admiral Kalbfus Rd., 401/847-2069, 6am-2pm Mon.-Fri., 6:30am-2pm Sat.-Sun., $4-9).

- **Snail Salad:** Sea snails, celery, onion, and olives sopped in garlic dressing, this Italian-influenced Rhode Island classic is getting harder to find, but you can still order a plate at Federal Hill's **Andino's Italian Restaurant** (171 Atwells Ave., 401/453-3164, Providence, www.andinositalianrestaurant.com, 11:30am-11pm daily, $14-25), as well as **Iggy's Doughboys** (1151 Point Judith Rd., Narragansett, 401/783-5608, www.iggysdoughboys.com, 11am-8pm daily, $4-15).
- **Pizza Strips:** For reasons lost to history, Rhode Islanders prefer their pizza devoid of cheese and cut into dense rectangular slivers. The chewy crust is topped with marinara sauce, and they're available at Italian bakeries around the state. One Providence favorite is **Buono's Italian Bakery** (559 Hartford Ave., Providence, 401/421-4554, 7am-5:30pm Tue.-Fri., 7am-4:30pm Sat., 7am-12:30pm Sun., $3-6, www.buonositalianbakery.com, where the pizza strips get a bit of extra crust from the brick oven.
- **Quahogs, Stuffies, and Clam Cakes:** Hard-shelled clams are called quahogs (pronounced koh-hogs) in the Ocean State, and there are dozens of ways to prepare the briny bivalves. Head to **Flo's Clam Shack** (4 Wave Ave., Middletown, 401/847-8141, www.flosclamshacks.com, 11am-9pm daily, $5-22) to try them as **stuffies**—the chopped clam meat is mixed with bread and spices, then baked in the shell. Some versions are spiced up with *chourica* sausage, a reminder of Rhode Island's Portuguese heritage. Flo's also does a brisk trade in **clam cakes,** deep-fried lumps of batter, spices, and clam meat that are perfect when dunked in a bowl of Rhode Island-style clam chowder, which is based on a clear seafood broth.

budget option for solo travelers and a convivial place to meet other visitors. The hostel's four-bed, single-gender dorms are slightly cramped but filled with light, and a cozy living room, kitchen, and outdoor porch are available for guest use. The hostel's friendly tone is set by the owner, an adventurous traveler who's generous with tips for exploring the area, sometimes offers spontaneous city tours, and has a fleet of bicycles available for rent. A simple breakfast of cereal, toast, tea, and coffee is provided, and the hostel has wireless Internet, but no parking.

$100-150

The compact rooms at ★ **Crow's Nest at the Seaman's Church Institute** (18 Market Sq., 401/847-4260, www.crowsnestnewport.com, $135-150) are neat as a pin, decorated with sweet quilts and images of the sea. This unique accommodation was designed as a haven for seamen and fishermen on shore leave, and the Seaman's Church Institute's profits still go to providing services for "the men and women of the sea," as well as other people in need. All rooms share clean communal bathrooms, and visitors have access to the extraordinary ocean-themed Seaman's Chapel and a library stocked with all the books you need to plan a round-the-world sailing trip. The Crow's Nest is a wonderful find in Newport; fishers, military, and mariners should inquire about discounts.

$150-250

Just a short walk from the harbor front, the **Burbank Rose** (111 Memorial Blvd. W., 401/849-9457, www.theburbankrose.com, $129-265, parking $15) feels like a glimpse into Newport's past—simple rooms are furnished with old-fashioned charm, and the owner prepares freshly baked pastries for the generous continental breakfast. Three suites are available with a small kitchen and sitting room, and every room has a coffeemaker, flat-screen television, and private bath. The steep, narrow stairs are as authentic as the hospitality, and 3rd-floor suites may be a challenge for some guests.

Over $250

With an unbeatable location on the Thames Street waterfront, LEED-certified **Forty 1° North** (351 Thames St., 401/846-8018, www.41north.com, $350-1,100) eschews Newport's beachy pastels for a palette of muted grays and iridescent highlights—the result is a kind of mermaid modernism. For travelers arriving in Newport on their own yachts, Forty 1° North has a private, full-service marina—for the rest of us, it's easy to while away an afternoon on the dock, enjoying a cocktail and watching the dock lines fly.

The ultraromantic ★ **Castle Hill Inn** (590 Ocean Dr., 401/849-3800, www.castlehillinn.com, $650-900) commands sweeping views of the water and feels like a world apart. Follow rocky footpaths to the Castle Hill Lighthouse, bring a drink down to Grace Kelly Beach, or cruise to downtown on the inn's motor launch. If a night at the Castle Hill Inn isn't in your travel budget, it's worth stopping by the inn's iconic lawn on a warm afternoon to sip a drink and watch the sails drift past.

Candy-colored decor offers a cheeky, modern take on Newport's over-the-top style at ★ **Gilded** (23 Brinley St., 401/619-7758, www.gildedhotel.com, $300-500). The irreverent design is refreshing and fun; rooms are stocked with iPads, plush linens, smart televisions, and kimono robes; and you can brush up your bank shot or wicket skills at the on-site billiard room and croquet green. Breakfast is a selection of small plates that's perfect for light appetites, but might send hungry travelers looking for more.

Guests at the historic **Admiral Fitzroy Inn** (398 Thames St., 866/848-8780, www.admiralfitzroy.com, $119-329, free parking) can escape the ruckus on Thames Street with a rooftop deck and thoughtfully decorated rooms that are light-filled and comfortable. Hot croissants and baked goods are served in an airy breakfast room, along with fresh fruit, yogurt, and granola. An elevator provides wheelchair access to all rooms (though not the rooftop terrace). Don't miss the Admiral Fitzroy barometer in the lobby—like the inn itself, the barometer was named for the British naval officer and scientist that captained the HMS *Beagle* during Darwin's famous expedition, and who revolutionized weather forecasting.

Camping

Twenty minutes north of downtown, the **Melville Ponds Campground** (181 Bradford Ave., Portsmouth, 401/682-2424, www.melvillepondscampground.com, Apr.-mid-Nov., tents $40, RVs $65-90) is a friendly place to put down stakes, with hot showers, picnic tables, fire rings, and a pretty stream through the property. Consult the map on the campground website before booking, as some sites are a fairly long walk from the bathhouses, and beware of holiday weekends and Newport's festival dates, as sites go up in price and have a two- or three-day minimum.

With an excellent location near Second Beach and the Sachuest Point NWR, **Second Beach Family Campground** (474 Sachuest Point Rd., Middletown, 401/846-6273, www.middletownri.com, May-Sept., RVs $60-70) has full hookups, but offers few other amenities. Tents are not allowed.

INFORMATION AND SERVICES

Stock up on brochures, maps, and any other kind of information on the area at the centrally located **Newport County Convention & Visitors Bureau** (23 America's Cup Ave., 401/845-9110, www.discovernewport.org, 9am-5pm daily). There's also parking on-site.

The area's major hospital is **Newport Hospital** (11 Friendship St., 401/846-6400, www.lifespan.org/newport). Local pharmacies include **Rite Aid** (268 Bellevue Ave., 401/846-1631, www.riteaid.com) and **CVS** (181 Bellevue Ave., 401/846-7800, www.cvs.com, pharmacy hours 8am-9pm Mon.-Fri., 8am-8pm Sat.-Sun.). A handful of banks are found on Thames Street, and several ATMs are located on Thames Street and on Bellevue Avenue, as well as at the bus station and in convenience stores. Free **Internet access** is available in several local cafés and at the majority of hotels (offered to guests only) in town. Faxing and shipping services are offered at **The UPS Store** (270 Bellevue Ave., 401/848-7600, www.theupsstore.com).

GETTING THERE AND AROUND

Newport's Thames Street area and Bellevue Avenue can get clogged with traffic during peak season, and **parking** can also be a challenge during summer months; the largest public lot is at **Gateway Center** (23 America's Cup Ave., $2 per half hour, $1.50 each additional half hour, $24.50 all-day maximum), and metered parking is available in the center for $2 per hour.

For visitors who prefer to leave their cars parked, it's easy to visit the main attractions on Bellevue Avenue on the #67 **RIPTA buses** (401/784-9500, ext. 2012, www.ripta.com/67, $2), which run frequently every day of the week. Another good way to get around is by **bicycle;** rent one at **Mansion Rentals** (113 Memorial Blvd. W., 401/619-5778, www.mansionrentalsri.com, 9am-7pm daily, $7 per hour, $25 full day). Taxi service is available from **Atlantic Taxi Service** (401/239-6600, www.atlantictaxinewport.com), or you can get squired around in a two-wheeled pedicab by **Newport Pedicab** (401/432-5498, www.newportpedicab.com).

South County

After winding through the folds of Narragansett Bay, the Rhode Island coast makes a run for it at the edge of the Atlantic, breezing past a series of sandy barrier beaches and clam shacks. The shoreline can fill to the brim on warm summer weekends, but head inland and the whole place retains a rural feel, with nature preserves and miles of farmland. Pack a beach blanket and some tanning oil, and find your stretch of sand—from the rollicking party feel of the Narragansett Town Beach to the gorgeous Napatree Point and everything in between.

NARRAGANSETT

Better known as a bay, beer, and Native American tribe, Narragansett was once America's first seaside resort, drawing Gilded Age tourists to frolic 'til dawn at its swanky beachfront casino. After the casino burned down in 1900, the community underwent a slow decline that left it overshadowed by neighboring Newport. These days it's all beach and is considered the best surfing destination in South County, with gentle, beginner-friendly waves and board rental places that pull up to the edge of the water.

★ Beaches

NARRAGANSETT TOWN BEACH

The migration to this swath of shore starts first thing in the morning, with groups laden down by blankets, umbrellas, and everything for a full day of serious beach time. The town beach is a great stop for novice surfers, as the waves tend to stay under shoulder high, and they're relatively gentle. Rent a board or sign up for lessons from **Warm Winds** (town beach south parking lot, 401/789-9040, www.warmwinds.com, rentals $25-55, group lessons from $50), which also has a **surf report hotline** (401/789-7020).

Pavilions by the entrance to the beach have food, first-aid, and restrooms, though they're

Narragansett Bay

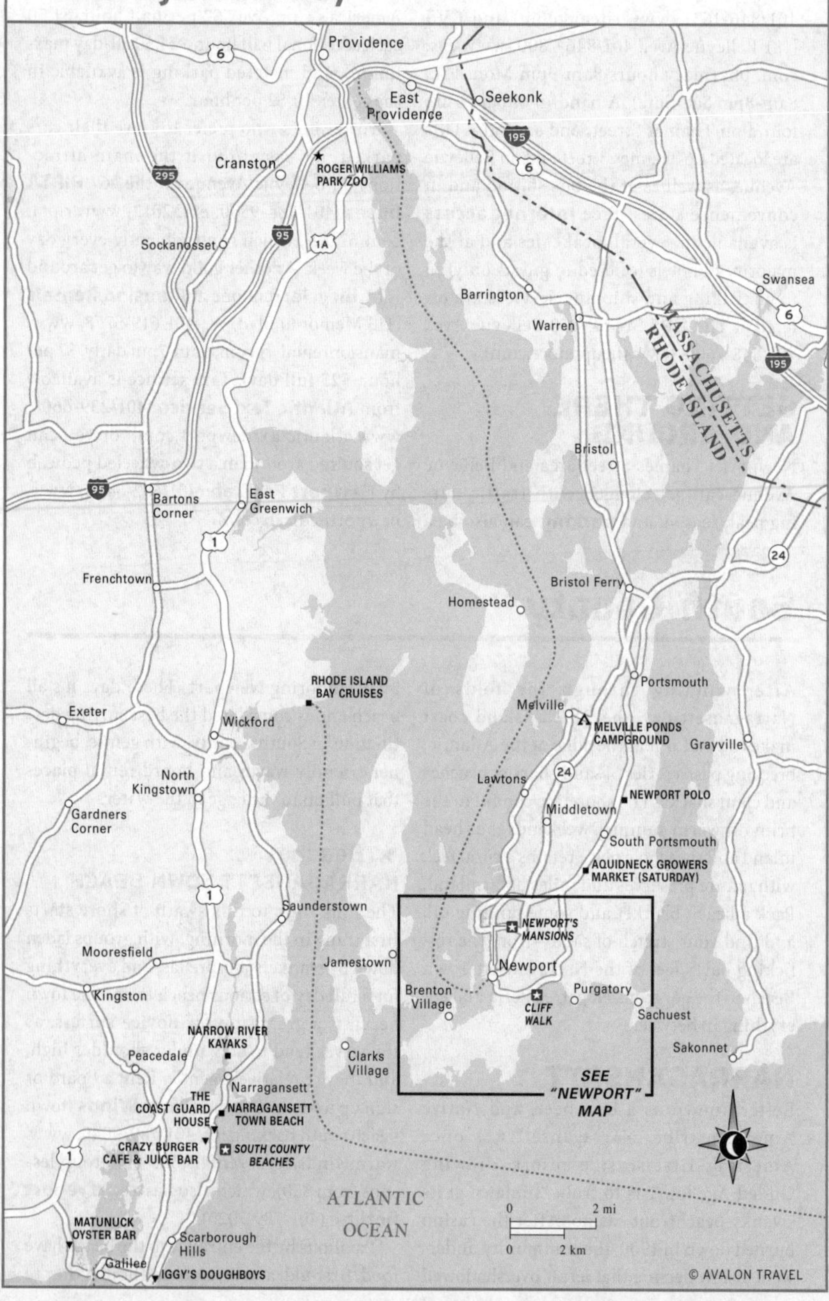
Providence
East Providence
Seekonk
Cranston
ROGER WILLIAMS PARK ZOO
Sockanosset
Barrington
Swansea
Warren
MASSACHUSETTS
RHODE ISLAND
Bristol
Bartons Corner
East Greenwich
Frenchtown
Bristol Ferry
Homestead
RHODE ISLAND BAY CRUISES
Portsmouth
Exeter
Wickford
Melville
MELVILLE PONDS CAMPGROUND
Grayville
North Kingstown
Lawtons
NEWPORT POLO
Gardners Corner
Middletown
South Portsmouth
AQUIDNECK GROWERS MARKET (SATURDAY)
Saunderstown
NEWPORT'S MANSIONS
Mooresfield
Jamestown
Newport
Kingston
Brenton Village
CLIFF WALK
Purgatory
Sachuest
NARROW RIVER KAYAKS
Peacedale
Clarks Village
Sakonnet
Narragansett
SEE "NEWPORT" MAP
THE COAST GUARD HOUSE
NARRAGANSETT TOWN BEACH
CRAZY BURGER CAFE & JUICE BAR
SOUTH COUNTY BEACHES
ATLANTIC OCEAN
0
2 mi
2 km
MATUNUCK OYSTER BAR
Scarborough Hills
Galilee
IGGY'S DOUGHBOYS
© AVALON TRAVEL
6
295
95
1A
195
1
24

only open when admission is charged mid-June-Labor Day ($8 adults, children under 12 free). Parking on-site is $10 on weekdays, $15 on weekends—if you're willing to walk, though, continue south from the beach along Ocean Road, where it's usually possible to find an unmetered parking spot at the edge of the road.

ROGER W. WHEELER STATE BEACH

Facing south from the village of Point Judith, this is one of the best beaches for families, with mild waves and a playground on-site. There are picnic tables, a pavilion with coin-operated showers, and food, and the fine sand is especially comfortable for lounging. Parking for nonresidents is $12 on weekdays and $14 on weekends, and lifeguards are on duty 9am-6pm daily in season.

Sports and Recreation

BOATING

To experience the real scope of Narragansett Bay, you have to get out on the water—**Rhode Island Bay Cruises** (1347 Roger Williams Way, North Kingstown, 401/295-4040, www.rhodeislandbaycruises.com, 1.5-hour cruises from $30 adults, $28 seniors, $16 youth under 13) runs a regular schedule of cruises that loop down through the bay, past 10 lighthouses, and over to Newport and Aquidneck Island. Some of the lighthouses are quite a distance away, so it's worth packing a pair of binoculars.

Set back on the river that flows out to Narragansett Town Beach, **Narrow River Kayaks** (94 Middlebridge Rd., 401/789-0334, www.narrowriverkayaks.com, kayaks/stand-up paddleboards from $25/35) has rental boats to take out on a very gentle river that's blissfully uncrowded even when the beach is packed. Go bird-watching in the warm shallows, paddle out to Gooseberry Island, or head upriver for a glimpse of a less developed side of the Rhode Island coast.

Food

Aside from the snack-bar style options at the Narragansett Town Beach pavilions, restaurants are a bit thin on the ground. One exception is the beloved **Crazy Burger Café and Juice Bar** (144 Boon St., 401/783-1810, www.crazyburger.com, 8am-9pm Sun.-Thurs., 8am-9:30pm Fri.-Sat., $5-13), which has a good selection of vegan entrées and solid breakfasts in addition to the namesake burgers and juice (as well as a fabulous key lime pie). This place tends to be busy, so come

South County beach

prepared for a wait on weekends. By the beach itself, **The Coast Guard House** (40 Ocean Rd., 401/789-0700, www.thecoastguardhouse.com, 11:30am-midnight Mon.-Thurs., 11:30am-1am Fri.-Sat., 10am-midnight Sun., $11-40) might not stand out for its menu of seafood and American fare, but views from the deck and terrace are so good it almost doesn't matter. This is prime territory for sunset drinks and snacks.

Just across from Point Judith, the ★ **Matanuck Oyster Bar** (629 Succotash Rd., South Kingston, 401/783-4202, www.rhodyoysters.com, 11:30am-10pm daily, $18-40) is worth the trip for refined seafood at the edge of the water. Above all, though, this place is all about bivalves, with a raw bar that uses oysters from the bar's own oyster farm, which is run by the marine biologist owner.

For a more down-home take on seafood, **Iggy's Doughboys** (1151 Point Judith Rd., 401/783-5608, www.iggysdoughboys.com, 11am-8pm daily, $4-15) is a Rhode Island classic. The "doughboys" themselves are bits of fried dough rolled in powdered sugar, and bowls of chowder come in red, white, and clear—those correspond to Manhattan style, the New England version, and Rhode Island's own take, with clams and potatoes swimming in a salty broth. The fish-and-chips is also excellent, super-flaky fresh cod in a crisp crust, and this is a good place to try stuffed quahogs, hard-shelled clams filled with minced clam meat. There's plenty of outdoor seating here, but for a quieter meal, take your food to the beach—continue down Point Judith Road until it takes a big swing to the left, and a small path heads straight to the shore.

Getting There and Around

The town of Narragansett, and the villages that extend from it, is accessible from Route 1, with the smaller Route 1A/Ocean Road running along the shore. To reach the beaches by public transit, the best bet is to travel to the **West Kingston Amtrak Station** (1 Railroad Ave., West Kingston, 800/872-7245, www.amtrak.com).

CHARLESTOWN

The most rural of the South County towns, a patchwork of farms and cottages runs right up to the incredible, seven-mile **Charlestown Town Beach** (557 Charlestown Beach Rd., 401/364-1222, www.charlestownri.org, nonresident parking $20, cash only). While the beach can get crowded, this is often the best place to go when other Rhode Island beaches are overflowing with out-of-towners—come early to stake out the best possible beachfront. The only food available is a little hot dog wagon, so bring a cooler if you're staying for the day.

On the other end of the big lagoon, **East Beach/Ninigret Conservation Area** (East Beach Rd., 401/322-0540) is one of the least developed beaches along the southern coast—three miles of sand that runs between the Atlantic Ocean and Ninigret Pond—and a favorite spot for bird-watching. Parking spots are very limited, so it's a bit of a risky bet in season.

Getting There

Charlestown is accessible from Route 1, which runs through the forest with spur roads to the coast. This area is not accessible by public transportation.

MISQUAMICUT

Another narrow stretch between a lagoon and the sea, **Misquamicut State Beach** (Atlantic Ave., 401/596-9097) is a summery vacation town that's popular with families, though the adjoining restaurants and services have seen better days.

Just about the only place on the south coast where you can get bar service from a beach chair, Misquamicut has several restaurants that extend all the way onto the sand, notably **The Andrea** (89 Atlantic Ave., 401/348-8788, www.andreaseaside.com, 11am-1am daily, $9-24), a landmark beach bar and restaurant with long rows of Adirondack chairs. The Andrea also has a webcam that's permanently trained on the beach, which is a good place to check if you want to see how packed the beach is.

Beach parking for nonresidents is $28, but it's usually possible to find cheaper options if you're willing to walk.

Getting There

Running parallel to Route 1A, Misquamicut's "strip" is Atlantic Avenue, with a series of beach access points and parking lots. This area is not accessible by public transportation.

WATCH HILL

Maybe it's the influence of nearby Connecticut that makes this village so much tonier than the rest of the southern coast, but Watch Hill is decidedly genteel. The finest beach here is the lovely **Napatree Point** (Westerly, 401/348-2500, www.oceanchamber.org, free 2-hour parking), a slender, sandy spit that points straight out into the sea before looping back onto itself.

It's easily among the loveliest beaches in Rhode Island, and you can walk with views of the ocean to each side, just a ruff of dune grass dividing the two shorelines. Though the most sought-after sighting in Watch Hill is Taylor Swift, whose sprawling beach house is a local landmark, this is a great place for watching birds, including piping plover and osprey.

On the way to the beach, you'll pass the **Flying Horse Carousel** (151 Bay St., 401/348-6007, www.watchhillbeachandcarousel.com, 11am-10pm Mon.-Fri., 10am-9pm Sat.-Sun., $1), a 19th-century beauty whose horses are outfitted with real horsehair tails and swing from long chains. To preserve the carousel's antique horses, it's only open to children under five feet and 100 pounds. If kids can snag the brass ring as they pass, it's good for a free ride. From the carousel, follow Bay Street 0.5 mile south to the **Watch Hill Lighthouse** (Lighthouse Rd., www.watchhilllighthousekeepers.org), a squat tower that's almost entirely surrounded by water. There's a small on-site **museum** (1pm-3pm Tues.-Thurs. July-Aug., free) that explores the life and work of a lighthouse keeper.

Getting There

To reach Watch Hill's main sights, turn onto Watch Hill Road from Route 1A, then follow it until it loops through the Watch Hill Historic District. This area is not accessible by public transportation.

Block Island

An isle of wild roses and coastal cliffs, Block Island offers a glimpse of the New England coast as it once was. The nonprofit Block Island Conservancy has preserved almost half the island from development, so it's free from the runaway vacation homes that crowd other coastal getaways.

And since humans aren't the only visitors that love Block Island's coast and wetlands, it's become a pilgrimage place for bird-watchers, who travel to the island each fall to spot some of the migratory birds that stop on their long flight south—even amateurs should pack a pair of binoculars.

The island's main town of Old Harbor is a compact cluster of shops and bike rental places that can get clogged with tourists during summer weekends, but it's always possible to escape the crowds on one of the trails that loop through the island interior. This is the place to leave your car on the mainland and explore by bike or moped, following the island's back roads to beaches, dunes, and coves. And when the sun sinks low above Block Island Sound, join the human migration toward outdoor decks in Old Harbor and by the Great Salt Pond, where sunset drinks kick off the island's laid-back nightlife.

SIGHTS

Southeast Lighthouse

Perched way up on the cliffs of Mohegan

Bluffs, this lighthouse has kept ships from the treacherous coast of Block Island since 1874. A National Historic Landmark, the lighthouse and attached keeper's house are brick red and rather elegant, with a blend of Gothic Revival and Victorian architecture. The modern-day light is mounted on a nearby steel tower, and the old-fashioned version is now a small museum that's open for **tours** (122 Mohegan Tr., 401/466-5009, 11am-5pm daily early July-mid-Sept., free). Though the grounds of the lighthouse are open each day sunrise-sunset, the volunteer-run museum has somewhat sporadic hours that are limited to the weekend during the shoulder season. For updated information about visiting the museum, call the Southeast Lighthouse phone number, or try the **Block Island Tourism Council** (800/383-2474).

Other Sights

Though its location isn't as dramatic as its southern cousin, the 55-foot-tall granite **North Lighthouse** (Corn Neck Rd., 401/466-3200, www.lighthouse.cc/blockinorth, early July-early Sept.) keeps watch over the northernmost point of the island at the end of a rocky beach. Inside, a small museum details the history of Block Island shipwrecks and rescues.

The island's agricultural past comes alive, sort of, at **Manisses Animal Farm** (Spring St. and High St., 401/466-2421, www.theinnatblockisland.com, dawn-dusk daily, free), an exotic animal farm at the Hotel Manisses with llamas, camels, fainting goats, and a zebu named Zeke.

For more about the history of the island, drop by the **Block Island Historical Society** (Old Town Rd., 401/466-2481, https://blockislandhistorical.org, 11am-4pm daily late June-early Sept., 11am-4pm Sat.-Sun. early Sept.-mid-Oct., off-season by appointment, $6 adults, $4 students and seniors), which maintains a series of well-labeled exhibits on 16th- and 17th-century farming and household life, as well as several rooms set up in the style of the island's heyday of Victorian tourism.

ENTERTAINMENT AND EVENTS

Sunset Drinks

The first thing you'll spot on the boat into Old Harbor are the broad decks that grace the front of downtown hotels, and decks are the place to be when the sun goes down. A standby in the middle of town is the **National Hotel** (36 Water St., 401/466-2901, www.nationalri.com, 7:30am-11pm daily high season, call for hours in the off- and shoulder-season), a grand dame hotel with a deep, shady deck that's ideal for early evening margaritas—and when the stars come out, head around the back to the hotel's fire pit. Hidden from view on the water side, the bar at **The Surf Hotel** (32 Dodge St., 401/466-2241, www.thesurfhotelbi.com, 5pm-11pm daily) has gorgeous views of Crescent Beach and catches delicious summer breezes from the ocean.

Half a mile from the strip in Old Harbor, the ★ **Spring House Hotel** (52 Spring St., 401/466-5844, www.springhouseblockisland.com, 3pm-sunset daily) lays out long lines of Adirondack chairs with gorgeous water views, and rolls out a menu of drinks and tapas that's just available on the lawn.

But for the very best sunset drinks on the island, make the (short) trek to the Great Salt Pond, where **The Oar** (221 Jobs Hill Rd., 401/466-8820, 11:30am-9pm daily) has perfect views of the placid boat basin. Grab a frozen drink and settle in on the deck, or at one of the picnic tables that dot the waterside lawn.

Events

The most exciting time on the island is during **Block Island Race Week** (914/834-8857, www.blockislandraceweek.com), held in June of odd-numbered years. Some 2,000 sailors and 200 boats from around the world vie for trophies during a week of regattas and onshore partying. An off-season highlight of the island calendar is the **Block Island Christmas Stroll** (800/383-2474, www.blockislandinfo.com, late Nov.), a post-Thanksgiving celebration that lights up the streets of Old Harbor with music and merriment.

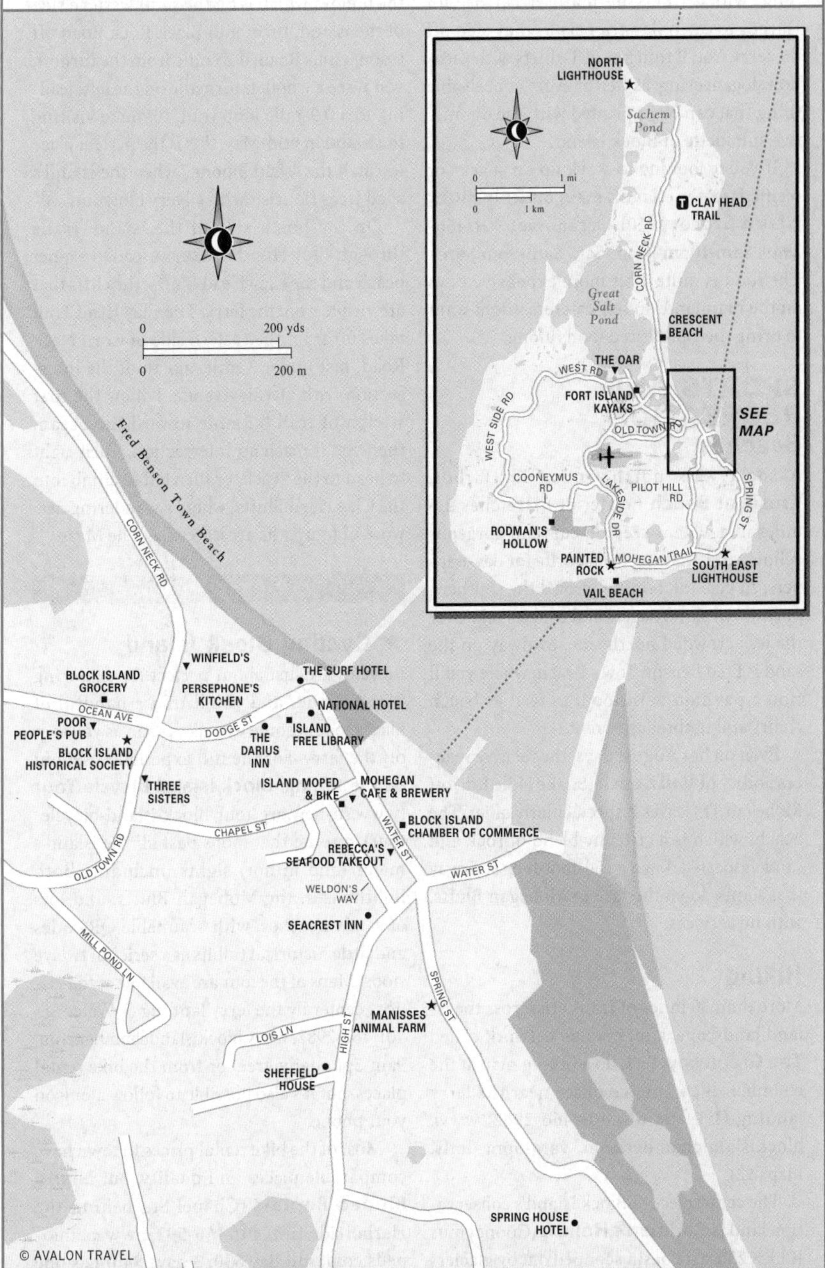
Block Island
0
200 yds
0
200 m
Fred Benson Town Beach
CORN NECK RD
WINFIELD'S
THE SURF HOTEL
BLOCK ISLAND GROCERY
PERSEPHONE'S KITCHEN
NATIONAL HOTEL
OCEAN AVE
POOR PEOPLE'S PUB
DODGE ST
THE DARIUS INN
ISLAND FREE LIBRARY
BLOCK ISLAND HISTORICAL SOCIETY
THREE SISTERS
ISLAND MOPED & BIKE
MOHEGAN CAFE & BREWERY
CHAPEL ST
WATER ST
BLOCK ISLAND CHAMBER OF COMMERCE
REBECCA'S SEAFOOD TAKEOUT
OLD TOWN RD
WATER ST
WELDON'S WAY
SEACREST INN
MILL POND LN
SPRING ST
MANISSES ANIMAL FARM
LOIS LN
HIGH ST
SHEFFIELD HOUSE
SPRING HOUSE HOTEL
© AVALON TRAVEL
NORTH LIGHTHOUSE
Sachem Pond
0
1 mi
0
1 km
CLAY HEAD TRAIL
CORN NECK RD
Great Salt Pond
CRESCENT BEACH
THE OAR
WEST RD
FORT ISLAND KAYAKS
WEST SIDE RD
OLD TOWN RD
SEE MAP
COONEYMUS RD
LAKESIDE DR
PILOT HILL RD
SPRING ST
RODMAN'S HOLLOW
PAINTED ROCK
MOHEGAN TRAIL
SOUTH EAST LIGHTHOUSE
VAIL BEACH

SHOPPING

It's impossible to miss Block Island's shopping, which lines the main street of Old Harbor to catch day-trippers as they step off the ferry. You'll find lots of T-shirts with vacation sloganeering, as well as every conceivable thing that can be imprinted with the distinctive silhouette of Block Island.

If you're looking to stock up on snacks or picnic fare, the island's main outlet is **Block Island Grocery** (101 Ocean Ave., 401/466-2949, 8am-10pm Mon.-Sat., 8am-9pm Sun.). The food is quite a bit more expensive than on the mainland, so self-caterers might want to bring their preferred foods along.

SPORTS AND RECREATION

Beaches

A short walk north from Old Harbor, **Crescent Beach** (Water St.) stretches 2.5 miles in a wide, sweeping curve of gorgeous yellow sand, making it a favorite for day-trippers. In general, families crowd the southern portion, while teenagers and couples take over the less crowded north side. Midway up the sand is Fred Benson Town Beach, where you'll find a pavilion with food, as well as beach chairs and umbrellas to rent.

Even on hot August days, the relative inaccessibility of **Vail Beach** (Snake Hole Rd., off Mohegan Tr.) leaves it spectacularly quiet. The beach, which is a crunchy blend of rock and sand, is located down a 150-foot-long stairway that slants down the face of Mohegan Bluffs, with no services.

Hiking

More than 30 miles of trails crisscross the island landscape, a marvelous network called **The Greenway.** Pick up a hiking map at the chamber of commerce office near the ferry landing (1 Water St., 401/466-2982, www.blockislandchamber.com, 9am-5pm daily, maps $2).

The centerpiece of Block Island's conservation land is **Rodman's Hollow** (Cooneymus Rd.), a 230-acre basin scooped out by glaciers 10,000 years ago and now filled with forested meadows and maritime shrub land. To enter the hollow, which is on the southwestern side of the island, turn onto Black Rock Road off Cooneymus Road; 0.25 mile from the turnoff, you'll see a wooden turnstile on the left, leading to a 0.9-mile loop trail. If you're visiting the island in mid-May, this is the perfect place to catch the "shad bloom," when the island's shad trees flourish with silvery blossoms.

On the north side of the island, trails through **Clay Head Preserve** lead to a quiet beach and the Clay Head Bluffs, the cliffs that are visible from the ferry. The Clay Head Trail takes off from the eastern side of Corn Neck Road, just under 3 miles north of the intersection with Ocean Avenue. Follow the first stretch of trail 0.3 mile toward the ocean, then you'll reach an intersection: Turn right to head to the beach, or turn left to climb into the Clay Head Bluffs, where a wandering network of footpaths are known as The Maze.

TOP EXPERIENCE

★ Cycling Block Island

Bicycles are just about perfect for exploring Block Island, and you'll find a handful of places to rent some wheels as soon as you step off the ferry. For the full experience, set out on the 16-mile **Block Island Bicycle Tour** (www.so-new.org/tour/block-island-bicycle-tour), a route that loops past all the island's major (and minor) sights, including both lighthouses, the Mohegan Bluffs, and lots of sandy beaches, with scannable QR codes and little historical tidbits at a series of twelve stops. Maps of the tour are available at the visitors center by the ferry landing (1 Water St., 401/466-2982, www.blockislandchamber.com, 9am-5pm daily, free) or from the bike rental places, but it's also possible to follow along on your phone.

Most of the bike rental places in town have comparable prices and quality, but **Island Moped Rentals** (Chapel St., behind the Harborside Inn, 401/466-5925, www.bimopeds.com, full day $30, 3 days $40) has one

bicycle rental shop on Block Island

of the biggest selections, including kid trailers and baby seats.

Boating

The sheltered Great Salt Pond makes for some of the best paddling—both kayaks and stand-up paddleboards—on the island, with oyster farms to explore and little coves that are ideal for nosing around. Rentals are available from **Fort Island Kayaks** (40 Ocean Ave., 401/466-5392, www.sandypointco.com, rentals from $25), and the company also offers guided kayak and stand-up paddleboard fishing tours, as well as longer charters. A handful of fishing charter companies are based in Block Island, and most run trips out to the big wind farm south of the island—the structures have created an artificial reef that attracts a remarkable variety of fish.

FOOD

The cute and compact ★ **Persephone's Kitchen** (235 Dodge St., 401/466-5070, www.persephoneskitchenbi.com, 7am-4pm daily, $5-12) is a fresh, vegetarian break from the fried fare and seafood served at many island restaurants. A menu of breakfast sandwiches, fancy varieties of toast, smoothies, and "bowls" leans healthy, and there's house-made baked goods to go with the café's strong coffee.

Owned by Molly, Brigid, and Maria Price, **Three Sisters** (443 Old Town Rd., 401/466-9661, 11:30am-2:30pm daily, $7-23) offers oversized sandwiches with funky names and soups like sweet potato-apple. On some evenings, the shop stays open for dinner under the name Mister Sister, and islanders congregate for barbecue ribs, the catch of the day, and live music under the stars.

Sidle up to the window at **Rebecca's Seafood Takeout** (435 Water St., 401/466-5411, www.rebeccasseafood.com, 7am-8pm Mon.-Tues. and Thurs., 7am-2am Wed. and Fri.-Sun., $5-15) for wraps, seafood sandwiches, fish-and-chips, and other snack bar fare, including a full range of fried seafood. Service is quick, and there are picnic tables outside, but it's just as easy to head down to the water and eat with a view.

In the middle of Old Harbor, **Mohegan Cafe and Brewery** (Water St., 401/466-5911, 11:30am-9:30pm Mon.-Thurs., 11:30am-10pm Sat., 11:30am-9pm Sun. May-Oct., hours vary in winter, $17.95-23.95) is in the middle of the road in other ways as well. With a big menu that includes burgers to fancy steaks, a wine list and decent beer selection, and a casual atmosphere, it's a family-friendly option that turns into a convivial drinking spot.

The laid-back **Poor People's Pub** (30 Ocean Ave., 401/466-8533, www.pppbi.com, 11:30am-1am daily, $11-25) specializes in mac and cheese with fancy fixings, served sizzling-hot in a skillet, but the menu runs to a solid selection of pub food, burgers, snacks, and a solid lobster and corn chowder.

While most of the island leans casual, **Winfield's** (214 Corn Neck Rd., 401/466-5856, www.winfieldsbi.com, 6pm-10pm daily, $26-37) is romantic and thoroughly grown-up. The kitchen consistently turns out the best food on Block Island, from filet mignon to lamb chops, squid salad, and duck confit prepared by a self-taught Texas chef.

ACCOMMODATIONS

Finding a place to stay on Block Island on a budget can be difficult, especially in the high season, when many accommodations have a three-night minimum. A good resource is the **Block Island Chamber of Commerce** (1 Water St., 800/383-2474, www.blockislandchamber.com), which maintains a list of any specials and discounted rates.

After a full overhaul for the 2017 season, the **Seacrest Inn** (207 High St., 401/466-5504, $80-240) is spic and span, and it's still one of the most inexpensive places to stay on the island. All rooms have private (though tiny) baths, televisions, air-conditioning, and reasonably comfortable queen beds, and the decor is updated and modern. There's no Wi-Fi available on the premises, and the inn is managed by the Harborside Inn by the ferry landing, where guests pick up their keys.

From the turret atop **Sheffield House** (351 High St., 401/466-2494 or 866/466-2494, www.sheffieldhousebi.com, shared bath $180-210, private bath $220-260), you get a picture-perfect view of the ocean (and the creatures at the adjoining animal farm). It's walking distance from the action in town, but far enough away to feel calm in the middle of the summer, and the innkeepers serve a hearty breakfast each morning. Rooms are old-fashioned and sweet, with quilts and flowered wallpaper, and the inn's blooming honeysuckle means that some rooms are infused with a heady fragrance.

Among all the old-fashioned choices, ★ **The Darius Inn** (62 Dodge St., 401/466-2722, www.dariusblockisland.com, rooms $150-400, suites $195-565) is downright cool, like visiting the beach house of an ultrahip friend. Bright and cheery decor pulls in many vintage and secondhand elements, with quirky art and tons of character. Rates include a hot, healthy breakfast and an evening cocktail hour, when guests gather on the back lawn. The inn is especially friendly to travelers with pets, though some rooms are designated animal free.

While many of the Victorian landmarks on the island are faded with time and salt air, the elegant **Spring House Hotel** (Spring St., 401/466-5844 or 800/234-9263, www.springhousehotel.com, $125-450) remains luxurious. Rooms are tastefully decorated with pastels and floral bedspreads, some with private baths as big as the bedrooms, but the gorgeous veranda is the real joy here, a big, shady porch made for whiling away a summer afternoon. The Spring House Hotel has a long history on the island, and notes on its website that it has hosted "notable guests such as President Ulysses S. Grant, Mark Twain, and Billy Joel." (Oh, Rhode Island.)

INFORMATION AND SERVICES

Brochures and advice are available from the **Block Island Chamber of Commerce** (1 Water St., 800/383-2474, www.blockislandchamber.com, 9am-5pm daily), which runs a visitors center at the ferry landing in Old Harbor.

There is no major hospital on the island, but **The Block Island Medical Center** (6 Payne Rd., 401/466-2974) offers daily care and emergency services. ATMs aren't easy to find, though there are a couple near the ferry terminal, as well as at the **Chamber Visitors Center** (Old Harbor, 800/383-2474, www.blockislandinfo.com), **Winfield's Restaurant** (214 Corn Neck Rd., 401/466-5856), and **Washington Trust Company** (123 Ocean Ave., 401/466-7710, www.washtrust.com).

Internet services on the island are often quite slow, but **Island Free Library** (Dodge St., 401/466-3233, www.islandfreelibrary.org) offers free access with no password, so you can pick up a signal even after the library is closed for the day.

GETTING THERE AND AROUND

Boat

The easiest way to get to the island is by ferry. **Block Island Ferry** (401/783-7996, www.blockislandferry.com) runs a **car ferry** year-round from **Point Judith** (34 Great Island Rd., Galilee, 55 min., round-trip $26 adults, $25 seniors, $13 children 5-11, $7 bicycles, $80 vehicles), as well as a **high-speed ferry** (May-Nov., 30 min., round-trip $38 adults, $22 children 5-11, $12 children under 5, $8 bicycles) from the same location.

Parking lots are a cottage industry in Point Judith, where most places charge $10 per day. There are, however, one or two places that charge $5, so it's worth circling the very small strip to look for options.

Summer ferry service is also available from **Newport** (Perrotti Park, 39 America's Cup Ave., late June-early Sept., 1 hr., round-trip $51 adults, $26 children 5-11, $12 bicycles) and **Fall River, Massachusetts** (State Pier, 1 Water St., late June-early Sept., 1 hr., round-trip $30 adults, $14 children 5-11, $6 bicycles).

From Connecticut, **Block Island Express** (2 Ferry St., New London, 860/444-4624 or 401/466-2212, www.goblockisland.com, 1.25 hrs., round-trip $53 adults, $27 children 5-11, $20 bicycles) runs a fast ferry from **New London.** And departing from **Montauk** is the **Viking Fleet** (462 W. Lake Dr., 631/668-6668, www.vikingfleet.com, 1.25 hrs., round-trip $80 adults, $50 children 5-12, children under 5 free, $10 bicycles).

Air

Block Island also sees a limited amount of air traffic. **New England Airlines** (56 Airport Rd., Westerly, 800/243-2460, www.blockislandsairline.com) has regular flights from Westerly Airport in South County.

Cars are not only unnecessary on Block Island, they are liable to be more hassle than they are worth, and renting a bicycle or moped is highly recommended. Lining up to meet each ferry, several taxis give tours of the island, including **Monica's Taxi** (401/742-0000) and **Mig's Rig** (401/480-0493, www.migsrigtaxi.com); most of the taxis charge about $75 for a tour that runs between 60-90 minutes for up to four people, with supplemental fares of $10 per person after that.

Vermont

Vermont's back roads and byways lead to picturesque villages, winding rivers, and orchards hung with heirloom fruit.

Among the most rural of the United States, Vermont can seem unchanged by passing time. More than half of Vermont's roads remain unpaved, simple dirt tracks that lead to dairy farms, villages, and leafy forests. The small state is divided by the spine of the Green Mountains, whose rocky peaks barely break above the tree line. And more than elsewhere in New England, it's a place defined by the seasons, from brilliant fall colors to snowy winters and springtime maple syrup.

But Vermont's true charm lies in a blend of traditional ways and innovation. In the Northeast Kingdom, generations-old dairy families partner with young cheese makers. Maple syrup producers collect sap on horse-drawn sleds, gathering it into state-of-the-art sugarhouses powered by the sun. Fiercely independent since the American Revolution, Vermonters have a politics all their own, with yearly town hall meetings and a legislature that was America's first to legalize gay marriage.

For a very Vermont blend of old and new, follow country roads to art-filled towns, craft breweries, and farm-to-table restaurants. Drive into the Green Mountains to summit rocky peaks and find the perfect line down a ski slope, or spend a weekend lingering in one of Vermont's many swimming holes. To experience the state's cultural capital, head to the lakeshore city of Burlington, where a colorful blend of students, old hippies, Yankees, and recent immigrants add a jolt of progressive energy to Vermont's country charm.

PLANNING YOUR TIME

You could breeze through Vermont in a couple of days, but travelers who slow down to the pace of this area will discover much to explore. Choose a home base in the south or the north—those regions are small enough to see on day trips from a single location. The southern mountains are gentler and a bit more touristy, while the north holds Vermont's highest peaks and most vibrant city, the cultural capital of Burlington.

Previous: skiing at Mad River Glen; grazing sheep. **Above:** sugar house and pails in Stowe.

Look for ★ to find recommended sights, activities, dining, and lodging.

Highlights

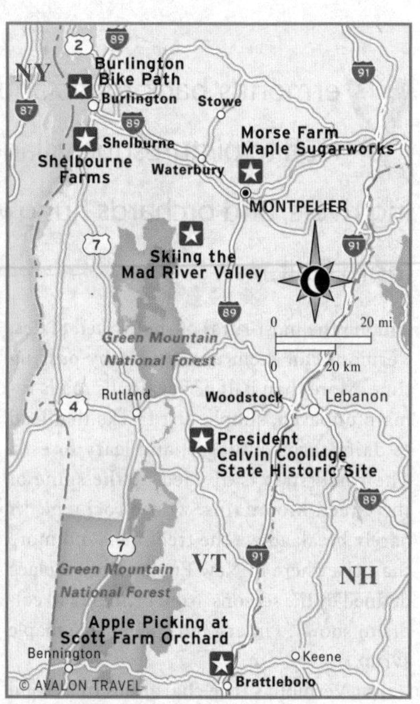

★ **Apple Picking at Scott Farm Orchard:** Fill up on heirloom fruit and literary history at this stunning property, where Rudyard Kipling's Vermont home presides over rolling lanes of apple trees (page 278).

★ **President Calvin Coolidge State Historic Site:** See the childhood home of the former president, who was sworn in by his father in the family parlor (page 292).

★ **Skiing the Mad River Valley:** Find some of Vermont's best lines in this northern valley, where Sugarbush and Mad River Glen offer two entirely different takes on Green Mountain riding (page 303).

★ **Morse Farm Maple Sugarworks:** See how the sweet stuff is made on a tour of a sugarhouse in the hills outside of Montpelier (page 310).

★ **Burlington Bike Path:** This lakeside bike path winds past art installations and perfect picnic spots, then extends into the middle of Lake Champlain on a three-mile-long raised causeway (page 326).

★ **Shelburne Farms:** Catch a springtime batch of baby lambs, eat ultra-local fare at a historic inn, then explore the sprawling farms on a network of walking trails (page 330).

Vermont

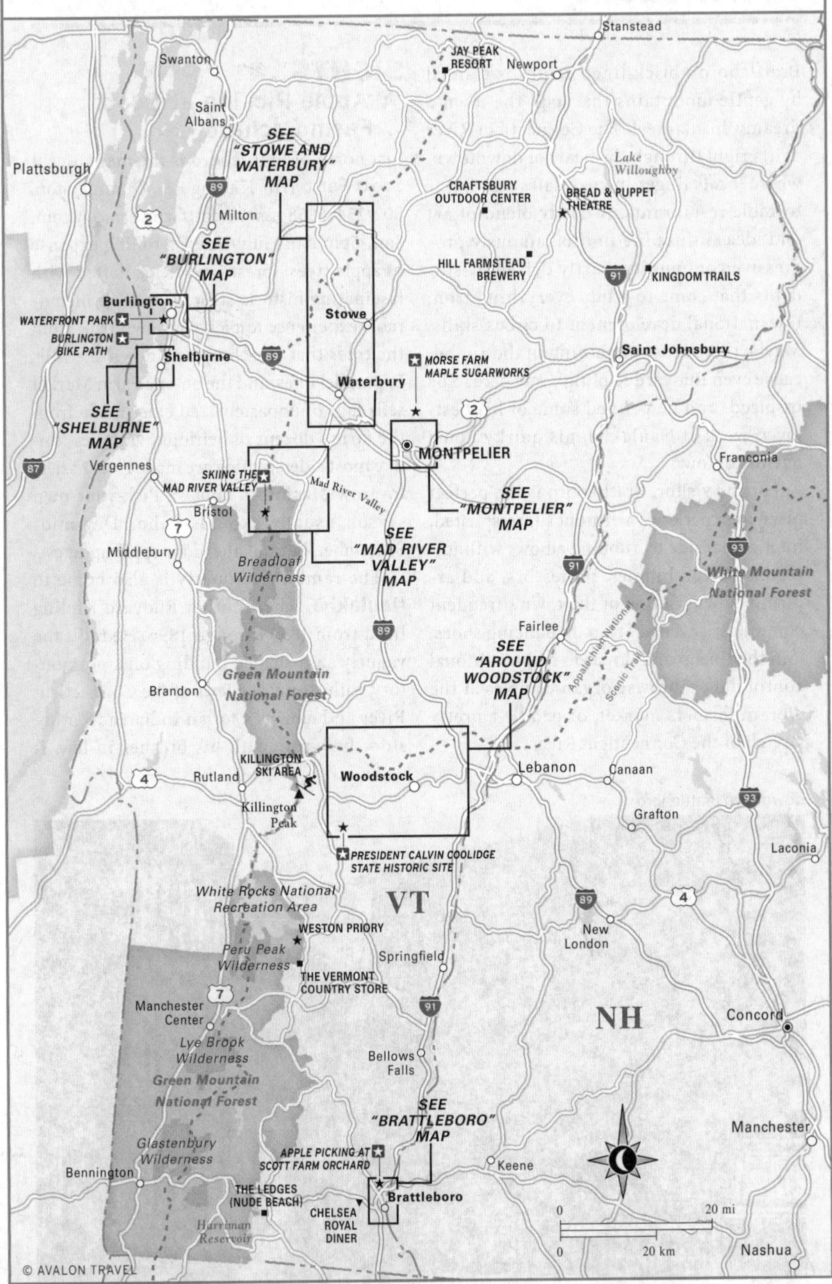

Stanstead
JAY PEAK RESORT
Newport
Swanton
Saint Albans
SEE "STOWE AND WATERBURY" MAP
Plattsburgh
Lake Willoughby
CRAFTSBURY OUTDOOR CENTER
BREAD & PUPPET THEATRE
Milton
SEE "BURLINGTON" MAP
HILL FARMSTEAD BREWERY
KINGDOM TRAILS
Burlington
WATERFRONT PARK
BURLINGTON BIKE PATH
Stowe
Shelburne
MORSE FARM MAPLE SUGARWORKS
Saint Johnsbury
Waterbury
SEE "SHELBURNE" MAP
MONTPELIER
Franconia
Vergennes
SKIING THE MAD RIVER VALLEY
Mad River Valley
SEE "MONTPELIER" MAP
Bristol
SEE "MAD RIVER VALLEY" MAP
Middlebury
Breadloaf Wilderness
White Mountain National Forest
Fairlee
Appalachian National Scenic Trail
SEE "AROUND WOODSTOCK" MAP
Green Mountain National Forest
Brandon
KILLINGTON SKI AREA
Woodstock
Lebanon
Canaan
Rutland
Killington Peak
Grafton
PRESIDENT CALVIN COOLIDGE STATE HISTORIC SITE
Laconia
White Rocks National Recreation Area
VT
WESTON PRIORY
New London
Peru Peak Wilderness
THE VERMONT COUNTRY STORE
Springfield
Manchester Center
NH
Concord
Lye Brook Wilderness
Bellows Falls
Green Mountain National Forest
SEE "BRATTLEBORO" MAP
Manchester
Glastenbury Wilderness
APPLE PICKING AT SCOTT FARM ORCHARD
Keene
Bennington
THE LEDGES (NUDE BEACH)
Brattleboro
CHELSEA ROYAL DINER
Harriman Reservoir
0
20 mi
0
20 km
Nashua
© AVALON TRAVEL

Brattleboro

Brattleboro's brick-lined center is framed by gentle mountains that lend the town a dreamy, insular feel. The Connecticut River drifts right through the heart of downtown, where locals linger in cozy cafés and farm-to-table restaurants. A heady blend of art and ideas infuse life in this famously progressive community, partly driven by students that come to study everything from international development to circus skills. Maybe there's just something in the air, because even Rudyard Kipling came here to be inspired, and he penned some of his best-loved work at Naulakha, his quirky home outside of town.

For the visitor, Brattleboro is the perfect place to experience Vermont's free-spirited, intellectual side by rubbing elbows with unreconstructed hippies, professors, and aspiring clowns at one of the town's frequent community events. Strap on dancing shoes, join the lineup and do-si-do in a traditional contra dance, browse organic apples at the vibrant farmers market, or paddle a pretty stretch of the Connecticut River.

SIGHTS

★ Apple Picking at Scott Farm Orchard

Just north of Brattleboro is the magnificent **Scott Farm** (707 Kipling Rd., Dummerston, 802/254-6868, www.scottfarmvermont.com, 8am-5pm daily July-Nov.), a rolling expanse of apple trees, forest, and fields dotted with fascinating historic structures. It's a memorable experience to pick your own fruit from the trees that march up and down the hills in parallel lines, and the on-site Farm Market sells jugs of unpasteurized cider made from the farm's dozens of heirloom varieties (unlike most ciders, which are made from easier-to-grow Macintosh apples). Pick-your-own season usually extends Labor Day-mid-September, but call ahead for apple updates.

The rambling property is also home to **Naulakha,** where author Rudyard Kipling lived from 1893 through 1896. He built the vaguely ship-shaped building on a promontory with stunning views of the Connecticut River and named it for an Indian adventure story he wrote with his brother-in-law. It

downtown Brattleboro

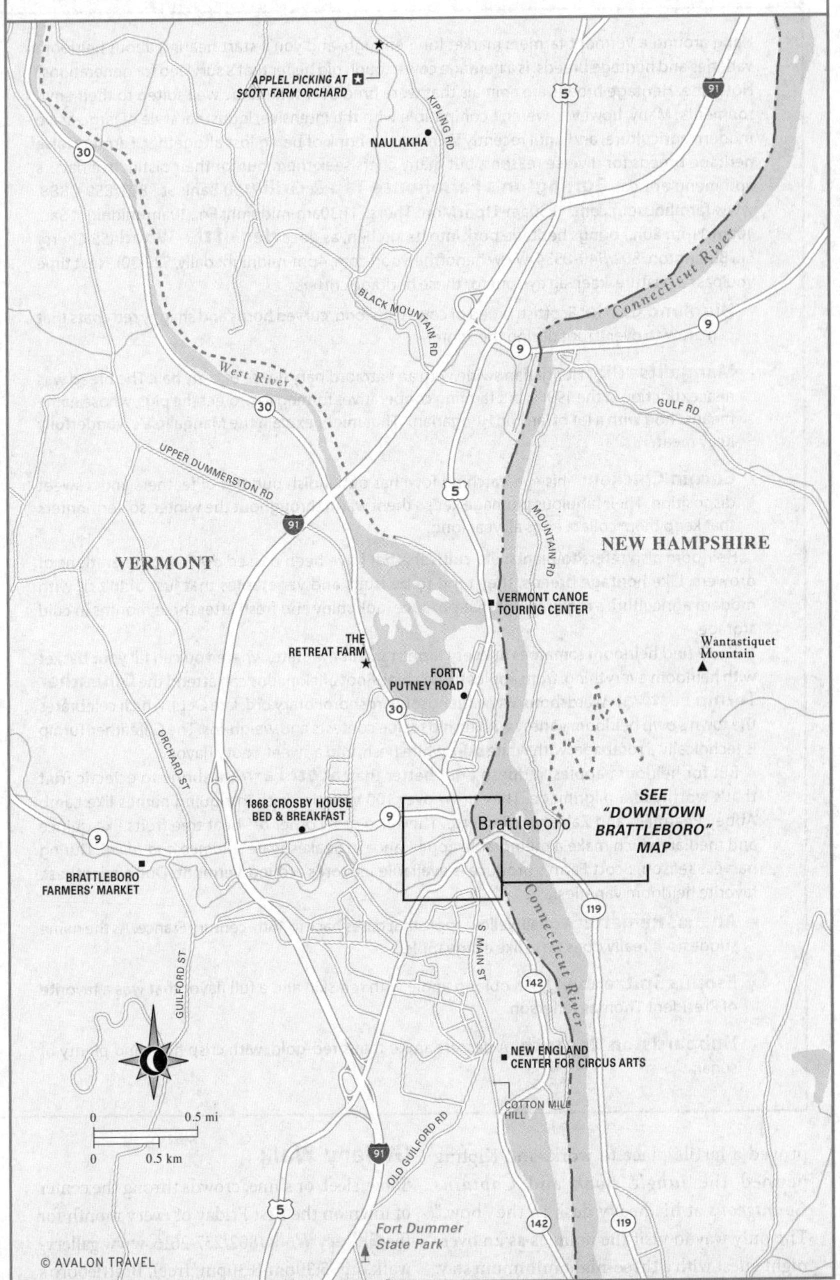
Brattleboro
APPLEL PICKING AT
SCOTT FARM ORCHARD
KIPLING RD
NAULAKHA
5
91
30
BLACK MOUNTAIN RD
Connecticut River
9
9
West River
30
GULF RD
UPPER DUMMERSTON RD
5
91
MOUNTAIN RD
NEW HAMPSHIRE
VERMONT
VERMONT CANOE
TOURING CENTER
THE
RETREAT FARM
Wantastiquet
Mountain
FORTY
PUTNEY ROAD
30
ORCHARD ST
1868 CROSBY HOUSE
BED & BREAKFAST
9
Brattleboro
SEE
"DOWNTOWN
BRATTLEBORO"
MAP
9
BRATTLEBORO
FARMERS' MARKET
Connecticut River
119
GUILFORD ST
S MAIN ST
142
NEW ENGLAND
CENTER FOR CIRCUS ARTS
COTTON MILL
HILL
0
0.5 mi
0
0.5 km
91
OLD GUILFORD RD
5
142
119
Fort Dummer
State Park
© AVALON TRAVEL

On Heritage and Heirlooms

Hang around a Vermont farmers market long enough, and you'll start hearing about heirloom varieties and heritage breeds. Is a heritage cow a tough old heifer that's survived for generations? Not quite. Heritage breeds are animals that were bred over time to be well suited to their environments. Many, however, weren't compatible with the intensive, industrial style of large-scale modern agriculture, and until recently were on the brink of being lost altogether. Farmers raise heritage breeds for diverse reasons, but many chefs seek them out for their distinctive flavors and menu appeal. **Burlington's Farmhouse Tap & Grill** (160 Bank St., 802/859-0888, www.farmhousetg.com, 11:30am-11pm Mon.-Thurs., 11:30am-midnight Fri., 10am-midnight Sat., 10am-11pm Sun.) brings heritage pork into its kitchen, as does **Hen of the Wood** (55 Cherry St., Burlington, 802/540-0534, www.henofthewood.com, 4pm-midnight daily, $22-30). Next time you pass a pasture, keep an eye out for these heritage critters:

- **Highland Cattle:** Scottish breed of cows with long, curved horns and shaggy red coats that can grow to over a foot during the winter.
- **Mangalitsa Pig:** Hungarian swine with an extraordinary fleece of curly hair. The breed was near extinction in the 1990s, but farming cooperatives formed to protect the pigs, whose name means "hog with a lot of lard" in Hungarian. (That might explain the Mangalitsa's wonderfully juicy meat.)
- **Cochin Chicken:** This eye-catching fowl has outlandish bundles of feathers and a sweet disposition. Their fabulous plumage keeps them warm throughout the winter, so Vermonters that keep them collect eggs all year long.

Heirloom also refers to plants: old cultivars that have been passed down by generations of growers. Like heritage breeds, they tend to be fruits and vegetables that just didn't fit with modern agriculture's requirement that produce look shiny and fresh after three months in cold storage.

You'll find heirloom tomatoes at every farm stand in the state, where you can fill your basket with heirloom everything, from apples to zucchini. Root aficionados can attend the **Gilfeather Turnip Festival** (Wardsboro, www.friendsofwardsborolibrary.org, late Oct.), which celebrates the town's own heirloom variety with turnip recipe contests and weigh-ins. The Gilfeather Turnip is technically a rutabaga, with white skin, white flesh, and a sweet, rooty flavor.

But for heirloom apples, it doesn't get better than **Scott Farm,** a shrine to eclectic fruit that's worthy of a pilgrimage. They grow over 100 varieties with intriguing names like Lamb Abbey Pearmain and Zabergau Reinette. They also grow other off-beat tree fruits like quince and medlar (which make a memorable appearance in Shakespeare's *Romeo and Juliet*). During harvest season, Scott Farm's produce is available in stores around Vermont. Don't miss these favorite heirloom varieties:

- **Ananas Reinette:** A small, yellow apple that dates back to 16th-century France. As the name suggests, it really does taste like a pineapple.
- **Esopus Spitzenberg:** An oblong apple with red skin and a full flavor that was a favorite of President Thomas Jefferson.
- **Hubbardston Nonsuch:** A dessert apple that's red-gold, with crisp flesh and plenty of sugar.

proved a fertile place to work, and Kipling penned the *Jungle Book* and *Captains Courageous* at his heavy desk in the "bow." The only way to visit the home is as an overnight guest with a three-night minimum stay.

Gallery Walk

Snow, sleet, or shine, crowds throng the center of town on the first Friday of every month for the **Gallery Walk** (802/257-2616, www.gallery-walk.org, 5:30pm-8:30pm, free), Brattleboro's

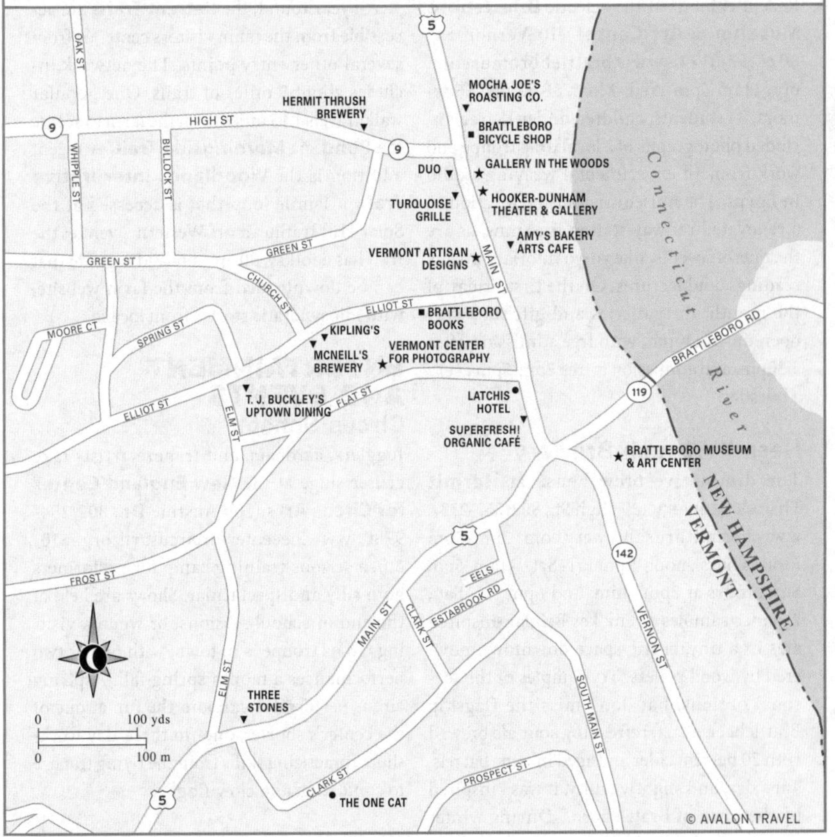

signature social event. Everyone in town comes out for it, and no other experience will give you a better feel for Brattleboro's unique spirit. The streets take on a festival atmosphere as neighbors catch up on news and pore over their friends' latest creations while juggling snacks and wine. A free map and guide (available online) will help you plot a course through the 50-some venues, which are mostly concentrated on Elliot and Main Streets.

Don't miss the exquisite **Gallery in the Woods** (145 Main St., 802/257-4777, www.galleryinthewoods.com, 11am-5:30pm Mon.-Sat., noon-5pm Sun.), whose focus on the "Visionary, Surreal, Fantastic and Sacred" results in surprisingly grounded and relatable exhibits that range from folk traditions to fine art. Another gem is the **Vermont Center for Photography** (49 Flat St., 802/251-6051, www.vcphoto.org, noon-5pm Fri.-Sun.), which hosts work by some of the region's most skilled and creative photographers. There's a broad range of mediums on display at **Vermont Artisan Designs** (106 Main St., 802/257-7044, www.vtart.com, 10am-5pm Sun.-Thurs., 10am-6pm Fri.-Sat.), and it's an ideal place to browse for unique handmade gifts.

Brattleboro Museum & Art Center

Recent exhibits at the eclectic **Brattleboro Museum & Art Center** (10 Vernon St., 802/257-0124, www.brattleboromuseum.org, 11am-5pm Wed.-Mon., $8 adults, $6 seniors, $4 students, children under 18 free) included photographs of a local drag troupe and work from an experimental weaving studio in Egypt. The museum's unusual location in a renovated railway station is a draw, as are the one-off events, like yo-yo tutorials, poetry readings, and lectures. On the first Friday of the month, the galleries and gift shop stay open until 8:30pm, with free admission after 5:30pm, and admission is free 2pm-5pm every Thursday.

Hermit Thrush Brewery

The diminutive brew house at **Hermit Thrush Brewery** (29 High St., 802/257-2337, www.hermitthrushbrewery.com, 3pm-8pm Mon.-Thurs., noon-9pm Fri.-Sat., 11am-6pm Sun., tours at 2pm, 4pm, and 6pm Fri.-Sat., 2-ounce samples $2) makes Belgian-inspired ales in a tiny, rustic space downtown powered by wood pellets. Try samples of the seasonal options, but don't miss the flagship Brattlebeer, a tart, refreshing sour ale brewed with 20 percent cider and aged in wine barrels. Tart, dry, and slightly fruity, it was "inspired by the town of Brattleboro." During winter months, the brewery closes one hour earlier.

The Retreat Farm

On the outskirts of town, the **Retreat Farm** (350 Linden St., 802/490-2270, www.retreatfarm.org, 10am-4pm Wed.-Sat., noon-4pm Sun. early June-Oct., $7 adults, $5 children 2-18) has a family-friendly "petting farm" with dozens of animals that range from familiar to exotic. The 475-acre property is still a working farm owned by the Windham Foundation, a private organization dedicated to preserving Vermont's rural traditions. In the spirit of being a "gateway farm," the Retreat offers plenty of ways to interact with the resident critters, so you can scratch a pig's belly, go eye-to-eye with a one-ton ox, and snag a selfie with an impossibly adorable dwarf goat.

All year round, the **Retreat Trails** are accessible from the main visitors center or from several other entry points. The network includes about 9 miles of trails. One popular walk travels 1.15 miles from the farm to scenic **Ice Pond** via **Morningside Trail.** A recent addition is the **Woodlands Interpretive Trail,** a 1-mile loop that is accessed at the Solar Hill trailhead off Western Avenue; the trail has a folksy, 30-minute audio guide that can be downloaded from the farm website, with idiosyncratic stories from locals.

ENTERTAINMENT AND EVENTS

Circus School

Jugglers, acrobats, and trapeze artists take center stage at the **New England Center for Circus Arts** (209 Austine Dr., 802/254-9780, www.necenterforcircusarts.org, $10-20), a serious training camp for performers both silly and spectacular. Shows are held at the end of school sessions, or when a visiting circus troupe is in town, with one or two performances a month spring-fall. Aspiring circus performers can join the fun at one of the center's shorter, one- to three-day workshops, practicing skills from the flying trapeze to contortion and clowning.

Nightlife

With in-house craft brews on tap and a prime riverside location, **Whetstone Station** (36 Bridge St., 802/490-2354, www.whetstonestation.com, 11:30am-10pm Sun.-Thurs., 11:30am-11pm Fri.-Sat.) is a year-round favorite. Take advantage of sunny weather on the rooftop deck or the beer garden: The main restaurant serves a slightly dressed up menu of pub fare, while the beer garden serves a slightly dressed down menu of pub fare.

There are bars named for Rudyard Kipling in places from Michigan to Mumbai, but **Kipling's** (78 Elliot St., 802/257-4848, 11:30am-8pm Mon.-Tues., 11:30am-2am Wed.-Fri., 3pm-2am Sat.) has a distinctively

Scenic Byways

DRIVING VERMONT'S ROUTE 100

Easily one of the prettiest roads in all of New England, **Route 100** winds north-south through quiet valleys, farmland, and historic villages. It sticks to the eastern side of the Green Mountains, and it's spectacular in foliage season, when bright colors illuminate the surrounding hills. Route 100 is ideal for a long weekend of exploration, as some of Vermont's most interesting destinations are right at the edge of the road. Starting at Route 9—the scenic byway that links Brattleboro and Bennington—here are some favorite stops from south to north.

Route 9 to Route 4

Route 100 bisects Route 9 just a few miles west of Hogback Mountain, a gentle peak that commands 100-mile views of the rolling hills to the south. Head north through a series of river valleys to the picture-perfect town of **Weston,** where the **Vermont Country Store** (657 Main St., Weston, www.vermontcountrystore.com, 802/824-3184) tends old-fashioned displays of everything from flannel nightgowns to penny candy. Time your visit to the morning, afternoon, or evening prayers at the Benedictine **Weston Priory** (58 Priory Hill Rd., Weston, 802/824-5409, www.westonpriory.org) to join the monks for a traditional sung service that's sometimes held outside during the summer months.

Continue north through the woods of Okemo State Forest, then duck onto the 100A cutoff that passes through Plymouth Notch and **President Calvin Coolidge State Historic Site** (3780 Rte. 100A, 802/672-3773, www.historicsites.vermont.gov/directory/Coolidge), where the president was raised and sworn into office. Pause to graze the samples at the Coolidge family's nearby cheese factory, **Plymouth Artisan Cheese** (106 Messer Hill Rd., 802/672-3650, www.plymouthartisancheese.com), then continue up Route 100A to the **Long Trail Brewing Company** (5520 Rte. 4, Bridgewater Corners, 802/672-5011, www.longtrail.com), a pioneer of Vermont craft brewing.

Route 4 to I-89

Get back on Route 100 where it rolls right to the base of **Killington Peak,** then continue north along the White River, passing through the pretty country towns of Stockbridge and Rochester, then entering the **Mad River Valley.** Duck off the road onto Warren's tiny Main Street, where you'll find a few artists' galleries, a covered bridge, and the **Warren Store** (248 Main St., Warren, 802/496-3864, www.warrenstore.com), an old-fashioned country store that's a community hub. In hot weather, don't miss the chance to cool off in one of Warren's spectacular **swimming holes,** then continue to the valley town of **Waitsfield** to taste locally made apple brandy at **Mad River Distillers** (114 Rte. 100, Waitsfield, 802/496-6973, www.madriverdistillers.com), or **rent an inner tube** for a float down the Mad River.

North of I-89

The mountains get bigger from here, so stop to fortify yourself with a scoop from the **Ben & Jerry's ice cream factory** (1281 Rte. 100, Waterbury, 802/882-2034, www.benjerry.com), or a freshly made **cider donut** from **Cold Hollow Cider Mill** (3600 Rte. 100, Waterbury Center, 800/327-7537, www.coldhollow.com), where you can watch apples turn into juice before your eyes. You'll cruise right through the resort town of **Stowe** as you head north—if you're traveling in the snow-free months, take a detour from Route 100 to drive Route 108 through **Smugglers' Notch,** a steeply winding and gorgeous stretch of road rimmed by granite boulders (watch out for rock climbers!).

When you get back onto Route 100 for the final stretch, you'll be in the Northeast Kingdom, where there are far more cows, mountains, and moose than people. Route 100 ends a bit unceremoniously by intersecting Route 105, but then you're just a hop away from the classic Kingdom town of Newport, where you can sample ice cider, artisan cheese, and other northern delights at the **Northeast Kingdom Tasting Center** (150 Main St., Newport, 802/334-1790, www.nektastingcenter.com).

Brattleboro feel, with a mashup of Irish bar, fish-and-chips joint, local hangout, and literary mecca (try the James Joyce burger). This is the sort of bar where regulars bang out tunes on the piano, and it's a good place to mingle with the locals.

The Arts

The landmark art deco building that houses the **Latchis Theatre** (50 Main St., 802/254-6300, http://theater.latchis.com, $9 adults, $7 children and seniors, $7 matinees) is as much a part of the show as anything on the screen. Its 750-seat main theater has an iridescent mural of the zodiac on the ceiling and frolicking Greeks along the walls. Three movie theaters show a mix of first-run and independent films. The 1938 building is also a hotel.

On the other end of the spectrum, patrons of the **Hooker-Dunham Theater & Gallery** (139 Main St., 802/254-9276, www.hooker-dunham.org, events $5-20, gallery admission free) enjoy its funky subterranean feel. This venue showcases art-house films, folk and chamber music, and avant-garde theater.

Festivals and Events

Follow step-by-step instructions from the caller, and you'll be twirling and swinging along with a crowd at **The Brattleboro Dance** (118 Elliot St., www.brattcontra.org, 7pm-10pm, $10-12 adults, $8 students), a bi-monthly traditional contra dance with live music and a welcoming set of regulars. Beginners can show up at 6:45pm for a bit of practice, and dancers should bring a pair of clean, soft-soled shoes to change into (though you'll likely spot some bare feet in the crowd).

Each June the cows take over for the **Strolling of the Heifers** (www.strollingoftheheifers.org, early June), a parade that celebrates the area's agrarian history and draws attention to the challenges faced by local farmers. In an opening parade, the pride of the pastures saunter down the street, followed by cow floats and kids in cow costumes. During the day, a Dairy Fest features free ice cream, cheese tastings, and a "celebrity" milking contest. Events recently added to the celebration include a Green Expo showcasing environmentally sustainable products and lifestyles, and a fiercely competitive Grilled Cheese Cook-Off, pitting professional and amateur chefs against each other for the coveted Golden Spatula. For a true taste of country living—and some enthusiastic swings and twirls—don't miss the evening community contra dance.

SPORTS AND RECREATION

Biking

With easygoing traffic and loads of scenic country roads, Brattleboro is the perfect place to ditch four wheels for two. If you've got your own bike, the Windham Regional Commission creates useful pdf bicycle suitability maps (www.windhamregional.org/bikemap), and 21-speed hybrid bikes are available to rent at **Brattleboro Bicycle Shop** (165 Main St., 802/254-8644, www.bratbike.com, $25 per day). The friendly staff is happy to suggest rides in the area, which are either flat out-and-backs in the Connecticut River Valley, or hilly climbs into the Green Mountains. As is the case throughout Vermont, some of the finest riding is on unpaved dirt roads, which outnumber the nearby asphalt options three to one, and are an ideal way to escape into quiet country hollows.

Boating

Canoes, kayaks, and tubes can be rented from the **Vermont Canoe Touring Center** (451 Putney Rd., 802/257-5008, www.vermontcanoetouringcenter.com, kayaks from $20, canoes from $25, tubes $20 per day, reservations required) at the intersection of the Connecticut and West Rivers. The stretch of the Connecticut above Vernon Dam is wide and pleasant, with some small islands along the way for paddlers to get out and explore; the West River is smaller but similarly peaceful, though it can also offer some great Class II and III whitewater in the early spring when the snow melts, or on one of a few release dates from the upstream dam each year.

Hiking

Three short, gentle nature trails leave from the Fort Dummer State Park Campground; the 1-mile **Sunrise Trail** and the 0.5-mile **Sunset Trail** loop through the forest, and the 0.5-mile **Broad Brook Trail** leads from the southern edge of the campground loop to a river swimming hole that's a pleasantly shady haven on a hot summer day.

Brattleboro's rolling skyline is dominated by **Wantastiquet Mountain,** but the trail to the top of the 1,368-foot peak starts in New Hampshire, just across the Connecticut River. To reach the trailhead, take Route 119 across the river from downtown Brattleboro and turn left onto Mountain Road just after the second bridge. The trailhead is 0.9 mile from downtown Brattleboro at a small parking area on the right side of the road. The 1.5 miles of switchbacks earn you sweeping views of the Connecticut valley from the summit, where an exposed granite slab makes an excellent picnic spot.

Swimming

The Connecticut River looks temptingly cool as it burbles past town, but there are cleaner, more peaceful options a short drive outside of the city limits. Though the river is generally too shallow for swimming, just flopping into a pool at **Stickney Brook Falls** is a delightful way to spend a hot afternoon. The series of gentle falls is on the left-hand side of Stickney Brook Road; from downtown Brattleboro, drive north on Route 30 and continue 3.7 miles past the I-91 underpass. Turn left on Stickney Brook Road and watch for cars parked along the road.

Stickney Brook is a tributary of the **West River,** which runs parallel to Route 30 north of Brattleboro. There are excellent swimming holes all along the waterway, notably just under the West Dummerston covered bridge (7.3 miles north of Brattleboro, with a sometimes strong current).

Half an hour west of Brattleboro, the sinuous **Harrington Reservoir** is pocked with pleasant spots to slip into the water. To reach the reservoir, drive west on Route 9 to the intersection with Route 100 in Wilmington. Access points and swimming beaches are located on the right side of Route 100, several with picnic areas and grills. The reservoir's most famous swim spot is **The Ledges,** a pristine, clothing-optional crook in the shoreline that's back in the buff after losing its nudist privileges in a hotly contested town vote. Thanks to support from groups like AANR—that's the American Association for Nude Recreation—the vote was eventually overturned.

SHOPPING

Downtown Brattleboro has an eclectic mix of shops that invites leisurely browsing, like **Boomerang** (12 Elliot St., 802/257-6911, www.boomerangvermont.com, 10am-6pm daily), which stocks new, used, and vintage clothing for men and women and many picks with flair.

Books tower from floor to ceiling at **Brattleboro Books** (36 Elliot St., 802/257-7777, www.brattleborobooks.com, 10am-6pm Mon.-Sat., 11am-5pm Sun.), an independent store with the best selection in town, including many used and out-of-print copies.

You can find one-of-a-kind gifts at **Vermont Artisan Designs** (106 Main St., 802/257-7044, www.vtart.com, 10am-6pm Mon.-Thurs. and Sat., 10am-8pm Fri., 10am-5pm Sun.), which features pottery, furniture, and other crafts made by artisans from across the state.

FOOD

The contrast between the thoughtful menus and the offbeat setting—a 1925 Worcester diner car—only heighten the experience at ★ **T. J. Buckley's Uptown Dining** (132 Elliot St., 802/257-4922, www.tjbuckleysuptowndining.com, 5:30pm-9:30pm Thurs.-Sun., open some Wed. summer, $40), a long-standing Brattleboro favorite. There are just eight tables, so chef-owner Michael Fuller gives personal attention to each dish and offers a handful of options nightly. All of them feature bold flavor combinations, such as venison with eggplant caponata, truffle oil, and fresh currants, or the quail with duck leg confit and root vegetables.

Exposed brick and an open kitchen make dining at ★ **duo** (136 Main St., 802/251-4141, www.duorestaurants.com, 5pm-9pm Mon.-Thurs., 5pm-10pm Fri., 9am-2pm and 5pm-10pm Sat., 9am-2pm and 5pm-9pm $18-24) a convivial and cozy experience. The fresh, farm-to-table menus bring diverse influences to bear on seasonal ingredients. Recent starters included fried pickled radishes and potted hot pastrami served with remoulade, sauerkraut, and rye. The pork chop is perfectly prepared and arrives alongside cornbread, bacon, and rhubarb chow chow.

With a brightly lit industrial-chic space right in the center of town, **Turquoise Grille** (128 Main St., 802/254-2327, www.turquoisegrille.com, 11am-3pm and 5pm-9pm Mon.-Sat., 9:30am-3pm Sun., $7-18) beckons on gray afternoons. The menu has global versions of meat on bread, with Turkish flair: kofte and kebabs alongside pulled pork, bratwurst, and burgers.

The unexpectedness of ★ **Three Stones Restaurant** (105 Canal St., 802/246-1035, www.3stonesrestaurant.com, 5pm-9pm Wed.-Sun., $12-16) is enchanting. A ramshackle exterior gives way to a warm and vivid interior with a decidedly casual feel. This family-run joint prepares classic foods of the Yucatán Peninsula in southern Mexico, like *panuchos*, a stuffed, refried tortilla; *salbutes*, fried maize cakes piled high with meat and vegetables; and *cochinita adobado*, slow-cooked pork that melts in your mouth. Don't miss the *onzicil*, a sauce made from toasted pepitas and tomatoes.

For those who love classic diner fare, but want their ingredients sustainably sourced, the **Chelsea Royal Diner** (487 Marlboro Rd., 802/254-8399, www.chelsearoyaldiner.com, 5:30am-9pm daily, $5-11) offers the best of both worlds, complete with blue plate specials.

Tucked into a cozy basement nook, **Mocha Joe's Roasting Co.** (82 Main St., 802/257-7794, www.mochajoes.com, 7am-8pm Mon.-Thurs., 7am-9pm Fri., 7:30am-9pm Sat., 7:30am-8pm Sun.) roasts coffee sourced from around the world, with direct trade programs in Cameroon and Nicaragua. The café serves pastries and snacks, but the brews are the real focus, and the friendly space may tempt you to while away the morning.

Vegetable lovers who've tired of Vermont's typically meat-heavy menus should head to ★ **Superfresh! Organic Café** (30 Main St., 802/579-1751, www.superfreshcafe.com, 10am-4pm Mon.-Wed., 10am-9pm Thurs., 10am-10pm Fri.-Sat., 10am-9pm Sun., $7-14), which fills plates with vibrant salads, filling sandwiches and wraps, and ample gluten-free options. You'll find plenty of smoothies, vegan "mylks," and elixirs for what ails you. The laid-back, artsy style is right at home in downtown Brattleboro, attracting a colorful crowd of locals.

Markets

The **Brattleboro Farmers' Market** (www.brattleborofarmersmarket.com, 9am-2pm Sat. May-Oct., 10am-2pm Tues. June-Oct.) is the best in southern Vermont, with piles of local produce, cheese, and meat from local farms, crafters, and producers. Snap up artisanal kimchi, gelato, and pasta, among many other things. The Saturday market is on Route 9 near the covered bridge; the Tuesday market is at Whetstone pathway, on lower Main Street.

ACCOMMODATIONS AND CAMPING

$100-150

Diminutive and homey, **The One Cat** (34 Clark St., 802/579-1905, www.theonecatvermont.com, $95-165) is as funky as Brattleboro itself. The two guest rooms—New England and Brighton—are named for the Anglo-American couple's homes, with respective decorative flourishes, as well as televisions,

DVD players, and coffeemakers. The tiny library is full of intriguing books and calls out for intimate wintertime reading. A full English breakfast is served, and a 20 percent discount is available for guests who arrive without cars.

$150-250

Despite the confusing name—which has led some guests to look for the wrong street address—**Forty Putney Road** (192 Putney Rd., 800/941-2413, www.fortyputneyroad.com, $100-240) is at 192 Putney Road, and the meticulous bed-and-breakfast couldn't be cuter. The pristine white house is surrounded by specimen trees and meticulous gardens outside, and filled with serenely decorated rooms evocative of the Provençal and English countryside. A full gourmet breakfast is included.

The lobby at the **Latchis Hotel** (50 Main St., 802/254-6300, www.latchis.com, $115-190) retains art deco flourishes from its heyday in the 1930s, and for some, it doesn't get any better than a room at a downtown movie theater. Period details like terrazzo floors and chrome fixtures maintain historical cool; ongoing renovations are sprucing up the down-at-the-heels rooms; and suites with small sitting rooms are available.

Sweet old-fashioned rooms have romantic appeal at the **1868 Crosby House Bed & Breakfast** (175 Western Ave., 802/257-7145, www.crosbyhouse.com, $160-199). Three individual rooms have queen-size beds and fireplaces; the largest has a double-whirlpool bath. Fans of dress-up will love the special afternoon tea at which the innkeepers lay out a selection of gloves and hats for guests, along with feathers and other accessories for decorating. The nearby Retreat Trails are perfect for morning walks.

Over $250

Slow down for a few days on the property that surrounds **Scott Farm Orchard** (707 Kipling Rd., Dummerston, 802/254-6868, www.scottfarmvermont.com), and you'll be rewarded with a sublimely peaceful retreat into scattered apple orchards and shady forests. The **Landmark Trust USA** (www.landmarktrustusa.org) maintains five historic buildings that are destinations worth planning a trip around, especially the exquisite **Naulakha** (sleeps 8, 3-night minimum stay, $390-450), Rudyard Kipling's scrupulously maintained home. The property favors historical preservation over modern-day comforts, but the grounds offer sweeping views of the Wantastiquet Range, where Kipling loved to watch Mount Monadnack break the clouds "like a giant thumb-nail pointing heavenwards." The other on-site rentals include the Kiplings' charming **Carriage House** (sleeps 4, 3-night minimum stay, $275), a renovated sugarhouse, and two historical farmhouses. All properties must be booked in advance, and have minimum stay requirements.

Camping

A 1908 dam on the Connecticut River flooded Fort Dummer—Vermont's first permanent European settlement—but the area around it has been preserved as **Fort Dummer State Park** (517 Old Guilford Rd., 802/254-2610, www.vtstateparks.com/htm/fortdummer.htm, mid-May-Labor Day, campsites and lean-tos $18-27). The 217-acre forest is just south of downtown, with a pleasant mix of oak, beech, and birch trees that shelter wild turkeys and ruffed grouse. The campground's 50 wooded tent sites are comfortable, if not particularly private, or you can spend the night in one of 10 more-secluded lean-tos. Hot showers and a dump station are available, but no hookups.

INFORMATION AND SERVICES

The **Brattleboro Area Chamber of Commerce** (180 Main St., 802/254-4565, www.brattleborochamber.org, 9am-5pm Mon.-Fri.) runs a visitors center downtown.

The area's premier hospital is **Brattleboro Memorial Hospital** (17 Belmont Ave., 802/257-0341, www.bmhvt.org). For pharmacy needs, there's **Rite Aid Pharmacy** (499 Canal St., 802/257-4204 and **Walgreens**

(476 Canal St., 802/254-5633). For nonmedical emergencies, contact the **Brattleboro Police** (230 Main St., 802/257-7946).

Banks are found all over the downtown area, particularly on Main Street. ATMs are plentiful around retail stores, in and around hotels, and in convenience stores. Most cafés have **wireless Internet.** Computers are available for public use at **Brooks Memorial Library** (224 Main St., 10am-9pm Wed., 10am-6pm Thurs.-Fri., 10am-5pm Sat.).

GETTING THERE AND AROUND

Just off the north-south I-91, Brattleboro is the eastern edge of Vermont's east-west Route 9, a scenic, two-lane highway that's known as the **Molly Stark Byway,** named for the wife of a Revolutionary-era general. Brattleboro is also on both of Vermont's Amtrak lines, the Ethan Allen Express from **New York City,** and The Vermonter, which travels from **Washington DC** (800/872-7245, www.amtrak.com, from NYC 5.5 hrs., from $65; from DC 8.75 hrs., from $135), and which now allow bicycles. **Greyhound Bus** (800/231-2222, www.greyhound.com) links Brattleboro with cities around the region, and taxi service is available from **Brattleboro Taxi** (802/254-6446, www.brattleborotaxi.com).

Metered parking is available all over downtown Brattleboro, and the town's small downtown is compact and easy to navigate. Three city bus lines connect at the Flat Street Transportation Center in downtown; rides within town are $1, buses operate Monday-Saturday, and a service map is available at www.crtransit.org.

Woodstock and Vicinity

With a bit of starch and a lot of history, this picture-book village is among the prettiest in New England. Rolling hills and farms are the perfect backdrop for Woodstock's covered bridges, elegant homes, and tiny town center. That "country gentleman" feel is no accident—this part of Vermont was a rural escape for some of the 19th century's most affluent U.S. families, and names like Rockefeller, Billings, and Marsh continue to define today's landscape of historic inns, parks, and farms.

In part due to its carefully maintained past, Woodstock attracts transplants from urban areas around the East. This blend of new and old lends an unusual vitality to the small town, where upscale restaurants, art galleries, and boutiques cheerfully coexist with farm stores and a quirky "town crier," a community blackboard listing contra dances and church suppers.

Just outside of Woodstock are a pair of appealing villages that are ideal for afternoon excursions. To the east, little Quechee has a renowned glassblowing studio and a deep, glacier-carved gorge. Southwest of Woodstock is the idyllic valley of Plymouth Notch, where the future President Coolidge was raised on the family farm—the creamery his father founded in 1890 makes award-winning cheese to this day.

SIGHTS

Woodstock

BILLINGS FARM & MUSEUM

One of Woodstock's most successful native sons was Frederick Billings, who made his money as a San Francisco lawyer in the heat of the gold rush. In the 1870s, he returned to Woodstock and bought the old Charles Marsh Farm, which he transformed into a model dairy farm complete with imported Jersey cows. Today visitors to the grounds of the **Billings Farm & Museum** (53 Elm St., 802/457-2355, www.billingsfarm.org, 10am-5pm daily Apr.-Oct., 10am-4pm Sat.-Sun. Nov.-Feb., $15 adults, $14 seniors, $8 children 5-15, $4 children 3-4, children under 3 free) can tour the property in wagons drawn by Percheron draft horses, meet the well-groomed herd of milking cows, and churn fresh cream into butter. The farm produces two varieties of cheddar from a herd of all Jersey cows: full-flavored and creamy sweet cheddar and butter cheddar, which is slightly salty with a rich, melting texture.

Next door, **Marsh-Billings-Rockefeller National Historical Park** (54 Elm St., 802/457-3368, www.nps.gov/mabi, 10am-5pm daily Memorial Day-Oct., $8 adults, $4 seniors, children 15 and under free) frames the mansion built by natural philosopher Charles Marsh 1805-1807 and bought by Billings in 1861. The mansion, open for tours by advance reservation, has a Tiffany stained-glass window and an extensive collection of American landscape paintings. In 1934, Billings's granddaughter married Laurance Rockefeller, and they donated the land to the National Park Service in 1992. The main visitors center is the former Carriage Barn, which houses a permanent exhibit about conservation history, a reading library, and a bookstore. **Combination tickets** ($20 adults, $15 seniors) include two-day admission to both Billings Farm and Marsh-Billings-Rockefeller National Historical Park.

SUGARBUSH FARM

Cows and other farm animals can be found at **Sugarbush Farm** (591 Sugarbush Farm Rd., 802/457-1757, www.sugarbushfarm.com, 8am-5pm Mon.-Fri., 9am-5pm Sat.-Sun. and holidays), which produces excellent cheddar cheese and keeps its maple sugar shack open all year (though syrup is generally made between February and April). To get here, take a right across the covered bridge at the small village of Taftsville and follow the signs to the farm. Call ahead for road conditions in winter and early spring.

DANA HOUSE MUSEUM

For a glimpse into Woodstock's nonagricultural past, visit the **Dana–Thomas House Museum** (26 Elm St., 802/457-1822, www.woodstockhistorical.org, 1pm-5pm Wed.-Sat., 11am-4pm Sun. June-mid-Oct., free), a federal-style home once owned by a prosperous local dry goods merchant. Now a museum run by the Woodstock Historical Society, it contains period rooms full of fine

Woodstock countryside

Woodstock

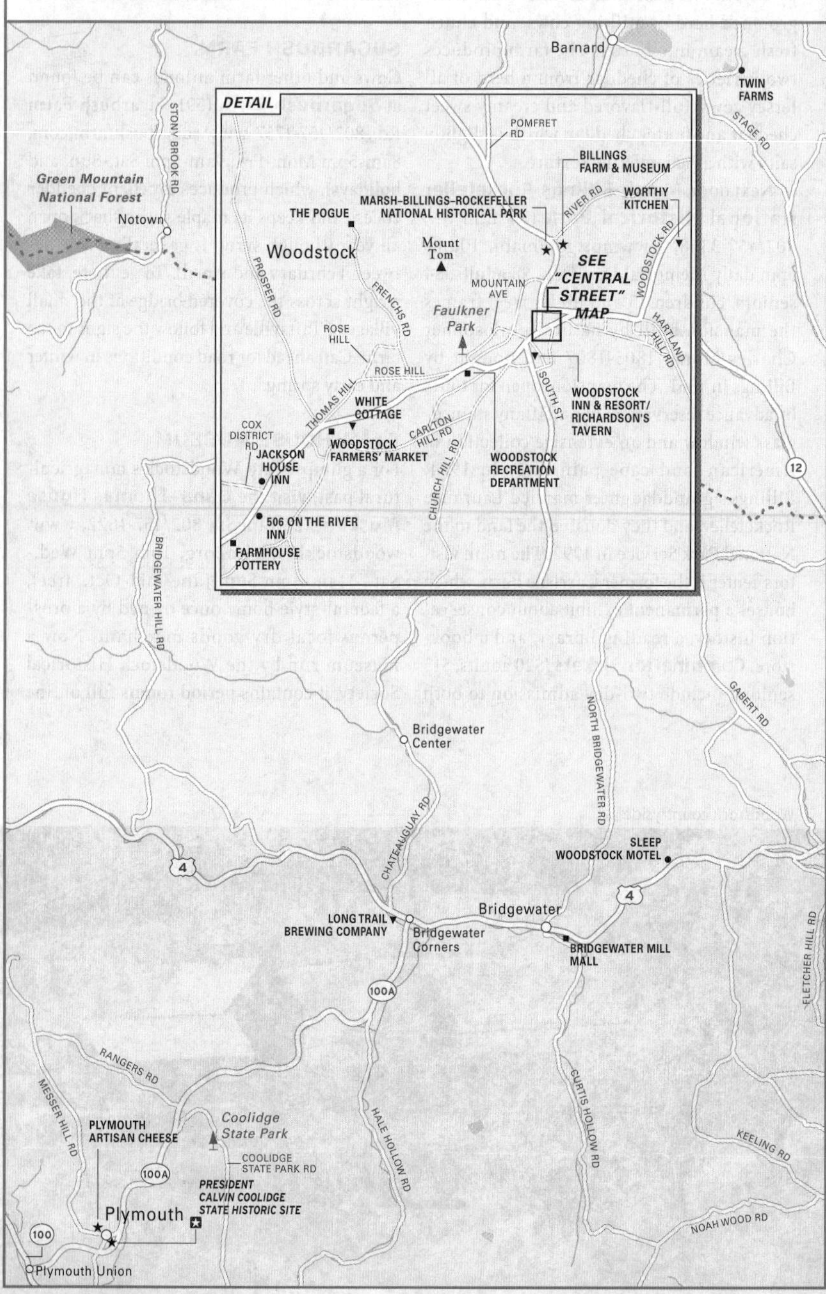
DETAIL
Barnard
TWIN FARMS
STAGE RD
POMFRET RD
STONY BROOK RD
Green Mountain National Forest
Notown
BILLINGS FARM & MUSEUM
WORTHY KITCHEN
RIVER RD
MARSH-BILLINGS-ROCKEFELLER NATIONAL HISTORICAL PARK
THE POGUE
Woodstock
Mount Tom
WOODSTOCK RD
SEE "CENTRAL STREET" MAP
MOUNTAIN AVE
PROSPER RD
FRENCHS RD
Faulkner Park
HARTLAND HILL RD
ROSE HILL
ROSE HILL
SOUTH ST
WOODSTOCK INN & RESORT/ RICHARDSON'S TAVERN
THOMAS HILL
WHITE COTTAGE
COX DISTRICT RD
CARLTON HILL RD
WOODSTOCK FARMERS' MARKET
JACKSON HOUSE INN
CHURCH HILL RD
WOODSTOCK RECREATION DEPARTMENT
12
506 ON THE RIVER INN
FARMHOUSE POTTERY
BRIDGEWATER HILL RD
NORTH BRIDGEWATER RD
GABERT RD
Bridgewater Center
CHATEAUGUAY RD
SLEEP WOODSTOCK MOTEL
4
4
Bridgewater
LONG TRAIL BREWING COMPANY
Bridgewater Corners
BRIDGEWATER MILL MALL
FLETCHER HILL RD
100A
RANGERS RD
MESSER HILL RD
CURTIS HOLLOW RD
Coolidge State Park
PLYMOUTH ARTISAN CHEESE
HALE HOLLOW RD
KEELING RD
COOLIDGE STATE PARK RD
100A
PRESIDENT CALVIN COOLIDGE STATE HISTORIC SITE
Plymouth
NOAH WOOD RD
100
Plymouth Union

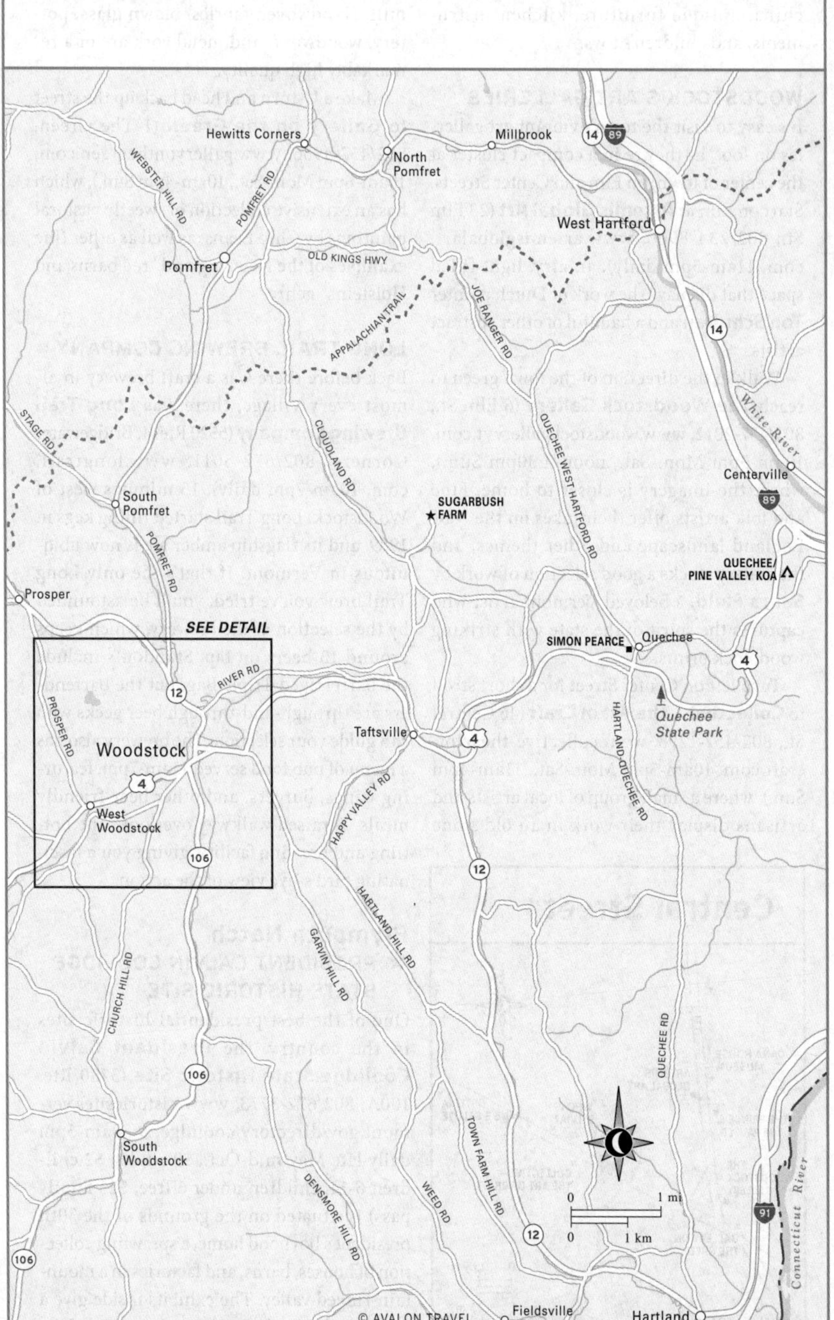
Hewitts Corners
North Pomfret
Millbrook
14
89
WEBSTER HILL RD
POMFRET RD
West Hartford
OLD KINGS HWY
Pomfret
JOE RANGER RD
APPALACHIAN TRAIL
14
STAGE RD
CLOUDLAND RD
QUECHEE WEST HARTFORD RD
White River
Centerville
89
South Pomfret
SUGARBUSH FARM
POMFRET RD
QUECHEE/ PINE VALLEY KOA
Prosper
SEE DETAIL
SIMON PEARCE
Quechee
4
RIVER RD
12
Quechee State Park
PROSPER RD
Woodstock
Taftsville
4
4
HARTLAND-QUECHEE RD
HAPPY VALLEY RD
West Woodstock
106
12
HARTLAND HILL RD
GARVIN HILL RD
CHURCH HILL RD
QUECHEE RD
106
TOWN FARM HILL RD
South Woodstock
DENSMORE HILL RD
WEED RD
0
1 mi
0
1 km
12
91
Connecticut River
106
© AVALON TRAVEL
Fieldsville
Hartland

china, antique furniture, kitchen instruments, and children's toys.

WOODSTOCK'S ART GALLERIES

It's easy to visit the town's vibrant art galleries on foot, as they're in a compact cluster at the center of town, on Elm and Center Streets. Start on Elm at **Artemis Global Art** (23 Elm St., 802/234-8900, www.artemisglobalart.com, 11am-5pm daily), an airy, light-filled space that displays the work of Dutch painter **Ton Schulten** and a handful of other abstract artists.

Walk in the direction of the town green to reach **The Woodstock Gallery** (6 Elm St., 802/457-2012, www.woodstockgalleryvt.com, 10am-5pm Mon.-Sat., noon-4:30pm Sun.), where the imagery is closer to home. Fine and folk artists offer their takes on the New England landscape and other themes, and the gallery stocks a good selection of work by **Sabra Field,** a beloved Vermont artist who captures the spirit of the state with striking woodblock prints.

Turn left on Center Street for a short stroll to **Collective—the Art of Craft** (46 Central St., 802/457-1298, www.collective-theartofcraft.com, 10am-5pm Mon.-Sat., 11am-4pm Sun.), where a small group of local artists and artisans display their work in an old stone mill. Handwoven fabrics, blown glass, pottery, woodwork, and metalwork are of a remarkably high quality.

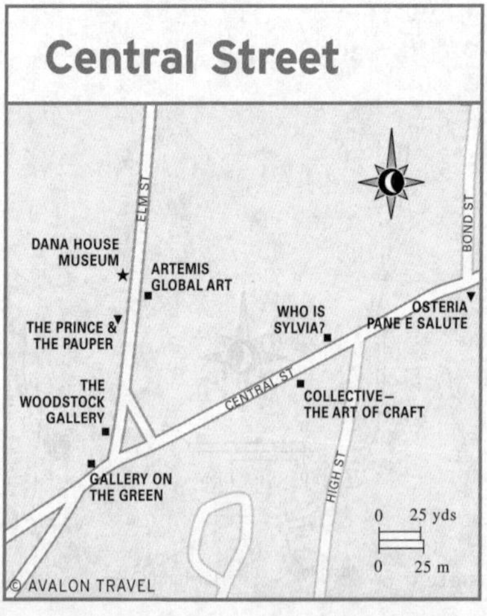

Make a U-turn and head back up the street to **Gallery on the Green** (1 The Green, 802/457-4956, www.galleryonthegreen.com, 10am-6pm Mon.-Sat., 10am-4pm Sun.), which has an extensive collection of sweetly pastoral paintings by Chip Evans, as well as other fine examples of the New England "red barns and Holsteins" genre.

Central Street

LONG TRAIL BREWING COMPANY

Back before there was a craft brewery in almost every village, there was **Long Trail Brewing Company** (5520 Rte. 4, Bridgewater Corners, 802/672-5011, www.longtrail.com, 10am-7pm daily), 15 minutes west of Woodstock. Long Trail started filling kegs in 1989, and its flagship amber ale is now ubiquitous in Vermont. If that's the only Long Trail brew you've tried, you'll be astounded by the selection at the brewery, which keeps around 13 beers on tap. Standouts include the barrel-aged Triple Bag, but the bartenders are through-and-through beer geeks who can guide your selection. The brewery also has a menu of pub food served 11am-7pm, featuring wings, burgers, and other beer-friendly meals. A raised walkway overlooks the bottling and brewing facility, giving you a fascinating bird's-eye view of the action.

Plymouth Notch

★ PRESIDENT CALVIN COOLIDGE STATE HISTORIC SITE

One of the best presidential historic sites in the country, the **President Calvin Coolidge State Historic Site** (3780 Rte. 100A, 802/672-3773, www.historicsites.vermont.gov/directory/coolidge, 9:30am-5pm daily late May-mid-Oct., $9 adults, $2 children 6-14, children under 6 free, $25 family pass) is situated on the grounds of the 30th president's boyhood home, a sprawling collection of houses, barns, and factories in a mountain-ringed valley. The exhibits inside give a rare intimate look into the upbringing of the

president known as Silent Cal for his lack of emotion, but who restored the dignity of the office during a time of widespread scandal. The family parlor preserves the spot where Coolidge was sworn into office—by his father, a notary public. Even in 1924, when Coolidge ran for reelection, the homestead swearing-in must have seemed like a scene from a simple, earlier time—one radio campaign ad described it in heavily nostalgic terms, pitching Cal as a rustic counterpoint to Washington DC's modernity and urban sophistication.

PLYMOUTH ARTISAN CHEESE

Nearby **Plymouth Artisan Cheese** (106 Messer Hill Rd., 802/672-3650, www.plymouthartisancheese.com, 10am-5pm daily) was founded in 1890 by John Coolidge, Calvin Coolidge's father. Its granular curd cheeses were once relatively common in the United States, but are now rare. Learn about the cheese-making process at the on-site museum, then sample everything from squeaky-fresh cheese curds to granular aged cheeses that have been hand-dipped in wax.

Quechee

The mission of the **Vermont Institute of Natural Science** (VINS, Rte. 4 just west of Quechee Gorge, 802/359-5000, www.vinsweb.org, 10am-5pm daily mid-Apr.-Oct., 10am-4pm daily Nov.-mid-Apr., $15 adults, $14 seniors, $13 children 4-17, children 3 and under free) is to rescue and rehabilitate birds of prey, including hawks, owls, and eagles, and display them for the education of visitors. Watching the raptors watch you is an unforgettable experience; the birds are released when fully healed, but a recent visit included a great horned owl, merlin falcons, and other fiercely captivating creatures.

Try to time your visit with one of the raptor educational programs, held at 11am, or their feeding time at 2:45pm. VINS puts on other educational programs throughout the day, and also has an hour-long interpretive nature trail that winds through the forested property.

Even if you're not in the market for the high-end glassware, **Simon Pearce** (1760 Main St., the Mill at Quechee, 802/295-2711, www.simonpearce.com, 10am-9pm daily) is a fascinating stop that's seven miles east of Woodstock in the village of Quechee. Located in an old mill building run entirely by hydroelectric power, the studio is open to the public, who can watch glassblowers blow bubbles into glowing orange balls of 2,400-degree silica. It's an extraordinary sight, especially the way multiple craftspeople coordinate individual components of a delicate wineglass, with precise timing and handiwork. If they slip up, of course, that's one more glass for the shelf of perfect-seeming "seconds" that are available for purchase at somewhat lower prices.

ENTERTAINMENT AND EVENTS

Each year toward the end of sugaring season (late Mar.-early Apr.), many of Vermont's sugarhouses open their doors for the **Maple Open House Weekend** (www.vermontmaple.org/events), which is an excellent chance to rub shoulders with sugarmakers and sample the state's sweetest treats, like sugar on snow (often served with a pickle, which is better than it sounds).

Billings Farm & Museum sponsors many special events throughout the summer, including **Cow Appreciation Day** every July, which includes a judging of the Jerseys, ice cream and butter making, and (always gripping) dairy trivia, as well as a **Harvest** celebration in October with husking competitions and cider pressing. In late July, Woodstock gets wordy during **Bookstock** (www.bookstockvt.org), a festival that attracts an intriguing lineup of writers. While the town maintains an events page, the best resource is kept up by the helpful owner of **Sleep Woodstock Motel** (www.sleepwoodstock.com/upcoming-events).

SHOPPING

Downtown Woodstock

Handmade pottery with a gorgeously modern aesthetic is the main draw at **Farmhouse**

Pottery (1837 Rte. 4, 802/774-8373, www.farmhousepottery.com, 10am-5pm Mon.-Sat., 10am-4pm Sun.), where you can watch the artisans at work. The store also stocks maple rolling pins, candles, and a seemingly endless array of beautiful things. Not your average vintage store, **Who Is Sylvia?** (26 Central St., 802/457-1110, 11am-5pm Sun.-Mon. and Thurs., 11am-6pm Fri.-Sat.) stocks flapper dresses, pillbox hats, brocade jackets, and other hard-to-find items dating back more than a century.

Bridgewater Mill Mall

Six miles west of Woodstock on Route 4, **Bridgewater Mill Mall** is filled with studio space for artisans and craftspeople. A highlight is **Shackleton Thomas** (102 Mill Rd., Bridgewater, 802/672-5175, www.shackletonthomas.com, 10am-5pm Tues.-Sat., 11am-4pm Sun.), where Charles Shackleton—a distant relation of Antarctic explorer Ernest Shackleton—crafts simple but elegant Shaker and modern-style furniture. It's fascinating to watch the woodcarvers, who train for years, and the display room is also stocked with eclectic gifts with unusual charm.

SPORTS AND RECREATION

Hiking

In addition to the exhibits at **Marsh-Billings-Rockefeller National Historical Park** (54 Elm St., 802/457-3368, www.nps.gov/mabi, 10am-5pm daily Memorial Day-Oct., $8 adults, $4 seniors, children 15 and under free), the preserve has 20 miles of walking trails, which are accessible from the park entrance on Route 12 and a parking lot on Prosper Road. The roads circle around the slopes of Mount Tom, which is forested with old-growth hemlock, beech, and sugar maples. Popular hikes include the 0.7-mile loop around the mountain pond called **The Pogue** and the gentle, 1-mile climb up to the **South Summit** of Mount Tom, which lords over Woodstock and the river below. No mountain bikes are allowed on the trails; in the winter, they are groomed for cross-country skiing.

It's also possible to walk 2.75 miles round-trip to the summit of **Mount Tom,** starting at the centrally located **Middle Covered Bridge** on Mountain Avenue. Cross the bridge and follow Mountain Avenue as it curves around to the left along a rock wall. An opening in the rock wall leads to the **Faulkner Trail** at Faulkner Park, where it begins to switchback up the gentle south flank of the peak. The last 300 feet of the trail get a bit steeper, giving wide views of the Green Mountains. Allow an hour for the hike.

Seven miles east of Woodstock, **Quechee State Park** (5800 Woodstock Rd., Hartford, 802/295-2990, www.vtstateparks.com/htm/quechee.htm, May 20-Oct. 16, free) has a pleasant 2.2-mile round-trip trail into Vermont's deepest gorge, which was carved by retreating glaciers. While the park's self-nomination as "Vermont's Little Grand Canyon" might set visitors up for a disappointment, the walk is lovely. The **Quechee Gorge Trail** hike takes about an hour and starts from the visitors center.

Swimming

There's an actual swimming pool inside the **Woodstock Recreation Department** (54 River St., 802/457-1502, www.woodstockrec.com, 6am-8pm Mon.-Fri., 8am-2pm Sat., 9am-1pm Sun.), but the real treat is a dip in the **Ottauquechee River.** There's a short path that leaves from right behind the Rec Department, descending to a gentle swimming area that's suitable for families. On the very hottest days, the finest place to swim is in the **Quechee Gorge,** where the water seems to stay cool through the heat of the summer. To reach the best swimming area, take the trail from the visitors center, turn left (downstream) as the Quechee Gorge Trail turns upstream, then follow the river for roughly 0.5 mile to a broad swimming hole.

FOOD

Dining on mostly fried, salty fare at a "snack bar" is a quintessential summer experience in Vermont, and **White Cottage** (863 Woodstock Rd., 802/457-3455, 11am-10pm daily May-Oct., $3-22, cash only) is a fine place to get your fix. Golden mounds of fried clams come with tartar sauce and lemon, maple creemees are piled high on sugar cones, and hamburgers are simple and to-the-point. Snack bar food doesn't vary much from place to place, but White Cottage's outdoor tables, riverside location, and friendly staff make it a favorite—and you can wade in the river while you wait for your order.

Pick up supplies at the confusingly named **Woodstock Farmers' Market** (979 W. Woodstock Rd., 802/457-3658, www.woodstockfarmersmarket.com, 7:30am-7pm Tues.-Sat., 8am-6pm Sun.), which turns out to be a specialty food shop that stocks plenty of locally made treats, cheese, beer, wine, and everything else you might need for a show-stopping picnic on the road.

Along with excellent espresso, **Mon Vert Cafe** (28 Central St., 802/457-7143, www.monvertcafe.com, 7:30am-4pm Mon.-Sat., 8am-4pm Sun., $8-11) has fresh breakfast and lunch in a sunny and stylish spot. Breakfast burritos and baked goods give way to a lunch menu of sandwiches and panini. The café also prepares food to go, which makes for great road tripping supplies.

Sedate and sophisticated, **The Prince & The Pauper** (24 Elm St., 802/457-1818, www.princeandpauper.com, 5:30pm-8:30pm Sun.-Thurs., 5:30pm-9pm Fri.-Sat., $18-25) serves fine dining classics—don't miss the restaurant's signature *carré d'agneau royale*, a tender dish of lamb, spinach, and mushrooms wrapped in puff pastry—in a candlelit country setting. Think high-backed wooden booths, exposed beams, and local art for sale on the wall. It's an ideal date setting, though families and groups are also welcome.

If you've had enough of Woodstock's white tablecloth scene, you may be ready for a meal at the relaxed and convivial ★ **Worthy Kitchen** (442 E. Woodstock Rd., 802/457-7281, www.worthyvermont.com, 4pm-9pm Mon.-Thurs., 4pm-10pm Fri., 11:30am-10pm Sat., 11:30am-9pm Sun., $8-15), a "farm diner" that has a hearty selection of pub food with flair, from fried chicken to poutine. Burritos, nachos, and burgers are other favorites, and there's an excellent beer selection.

ACCOMMODATIONS AND CAMPING

Woodstock has some of the most appealing accommodations in the state. Prices tend to be higher than elsewhere and rise dramatically during peak foliage season, while off-season prices may be significantly lower than those listed.

$100-150

There's nothing fancy about **Sleep Woodstock Motel** (4324 W. Woodstock Rd., 802/332-6336, www.sleepwoodstock.com, $88-178, 2-bedroom suite $250-450), but a 2017 renovation has revitalized the property. The roadside motel was built in 1959, and rooms retain a retro feel, but bathrooms are new and everything feels fresh and sunny. The motel is a short drive west of the center.

$150-250

Elegant, well-appointed rooms at the ★ **Jackson House Inn** (43 Senior Ln., 802/457-2065, www.jacksonhouse.com, $189-339) manage to avoid fussiness. Quarters in the main house are somewhat more in keeping with the old-fashioned style of the place, but new additions come with perks like massage tubs. Each one is different, so peek into a few before making your choice. The crackling fire is an appealing place to thaw, but in summer months the broad porch entices. The congenial owners, Rick and Kathy, are devoted to local food, and Rick prepares sumptuous breakfasts with ingredients from area farms.

The **506 on the River Inn** (1653 Rte. 4, 802/457-5000, www.ontheriverwoodstock.com, $139-379) was renovated in 2014 and has an appealingly chic take on Woodstock's genteel country style. Throw pillows are emblazoned with folksy Vermont expressions, antiques are used with restraint, and welcome extras include a game room, library, and toddler playroom. Breakfast is well prepared and lavish, served in a dining room and bar that open to the public at night. The inn's bistro menu covers classed-up pub food and child-friendly diner standbys like mac and cheese.

Over $250

You can't miss the grand ★ **Woodstock Inn & Resort** (14 The Green, 802/457-1100 or 800/448-7900, www.woodstockinn.com, $235-820), which dominates the green in the heart of the village. The rooms and facilities are some of the prettiest in Vermont, full of thoughtful touches and design. This location has been a tourist destination since a tavern with accommodations was established in 1793, but Laurance Rockefeller built the current structure in the 1970s. There are seemingly endless facilities: spa, fitness center, cruiser bikes for exploring the town, organic gardens, and a celebrated 18-hole golf course. You can come take courses on farming and falconry, or just watch the weather from the glassed-in conservatory.

The exquisite and extravagant **Twin Farms** (452 Royalton Turnpike, Barnard, 800/894-6327, www.twinfarms.com, $1,450-2,800) is the former home of journalist Dorothy Thompson and Nobel laureate Sinclair Lewis, who was known for his stirring critiques of capitalism and materialism. Even he might be tempted by this alluring and romantic resort, where the rooms are kitted out with four-poster beds, fireplaces, whirlpool tubs, rare woods, and museum art, with views over a breathtaking property. Twin Farms is all-inclusive and offers an impressive suite of activities, along with remarkable food and drink.

Camping

Quechee State Park (5800 Woodstock Rd., Hartford, 802/295-2990, www.vtstateparks.com/htm/quechee.htm, mid-May-mid-Oct.) has some excellent spots for river **swimming** near a bustling, friendly **campground,** with lean-tos and 45 RV and tent sites along a forested loop (tents $18-24, lean-tos $25-29). There is a dump station, but no hookups; fully powered sites in this area are limited, and the closest option is 2.6 miles farther east, at the **Quechee/Pine Valley KOA** (3700 E. Woodstock Rd., White River Junction, May 1-Oct. 15, tents $28-36, RVs $45-70).

INFORMATION AND SERVICES

The **Woodstock Area Chamber of Commerce** (888/469-6378, www.woodstockvt.com) runs a **welcome center** (3 Mechanic St., 802/432-1100, 9am-5pm daily) and an information booth (on the green). The well-stocked, independent **Woodstock Pharmacy** (19 Central St., 802/457-1306) is conveniently located in the center of town, as are the ATM machines at **People's United Bank** (2 The Green, 802/457-2660) and **Citizens Bank** (431 Woodstock Rd., 802/457-3666,). In an emergency, contact the **Woodstock Police** (454 Rte. 4, 802/457-1420).

GETTING THERE AND AROUND

Route 4 runs straight through the heart of Woodstock, which is easily walkable once you arrive. There's **Amtrak** service to **White River Junction,** 15 miles to the east of Woodstock (800/872-7245, www.amtrak.com), and it's possible to continue to Woodstock on **Vermont Translines** (844/888-7267, www.vttranslines.com), which has daily service from White River Junction to Woodstock, Killington, and Rutland.

Parking in the village is metered 10am-4pm Monday-Saturday, but it's often possible to find free parking on the west side of town. Woodstock also has an unusual parking validation policy—if you get a ticket in a metered spot, you can bring it to any merchant or restaurant, who can validate it (cancel it) for free.

Killington

Following the Ottauquechee River through the southern Green Mountains, Route 4 rolls right to the foot of the imposing Killington Peak. It's been a ski resort since 1958, and was ambitious from the first chair—Killington strung lift after lift on the neighboring peaks and became one of the first mountains to install snowmaking equipment. (It's still known as the first resort to open and last to close each year, though springtime skiing may require dodging patches of grass.)

The mountain's very size and popularity led to some unattractive development on its flank—and the long, twisting Killington Road is now a very un-Vermont stretch of hotels, restaurants, and nightclubs extending up to the summit. Locals may roll their eyes, but for some it's a welcome bit of civilization and fun in the middle of the woods.

The mountain can get crowded on big winter weekends, though Killington's scale offers notable advantages: varied terrain, 3,000 feet of vertical drop, and its unique "good snow guarantee." If you don't like the conditions, you can return your lift ticket. In recent years, Killington has added a popular downhill mountain biking area, with lift service and Vermont's most challenging terrain.

SIGHTS

Skiing and Riding

The mountain that gives Killington its name is only one of six peaks that make up **Killington Resort** (4763 Killington Rd., 800/621-6867, www.killington.com, $105 adults, $89 seniors, $81 youth 7-18, children under 7 and seniors over 80 ski free), a massive ski resort that boasts more than 200 trails. But the main event is still Killington Peak, where most of the toughest trails start their descent. The peak is accessible from the express gondola from the K-1 Lodge at the top of Killington Road.

Ten minutes west of Killington, the co-owned **Pico Mountain** (Rte. 4, 2 miles west of Killington Rd., 866/667-7426, www.picomountain.com, $76 adults, $59 seniors, $65 youth 7-18, children under 7 and seniors over 80 ski free) is a quieter and less crowded mountain, with 50-some trails and

Killington Resort

Killington

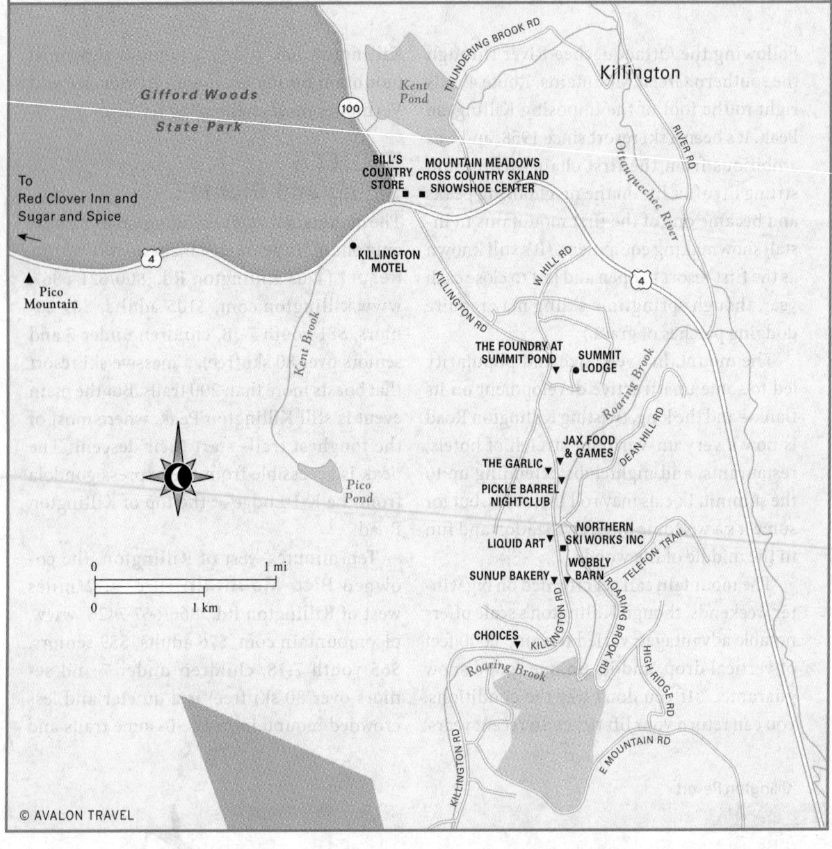

a family-friendly reputation. Pico is closed Tuesday-Wednesday outside of peak skiing weeks.

As might be expected, skiing is not the only way to hit the hill. **Killington Snowmobile Tours** (802/422-2121, www.snowmobilevermont.com) offers one-hour gentle rides along groomed ski trails ($99 single/$139 double), as well as a more challenging 25-mile, two-hour backcountry ride through Calvin Coolidge State Forest ($154/$199).

Both skate and classic skiers will love the gentle terrain at **Mountain Meadows Cross Country Ski and Snowshoe Center** (Rte. 4 at Rte. 100, 802/775-7077, www.xcskiing.net, $19 adults, $16 seniors, $8 youth, children under 6 free), where you can rent skis and snowshoes.

In the summer months, Killington has **mountain biking** on trails served by the K-1 Express Gondola and the Snowshed Express Quad, which ranges from relatively approachable beginner trails to serious and challenging downhilling. A full day of lift and trail access is $55 for adults, or you can sweat your way up the hill and ride the trails for $20. The resort also rents protective gear and full-suspension bikes.

ENTERTAINMENT AND EVENTS

Nightlife

For 50 years, the classic Killington spot has been the **Wobbly Barn** (2229 Killington Rd., 802/422-6171, www.wobblybarn.com, 8pm-2am daily Nov.-Apr., $20 cover for events), where there's a consistently boisterous crowd watching live music and dancing.

Toward the bottom of the access road, **JAX Food & Games** (1667 Killington Rd., 802/422-5334, www.supportinglocalmusic.com, 3pm-2am daily) is a fun venue with plenty of live music and a game room containing air hockey, arcade games, and pool. The **Pickle Barrel Night Club** (1741 Killington Rd., 802/422-3035, www.picklebarrelnightclub.com, 8pm-2am Thurs.-Sun. Oct.-Apr., $20 cover for events) has three levels of dancing space, each with its own bar and loud music that tends to attract a young party crowd.

Festivals and Events

Most months feature at least one or two festivals at Killington, so check the resort's **Events Calendar** (www.killington.com). Every summer, the **Killington Music Festival** (802/773-4003, www.killingtonmusicfestival.org) stages a series of classical music events called Music in the Mountains, with musicians from around the country. The weekend before Labor Day, a thousand motorcyclists invade town for the **Killington Classic Motorcycle Rally** (518/798-7888, www.killingtonclassic.com). Events include a cycle rodeo and bike judging.

The **Killington Foliage Weekend** and **Brewfest Weekend** (802/422-6237, www.killington.com) overlap in the town center and on the local slopes every year, getting under way in late September and early October. Family activities, from hayrides to gondola tours, are a highlight, as are the handcrafted beers served.

SPORTS AND RECREATION

Hiking

In addition to the hiking trails at Killington, a popular short trek is the one up to the scenic overlook on Deer Leap Mountain, located in **Gifford Woods State Park** (34 Gifford Woods Rd., 802/775-5354, www.vtstateparks.com). The trail starts behind the Inn at Long Trail on Route 4 and is two miles round-trip to fantastic views of Pico Peak and Killington Mountain.

To summit the main attraction, trek the **Bucklin Trail** to the top of Killington Peak. The 7.2-mile out-and-back starts from the Bucklin Trailhead (20 Wheelerville Rd., Mendon) and follows a west-facing ridgeline for 3.3 miles before intersecting with the Long Trail. A 0.2-mile spur from the Long Trail leads to the rocky, exposed peak, where you can see all the way to Mount Mansfield on a clear day.

Swimming and Fishing

The Appalachian Trail runs right past **Kent Pond** (access on Thundering Brook Rd., off Rte. 4), but you don't have to be a "thru-hiker" to enjoy the scenic swimming spot. The pond is ringed by low mountains and stocked with both brook and rainbow trout.

SHOPPING

Each of the resorts have ski shops with everything you need for a day in the snow, but one of the best off-mountain stores is **Northern Ski Works** (2089 Killington Rd., next to the Wobbly Barn, 802/422-9675, www.northernski.com, 8am-8pm Mon.-Thurs., 8am-11pm Fri., 7:30am-9pm Sat., 7:30am-8pm Sun. Oct.-Apr.). It's where to head for all manner of equipment, from snowshoes and helmets to boards and, of course, skis.

FOOD

For classic American fare done with flair, **The Foundry at Summit Pond** (63 Summit Path, 802/422-5335, www.foundrykillington.

TOP EXPERIENCE

Skiing and Snowboarding in the Green Mountains

Killington might be the most accessible mountain resort from southern New England, but skiers and riders will find great places to play in the snow up and down the spine of the Green Mountains. Each resort has its own personality, from Killington's "Beast of the East" bravado to the far-flung slopes of Jay Peak. Here are some favorite places to get in some turns:

Tucked into the hills of the Mad River Valley, **Sugarbush** and **Mad River Glen** offer two entirely different takes on the resort experience. **Sugarbush** (1840 Sugarbush Access Rd., Warren, 802/583-6300 or 800/537-8427, www.sugarbush.com, $84-91 adults, $65-71 seniors and youth 7-18, children under 7 free) has more than 100 trails descending from two main peaks, with high-speed chairs, extensive grooming, and terrain for everybody. **Mad River Glen** (Rte. 17, 5 miles west of Waitsfield, 802/496-3551, www.madriverglen.com, $60-75 adults, $55-59 seniors and youth 6-18) is the crusty old-timer of the Vermont world—keep your eyes out for leather telemark boots on the trails, where no snowboards are allowed. The cooperatively owned Mad River Glen calls itself a place where "skiing is still a sport, not an industry," which means limited grooming or snowmaking.

The mountains get bigger and more dramatic as you head north, and **Stowe** (7416 Mountain Rd., Stowe, 800/253-3000, www.stowe.com, $92-124 adults, $82-114 seniors, $72-104 children) towers above them all, climbing the slopes of Mount Mansfield, the highest peak in Vermont. Fancy base lodges and resort amenities make this Vermont skiing at its most elegant, but the mountain itself is the real draw: There are 40 miles of riding, a superfast gondola, and extensive snowmaking that smooths over the pesky Eastern thaws. Just on the other side of the mountains, **Smugglers' Notch** (4323 Rte. 108, Jeffersonville, 800/370-3186, www.smuggs.com, $72 adults, $54 youth 6-18 and seniors) has positioned itself as the family-friendly mountain, with lots of kids classes and a money-back "fun guarantee."

As far north as you can go, **Jay Peak Resort** (4850 Rte. 242, Jay, 802/988-2611, www.jaypeakresort.com, $72 adults, $47 seniors, $57 youth 6-18, $16 children 5 and under) gets a massive amount of snow on 50 miles of trails, with legendary glades and lots of backcountry terrain just beyond the patrolled boundaries.

And the skiing doesn't stop with the downhill resorts—many resorts have cross-country areas, and there are purpose-built destinations for cross-country skiers around the state. Two great options are the 60 miles of trails at **Trapp Family Lodge** (700 Trapp Hill Rd., Stowe, 802/253-8511 or 800/826-7000, www.trappfamily.com, $25 adults, $20 seniors, $15 youth 12-18, $10 children 6-11, children under 6 free), or the Northeast Kingdom's **Craftsbury Outdoor Center** (535 Lost Nation Rd., Craftsbury Common, 802/586-7767, www.craftsbury.com, $10 adults, $5 students and seniors, children 6 and under free), whose massive network of trails is popular with both skate and classic skiers.

com, 3pm-10pm Mon.-Thurs., 11:30am-11pm Fri.-Sat., 11am-10pm Sun., $18-50) is a popular spot. Its steaks are superlative, there's an appealing raw bar, and the apple pie is a delight. The Tavern bar menu includes a more relaxed selection of sandwiches. Don't miss the ice-skating pond, just beside the restaurant.

You won't miss **Liquid Art** (37 Miller Brook Rd., 802/422-2787, www.liquidartvt.com, mid Nov.-May 8am-9pm Mon.-Tue., 8am-10pm Wed.-Fri., 7am-10pm Sat., 7am-9pm Sun.; hours vary in off-season, $4-10) in an eye-catching blue building beside Killington Road. It always opens an hour before the lifts and has a hearty breakfast menu and locally roasted coffee. The menu is available all day, and the sandwiches and light fare include the most plentiful vegetarian options in town.

With a cozy feel and a popular bar, **The Garlic** (1724 Killington Rd., 802/422-5055, www.thegarlicvermont.net, 5pm-10pm Mon.-Fri., 4pm-10pm Sat.-Sun., $10-30) serves Italian classics like osso buco and pasta puttanesca that are perfect for a post-ski meal. It's cozy, dim, and the closest that Killington's eateries get to subdued.

The cheerful early birds at **Sunup Bakery** (2250 Killington Rd., 802/422-3865, www.sunupbakery.com, 7am-5pm Mon.-Fri., 6:30am-5pm Sat.-Sun. Nov.-Apr., 7am-3pm Fri.-Sun. May-June, 7am-3pm Thurs.-Mon. July-Oct., $3-8) will get you adventure-ready with a carb-loaded lineup of pastries (seriously, try the espresso bread pudding muffin), soups, and sandwiches of every stripe. The café uses plenty of local ingredients and is housed in a perky chalet on the main road.

ACCOMMODATIONS AND CAMPING

$100-150

The rooms at the **Killington Motel** (1946 Rte. 4, 800/366-0493, www.killingtonmotel.com, $119-240) are clean and comfortable, and the owners, Robin and Steve, are friendly enough to inspire a loyal following who return year after year. The place has an unselfconsciously retro vibe, and is one of the best places for value in the area. Steve roasts coffee beans on-site, and wintertime rates include an appealing breakfast.

Several generations of Saint Bernards have greeted guests at the **Summit Lodge** (200 Summit Rd., off Killington Rd., 800/635-6343, www.summitlodgevermont.com, $99-219), which is as famous for its canine companions as it is for its congenial staff. Even though the lodge is only a few minutes away from Killington Resort, its position at the top of a steep hill makes it feel secluded. Rooms are nothing fancy but are quiet and clean, with friendly service. A pool and reading room offer extra relaxation.

$150-250

Twenty minutes away from the ski lifts, the **Red Clover Inn** (7 Woodward Rd., Mendon, 802/775-2290, www.redcloverinn.com, $199-340) feels a world away from Killington's bustling scene. Set on a rambling property that once housed a goat farm, the guest rooms retain a country charm and quiet that's enhanced by the lack of in-room televisions. The inn's restaurant and diminutive bar are enough to keep you in for the evening, with local beers, cocktails, and a well-crafted menu that makes the dining room a destination.

Over $250

If you book a slope-side room at the **Killington Grand Resort Hotel** (228 E. Mountain Rd., 802/422-5001, www.killington.com, $350 and up), you can spend your evening watching the grooming machines crawl up and down the mountain like glowworms. The comfortable rooms include access to the excellent health club, and there's a spa and restaurant on-site.

Camping

Gifford Woods State Park (34 Gifford Woods Rd., 802/775-5354, www.vtstateparks.com) has 4 cabins, 22 tent sites, and 20 lean-tos for overnights (campsites $18-29, cabins $48-50). The northern tent loop is much more secluded than the southern one. Several "prime" lean-tos are especially secluded in one of Vermont's only old-growth hardwood forests, made up of giant sugar maple, white ash, and beech trees.

INFORMATION AND SERVICES

The **Killington Chamber of Commerce** (2026 Rte. 4, 802/773-4181, 9am-5pm Mon.-Fri., 10am-5pm Sat.-Sun. June-Nov., 9am-5pm Mon.-Fri., 10am-2pm Sat.-Sun. Dec.-May, www.killingtonchamber.com) operates a visitors information center at the intersection of Route 4 and Killington Road. Near the same intersection is a branch of **Lake Sunapee Bank** (1995 Rte. 4, 802/773-2581). Additional ATM machines are available at **Merchants Bank** (286 Rte. 7 S., Rutland, 802/747-5000,

9am-5pm Mon.-Thurs., 9am-6pm Fri.) as well as at Killington Resort's base lodge. For condos and hotel reservations, you can also try the helpful **Killington Resort's Central Reservations** (800/621-6867), which is especially useful for large groups.

GETTING THERE AND AROUND

Killington is the high point of Route 4, and towers over the intersection with Route 100. For such a popular destination, public transport options are limited. It's possible to schedule pickup service with **Killington Transportation** (802/770-3977) from Rutland or White River Junction. Within Killington, the resort offers shuttle bus service between the various base lodges and nearby lodging. Ski buses depart for Killington from **Boston** (508/340-1034, www.newenglandsnowbus.com, $50-89) and **New York City** (www.ovrride.com, from $129), which can be a great deal as a transport/lift tickets/lodging package.

Mad River Valley

The peaks that flank the Mad River Valley seem to protect it from passing time. A blend of pastoral beauty and culture have made it a haven for artists, farmers, and eccentrics, while the valley's two ski resorts have grown into serious skiing destinations.

It's a compact place—just 30 minutes from one end to the other—and nowhere else in Vermont can you find such iconic, varied scenery and activities so close together. Incredible skiing, vibrant agriculture, forested hikes to waterfalls, and impeccable food and drink make this spirited region a perfect distillation of the state.

WARREN

Not a shingle is out of place in Warren's achingly cute center, whose general store, artists' studios, and single elegant inn look more like a movie set than a real town. But this rural community is also home to Sugarbush resort, a sprawling cluster of six peaks with 53 miles of trails, not to mention an additional 2,000 acres of wild backcountry.

And while Warren might seem a bit prim at first glance, there's serious verve behind the colonial facade. Immerse yourself in it during Warren's justifiably famous Fourth of July parade, an unrestrained celebration that is among the most independent of Vermont's Independence Day events. Locals spend the year constructing complicated floats with themes that range from politics to all-purpose Vermont pride, and accompany them through town in sundry dress (and undress).

There are no banks or ATMs in the tiny Warren center. The closest one is at the gas station two miles north of town: Mac's Market (114 Route 100, Warren, 802/496-3366, 9am-6pm daily).

Sights

Warren has its own covered bridge, the 55-foot-long **Warren Bridge,** which sports an unusual asymmetrical design. (The angles on the eastern and western sides are slightly different.) The bridge is off Route 100, just below downtown.

Events

Warren's Fourth of July parade is an unorthodox event that always seems more about the independence of small-town Vermont than the United States. Eye-catching floats and costumes often have a political theme that set this parade apart from simple flag waving, but it's also a welcoming and thoroughly entertaining glimpse of life in the Mad River Valley. The parade starts at 10am on Main Street, and festivities wrap up by 8:30pm. Fireworks are held at Sugarbush resort in the evening. The parade is free to attend, but a $1 donation is requested at the entrance to the town; in return, you'll receive a numbered "buddy badge." There's two of every number, and the badges are given out randomly. If you find your matching pair, the two of you can head to the village gazebo to collect a prize. Parking can be a challenge, but a free shuttle bus is available (www.madrivervalley.com/4th).

Sports and Recreation

★ SKIING

Once known as Mascara Mountain for its tendency to draw the jet-setting crowd, **Sugarbush** (1840 Sugarbush Access Rd., 802/583-6300 or 800/537-8427, www.sugarbush.com, $84-91 adults, $65-71 seniors and youth 7-18, children under 7 free) has come a long way to rightly earn its place as Vermont's "Second Slope," often favorably described as a more welcoming "alternative" to Killington. It's second to Killington in the number and difficulty of the slopes it offers. Sugarbush boasts 111 trails descending from two summits, Lincoln Peak and Mount Ellen. But it may have the most difficult trail in the East: the rock-and-glade ride known as the Rumble. Sugarbush is also prized for the high amount of natural snow it gets each year, as storms from Lake Champlain unload their cargo after passing over the mountains. Not that it needs it—the Bush has one of the most sophisticated snowmaking systems around. As a bonus, Sugarbush and Mad River Glen have worked out lift packages that include both mountains—so you can experience big-mountain skiing on Sugarbush then head up-valley to ride Mad River Glen's gnarly glades.

In the shadow of Sugarbush and the surrounding mountains, **Ole's Cross Country Center** (Airport Rd., 802/496-3430, www.olesxc.com, $18 adults, $15 youth and seniors) has 30 miles of trails through deep woods and farm country. Another great spot for forested skiing is **Blueberry Lake Cross Country and Snowshoeing Center** (Plunkton Rd., 802/496-6687, www.blueberrylakeskivt.com, $14), with 19 miles of trails. Both ski areas have rentals and lessons and are groomed for both Nordic and skate skiing.

SWIMMING

With crystal clear pools and a natural rock slide, **Warren Falls** is one of the best swimming holes in the state, though it can be very crowded on summer weekends. To get there, travel south on Route 100 from Warren; the parking area is 0.75 mile south of the intersection of Warren's Main Street and Route

skiing at Mad River Glen

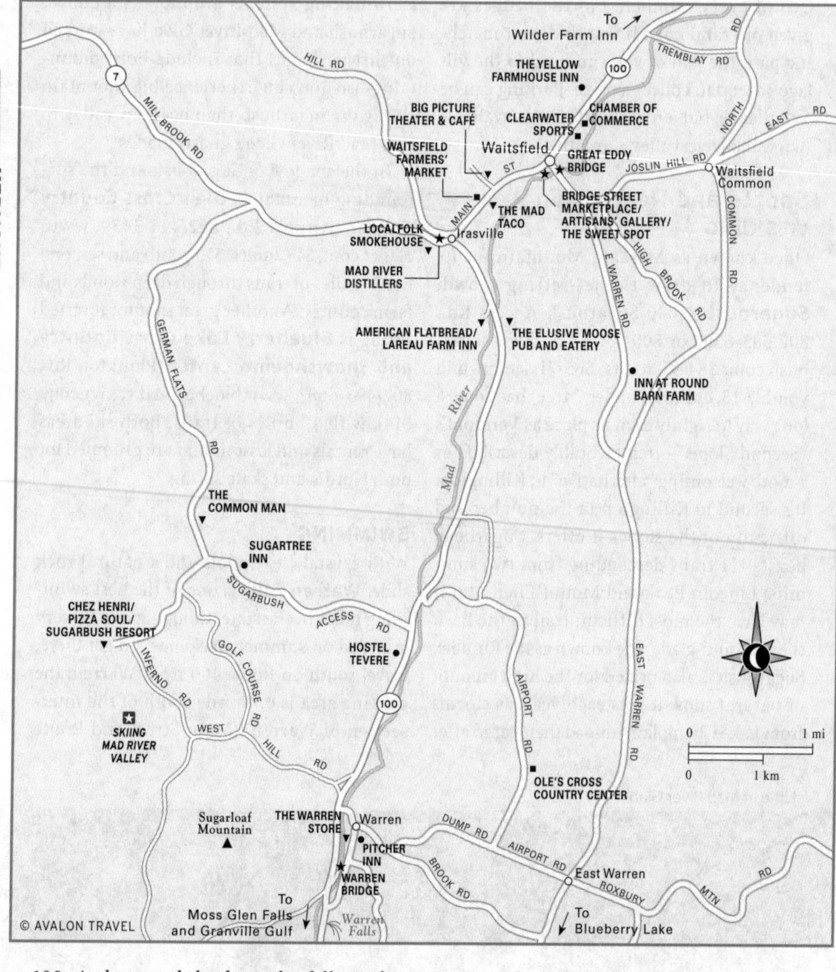

100. A short path leads to the falls. A few miles farther south in Granville (population 309), **Moss Glen Falls** is another scenic spot (without swimming, however). A multi-pitched cataract that drops 125 feet through a narrow gorge, the waterfall is just as beautiful frozen in winter as it is gushing in summer. A viewing platform is accessible from the highway. The falls themselves are part of the **Granville Gulf State Reservation,** a seven-mile stretch of pathless wilderness that is among the most scenic drives in the Green Mountains. Keep an eye out for the moose that frequent the area's streams and beaver ponds.

Shopping

For food, provisions, and local gossip, everyone heads to **The Warren Store** (284 Main St., 802/496-3864, www.warrenstore.com, 8am-7pm Mon.-Sat., 8am-6pm Sun.). Spend a few days here, and you'll be on a first-name basis with the friendly staff at this eclectic provisions shop, full of Vermont-made odds and ends (from pillows to salad bowls). The shop has a nice selection of unusual wines for sale and churns out excellent, creative sandwiches from the deli—all with bread baked on-site.

Food

Warren has appealing—but limited—dining options. Breakfast means a trip into Waitsfield or pastries at The Warren Store.

The elegant and refined **275 Main at The Pitcher Inn** (275 Main St., 802/496-6350, www.pitcherinn.com, 6pm-9pm Wed.-Mon., $26-36) boasts a superlative and hefty international wine list, and a menu to match. Global in its influences but local in most of its ingredients, the kitchen emphasizes organic seasonal produce and fresh game such as grilled Vermont-raised lamb. For a particularly memorable experience, reserve a private dinner for two in the restaurant's wine cellar.

An unlikely morsel of Paris in a mountain setting, **Chez Henri** (80 Sugarbush Village Dr., 802/583-2600, www.chezhenrisugarbush.com, 11:30am-11pm Mon.-Fri., 4:30pm-11pm Sat.-Sun., $19-43) makes dining a transporting experience. Classic bistro meals like *canard aux fruits* and onion soup *gratinée* are served in an intimate setting warmed by an open fire.

Snag thin-crust pizzas with all the fixings at **Pizza Soul** (Sugarbush Village, 802/496-6202, www.pizzasoul.com, 11:30am-8:30pm Sun. and Tues., 11:30am-4pm Wed., 11:30am-8:30pm, Thu., 11:30am-11pm Fri.-Sat., pizzas $14-23), a quirky joint right at the base of the mountain.

Accommodations

UNDER $100

If the valley's ubiquitous antiques and romance aren't for you, try the stylish ★ **Hostel Tevere** (203 Powderhound Rd., 802/496-9222, www.hosteltevere.com, dorm beds $38 summer, $40 winter). It's a convivial place to land after a day on the slopes or floating the Mad River, and the hostel's bar keeps some of the best local brews on tap. There's also a winter dart league on Thursday nights that's open to visitors, and the bar regularly hosts live music on Friday (early-to-bed types should request a dormitory that's farther from the stage). All dorms are mixed gender, with 5-7 beds; linens are provided, and towels are available for rent ($2).

$150-250

Right at the base of the Sugarbush access road, **The Warren Lodge** (731 Rte. 100, 802/496-3084, www.thewarrenlodge.com, $99-175) was entirely renovated in 2016 with a blend of rustic design and modern comfort. Motel-style standard rooms have refrigerators and flat-screen televisions, and there are a range of suites, a cottage, and an efficiency that are a good deal for groups.

OVER $250

Exquisitely decorated, the Relais & Chateaux-designated **Pitcher Inn** (275 Main St., 802/496-6350, www.pitcherinn.com, $425-800) houses 11 rooms and suites—each individually decorated in a Vermont theme and with Wi-Fi, CD players, TVs, whirlpool tubs, and radiant floor heating; a few have wood-burning fireplaces. There's also a stand-alone spa on the property, offering everything from hair care and pedicures to facials.

WAITSFIELD

Of this village's original settlers, 11 of 13 were veterans of the Battle of Lexington, the kick-off to the Revolutionary War. Bits of the original colonial architecture remain sprinkled throughout the town, which is the cultural center of the valley. Beyond the picture-perfect historical facades are start-up technology companies, artisans, and artists. It's a sophisticated community that enjoys an extraordinary quality of life.

Waitsfield's restaurants and accommodations make it a logical base for exploring the valley, and even if you're just passing through, it's a compelling place to pass an afternoon visiting little shops and enjoying the sunny beach by the town's covered bridge.

Sights

MAD RIVER GLEN

In an era of ski-resort consolidation, rising lift-ticket prices, and runaway base-lodge development, **Mad River Glen** (MRG, Rte. 17, 5 miles west of Waitsfield, 802/496-3551, www.madriverglen.com, $60-75 adults, $55-59 seniors and youth 6-18) has its own agenda. MRG is the only cooperatively owned ski resort in the United States, and the only one on the National Register of Historic Places. The 1,800 skier-owners still staunchly ban snowboards and limit grooming to about half the trails, mostly novice and intermediate pistes.

It's an unfashionable outlook that has earned passionate supporters, including a devoted set of lift-served telemark skiers, whom you can spot dropping their knees all over the hill. Mad River Glen's motto is "Ski it if you can," and the mountain's steep, narrow, and notoriously hairy advanced trails (about half the runs) are truly challenging. Experts should take a run at Paradise, a precipitous tumble down exposed ledges, rocky moguls, and a frozen waterfall to get to the bottom. In practice, though, the resort is a friendly, community-oriented place where families and skiers of all abilities are welcomed. Just don't try to sneak in a snowboard.

MAD RIVER DISTILLERS

Sample maple rum, bourbon whiskey, and other spirits at the Waitsfield tasting room of **Mad River Distillers** (Rte. 100 and Rte. 17, 802/496-3330, www.madriverdistillers.com, noon-6pm Wed.-Sun.). This Warren-based distillery sources many of its ingredients from within the state, and the bottles have been racking up awards. Don't miss the Malvados, a Calvados-inspired apple brandy made with fruit from Shoreham's Champlain Orchards.

COVERED BRIDGE

Waitsfield's historical downtown is anchored by the 1833 **Great Eddy Bridge**, the second-oldest operating covered bridge in the state, which crosses the Mad River at the intersection of Route 100 and Bridge Street. (Only the Pulp Mill Bridge in Middlebury is older.) During the flooding following Hurricane Irene in 2011, the water line came up all the way to the base of the bridge, but the span stood, a testament to the nearly 200-year-old construction. There's also a little beach and swimming hole right under the bridge.

Entertainment and Events

The sophisticated, artsy vibe at **Big Picture Theater and Cafe** (48 Carroll Rd., off Rte. 100, 802/496-8994, www.bigpicturetheater.info, 8am-9pm daily) makes for one-stop evening fun—cutting-edge movies, film series, even an on-site restaurant where you can dine before the show ($9-18, reservations recommended).

During August, the whole valley comes alive for the month-long **Festival of the Arts** (802/496-6682, www.vermontartfest.com), in which the area's many artisans hold art shows and classes, and local restaurants and lodgings offer special rates and events.

Sports and Recreation

The Mad River Valley abounds with recreational activities. In addition to the suggestions below, the Mad River Glen ski area runs the **Mad River Glen Naturalist Program** (802/496-3551, www.madriverglen.com/naturalist), with guided tours that range from moonlit snowshoeing expeditions to wildlife-tracking trips to rock climbing.

HIKING AND BIKING

With a bit of a drive there's great hiking based out of Waitsfield, and three out of five of the peaks in Vermont above 4,000 feet rise from the Mad River Valley. While not the highest mountain in Vermont, the distinctly shaped **Camel's Hump** is one of the best loved. Originally named "Camel's Rump," its shape is identifiable for miles around, and its summit is a great chance to see the unique (and uniquely fragile) eastern alpine ecosystem.

The most popular ascent is up the seven-mile **Monroe Trail,** a rock-hopping ascent from a birch-and-beech forest up to the unique alpine vegetation zone of its undeveloped summit. The parking area for the trail is at the end of Camel's Hump Road in Duxbury. There is a trail map available on the website for **Camel's Hump State Park** (www.vtstateparks.com/camelshump.html). The state park itself doesn't have a visitors center or services, but ample information on access is available on the website.

Two more peaks, **Mount Ellen** and **Mount Abraham,** can be hiked singly or together, following the Long Trail along the 4,000-foot ridge between them. For information on all of these hikes, contact the **Green Mountain Club** (802/244-7037, www.greenmountainclub.org), or pick up a copy of the club's indispensable *Long Trail Guide,* available at most bookstores and outdoors stores in Vermont.

This is an idyllic area for cycling, and you can take your pick of the Mad River Valley's beautiful back roads. If you're feeling ambitious, you can tackle the "gaps," the steep mountain passes that lead to the neighboring Champlain Valley. Lincoln Gap and Appalachian Gap, two of the steepest in the state, can be connected in a leg-punishing loop that does a staggering amount of climbing in 35 miles.

If the mountains seem too daunting, the **Mad River Path Association** (802/496-7284, www.madriverpath.com) manages several walking and biking trails that weave in and out of the villages of the valley, taking in farms, woodlands, and bridges along the way. Bicycles can be rented from **Clearwater Sports** (4147 Main St., Rte. 100, Waitsfield, 802/496-2708, www.clearwatersports.com, bike rental from $25/day).

BOATING AND TUBING

With a steady flow and the occasional patch of white water, the Mad River is ideal for anything that floats. **Clearwater Sports** (4147 Main St., Rte. 100, Waitsfield, 802/496-2708, www.clearwatersports.com) leads affordable all-day tours on the Mad and Winooski Rivers ($80 per person), as well as moonlight paddles. It also offers canoe and kayak rentals ($40-90) and inner tubes ($18), with an optional shuttle service. Book ahead when possible. For a quick dip, there's also swimming beneath the **Great Eddy Bridge** in downtown Waitsfield.

ICE-SKATING

Waitsfield's outdoor skating rink, the **Skatium** (Village Sq., 802/496-8909) is a community gathering place in winter. The rink has skate rentals during public skating hours, generally all day on Saturday and Sunday from early December to as long as the ice lasts, as well as other hours during the week that vary by season. During the winter, call the rink directly for a full schedule.

HORSEBACK RIDING

Ride in Viking style on an Icelandic horse. In addition to the usual walk, trot, canter, and gallop, they've got a fifth gait, the tölt, a fluid, running walk. The **Vermont Icelandic Horse Farm** (3061 N. Fayston Rd., 802/496-7141, www.icelandichorses.com, rides $60-200) breeds well-mannered purebreds for rides that last an hour or all day.

Shopping

Step into the **Artisans' Gallery** (20 Bridge St., 802/496-6256, www.vtartisansgallery.com, 11am-6pm daily), in the Old Village area of Waitsfield, and prepare to feel bewildered by the enormous selection. Upward of 175 local craftspeople sell their goods here, which means you'll have no problem finding jewelry, woodblock prints, hand-painted wooden bowls, and stoneware.

The most respected outdoors outfitter in the area, **Clearwater Sports** (4147 Main St., 802/496-2708, www.clearwatersports.com, 10am-6pm Mon.-Fri., 9am-6pm Sat., 10am-5pm Sun.) offers scads of gear and all the equipment rentals and guided tours you need to put it to proper use.

As in many of Vermont's small towns, the **Waitsfield Farmers' Market** (Mad River Green, 802/472-8027, www.waitsfieldfarmersmarket.com, 9am-1pm Sat. May-Oct.) is one of the week's most important social events, where residents come down from the hills and stock up on community (and gossip) along with fresh produce and prepared foods. There is perhaps no better way to clue into the spirit of the valley than the boisterous event full of craft booths, organic produce from local farms, and stages full of folk, Latin, and Celtic musical performers.

Food

★ **American Flatbread** (48 Lareau Rd., 802/496-8856, www.americanflatbread.com, 5pm-9:30pm Thurs.-Sun., $7-16) has a devoted following, and deservedly so. Thursday-Sunday nights, the unassuming farmhouse setting turns into a party, swarmed by lovers of the organic menu of wholesome and gourmet pies, salads, and desserts made entirely from sustainable, farm-fresh Vermont ingredients. Reservations aren't accepted, but do as the locals do and show up at 5pm to put your name on the wait list. You can request a specific time to come back, or just wait by the bonfire with a pint until your name is called.

There's usually a crowd at **Localfolk Smokehouse** (Rte. 17 and Rte. 100, 802/496-5623, www.localfolkvt.com, 4pm-close Tues.-Sat., $6-17), a ramshackle-looking barbecue joint in an old Waitsfield barn. The menu has barbecue classics, tacos, and pub snacks, but regulars head straight for the meats: pulled pork, ribs, and chicken, smoked on-site and served with Southern-style sides. There's often music on weekends, and the late night local scene can be boisterous.

Tucked into an unpromising-looking cluster of shops on Route 100, ★ **The Mad Taco** (5101 Main St., 802/496-3832, www.themadtaco.com, 11am-9pm daily, $9-11) serves Mexican favorites with rebellious flair. Snag a burrito or taco loaded up with carnitas or yams, and head straight for the assortment of house-made salsas and hot sauces. They come in squeeze bottles marked with a heat rating of 1-10—the spicy stuff is no joke. The Mad Taco also has a bar stocked with favorite local brews on draft and a few Mexican options in bottles.

In an adorable riverside shop, **The Sweet Spot** (40 Bridge St., 802/496-9199, 8am-4pm Mon.-Thurs., 8am-6pm Fri.-Sat., 8am-2pm Sun., $2-8) is exactly that. Creative homemade tarts and cookies and quality espresso drinks, as well as a dreamy assortment of house-made ice creams make this a perfect place to fortify yourself for an afternoon's adventures. If you're looking for something a bit more bracing to go with your brownie, The Sweet Spot also serves a nicely chosen list of cocktails, including some classic ice cream drinks.

Accommodations

$100-150

Under the same ownership—and on the same property—as the lovably bohemian American Flatbread, **Lareau Farm Inn** (48 Lareau Rd., 802/496-4949, www.lareaufarminn.com, shared bath $100, private bath $125-145) names its rooms after principles its management holds dear—love, patience, and respect among them. The inn has the rambling feel of a family farmhouse and is enjoyably relaxed. With delicious breakfasts and free wireless Internet included—not to mention the attention of a genuinely warm staff—Lareau couldn't offer better value.

Bright, creative touches make the vibrant rooms at the ★ **Wilder Farm Inn** (1460 Rte. 100, 800/496-8878, www.wilderfarminn.com, $152-192) as appealing as the homey common areas and rambling grounds. The owners, Linda and Luke, have decorated each one in a different style—from shabby chic to contemporary—so check out the options before choosing where to lay your head. The inn lends guests snowshoes for winter outings and inner tubes for trips down the Mad River, just across the street.

On a quiet property just outside of town, the **Yellow Farmhouse Inn** (550 Old Country Rd., 802/496-4623, https://yellowfarmhouseinn.com, $149-159) is as comfortable as it is lovely: With woodstoves in the guest rooms, it is especially cozy in the winter. Home-baked cookies, lavish breakfasts, and friendly hosts make this a spot that many travelers come to year after year.

OVER $250

The ultraromantic ★ **Inn at the Round Barn Farm** (1661 E. Warren Rd., 802/496-2276, www.theroundbarn.com, $205-330) is a harmonious blend of old-fashioned style and thoughtful modern luxuries. Most rooms in the 19th-century farmhouse have skylights, king-size beds, whirlpool tubs, gas fireplaces, and jaw-dropping mountain views. Executive chef Charlie Menard prepares a multicourse breakfast that is both generous and refined, a memorable experience.

GETTING THERE AND AROUND

Waitsfield and Warren are both on Route 100, which is easily accessed from I-89. The **Mad Bus** (802/496-7433, www.madrivervalley.com) shuttle stops at various locations in Waitsfield and Warren, with connections to Sugarbush, Mad River Glen, and Montpelier.

INFORMATION AND SERVICES

The **Mad River Valley Chamber of Commerce** (4061 Rte. 100/Main St., 800/828-4748, www.madrivervalley.com) runs a small visitors information center with maps, brochures, and sporadic staffing. An ATM is located at **Chittenden Bank** (Mad River Shopping Center, 802/496-2585).

Montpelier

Wrapped by forested hills and bisected by the Winooski River, America's tiniest capital city has a small-town soul. Everyone seems to know each other in the downtown cafés, the natural food co-op, and at the traditional contra dances held at the Capital City Grange.

It's an easy place to explore on foot, and federal-style brick buildings and Victorian mansions lend a bit of pomp to the capital's diminutive downtown. At the center of it all is the gold-capped capitol, dramatic against a leafy backdrop that changes with the seasons. Just as America's founders intended, most of Vermont's representatives undertake political life as a kind of community-serving side hustle, so if the politicians look more like farmers, professors, and retirees than the average DC politico, that's because they are.

SIGHTS

State House

Montpelier's impressive **State House** (115 State St., 802/828-2228, www.legislature.vermont.gov, 7:45am-4:15pm Mon.-Fri., 11am-3pm Sat. July-Oct., guided tours every half hour 10am-3:30pm Mon.-Fri. late June-Oct.) dominates State Street with a 57-foot golden dome above a columned Renaissance Revival building that was built in 1859.

Fittingly for the state, the dome is topped by a wooden statue of Ceres, the goddess of agriculture. Look for a **statue of Ethan Allen,** the Revolutionary War figure, in the Greek Revival front portico, and a **cannon** that was seized at the Battle of Bennington (having completed Revolutionary service, it's now permanently trained on the Department of Motor Vehicles across the street). Tours of the building's interior take in statues and paintings of Vermont politicians who figured in state and national history, including Presidents Coolidge and Chester A. Arthur. You can also explore on your own, by accessing a cell phone **audio guide** (802/526-3221, vermontstatehouse.toursphere.com) that corresponds to numbered locations within the State House.

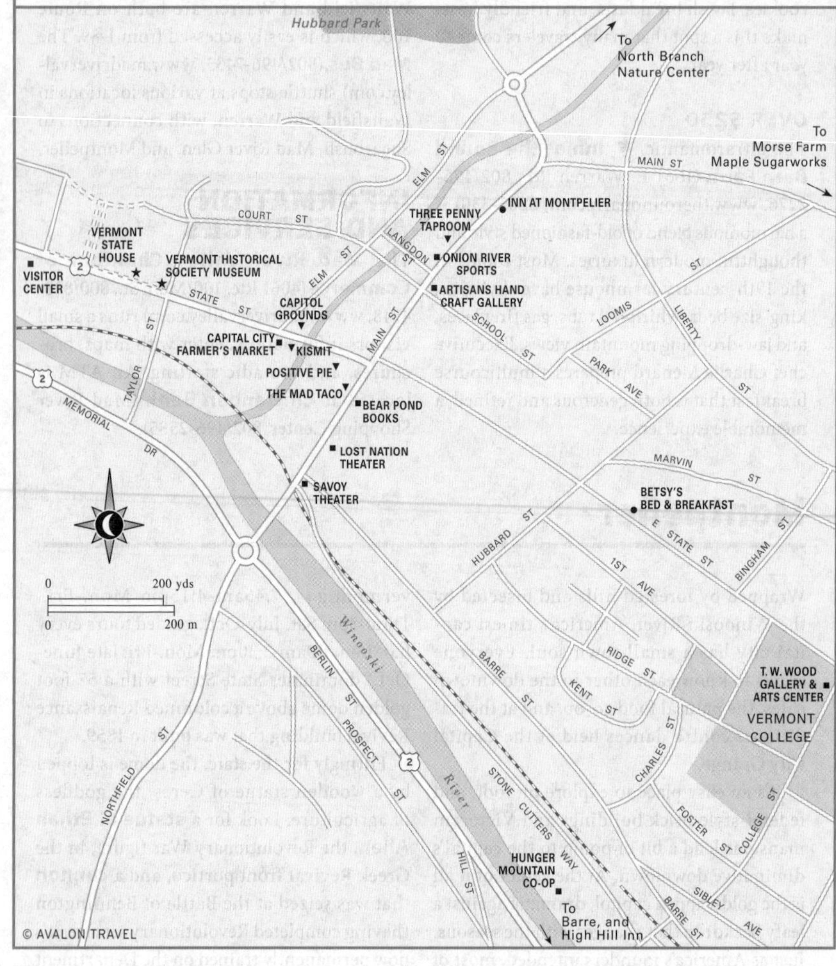

★ Morse Farm Maple Sugarworks

In Vermont, you are never far from a sugarhouse. On the edge of the city, seventh-generation Burr Morse has turned his farm into one of the premier maple syrup producers in the state. **Morse Farm Maple Sugarworks** (1168 County Rd., 800/242-2740, www.morsefarm.com, 9am-8pm daily late May-early Sept., 9am-6pm daily early Sept.-Christmas, 9am-5pm daily Christmas-late May, donations accepted) is a virtual museum of the industry, with old photographs and a "split-log" movie theater that shows a film of the sugaring process. A cavernous gift shop sells maple kettle corn and that most Vermont-y of treats, maple creemees (soft-serve maple ice cream cones).

Sugaring Off

Maple sap flows from a tap on a maple tree to produce maple syrup.

Spring in Vermont is better known as mud season, when frozen back roads melt into quagmires, and precipitation falls as a slushy wintry mix. But the period from mid-March until early April is also sugaring season, when a precise cycle of alternating freezes and thaws kick-starts the sugar maples' vascular systems and causes sap to flow. When that happens, sugarmakers collect the slightly sweet liquid by drilling tap holes in each tree and collecting the runoff in metal buckets or plastic tubing that runs through the forest like spider webs.

When they have enough sap, sugarmakers boil it in wide, shallow pans called evaporators, usually heated by wood gathered in the surrounding hills, and cook it down until it turns thick and golden—the ratio of sap to syrup varies from tree to tree, but averages around 40:1.

Sugaring is a social event in Vermont, and neighbors have a sixth sense for when someone's boiling. Over the course of an evening in the sugarhouse, friends will drop by for beer and conversation, along with shots of hot, fresh syrup, right out of the pan. Everyone's got a favorite sugaring snack, from hot dogs boiled in sap to syrup poured over vanilla ice cream, and you can discover yours at the yearly Maple Open House Weekend (www.vermontmaple.org, mid-Mar.), when sugarhouses around the state open their doors to visitors and prepare all the traditional treats. Don't miss sugar on snow, where syrup is cooked to a taffy-like consistency and served with a pickle.

Vermont Historical Society Museum

From the beginning of Vermont's history as an independent republic, its residents have struggled with the tension between "Freedom and Unity," the state motto that became a starting point for the complete renovation of the **Vermont Historical Society Museum** (109 State St., 802/828-2291, www.vermonthistory.org, 10am-4pm Tues.-Sat. May-mid-Oct., $7 adults, $5 students and seniors, children under 6 free, $20 families), a notably thoughtful journey back into the story of the state. Exhibits start with full-scale reconstructions of an Abenaki dwelling and the Revolutionary-era Catamount Tavern, and continue on to include Civil War artifacts, a room dedicated to Vermont-born president Coolidge, and even a collection on the early history of skiing. The gift shop has an extensive selection of books on Vermont history and culture.

Galleries

One of the best of Montpelier's galleries is also the oldest. The **T.W. Wood Gallery & Arts Center** (46 Barre St., 802/262-6035, www.twwoodgallery.org, noon-4pm Tues.-Sun.) has been showcasing the work of Vermont artists for more than 100 years, with a permanent collection of modern art and rotating shows by local contemporary artists.

Mary Stone's hand-sculpted clay animal whistles are just one of the unique crafts on display at the **Artisans Hand Craft Gallery** (89 Main St., 802/229-9446, www.artisanshand.com, 10am-6pm Mon.-Sat., noon-4pm

Sun.), a hub for jewelry, pottery, woodwork, and metalwork from Vermont artisans.

ENTERTAINMENT AND EVENTS

With a destination-worthy beer list and a laid-back atmosphere, **Three Penny Taproom** (108 Main St., 802/223-8277, www.threepennytaproom.com) is Montpelier's best bar, and the adjoining restaurant serves appealing, dressed-up pub fare.

Montpelier's professional theater company, **Lost Nation Theater** (39 Main St., 802/229-0492, www.lostnationtheater.org) performs an eclectic mix of musicals, contemporary drama, and an annual fall Shakespeare production. The **Savoy Theater** (26 Main St., 802/229-0509, www.savoytheater.com) screens first-run and classic art films.

FOOD

Moody decor and sophisticated food have made **Kismet** (52 State St., 802/223-8646, www.kismetkitchens.com, 5pm-9pm Wed.-Fri., 8am-2pm and 5pm-9pm Sat., 9am-2pm Sun., $20-27, prix fixe $40) Montpelier's classic date-night restaurant; couples dine on tortellini with baked ricotta and pistachio butter, or crimini en croute (crimini bathed in garlic butter). Brunch is served on the weekends and is sublime: Think savory bread pudding with bone marrow broth, and eggs *en cocotte*.

Like its fraternal twin in Waitsfield, ★ **The Mad Taco** (72 Main St., 802/225-6038, www.themadtaco.com, 11am-9pm daily, $9-11) serves Mexican fare with an anarchic Yankee streak. The menu is the same as at the Waitsfield location, and tortillas come filled with classics like carnitas and pork *al pastor*, or culinary mashups: Try the smoked pork with kimchi and cilantro. The beer and the food are often local, and the hefty burritos are memorable.

Bringing a welcome serving of Southern cuisine to Montpelier's restaurant scene, **Down Home Kitchen** (100 Main St., 802/225-6665, www.downhomekitchenvt.com, 8am-2pm daily, $10-15) serves hearty, comforting food in a cheery space downtown. Meat and three, griddle cakes, and fried chicken are based in fresh, often local ingredients, with excellent coffee and beer to go alongside.

For years, **Bohemian Bakery** (78 Barre St., 802/461-8119, www.bohemianbakeryvt.com, 7:30am-1:30pm Wed.-Fri., 8am-2pm Sat.-Sun., $2-9) was based out of a tiny house in the northern woods, open to the public just one day a week, so sweets-lovers rejoiced when Bohemian opened a Montpelier shop in 2017. Favorites include the wonderfully flaky croissants, caramel-crispy kouign amann, and palm-sized fruit tarts, and there are savory pastries and hearty quiche for lunch.

FARMERS MARKETS

Artisans and growers come out of the woodwork for the **Capital City Farmers Market** (State St. at Elm St., 9am-1pm Sat. May-Oct.), one of the best in the state. Vendors include the highly sought-after (and scarce) **Lawson's Finest Liquids** brewery, which isn't open to the public.

ACCOMMODATIONS

$100-150

In the heart of downtown, **Betsy's Bed & Breakfast** (74 E. State St., 802/229-0466, www.central-vt.com/web/betsybb, $85-190) has 12 guest rooms spread between two Victorian mansions decorated with period antiques. The interiors are a bit timeworn and dark, but the friendly owners, Betsy and Jon, serve delightful breakfasts.

Drift off to the sounds of crickets and frogs (or falling snow) at ★ **High Hill Inn** (265 Green Rd., East Montpelier, 802/223-3623, www.highhillinn.com, $132-170). Comfortable rooms and a relaxed country setting make this hilltop inn feel like a getaway. The generous breakfast spread is a highlight.

$150-250

Two gracious federal-style buildings (with no

Vermont's Northeast Kingdom

Wilder and more rural than the rest of the state, the northern part of Vermont between Jay Peak and New Hampshire is the Northeast Kingdom, often called simply The Kingdom. There's deep, dark forests here, mountains that rake huge piles of snow from the clouds, hippie communities, and some serious redneck credentials. Sights are scattered across the landscape, but this is the place to go for Vermont's best mountain biking, hallucinogenic performance art, beautiful scenery, and a small-town library with world-class art. Here are the very top picks for exploring the Kingdom.

Go Mountain Biking at Kingdom Trails (Kingdom Trail Association, 478 Rte. 114, East Burke, 802/626-0737, www.kingdomtrails.org, $15). Carriage paths, railroad right-of-ways, and single-track have been stitched together into a cyclist's wonderland, more than 100 miles of riding that ranges from fast and flowy to rocky and technical. There are trails for every ability, and it's easy to rent bikes on-site.

Line Up for the "World's Best Beer" at Hill Farmstead Brewery (403 Hill Rd., Greensboro Bend, 802/533-7450, www.hillfarmstead.com, noon-5pm Wed.-Sat.). True believers come from around the country to this rural brewery, bringing empty growlers to fill with Shaun Hill's creations. The brewery has repeatedly snagged the title of "best in the world," though many would dispute the honor, and the beer is undeniably fabulous.

Catch a Show at Bread and Puppet (753 Heights Rd., Glover, 802/525-3031, www.breadandpuppet.org, 10am-6pm daily June-Oct., free). Giant puppets, progressive politics, and a fierce ethos of "cheap art" have kept this wild and rural theater fresh since the 1970s. Bring a lawn chair and a sun hat, and join the crowd at Bread and Puppet's outdoor amphitheater.

Paddle Lake Willoughby (96 Bellwater Ave., Barton, 802/525-6205, www.vtstateparks.com/htm/crystal.htm, late May-early Sept.). A glacially carved lake flanked with high cliffs, this is a stunning body of water, especially when autumn foliage lights up the surface of the lake.

Browse the Stacks at the St. Johnsbury Athenaeum (1171 Main St., St. Johnsbury, 802/748-8291, www.stjathenaeum.org, 10am-5:30pm Mon., Wed., and Fri., 2pm-7pm Tues. and Thurs., 10am-3pm Sat.). A tiny library with lofty aspirations, this is one of a handful of athenaeums in New England—loaning libraries that take their name from ancient temples to Athena, the Greek goddess of wisdom. Hidden in the back is a magnificent art collection, including some fine examples from the Hudson School.

Eat and Drink at the Northeast Kingdom Tasting Center (150 Main St., Newport, 802/334-1790, www.nektastingcenter.com, 8am-8pm Mon.-Sat., 9am-3pm Sun.). Try cheese, locally brewed beer, and Kingdom-baked bread, but the real highlight of a trip to this tasting center is sampling ice cider, a sweet, nectar-like answer to old-world ice wine, made from frozen cider.

fewer than 10 fireplaces) comprise the **Inn at Montpelier** (147 Main St., 802/223-2727, www.innatmontpelier.com, $150-250). The antiques-filled common areas lead into 19 neat rooms, with canopy beds, colonial-style bureaus, and walls ranging from tomato-red to bold floral. A simple breakfast is served in the old-fashioned dining room, and in warm months, the gracious porch is the perfect place to watch the town drift by. Book well ahead during the legislative session (Jan.-Apr.).

INFORMATION AND SERVICES

Across from the State House, the **Capital Region Visitors Center** (134 State St., 802/828-5981, 6am-5pm Mon.-Fri., 9am-5pm Sat.-Sun.) has lots of brochures, maps, and advice on area attractions.

ATMs are available at many downtown locations, including at **Citizens Bank** (7 Main St., 802/223-9545). In an emergency, contact **Vermont State and Montpelier City Police** (1 Pitkin Ct., 802/223-3445).

GETTING THERE AND AROUND

Montpelier is located directly off I-89 at exit 8, and at the confluence of Route 2 and Route 302 from New Hampshire.

Amtrak (800/872-7245, www.amtrak.com) runs trains to Junction Road in Montpelier. Buses from **Green Mountain Transit** (802/864-2282, www.ridegmt.com) link Montpelier with Burlington on weekdays only. Taxi service is available from **Green Cab** (802/864-2424, www.greencabvt.com), and the **Green Mountain Transit Agency** (802/223-7287, www.gmtaride.org) operates bus routes around Montpelier and Barre.

Stowe

Upon arrival in Stowe's center, you might find that the curated cuteness of downtown—white church spire, alpine-style buildings, boutique shops—seems slightly clichéd. But this particular New England town is an original, the real deal, and helped define the genre of adorable mountain resorts. Tourists have been coming here since the Civil War, drawn to the remarkable scenery, rugged culture, and endless opportunities for outdoor adventure that continue to attract visitors from around the world. This is mountain living gone upscale, and if Stowe has acquired a commercial sheen since its founding in 1763, it's still got deep Vermont roots, with great dining and appealing accommodations that make it an excellent base for exploring the northern Green Mountains.

SIGHTS

Stowe Mountain Resort

Climbing the slopes of Mount Mansfield, Vermont's highest peak, **Stowe Mountain Resort** (7416 Mountain Rd., 800/253-3000, www.stowe.com, $92-124 adults, $82-114 seniors, $72-104 children) is one of the state's best downhill destinations. The base lodge is chic, the lifts are fast, and there's a massive snowmaking operation that keeps the mountain chugging even in chancy weather. A gondola links Mount Mansfield with the neighboring Spruce Peak, and even on busy

Route 108 near Smugglers' Notch

weekends, the massive trail system means there's always some clear space to get in some turns.

In the summer, Stowe Mountain Resort operates an eight-person, high-speed **gondola skyride** (Mountain Rd./Rte. 108, 800/253-4754, www.stowe.com, 10am-4:30pm late June-mid-Oct., round-trip $28 adults, $17 youth 6-12, $84 families) up to the summit that takes in views of the village and surrounding mountains on the way.

Stowe Mountain Toll Road and Smugglers' Notch

It's also possible to drive to the summit of Mount Mansfield on the winding, unpaved **Stowe Mountain toll road,** which takes off from Route 108 at the **Toll House Conference Center** (5781 Rte. 108/Mountain Rd., tolls $23 car and driver, $8 each passenger, children 4 and under free). The 4.5-mile-long road is closed to motorcycles, RVs, and bicycles, and climbs steeply to the "nose" of Mount Mansfield, where it's possible to park and continue to the "chin," the highest summit, on a 1.3-mile, one-way walking trail.

The views are spectacular, but for a scenic drive without the toll, just keep winding up **Route 108,** an incredibly twisty, curving road that's hemmed in by high cliffs, granite boulders, and trees that turn bright gold in the fall. Route 108 climbs through Smugglers' Notch, a mountain pass said to have been used to bring contraband from Canada during the years of Prohibition. Oversized vehicles should stay away, and all drivers should approach this road with great care, as hikers, rock climbers, and cyclists are often hidden behind the sharp corners.

Brewers and Distillers

Stowe is blessed with a wealth of locally made craft alcohols, starting with the Austrian lager beers at **Von Trapp Brewery & Bierhall** (1333 Luce Hill Rd., 802/253-5750, www.vontrappbrewing.com, 11:30am-9pm daily). Favorites include the malty Vienna Style Lager

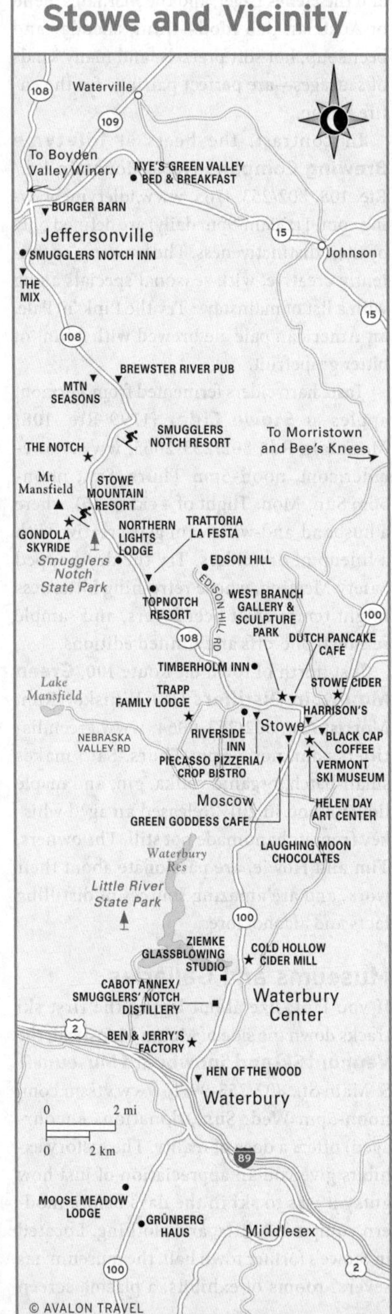

and the Helles Lager, and the Bierhall's menu of Austrian pub food—think cheddar and beer soup, hot soft pretzels, and many kinds of sausages—are perfect pairings for the entire lineup.

In contrast, the beers at **Idletyme Brewing Company** (1859 Mountain Rd./Rte. 108, 802/253-4765, www.idletymebrewing.com, 11:30am-9pm daily) are defined only by their distinctiveness. The brewer is consistently creative, with seasonal specials along with a list of mainstays: Try the Pink 'n' Pale, an American pale ale brewed with a hint of bitter grapefruit.

Taste hard ciders fermented from Vermont apples at **Stowe Cider** (1799 Rte. 108/Mountain Rd., 802/253-2065, www.stowecider.com, noon-6pm Thurs.-Sat., noon-5pm Sun.-Mon., flight of 4 ciders $6), where a husband-and-wife team gets creative with a lineup of dry ciders. Try the dry-hopped Safety Meeting, whose refreshing bitterness might tempt craft beer lovers, and sample seasonal one-offs and limited editions.

Just north of town on Route 100, **Green Mountain Distillers** (171 Whiskey Run, Morristown, 802/253-0064, www.greendistillers.com, noon-5pm Thurs.-Sat.) makes small-batch, organic vodka, gin, and maple liqueur, and in 2017, released an aged whiskey from its handmade pot still. The owners, Tim and Howie, are passionate about their work, and are amazing sources of distilling facts and alcohol lore.

Museums and Galleries

If you fantasize about laying the first ski tracks down the side of Mount Mansfield, the **Vermont Ski and Snowboard Museum** (1 S. Main St., 802/253-9911, www.vtssm.com, noon-5pm Wed.-Sun., donations encouraged) offers a dose of reality. The history exhibits give you an appreciation of just how gutsy it was to ski in the days before modern equipment, lifts, and clothing. Located in Stowe's former town hall, the museum has several rooms of exhibits, a plasma screen with ski videos, and a hall of fame of great names in Vermont skiing history.

The community-supported **Helen Day Art Center** (90 Pond St., 802/253-8358, www.helenday.com, 10am-5pm Tues.-Sat. year-round, donations accepted) has been dedicated to showcasing local art for more than 25 years. It inhabits the 2nd floor of a Greek Revival building in the center of town, with a sculpture garden out back.

A more extensive sculpture garden fills the grounds of the **West Branch Gallery and Sculpture Park** (17 Towne Farm Ln., 802/253-8943, www.westbranchgallery.com, 10am-5pm Tues.-Sun. year-round, free), where contemporary art has a bucolic backdrop about a mile north of town.

ENTERTAINMENT AND EVENTS

Nightlife

Mountain Road is lined with lively bars and restaurants for après-ski recovery, and most sport fireplaces, rustic decor, and the kind of comforting snacks that go well with beer. In addition to **Doc Ponds** and **The Bench** (see the *Food* section for listings), **Piecasso Pizzeria & Lounge** (1899 Mountain Rd., 802/253-4411, 11am-11pm daily, www.piecasso.com) is a local favorite, with lots of seats at the bar, creative pizza, and undeniably scrumptious chicken wings. This is the kind of bar where kids are welcome and comfortable.

Festivals and Events

The Trapp family keeps the hills alive (with the sound of classical music) by hosting **Music in our Meadow,** a series of outdoor performances in partnership with **Stowe Performing Arts** (802/253-7729, www.stoweperformingarts.com). And the **Stowe Theatre Guild** (67 Main St., 802/253-3961, www.stowetheatre.com) presents crowd-pleasing musicals throughout the year at the Stowe Town Hall Theatre.

Ski jumping and ice-sculpture carving

shake Stowe out of the winter doldrums during the **Stowe Winter Carnival** (www.stowecarnival.com, late Jan.). A highlight is the Village Night Block Party, which fills the streets with bulky parkas and merriment.

SHOPPING

Sweets lovers can follow their noses to **Laughing Moon Chocolates** (78 S. Main St., 802/253-9591, www.laughingmoonchocolates.com, 9am-6pm daily), where confections are handmade on-site. True devotees can sign up for chocolate-dipping workshops ($125 for 2 people).

Artist Susan Bayer Fishman owns and runs **Stowe Craft Gallery** (55 Mountain Rd., 802/253-4693, www.stowecraft.com, 10am-6pm daily, until 7pm holiday season), an epic collection of many other artists' works—knickknacks like pewter measuring cups, glazed vases, and hand-carved backgammon sets.

SPORTS AND RECREATION

Winter Sports

Behind the Trapp Family Lodge, the **Trapp Family Lodge Touring Center** (700 Trapp Hill Rd., Stowe, 802/253-8511 or 800/826-7000, www.trappfamily.com, $25 adults, $20 seniors, $15 youth 12-18, $10 children 6-11, children under 6 free) has some 100 kilometers of cross-country ski trails through both groomed and ungroomed forest and meadowland. Plan your ski to pass by the **Slayton Cabin,** Trapp's hilltop warming hut, where you can cozy up with hot chocolate by the fire. Rentals are available on-site.

Or you can dash through the woods to the sound of sleigh bells and draft horses, as Trapp Family Lodge offers open sleigh rides each weekend ($25 adults, $15 children 4-12, children under 4 free), or book a private sleigh ride ($95 couple, $22 child).

For gravity-powered entertainment, rent a toboggan from **Shaw's General Store** (54 Main St., 802/253-4040, www.heshaw.com, 9am-6pm Mon.-Fri., 9am-5pm Sun.), or a more extreme sled from **Umiak Outdoor Outfitters** (849 S. Main St., 802/253-2317, www.umiak.com, 9am-6pm daily, $25 per day), which features the latest from Mad River Rockets and Hammersmith, and will point you to the vertiginous heights on which to test them. The best spot for sledding right in Stowe is Marshall's Hill, just behind the elementary school; to get there, turn onto School Street at **Black Cap Coffee** (144 Main St.).

Hiking and Biking

Leaving from the top of the Smugglers' Notch road, a steep, 1.1-mile hike leads to scenic **Sterling Pond,** a scenic body of water that is dazzling in autumn. To reach the trailhead from Stowe village, drive 8.9 miles north on Route 108, then park in the Smugglers' Notch Visitor Center parking lot on the left. The trail departs from just across the street, following blue blazes to the lake. Once there, an additional loop trail continues around the 1.4-mile perimeter of Sterling Pond.

An easier hike is the 1-mile walk to **Moss Glenn Falls,** which flows into a series of swimming holes that are perfect for hot afternoons. From Stowe village, drive 3 miles north on Route 100, then turn right on Randolph Road. Take the first right, on Moss Glenn Falls Road, then continue 0.6 mile to a parking lot on the left. Another great swimming hole (at the end of an even shorter trail) can be found at **Bingham Falls.** To reach the falls from Stowe village, drive north on Route 108 for 6.4 miles, and watch for the trailhead and pullouts to the east of the road. It's a 0.5 mile hike to the falls.

Stretching 5.3 miles from Stowe village to Top Notch Resort on Mountain Road, the paved **Stowe Recreation Path** (802/253-6148, www.stowerec.org) twists back and forth across the West Branch River, with plenty of places to stop to swim and picnic along the way. The access point in Stowe village is behind the Stowe Community Church at 137 Main Street, and dogs are allowed on leash.

Bikes are available for rent at several locations in town, including **AJ's Ski and Sports** (350 Mountain Rd., 800/226-6257, www.stowesports.com, $9 per hour, $19 for 4 hours).

For biking that's more dirt, less asphalt, head to the excellent **Cady Hill Forest** (parking lot on Mountain Rd. across from Town and Country Resort, 876 Mountain Rd., www.stowelandtrust.org), with 11 miles of singletrack that ranges from moderate and flowy to technical and rocky. Maps of the trails can be found on the Stowe Land Trust parking lot, and paper versions are for sale at most of the town's bicycle shops. Some sections of Cady Hill are groomed for fat biking during the winter months.

FOOD

With a fabulous beer list and lots of polished copper, **The Bench** (492 Mountain Rd., 802/253-5100, www.benchvt.com, 4pm-close Mon.-Fri., 11:30am-close Sat.-Sun., mains $15-20) serves pizzas, salads, and grown-up comfort food in a relaxed setting. There are 25 beers on tap, and in the snowy months it's hard to beat a seat at the bar, where you'll have a view of the wood-fired brick oven that's used for much of the menu (including the delightful roast duck).

Run by the chefs behind the James Beard Award-winning Hen of the Wood in Burlington, ★ **Doc Ponds** (294 Mountain Rd., 802/760-6066, www.docponds.com, 4pm-midnight Tues.-Thurs., 11:30am-midnight Fri.-Mon., $7-19) serves a menu of hearty snacks and comfort food, with burgers, smoked meats, and ample pickled vegetables.

Excellent espresso, teas, and filling breakfast sandwiches make **PK Coffee** (1880 Mountain Rd., 802/760-6151, www.pkcoffee.com, 7am-5pm daily) a good stop on the way up to the mountain, and the counter is stocked with locally made pastries, granola, and other treats.

Ten minutes south of the village, **Michael's on the Hill** (4182 Rte. 100, 802/244-7476, www.michaelsonthehill.com, 5:30pm-9pm Wed.-Mon., $28-43) is worth the trip for a special dinner. An elegant menu of European-influenced food prepared with many local ingredients is served in a converted farmhouse.

If you're detoxing from all that comfort food, seek out the **Green Goddess Café** (618 S. Main St., 802/253-5255, www.greengoddessvt.com, 7:30am-3pm Mon.-Fri., 8am-3pm Sat.-Sun., mains $6-10), where breakfast and lunch include great salads, fresh juice, and plenty of vegetarian options alongside hearty sandwiches and egg dishes.

Also, it's worth nothing that many of the listings in other sections of this chapter—notably the **Von Trapp Brewery & Bierhall, Piecasso Pizzeria & Lounge,** and **Idletyme Brewing Co.**—are also very worthwhile restaurants.

ACCOMMODATIONS AND CAMPING

Under $100

For travelers on a budget, you can't beat a room at the **Riverside Inn** (1965 Mountain Rd., 802/253-4217, www.rivinn.com, $69-139), a homey, somewhat ramshackle farmhouse with charming owners and a great location. Motel-style rooms out back are newer and have coffeemakers and microwaves. It's a good choice for families and groups, as some rooms come equipped with several beds.

$100-150

The rustic and comfortable **Timberholm Inn** (452 Cottage Club Rd., 802/253-7603, www.timberholm.com, $110-235) is convenient to the mountain and village and includes a three-course homemade breakfast and warm cookies in the afternoon. A hot tub, shuffleboard, and movie area make this a welcoming haven when the weather doesn't cooperate. If you're planning to ski, ask about packages with lift tickets.

Even closer to the slopes is **Northern Lights Lodge** (4441 Mountain Rd., 802/253-8541, www.stowelodge.com, $99-200), which offers hot breakfasts, a hot tub, and a sauna to help you prepare for (and recover from) your activities of choice.

Over $250

★ **Edson Hill** (1500 Edson Hill Rd., 802/253-7171, www.edsonhill.com, $175-500), which was redesigned in 2014, is drop-dead gorgeous, from the picture-perfect interior to its setting on a hill with killer views. Rooms include breakfast in an enchanting dining room, and with a plush tavern, craft drinks, and a menu of creatively wrought comfort food, you many never want to leave. The 38-acre property includes stables and hiking trails, as well as cross-country skiing (equipment is provided).

With loads of pampering and fantastic recreation for adults and kids, ★ **Topnotch Resort** (4000 Mountain Rd., 800/451-8686, www.topnotchresort.com, $385-535) wins the luxury-for-families award, hands down. Grown-ups can chill out on the slopes at either of the beautifully kept mountainside pools (one indoors, one outdoors) or in the glorious new spa's treatment rooms. Meanwhile, the children's activity program is extensive and well organized, so both they and mom and dad feel entertained by the day's end. Not for families only, the resort also manages to make couples feel catered to, with romantic dining at Norma's, sumptuously decorated suites with oversized tubs, and couples' massages.

Camping

With 20 walk-in sites and 14 lean-tos, the campground at **Smugglers' Notch State Park** (6443 Mountain Rd., 802/253-4014, www.vtstateparks.com/smugglers.html, tent sites $18-20, lean-tos $25-27) has a great location on Mountain Road and historic structures built by the Civilian Conservation Corps (CCC).

INFORMATION AND SERVICES

The **Stowe Area Association** (51 Main St., 877/467-8693, 9am-6pm Mon.-Sat., 11am-5pm Sun., www.gostowe.com) runs a welcome center at the crossroads of Main Street and Mountain Road. Wi-Fi Internet can be accessed around the corner at **Stowe Free Library** (90 Pond St., 802/253-6145, 9:30am-5:30pm Mon., Wed., Fri., noon-7pm Tue. & Thu., 10am-3pm Sat.). Also at Main and Mountain is a branch of **People's United Bank** (1069 Mountain Rd., 802/253-8525, 8:30am-4:30pm Mon.-Fri.).

Medical needs can be filled at **Heritage Drugs** (1878 Mountain Rd., 802/253-2544) as well as **Kinney Drugs** (155 S. Main St., Cambridge, 802/644-8811, 8:30am-8pm Mon.-Fri., 8:30am-7pm Sat., 9am-5pm Sun., pharmacy 8:30am-7pm Mon.-Fri., 8:30am-4pm Sat.). In an emergency, contact the **Stowe Police Department** (350 S. Main St., 802/253-7126).

GETTING THERE AND AROUND

Stowe village is at the intersection of Route 108 and Route 100, 15 minutes north of I-89. **Amtrak** has service to Waterbury, where you can catch one of the frequent buses to Stowe with **Green Mountain Transit** (802/864-2282, www.ridegmt.com).

During the winter months, the free **Mountain Road Shuttle** (www.gostowe.com) connects the village and the resort, with stops at major hotels along the way.

Burlington

With a mix of small-town reserve and urban sophistication, Vermont's largest city is the state's cultural heart. There are forested trails, organic farms, and beaches within the city limits, and on snowbound winter mornings you can spot cross-country skis lined up outside the coffee shops.

Throughout the summer, the waterfront fills up with sailboats and kayaks, and locals ditch work to cool off at their favorite swimming spots. The warm months are a frenzy of activity in Burlington, with almost-weekly festivals that flood the town with music, art, and food lovers.

Perched above it all is the stately University of Vermont, whose 12,000 students swell the population by almost 30 percent. The school was founded in 1791 by Ira Allen (Ethan's brother), and academic life remains an important source of energy for the town. This is not a place with a town-gown divide—on a Saturday night in Burlington you can raise a glass, cut a rug, or take a moonlight ski with sugarmakers, sociologists, and senators.

SIGHTS

★ Waterfront Park

A few decades of renovations have turned the **Burlington Waterfront** (1 College St., 802/865-7247), once a bustling lumber port, into a pedestrian-friendly park filled with art and native plants. The view is dramatic when the sun sets over the Adirondacks, so bring a picnic and watch as sailboats, paddleboards, and kayaks drift by. The bike path runs right through the middle of things, so if you've got two wheels or want to rent them, the waterfront is a great starting point. While you're exploring, see if you can find the statue of ***The Lone Sailor*** tucked behind the **ECHO Leahy Center for Lake Champlain.** The monument was cast with bronze from eight U.S. Navy ships, a fitting tribute on the shores of Lake Champlain, which saw key naval battles in the Revolutionary War and the War of 1812.

On summer days when the city is stifling, the best seat in town may be at the easy-to-miss **Splash at the Boathouse** (0 College St., 802/343-5894, www.splashattheboathouse.com, 11am-10pm daily May-Oct.,

the Burlington Waterfront

Burlington

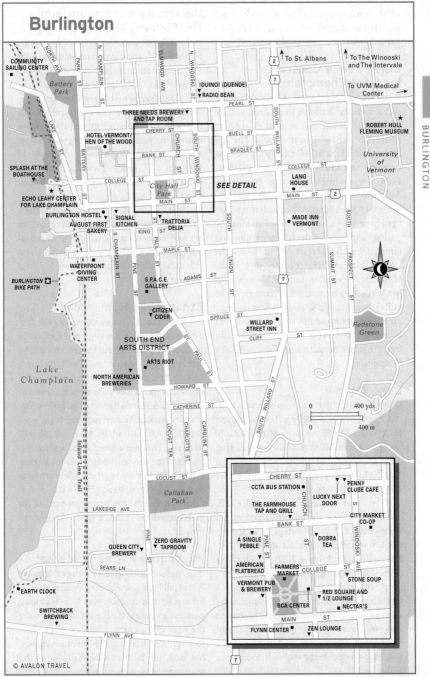

COMMUNITY SAILING CENTER
Battery Park
NORTH AVE
PARK ST
N CHAMPLAIN ST
ELMWOOD AVE
N WINOOSKI ST
To St. Albans
To The Winooski and The Intervale
To UVM Medical Center
¡DUINO! (DUENDE)
RADIO BEAN
PEARL ST
THREE NEEDS BREWERY AND TAP ROOM
CHERRY ST
BUELL ST
BRADLEY ST
CHURCH ST
SOUTH WINOOSKI ST
SOUTH WILLARD ST
HOTEL VERMONT/ HEN OF THE WOOD
BANK ST
BATTERY ST
LAKE ST
ROBERT HULL FLEMING MUSEUM
University of Vermont
COLLEGE ST
SPLASH AT THE BOATHOUSE
City Hall Park
SEE DETAIL
LANG HOUSE
ECHO LEAHY CENTER FOR LAKE CHAMPLAIN
MAIN ST
BURLINGTON HOSTEL
SIGNAL KITCHEN
TRATTORIA DELIA
AUGUST FIRST BAKERY
KING ST
MADE INN VERMONT
SOUTH UNION ST
SOUTH PROSPECT ST
S CHAMPLAIN ST
PAUL ST
MAPLE ST
SUMMIT ST
WATERFRONT DIVING CENTER
BURLINGTON BIKE PATH
PINE ST
ADAMS ST
S.P.A.C.E. GALLERY
CITIZEN CIDER
SPRUCE ST
WILLARD STREET INN
Redstone Green
CLIFF ST
SOUTH END ARTS DISTRICT
ARTS RIOT
Lake Champlain
NORTH AMERICAN BREWERIES
HOWARD ST
CATHERINE ST
0 400 yds
0 400 m
LOCUST TER
CHARLOTTE ST
CAROLINE ST
Island Line Trail
LOCUST ST
Callahan Park
LAKESIDE AVE
ZERO GRAVITY TAPROOM
QUEEN CITY BREWERY
SEARS LN
EARTH CLOCK
SWITCHBACK BREWING
FLYNN AVE

CHERRY ST
CCTA BUS STATION
PENNY CLUSE CAFÉ
LUCKY NEXT DOOR
THE FARMHOUSE TAP AND GRILL
CITY MARKET CO-OP
BANK ST
A SINGLE PEBBLE
DOBRA TEA
AMERICAN FLATBREAD
FARMERS' MARKET
COLLEGE ST
STONE SOUP
S WINOOSKI AVE
VERMONT PUB & BREWERY
RED SQUARE AND 1/2 LOUNGE
BCA CENTER
NECTAR'S
MAIN ST
FLYNN CENTER
ZEN LOUNGE

$8-15) restaurant at the end of a dock on the waterfront. Snag an Adirondack chair for a stellar sunset view.

ECHO Leahy Center for Lake Champlain

With ancient coral reefs, whale skeletons, and a mythical monster in its depths, Lake Champlain is one of the most distinctive bodies of freshwater in the world. The scientists behind the **ECHO Leahy Center for Lake Champlain** (1 College St., 802/864-1848, www.echovermont.org, 10am-5pm daily, $16.50 adults, $14.50 seniors and students, $13.50 children 3-17, children under 3 free) have done a bang-up job of making the geology and fauna of the lake accessible and family friendly. "Hands-on" is the watchword at this small science center, with plenty of interactive exhibits to get kids good and wet while they learn about river currents or pull critters out of lake pools. There is plenty for nature-loving adults, too, like aquarium tanks full of the fish, turtles, snakes, and frogs that live beneath the surface of Lake Champlain.

Lake Tours

Check out Burlington from the water on the ***Spirit of Ethan Allen III*** (Burlington Boathouse, 348 Flynn Ave., 802/862-8300, www.soea.com, 10am, noon, 2pm, and 4pm daily May-Oct., $21 adults, $8.43 children 3-11), which has piped-in narration for its 1.5-hour sightseeing cruise.

If you prefer to hit the lake under sail, consider a trip on the beautiful gaff-rigged sloop ***Friend Ship*** (1 College St., 802/598-6504, www.whistlingman.com, May-Oct., $50 adults, $35 children 2-12), which offers three daily sailing cruises as well as two-, four-, and eight-hour private charters. It's a sublime experience when a steady breeze allows Captain Mike to shut off the engine and you travel to the sounds of water and wind alone. The cruises are two hours, and water is provided; bring your own food, beer, and wine.

University of Vermont and the Fleming Museum

University of Vermont (194 S. Prospect St., 802/656-3131, www.uvm.edu) educates some 12,000 students on a stately campus filled with historic brick buildings. Chartered in 1791 by a group of Vermonters, including Ira Allen, it was the fifth college in the country (after Harvard, Yale, Dartmouth, and Brown). For visitors, its prized attraction is the **Robert Hull Fleming Museum** (University of Vermont, 61 Colchester Ave., 802/656-0750, www.flemingmuseum.org, 10am-4pm Tues. and Thurs.-Fri., 10am-7pm Wed., noon-4pm Sat.-Sun., $5 adults, $3 students and seniors, children 6 and under free, $10 families), an art and archaeology museum with mummies, Buddhas, Mesoamerican pottery, and other artifacts from some of the world's great civilizations.

Ethan Allen Homestead

Today, Ethan Allen's name recalls the furniture company that was named for him in 1932, but Allen was one of the most colorful—and enigmatic—characters of early Vermont history. His modest Cape Cod-style home, known as the **Ethan Allen Homestead** (1 Ethan Allen Homestead Way, 802/865-4556, www.ethanallenhomestead.org, 10am-4pm daily May-Oct., $10 adults, $9 seniors, $6 children 5-17, children under 5 free), has been restored to the period, though only his kitchen table and a few other small Allen artifacts survive. The homestead offers a low-budget film exploring the conflicting accounts of the man himself, as well as a guided tour of the property.

Burlington Farmers' Market

The outdoor **Burlington Farmers' Market** (City Hall Park, www.burlingtonfarmersmarket.org, 8:30am-2pm Sat. May-Oct.) is a foodie paradise and one of the biggest social events of the week in the Queen City. Locals and visitors fill their baskets with fresh vegetables, hot food, and pastries while listening to live music and lounging on the grass. With dozens of vendors, you could browse all day, but don't miss the home-brewed soda at **Rookie's Root Beer** (the Dark Side is an addictive blend of espresso and root beer topped with molasses cream). If you're planning a picnic, pick up some excellent goat cheese at **Doe's Leap** to go with rye bread from **Slow Fire Bakery** or savory biscuits from **Barrio Bakery.** There are lots of sweet treats to choose from, but on a hot day you can follow the lines to **Adam's Berry Farm** for popsicles made from organic fruit, or to **The Farm Between** for what may be the world's best snow cones—try the black currant.

BCA Center

Art at the **BCA Center** (135 Church St., 802/865-7166, www.burlingtoncityarts.org, 11am-5pm Tues.-Thurs., 11am-8pm Fri.-Sat., also Sun. 11am-5pm May-Oct., free) explores contemporary themes with multimedia and interactive exhibitions in oversized gallery spaces. Some of its shows are more successful than others; all are provocative. A recent exhibit, for example, looked at perspectives from Iraq vets-turned-artists working in media including U.S. currency and flags and their own uniforms, to come to grips with their experiences in war.

Farm Tours

When flying into Burlington's airport, the city looks tiny, a tidy cluster of buildings surrounded by farms. It's worth getting out to one, because agriculture continues to be the cultural and financial mainstay of the state, and once you meet a few farmers you'll notice their names on menus all over town and leave with a deeper sense of place. Dairy continues to be the most significant agricultural product in the Champlain Valley, but locavore culture has made this fertile ground for a thriving community of small farmers who cultivate everything from grapes to grains.

A good place to start is **Vermont Farm Tours** (802/922-7346, www.vermontfarmtours.com, $75-125), which organizes visits to vintners, cheese makers, and other horticultural hot spots, as well as farm-oriented bike tours in the area. Chris Howell, the affable owner, also runs a monthly **Cocktail Walk** ($45) in Winooski that pairs local distillers and mixologists.

In July and August, the urban farming nonprofit **Intervale Center** (180 Intervale Rd., 802/660-0440, www.intervale.org) hosts **Summervale,** an agricultural hoedown each Thursday with music and food. They also organize free monthly tours of the on-site organic farms (call for details). Every Friday during the summer, the organic **Bread and Butter Farm** (200 Leduc Farm Dr., Shelburne, 802/985-9200, www.breadandbutterfarm.com) throws festive **Burger Nights,** with music, burgers (veggie and beef), hot dogs, and fixings from its cows and on-site bakery. The gorgeous spread is a 15-minute drive from downtown Burlington.

ENTERTAINMENT AND EVENTS

The best place to find out what's happening in the Queen City's nightclubs, theaters, and concert halls is in the free weekly paper *Seven Days* (www.7dvt.com) or on the Lake Champlain Region Chamber of Commerce website (www.vermont.org).

Bars

The last several years have seen an explosion of craft cocktail culture in Vermont, as creative bartenders bring the farm-to-table approach to mixing drinks using locally distilled spirits, artisanal bitters, and fresh ingredients of all kinds. Some of the best cocktail bars are also restaurants, like the superb **Juniper Bar at Hotel Vermont** (41 Cherry St., 802/651-0080, www.hotelvt.com, 7am-midnight daily), which stocks every single spirit made in Vermont and blends them into thoughtful drinks. Another fabulous restaurant bar is the one at **Pizzeria Verità** (156 St. Paul St., 802/489-5644, www.pizzeriaverita.com, 5pm-10pm Sun.-Thurs., 5pm-11pm Fri.-Sat.), whose Italian-inflected cocktails blend in a wide range of *amaro* liqueurs.

And though it's not exactly a mixology destination, there is something transporting about a lazy afternoon at **Splash at the Boathouse** (0 College St., 802/658-2244, www.splashattheboathouse.com, 11am-10pm daily May-Oct.), where generic tropical bar decor complements the best views in town. Since Splash is built on a floating dock, you can drink your beer with your toes in the water while watching bare-chested yachties maneuver their powerboats in the marina's close quarters. (For Burlington's many beer-focused bars, see Callout.)

Live Music and Dancing

You can find something to shimmy to every day of the week in Burlington, where most bars stay open until 2am. There's always a full lineup at **Radio Bean** (8 N. Winooski Ave., 802/660-9346, www.radiobean.com), a bar and coffee shop packed with hipsters watching acts that range from traditional Irish to experimental jazz. **Honky Tonk Night** (10pm Tues.) is a good bet for swinging neo-country music.

On weekend nights, **Church Street Marketplace** is thronged with a lively college crowd that heads to **Red Square** (136 Church St., 802/859-8909, www.redsquarevt.com) or **Nectar's** (188 Main St., 802/856-4771, www.liveatnectars.com) to shake it off to DJ and live music.

It's always worth checking the lineup of high-quality indie groups that play at **Signal Kitchen** (71 Main St., 802/399-2337, www.signalkitchen.com) and **ArtsRiot** (400 Pine St., 802/540-0406, www.artsriot.com), who further their mission of "destroying apathy" by cooking up great shows and tasty, creative pub food. When bigger acts come through Burlington, though, they usually land at **Higher Ground** (1214 Williston Rd., South Burlington, 802/652-0777, www.highergroundmusic.com).

The Arts

A former vaudeville house, the **Flynn Center for the Performing Arts** (153 Main St., 802/863-5966, www.flynncenter.org) was restored to its art deco grandeur in 2000. It now serves as the cultural hub of the city, with musicals, dance performances, and shows by mainstream jazz and country acts from Diana Krall to Pink Martini.

The **South End Arts District** (802/859-9222, www.seaba.com) is home to many collective studios and galleries. They throw open their doors for the **First Friday Art Walk** (802/264-4839, www.artmapburlington.com) each month, which is free to attend; most galleries stay open 5pm-8pm. Don't miss the **S.P.A.C.E. Gallery** (266 Pine St., Ste. 105, 802/578-2512, noon-5pm Wed.-Sat.), which has a quirky mix of artist spaces that run the gamut from fine oil paintings to scary dolls.

Events

Burlington hosts a festival almost every weekend during the summer, and it's worth booking far ahead during those times, as hotels fill up quickly. For 10 days in early June, music lovers from around the region flock to the **Burlington Discover Jazz Festival** (www.discoverjazz.com, June). The town is filled with tunes, from ticketed events featuring big-name artists to free daily jazz sets in many restaurants, bars, and parks. And if you prefer brews to blues, don't miss July's **Vermont Brewers Festival** (802/760-8535, www.vtbrewfest.com, July), when a who's who of local and regional brewers sets up shop right in Waterfront Park. If you'd like to attend, check the website well in advance of your trip, as tickets often sell out the day they go on sale (usually in May).

One of the most energetic days on the lake is the picturesque **Dragon Boat Festival** (802/999-5478, www.ridethedragon.org, Aug.), a boat race in which teams of 20 paddle 40-foot brightly painted canoes to raise money for local charities. The winner is invariably the team that works the best together, not necessarily the strongest.

The summer wraps up with the **Grand Point North** (www.grandpointnorth.com, mid-Sept) festival, put on by hometown

Burlington Breweries

Vermont has more breweries per capita than any other state, and many of its award-winning craft beers (and ciders!) are only available locally. It's a source of pride to beer-loving residents, who are always ready to debate the finer points of hop varieties and snap up tickets to Burlington's **Vermont Brewers Festival** (www.vtbrewfest.com, third weekend of July, $35) as fast as a case of Heady Topper (a notoriously hard-to-find canned beer made in Waterbury).

Conveniently, the downtown breweries are next door to one another, and the **Pine Street Arts District** is home to a cluster of young breweries that are easily reached by car or bus from the center. If all the options leave you thinking that you'd like a tour guide (and chauffeur), you can hop on the bus with **Burlington Brew Tours** (261 S. Union St., 802/760-6091, www.burlingtonbrewtours.com, $85), whose itineraries take you behind the scenes at some of the best breweries in town. Here are some favorites:

Zero Gravity Craft Brewery (115 St. Paul St., 802/861-2999, www.zerogravitybeer.com, 11:30am-close daily) has something for most beer lovers, starting with the flagship **Conehead,** a single hop wheat India pale ale that's brewed with Citra hops and is aromatic and hoppy without being overpowering. Another favorite is the **London Calling,** an English ordinary bitter that's malty and mellow—and not particularly bitter. The main location is tucked into the American Flatbread restaurant, but there's a newer outpost on Pine Street, **Zero Gravity Taproom** (716 Pine St., 802/497-0054, www.zerogravitybeer.com, noon-9pm Sun.-Mon. and Wed.-Thurs., noon-10pm Fri.-Sat.), which has all the same beers with an industrial-chic vibe.

Citizen Cider (316 Pine St., 802/448-3278, www.citizencider.com, noon-9pm Mon.-Thurs.) serves many varieties made from Vermont apples in a beautifully designed taproom. Tours tend to be impromptu but are a fascinating glimpse of the cider-making process. The five-glass flights are an excellent introduction to these unusual ciders: The sweetest of the bunch is the flagship **Unified Press,** but the ginger-spiked **Dirty Mayor** has a passionate following, as does the **Full Nelson,** which is dry hopped with Nelson Sauvin hops that give it a beer-like edge.

Queen City Brewery (703 Pine St., 802/540-0280, www.queencitybrewery.com, 2pm-7pm Wed.-Thurs., 2pm-9pm Fri., noon-7pm Sat., 1pm-5pm Sun.) makes European-style beers in a nondescript industrial building. The tasting room has more charm and is lined with old beer cans and historical images of Burlington. Try the hugely popular **Yorkshire Porter,** an English dark ale that's rich and full bodied, or **Argument,** an English India pale ale that's brewed true to style: strong and bitter.

Foam Brewers (703 Pine St., 802/540-0280, www.foambrewers.com, noon-10pm Mon.-Thurs., 11am-midnight Fri.-Sat., 11am-7pm Sun.) is a relatively recent addition to Burlington's beer scene, with hoppy, aromatic beers made by passionate beer geeks. A prime location on the Burlington waterfront, as well as pleasant outdoor seating, makes this a great place to linger over a flight, and the brewery serves charcuterie platters that make for perfect pairings.

musical heroes **Grace Potter and the Nocturnals.** Two days of music feature an impressive lineup of bands on open-air stages on the Burlington Waterfront, and Sunday's final show is usually attended by a flotilla of kayaks and sailboats getting their tunes for free.

SHOPPING

Church Street Marketplace (2 Church St., 802/863-1646, www.churchstmarketplace.com, 10am-7pm Mon.-Thurs., 10am-8pm Fri.-Sat., 10am-6pm Sun.) is the pedestrian heart of Burlington, lined with restaurants, bars, and a blend of local and national stores. There's a handful of excellent outdoors gear stores, like **Outdoor Gear Exchange** (37 Church St., 802/860-0190, www.gearx.com, 10am-8pm Mon.-Thurs., 10am-9pm Fri.-Sat., 10am-6pm Sun.), which sells new and used equipment for every adventure imaginable, and the **Ski Rack** (85 Main St., 800/882-4530, www.skirack.com, 10am-7pm Mon.-Sat., 11am-5pm Sun.), whose collection of cross-country, backcountry, and alpine skis are the best in town. Both stores offer rental equipment for winter and summer sports.

Downtown Burlington also has two excellent locally owned bookstores: **Crow Bookshop** (14 Church St., 802/862-0848, www.crowbooks.com, 10am-9pm Mon.-Wed., 10am-10pm Thurs.-Sat., 10am-6pm Sun.) has a nice collection of used books and many local authors. **Phoenix Books** (191 Bank St., 802/448-3350, 10am-7pm Mon.-Wed., 10am-8pm Thurs.-Sat., 11am-5pm Sun., www.phoenixbooks.biz) has a broader selection of new books, including many options for regional travel.

SPORTS AND RECREATION

Walking and Biking

★ BURLINGTON BIKE PATH

Burlington is a great place to be a cyclist. If you've got wheels, the logical place to start is the **Burlington Bike Path** (Burlington Parks and Recreation, 802/864-0123, www.enjoyburlington.com), an eight-mile path that runs along the lake and connects several parks perfect for picnicking. A spur can connect via surface streets to **Ethan Allen Homestead** (1 Ethan Allen Homestead, 802/865-4556, www.ethanallenhomestead.org), where cyclists with dirt-appropriate tires can follow paths to the **Intervale,** a cluster of 11 organic farms strung out along the Winooski River.

At the far northern end of the path, you can continue onto the **Causeway,** an elevated path that has unparalleled views of the lake. On most summer weekends you can catch a **bicycle ferry** from the end of the causeway that will drop you and your bike on **South Hero Island.** For more information about the ferry, or to rent bikes, contact the nonprofit **Local Motion** (1 Steele St., 802/861-2700, www.localmotion.org, 10am-6pm daily May-Oct.), which is a great source of cycling maps, gear, and advice on where to ride.

WALKING TRAILS

You could stroll around downtown all day, but if you want to get your feet on some dirt there's some excellent natural areas right in town. The **Rock Point Center** (20 Rock Point Rd., 802/658-6233, www.rockpointvt.org, donations accepted) is owned by the Episcopal Church, which invites visitors to stroll around its forested property that juts dramatically out into the lake, making for showstopping sunsets. Stop by the diocese office for a free pass.

Rock Point's main rival for sunset watching

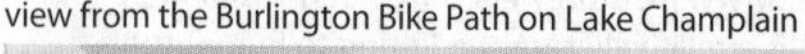
view from the Burlington Bike Path on Lake Champlain

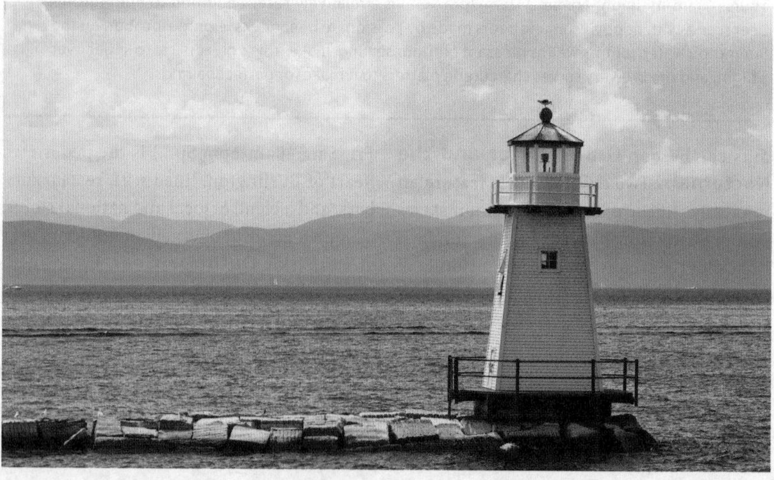

is **Red Rocks Park** (Central Ave., South Burlington, 802/846-4108), which has well-maintained trails with great lake views. But in springtime, at least, you won't take your eyes off the ground, which is carpeted in wildflowers: look for Dutchman's-breeches, trillium, and columbine. For more information about parks, visit the **Burlington Parks and Recreation Department** website (www.enjoyburlington.com, 802/864-0123).

Boating

On sunny summer days, the lakefront fills with a cheerful flotilla of kayaks, canoes, and stand-up paddleboards, as locals and tourists alike head for the water. It's a wonderful way to explore the ins and outs of the shoreline, like the crags at Lone Rock Point and the forested peninsula just to the north of **North Beach** (60 Institute Rd. 802/862-0942). Look carefully at the rocks on the northern side of the outcropping and you'll see a clear divide between the pale, smooth dolomite rock that makes up the top of the cliff and the dark, crumbling shale at the base. It's an exposed thrust fault, where continental plates are colliding. You can rent a kayak or paddleboard right on the beach from **Umiak Outfitters** (802/651-8760, 11am-6pm daily mid-June-Labor Day, $20-30 for 2 hours).

Closer to downtown, the **Community Sailing Center** (234 Penny Ln., 802/864-2499, www.communitysailingcenter.org, hours vary, May-Oct, $15-55 per hour) has kayaks, paddleboards, and sailboats for use in Burlington Bay, and offers private and group classes if you want to brush up on your boat handling. Yogis ready to take their boat pose out for a spin should consider attending "Floating Yoga" classes taught on paddleboards (call for dates, $35).

FOOD

Before opening on the site of a national hamburger chain, **The Farmhouse Tap & Grill** (160 Bank St., 802/859-0888, www.farmhousetg.com, 11:30am-11pm Mon.-Thurs., 11:30am-midnight Fri., 10am-midnight Sat., 10am-11pm Sun., $16-24) asked the community to suggest names, and then held a vote on its favorites. The winner was "The Old McDonalds Farmhouse." Now known simply as The Farmhouse, this farm-to-table gastropub is popular for creative and comforting fare. The burgers are celebrated, but the starters, like the beef tartare with freshly made potato chips, are often standouts.

Right next door to the Zero Gravity Taproom, **The Great Northern** (716 Pine St., 802/489-5102, www.thegreatnorthernvt.com, 7am-9pm Mon.-Thurs., 7am-10pm Fri., 10am-10pm Sat., 10am-3pm Sun., $11-20) serves creative cuisine that pulls on local ingredients and global flavors. Brunch is a highlight here, with a lineup of hearty savory plates and stacks of pancakes topped with generous maple syrup.

Zabby & Elf's Stone Soup (211 College St., 802/862-7616, www.stonesoupvt.com, 7am-9pm Mon.-Fri., 9am-9pm Sat., $7-12), an intimate, sunlit café, serves hearty soups, salads, and excellent sandwiches on its own bread, along with an eclectic buffet with plenty of vegan and gluten-free options. The large front window is made for people-watching, and there's a decent wine and beer selection. When you add in one of the almond macaroons, you've got all the ingredients for a perfect afternoon.

★ **Hen of the Wood** (55 Cherry St., 802/540-0534, www.henofthewood.com, 4pm-midnight daily, $22-30) is the second location of Chef Eric Warnstedt's award-winning restaurant, and both turn out inspired, thoughtful food that draws diners from around the region. Chef Warnstedt blends a refined aesthetic with a serious throw-down of New England flavors. He places agriculture front and center, and the menu changes frequently, but oysters are a standout, as is the house-made charcuterie (Hen of the Wood offers a popular happy hour special of $1 oysters 4pm-5pm).

The food is as whimsical as the hosts are at ★ **Penny Cluse Cafe** (169 Cherry St., 802/651-8834, www.pennycluse.com,

6:45am-3pm Mon.-Fri., 8am-3pm Sat.-Sun., $6-12), named for the owner's childhood dog and decked out with an ever-rotating collection of posters and local art. Dig into gingerbread pancakes at breakfast, or hang out until lunch and order up Baja fish tacos and a Bloody Mary.

Butch + Babes (258 N. Winooski, 802/495-0716, www.butchandbabes.com, 5pm-9pm Sun.-Wed., 5pm-10pm Thurs.-Sat., brunch 9:30am-2pm Sun., $12-16) is a collaboration between a Chicago-raised restaurateur and a New England Culinary Institute-trained chef from Bangkok, with a pub-inspired menu that pulls from those sources willy-nilly. The results are surprisingly harmonious and refreshingly laid-back, in an atmosphere that channels the vitality and diversity of the Old North End neighborhood where it's located.

The folks at **American Flatbread** (115 St. Paul St., 802/861-2999, 11:30am-close daily, www.americanflatbread.com, pizzas $12-20) bought local before it was cool. This beloved pizza joint still serves thin-crust pizza topped with cheese, veggies, and meats from area farms. The specials are always worth a try, but the basic menu is filled with excellent options like the Punctuated Equilibrium, with olives, red peppers, and goat cheese. Wait times can get long on weekend nights, but if you can wedge yourself into the crowd at the bar, it's a convivial place to while away an evening.

On evenings that call for low light and house-made banana ketchup, atmospheric **¡Duino! (Duende)** (10 N. Winooski Ave., 802/660-9346, www.duinoduende.com, 4pm-midnight Sun.-Thurs., 4pm-1am Fri.-Sat., brunch 10am-4pm Sat.-Sun., $10-15) beckons. Its concept of "international street food" is interpreted loosely and with a taste for cultural mashups: Korean tacos with kimchi and coconut rice is a standout example. Duino is connected by an internal door to the **Radio Bean** bar, so check the music lineup before settling in for dinner.

Taiwanese chef Duval brings her fresh, local approach to cooking classic and regional Chinese dishes at this excellent restaurant, **A Single Pebble** (133 Bank St., 802/865-5200, www.asinglepebble.com, dim sum 11:30am-1:45pm Sun.; lunch 11:30am-1:45pm Mon.-Fri., 11:30am-3pm Sat.; dinner 5pm-late daily, $10-25), to ongoing acclaim. This is a favorite for special occasions and holidays, and the mock eel is legendary.

In the Old North End neighborhood, **Scout & Co.** (237 North Ave., www.scoutandcompanyvt.com, 7am-5pm Mon.-Fri., 8am-6pm Sat.-Sun.) serves excellent espresso alongside creative house-made ice cream in an airy space equipped with a browsing library of esoteric cookbooks.

ACCOMMODATIONS AND CAMPING

Under $100

A welcome exception to the lack of budget options downtown, the no-frills **Burlington Hostel** (50 Main St., 802/540-3043, www.theburlingtonhostel.com, May-Oct., $44-60 per person) is clean, safe, and walking distance from everything. Three of the eight-bed dorms are single gender, and several four-bed dorms are set aside for groups and families. There's Wi-Fi and a public computer, and weekly rates are available.

$150-250

In a sweet residential neighborhood overlooking the lake, **One of a Kind BNB** (53 Lakeview Terrace, 802/862-5576, www.oneofakindbnb.com, $175-275) is still walking distance from downtown. The owner, artist Maggie Sherman, has thoughtfully renovated the home, and the relaxed breakfasts are full of local options. There's no television or air-conditioning, but there is a friendly cat, an excellent garden, and a backyard tree swing.

The Willard Street Inn (349 S. Willard St., 802/651-8710, www.willardstreetinn.com, $150-265) is as beautiful inside as it is outside; the sprawling Victorian manse lays claim to impeccably decorated rooms. Each is filled with thoughtful details—a hand-carved antique chest here, a gas fireplace with antique mosaic tile there. Terry bathrobes and a full breakfast served in the marble-floored solarium come with every stay. Children over 12 are welcome.

Over $250

The newest, chicest digs in town are surely at ★ **Hotel Vermont** (41 Cherry St., 802/651-0080, www.hotelvt.com, from $275), an urban oasis that blends a rustic aesthetic with Scandinavian-influenced modern style. From woolly blankets to rough-hewn granite, seemingly everything you touch here is sourced regionally and with beautiful taste. The friendly staff includes a beer concierge and an outdoor activities director, and there are bicycles, snowshoes, and even an ice fishing shack available for guest use.

Made INN Vermont (204 S. Willard St., 802/399-2788, www.madeinnvermont.com, from $230) is perched on a hill above downtown, a bed-and-breakfast that's a temple of curated quirk with artistic flair and a contemporary sensibility. Owner Linda Wolf has filled her historical home with curiosities and comforts, and rooms are stocked with cans of Heady Topper, chalkboard walls, and views of the lake below. Atop the peaked roof and equipped with a telescope, the enclosed widow's walk is where you can watch stars and sails drift by. Breakfast is sumptuous. And well-behaved pets are welcome.

Camping

With a prime location by the lake and the bike path, **North Beach Campground** (60 Institute Rd., 802/862-0942, www.enjoyburlington.com, tent sites $37, hookups $41-45) is also just two miles north of downtown, making it an excellent base for exploring the city.

INFORMATION AND SERVICES

The **Lake Champlain Chamber of Commerce** (877/686-5253, www.vermont.org) runs an information booth (9am-9pm daily, mid May-mid Oct.) during summer months on Church Street at the corner of Bank Street. Also look for a copy of the **Blue Map** (www.bluemap.com), a detailed tourist map of downtown and the Greater Burlington Area.

For emergency and hospital services, head to **Fletcher Allen Hospital** (Colchester Ave., 802/847-0000), but **Vermont Children's Hospital** (111 Colchester Ave., 802/847-5437) is equipped to handle younger patients' needs. Fill prescriptions at **Lakeside Pharmacy** (242 Pearl St., 802/862-1491, www.lakerx.org, 8:30am-7pm Mon.-Fri., 9am-3pm Sat.) or **Rite Aid** (158 Cherry St., 802/862-1562, 8am-9pm Mon.-Fri., 9am-6pm Sat., 9am-5pm Sun.), which also offers faxing services and has a second location (1024 North Ave., 802/865-7822). A handful of banks are in the downtown blocks of Burlington's retail area along Church Street. In that same area, ATMs seem to be on every block. In nonmedical emergencies, contact the headquarters for the **Burlington Police Department** (1 North Ave., 802/658-2704).

Internet access is offered at almost all cafés and at the **Fletcher Free Library** (235 College St., 802/863-3403, www.fletcherfree.org, 10am-6pm Mon. and Thurs.-Sat., 10am-8pm Tues.-Wed., noon-6pm Sun.). **FedEx Office Center** (199 Main St., 802/658-2561, 6am-midnight Mon.-Fri., 8am-9pm Sat., 9am-9pm Sun.) also offers fax services and shipping services.

GETTING THERE AND AROUND

Burlington is on I-89, and flights from many major cities land at **Burlington International Airport** (BTV, 1200 Airport Dr., South Burlington, 802/865-7571, www.btv.aero), which is served by half a dozen airlines. Reservation desks for major rental car companies are available at the airport.

Amtrak (800/872-7245, www.amtrak.com) sells tickets for trains to Burlington, but the station is 20 minutes away in Essex Junction (29 Railroad Ave., Essex Junction). **Greyhound Bus Lines** (800/231-2222, www.greyhound.com) runs buses to Burlington from Montreal and Boston that arrive at the airport, and **Megabus** (www.us.megabus.com) has regular service to several cities around the Northeast,including Boston and New York City.

Green Mountain Transit (802/864-2282, www.ridegmt.org) has bus routes throughout Burlington and the surrounding area, including buses downtown from the airport and train station. Bus fare is $1.25. Taxi stands are also available at the airport and the train station; to call a cab from other locations, contact **Green Cab VT** (802/864-2424, www.greencabvt.com). Burlington is also served by **Uber** (www.uber.com) and **Lyft** (www.lyft.com), mobile-app services connecting riders with private drivers/vehicles, but coverage is less complete than in bigger cities.

Ferry

From New York, it's possible to get to Burlington via ferry from Port Kent. Several boats a day are run by **Lake Champlain Transportation** (King Street Dock, 802/864-9804, www.ferries.com, mid-June-late Sept., $8 adults, $3.10 children, children under 6 free, $30 vehicle and driver one-way), which take about an hour to cross the lake. The round-trip threading through the lake's islands is also one of the most economical ways to enjoy Champlain's scenery.

SHELBURNE

A sweet cluster of inns and shops, it would be easy to miss Shelburne entirely, but beyond the picturesque downtown is a gracious landscape of well-kept farms and vineyards. The sprawling Shelburne Farms is a grand example of a historic agricultural estate, with walking trails and barns, and Shelburne Museum is a trove of art and ephemera. And even without visiting the major sites, it's a pleasant place to spend a fall day picking apples and tasting wine.

Sights

★ SHELBURNE FARMS

Shelburne Farms (1611 Harbor Rd., 802/985-8686, www.shelburnefarms.org, 9am-5:30pm daily mid-May-Oct., $8 adults, $6 seniors, $5 children 3-17, children under 3 free) is a bewitching property that's a wonderful stop for a stroll through the wooded paths and rolling farm fields, past elegant barns with patinated copper roofs. The farm was the country retreat of the Webb family, and if you find it inspires hazy historical fantasies about roaming the estate with members of the American aristocracy and their glamorous guests, you're not the only one.

Shelburne Farms' head cheesemaker, Kate Turcotte

These days, though, you're more likely to bump into school kids than scions, as Shelburne Farms is now a nonprofit that works for sustainability in the food system. All income from the property goes to education and conservation efforts, including those from the inn and on-site restaurant. Sights change with the season: Spring means maple sugaring and lambing, and you can bundle up for horse-drawn sleigh rides in the winter. The on-site cheese-making operation is active year-round, however.

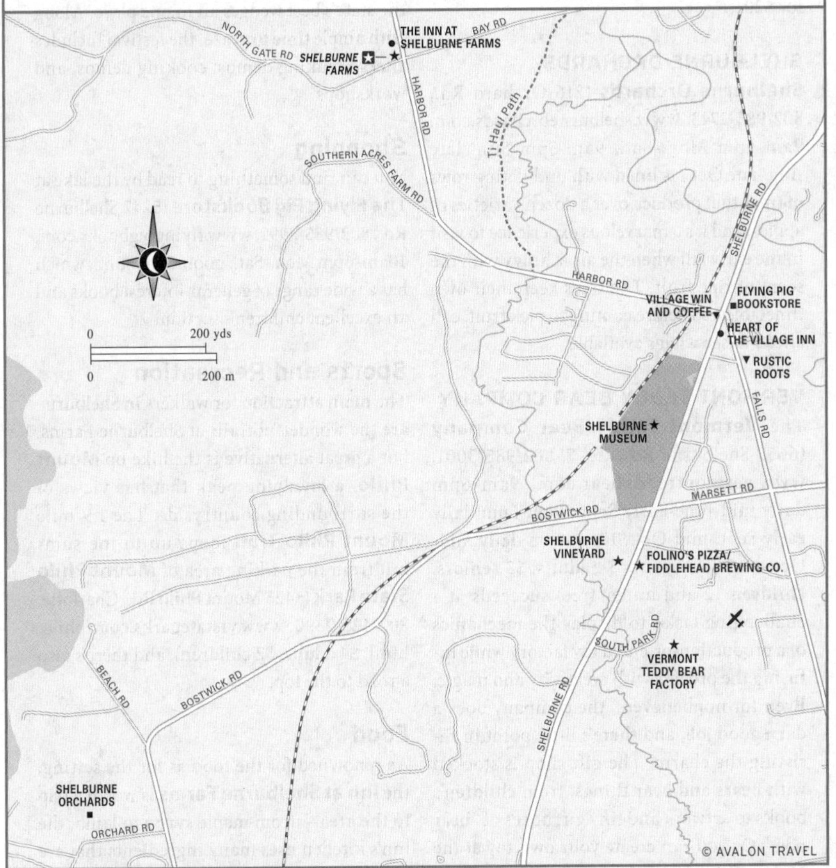

SHELBURNE MUSEUM

The **Shelburne Museum** (5555 Shelburne Rd., 802/985-3346, www.shelburnemuseum.org, 10am-5pm daily May-Dec., 10am-5pm Wed.-Sun. Jan.-Apr., $24 adults, $14 youth 13-17, $12 children 5-12, children under 5 free, $58 family day pass, Nov.-Apr. $10 adults, $5 youth 5-17, children under 5 free) is less a museum than a city-state founded by a hoarder with exquisite taste. Its 38 buildings are full of extraordinary art and historical gewgaws, not to mention a Lake Champlain steamship and its own covered bridge. This is the work of art collector Electra Havemeyer Webb, who relocated buildings from across the country to display her collection, opening the museum in 1947. The buildings are as intriguing as their contents, and include a 19th-century jailhouse, a Methodist meetinghouse, and a beautifully restored round barn, one of just two dozen built in Vermont. While the entire campus is open from May through October, access to limited exhibits is now possible from November through April.

Webb's own home was a Greek Revival mansion that now holds first-rate paintings by Cassatt, Degas, Monet, Corot, and Manet, including the first impressionist painting brought to America, a Monet painting of a drawbridge, which Webb purchased in Paris for $20.

SHELBURNE ORCHARDS

Shelburne Orchards (216 Orchard Rd., 802/985-2743, www.shelburneorchards.com, 9am-6pm Mon.-Sat., 9am-5pm Sun. late Aug.-late Oct.) is lined with undulating rows of trees that produce over a dozen varieties of apples, and it's a marvelous experience to visit in the early fall when the air is heavy with the scent of ripe fruit. The trees keep their own timetables, so before coming to pick fruit, call ahead to see what's available.

VERMONT TEDDY BEAR COMPANY

The **Vermont Teddy Bear Company** (6655 Shelburne Rd./Rte. 7, 802/985-3001, www.vermontteddybear.com, 9am-6pm daily mid-June-early Sept., 9am-5pm daily early Sept.-mid-Oct., 10am-2pm daily mid-Oct.-mid-June, tours $4 adults, $3 seniors, children 12 and under free) succeeds at a challenging task—to display the mechanics of a production-oriented toy factory while infusing the process with creativity and magic. Even for nonbelievers, the company does a darn good job, and there's little point in resisting the charm. The gift shop is stocked with bears and bear things, from children's books to artwork and tiny gift boxes of "bear poo." Or you can create your own toy at the Make a Friend for Life station, where you select a bear body, then fill it with fluff from a machine whose settings include Joy, Giggles, and Imagination.

Events

Past performers at the **Concerts on the Green** (5555 Shelburne Rd., 802/985-3346, www.shelburnemuseum.org) music series include Willie Nelson, Emmylou Harris, and Crosby, Stills, and Nash. Musicians play on select summer weekends on the grounds of the Shelburne Museum.

Shelburne Farms hosts the annual **Vermont Cheesemakers Festival** (1611 Harbor Rd., 802/986-8686, www.vtcheesefest.com, late July), where you can sample the state's best wedges all in one place. Along with ample time to graze, the festival includes cheese-making demos, cooking demos, and workshops.

Shopping

You can find something to read by the lake at **The Flying Pig Bookstore** (5247 Shelburne Rd., 802/985-3999, www.flyingpigbooks.com, 10am-6pm Mon.-Sat., noon-5pm Sun.), which has a wide range of general-interest books and an excellent children's section.

Sports and Recreation

The main attraction for walkers in Shelburne are the wonderful trails at Shelburne Farms, but a great alternative is the hike up **Mount Philo,** a low-lying peak that has views of the surrounding countryside. The 1.9-mile **Mount Philo Trail** loops up to the summit from the parking area of **Mount Philo State Park** (5425 Mount Philo Rd., Charlotte, 802/425-2390, www.vtstateparks.com/philo.html, $4 adults, $2 children), and there's also a road to the top.

Food

As renowned for the food as for the setting, the **Inn at Shelburne Farms** is worth a trip to the area— from maple syrup to lamb, the inn's kitchen uses many ingredients that are produced onsite, and the menu changes with the unfolding summer season. Dinners are spectacular, but stopping by for breakfast is a good way to experience the inn without splashing out for an expensive treat... and the inn's light-as-a-feather scones are a local legend. Shelburne has a handful of restaurants clustered in the downtown area, but it's worth heading to the southern edge of town to find **Folino's Pizza** (6305 Shelburne Rd., 802/881-8822, www.folinopizza.com, noon-9pm daily, $10-18), which serves crisp, wood-fired pizza with views of the vineyard next door. Try the rhapsody-inspiring flatbread with bacon, scallops, and lemon zest.

Folino's is strictly BYO, but it's got a freezer full of pint glasses and shares a building with **Fiddlehead Brewing** (802/399-2994, www.fiddleheadbrewing.com, noon-9pm Sun.-Fri., 11am-9pm Sat.), which offers free tastings of its beers on tap as well as growler and growlette fills.

Right across the street is **Shelburne Vineyard** (6308 Shelburne Rd., 802/982-8222, www.shelburnevinyard.com, 11am-6pm daily May-Oct., 11am-5pm daily Nov.-Apr.), where the $7 tastings include a souvenir wineglass and a taste of 8-10 wines. Don't miss the award-winning Marquette Reserve.

In the village center, **Rustic Roots** (195 Falls Rd., 802/985-9511, www.rusticrootsvt.com, brunch 9am-3pm Wed.-Sun., dinner 6pm-7:30pm Fri.-Sat., $14-25) serves thoughtful food with European flair in a restored home, using many local ingredients. For a coffee with something sweet, **Village Wine and Coffee** (5288 Shelburne Rd., 802/985-8922, www.villagewineandcoffee.com, 7am-6pm Mon.-Sat., 8:30am-4pm Sun.) is a favorite stop by the town's main intersection.

Accommodations

The gorgeously preserved ★ **Inn at Shelburne Farms** (1611 Harbor Rd., 802/985-8498, www.shelburnefarms.org, May-Oct., $160-525) is situated right on the lake and may have the best sunset views in the Champlain Valley. The inn's restaurant prepares beautiful meals with ingredients grown organically on-site.

Tucked into a sweet Victorian in the center of town, **Heart of the Village Inn** (5347 Shelburne Rd., 802/985-9060, www.heartofthevillage.com, $220-400) charms with thoughtful touches like locally made chocolates. The homemade breakfasts are sumptuous, with hot and cold options available daily.

Information and Services

The **Shelburne Museum** (5555 Shelburne Rd., 802/985-3346, www.shelburnemuseum.org, 10am-5pm daily May-Dec., 10am-5pm Wed.-Sun. Jan.-Apr.) has a visitor information center stocked with maps and brochures; no admission fee is required.

A **Rite Aid Pharmacy** (30 Shelburne Shopping Park, 802/985-2610, 9am-6pm Mon.-Sat. for both store and pharmacy) is located in the center of downtown. In an emergency, contact the **Shelburne Police** (5420 Shelburne Rd., 802/985-8051).

Getting There and Around

Shelburne is on Route 7, a two-lane highway that runs parallel to Lake Champlain. **Green Mountain Transit** (802/864-2282, www.ridegmt.org) has frequent bus service between Burlington and Shelburne Monday-Saturday, with stops at the Shelburne Museum and Vermont Teddy Bear Company.

New Hampshire Seacoast and Lakes Region

A perfect sliver of coast leads to a thick, inland forest dotted with lakes, a varied region with deep history, a fascinating natural world, and a laid-back vacation culture.

Craggy peaks and fierce politics are the face New Hampshire turns toward the world, so the lakes and seacoast can come as a bit of a surprise.

And with just 18 miles of coastline, there's a lot to see and do by the water. Portsmouth is a stately blend of colonial history and Yankee grit, equally appealing for a trip through New England history as for an afternoon of "deck punch" and sunshine by the Piscataqua River, with the town's active fishing fleet bobbing at your feet.

All the pomp and tradition are offset by the hubbub of nearby Hampton Beach, where Portsmouth's brick architecture gives way to an oceanside strip scented with fried dough and teenage hormones.

Leave the coast behind, and the landscape closes into a rolling forest, broken by some of New Hampshire's endless lakes—the state claims nearly 1,000. Ranging from thumbprint ponds to vast bodies of water, they're pure nostalgia, lined with ice cream shops, lakeside cottages, penny arcades, and old-fashioned bandstands.

PLANNING YOUR TIME

Unless you're a die-hard history buff, two days is enough to see Portsmouth's main sites, though it's worth adding in a third if you'd like to explore the nearby Isles of Shoals. Since Hampton Beach is a love-it-or-hate-it sort of destination, opt for a couple of wild days or skip it altogether. And while there's plenty of lakes for a lifetime of puddle jumping, a few days will suffice for most, time enough to swim, take in a drive-in movie, and listen to the sounds of loons or power boats (depending on your lake of choice).

Previous: Hampton Beach; Lake Wentworth. **Above:** lobsters in Portsmouth.

Look for ★ to find recommended sights, activities, dining, and lodging.

Highlights

★ **Strawbery Banke Museum:** A whole neighborhood of historic homes brings colonial-era America to life with costumed docents and fascinating stories (page 340).

★ **Cruising the Isles of Shoals:** Shrouded in mist and a bit of historic mayhem, this cluster of rocky islands has long drawn pirates, dreamers, and outcasts (page 342).

★ **Lake Winnipesaukee Cruises:** People come from all over to take in the breathtaking views of Lake Winni aboard impressive vessels (page 349).

★ **Squam Lakes Natural Science Center:** Among New England's best places to learn about the natural world, families can meet mountain lions, bears, and more at this rambling outdoor nature center (page 356).

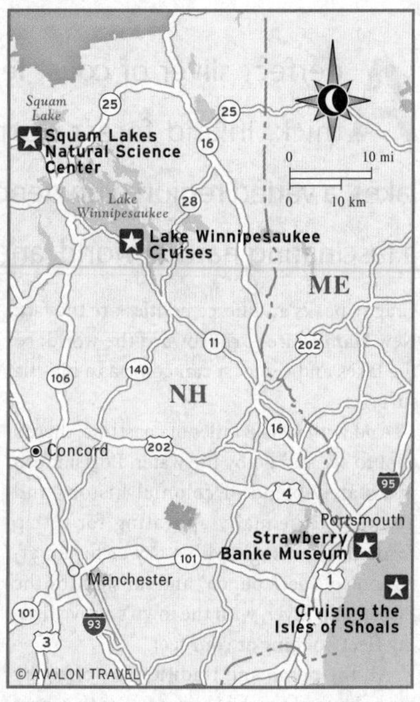

New Hampshire Seacoast and Lakes Region

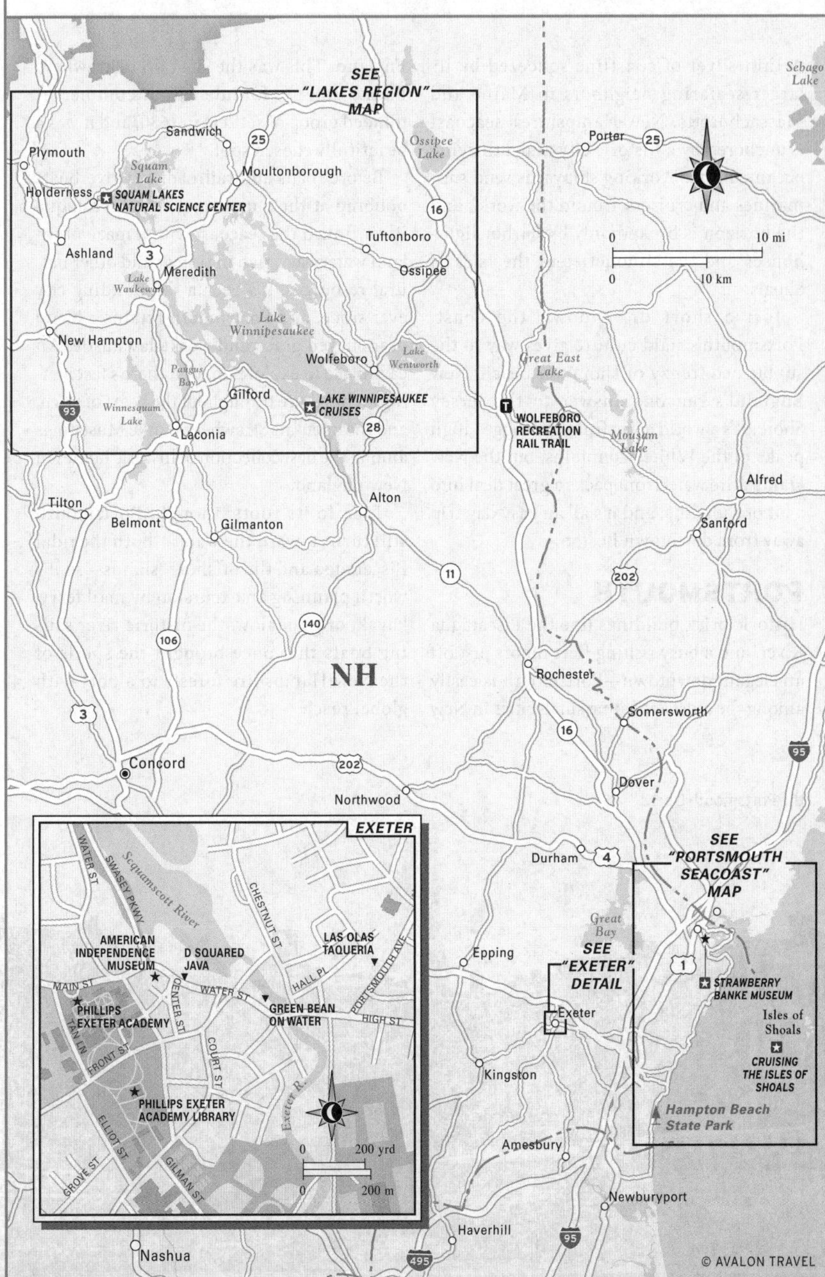

Portsmouth and the Seacoast

A thin sliver of coastline squeezed by its larger seafaring neighbors in Maine and Massachusetts, New Hampshire's seacoast is anchored by a historic city and a thriving ocean culture. Working shipyards send submarines and cruisers around the world, and the horizon is broken only by harbor lighthouses and the silhouettes of the Isles of Shoals.

Just a short drive down the coast, Portsmouth's staid culture gives way to the sunburned frenzy of Hampton Beach, New England's raucous answer to the Jersey Shore. It's a world away from the rugged high peaks of the White Mountains, but the New Hampshire waterfront packs a great deal into a bit of shoreline, and it's all an easy day trip away from downtown Boston.

PORTSMOUTH

Historic brick buildings line the Piscataqua River, and a busy fishing fleet moors just off an elegant downtown—Portsmouth is easily among the most appealing small cities in New England. This was the site of the Strawbery Banke colony, founded by a commerce-minded group of settlers in 1630, and it was a beautifully chosen spot.

Before roads and railroads left riverboats bobbing at their moorings, the Piscataqua River linked the seacoast with a maze of inland waterways, rich in timber and other natural resources. It's been a shipbuilding city ever since, and Portsmouth retains a blend of moneyed grace and workaday hustle. An easy place to explore on foot, there's fascinating architecture throughout the heart of town, and the open-air Strawbery Banke Museum is among the best collection of historic homes in New England.

True to its roots, though, Portsmouth still turns toward the water—both the tidal Piscataqua and the offshore islands—so it's worth planning an excursion by mail ferry, kayak, or gundalow, the historic river sailing boats that once brought the spoils of the New Hampshire forests to a port with global reach.

the Portsmouth Decks

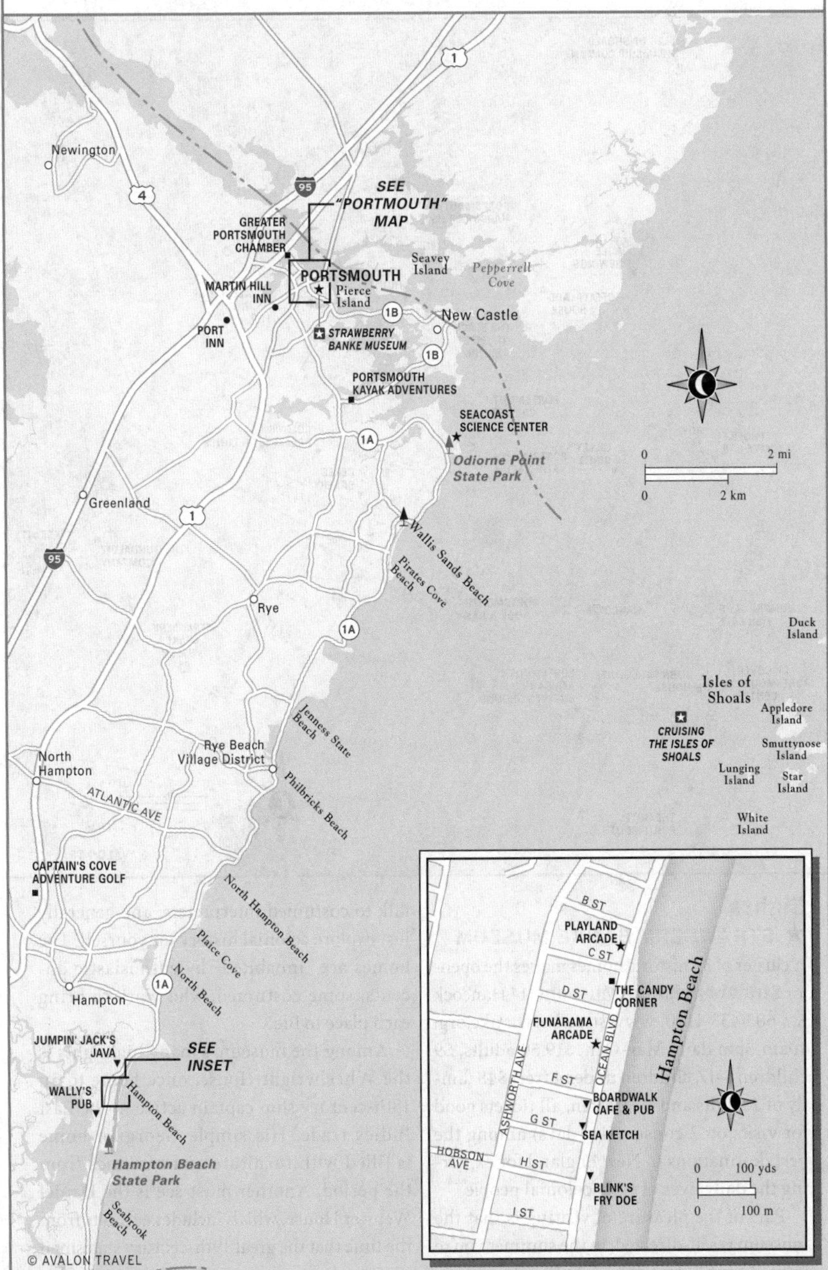
Portsmouth Seacoast
Newington
SEE "PORTSMOUTH" MAP
GREATER PORTSMOUTH CHAMBER
PORTSMOUTH
Pierce Island
MARTIN HILL INN
PORT INN
Seavey Island
Pepperrell Cove
New Castle
STRAWBERRY BANKE MUSEUM
PORTSMOUTH KAYAK ADVENTURES
SEACOAST SCIENCE CENTER
Odiorne Point State Park
0
2 mi
0
2 km
Greenland
Wallis Sands Beach
Pirates Cove Beach
Rye
Duck Island
Isles of Shoals
Appledore Island
CRUISING THE ISLES OF SHOALS
Smuttynose Island
Lunging Island
Star Island
White Island
Jenness State Beach
Rye Beach Village District
North Hampton
ATLANTIC AVE
Philbricks Beach
CAPTAIN'S COVE ADVENTURE GOLF
North Hampton Beach
Plaice Cove
North Beach
Hampton
JUMPIN' JACK'S JAVA
SEE INSET
WALLY'S PUB
Hampton Beach
Hampton Beach State Park
Seabrook Beach
© AVALON TRAVEL
B ST
PLAYLAND ARCADE
C ST
THE CANDY CORNER
D ST
FUNARAMA ARCADE
OCEAN BLVD
ASHWORTH AVE
F ST
BOARDWALK CAFE & PUB
G ST
SEA KETCH
HOBSON AVE
H ST
BLINK'S FRY DOE
I ST
0
100 yds
0
100 m

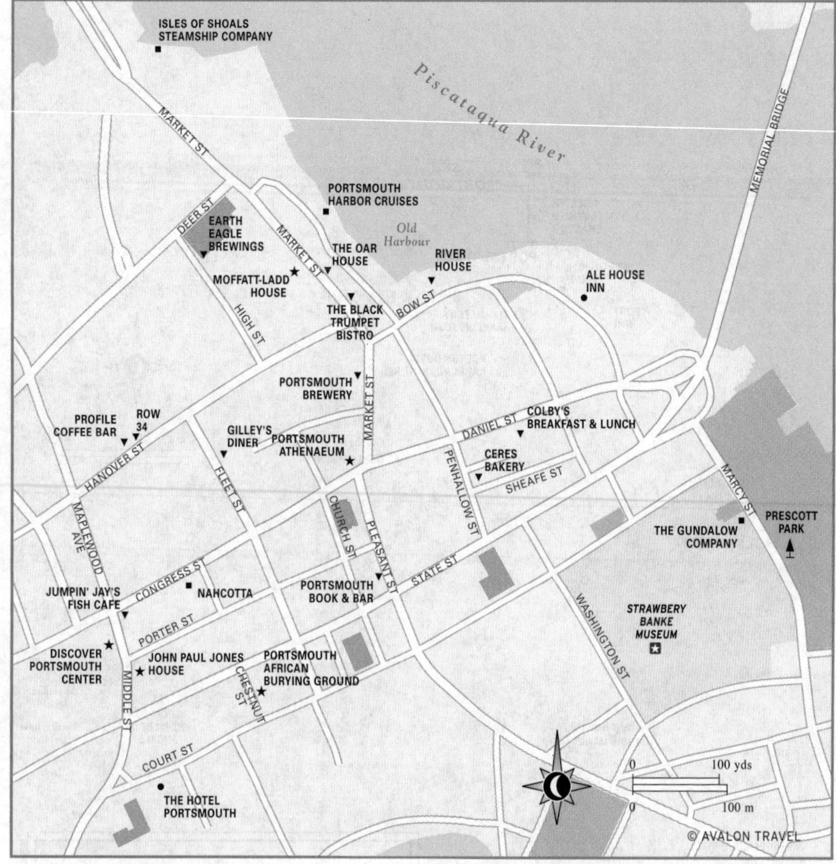

Sights

★ STRAWBERY BANKE MUSEUM

A cluster of 32 historic homes makes the open-air **Strawbery Banke Museum** (14 Hancock St., 603/433-1100, www.strawberybanke.org, 10am-5pm daily May-Oct., $19.50 adults, $9 children 5-17, children under 4 free, $48 family of 2 adults and 2 children, all tickets good for visits on 2 consecutive days) among the best destinations in New England for exploring the daily lives of early colonial people.

Part of the pleasure of visiting is that the museum is self-directed; in the summer you're invited to wander around, poke into houses, talk to costumed interpreters, and generally just explore colonial history for yourself. The homes are "inhabited" by enthusiastic docents, some costumed, who work to bring each place to life.

Among the museum's many highlights is the Wheelwright House, once home to an 18th-century ship captain active in the East Indies trade. His simple Georgian home is filled with furniture and ceramics from the period. Another must-see is the Daniel Webster House, which includes exhibits from the time that the great 19th-century statesmen spent in Portsmouth in the early part of his career. And if you are interested in seeing the actual items unearthed in the restoration of all the homes in the museum, stop by the **Jones Center,** which displays the findings from archaeological work on the neighborhood.

PORTSMOUTH HARBOR TRAIL

Strawbery Banke is just the beginning of historic properties on view in the city; if house museums are your thing, you could easily spend a week marveling at the variety and quality of those preserved here. The **Greater Portsmouth Chamber of Commerce** (500 Market St., 603/610-5510, www.goportsmouthnh.com) has linked up some of the highlights on the Harbor Trail, a walking path that loops through the historic downtown—pick up a map at the chamber of commerce office, or at the information booth on Market Square.

While it's easy enough to explore on your own, the **walking tours** offered by the **Portsmouth Historical Society** (10 Middle St., 603/436-8433, www.portsmouthhistory.org, $15) are very worthwhile. Led by knowledgeable, local docents, the tours offer broad context for the sites along the way. If you're planning to visit historic homes, it's a good introduction before exploring each place. Tours depart from the Portsmouth Historical Society, which maintains rotating exhibits on local history.

One fascinating stop on the Harbor Trail is the **Portsmouth Athenaeum** (9 Market Sq., 603/431-2538, www.portsmouthathenaeum.org, 1pm-4pm Tues. and Thurs., 10am-4pm Sat., free), one of New England's most fascinating private libraries, with a collection that illustrates the founders' broad-minded approach to documenting history. Treasures include the hatchet from the infamous Smuttynose murders and a purported whale eyeball that's rumored to be a whale testicle, but the building itself is gorgeous.

And if you're visiting just one historic house in the city, make it the **Moffatt-Ladd House** (154 Market St., 603/436-8221, www.moffattladd.org, 11am-5pm Mon.-Sat., 1pm-5pm Sun. June-mid-Oct., $8 adults, $2.50 children), built by a wealthy colonial merchant. The Georgian-style mansion is carefully restored, with wallpaper, paint, and decor much like those used by generations of inhabitants. And if you didn't know that there was a National Register of Historic Trees, the docents will fill you in—the enormous horse chestnut tree in front of the house was planted in 1776 by a signer of the Declaration of Independence.

A pleasant place to end the walk is at the riverside **Prescott Park** (105 Marcy St., www.prescottpark.org), which overflows with perennial blooms throughout the summer months. It's also the location for many free, outdoor movies, concerts, and other events—you can even go on the website to reserve blanket space right in front of the stage.

PORTSMOUTH BLACK HERITAGE TRAIL

In recent years, Portsmouth has worked to acknowledge the history of enslaved people who lived and worked in the city through colonial times and beyond. Focusing on their stories, the **Portsmouth Black Heritage Trail** (www.blackheritagetrailnh.org) visits taverns, homes, and two burial grounds, including the moving **Portsmouth African Burying Ground** (1 Junkins Ave., 603/610-7226, www.africanburyinggroundnh.org), which was rediscovered in 2003. The site is now inscribed with words from the 1799 Freedom Petition that a group of enslaved Africans submitted to the New Hampshire legislature, an eloquent document requesting that "we may regain our liberty and be rank'd in the class of free agents, and that the name of SLAVE be no more in a land gloriously contending for the sweets of freedom." A self-guided tour is available from the website, and the Portsmouth Historical Society also leads walking tours of the Black Heritage Trail.

SEACOAST SCIENCE CENTER

Kids can get their hands salty at the coastal **Seacoast Science Center** (570 Ocean Blvd.,

Rye, 603/436-8043, www.seacoastscience-center.org, 10am-5pm daily, $13 adults, $8 seniors and military, $5 children 3-12, children under 3 free), with indoor exhibits and outdoor programs that take advantage of the rocky tide pools that are just outside. Indoor tanks and touch pools explore the wildlife of the Gulf of Maine, as well as the researchers who work with marine wildlife. One advantage of the Seacoast Science Center's long-established marine rescue program is that when local fishermen and lobstermen find odd creatures—like the rare blue, yellow, or calico lobsters—they will often land on public display in one of the center's rotating tanks, so there's usually something remarkable for even repeat visitors. Memorial Day-Columbus Day, visitors in cars must also pay admission to **Odiorne State Park** (603/436-7406, www.nhstateparks.org, $4 adults, $2 children), where the science center is located.

★ ISLES OF SHOALS

A haven for fishermen, pirates, artists, and Unitarians, the nine rocky islands scattered off Portsmouth Harbor are thick with legend. This was a colonial-era escape from the Puritan strictures of the mainland, a prime spot for buried pirate treasure, and, they say, where Blackbeard honeymooned with his final bride. The 19th-century poet Celia Thaxter was raised in the Isles of Shoals, and later wrote of the islands that "there is a strange charm about them, an indescribable influence in their atmosphere, hardly to be explained, but universally acknowledged."

But the islands' most famous event is of the true crime genre—in 1873 two sisters were brutally murdered by an axe-wielding itinerant fisherman on the island of Smuttynose. A third woman managed to elude the killer and bring him to justice, but the story continues to haunt the area, inspiring florid books and movies ever since (for the best account, look up Celia Thaxter's contemporary piece in *The Atlantic*).

Tours of the islands with the **Isles of Shoals Steamship Company** (315 Market St., Portsmouth, 603/431-5500, www.islesofshoals.com, several tours daily, 2.5-4.5-hour cruises, $28-35 adults, $25-35 seniors, $18-25 children) milk all of the mist-enshrouded legends, and some include time to explore Star Island. You're free to wander off, but guided tours cover the stories, from the 1614 arrival of Captain John Smith to a lineup of local ghosts.

Entertainment and Events

There's often live music at the laid-back **Portsmouth Book & Bar** (40 Pleasant St., 603/427-9197, www.bookandbar.com, 10am-10pm Sun.-Thurs., 9am-midnight Fri.-Sat.), a bookstore with comfortable seats, strong coffee, and a solid menu of local beers and wine. In a cavernous space downtown, **The Portsmouth Brewery** (56 Market St., 603/431-1115, www.portsmouthbrewery.com, 11:30am-12:25am daily) has held court for years with a range of well-executed beers that range from traditional to highly creative. There's a full menu and bar snacks, and there's usually food specials during the 5pm-7pm Mon.-Fri. happy hour. Smaller and infinitely funkier, **Earth Eagle Brewings** (165 High St., 603/502-2244, www.eartheaglebrewings.com, 11:30am-10pm Sun.-Thurs., 11:30am-midnight Fri.-Sat.) specializes in gruits, beers that use herbs to provide the bitter background usually supplied by hops. An outdoor patio and live music on weekends make this a friendly, offbeat place to while away the night.

In the summer months, though, evenings in Portsmouth start at **The Decks,** a series of patios that jut out above the Piscataqua River, a great spot for catching the breeze and lovely sunset views. Most of the restaurants near the junction of Bow Street and Ceres Street have great decks, and many have their own version of "deck punch," usually a tropically inspired blend of rum and something sweet. One favorite is **The River House** (53 Bow St., 603/431-2600, www.riverhouse53bow.com, 11am-9pm daily), which also has a very respectable seafood chowder. Just around the corner, **The Oar House** (55 Ceres St., 603/436-4025, www.portsmouthoarhouse.

com, 11:30am-9pm Mon.-Fri., 11:30am-10pm Sat., 10am-3pm Sun.) commands equally great views, with live music on Friday and Saturday nights. The website **Seacoast Happy Hours** (www.seacoasthappyhours.com) is a great resource for daily drinks and food specials.

On the first Friday of every month, the local art association sponsors a **Gallery Walk** (www.artroundtown.org), in which galleries around downtown break out wine and cheese for simultaneous openings. Additionally, Strawbery Banke Museum sponsors several different theme weekends throughout the year, including a summer Maritime Weekend, Halloween ghost tours, and the popular **Candlelight Stroll** (603/433-1100, www.strawberybanke.org, Dec.), in which the streets of the museum are filled with hundreds of lit candles, and interpreters lead visitors in traditional holiday festivities.

Shopping

Downtown Portsmouth is packed with shops, with many clustered around Market Square, then following Market Street to the water. Just off that route is the stylish gallery-boutique **Nahcotta** (110 Congress St., 603/433-1705, www.nahcotta.com, 10am-6pm Mon.-Sat., 11am-5pm Sun.), which features a great deal of work by New England artists. When it comes to shopping in Portsmouth, visitors are divided between the browsable shops in the historic center and the outlet stores just across the Piscataqua River in Kittery.

Sports and Recreation

HIKING AND BIKING

Following the coast through a former military installation, **Odiorne State Park** (570 Ocean Blvd., Rye, 603/436-7406, www.nhstateparks.org, $4 adults, $2 children) has a network of walking trails that weave between salt marsh, beaches, and rocky outcroppings. On the western side of the park, there's a breakwater and pleasant sandy beach looking across the harbor, while the northeastern extreme has a picnic area surrounded by water.

In 2017, Portsmouth launched a **city bike program** (202/999-3924, bike.zagster.com/portsmouthnh) with six bike stations in the downtown area. To access the bikes, users download a free app, then pay a small membership fee. Bikes are free for up to two hours, then $3 per hour for the rest of the day. They're great for cruising around town, and there are some good, longer rides from Portsmouth—one favorite is the New Castle Loop, an eight-mile route that follows Route 1B from downtown across a series of linked islands, the largest being New Castle.

BOATING

The Piscataqua River once bristled with sails, as merchants brought lumber and other goods between the seaport and inland communities. Many of the boats were cargo barges with a shallow draft, and a mast that could be lowered to slide under bridges. That tradition lives on at **The Gundalow Company** (60 Marcy St., 603/433-9505, www.gundalow.org, $25-35), whose *Piscataqua* is a floating lesson in local sailing heritage. Trips range from history sails along the Portsmouth waterfront to longer, upriver sails, and some scheduled trips include free admission for children.

Less expensive and with multiple departures each day through the summer, **Portsmouth Harbor Cruises** (64 Ceres St., 800/776-0915, www.portsmouthharbor.com, $15-25 adults, $13-22 seniors, $11-18 children) has fully narrated trips aboard the comfortable *Heritage*, including history cruises, upriver cruises, and sunset tours that catch the city at its most enchanting.

You can get out on the water in decidedly smaller craft through **Portsmouth Kayak Adventures** (185 Wentworth Rd., 603/559-1000, www.portsmouthkayak.com, 2- to 3-hour guided tours $45-75, kayak rentals from $45), which leads guided trips around the Piscataqua River estuaries as well as out on the open ocean of Portsmouth Harbor.

BEACHES

Ten minutes outside of Portsmouth, **New Castle Beach** (301 Wentworth Rd., New

Castle, admission $4) has sand for lounging and picnic tables, as well as great views of Portsmouth Harbor boat traffic and a pair of pretty lighthouses. Restrooms are available through the summer months, and a small playground is on-site.

With somewhat warmer water and more facilities, **Wallis Sands State Beach** (1050 Ocean Blvd., Rye, 603/436-6404, www.nhstateparks.org, parking $15) is a favorite with families. A long stretch of sand looks out toward the Isles of Shoals, a lifeguard is on duty 10am-5pm, and the park is stocked with snack bars, showers, and a bathhouse. Low tide reveals a network of tidepools among beds of glistening seaweed.

Food

In a sleekly hip space downtown, ★ **Row 34** (5 Portwalk Pl., 603/319-5011, www.row34nh.com, 11:30am-10pm Mon.-Thurs., 11:30am-11pm Fri.-Sat., 10:30am-10pm Sun., $15-35) is a shrine to the raw bar, with piles of glistening ice mounded under fresh oysters, clams, and shrimp. Some of the oysters come from the restaurant's own farm in Duxbury, Massachusetts, and the servers are uncommonly knowledgeable about the subtleties of oyster provenance and flavor. It's fascinating to try a lineup of oysters from neighboring farms, as the bivalves vary dramatically, but the regular menu is solid as well, with classic seafood preparations and a few non-maritime options. Every day until 5pm, $1 oysters are on special.

Another favorite for seafood is **Jumpin' Jay's Fish Café** (150 Congress St., 603/766-3474, www.jumpinjays.com, 5pm-9pm Sun.-Thurs., 5pm-10pm Fri.-Sat., $20-30), whose careful preparations belie the casual atmosphere. The crab cakes are superb, and the haddock piccata is something of a legend around town, with a bright lemon, caper, and white wine sauce served over mashed potatoes.

A sip of Portland (Oregon) in the middle of Portsmouth, **Profile Coffee Bar** (15 Portwalk Pl., 603/501-1801, www.profilecoffeebar.com, 6:30am-6pm daily, $2-9) serves the best cups in town. Cold brew nitro, espresso, and pour overs are made with Counter Culture coffee beans, and the small menu of breakfast sandwiches, soups, and salads is excellent. If you're looking for a place to settle in with a laptop, this is the spot.

Not a gourmet destination, per se, **Gilley's Diner** (175 Fleet St., 603/431-6343, www.gilleyspmlunch.com, 11am-2am daily, $2-6) is all about steamed hot dogs and nostalgia. The tiny diner is in a lunch cart built by the Worcester Lunch Car Co., the original 1940 structure banged onto a trailer-like extension. Order your dog "with everything" and it will come buried in a delightfully sloppy pile of mustard, relish, onions, mayonnaise, ketchup, and pickles.

For a romantic night out, it's hard to beat the **Black Trumpet Bistro** (29 Ceres St., 603/431-0887, www.blacktrumpetbistro.com, 5pm-9:30pm Sun.-Thurs., 5pm-10pm Fri.-Sat., $19-35), which has been a leader in bringing sustainable seafood to New England restaurants. It's in an atmospheric building by the waterfront that's all brick and polished wood, while the menu brings broad influences to bear on local fish and meat. Seafood paella is very well done here, and the hangar steak wins raves.

A bright, casual eatery with very hearty servings, **Colby Breakfast & Lunch** (105 Daniel St., 603/436-3033, 7am-2pm daily, $5-12) is cozy and compact. You might have to wait for a table on busy mornings, but piles of blueberry pancakes, generously sauced huevos rancheros, and classic sandwiches make it worth your while.

With a bakery case full of goodies and a menu of sandwiches, soups, and wraps, **Ceres Bakery** (51 Penhallow St., 603/436-6518, www.ceresbakery.com, 7am-5pm Mon.-Sat., 7am-4pm Sun., $2-9) is a long-time local favorite with colorful charm. Sometimes the seating fills up, but the bakery is a short walk away from Prescott Park, making this an excellent spot to pick up picnic fare on a sunny day.

Accommodations

Hotels and inns in central Portsmouth tend to be quite expensive, especially those that are walking distance from downtown sights. Airbnb is a good alternative here, and many owners of historic homes rent out a room or two during high season. Finding a place to park on the street, however, can be a challenge, so it's worth ensuring that your rental has a spot for guests. A cluster of chain hotels by the interstate is another option for travelers on a budget.

$150-250

Outside of the crush of the center, **Port Inn** (505 Rte. 1 Bypass, 855/849-1513, www.portinnportsmouth.com, $159-259) is a good option for families who don't lean toward inns—motel-style rooms are spacious, and the inn is equipped with a heated, outdoor pool. The dog-friendly property has a self-serve breakfast bar that's a solid step above the average motel options, with local granola, cappuccinos, and Belgian waffles.

A 0.5 mile stroll from downtown sights, ★ **Martin Hill Inn** (404 Islington St., 603/436-2287, www.martinhillinn.com, $145-220) is a pair of historic homes surrounded by pretty gardens. Decor leans toward B&B-traditional, with judicious flounces, throw pillows, and the occasional four-poster bed, but rooms are comfortable and updated, each with private bath and flat-screen television. The innkeepers serve a hearty, two-course breakfast between 8:30 and 9:30 in the morning, and set out treats like freshly baked cookies, chocolates, and a decanter of sherry, along with fixings for tea and coffee.

The stylish **Ale House Inn** (121 Bow St., 603/431-7760, www.alehouseinn.com, $129-600) is built into a former brewery warehouse that's over a century old, and it has the feel of a beautifully renovated loft (as well as the very recognizable put-a-bird-on-it aesthetic of the Lark Hotel chain). Amenities include use of the hotel's bicycles, parking, air-conditioning, and in-room iPads, and the downtown location is unbeatable. The same hotel group owns **The Hotel Portsmouth** (40 Court St., 603/433-1200, www.thehotelportsmouth.com, $169-500), which combines the same amenities and design focus with an inn-like feel (rates at this property also include breakfast).

Information and Services

For more information on the city, contact the **Greater Portsmouth Chamber of Commerce** (500 Market St., 603/610-5510, 9am-5pm Mon.-Fri., 10am-5pm Sat.-Sun. mid May-mid Oct.; 9am-5pm Mon.-Fri. mid Oct.-mid May, www.goportsmouthnh.com) which also runs an information booth (10am-5pm daily mid May-mid Oct.) on the main corner of Market Square. Portsmouth offers free Wi-Fi Internet access throughout the downtown Market Square area.

Getting There

Portsmouth is located off I-95, on the northern border of the New Hampshire seacoast. **C & J Bus** (800/258-7111, www.ridecj.com) has service between Portsmouth and **Boston** (from 1 hr., 20 min., one-way ticket $17) and **New York City** (5 hrs., one-way ticket $79).

HAMPTON BEACH

Fried clams, penny arcades, sunburns, and mini golf—Hampton Beach is a rowdy and ramshackle beach town with the volume cranked to 11. Go for the people-watching or just dive into the honky-tonk fun, drifting up and down the main drag alongside a crowd of slow-cruising teenagers checking out each other's tans.

And when you've got enough sun, hit the arcades for some skee-ball, pinball, and vintage video games, then get your fortune told by a beachfront psychic.

Sights

HAMPTON BEACH STATE PARK

Miles of sandy beach are the starring attraction at **Hampton Beach State Park** (Ocean Blvd., 603/926-8990, www.nhstateparks.org), and on sunny days, the waterfront fills with families. Restroom facilities are dotted along the street side of the beach, and there's a huge parking lot on the south end of the beach that is a good alternative to searching for street parking (160 Ocean Blvd., 603/227-8700, all-day parking $15).

PENNY ARCADES

There used to be far more, but the Hampton Beach arcade scene has been reduced to two holdouts. The 1905 **Funarama Arcade** (169 Ocean Blvd., 603/926-2381, 10am-11pm daily) is the largest arcade in Hampton Beach, with a good mix of newer games and nostalgic favorites. A bit grimy and neglected, this is the land of Skee-Ball and PAC-MAN, and includes some one-off treasures like a vintage, coin-operated puppet show. Pinball aficionados should opt for **Playland Arcade** (211 Ocean Blvd., 603/926-3831, 10am-11pm daily), which has a huge collection of games and a classic selection of chintzy prizes.

MINI-GOLF

Shipwrecks, waterfalls, and a full 18 holes makes **Captain's Cove Adventure Golf** (814 Lafayette Rd., 603/926-5011, www.smallgolf.com, 10am-10pm daily in season) a favorite with the mini-golf crowd, and there's a concession stand that doles out mammoth servings of ice cream (there's often golfing discounts available online).

Entertainment and Events

Back in the 1930s, the historic **Hampton Beach Casino Ballroom** (169 Ocean Blvd., 603/929-4100, www.casinoballroom.com) featured big-band headliners from Count Basie to Duke Ellington. It's been a bit of a downhill journey, but the historic 2,000-seat ballroom is still a great place to see a show. Locals play live at **Wally's Pub** (144 Ashworth Ave., 603/926-6954, www.wallyspubnh.com), where you'll never have difficulty securing a seat or a cold beer. Some nights can get a little raucous (the tail end of Monday night beer pong tournaments, for example).

The strip is home to countless events over the course of the summer. Perhaps the most eagerly anticipated is the **Master Sand Sculpting Competition** (603/929-6301, www.greggrady.com, late June), in which 250 tons of sand are delivered to the beach for sculptors to turn into castles, mermaids, and pop stars.

Shopping

There are souvenir shops up and down Ocean Boulevard, but the classic Hampton Beach

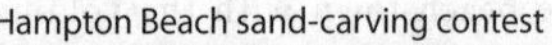
Hampton Beach sand-carving contest

souvenir would be a pile of saltwater taffy and caramel corn from **The Candy Corner** (197 Ocean Blvd., 603/926-1740, 9am-11pm daily), which also does a brisk trade in fudge of all varieties.

Food

Beachgoers line up for great slabs of golden fried dough from **Blinky's Fry Doe** (191 Ocean Blvd., 603/926-8933, 9am-1am daily, $2-9), a longtime institution across the street from the beach. The standard offering comes showered with powdered sugar and cinnamon, but there's a laundry list of options, including several savory varieties.

Find coffee and a menu of light breakfast items at **Jumpin' Jack's Java** (333 Ocean Blvd., 603/758-1559, www.jumpinjacksjava.com, 5am-6pm Mon.-Sat., 6am-3pm Sun., $2-8), which also has decent non-fried takeout options that are convenient for ocean-side picnics.

A big, shady porch is the draw at **Boardwalk Café and Pub** (139 Ocean Blvd., 603/929-7400, www.boardwalkcafe.net, 11am-late daily, $10-32), whose huge menu has something for everyone. This is a prime place to stake out for watching the crowd, and there are some healthy options to offset the fried seafood mainstays.

Slightly more sedate, **Sea Ketch** (127 Ocean Blvd., 603/926-0324, www.seaketch.com, 7:15am-11:45pm daily, $11-25) serves classic surf and turf dinners and straight-from-the-market seafood on outdoor porches and a rooftop deck.

Information

The **Hampton Area Chamber of Commerce** (603/926-8717, www.hamptonchamber.com) runs a visitors information center located at the Seashell (180 Ocean Blvd.). More information is available from the **Hampton Village District** (22 C St., 603/926-8717, www.hamptonbeach.org).

Getting There and Around

Ocean Boulevard is the heart of Hampton Beach, but the center of town can get terribly snarled with traffic and crowds. Parking is a major cottage industry here, with small lots on every street that range $5-15 for the day, depending on proximity to the strip. There's no direct public transit from Boston to Hampton Beach, but it's possible to catch a **Coach Company** (800/874-3377, www.coachco.com, one-way $13) bus to the Newburyport Park and Ride, then take a taxi for the remaining 10-mile trip to Hampton Beach. Taxi service is available from **Merrimack Taxi Co.** (978/687-0911).

EXETER

For a brief period between 1775 and 1789, the attractive town of Exeter was the capital of New Hampshire. To this day, the town celebrates its link to the colonial period, when it was a bustling trade center and hotbed of Revolutionary sentiment. Nowadays, the town is best known as the site of Phillips Exeter Academy, one of the best private high schools in the country and the archetype of the New England prep school.

Sights

PHILLIPS EXETER ACADEMY

It's difficult to tell where the town ends and the prestigious **Phillips Exeter Academy** prep school (20 Main St., 603/772-4311, www.exeter.edu) begins. The academy was founded in 1781 by local doctor and Harvard graduate John Phillips, under the sound principle, "Goodness without knowledge is weak and feeble, yet knowledge without goodness is dangerous." With a campus more impressive than many small colleges, the school is a mix of Georgian colonial buildings and more modern structures radiating out in waves from downtown Exeter.

If you're wandering through the campus, don't miss the **Philips Exeter Academy Library** (2-36 Abbot Hall, 603/777-3328, 8am-4pm Mon.-Fri.), whose spectacular design was created by the architect Louis Kahn (it's also the second-largest secondary school library in the world).

AMERICAN INDEPENDENCE MUSEUM

The smart little **American Independence Museum** (1 Governors Ln., 603/772-2622, www.independencemuseum.org, 10am-4pm Tues.-Sat. May-Nov., $6 adults, $5 seniors, $3 students, children under 6 free) brings America's fight for independence to life. It includes two historic properties: the home of one of Exeter's rebel families and the tavern where many political theories were hashed out at the time. Inside are interactive exhibits exploring the causes and characters of the Revolution. The stars of the museum's collection are an original draft of the Constitution and a Dunlap copy of the Declaration of Independence, but they're only on display during the yearly Independence Day festivities.

Entertainment and Events

"George Washington" addresses the crowds at the annual **American Independence Festival** (603/772-2622, www.independencemuseum.org, mid-July), which takes place on the grounds of the American Independence Museum and is held in mid-July to celebrate the date that the Declaration of Independence was first read in Exeter, on July 16, 1776. Costumed interpreters also circulate through the event, which features helicopter rides, fireworks, music, craft vendors, and a specially brewed Independence Ale from Redhook Brewery.

Food

A downtown coffee shop that's popular with students, **D2 Java** (155 Water St., 603/583-5646, www.dsquaredjava.com, 7am-8pm Mon.-Sat., 8am-6pm Sun., $2-7) has the best espresso in town, a short menu of breakfast items, and a case stocked with treats from local bakers, including gluten-free and vegan options.

Mexican American staples like burritos and nachos are the draw at **Las Olas Taqueria** (30 Portsmouth Ave., 603/418-8901, www.lasolastaqueria.com, 11am-9pm Mon.-Sat., 11am-8pm Sun., $7-10), a bright, basic space with counter service. Build-your-own options include organic pork and locally sourced chorizo, and servings are generous.

A favorite for super-fresh lunches, **Green Bean on Water** (33 Water St., 603/778-7585, www.nhgreenbean.com, 11am-7pm daily, $8-12) specializes in sandwiches on house-baked ciabatta, big salads, and soups—there's a rotating menu of more than 60 varieties. The outdoor seating is welcome on sunny days, with views to the Exeter River from the back patio.

Getting There

Exeter is located on Route 101, inland from Hampton Beach and Portsmouth. It's on the Downeaster rail line from **Amtrak** (800/872-7245, www.amtrakdowneaster.com), linking the city with **Boston** (1 hr., one-way ticket $11) and **Brunswick,** Maine (2 hrs., one-way ticket $26), with several stops in between.

The Lakes Region

Hundreds of lakes are scattered through the forested landscape of central New Hampshire, from tiny fishing ponds to the sprawling shoreline of Lake Winnipesaukee. The lakeshore communities are just as varied, and include tranquil getaways, historic villages, and old-school vacation towns soaked in tanning oil and beer. A getaway for New Englanders since the 19th-century, the Lakes Region retains a nostalgic charm, but most visitors come to whip around the lakes on speedboats, snap up souvenir T-shirts, and hit the boardwalk at Weirs Beach.

If that's not your box of fudge, it's easy to get beyond the crowds to search for loons, explore the natural world, or hike one of the many low-lying mountains that rise up between the lakes, where it's easy to get away from the crowds.

PLANNING YOUR TIME

Visting the Lakes Region isn't about bagging sites per se; it's more about getting out on the water—whether that means by inner tube, canoe, speedboat, or cruise ship. As far as that goes, you can't go wrong with the **M/S *Mount Washington,*** the queen of Winnipesaukee and the best way to get a feel for the history of the lake. If you want to experience all the bustle and excitement of Lake Winni, base yourself in the quaint town of Meredith, which is close enough to the action of Weirs Beach without being *too* close. If it's solitude you're after, go straight to Squam Lake—and while you are there, take in the excellent live animal displays and nature cruises offered by the **Squam Lakes Natural Science Center.**

LAKE WINNIPESAUKEE

Four-season, water-bound activities are everywhere you look around Winnipesaukee, the largest lake in New Hampshire and the third-largest in New England (after Champlain and Moosehead). Known universally to residents as Lake Winni, the lake is a full 72 square miles of spring-fed water, with upwards of 200 miles of shoreline. Come summer, tourists descend on the lake from all over New England for boating, swimming, and cruises.

The villages surrounding the lake help everyone self-sort: Families and packs of Harley riders know just where to go. If you're looking for kitschy fun, the boardwalks of Weirs Beach have more than their fair share of waterslides, public beaches, arcades, and a great drive-in theater. Meanwhile, spots like Meredith and Wolfeboro offer quieter pleasures like antiquing, searching out galleries, and simply enjoying the scenery.

Laconia and Weirs Beach

If the villages clustered around Lake Winnipesaukee were a family, Weirs Beach would be the fun-loving cousin who gets a little wild on the weekends. Throngs gather on its beach and boardwalk every summer, and it buzzes all through the warm months. It's been that way since about 1848, when the railroad running from Boston to Montreal reached Weirs Beach. By the turn of the 19th century, four express trains left Boston's Union Station each day for Weirs Beach. The train service ended in 1960, but the annual migration did not: Each year, thousands of tourists still make their way here to ride the lake steamship, eat glorious piles of fried food, and pick up a tan or tattoo.

★ LAKE WINNIPESAUKEE CRUISES

The feeling strikes almost as soon as you catch a glimpse of Lake Winni's vast, folded shoreline—*why am I on dry land right now?* The grande dame of the lake is the **M/S *Mount Washington*** (211 Lakeside Ave., Weirs Beach, 603/366-5531 or 888/843-6686, www.cruisenh.com, May-Oct., $32-50 adults, $16-25 children 5-12, children under 5 free), so named—the tour guides will tell you—because when the sky is clear you can see New Hampshire's tallest peak from the deck (M/S stands for motor ship). The current cruise ship is actually the second *Mount Washington* to cruise the lake. The first ship, built in 1872, was destroyed by a fire in 1939. Her replacement is an 1888 steamship that was completely overhauled and rebuilt in 1940. The ship is a whopping 230 feet long, and re-creates the era of the old paddlewheel steamships, even though she is now propelled by twin diesel engines.

The same company also has two smaller boats in its fleet that are ideal for those wanting to avoid crowds or poke into some of the smaller bays the *Mount* can't get into. The **M/S *Sophie C.*** ($28 adults, $14 children) is the only U.S. Mail Boat on an inland waterway, and passengers can hitch a ride on the two-hour run to a scattering of island communities and summer camps.

SIGHTS

Part of the original Boston & Maine Railroad that used to bring tourists to the region has been preserved and turned into the **Winnipesaukee Scenic Railroad** (154

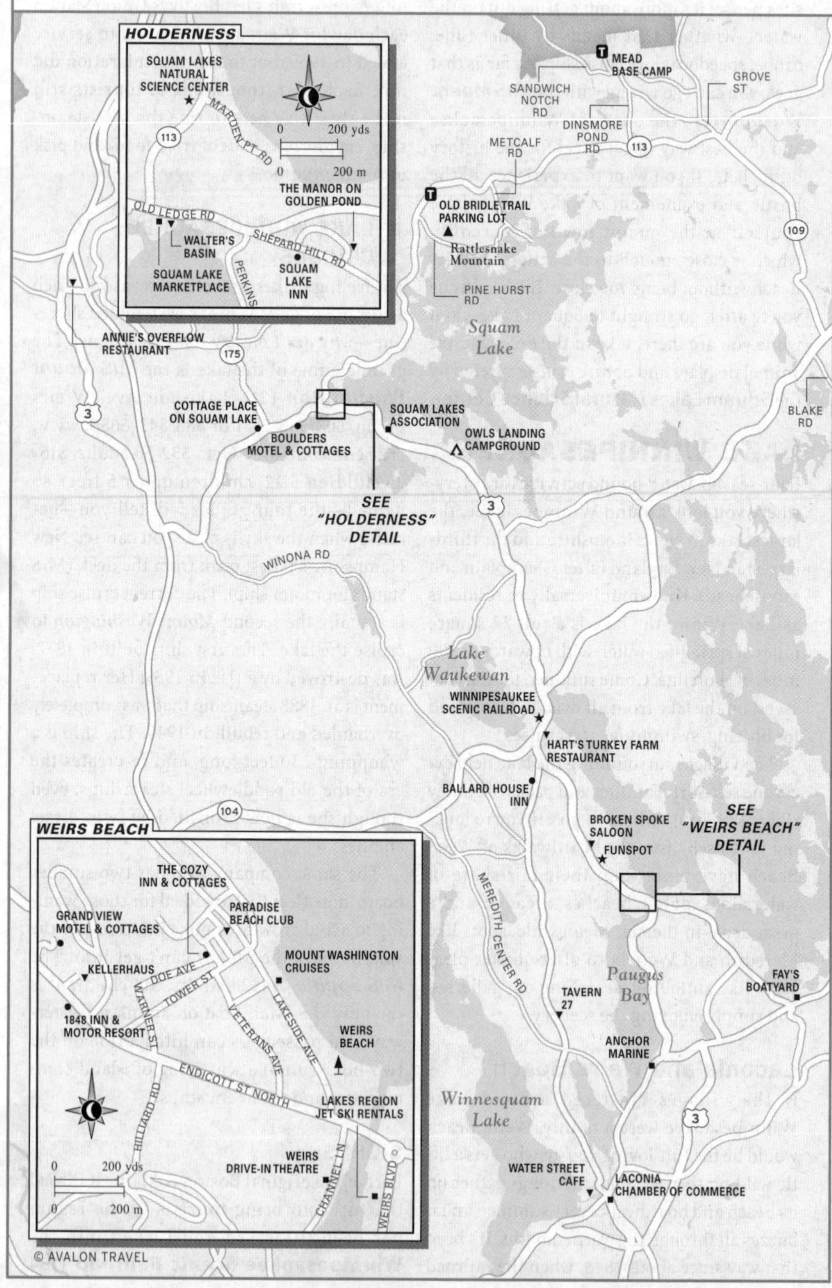
New Hampshire Seacoast and Lakes Region
HOLDERNESS
SQUAM LAKES NATURAL SCIENCE CENTER
MARDEN PT RD
113
0 200 yds
0 200 m
THE MANOR ON GOLDEN POND
OLD LEDGE RD
SHEPARD HILL RD
WALTER'S BASIN
SQUAM LAKE MARKETPLACE
PERKINS
SQUAM LAKE INN
MEAD BASE CAMP
SANDWICH NOTCH RD
GROVE ST
DINSMORE POND RD
METCALF RD
113
OLD BRIDLE TRAIL PARKING LOT
Rattlesnake Mountain
109
PINE HURST RD
Squam Lake
ANNIE'S OVERFLOW RESTAURANT
175
3
COTTAGE PLACE ON SQUAM LAKE
BOULDERS MOTEL & COTTAGES
SQUAM LAKES ASSOCIATION
OWLS LANDING CAMPGROUND
BLAKE RD
SEE "HOLDERNESS" DETAIL
3
WINONA RD
Lake Waukewan
WINNIPESAUKEE SCENIC RAILROAD
HART'S TURKEY FARM RESTAURANT
BALLARD HOUSE INN
104
BROKEN SPOKE SALOON
FUNSPOT
SEE "WEIRS BEACH" DETAIL
MEREDITH CENTER RD
WEIRS BEACH
THE COZY INN & COTTAGES
PARADISE BEACH CLUB
GRAND VIEW MOTEL & COTTAGES
MOUNT WASHINGTON CRUISES
KELLERHAUS
DOE AVE
TOWER ST
WARNER ST
VETERANS AVE
LAKESIDE AVE
1848 INN & MOTOR RESORT
WEIRS BEACH
ENDICOTT ST NORTH
HILLIARD RD
LAKES REGION JET SKI RENTALS
CHANNEL LN
WEIRS BLVD
WEIRS DRIVE-IN THEATRE
0 200 yds
0 200 m
Paugus Bay
FAY'S BOATYARD
TAVERN 27
ANCHOR MARINE
Winnesquam Lake
3
WATER STREET CAFE
LACONIA CHAMBER OF COMMERCE
© AVALON TRAVEL

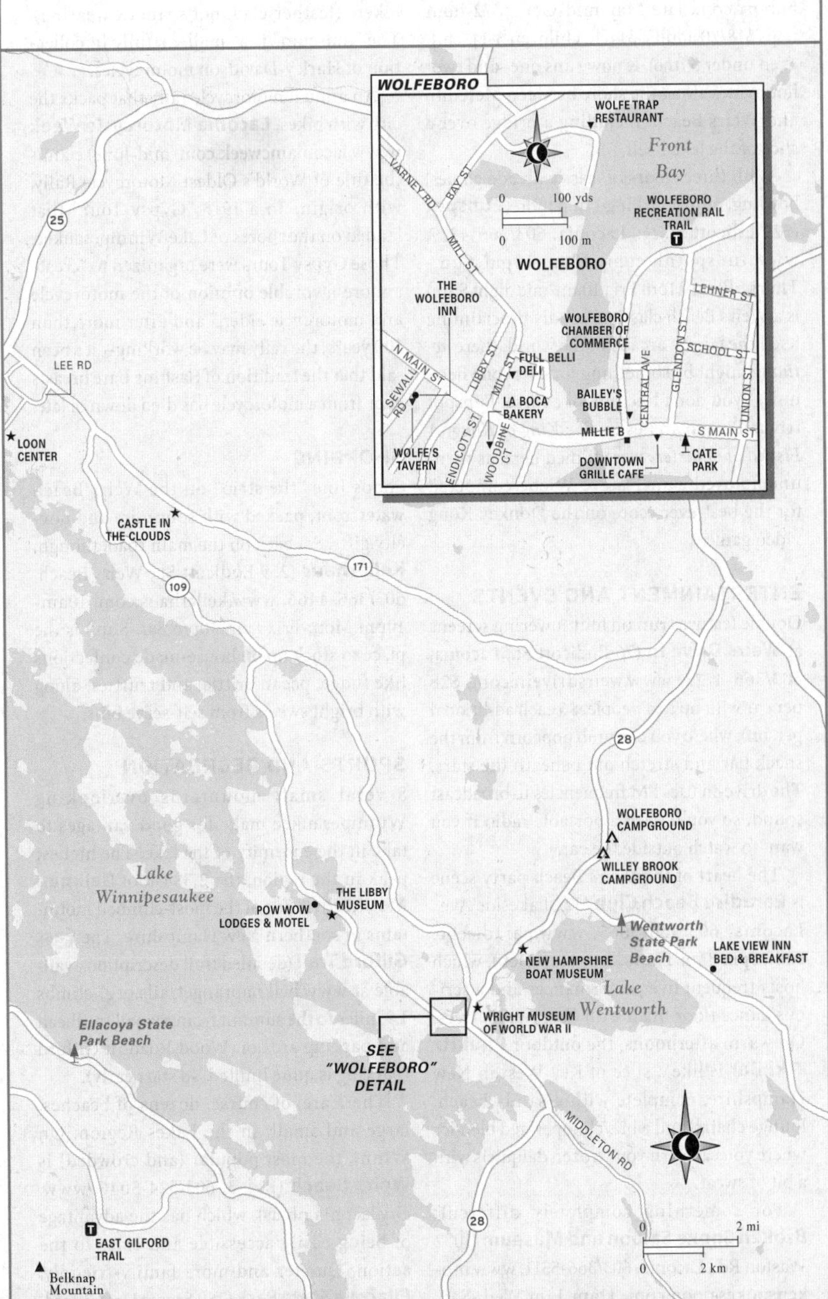
WOLFEBORO
WOLFE TRAP RESTAURANT
Front Bay
VARNEY RD
BAY ST
0 100 yds
0 100 m
WOLFEBORO RECREATION RAIL TRAIL
MILL ST
WOLFEBORO
THE WOLFEBORO INN
LEHNER ST
WOLFEBORO CHAMBER OF COMMERCE
N MAIN ST
LIBBY ST
MILL ST
FULL BELLI DELI
SCHOOL ST
CENTRAL AVE
GLENDON ST
SEWALL RD
LA BOCA BAKERY
BAILEY'S BUBBLE
UNION ST
ENDICOTT ST
WOODBINE CT
MILLIE B
S MAIN ST
WOLFE'S TAVERN
DOWNTOWN GRILLE CAFE
CATE PARK
LEE RD
LOON CENTER
CASTLE IN THE CLOUDS
WOLFEBORO CAMPGROUND
WILLEY BROOK CAMPGROUND
Lake Winnipesaukee
POW WOW LODGES & MOTEL
THE LIBBY MUSEUM
Wentworth State Park Beach
LAKE VIEW INN BED & BREAKFAST
NEW HAMPSHIRE BOAT MUSEUM
Lake Wentworth
WRIGHT MUSEUM OF WORLD WAR II
Ellacoya State Park Beach
SEE "WOLFEBORO" DETAIL
MIDDLETON RD
0 2 mi
0 2 km
EAST GILFORD TRAIL
Belknap Mountain

Main St., Wiers Beach, 603/745-2135, www.hoborr.com, late May-mid-Oct., 1-/2-hour trips $18/20 adults, $14/16 children 3-11, children under 3 free). It now runs one- and two-hour rides along the shore between Meredith and Weirs Beach, including a bridge over a slice of the lake itself.

With three floors of classic arcade games, bowling, mini golf, bingo, and more, **Funspot** (579 Edicott St. N., Laconia, 603/366-4377, www.funspotnh.com, 10am-10pm Sun.-Thurs., 10am-11pm Fri., 10am-midnight Sun.) is a Weirs Beach classic. Proudly proclaiming itself the largest arcade in the world, there *actually* might be something for everyone here, unless you don't like fun, of course. Funspot trivia: Pivotal scenes in *The King of Kong: A Fistful of Quarters* were filmed here, as then-unemployed gamer Steve Wiebe competed for the best-ever score on the Donkey Kong video game.

ENTERTAINMENT AND EVENTS

Double features run on four towering screens at **Weirs Drive In** (76 Endicott St., Laconia, 603/366-4723, www.weirsdrivein.com, $28 per car with up to 4 people, $6 each additional person), where you can grab popcorn from the snack bar and stretch out beneath the stars. The drive-in uses FM frequencies to broadcast sound, so you'll need a portable radio if you want to watch outside the car.

The heart of the Weirs Beach party scene is **Paradise Beach Club** (322 Lakeside Ave., Laconia, 603/366-3665, www.paradisebc.com, 8pm-1am Thurs.-Sat. May-Oct.), which hosts frequent live performances and a serious dance floor lined with (faux) palm trees. On warm afternoons, the outdoor **Phukitz Tiki Bar** is like a slice of Key West in New Hampshire, complete with a sandy beach, lounge chairs, and a bicycle-operated blender where you can earn your frozen daiquiris with a bit of sweat.

For something completely different, **Broken Spoke Saloon and Museum** (1072 Waston Rd., Laconia, 603/366-5511, www.brokenspokesaloon.com, 11am-1am Wed.-Sat., 11am-10pm Sun. June-Oct.) is a favorite with bikers (leather-clad, not spandex-wearing). The "museum" is a small, artfully lit collection of Harley-Davidson motorcycles.

An annual motorcycle rally that packs the city with bikes, **Laconia Motorcycle Week** (www.laconiamcweek.com, mid-June) claims the title of World's Oldest Motorcycle Rally, with origins in a 1916 "Gypsy Tour" that landed on the shores of Lake Winnipesaukee. Those Gypsy Tours were organized to "create a more favorable opinion of the motorcycle and motorcycle rider," and after more than 100 years, the rally may be working—it's been said that the tradition of flashing bare breasts at or from a motorcycle has died down of late.

SHOPPING

Shops line "the strip" on the Weirs Beach waterfront, packed with souvenirs and novelty gifts. Set back on the main road, though, **Kellerhaus** (259 Endicott St., Weirs Beach, 603/366-4466, www.kellerhaus.com, 10am-10pm Mon.-Fri., 8am-10pm Sat.-Sun.) is the place to stock up on house-made confections like fudge, pecan brittle, and truffles, along with bright sweets from self-serve bins.

SPORTS AND RECREATION

Several small mountains overlooking Winnipesaukee make for good vantages to take in the enormity of the lake. The highest peak in the region, the 2,384-foot **Belknap Mountain** is one of the most-climbed mountains in southern New Hampshire. The **East Gilford Trail** (detailed trail description available at www.belknaprangetrails.org) climbs 1.9 miles to the summit from a small trailhead and parking area on Wood Road in Gilford (parking is quite limited, so start early).

There are, of course, dozens of beaches, large and small, in the Lakes Region. On Winni, the most popular (and crowded) is **Weirs Beach** (Rte. 3, 603/524-5046, www.city.laconia.nh.us), which has the advantage of being easily accessible and close to the action. Quieter and more family-friendly, **Ellacoya State Park** (280 Scenic Dr., Gilford,

603/293-7821, www.nhstateparks.org, $5 adults, $2 children 6-11) has a long, sandy beach with views of the mountains and welcome patches of shade beneath stands of trees. Admission is capped, and on busy weekends, the beach can fill to capacity.

If it floats and it's fun, you can probably rent it in Weirs Beach. Zip around on a **Jet Ski** from **Lakes Region Jet Ski Rentals** (1184 Weirs Rd., Laconia, 603/366-5566, www.lakesregionjetski.com, 1 hour from $85, half day from $299), or opt for a more sedate **pontoon boat** from **Anchor Marine** (1285 Union Ave., Laconia, 603/366-4311, www.anchormarine.net, 2-hour pontoon boat rental $135). A short drive south in Gilford, **Fay's Boat Yard** (71 Varney Point Rd., Gilford, 603/293-8000, www.faysboatyard.com, half-day rentals from $25) is the place to go for canoes, kayaks, and sailboats.

FOOD

Ten minutes north of Weirs Beach, you can tuck into year-round Thanksgiving dinners at ★ **Hart's Turkey Farm Restaurant** (233 Daniel Webster Hwy., Jct. Rtes. 3 and 104, Meredith, 603/279-6212, www.hartsturkeyfarm.com, 11:15am-8:30pm daily, $10-28), where dark and light meat come with all the fixings, from cranberry sauce to gravy and stuffing. The regular menu is long and features an astonishing variety of turkey items: turkey nuggets, turkey marsala, turkey livers, turkey croquettes, turkey tempura . . .

Beyond the gift shop at **Kellerhaus** (259 Endicott St., Weirs Beach, 603/366-4466, www.kellerhaus.com, 10am-10pm Mon.-Fri., 8am-10pm Sat.-Sun.) is an ice cream wonderland. The self-serve ice cream sundae bar features a laundry list of flavors, but the joy is in the toppings, from house-made marshmallow fluff to fudge and caramel sauce.

A tapas bar with live piano music, **Tavern 27** (2075 Parade Rd., Laconia, 603/528-3057, www.tavern27.com, 5pm-9pm Wed.-Thurs., 11am-9pm Fri.-Sun., $17-22) has a menu of small plates that use many locally sourced ingredients, some from the restaurant's own organic vegetable garden. Save room for dessert—the bread pudding comes highly recommended.

Every Friday, seemingly all Laconia turns up at **Water Street Cafe** (141 Water St., Laconia, 603/524-4144, www.water-street-cafe.com, 6am-2pm Mon.-Thurs. and Sat., 6am-8pm Fri., 7am-1pm Sun., $5-25) for all-you-can-eat fresh haddock or clams. It's a great deal—as are the homemade seafood chowders and farm-fresh egg omelets at breakfast.

ACCOMMODATIONS

Decorated with grandfather clocks, maple wood floors, and tufted sofas, **The Cozy Inn & Cottages** (12 Maple St., Weirs Beach, 603/366-4310, www.cozyinn-nh.com, cottages $135-245, rooms $60-125) offers 16 cottages (either poolside or with lake views) and rooms in two separate buildings. Cottages have kitchens, air-conditioning, and grills, and the rooms in the main houses are simple but tidy and comfortable. It's a short downhill walk to the center of Weirs Beach.

The family-owned **1848 Inn and Motor Resort** (258 Endicott St., North Weirs Beach, 603/366-4714, www.1848inn.com, Apr.-Nov., $79-125) has clean rooms as well as cottages with kitchens and an outdoor swimming pool, a game room, and a picnic area. It's located within walking distance to Weirs Beach. Another good option for cottages is **Grand View Motel & Cottages** (291 Endicott St., North Weirs Beach, 603/366-4973, www.grandviewmotel-nh.com, Apr.-Oct., $129-189), which also offers neatly kept cottages with views of the lake, and grounds with grills, fire pits, and a fenced-in pool.

Simple and tranquil, **Ballard House Inn** (53 Parade Rd., Meredith, 603/279-3434, www.ballardhouseinn.com, $129-239) is a welcome break from the action in Weirs Beach without going too far away—it's just a few miles north of town. The house-made breakfast is a highlight, and the innkeepers furnish the common spaces with cookies, hot drinks, beer, and wine for guests. Some rooms have gorgeous views of the lake and mountains.

INFORMATION

The **Lakes Region Chamber of Commerce** (383 S. Main St., Laconia, 603/524-5531, 9am-3pm Mon.-Fri., www.lakesregionchamber.org) has year-round travel information in its main office, as well as a self-serve rack of brochures on Weirs Boulevard in Weirs Beach.

GETTING THERE

Laconia and Weirs Beach are located on Route 3, on the western shore of Lake Winnipesaukee. **Concord Coach Lines** (800/639-6317, www.concordcoachlines.com) links Meredith, a few miles north of Weirs Beach, with **Boston** (2 hrs., 30 min., $24.50), **Portland** (5 hrs., 10 min., $45.50), and **Concord** (1 hr., $12).

Wolfeboro

Waving flags, white churches, and a compact main street make Wolfeboro a nostalgic place to while away a summer weekend on Lake Winnipesaukee. Locals like to call the town the "oldest summer resort in America"—Governor John Wentworth drew a fashionable crowd to the area after building a summer home in 1769—and it retains an old-fashioned charm.

Catch a concert in a lakeside gazebo, see a stars-and-stripes take on World War II, or take a cruise on a vintage wooden lake boat, while slowing down to the pace of life on the "quiet side" of the lake.

SIGHTS

The tank bursting out of the brick facade of the **Wright Museum of World War II** (77 Center St., 603/569-1212, www.wrightmuseum.org, 10am-4pm Mon.-Sat., noon-4pm Sun. May-Oct., $10 adults, $8 seniors and veterans, $6 students, children under 8 free) sets the tone for the museum's extensive collection, which offers a more upbeat take on the era than the average war museum. There's an impressive array of cars, motorcycles, tanks, and airplanes, as well as ephemera that helps illustrate daily life in the United States during the conflict.

Gleaming vintage boats are the starring attraction at the diminutive **New Hampshire Boat Museum** (395 Center St./Rte. 28, Wolfeboro Falls, 603/569-4554, www.nhbm.org, 10am-4pm Mon.-Sat., noon-4pm Sun. late May-mid-Oct., $7 adults, $5 seniors, $3 students, children under 7 free), whose collection includes some of the glamorous vessels that cruised Lake Winnipesaukee a century ago.

Twenty-five minutes outside of Wolfeboro, **Castle in the Clouds** (455 Old Mountain Rd., Moultonborough, 603/476-5900, www.castleintheclouds.org, 10am-5:30pm daily mid-May-late Oct., $17 adults, $14 seniors, $10 children 5-17, children under 5 free) is a spectacular Arts and Crafts mansion set high on a hilltop with views of the entire Lakes Region. It's the former home of a shoe mogul, whose original estate once covered 6,300 acres, stretching from the mountains to the edge of the lake. The view itself is worth the trip to the house, but the interior is beautifully restored, with decor and furnishings based on images of the original house or on written descriptions. The surrounding grounds are now managed by the **Lakes Region Conservation Trust** (LRCT, www.lrct.org), with 30 miles of hiking trails that are accessible without paying the entrance fee to the house. Maps of the hiking trails are available on the LRCT website, or can be purchased at the Castle in the Clouds gift shop. Hiker parking is by Shannon Pond on Ossipee Park Road.

A quirky natural history museum built from the collection of an early 20th-century doctor, **The Libby Museum** (755 N. Main St., 603/569-1035, www.thelibbymuseum.org 10am-4pm Tues.-Sat., noon-4pm Sun. June-mid-Oct., $5 adults, youth under 17 and veterans free) has a fascinating rainy-day collection of stuffed animals and Native American artifacts. Free wild animal shows are held at 2pm each Wednesday in July and August.

ENTERTAINMENT AND EVENTS

Nighttime entertainment can be tough to come by in these quiet parts, but there's usually a good crowd at **Wolfe's Tavern** (90 N. Main St., 603/569-3016, www.wolfeboro-inn.com, 7am-9pm daily) at the Wolfeboro Inn. The authentic New England-style pub (with several fireplaces, and pewter beer mugs strewn across the ceiling) serves food, but later in the evening, it's all about the beer. If you drink all 70 kinds available—no more than two per visit, alas—you'll get to kiss the moose head and hang your own personalized pewter mug on the ceiling.

Saturday evenings July-early September, a crowd gathers near the water for the **Wolfeboro Community Bandstand Concerts** (Cate Park, www.wolfebrorobandstand.org, 7pm-9pm, free), featuring a range of performers that lean local. Held by the New Hampshire Boat Museum, the **Vintage Race Boat Regatta** (603/569-4554, www.nhbm.org, Sept.), features dozens of boats that range from magnificent to strange, a rare chance to see the historic vessels in action.

SPORTS AND RECREATION

Running 11 miles from Wolfeboro to the village of Wakefield, the **Wolfeboro Recreation Rail Trail** (trailhead on Depot St. by the Wolfeboro Chamber of Commerce, www.nhstateparks.org) leaves right from the center of town, following the mostly flat rail bed through the forest. The trail surface is crushed gravel that's easy to ride even with narrow tires, and highlights of the trail are a pair of causeways that cross Lake Wentworth and Crescent Lake. Bikes are available to rent at **Nordic Skier Sports** (47 N. Main St., 603/569-3151, www.nordicskiersports.com, 9am-5pm Mon.-Sat., half-day rental $20).

On a small lake just east of Winni, **Wentworth State Park** (Rte. 109, 603/569-3699, www.nhstateparks.org, $4 adults, $2 children 6-11, children under 6 free) features a sandy beach on the land where Governor Wentworth once spent summer vacations. There are picnic tables and a bathhouse, and the water tends to be warmer than Lake Winnipesaukee, making this an excellent place to swim.

With a design based on a 1928 Hacker-Craft, the ***Millie B*** (11 S. Main St., 603/569-4554, www.nhbm.org, 45-minute tour $22 adults, $20 seniors, military, and youth 13-16, $10 children 5-12, children under 5 free) is 28 feet of sleek mahogany with an unusual triple cockpit, and is owned and operated by the New Hampshire Boat Museum. The tours combine local sights with wildlife watching and a bit of history, but the real highlight is just cruising around in a gorgeous boat that's a throwback to the glory days of wooden boats.

FOOD

It's all ice cream, all the (summer)time at **Bailey's Bubble** (5 Railroad Ave., 603/569-3612, www.baileysbubble.com, 11am-9pm Mon.-Fri., 11am-10pm Sat.-Sun., $2-4). Open May-September, the locally loved stand scoops up banana splits, brownie sundaes, and flavors like maple walnut and cherry chip, plus homemade hot fudge. A New Hampshire classic is Moose Tracks, with a blend of vanilla ice cream, peanut butter, and chocolate.

With a menu of hefty sandwiches, **Full Belli Deli** (15 Mill St., 603/569-1955, 10:30am-6pm Mon.-Fri., 10:30am-4pm Sat., 10:30am-3pm Sun., $8-12) is a good option for lunch or a picnic. You might find that the sandwiches are big enough to share, and it's worth calling in an order on busy days, when the line can stretch to the door.

Simple egg breakfasts, wraps, and waffles bring in a steady crowd for breakfast at the **Downtown Grille Café** (33 S. Main St., 603/569-4504, www.downtowngrille.cafe, 7am-3pm daily, $5-11), while lunch is a lineup of sandwiches and burgers. It's an easygoing spot with counter service, and if you're lucky you'll snag a table on the back deck with views of the lake.

A short distance outside of the compact downtown, **Wolfetrap** (19 Bay St., 603/569-1047, www.wolfetrapgrilleandrawbar.com, 11am-late daily, $9-25) is an escape from the crush on busy days, with waterfront seating on a back bay of Lake Winnipesaukee. There's a reasonable raw bar with shucked oysters and clams, but the main draw is a menu of fried and grilled seafood (the crab cakes win raves).

Scratch-baked pastries and breads at **La Boca Bakery** (50 N. Main St., 603/569-5595, www.labocabakery.com, 9am-4pm Wed.-Sat., 8am-1pm Sun., $3-8) are well made and not too sweet, with croissants, cupcakes, and personal-size cheesecakes.

ACCOMMODATIONS AND CAMPING

With a gorgeous location between two lakes, ★ **Pow-Wow Lodges & Motel** (19 Governor Wentworth Hwy., 603/515-7011, www.powwowlodges.com, suites $145-165, cottages from $1,250 per week) is a great place to get out on the water, and rowboats, canoes, kayaks, and paddleboards are available for guest use. Suites each come with two beds and a private deck, microwaves, refrigerators, coffeemakers, and air-conditioning, while some have a full kitchenette. When things quiet down for the evening, you may hear calling loons from nearby Mirror Lake.

A good value that's 10 minutes away from the center of Wolfeboro, **Lake View Bed & Breakfast** (20 Martin Hill Rd., 603/515-6415, www.lakeview-inn.com, $160) certainly delivers on the promise of lake views, with spectacular vistas from some rooms. Big breakfasts of scones, with cooked-to-order plates of eggs and French toast, are highlights. The innkeepers have six friendly dogs, and some guests have been bothered by their sometimes energetic barking.

Lines of Adirondack chairs line the private beach at **The Wolfeboro Inn** (90 N. Main St., 603/569-3016, www.wolfeboroinn.com, $150-300), which is walking distance from the center of town. Rooms are smart, if unremarkable, and there's plenty of room to linger on the property—around fire pits, by the shore, and over cookies, lemonade, and tea each day in the lobby.

Set back in the forest behind Lake Wentworth, **Wolfeboro Campground** (61 Haines Hill Rd., 603/569-9881, www.wolfeborocampground.com, $29-33) has wooded sites, clean restrooms, and a group campfire area, as well as a screened-in gazebo in a pleasant garden. If that's full, the nearby **Willey Brook Campground** (883 Center St., 603/569-9493, www.willeybrookcampground.com, $29-37) is just about the same, with perhaps a shade more lawn than forest.

INFORMATION

The **Wolfeboro Area Chamber of Commerce** (32 Central Ave., 603/569-2200, www.wolfeboro.com, 10am-3pm Mon.-Sat., 10am-noon Sun.) runs a comprehensive information center in the town's historic old train station.

GETTING THERE

Wolfeboro is at the intersection of Route 28 and Route 109, on the eastern shore of Lake Winnipesaukee. There's no direct public transit to Wolfeboro, but buses from **Concord Coach Lines** (800/639-3317, www.concordcoachlines.com) link **Boston** with **Meredith** (2 hrs., 30 min., $23.50). From there, taxi service to Wolfeboro is available from **Big Lake Taxi & Limousine** (603/875-3365, www.biglaketaxiandlimo.com, $125).

Squam Lakes

Beyond the bustle of Lake Winnepesaukee, the forest closes in around a scattershot of ponds, lakes, and potholes—New Hampshire has almost 1,000 lakes altogether. Of these, Squam Lakes are among the most appealing. Morning breaks with the eerie loon call, or with the shushing rhythm of canoe paddles.

There's not much to the town itself—a stamp-sized post office and a general store hold down the main crossroads—but that's just the idea. It's a place to pack a picnic lunch, maybe pick up some bait, then spend the day exploring the shoreline, spotting birds, or visiting the rambling outdoor science museum.

★ SQUAM LAKES NATURAL SCIENCE CENTER

New England's last known mountain lion was killed in Maine in 1938, but you can still see one of the beautiful cats at the excellent

Squam Lakes Natural Science Center (23 Science Center Rd./Rte. 113, Holderness, 603/968-7194, www.nhnature.org, 9:30am-5pm daily May-Oct., $19 adults, $16 seniors, $14 youth 3-15, children under 3 free), hands-down the best in New England. The center has dozens of local animals, including a bobcat, several black bears, otters, and flying raptors arranged in spacious enclosures along a 0.75-mile wooded nature trail. (Most of the animals were injured and unable to survive in the wild.)

Where it really excels, though, is in the interactive exhibits that accompany each animal—they're imaginative and educational for kids and adults alike. (Case in point is the "long jump" that compares your personal best with the mountain lion's.) The center also has an informative exhibit on the star of the northern lakes: the common loon.

The science center also runs a series of highly regarded, 90-minute **lake cruises** ($27 adults, $25 seniors, $23 youth, children 3 and under free) that focus on everything from bald eagles to loons, geography, and lake ecosystems. Combo tickets for the science center and lake cruises are also available ($40 adults, $35 seniors, $31 youth).

If hanging out on the lakes for a while makes you suddenly crazy for loons, learn more about the water bird with the eerie call at the **Loon Center** (183 Lee's Mill Rd./off Rte. 25, Moultonborough, 603/476-5666, www.loon.org, 9am-5pm Mon.-Sat. mid-May-June, 9am-5pm daily July-early Oct., 9am-5pm Thurs.-Sat. early Oct.-mid-May, free), a half-hour drive from Holderness. This homegrown museum explains such mysteries as why loons' eyes are red, why chicks ride on their parents' backs, and what that ghostly cry actually means. A 1.5-mile nature trail along the shores of Moultonborough Bay, a branch of Lake Winni, takes in coves where loons are known to nest in spring.

SHOPPING

In small New England communities, a good general store can make the town, and **Squam Lake MarketPlace** (862 Rte. 3, Holderness, 603/968-8588, www.squammarket.com, 7am-5pm daily) is a one-stop destination for gossip, advice, food, and cabin-cutesy souvenirs. The made-to-order breakfast sandwiches are a treat, and the store packs customized picnic boxes that range from a simple lunch of sandwiches and canned drinks to more elaborate

river otter at the Squam Lakes Natural Science Center

spreads including lobster rolls, bottles of bubbly, and cheese boards (with a loaner cooler for the day).

Dozens of artists display their work at **Squam Lakes Artisans** (900 Rte. 3, Holderness, 603/968-9525, www.squamlakesartisans.com, 10am-5pm daily mid-May-early Sept., 10am-5pm Fri.-Mon. early Sept.-mid-Oct.), whose collection ranges from elegant canvases to folksy quilts and crafts.

SPORTS AND RECREATION

The nonprofit **Squam Lakes Association** (534 Rte. 3, Holderness, 603/968-7336, www.squamlakes.org, 9am-5pm daily) rents canoes, kayaks, and paddleboards by the hour and the day ($15-20 per hour, $50-65 per day), and the staff is happy to help with paddling basics. The Squam Lakes Association also operates a series of backcountry and island campsites that are amazing for overnight canoe trips if you're equipped for sleeping out of doors.

The most popular hike near Squam Lakes is the 2-mile round-trip to the summit of **West Rattlesnake Mountain,** which departs from the Old Bridle Path trailhead on Route 113. To reach the trailhead, travel 5.5 miles north from the intersection of Route 113 and Route 3, parking on the right-hand side of the road in a small pullout. The yellow-blazed trail leads through a forest of red oaks and red pines, then breaks from the trees for gorgeous views of Squam Lakes from a rocky summit.

For a longer day on the trail, the **Squam Range Traverse** is a classic, 13.1-mile point-to-point that summits the seven named peaks in the Squam Range, starting from Mead Base Camp to the north of Squam Lakes, and describing an arc that moves south and west on the Crawford Ridgepole Trail. Hiking maps and guides can be purchased at the **Squam Lakes Association,** and an excellent trail description is available at **Hike New England** (www.hikenewengland.com).

FOOD

Laid-back and sunny, the dining room at the ★ **Squam Lake Inn** (28 Shepard Hill Rd., Holderness, 603/968-4417, www.squamlakeinn.com, 5pm-8pm Wed.-Sun., $18-33) turns out consistently excellent meals that are among the most appealing in the region. The well-balanced menu blends seafood and classic meat dishes, including oysters fresh from the coast, salmon grilled on a cedar plank, flatiron steak, and ribs. The meltingly tender scallops are a highlight, as is the bright and refreshing frozen key lime pie.

The only waterfront dining on Squam is at **Walter's Basin** (Rte. 3, Holderness, 603/968-4412, www.waltersbasin.com, 11:30am-9:30pm Sun.-Thurs., 11:30am-10pm Fri.-Sat., $11-26), a restaurant and pub serving a mish-mash of comfort foods, including great piles of fried fish, meatloaf, and hearty sandwiches. The dining room inside is open year-round, whereas outdoor seating runs May-October, and is as apt to see guests arrive by boat as by foot.

Ten minutes from the edge of Squam Lakes, **Annie's Overflow Restaurant** (138 Rte. 175A, Holderness, 603/536-4062, www.overflowrestaurantplymouth.com, 6am-2pm daily, $4-10) is a cheerful little diner with hearty servings. Breakfasts are egg classics and piles of pancakes, while the lunch menu ranges from Reuben sandwiches to old-fashioned beef liver and onions.

For formal occasions in the New Hampshire forest, ★ **The Manor on Golden Pond** (Rte. 3, Holderness, 603/968-3348, www.manorongoldenpond.com, seatings 6pm-8pm daily, reservations recommended, $28-41) is the place to be. The elegant estate house serves grand, European-style cuisine in the white linen-filled Van Horn room, with a refined wine list to accompany meals.

ACCOMMODATIONS AND CAMPING

Sweet and welcoming, ★ **Cottage Place on Squam Lake** (1132 Rte. 3, Holderness, 603/968-7116, www.cottageplaceonsquam.com, $129-269) is the kind of place families return to year after year, setting up shop in compact cabins just across the road from a private beach. The units are being overhauled one by one with plenty of antiques, but the feel is more old-fashioned than fussy. Perks include an outdoor fire pit, grills for guests to use, and inexpensive kayak and canoe rentals. While the cottages are the starring attraction, the property also includes a handful of more modern motel units and a lodge for larger groups.

You'll find 10 very pretty guest rooms (each with lake-themed decor) at **Squam Lake Inn** (Rte. 3 and Shepard Hill Rd., Holderness, 603/968-4417, www.squamlakeinn.com, $160-300). The century-old Victorian farmhouse building outfits each chamber with exceptional linens and Wi-Fi, and offers a full breakfast (from four-grain blueberry pancakes to eggs Benedict). Common areas include a charmingly decorated library and a lovely wraparound porch.

The rustic (and rather outdated) **Boulders Motel** (981 Rte. 3, Holderness, 603/968-3600, www.bouldersmotel.com, $79-299) gets mixed reviews, but snagging a cottage with a screened-in porch means you can enjoy your morning coffee overlooking the lake. There's a fire pit on the beach, grills, and a swimming raft that make this an especially good choice for families, and muffins and hot drinks are included in the price.

Somewhat rundown and dominated by season-long RVers, **Owls Landing Campground** (245 Rte. 3, Holderness, 603/279-6266, www.owlslanding.com, sites $30-40) is nevertheless a serviceable and affordable place to sleep. A campground store on-site is good for stocking up on campfire marshmallows, and kid-friendly perks include a swimming pool and rec room with pool tables.

INFORMATION

For more information on the area, contact the **Lakes Region Tourism Association** (603/286-8008, www.lakesregion.org).

GETTING THERE

Squam Lakes are a pair of lakes linked by a short outlet at Holderness, flanked by Route 3 and Route 113. No public transportation is currently available to Squam Lakes.

New Hampshire's White Mountains

Alpine peaks tower over wooded valleys, mountain rivers, and a lifetime of hiking trails in New Hampshire's White Mountains.

It's a place of howling winter storms, fiercely pitched trails, and flowers that grow nowhere else in the world. A highlight of the 2,200-mile Appalachian Trail, the White Mountains are New England's top wilderness destination.

What really sets these mountains apart, though, is how easy it is for visitors of any ability (or motivation) to get to a peak. In the 19th century, Americans fell hard for the wilderness of New Hampshire, which became a favorite destination for escaping hot, crowded cities. They took to the hills in woolen knickers and hiking gowns, capturing images of the sublime landscape and weather on portable easels and with early cameras. Those first tourists left paths that can still be followed today: They forged scenic roads that wind to mountain peaks, built a railway that runs straight to the top of Mount Washington, and slept in grand hotels offering all the views with none of the sweat. Another legacy is a series of backcountry huts maintained by the Appalachian Mountain Club (AMC), off-grid stations that in the summer become small communities that welcome hikers from around the world.

To discover the best of the White Mountains, simply choose a trail, pick a road, or take a seat on the cog railway to get a taste of New England rock laid bare.

PLANNING YOUR TIME

Two great ranges hold down opposite sides of the White Mountains, and a series of valley highways wind from peak to peak. On the northeastern side is Mount Washington and the Presidential Range, mountains that are most easily accessed from Gorham or the Conways, where many of the region's services, hotels, and attractions are based.

On the west side, along I-93, is the Franconia Range. Here the peaks are smaller (though by no means unimpressive), and the highway is studded with family-style attractions and trailheads. Running along the southern edge of both ranges, the Kancamagus Highway—or "the Kanc"—cuts

Previous: horses in Franconia; covered bridge over Pemigewasset River. **Above:** Flume Gorge.

New Hampshire's White Mountains

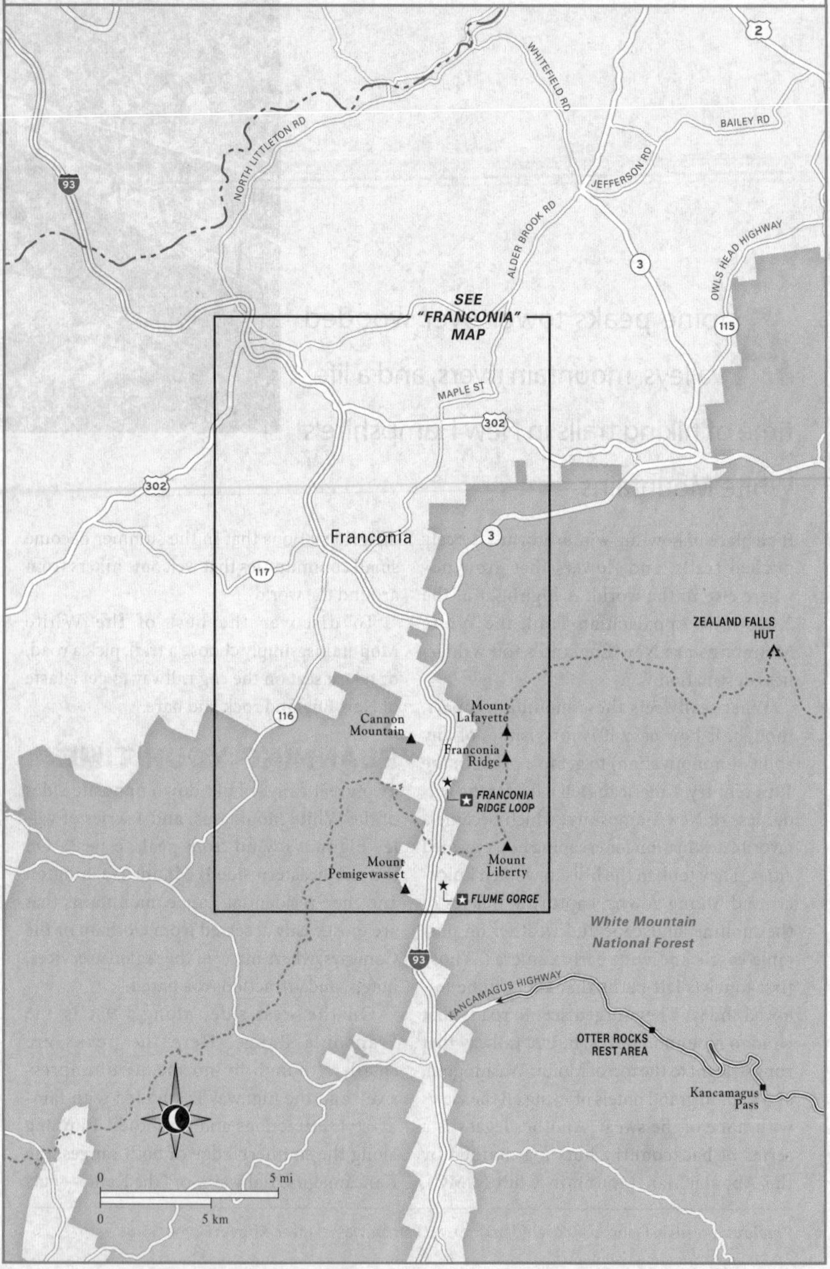

2
WHITEFIELD RD
BAILEY RD
NORTH LITTLETON RD
JEFFERSON RD
93
ALDER BROOK RD
OWLS HEAD HIGHWAY
3
115
SEE "FRANCONIA" MAP
MAPLE ST
302
302
Franconia
3
117
ZEALAND FALLS HUT
116
Mount Lafayette
Cannon Mountain
Franconia Ridge
FRANCONIA RIDGE LOOP
Mount Liberty
Mount Pemigewasset
FLUME GORGE
White Mountain National Forest
93
KANCAMAGUS HIGHWAY
OTTER ROCKS REST AREA
Kancamagus Pass
0
5 mi
0
5 km

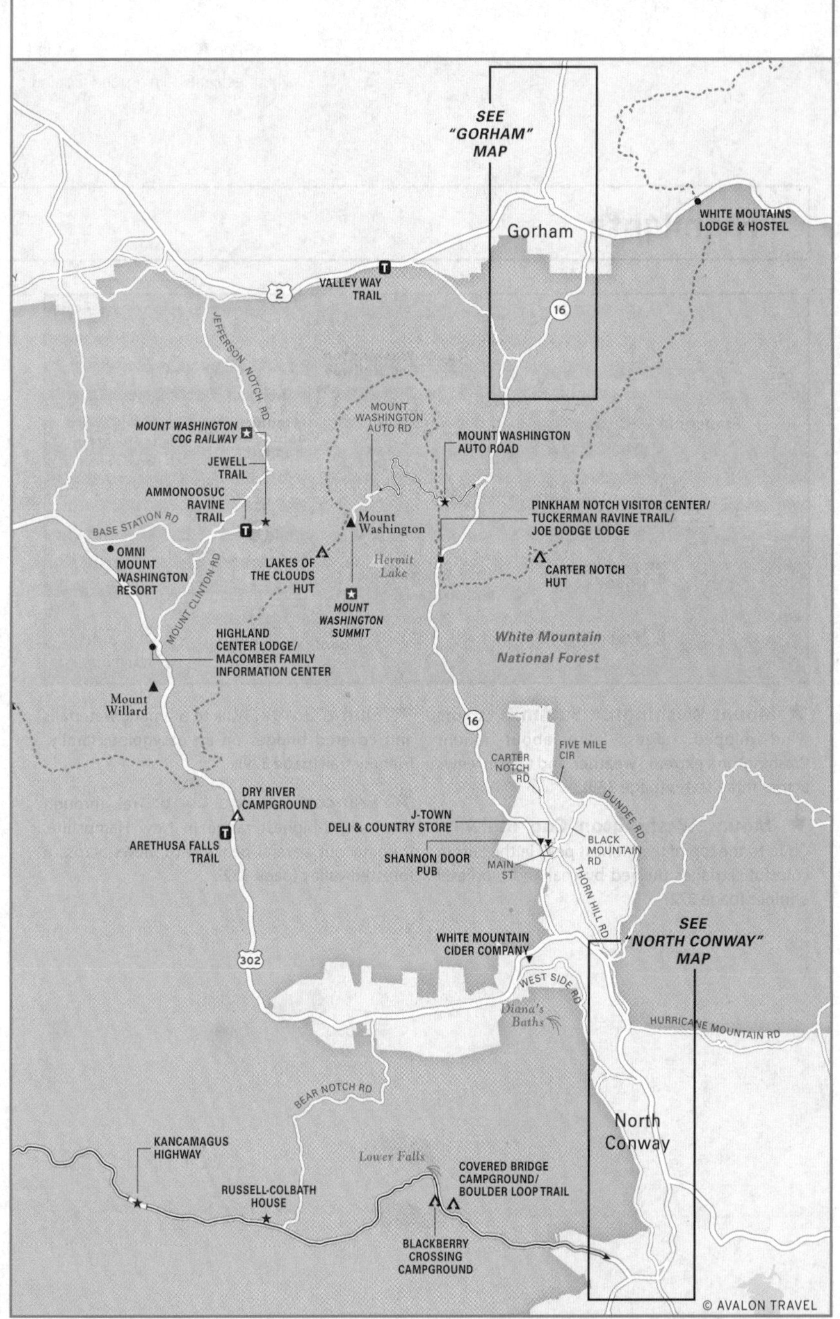
SEE
"GORHAM"
MAP
Gorham
WHITE MOUTAINS
LODGE & HOSTEL
2
VALLEY WAY
TRAIL
16
JEFFERSON NOTCH RD
MOUNT
WASHINGTON
AUTO RD
MOUNT WASHINGTON
COG RAILWAY
MOUNT WASHINGTON
AUTO ROAD
JEWELL
TRAIL
AMMONOOSUC
RAVINE
TRAIL
BASE STATION RD
Mount
Washington
PINKHAM NOTCH VISITOR CENTER/
TUCKERMAN RAVINE TRAIL/
JOE DODGE LODGE
OMNI
MOUNT
WASHINGTON
RESORT
MOUNT CLINTON RD
LAKES OF
THE CLOUDS
HUT
Hermit
Lake
CARTER NOTCH
HUT
MOUNT
WASHINGTON
SUMMIT
White Mountain
National Forest
HIGHLAND
CENTER LODGE/
MACOMBER FAMILY
INFORMATION CENTER
Mount
Willard
16
FIVE MILE
CIR
CARTER
NOTCH
RD
DUNDEE RD
DRY RIVER
CAMPGROUND
J-TOWN
DELI & COUNTRY STORE
ARETHUSA FALLS
TRAIL
SHANNON DOOR
PUB
BLACK
MOUNTAIN
RD
MAIN
ST
THORN HILL RD
SEE
"NORTH CONWAY"
MAP
WHITE MOUNTAIN
CIDER COMPANY
302
WEST SIDE RD
Diana's
Baths
HURRICANE MOUNTAIN RD
BEAR NOTCH RD
North
Conway
KANCAMAGUS
HIGHWAY
Lower Falls
COVERED BRIDGE
CAMPGROUND/
BOULDER LOOP TRAIL
RUSSELL-COLBATH
HOUSE
BLACKBERRY
CROSSING
CAMPGROUND
© AVALON TRAVEL

Look for ★ to find recommended sights, activities, dining, and lodging.

Highlights

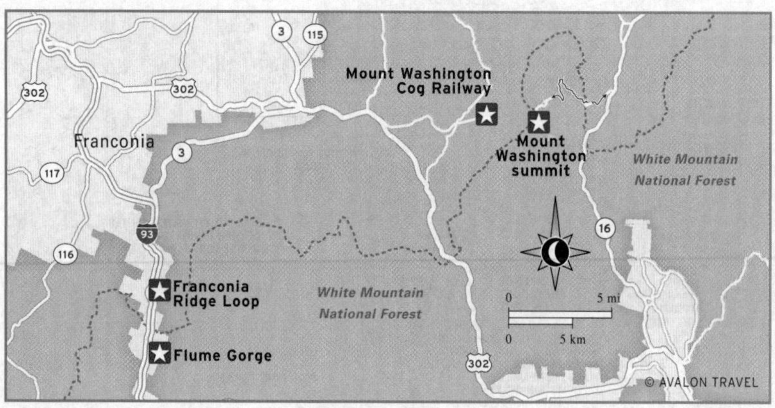

★ **Mount Washington Summit:** Explore wind-whipped ridges, learn about Mount Washington's extreme weather, and take in views across three states (page 369).

★ **Mount Washington Cog Railway:** Chug to the top of the highest peak in the East in colorful carriages pushed by coal and biodiesel engines (page 372).

★ **Flume Gorge:** Walk to dramatic waterfalls and covered bridges on an easygoing, family-friendly trail (page 379).

★ **Franconia Ridge Loop:** Trek through the second-highest range in New Hampshire, topping out several peaks with views across a forested valley (page 382).

through the most dramatic terrain in the White Mountains, following the Swift River past rolling hills and notches. The towns of Franconia and Littleton are the principal gateways to the Franconia Range, with trailheads, campgrounds, and accommodations.

Mount Washington and the Presidential Range

A series of bare peaks pushing high above the tree line, the Presidential Range is the heart of White Mountain National Forest, a rugged spine that culminates in Mount Washington, the highest summit in the northeastern United States. While the area isn't vast—the entire Presidential Range can be hiked in one punishing 23-mile day—it has the feel of true wilderness.

Even in summer, the temperature difference between the peak of Mount Washington and neighboring valleys averages around 30 degrees. The tree line, the elevation where trees go from stunted to nonexistent, is around 4,400 feet in the White Mountains, in contrast to 11,000-12,000 feet in Colorado's Rocky Mountains; that difference shows how harsh the conditions are in New Hampshire's relatively low-lying alpine areas. The weather observatory on that peak has recorded some of the world's most extreme weather, including the highest wind speeds on record, and the Presidentials get hammered by winter storms that coat them in thick layers of rime ice, snow, and frost.

Anyone with time and strong legs can find lonely trails and solitude in the White Mountains, and it can be a sublime experience. But it's delightfully fun to enjoy the Presidential Range in 19th-century style, chugging up the slope in "The Cog," bagging a few stony summits, then taking high tea in the Princess Room at Bretton Woods.

NORTH CONWAY AND CONWAY

In the shadow of the towering Presidential Range, this pair of mountain towns is the gateway to White Mountain adventures. North Conway's cute and historic downtown quickly gives way to an uninspiring cluster of outlet stores and inns, and it can get jammed on busy hiking and skiing weekends. But it's not really about the town—above all, this is the place to stock up on gear, plan your route, and rise early for a trip into New Hampshire's high places, then come back to recover over hearty mountain food and beer. North Conway and Conway are just five miles apart, with services stretching along Route 16, so this section includes listings for both towns.

Sights

A beloved destination for New Hampshire's rock climbers, **Cathedral Ledge** is a spectacular band of granite cliffs within **Echo Lake State Park** (68 Echo Lake Rd., Conway, 603/356-2672, www.nhstateparks.org, 9am-7pm daily mid-May-mid-Oct., $4 adults, $2 children 6-11) that have wonderful views of the surrounding mountains—it's a prime spot for picnics. To reach the top of the ledge, visitors can drive a scenic, mile-long road, or hike up the steep **Bryce Path** from the same parking lot (2.4-miles round-trip). An easier hike within the park is the mostly flat, mile-long loop around **Echo Lake,** which departs from the visitors center (with a beach that's perfect for cooling off).

During the heyday of 19th-century travel to the White Mountains, rail lines threaded around the range, with spurs to each of the grand hotels. Most of the tracks are quiet, but the **Conway Scenic Railway** (38 Norcross Circle, North Conway, 603/356-5251, www.conwayscenic.com, $17.50-140) sends vintage

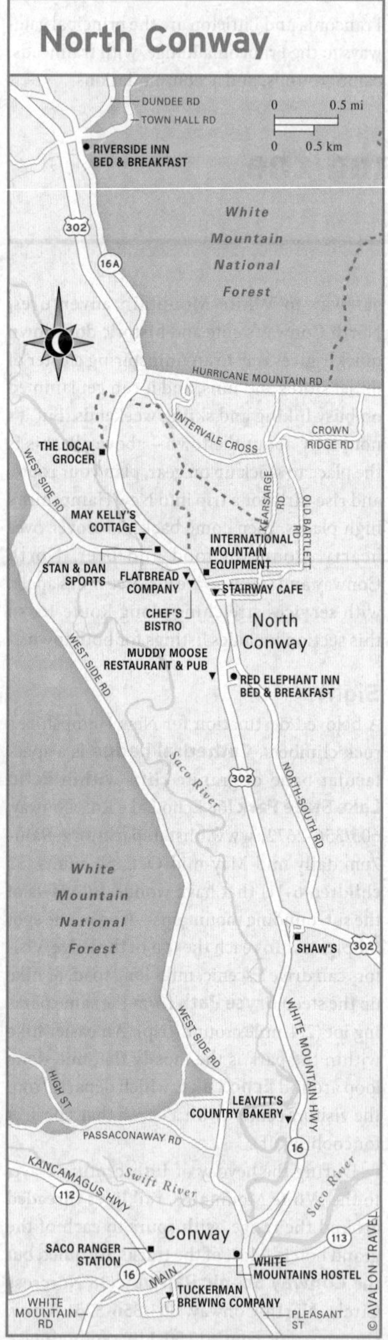

passenger trains from the charming, 1874 train station in North Conway Village. For rolling terrain and the finest views, opt for the five-hour round-trip on the **Notch Train** to Crawford Notch. Trips on the **Valley Train** range about 1-1.75 hours, linking North Conway with Conway or Bartlett. Some trips include lunch or dinner.

Entertainment and Events

What nightlife there is in this corner of the mountains is firmly based in the Conways, the cultural hub of the Whites. It's not really "night" life, but you can try local beers well into the early evening at **Tuckerman Brewing Company** (66 Hobbs St., Conway, 603/447-5400, www.tuckermanbrewing.com, noon-6pm daily, tours 2pm and 4pm daily), which brews a lineup of stouts, ales, and IPAs. A good way to meet some locals is at the Sunday night Irish session at **May Kelly's Cottage** (3002 Rte. 302, Conway, 603/356-7005, www.maykellys.com, 4pm-9pm Tues.-Thurs., noon-10pm Fri.-Sat., noon-8pm Sun.), which has a pleasant porch for afternoon beers and a convivial feel.

A favorite watering hole is **Muddy Moose Restaurant & Pub** (2344 Rte. 302, North Conway, 603/356-7696, www.muddymoose.com, 11:30am-9pm Sun.-Thurs., 11:30am-10pm Fri.-Sat.), whose antler chandelier and raw wood interior evoke an oversized summer cottage. Up the road in little Jackson, the **Shannon Door Pub** (Rte. 16, Jackson, 603/383-4211, www.shannondoor.com, 4pm-10pm Mon.-Wed., 4pm-11pm Thurs. and Sun., 4pm-midnight Fri.-Sat.) has live music nightly Thursday-Saturday and a fun, country Irish atmosphere.

Shopping

While there are plenty of shops for poking around in the Conways, the most useful stores in the White Mountains are gear shops stocked with everything you need to walk, ride, or climb your way into the hills. The Conways have a plethora: **International Mountain Equipment** (2733 Rte. 302, North

Conway, 603/356-7013, www.ime-usa.com, 9am-6pm Sun.-Thurs., 9am-9pm Fri., 8am-8pm Sat.) is a well-stocked gear shop run by the International Mountain Climbing School, which also rents hiking and camping equipment. **Stan & Dan Sports** (2936 Rte. 302, North Conway, 603/356-6997, www.stanandansports.com, 9am-6pm Mon.-Sat., 9am-5pm Sun.) is a go-to for bike and ski gear.

Sports and Recreation

HIKING

A good choice for hiking with kids, the gentle, 0.6-mile walk to **Diana's Baths** between North Conway and Bartlett ends in an enchanting series of waterfalls ideal for cooling off in wading pools (the baths vary greatly with water level, though, and by late summer the waterfalls can be mere trickles). To reach the parking area from North Conway, take Route 302 north out of town, then turn left on River Road (which becomes West Side Rd. after a mile) for 2.5 miles. A large parking lot is on the left with a self-service, cash-only parking fee station ($5).

Steeper and a bit more ambitious is the **Black Cap Hiking Trail** (Hurricane Mountain Rd., Intervale), a 2.4-mile round-trip that passes through a forest of beech and spruce trees on the way to a rocky summit with great views of the surrounding mountains (it's particularly spectacular in fall).

Food

A year-round favorite is ★ **May Kelly's Cottage** (3002 Rte. 302, 603/356-7005, www.maykellys.com, 4pm-9pm Tues.-Thurs., noon-10pm Fri.-Sat., noon-8pm Sun., $9-22), which serves hearty Irish classics and American pub fare in a relaxed, old-world setting. With fabulous mountain views and shaded tables, the outdoor patio is perfect for an early evening meal, while the interior is decked with a pleasant jumble of Americana and Irish bric-a-brac. Shepherd's pie, soups, and hearty salads all come with homemade, grainy bread, and regulars love the fried potato cakes with spinach and horseradish sauce. On Sunday evenings, a fun group of Irish musicians holds a relaxed live session, playing around a table over beers.

Fresh, simple breakfasts and hearty lunches at ★ **Stairway Café** (2649 Rte. 302, North Conway, 603/356-5200, www.stairwaycafe.com, 7am-3pm daily, $7-18) are the main draw, but the atmosphere is pretty great too—the decor strikes a curious balance between country kitchen and rock and roll (imagine a bacon-and-egg skull on a floral print menu). Both the breakfast and lunch menus are served all day and include plenty of basic egg plates, burgers, and sandwiches, along with offbeat additions like wild game sausage and Maine lobster Benedict.

The unassuming **Leavitt's Country Bakery** (564 Rte. 302, Conway, 603/447-2218, 4am-5pm Mon.-Sat., 4am-1pm Sun., $2-7) turns out great piles of doughnuts, fritters, and Bismarck pastries—regular visitors fill boxes full of sweets before leaving the Whites. With no seating and little fuss, Leavitt's is perfect for picking up pre-hike treats and coffee, and it also prepares a mean breakfast sandwich to go.

Part of a small chain of earthy pizza joints with a focus on natural, organic ingredients, **Flatbread Company** (2760 Rte. 302, North Conway, 603/356-4470, www.flatbreadcompany.com, 11:30am-9pm Sun.-Thurs., 11:30am-9:30pm Fri.-Sat., $9-13) pulls thin-crust pies from a wood-fired oven, topped with homemade pepperoni and sausage, piles of fresh vegetables, and tomato sauce that bubbles away in a cauldron by the fire. The very casual spot is rustic and a little loud, a good choice for larger groups and families with children.

With a bit more polish and creative food, **Chef's Bistro** (2724 Rte. 302, North Conway, 603/356-4747, www.chefsbistronh.com, 11am-9pm daily, $9-28) serves eclectic dinners ranging from a vegetarian Thai curry to Asian beef salad and bistro-style steaks with great piles of hand-cut fries. Lunch is simpler, with unfussy and appealing sandwiches, burgers, and salads. This is an especially good place for those with dietary restrictions, and the restaurant has a basic kids' menu.

Conway is the main base for services in the area, with a **Shaw's grocery store** (1150 Eastman Rd., Conway, 603/356-5471, 7am-11pm Mon.-Sat., 7am-10pm Sun.); **The Local Grocer** (3358 Rte. 302, North Conway, 603/356-6068, www.nhlocalgrocer.com, 8am-7pm daily) is a smaller store that stocks natural and organic options.

Accommodations

UNDER $100

Compare blisters with fellow travelers at the **White Mountains Hostel** (36 Washington St., Conway, 866/902-2521, www.wmhostel.com, dorms $34, private rooms $64), a super-friendly spot with a communal kitchen, comfortable common areas, and very clean (if rather plain) quarters. The six-bed dorms include female-only, male-only, and coed options, and the private rooms are an excellent choice for families—each has a full bed, and some have an additional twin or bunk bed (prices are for two adults, and there's a supplemental charge of $20 per adult or $10 per child).

$100-150

A family-owned motel with plain and tidy rooms, **Colonial Motel** (2431 Route 16, North Conway, 603/356-5178, www.thecolonialmotel.com, $80-160) is a convenient choice (and a pretty solid deal). Rooms have mini fridges; hot drinks are served in the morning; and the motel is easy walking distance from downtown and the railway station. Dogs are welcome for an additional $10 per night.

$150-250

With a central location in North Conway, the ★ **Red Elephant Inn Bed & Breakfast** (28 Locust Ln., North Conway, 603/356-3548, www.redelephantinn.com, $129-239) combines the best of a classic bed-and-breakfast—giant breakfast spread, a friendly atmosphere, and cozy common spaces—with the amenities and style of a more luxurious inn. Complimentary afternoon wine and snacks are just the thing after a day spent on the trails, and the big library is stocked with local maps and books to read by the unheated outdoor pool. A hot drink and snack bar is available throughout the day for guests to help themselves, and rooms balance a warm wood-and-plaid White Mountains aesthetic with bits of art deco flair that keep things fresh and contemporary.

Fireplaces in every room and elegant four-poster beds make the **Riverside Inn Bed & Breakfast** (372 Rte. 16, Intervale, 866/949-0044, www.riverside-inn-bed-breakfast.com, $119-225) one of the more romantic places to stay in the White Mountains, with a central location that's four miles outside of North Conway. A river runs through the serene backyard, which is stocked with well-placed lawn chairs and a hammock, and the cooked-to-order breakfasts use lots of local ingredients, organic veggies, and seasonal fruits. Fresh cookies are served at afternoon teas in the old-fashioned sitting room.

Information

The White Mountain National Forest **Saco Ranger Station** (33 Rte. 112, Conway, 603/447-5448, 8am-5pm daily late May-mid-Oct., 8am-4:30pm daily Oct.-May) has maps, advice, and updated weather reports. Small visitors information centers cover non-trail-related questions in **North Conway** (2617 Rte. 16, North Conway, 603/356-5947, 10am-6pm daily) and **Conway** (250 Main St., Conway, 603/447-2639, 10am-5pm Sun.-Thurs., 10am-2pm Fri.-Sat.).

Getting There

The Conways are at the junction of several main access roads: Route 302 from Maine, Route 16 from southern New Hampshire, and the eastern end of the Kancamagus Highway. **Concord Coach Lines** (800/639-3317, www.concordcoachlines.com) links North Conway by bus with **Boston** (3 hrs., 50 min., round-trip $59).

The Presidential Traverse

Strictly for extremely fit, experienced hikers, the **Presidential Traverse** is a 23-mile hike that goes up and over every peak in the Presidential Range—tellingly, this hike is often referred to as the **Death March.** Many hikers begin and end in the dark (although the classic Death March is a long day hike, it's possible to break it up with a night in the **Lakes of the Clouds** hut). Most hikers go north to south, taking the **Valley Way Trail** from the Appalachia parking lot (Rte. 2, 5 miles west of the intersection with Rte. 16) up Mount Madison before ticking off a who's who of American presidents, ending with Mount Jackson, then descending into Crawford Notch. The one-way hike requires a car on either end, or you can use the **AMC Hiker Shuttle** (603/466-2727, www.outdoors.org, early June-Oct., $23). More information can be obtained at the **Pinkham Notch Visitor Center** (361 Rte. 16, 603/466-8116, www.outdoors.org, 6:30am-10pm daily).

PINKHAM NOTCH

A scenic pass at the base of Mount Washington, Pinkham Notch is wrapped in peaks, with the Presidential Range commanding the western horizon and the ski slopes of Wildcat Mountain and the Carter Range to the east. More mountain outpost than actual town, this is a starting point for peak-bagging hikes and time above tree line, with an Appalachian Mountain Club hiker information center to get you safely on the trail.

Sights

MOUNT WASHINGTON AUTO ROAD

You'll see the bumper stickers as soon as you start driving around New England: "This Car Climbed Mount Washington." And you'll earn breathtaking views with every turn of the **Mount Washington Auto Road** (Rte. 16, Pinkham Notch, 603/466-3988, www.mountwashingtonautoroad.com, variable hours early May-late Oct., $29 car and driver, $9 each adult, $7 each child, children under 5 free, $17 motorcycle and driver, no bicycles or hitchhiking). The 7.6-mile trip goes by at a snail's pace, taking about 30 minutes on the way up, 40 on the way down, and it's not for everyone—both drivers and passengers who are unnerved by heights may be better off in one of the guided van tours (from $36 adults, $31 seniors, $16 children 5-12, children under 5 free).

For hikers who'd like to make a one-way trip up or down Mount Washington, there's an annoyingly expensive **one-way shuttle** ($31 adults, $26 seniors, $13 children 5-12); hitchhiking is prohibited. At the bottom of the road, the **Red Barn Museum** (1 Mount Washington Auto Rd., 603/466-3988, 10am-4pm daily late May-early Oct., free) displays objects relating to the auto road's past, including antique cars and a carriage that used to climb the mountain.

★ MOUNT WASHINGTON SUMMIT

Learn about the scientists who live and work at the top at the **Mount Washington Observatory Weather Discovery Center** (summit building, 10am-5pm daily, $2 adults, $1 children 7-17, children under 7 free), which has interactive displays explaining the mountain's wild weather and telling the story of the day in 1934 when a record-breaking 231 miles-per-hour wind was recorded at the summit. There's also a good visual guide to the alpine plants that grow on the summit, including the dwarf cinquefoil, a tiny flower that grows only in the alpine zones of the Presidential Range and Franconia Ridge.

Those willing to join the observatory's membership program can register for a tour of the **weather station** (www.mtwashington.org, 603/356-2137, ext. 211, membership $50 individual, $75 couple or family) itself; unfortunately, the station is closed to the public, though the observatory recently began partnering with the Mount Washington Cog

Railway so that several railway trips a week include a tour of the weather station (call for details).

The oldest surviving building on the summit is the **Tip Top House,** a rustic stone lodge built in 1853 as a hotel, which then became the office for *Among the Clouds*, a mountain newspaper that chronicled social events, train schedules, weather, and gossip in 1888-1915. Tiny bunks, communal tables, and a few dusty reproductions of the newspaper are on display.

Sports and Recreation

TOP EXPERIENCE

HIKING

The most iconic hike in the White Mountains may be the **Tuckerman Ravine Trail,** a 4.2-mile route to the summit of Mount Washington that leaves from the **Pinkham Notch Visitor Center** (361 Rte. 16). Doing this hike as a round-trip is a full-day outing of at least six hours, and it's especially important to bring extra clothes, water, and a headlamp for this strenuous trail. After some initial switchbacks through thick forest, the trail rises fairly gradually to **Hermit Lake Shelter** after 2.4 miles, where you'll find lean-tos, tent platforms, and potable water from a hand-operated pump.

After the lake the trail begins to climb in earnest, then aims straight up the western edge of Tuckerman Ravine, earning elevation and views with every step. Upon cresting the valley headwall, the trail reaches a junction that's clearly signed for the Mount Washington summit (0.6 mile) and Lakes of the Clouds (0.8 mile), the most spectacular of the White Mountains' AMC huts and a pleasant spot to stop for hot drinks (and sometimes freshly baked treats from the hut staff). For a return trip to Pinkham Notch that's easier on the knees, it's possible to descend via the more moderate **Boott Spur** or **Lion Head Trails,** or just book a spot on the one-way hiker shuttle from the top.

Before setting out, it's important to stop by the **Pinkham Notch Visitor Center** (361 Rte. 16, 603/466-8116, www.outdoors.org, 6:30am-10pm daily) to pick up detailed maps and get the most recent updates about weather and trail conditions.

SKIING

A ski resort with broad exposure to the northwest, **Wildcat Mountain** (542 Rte. 16, Pinkham Notch, 603/466-3326, www.

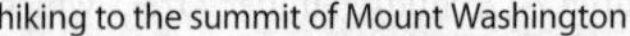

hiking to the summit of Mount Washington

skiwildcat.com, $75-79 adults, $50-54 seniors and youth 7-17, children under 7 free with adult) is known for snagging the area's biggest snowfalls. There's 2,112 feet of vertical drop and 48 runs dominated by intermediate options, and many of the trails have spectacular views across the valley to Mount Washington.

Food

Family-style meals at the **Pinkham Notch Visitor Center** (361 Rte. 16, 603/466-8116, www.outdoors.org, breakfast 6:30am-9am $15, lunch 9:30am-4pm $5-12, dinner Mon.-Thu. 6pm, Fri.-Sun. 5:30pm-7:30pm $29, open seven days) are just about the only game in town, but the food is plentiful and it's a great way to meet fellow hikers. Breakfast and dinner are all-you-can-eat affairs—weekend dinners are buffets, and weeknights are served family-style with a single seating. The à la carte lunch menu is deli style and designed for the trail, with packable sandwiches and snacks.

Accommodations and Camping

$100-150

One of the two front-country lodges operated by the AMC, the **Joe Dodge Lodge** (Rte. 16, Pinkham Notch, 603/466-2727, www.outdoors.org, room with dinner and breakfast from $92 pp) is something of a hostel experience, and a good fit for families. Both private rooms and bunk rooms share bathrooms, and there's often a blazing fire in the living room and library. Meals are served family style at big tables, and knowledgeable staff members lead guided hikes and give talks on the natural world.

CAMPING

In the White Mountain National Forest, backcountry camping is allowed below the tree line, as long as tents are over 200 feet from trails and water. The national forest also operates a number of excellent campgrounds: Six miles south of Gorham, **Dolly Copp Campground** (Rte. 16, 877/444-6777, mid-May-mid-Oct., reservations accepted, some sites first-come, first-served, $22) is one the largest in the forest, with vault toilets, campfire rings, and ranger-run programs. No showers are on-site, but coin-operated showers are available five miles south at the AMC's **Pinkham Notch Visitor Center** (361 Rte. 16).

Information and Services

On Route 16, the AMC's **Pinkham Notch Visitor Center** (361 Rte. 16, 603/466-8116, www.outdoors.org, 6:30am-10pm daily) has plenty of the same, along with a small trading post for supplies. If you're coming to use the visitors center's coin-operated showers, plan to bring a stack of quarters.

Getting There and Around

Roughly 40 minutes north of Conway, Pinkham Notch is on Route 16. Parking is available at the visitors center, and **Concord Coach Lines** (800/639-3317, www.concordcoachlines.com) links Pinkham Notch by bus with **Boston** (4 hrs., 14 min., round-trip $64).

Pinkham Notch Visitor Center is the starting point for one of the two **AMC Hiker Shuttle** (www.outdoors.org, early June-Oct., $23, $19 AMC members) routes, which access many popular trailheads in the area, especially those that lead to the AMC's mountain huts.

BRETTON WOODS AND CRAWFORD NOTCH

Look carefully at the southern flank of Mount Washington, and you may see tiny puffs of smoke and steam emerging from a toy-sized train—the Mount Washington Cog Railway is climbing to the summit. Along with a grand, 19th-century hotel, the cog railway is a remnant of the heyday of White Mountain tourism, when New England's urban residents fell for big peaks and wilderness.

But if the name Bretton Woods sounds familiar, it's likely due to a financial accord that involved the world's leading economists and (reportedly) a great deal of alcohol. In July 1944, the Bretton Woods Conference was held in the Mount Washington Hotel as World War II still raged. With a spectacular view of Mount Washington, delegates from 44 Allied Nations fought a series of bloodless battles that determined the postwar financial landscape, drank late into the night, and established the dollar as the world's standard reserve currency.

It's fascinating to explore that history in the hotel—now with the drably corporate name of Omni Mount Washington Resort—and on the cog, which makes several chugging trips up Mount Washington each day. And for those who'd prefer to hike the mountain, this is an excellent place to set out, with trails leaving from Bretton Woods and Crawford Notch State Park.

Sights

★ MOUNT WASHINGTON COG RAILWAY

When Chicago meatpacking baron Sylvester Marsh first presented his idea for a railway to the top of Mount Washington, the state legislature told him he might as well "build a railway to the moon." In the spirit of the times, he was undeterred and began work on the world's first mountain-climbing train using materials hauled through thick forest by oxen teams. When the railway began service in 1869, it was the first in the world to employ toothed gears, or cogs, that meshed with a pinion on the track to prevent the train from slipping backward. In those early years, the railway was powered with staggering quantities of wood, which gave way to coal in 1908.

These days the historic coal-fired trains alternate with more eco-friendly biodiesel engines, and though the railway is slower (and more expensive) than the auto road, it's wonderfully fun to chug your way up Mount Washington as the steam whistle echoes off the surrounding peaks. The trains of the **Mount Washington Cog Railway** (Base Rd., off Rte. 302, Bretton Woods, 603/278-5404, www.thecog.com, 3-hour round-trip on steam/biodiesel, $75/$69 adults, $69/65 seniors, $39 children 4-12, children under 4 free, one-way tickets $48, discount with military ID) run late April-November; daily service June-October tapers to weekends during April-May and November. After reaching the top of Mount Washington, it's worth asking the engineer for a peek inside the engine to see the coal bin, brakes, levers, and gauges. Trips allow for one hour on the summit, so if you'd like to spend the day hiking, you'll

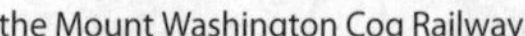
the Mount Washington Cog Railway

have to book a standby return ticket—though you're guaranteed to get down by the end of the day, it's not possible to reserve a spot on any given train.

Entertainment and Events

The **Omni Mount Washington Resort** (Rte. 302, Bretton Woods, 603/278-1000, www.mountwashingtonresort.com) has a suite of restaurants with varying quality, but it's the hotel's high tea and cocktail hours that are destination worthy. For alpine elegance, you can't beat tea in the **Princess Room** (3pm Fri.-Sat., $20 adults, $12 children 10 and under): Grown-ups sip their brews along with ceviche, savory tartlets, scones, and sweets, while kids get mini marshmallows in their hot chocolate, and a menu of tiny sandwiches, savory muffins, macarons, and strawberry tarts. The elegant room is named for Princess Caroline, the eccentric, glamorous wife of the hotel's original owner.

As charming as those princess-worthy tea parties can be, though, the finest seats in the hotel are on the broad back veranda, where comfortable wicker chairs are pointed straight at the southern slope of Mount Washington. Sunsets are spectacular here, and sharp-eyed visitors can spot the glint and smoke of the cog railway as it chugs up the slope. Guests on the veranda can order from the ★ **Rosebrook Bar** (noon-10pm, $9-15), and sip wine, beer, and cocktails along with savory nibbles that would seem overpriced in a different venue.

Sports and Recreation

TOP EXPERIENCE

HIKING

Two trails ascend Mount Washington from the cog railway station; allow a full day for a round-trip hike on either. The most direct route is the 4.4-mile **Ammonoosuc Ravine Trail,** which climbs steeply to Lakes of the Clouds, then continues up a rocky path to the summit; in addition to passing scenic ponds and the AMC hut, this trail has gorgeous views as it works its way up the southwest face of the mountain. Somewhat longer and more gradual, the 5.1-mile **Jewell Trail** ascends the western slope of Mount Clay, then skirts the summit to join a ridge trail to the top of Mount Washington. This is another stunner on clear days; it's delightful to hike parallel to the cog railway for views of the brightly colored trains with an endless backdrop.

Not all the hikes in the White Mountains are quite so strenuous. One favorite option for families is the 3.2-mile round-trip hike up **Mount Willard,** which earns fabulous views of Crawford Notch, with more gradual slopes (for that reason, this hike tends to be crowded on busy days in the Whites, so don't expect solitude). Park at the railroad depot information center adjacent to the **AMC Highland Center** on Route 302.

Find the highest single-drop waterfall in New Hampshire at the end of the **Arethusa Falls Trail,** a 2.6-mile round-trip hike along Bemis Brook. Park on the west side of Route 302 about a mile south of Dry River Campground in Crawford Notch State Park. The hike is fairly steep but well suited for families with older kids, and it's possible to extend it into a 4.7-mile loop by returning via **Frankenstein Cliff Trail,** which has lovely views of the valley. The falls' musical name is said to be taken from a poem by Percy Bysshe Shelley about a Greek nymph who was transformed into a flowing spring, and the lines evoke the spot beautifully:

Arethusa arose
From her couch of snows
In the Acroceraunian mountains,
From cloud and from crag,
With many a jag,
Shepherding her bright fountains.
She leapt down the rocks,
With her rainbow locks
Streaming among the streams;
Her steps paved with green
The downward ravine
Which slopes to the western gleams

SKIING

New Hampshire's biggest ski area is **Bretton Woods Mountain Resort** (99 Ski Area Rd., Bretton Woods, 603/278-3320, www.brettonwoods.com, lift tickets $78-89 adults, $25-89 seniors, $58-68 youth 13-17, $43-53 children 5-12), which looks out at the southern edge of Mount Washington and the Presidential Range, with 97 trails, from beginner to expert. There's 464 acres of terrain here and 10 lifts, which usually run mid-November-mid-April. The ski hill is part of the Omni Mount Washington Resort group, and tickets are discounted for hotel guests.

Food

Nonguests can join the convivial dining hours at the AMC's **Highland Center at Crawford Notch** (Rte. 302, Crawford Notch, 603/278-4453, www.outdoors.org, breakfast 6:30am-10am, $15 adults, $10.50 children 3-12, à la carte lunch 11am-4pm, dinner 6pm-8pm, $29 adults, $14 children 3-12). Breakfast is an all-you-can-eat buffet spread that's aimed at hikers heading into the hills, and dinner is either buffet-style or family-style (on family-style nights, dinner is at 6pm sharp). For breakfast and dinner, it's important to call ahead, as meals can book up on busy nights—lunch is for stocking up on trail food, with no reservations required.

Another solid choice is **Fabyan's Station** (Rte. 302, 603/278-2222, www.brettonwoods.com, 11:30am-9pm daily, hours may be limited in off-season, $11-14), which serves basic pub fare in a historic railroad station that was once the depot for Crawford Notch. Burgers, sandwiches, and salads aren't standout, but the atmosphere is good and the alternatives are sparse. Like almost everything else in Bretton Woods, the restaurant is owned by Omni Mount Washington Resort, which also operates a fancy dining room and an on-site pub (which are decent options if you're staying, but aren't really worth the trip).

Accommodations and Camping

$100-150

Adjacent to the Appalachian Mountain Club's visitors center is the **Highland Center at Crawford Notch** (Rte. 302, Crawford Notch, 603/278-4453, www.outdoors.org, pp with shared bath, dinner and breakfast included, from $90 adults, $80 youth 12-17, $45 children 11 and under), the sibling to the Joe Dodge Lodge in Pinkham Notch. It's friendly and rustic, with fireplaces for post-hike lounging,

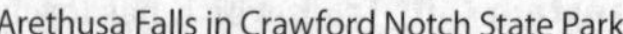
Arethusa Falls in Crawford Notch State Park

The Appalachian Mountain Club's White Mountain Huts

The Appalachian Mountain Club (AMC) has maintained a system of nine backcountry huts in the White Mountains since 1888, making the wilderness accessible for hikers without the gear and experience to rough it on their own. Spending a night at one of the AMC huts is a great deal like alpine summer camp, with bunk beds, communal meals, and a convivial atmosphere among the tired hikers. While rates can seem high (especially given the rustic experience), you're paying for meals hiked in by hardy college students in a wild, scenic place, and staying in the backcountry is an unforgettable experience.

The most famous—and perhaps most spectacular—among the AMC huts is **Lakes of the Clouds,** set by a cluster of alpine ponds just a ridgeline away from the top of Mount Washington. The trail to pretty **Zealand Falls Hut** is far less challenging, a relatively gradual 2.8-mile hike that ends at a perfect river swimming spot. Less popular (and crowded) than those two all-stars, **Carter Notch Hut** is the easternmost hut in the AMC system, a 1914 stone structure set between Wildcat Dome and Carter Mountain.

One of the AMC's most easily accessible huts from the Franconia Range side is **Lonesome Lake Hut,** which is a 1.6-mile hike from the trailhead in Lafayette Campground, with fabulous views of the mountains, naturalist programs, and rustic coed bunk rooms. Another favorite in the Franconia area is **Greenleaf Hut,** which is at the end of a moderate, 2.7-mile walk and offers an equally spectacular perspective on the rugged terrain.

Rates include dinner the night of arrival and breakfast the morning after, and **reservations** (603/466-2727, www.outdoors.org, $105-131) can be made online or by phone. Visitors must bring their own sleeping bags, though additional wool blankets are provided, and guests share simple, often solar-powered bathrooms with cold running water. The most popular huts, and especially Lakes of the Clouds, are often booked months in advance, but there's almost always last-minute space if you're flexible about where you stay.

and a cafeteria where meals are served family style. Most rooms at the lodge use shared baths, but there are a few private bathrooms available for those who prefer not to share sinks. If you're staying at the Highland Center, you get free access to the gear room, which has all the warm layers and hiking boots you need for tackling some peaks.

OVER $250

Of the dozens of grand hotels that dotted the mountains at the turn of the 20th century, the 1902 ★ **Omni Mount Washington Resort** (Rte. 302, Bretton Woods, 603/278-1000 or 800/843-6664, www.mountwashingtonresort.com, $179-469) is the most perfectly preserved, and discovering the gorgeous historical touches throughout the building could easily occupy a rainy afternoon. A gracious veranda runs the length of the rambling hotel, with comfortable chairs that look straight out on Mount Washington. Even if you're not staying here, stopping by for a drink on the deck—or an utterly charming high tea in the Princess Room—is a wonderful experience, and a gracious counterbalance to the White Mountains' rugged scenery.

If you come for the night, be sure to head outside to watch the stars from the outdoor fireplace or pool, and enjoy the period feel of the rooms—while the usual contemporary amenities have been added, the rooms are still thoroughly old-fashioned. For much of the year, the most desirable are those facing the mountain, which get stunning sunrise views, but for trips during foliage season, book the front of the hotel, which looks across the valley at a slope crowded with flaming maple trees. Bretton Woods, as it's still called by many, is a city unto itself, complete with a post office in the basement, golf courses, a zip line, riding stables, and a handful of restaurants on-site. While much of Bretton Woods is beautifully done, meal service is inconsistent, and the main dining room seems overpriced for quality. Many visitors prefer to duck into the downstairs pub, which is less grand but more reliable.

CAMPING

For good access to the cog railway and hikes on the Crawford Notch side of Mount Washington, Crawford Notch State Park's **Dry River Campground** (2057 Rte. 302, Bartlett, 877/647-2757, www.nhstateparks.org, May-Oct., $23) is a good option, with 36 primitive sites, good bathroom facilities, and showers.

Information

The AMC **Macomber Family Information Center** (3575 Rte. 302, Crawford Notch, 603/466-2727, 9am-4pm daily, closes earlier in off-season) is a popular trailhead and hiker information spot. The AMC also has a trail information and weather hotline (603/466-2721).

Getting There and Around

Both Crawford Notch and Bretton Woods are located on Route 302, and visitors need their own form of transportation to get there. For hikers who want to do longer, one-way hikes, it's worth looking into the **AMC Hiker Shuttle** (www.outdoors.org, early June-Oct., $23), which has a fixed route that accesses many popular trailheads in the area, especially those that lead to the AMC's mountain huts. There's also local service from **Garey's Taxi** (603/991-4546, www.gareystaxi.weebly.com).

GORHAM

A useful stop for food and supplies on the way to the Whites, Gorham is also a reasonable home base for trips into the mountains. Though the sprawling downtown is a bit faded, the northern edge of the Presidential Range provides a dramatic backdrop. Gorham has taken the moose as an unofficial mascot—the rest of New Hampshire might contest its claim—and tours set out daily in search of the lumbering creatures.

Sights

As wary New England drivers know, moose come out at dusk. With that in mind, **Gorham Moose Tours** (69 Main St., 603/466-3103, www.gorhammoosetours.org, 2.5-3-hour tours depart 7pm daily, $25 adults, $15 children 5-12, $5 children under 5) strikes out into the forest as the sun goes down. Tours are on 14-person vans, and the odds of spotting moose are high—in a good year with plentiful moose, the animals are sighted on every outing. A driver will search out moose-y spots and share an encyclopedia of moose facts along the way, but here are a few good ones: The animals weigh in at 1,500 pounds and can measure nine feet long, and a moose can carry up to 120,000 ticks.

In many ways, the White Mountains were easier to reach a century ago than today—frequent trains made the trip from Boston a breeze, with whistle stops at lodges and hotels. The small, volunteer-run **Gorham Historical Society & Railroad Museum** (25 Railroad St., 603/466-5338, www.gorhamnewhampshire.com, 10am-3pm Tues.-Sat. May-Oct., free) preserves artifacts from that era in Gorham's 1907 railway station. Call before visiting, as hours can vary with volunteer availability.

Shopping

In Gorham, stop by **Gorham Hardware & Sport Center** (96 Main St., 603/466-2312, www.nhhockeyshop.com, 8am-5pm Mon.-Fri., 8am-4pm Sat., 8am-1pm Sun., hours may vary seasonally) for hiking, climbing, skiing, and camping setups.

For groceries in Gorham, you'll find a **Save-A-Lot** (491 Main St., 603/752-1248, 8am-8pm daily) discount grocery and **Walmart Supercenter** (561 Main St., 603/752-4621, 7am-10pm daily).

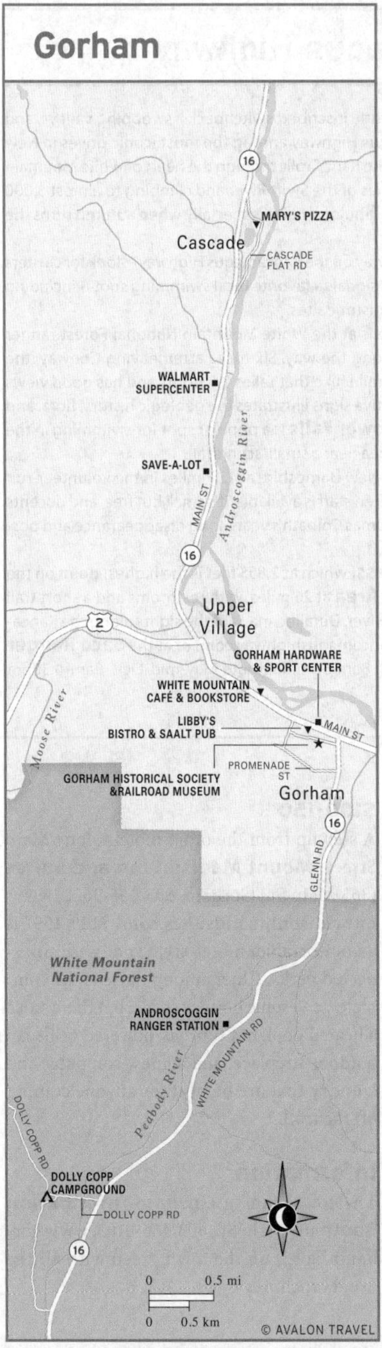

Food

Amid the generic chains lining Route 2 through Gorham, **White Mountain Café & Bookstore** (212 Rte. 2, 603/466-2511, www.whitemountaincafe.com, 7am-4pm daily, $4-11) stands out with personality and charm. Head to the counter for sandwiches, burritos, pastries, and salads, then settle in at a small café table or the sunny front lot. The café also has solid espresso and wireless Internet, making it a good spot to sit a spell and catch up on emails.

For pizza lovers of a certain age, it's hard not to love **Mary's Pizza** (9 Cascade Flats Rd., 603/752-6150, www.maryspizzanh.com, lunch 11am-2pm Wed.-Sat., dinner 4pm-9pm Mon.-Sat., $6-18), an old-school Italian American joint that recalls the years before "flatbread" began to appear covered with gourmet toppings. Pizzas and pastas are simple and come piled with lots of cheese, meat, and vegetables, with decor to match—think red and white-checkered vinyl tablecloths, red Coke glasses, and a jukebox stocked with country and rock-and-roll CDs.

If you've taken some time to explore Gorham, then ★ **Libby's Bistro & SAaLT Pub** (111 Rte. 16, 603/466-5330, www.libbysbistro.org, bistro 5pm-8pm Fri.-Sat., $10-24, pub 5pm-9pm Wed.-Sun., $9-15) will come as something of a surprise. The more upscale bistro and the clubby, convivial pub both have outstanding food, as well as a full bar menu. Even the burgers have creative flair, like the Korean burger topped with kimchi coleslaw and chili mayo or the Peruvian fish sandwich daubed with spiced tartar sauce, but the kitchen really gets going with the global mains: Ricotta gnocchi with veal meatballs, Mumbai cakes, and Middle Eastern-spiced fried chicken strike a balance between thoughtful and satisfying.

Accommodations

UNDER $100

Four miles east of Gorham, ★ **Rattle River Lodge and Hostel** (592 Rte. 2, Shelburne, 603/466-5049 or 715/557-1736, www.whitemountainslodgeandhostel.com, $35 with

Driving the Kancamagus Highway

Between Conway and Lincoln, 35 miles of tightly inscribed switchbacks, swooping valleys, and perfect mountain views make the Kancamagus Highway among the most iconic drives in New England. Route 112, affectionately known as "the Kanc," rolls through the heart of White Mountain National Forest, following the twists and curves of the Swift River and climbing to almost 3,000 feet—at 2,855 feet, the Kancamagus Pass has fabulous views, especially when autumn turns the surrounding forest into a riot of color.

There are plenty of places to stop along the way on the Kancamagus Highway—look for clusters of cars along the side of the road, which often signals a favorite local swimming spot—including a series of scenic overlooks, hiking trails, and historic sites.

Driving from Conway to Lincoln, mile zero is at the White Mountain National Forest ranger station, making it easy to find landmarks along the way. Six miles after leaving Conway, the **Boulder Loop Trail** is a moderate, three-mile hike that takes 2-3 hours and has good views of rocky ledges and forest. A series of interpretive signs illustrates the geologic history, flora, and fauna of the White Mountains. At 7.0 miles, **Lower Falls** is a popular spot for swimming in the Swift River, and has bathrooms and a picnic area near a small, scenic fall.

You can peer into daily life in 19th-century New Hampshire at 12.7 miles in the volunteer-run **Russell-Colbath House,** which is open when staff is available. It's small but free, and docents are happy to share the mysterious story of Thomas Colbath's years-long disappearance and possible reappearance.

Keep winding up to the **Kancamagus Pass,** which at 2,855 feet is the highest point on the road, then you'll find the **Otter Rock Rest Area** at 26 miles, with restrooms and a short trail to another lovely swimming area in the Swift River. Detailed maps of the sights along the Kancamagus Highway are available online (www.kancamagushighway.com) or at the **Saco Ranger Station** (33 Rte. 112, Conway, 603/447-5448, 8am-5pm daily late May-mid-Oct., 8am-4:30pm daily Oct.-May).

breakfast) is an excellent option for budget travelers, and as it's popular with thru-hikers on the Appalachian Trail, it's a good place to hear tales from the woods. The coed rooms have 2-6 beds, and the huge, home-cooked Belgian waffle breakfasts are perfect fuel for a day on the trail. The rambling 19th-century building is both gracious and homey, with a patio, pond, and fire pit.

The basic **Moose Brook Motel** (65 Lancaster Rd., Gorham, 603/466-5400, www.moosebrookmotel.com, $79-109) has simple, clean accommodations with nostalgic wood paneling. Each room is stocked with a coffeemaker, there's (slow) wireless Internet, and the pool looks pretty inviting after a day on the trail. Children are free, and dogs are an additional $5.

$100-150

A step up from the other motels along Main Street, **Mount Madison Inn and Suites** (365 Main St., Gorham, 603/466-3622, www.mtmadisoninnandsuites.com, $129-159) is a comfortable, motel-style spot with unexpected perks. Chief among those is the completely awesome bouncy castle, but there's also a heated pool, hot tub, gas-powered grills, an outdoor fireplace, and a guest computer and laundry that are helpful for anyone coming off the trail.

Information

The town runs a **Gorham Information Booth** (69 Main St., 603/466-3103, www.gorhamnh.org) on the town green with all the usual brochures.

Getting There and Around

At the intersection of the east-west Route 2 and the north-south Route 16, Gorham is the entry point to the Mount Washington Valley for visitors arriving from northern Maine and Vermont.

Concord Coach Lines (800/639-3317, www.concordcoachlines.com) links Gorham by bus with **Boston** (4 hrs., 30 min., round-trip $67). The **AMC Hiker Shuttle** (www.outdoors.org, early June-Oct., $23) connects the Gorham gas station (350 Main St.) with trailheads throughout the mountains.

The Franconia Range

A north-south ridgeline running from Mount Lafayette to Mount Flume, the Franconia Range is second only to the Presidential Range among New Hampshire's peaks. While the Presidential Range outdoes the highest of these by a cool 1,000 feet, the Franconia Range is just as rugged. And there's no road to the top of these mountains, so if you sweat to the Mount Lafayette summit, you won't need to share the view with crowds in flip-flops.

In the valley below, Franconia Notch State Park offers easy access to hiking trails, waterfalls, and a deep, natural gorge. This was the home of New Hampshire's most recognizable landmark, the "Old Man of the Mountain," but the series of granite ledges came tumbling down in 2003, despite elaborate efforts to hold the stony face together.

The towns of Littleton and Franconia are the main bases for visiting Franconia Notch, and the road into the park is high drama, twisting between high peaks and cliff faces. Franconia Notch itself is a bustling vacation spot, with an enormous campground, a lake with a swimming beach, a mountain tram, and trail after trail heading up into the hills.

FRANCONIA

Sights

FRANCONIA NOTCH STATE PARK

Following the valley (and highway) between the Kinsman Range and the Franconia Range, this beautiful state park has a bit of everything—including beaches, a campground, lots of hiking, and kid-friendly trails. Set just at the base of Cannon Mountain, **Echo Lake Beach** (Exit 34C, Franconia Notch State Park, 603/823-8800, $4 adults, $2 children 6-11, children under 6 free) is sandy and scenic, with a lifeguard on duty during the day; it's possible to rent canoes, kayaks, and paddleboats here for $20 per hour.

The fast-moving traffic through the valley doesn't give much time for taking in the views, but you can move at your own pace on the **Franconia Notch State Park Recreation Path,** an 8.8-mile bike and pedestrian trail that slopes gently downhill from the base of Cannon Mountain to the Flume Gorge. There's trailhead parking at both ends—to reach the Cannon Mountain trailhead, take exit 34B; you'll see the trailhead on the left. Bike rentals are available at each end from **Sport Thoma** (371 Rte. 3, Lincoln, 603/745-8151 *or* Aerial Tramway Lodge, Exit 34B, Franconia, 603/823-8800, www.sportthoma.com, bike rental half-day $35, full-day $50, shuttle-only $20), whose prices include transfer on the one-way shuttle. (Most people drop a car at Flume Gorge, take a shuttle to the top, then ride back down.)

★ FLUME GORGE

Narrow, wooden walkways lead through this natural chasm, accessible from a **visitors center** (852 Rte. 3, Lincoln, 603/745-8391, www.nhstateparks.org, 8:30am-5pm daily early May-late Oct., until 5:30pm mid-June-early Sept., $16 adults, $13 children 6-12, children under 6 free) just a few minutes south of Franconia Notch State Park. Its high Conway granite walls shelter covered bridges, mossy

Franconia

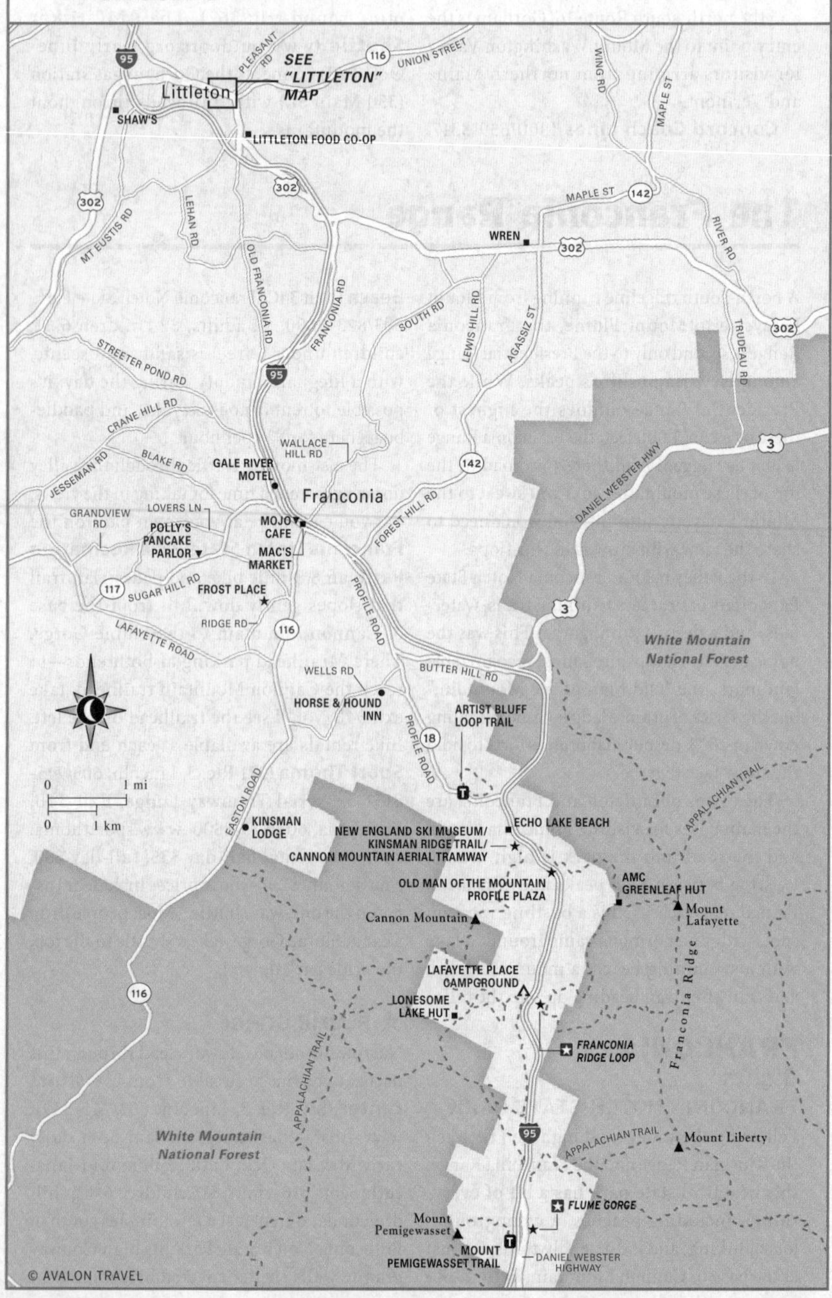

SEE "LITTLETON" MAP
Littleton
SHAW'S
LITTLETON FOOD CO-OP
PLEASANT RD
UNION STREET
WING RD
MAPLE ST
MAPLE ST
RIVER RD
WREN
MT EUSTIS RD
LEHAN RD
OLD FRANCONIA RD
FRANCONIA RD
SOUTH RD
LEWIS HILL RD
AGASSIZ ST
TRUDEAU RD
STREETER POND RD
CRANE HILL RD
WALLACE HILL RD
BLAKE RD
JESSEMAN RD
GALE RIVER MOTEL
Franconia
FOREST HILL RD
DANIEL WEBSTER HWY
GRANDVIEW RD
LOVERS LN
POLLY'S PANCAKE PARLOR
MOJO CAFE
MAC'S MARKET
SUGAR HILL RD
FROST PLACE
RIDGE RD
LAFAYETTE ROAD
PROFILE ROAD
White Mountain National Forest
BUTTER HILL RD
WELLS RD
HORSE & HOUND INN
ARTIST BLUFF LOOP TRAIL
PROFILE ROAD
0 1 mi
0 1 km
EASTON ROAD
KINSMAN LODGE
ECHO LAKE BEACH
NEW ENGLAND SKI MUSEUM/ KINSMAN RIDGE TRAIL/ CANNON MOUNTAIN AERIAL TRAMWAY
APPALACHIAN TRAIL
OLD MAN OF THE MOUNTAIN PROFILE PLAZA
AMC GREENLEAF HUT
Mount Lafayette
Cannon Mountain
Franconia Ridge
LAFAYETTE PLACE CAMPGROUND
LONESOME LAKE HUT
FRANCONIA RIDGE LOOP
APPALACHIAN TRAIL
White Mountain National Forest
APPALACHIAN TRAIL
Mount Liberty
FLUME GORGE
Mount Pemigewasset
MOUNT PEMIGEWASSET TRAIL
DANIEL WEBSTER HIGHWAY
© AVALON TRAVEL

walls, and waterfalls, including the spectacular 45-foot-high Avalanche Falls. The gorge was formed before the last ice age, when a fin of basalt was forced into the vertically fractured granite; the basalt weathered away more quickly than the surrounding granite, leaving a winding slot in its place. A two-mile trail leads through the gorge, with a few places to duck off the path and explore, such as the Wolf's Den, a narrow, one-way route that involves squeezing yourself through cracks in the rock and crawling on hands and knees. As the story goes, Flume Gorge was discovered by 93-year-old Jess Guernsey when she was looking for a new spot to drop a fishing line, and it still holds the thrill of discovery: It's cool between the rock walls, and birch trees worm out of stony cracks. Don't miss the visitors center's display case full of old-timey Flume Gorge postcards that 19th-century vacationers sent to their friends back home.

CANNON MOUNTAIN

Get your bearings from the top of this bare granite dome—on a clear day, views stretch to four states and Canada, and you can enjoy the scene from an observation deck. You'll also find a café at the top of Cannon Mountain and walking trails that cross the 4,080-foot summit. Zip up to the top in fewer than 10 minutes on the **Aerial Tramway** (260 Tramway Dr., 603/823-8800, www.cannonmt.com, 9am-5pm daily late May-mid-June, 8:30am-5:30pm daily mid-June-mid-Oct., round-trip $18 adults, $16 children 6-12; one-way $13 adults, $10 children 6-12, children under 6 free), or you can hike to the top on the **Kinsman Ridge Trail,** a 2.2-mile one-way hike that leaves from the tramway parking lot and has great perspectives on Franconia Notch.

FROST PLACE

From 1915 to 1920, Robert Frost lived in a small house with views of the mountains, and his spirit lives on at the secluded farmstead, now a museum and poetry center. Each year, the museum invites a poet to live in the house for six weeks, writing and working in Frost's former home of **Frost Place** (Ridge Rd., 603/823-5510, www.frostplace.org, 1pm-5pm Thurs.-Sun. late May-June, 1pm-5pm Wed.-Mon. July-mid-Aug., 10am-5pm Wed.-Mon. Sept.-mid-Oct., $5 adults, $4 seniors, $3 students 12 and above, children under 12 free), which retains a peaceful, contemplative feel. The museum has signed first editions of Frost's poetry, as well as other memorabilia from his life, and there's a 0.5 mile nature trail winding through the property with poems from the Franconia years. The trail, grounds, and peaceful front porch of the house are always open to the public.

OTHER SIGHTS

Relive the glory days and the fall of New Hampshire's rocky mascot at the **Old Man of the Mountain Profile Plaza** (Tramway Dr., Exit 34B from I-93), where you can line up just right and get a glimpse of what the cliffs looked like before they collapsed in 2003. You can watch ski technology progress from furry boots and wool knickers to high-tech jumpsuits at the diminutive **New England Ski Museum** (Tramway Dr., 603/823-7177, www.newenglandskimuseum.org, 10am-5pm daily late May-end of ski season, free), whose koan-like motto is "preserving the future of skiing's past." The museum has medals and trophies from New Hampshire-native skier Bode Miller and a short movie about his career.

Entertainment and Events

The mountain meadows north of the notch are filled with violet blossoms every year in time for the **Lupine Festival** (603/823-8000, www.franconianotch.org, mid-June), a street festival and art show with events throughout the region. By governor's decree, each year in early July, Frost Place holds **Frost Day** (603/823-5510, www.frostplace.org), with readings of poetry by the poet-in-residence and musical performances at the farmstead.

Hiking

For hikes in the area, stop by the hiker cabin at

Lafayette Place Campground (Franconia Notch State Park, 603/823-5884, www.nhstateparks.org, 8am-3pm daily) for updated trail conditions, maps, and alpine weather reports—even when valley weather is blissful, the exposed alpine trail can get howling wind and whiteout fog.

★ FRANCONIA RIDGE LOOP

For the ultimate Franconia hike, plan for at least six hours on the 8.2-mile **Franconia Ridge Loop,** a rugged New Hampshire classic that goes up and over three peaks: Little Haystack Mountain, Mount Lincoln, and Mount Lafayette. The trail starts on the east side of I-93, opposite Lafayette Place Campground, and starts straight up the fall line, climbing 3,480 feet in around four miles, passing a series of scenic waterfalls on the way up Little Haystack. The ridgeline trail between Mount Lincoln and Mount Lafayette is a highlight, a knife-edge ridge that's all exposed rock and perfect views.

Earn your views with (somewhat) less work on the **Mount Pemigewasset Trail,** a moderate, 3.3-mile out-and-back that takes roughly 2-3 hours to complete from the Flume Gorge Visitor Center parking lot. Much of the way is wooded and shady, and the trail crosses a series of pretty brooks, but the summit is bare rock, and though the mountain tops out at 2,557 feet, it feels like a real adventure. For more information on this hike, ask at the on-site visitors center.

Easy enough for younger children, the 1.5-mile **Artist Bluff Loop Trail** looks out toward Cannon Mountain and Franconia Notch from the valley floor. To access the trailhead from Littleton or Franconia, take exit 34C from I-93, then take Route 18 west for 0.5 mile and park in the large lot on the right. This trail is particularly nice in early spring, when wildflowers bloom along the edge of Echo Lake.

Skiing

With the longest vertical drop in New Hampshire, **Cannon Mountain** (Exit 34C, 603/823-7771, www.cannonmt.com, lift tickets $75 adults, $62 youth 13-17, $52 seniors and children 6-12) has a mix of groomed trails and glades that are dominated by intermediate runs. The aerial tramway means riders get to the top with a bit less windchill than elsewhere in the White Mountains, but Cannon is very exposed to harsh weather, and can be an extremely cold place to ski and ride when the temperatures drop.

Artist Bluff Loop Trail

Food

For takeout sandwiches, strong coffee, ice cream, and pizza, the colorful **Backpack Cafe** (334 Main St., 603/823-5697, www.backpackcafenh.com, 7am-4pm Tues.-Thurs., 7am-7pm Fri.-Sat., 8am-11:30am Sun., $3-12) is the place in town. Limited counter seating is available inside, and there are a few tables on the sunny front porch.

The elegant dining room at the ★ **Horse & Hound Inn** (205 Wells Rd., 800/450-5501, www.horseandhoundnh.com, reservations recommended, 5pm-8pm Wed.-Sun. late May-late Oct., 5pm-8pm Fri.-Sun. late Nov.-Apr., $20-33) has a refined menu that changes with the season, using plenty of fresh, local ingredients, some of which come from the on-site garden. A recent menu included lobster corn custard, fresh handkerchief pasta with wild mushrooms, and a roasted half rack of lamb with mint pesto. On warm days, the outdoor terrace is serene and sunny, and the more casual tavern has a full bar and wonderfully cozy, historical feel.

Two miles west of Franconia, ★ **Polly's Pancake Parlor** (672 Rte. 117, Sugar Hill, 603/823-5575, www.pollyspancakeparlor.com, 7am-3pm daily, $7-13) serves legendary stacks of three-inch cakes with house-made maple syrup (the "fake stuff" is available on request, but it's sure to come with a tart helping of side eye). Buckwheat, cornmeal, and whole wheat flours are stone-ground on-site, and while some nostalgic visitors note that the newly renovated building doesn't have the down-home charm of the original, it has loads of seating, which reduces the impressive lines on weekend mornings.

Find basic groceries in Franconia at **Mac's Market** (347 Main St., 603/823-7795, 7am-8pm daily), which is small, but has beer, wine, and deli products.

Accommodations and Camping

UNDER $100

Find country hospitality at the ★ **Kinsman Lodge** (2165 Easton Rd., 603/823-5686, www.kinsmanlodge.com, $55 s, $95 d), which Chet and Sue Thompson run with a minimum of fuss in a rambling historic building. Guest rooms share superclean bathrooms in the hallway, and the accommodations are simple but comfortable. After a hot day of hiking, it's hard to beat a rocking chair on the broad, shady porch, or a seat in the library, which is stocked with books and games. A big breakfast is served in the sunny dining room.

$100-150

Simple motel rooms and cottages have views of Mount Lafayette and Franconia Notch at **Gale River Motel** (1 Main St., 603/823-5655, www.galerivermotel.com, rooms $90-105, cottages $140-220), where fairly basic accommodations are set on a six-acre property with a shuffleboard, pool, and barbecue area. Rooms have coffeemakers, fridges, wireless Internet, and televisions; the lobby always has freshly baked cookies, cocoa, and tea; and the friendly owner is happy to lend out a DVD player and board games. This motel attracts many guests with pets and kids.

Six miles south of Cannon Mountain, the rustic and pet-friendly **Pemi Cabins** (460 Rte. 3, Lincoln, 800/865-8323, www.pemicabins.com, $72-130) are right on the Pemigawasset River, and some cabins have screened-in porches that look out over the water. Each one is a little different, but most have wood-burning fireplaces, a small sitting area, and cable television, while some have little kitchenettes. The owners can provide home-baked muffins or s'more fixings upon request.

$150-250

As in the wonderful restaurant on-site, lodgings at the ★ **Horse & Hound Inn** (205 Wells Rd., 800/450-5501, www.horseandhoundnh.com, $130-195) are full of well-polished rustic charm. Hardwood floors, locally handmade maple furniture, organic soaps, and beautiful linens are right in keeping with the inn's nostalgic, lodge-like feel. There's a bottle of brandy for nightcaps, a library stocked with books and games, and a fireplace that roars away on cold nights; a breakfast of freshly baked pastries, egg dishes, granola, and fruit is served.

CAMPING

The sites at **Lafayette Place Campground** (1 Franconia Notch State Park, 603/823-9513, www.nhstateparks.org, $25) are right in the heart of the action, with quick access to the trails and destinations within Franconia Notch State Park and hiker information on-site. The location also means the campground has quite a bit of road noise, contained by the high valley walls, but the 97 sites have showers, a camp store, and fire rings, and are ideal for an early start up the Franconia Ridge.

Information and Services

The **Franconia Notch Chamber of Commerce** (603/823-8000, www.franconianotch.org), on I-93 just north of the notch, runs an unstaffed **information center** stocked with brochures, open 24 hours a day. The booth is right next door to the **Abbie Greenleaf Library** (439 Main St., 603/823-8424, 2pm-6pm Mon.-Tues., 10am-noon and 2pm-6pm Wed., 2pm-5pm Thurs.-Fri., 10am-1pm Sat.). Another good source of outdoors info is the hiker cabin at **Lafayette Place Campground** (Franconia Notch State Park, 603/823-5884, www.nhstateparks.org, 8am-3pm daily).

Getting There

Franconia is located off I-93, which continues south through Franconia Notch State Park. **Concord Coach Lines** (800/639-3317, www.concordcoachlines.com) links Franconia by bus with **Boston** (3 hrs., 20 min., round-trip $58).

LITTLETON

With a sweetly old-fashioned Main Street that runs along the Ammonoosuc River, Littleton is farther from the action in Franconia Notch, but there's (a little) more to do here after a day in the mountains. The town's claim to fame may be fading from memory—this was the hometown of writer Eleanor H. Porter, author of the book *Pollyanna*—but Littleton keeps the spirit alive with a yearly festival that celebrates the famously chipper main character.

Sights

Littleton's not big on sights, per se, but if you're walking around downtown there's two small-town landmarks worth the stroll. The **Riverwalk Covered Bridge** (18 Mill St.) was built in 2004, but has the elegant trusswork of the original variety, and the **Pollyanna Statue** (92 Main St.) is a permanent monument to exuberance and joy.

Entertainment and Events

The **Schilling Beer Co.** (18 Mill St., 603/444-4800, www.schillingbeer.com, noon-11pm Sun.-Thurs., noon-midnight Fri.-Sat.) brews small-barrel batches of European-style beers that range from more familiar Hefeweizens to offbeat pours; on a recent summer afternoon, the family-owned brewery was pouring a sour brown wild ale, Leipzig-style gose, and Czech black lagers in a historic riverside barn.

Littleton author Eleanor H. Porter created the super-chipper Pollyanna in a pair of children's novels, and the town has adopted the character as a kind of local mascot. The official **Pollyanna Glad Day** (www.golittleton.

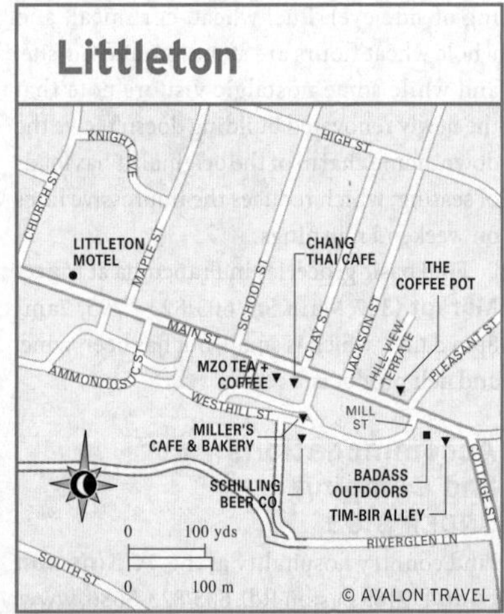

com, early June) celebrates her optimistic legacy with readings, awards, and festivities.

Shopping

Shopping in this area usually means picking up an extra layer for a hike, so stores lean more toward gear than souvenirs. In Littleton, stop by the little, employee-owned **Badass Outdoors** (17 Main St., 603/444-9445, 11am-5pm Tues.-Thurs. and Sun., 10am-6pm Fri.-Sat.). Bethlehem, a cute little town five miles down Route 302 from Littleton, has a supercool shop stocked with work by local artists and artisans, a worthwhile exception to the mostly gear rule; visit **WREN** (2011 Main St., Bethlehem, 603/869-9736, www.wrenworks.org, 10am-5pm daily) to pick up truly local gifts, which are otherwise hard to find in the area.

Food

In addition to its brews, the ★ **Schilling Beer Co.** (18 Mill St., 603/444-4800, www.schillingbeer.com, noon-11pm daily, $9-18) serves Neapolitan-style pizza from a wood-fired oven, and when the riverside patio is open, it's easily the most pleasant, relaxing place to eat in town.

For hearty American breakfasts and lunch at old-fashioned prices, ★ **The Coffee Pot** (30 Main St., 603/444-5722, www.thecoffeepotrestaurant.com, 6:30am-4pm Mon.-Fri., 6:30am-2pm Sat., 6:30am-noon Sun., $4-10) is beloved, with tightly packed tables, a diner counter, and paper place mats advertising local lawn mower repair services. The blueberry pancakes are chock-full of fruit and served with maple syrup, hearty sandwiches are made using house-baked bread, and a fresh fruit pie is always on the menu.

Exposed brick walls, white tablecloths, and refined service make **Tim-Bir Alley** (7 Main St., 603/444-6142, 5pm-9pm Fri.-Sun., $19-30) the most romantic place to eat in Littleton, and the small, handwritten menu changes frequently to reflect the season. Tournedos of beef, ocean fish with fresh herbs, and wild mushroom soup were included on a recent springtime menu, and it's a genuine challenge not to fill up on the breadbasket full of fresh-baked biscuits and butter.

The back porch of **Miller's Cafe and Bakery** (16 Mill St., 603/444-2146, www.millerscafeandbakery.com, 9am-3:30pm Sun. and Tues.-Fri., 9am-9pm Sat., $5-9) overlooks the Ammonoosuc River just as it makes its way under a bright-red covered bridge, so the views alone make this a charming place for breakfast or lunch. Sandwiches, quiche, salads, and a bakery case full of toothsome, old-fashioned sweets are hearty and simple.

Find big-city style and beans from a local roaster at **Blue Jay Coffee & Tea Bar** (81A Main St., 603/575-5433, 9am-6pm Mon.-Sat., 9am-5pm Sun., $3-8), along with a long menu of loose leaf teas and locally baked pastries. Comfy chairs and wireless Internet make this a good place to catch up on the world outside the White Mountains.

A few doors down, **Chang Thai Café** (77 Main St., 603/444-8810, www.changthaicafe.com, 11:30am-3pm and 4:40pm-9pm daily, lunch $9-13, dinner $9-19) is a casual, laid-back place with a menu that includes the American Thai classics—pad thai, drunken noodles—as well as some unexpected additions, like Massaman avocado curry with black tiger shrimp. Lunch specials are a great deal, and the café serves bento boxes with teriyaki and sushi.

Stock up on groceries at **Shaw's** (625 Meadow St., 603/444-1017, 7am-9pm daily) or the **Littleton Food Co-Op** (43 Bethlehem Rd., 603/444-2800, www.littletonfoodcoop.com, 8am-8pm daily), which has a very good selection of local and organic products, a bulk department, and prepared foods.

Accommodations and Camping

UNDER $100

Just off I-93, the pragmatically named **Exit 41 Travel Inn** (337 Cottage St., 603/259-3085, www.exit41travelinn.com, $90-110) is designed as a decent place to get off the road—but that said, the motel is friendly, clean, and kempt, with an outdoor swimming pool and a (very) small continental breakfast.

Walking distance from downtown restaurants, the **Littleton Motel** (166 Main St., 603/444-5780, www.littletonmotel.com, $68-108, 2-room suites $98-158) has old-fashioned, wood-paneled rooms and country charm. Guests gather around the fire pit, and the rooms all have flat-screen televisions and coffeemakers. Children under the age of 16 are free.

$100-150

In a mauve-colored historic home on Main Street, you can't miss **The Beal House** (2 W. Main St., 603/444-2661, www.thebealhouse-inn.com, $129-169), a friendly inn with quaint and pleasant rooms. There's an appealing tavern on-site, and rates include a self-serve continental breakfast of fruit, fresh pastries, and granola.

CAMPING

Five miles from downtown, the forested **Crazy Horse Family Campground** (788 Hilltop Rd., 603/444-2204, www.crazyhorsenh.com, tent sites from $35, sites with hook-ups from $39, 2-bedroom trailer $110) is open year-round, with a summer camp's worth of amenities—a swimming pool, nature trails, a playground, and fire pits—and there's wireless Internet on-site. Pets are welcome (dogs on leash).

Information

In downtown Littleton, stop by the **information center** (124 Main St., 603/444-0616, 9am-4pm Fri.-Sat., 11:30am-3pm Sun. late May-June, 9am-4pm Mon.-Sat., 11:30am-3pm Sun. July-Oct.) run by the **Littleton Area Chamber of Commerce** for a self-guided walking tour of town and information on area businesses. During the months the center is closed, information is available at the **chamber office** (2 Union St., 603/444-0616, www.littletonareachamber.com, 9am-5pm Mon.-Fri.).

Getting There

Littleton is located off I-93, Route 302, and Route 116. **Concord Coach Lines** (800/639-3317, www.concordcoachlines.com) links Littleton by bus with **Boston** (3 hrs., 30 min., round-trip $60.50).

Coastal Maine

Look for ★ to find recommended sights, activities, dining, and lodging.

Highlights

★ **Portland Museum of Art:** This excellent museum houses an extensive collection of impressionist and American art, including nautical themed paintings by Winslow Homer (page 405).

★ **Popham Beach State Park:** Stretch out on a dreamy swatch of sand, or plot a low-tide walk across the flats to tiny Fox Island (page 424).

★ **Lobster Feast:** Dig into great piles of steamed lobster and clams and get a taste of Maine (page 433).

★ **Pemaquid Point Light:** Every rocky peninsula and outcropping's got its very own lighthouse, from hidden gems to crowd favorites (page 435).

★ **Farnsworth Art Museum:** See the Maine coast through the eyes of the state's most beloved painter, Andrew Wyeth, who captured the moods and melancholy of Penobscot Bay and beyond (page 438).

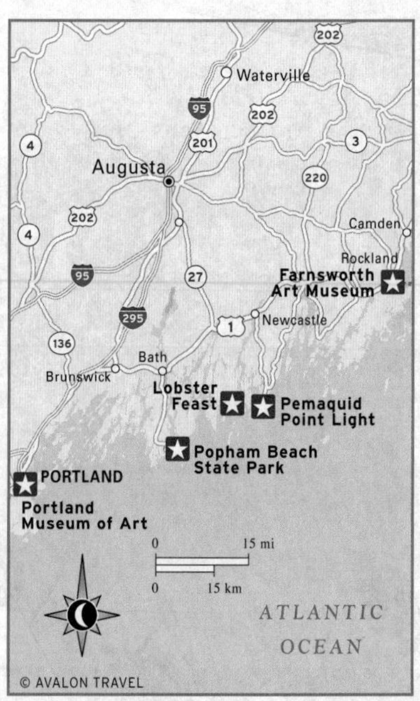

Trace a route along Maine's 3,500-mile waterfront, and you'll find fishing towns, far-flung beaches, and one of New England's most vibrant small cities.

Within day-tripping distance from Boston, the south coast is a classic vacation getaway for city crowds who come to sail and socialize in grand seaside inns. This is the pinnacle of Maine beach chic, with perfect sand, gentle surf breaks, and elegant waterside dining. A few lighthouses up the coast, Portland is the cultural capital of the state, with a fabulous setting and quality of life that draw creative talent from around the country. Framed by a pair of scenic parks, downtown overflows with boat-to-table restaurants, microbreweries, and art.

After Portland, the shoreline goes wild, fracturing into deep coves and bays; proud shipwright towns stand back from the sea on tidal rivers that sent merchant vessels and warships to every corner of the globe. Roads to the shore dead-end at seasonal lobster shacks where you can dine "in the rough" as fishers unload the day's catch.

From Rockland's working waterfront to pretty Camden, the towns lining Penobscot Bay are home to lobster-boat captains, sailors, and summer people, and their harbors shelter grand old schooners and elegant luxury yachts. This is the beginning of Down East, the far stretch of the Maine coast that extends to the most easterly point in the United States. From Penobscot Bay, the coast gets increasingly remote, the towns divided by long passages of deep forest and rugged shoreline leading onward to the scenic jewel of Acadia National Park.

PLANNING YOUR TIME

Even more than other destinations in New England, the true high season in Maine is during schools' summer vacation, when families descend on beaches in hordes. Visiting in late June or late August offers the best weather without the crowds, though many locals say September is the finest month, with still-warm days and cooler nights. At any time of year, however, the weather can be unpredictable, and Maine can seemingly pass through multiple seasons in a single day, with sunshine giving way to fog and rain before turning again.

Previous: York Beach; Ogunquit Coast. **Above:** statue of Paul Bunyan in Bangor.

Experiencing the highlights of coastal Maine takes at least a week, especially when summer crowds turn Route 1 into a series of bottlenecks. Allot this much time and you can take in the region in a series of clusters (with less time, perhaps focus on one, and avoid Route 1 when possible for expediency).

Spend a couple of days exploring south coast lighthouses, beaches, and restaurants from the Kennebunks—Kennebunkport and Kennebunk—or Portland, with time to visit the outdoors or go outlet shopping in Freeport. Make your second destination one of the towns of Maine's Mid-Coast, such as Brunswick, Bath, Wiscasset, and Damariscotta. Plenty of museums and historic downtowns are along Route 1, but don't miss the chance to get off the main road, following quiet highways to island communities and seaside lobster shacks.

After making its way through inland forests, Route 1 finds the coast in Penobscot Bay, where a trio of wonderful towns is perched on picturesque harbors: Rockland, Rockport, and Camden are ideal places to trade your car for a kayak or a berth on a historic schooner and explore the islands dotting the coast.

ORIENTATION

Perched just before the coastline crumbles into a squiggly line of bays and peninsulas, Portland is the cosmopolitan hub and gateway to Maine's endless shoreline. Beyond the city, other destinations on the Maine coast lie along Route 1, a two-lane highway lined with banks of wildflowers and thick forest. Traffic slows to a crawl in each of the towns along the way, where coastal roads sheer off into fishing villages and deep inlets.

The Southern Coast

A beach-lover's utopia, this region more than doubles its population in summer—and for good reason. Its shoreline is peppered with craggy beaches boasting soft sand and unforgettable sunsets, nature preserves, and bird and wildlife sanctuaries.

But there are plenty of man-made reasons to visit, too. The area was originally settled not two decades after the *Mayflower* hit Plymouth Rock, and that shows in its pervasive sense of history, from Kennebunkport's 17th-century homes to Kittery's old naval museums. More modern treasures are abundant, too, from Kennebunk's clam shacks to the antiques shops of Wells, the cafés and top-notch restaurants of Ogunquit, and the bargain outlets of Kittery. June-October, the region's streets get congested with vacationing families and urbanites; the best times to soak up the area's pleasures are in early to mid-autumn.

KITTERY

Just across the Piscataqua River from downtown Portsmouth, Kittery is mostly a destination for shoppers—there's a massive collection of outlet stores and malls sprawling along Route 1. If you're looking for classic Maine, keep heading up the coast, but Kittery's got a few interesting spots beyond the bargain-seeking mayhem, including a small naval museum that explores the town's seafaring past. For a pleasant drive that feels a world away from Route 1, simply duck off the main road onto Route 103, which winds through coast and forest on the scenic route to York Harbor.

Sights

Nautical buffs ought not miss the **Kittery Historical and Naval Museum** (200 Rogers Rd. Extension, 207/439-3080, www.kitterymuseum.com, 10am-4pm Wed.-Sat.,

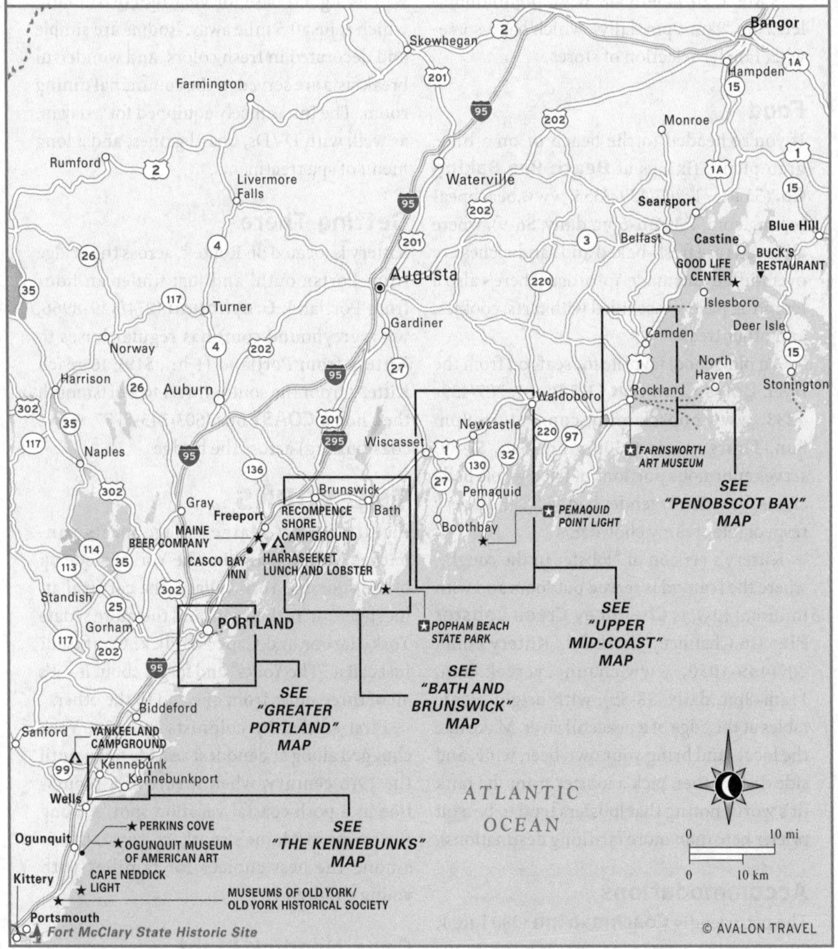

1pm-4pm Sun. June-Oct., $5 adults, $3 children 7-15, children under 7 free, $10 families,), full of seafaring gear, loads of intricate scrimshaw, ship models, and a collection of painted seascapes.

Armed and ready through the colonial period, the American Revolution, the War of 1812, the Civil War, and the Spanish American War, **Fort McClary** (Rte. 103, Kittery Point, 207/490-4079, www.fortmcclary.org, 10am-sunset daily Memorial Day-Columbus Day, $4 adults, $1 seniors) is perfectly situated to protect the Portsmouth Harbor from naval attacks, but these days it's mostly a good spot for a walk, or a picnic with views across the water to the Portsmouth Naval Shipyard.

Shopping

You can't miss **Kittery Outlets** (306 Rte. 1, 207/439-4367, www.thekitteryoutlets.com, 9am-9pm daily), where more than 120 stores draw bargain-minded shoppers from around the region, and which shouldn't be confused with the adjacent **Kittery Premium Outlets** (375 Rte. 1, 207/439-6548, www.premiumoutlets.com, 9am-9pm daily), which has a somewhat fancier selection of stores.

Food

If you're headed to the beach or on a hike, grab picnic fixings at **Beach Pea Baking Co.** (53 Rte. 1, 207/439-3555, www.beachpeabaking.com, 7:30am-6pm daily, $6-9), where all breads are fresh-baked and sandwiches are overstuffed and made-to-order. There's also a tempting pastry case filled with tarts, cookies, and other treats.

An old-school favorite for seafood from the fryer, **Bob's Clam Hut** (315 Rte. 1, 207/439-4233, www.bobsclamhut.com, 11am-9pm Sun.-Thurs., 11am-9:30pm Fri.-Sat., $7-29) serves enormous portions of fried whole belly clams, beautifully tender haddock, and a very respectable creamy chowder.

Kittery's version of "lobster in the rough," where the seafood is served outdoors and with minimal fuss, is **Chauncey Creek Lobster Pier** (16 Chauncey Creek Rd., Kittery Point, 207/439-1030, www.chaunceycreek.com, 11am-8pm daily, $8-35), with bright picnic tables at the edge of a peaceful river. Make like the locals and bring your own beer, wine, and side dishes, then pick a lobster from the tank (it's worth noting that lobsters tend to be a bit pricier here than more far-flung destinations).

Accommodations

The pet-friendly **Coachman Inn** (380 Rte. 1, 800/824-6183, www.coachmaninn.net, $120-200) is a basic motel that's a good alternative to pricier accommodations in neighboring Portsmouth and York. It's walking distance from the Kittery outlets and several fast-food chains, and there's a useful family suite, with a pair of twin beds in the second bedroom. A basic continental breakfast is served in the lobby, and fully accessible rooms are available upon request.

With views across the Piscataqua River, the ★ **Portsmouth Harbor Inn & Spa** (6 Water St., 207/439-4040, www.innatportsmouth.com, $150-250) is an inviting place to land, as well as a good base for visiting Portsmouth, which is just 0.5 mile away. Rooms are simple and decorated in fresh colors, and wonderful breakfasts are served in the communal dining room. The inn is nicely equipped for a day in, as well, with DVDs, board games, and a long menu of spa treatments.

Getting There

Kittery is located on Route 1, across the bridge from Portsmouth, and just under an hour from Portland. **Greyhound** (214/849-8966, www.greyhound.com) has regular buses to Kittery from Portland (1 hr., $19); to reach Kittery from the south, travel to Portsmouth then hop a **COAST** bus (603/743-5777, www.coastbus.org) across the bridge.

THE YORKS

Picture-perfect Maine village meets sunburned Vacationland in The Yorks, made up of the adorable York Village, the carnival atmosphere at York Beach, and the more sedate York Harbor and Cape Neddick. Confused? Just call it "The Yorks" and forget about it—it's all of three miles from one end to the other.

First settled by colonists in 1624, York chugged along as a modest seaside town until the 19th century, when it earned a reputation as a posh coastal vacation spot. Among the towns of Maine's southern coast, this is among the best choices for families with young children.

Cape Neddick Light

Otherwise known locally as Nubble Light, the stark-white **Cape Neddick Light** (Nubble Rd., Rte. 1A, off Short Sand Beach, York Beach, 207/363-1040, www.lighthouse.cc/capeneddick) and rocky grounds are a favorite with photographers, as it's easy to capture dramatic shots with a big sweep of ocean and sky. The lighthouse itself is on a small, rocky island some dozen yards off the coast, and is off-limits to the public. Viewers congregate on the grounds of Sohier Park (Nubble Rd.,

York) instead, snacking on ice cream, scrambling over the rocks, or just gazing past the lighthouse to the horizon.

Museums of Old York

Small and meticulous, York Village is a historian's dream, filled with colonial homes, a library and schoolhouse, and a cemetery. Many landmarks are open for tours through the **Old York Historical Society** (3 Lindsay Rd., York, 207/363-4974, www.oldyork.org, 10am-5pm Tues.-Sat., 1pm-5pm Sun. late May-early Sept., 10am-5pm Thurs.-Sat., 1pm-5pm Sun. early Sept.-mid-Oct., all-day/one site tickets $15/8 adults, $10/5 children under 16). Start at the historical society, where you can purchase tickets and pick up a map of town, then walk to the landmarks, many of which are staffed by local docents.

York Beaches

LONG SANDS BEACH

Easily walkable from the shops and restaurants that line Route 1A, **Long Sands Beach** is a 1.5-mile stretch of pale sand that invites daylong beach planet sessions. Bring quarters for the metered parking that's available along the waterfront—it's $1 per hour south of **Sun and Surf Restaurant** (264 Rte. 1A), and $2 per hour north of the restaurant. Sheltered from the wind by Cape Neddick, the beach is among the best around for **surfing,** with (often) gentle waves that are good for beginning riders. Rent a board and 3/2 wetsuit from **Liquid Dreams Surf Shop** (171 Long Beach Ave., 207/351-2545, www.liquiddreamssurf.com, 8am-8pm daily, rentals $8 per hour, $20 half day), which also offers **surf lessons** (2-hour group lessons $70, private $105, includes board and wetsuit). During the hours of 9am-5pm Memorial Day-Labor Day, surfing is limited to the marked "surf zone," but it's a free-for-all after hours or in the off-season.

SHORT SANDS BEACH

A quarter mile of sand between the cliffs in York, **Short Sands Beach** is a favorite with young families, who love the sheltered water and adjoining playground. Every handful of years, rough tides will expose a historic shipwreck that's (mostly) buried beneath the sand here, thought to be a "pinky," a maneuverable square-rigged fishing boat that was popular along the coast in the 18th century. If you're lucky enough to see the ship appear, keep your distance, as it's considered an archaeological site. Parking in the on-site lot is $1 per hour, though it's worth arriving early during the summer months if you're hoping for a spot.

Both of the beaches are on the route of the **Beach Trolley** (207/363-9600, www.yorktrolley.com, $4), making this a great spot to park the car for the day and explore on foot.

Food

No pilgrimage to Nubble Light is complete without a stop off at **Dunne's Ice Cream** (214 Nubble Rd., York Beach, 207/363-1277, noon-9pm daily), formerly known as Brown's Ice Cream, whose enormous list of flavors includes New England treats like Maine blueberry, Indian pudding, and Maine whoopie pie.

The other classic stop for vacation food is **Flo's Hot Dogs** (1359 Rte. 1, Cape Neddick, www.floshotdogs.com, 11am-3pm Thurs.-Tues., $2-5), an unassuming little shack at the edge of Route 1. Like the sign says, though, Flo's has "the most famous hot dogs with hot sauce on Route 1 from Maine to Key West," and there's often a line—locals say the secret is in the tasty relish that tops the "house special," along with mayonnaise and celery salt. Cash only.

Tucked in a basement with a nautical theme, the **Ship's Cellar Pub** (480 York St., York, 207/363-5119, www.yorkharborinn.com, 11:30am-11:30pm Mon.-Thurs., 11:30am-midnight Fri.-Sat., 3pm-11:30pm Sun., $24-35) is a cozy spot to while away an evening over classic dishes like broiled scallops or seafood pie. All portholes and glossy wood, it's the next best thing to dinner on a boat, and the pub has frequent live music during the busy months, as well as a popular happy hour 4pm-6pm weeknights.

With a welcome emphasis on fresh ingredients and preparations, ★ **Frankie & Johnny's** (1594 Rte. 1, Cape Neddick, 207/363-1909, www.frankie-johnnys.com, 5pm-9pm Thurs.-Sun., $27-40) has beautiful vegan and vegetarian options on an eclectic menu that pulls from all over the globe. Meat eaters rave about the rack of lamb and the chicken piccata, and even the house salad impresses with a rainbow of veg. Cash and reservations only; bring-your-own beer and wine.

Accommodations and Camping

No frills but with an unbeatable location, **Seaturn Motel** (55 Longbeach Ave., York, 207/363-5137, www.seaturnmotel.com, $95-245) offers a clean, tidy place to recover from trips to the beach, which is right across the street. Rooms are compact, but stocked with a mini fridge and microwave, and rates include parking on-site. Oh, and there's a pool.

In a quiet spot that's still walking distance to Long Sands Beach, ★ **The Lighthouse Inn & Carriage House** (20 Nubble Rd., York Beach, 207/363-6072, www.thelighthouseinn.com, $89-199) is a great base for exploring the Yorks, with a pool and hot tub to retreat from the crowded beach. Decor is bright and updated, and the thoughtful owners supply extras like "beach wagons," so you can hit the sand with all your gear. Rates include an above-par continental breakfast.

Staking out its own peninsula, the **Stage Neck Inn** (8 Stage Neck Rd., York, 207/363-3850, www.stageneck.com, $175-450) has a small private beach, with lots of cozy places to watch the ocean rise and fall. There are tennis courts and walking paths on-site, and rates include an ample, if forgettable, self-serve buffet breakfast.

Exclusively for RVs and trailers, **Libby's Oceanside Camp** (725 York St., York, 207/363-4171, www.libbysoceancamping.com, sites with hook-ups $60-100) looks right out over the water, with picnic tables and fire pits that are perfect for long ocean sunsets. The **Beach Trolley** passes right by, so you can leave your rig parked and explore on foot. Adjacent to the bridge between York and Ogunquit, **Cape Neddick Oceanside Campground** (63 Shore Dr., Cape Neddick, 207/363-4366, 2-person tent sites $41) has tightly packed spaces with some shade, reasonably clean facilities with coin-operated showers, and a pleasantly rocky waterfront to explore.

Getting There and Around

The Yorks are linked by Route 1A, paralleled by both Route 1 and I-95. While Route 1A is indisputably the scenic route, it can get terribly clogged during the summer season, so expect delays. If at all possible, it's worth parking your car and getting around on the **Beach Trolley** (207/363-9600, www.yorktrolley.com, $4), which links up many of the towns' sites and beaches. There is currently no bus or train transport to York.

OGUNQUIT AND WELLS

Neighboring Ogunquit and Wells used to be a single town, until a knock-down, drag-out fight about streetlights caused the people of Ogunquit to rise up and secede. Things have simmered down since then, and the two towns have distinctive personalities—Ogunquit's gorgeous beachfront has become a favorite escape for New England's LGBT community, while Wells moves at a more relaxed pace, with nature preserves that ramble through pine forest and salt marsh.

That 1980 secession vote aside, it's really a nice combination. Ogunquit has a party scene that doesn't quit all summer, and sunny days bring a crowd to the three-mile sandy beach. Just up the coast, then, the Rachel Carson National Wildlife Refuge is a welcome break, with plenty of walking trails and paddling for afternoons of exploring.

Marginal Way

The 1.25-mile paved walking path that skims Ogunquit's harbor was bequeathed to the town in 1923, winding from Ogunquit beach to a rocky cove. It's a dramatic walk, with crashing surf to one side and salt-kissed coastal plants to the other. Bayberry bushes and roses, in white and seemingly every shade of pink, perfume the path in summertime, when it's one of Ogunquit's most popular destinations.

Perkins Cove

Known in its early days as Fish Cove, this stubby peninsula was once the focal point of the area's fishing and trade industry—one holdover from the era is a footbridge that cranks up and down to allow ships to pass beneath. These days it's pure vacationland, with art galleries, chowder houses, gift shops, and studios, all with lovely views of the water. This is the place to pick up salt water taffy and watch the lobster boats come and go—preferably early or late in the day, when the area isn't so crowded. Parking can be difficult in busy summer months, so it's worth parking downtown and catching a trolley to the cove.

Ogunquit Museum of American Art

This jewel of a museum, the **Ogunquit Museum of American Art** (542 Shore Rd., 207/646-4909, www.ogunquitmuseum.org, 10am-5pm daily, $10 adults, $9 seniors and students, children under 12 free) is displayed like a work of art, perched on a cliff above the ocean. The temporary exhibits often feature some of Maine's great painters like Andrew Wyeth and Rockwell Kent, and the permanent collection includes a beautifully chosen selection of watercolors, oils, sculpture, and drawings. Save some time to see the outdoor sculpture garden.

Sports and Recreation

RACHEL CARSON NATIONAL WILDLIFE REFUGE AND WELLS RESERVE

Stretching 50 miles along the coast, the remarkable **Rachel Carson National Wildlife Refuge** protects salt marshes and estuaries that are essential for the migratory birds that travel the Atlantic seaboard on their yearly journeys. Stop by the refuge's **visitors center** (321 Port Wells Rd., Wells, 207/646-9226, www.fws.gov, office hours 8am-4:30pm Mon.-Fri.) to learn about the wildlife that thrives here, then hike the mile-long **Carson Trail,** which has a series of overlooks across the salt marsh, with signs that explore local species and conservation.

The adjacent **Wells Reserve** (342 Laudholm Farm Rd., Wells, 207/646-1555,

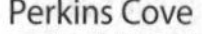
Perkins Cove

www.wellsreserve.org, 7am-sunset daily, $5 adults, $1 children 6-16, children under 6 free) is smaller, but has more ways to get around. A network of trails extends from the main entrance through the forest and salt marshes to Laudholm Beach, which narrows to a sliver at high tide, then widens into an expanse of nubbly rocks and tidepools. There are guided walks on many days, covering themes from the intertidal zone to the history of waterfront farming in Maine.

BEACHES

Ogunquit's crowning glory is the 3.5-mile-long **Ogunquit Beach** (Beach St., Ogunquit, parking $4 per hour, $30 per day), among New England's very finest. Soft sand is fringed by low dunes on a long peninsula that runs between the sea and the Ogunquit River. The southern end of the beach is the main access point, but there's also parking and an access road at the opposite end, called **North Beach** (Ocean Ave., Ogunquit, parking $4 per hour, $25 per day), which tends to be a bit quieter. There are bathroom facilities at both ends.

On the other side of the town line, Wells's beaches hold their own. The main destination is **Wells Beach** (Atlantic Ave., Wells, parking $12 half day, $20 full day), a long, sandy stretch that's popular with families and has lifeguards and restroom facilities in several locations. (If you can find a spot, there's free parking for Wells Beach at the ocean end of Mile Road, near Forbes Restaurant.) For fewer crowds and a bit more distance from the downtown shops, head to **Drake's Island Beach** (Island Beach Rd., Wells, parking $12 half day, $20 full day), which also has lifeguards and restrooms.

Food

OGUNQUIT

Excellent coffee and pastries make **Bread and Roses Bakery** (246 Main St., 207/646-4227, www.breadandrosesbakery.com, 7am-9pm daily, $2-7) a favorite for breakfast, but it's an equally worthwhile stop for picnic sandwiches. If you haven't tried pie made from wild Maine blueberries, this is the perfect place to get initiated.

Eat outside a little flotsam-covered shack at **Beach Plum Lobster Farm** (615 Main St., 207/646-7277, 9am-7pm daily, $5-25), which keeps it simple with lobsters and steamers (clams) served alongside corn on the cob and copious melted butter. Call ahead and the shop will package up your order to go, the fixings for a pretty luxe seaside picnic.

The food at ★ **The Front Porch Piano Bar & Restaurant** (9 Shore Rd., 207/646-4005, www.thefrontporch.com, 5pm-11pm daily, bar open late, $13-38) is every bit as good as it needs to be—think solid entrées like baked salmon, steak, and hearty salads. But the real draw is the piano bar atmosphere, which invites increasingly raucous show tune sing-alongs as the night wears on. There are no reservations at this popular spot, but you can call 45 minutes ahead to get your name on the waiting list.

WELLS

The classic seafood at **Fisherman's Catch** (134 Harbor Rd., 207/646-8780, www.fishermanscatchwells.com, 11:30am-9pm daily, $7-20) keeps it bustling through the summer months, when diners gather around picnic tables on the restaurant's large, screened-in porch. The restaurant has all the usual orders, but the chowder and the blueberry pie win raves.

Meet local policemen (or local anyone, for that matter) at **Congdon's Doughnuts** (1090 Post Rd., 207/646-4219, www.congdons.com, 6am-2pm daily, $2-9), which has been slinging vast quantities of the sweet treats since 1945. There's also a hearty breakfast and lunch menu, including some of the best breakfast sandwiches in town.

Set in a charming 18th-century house, ★ **Joshua's** (1637 Post Rd., 207/646-3355, www.joshuas.biz, 5pm-10pm daily, $27-35) creates special meals using locally sourced ingredients, and is a wonderful choice for an evening out. The menu changes frequently, but always features some good vegetarian options, as well as truly phenomenal crab cakes.

Accommodations and Camping

An impeccable budget option that's a fabulous deal in the shoulder season, **Towne Lyne Motel** (747 Main St., Ogunquit, 207/646-2955, www.townelynemotel.com, $69-214) is right on the trolley line, making it an easy spot for hitting the beach or the town. Rooms are stocked with fridges, microwaves, and coffeemakers, and updated bathrooms and decor make this a cut above the average motel.

The welcoming **Dragonfly Guest House** (254 Shore Rd., Ogunquit, 207/216-4848, www.dragonflyguesthouse.com, $125-275) is walking distance from Perkins Cove, Marginal Way, and the beach, but still manages to feel relaxed in the heart of the summer season. Perks include afternoon cookies and a great breakfast, and the bed-and-breakfast runs frequent specials with discounted massages and theater tickets.

Pet-friendly and simple, **The Beaches Motel & Cottages** (773 Post Rd., Wells, 207/216-4065, www.beachesofmaine.com, motel rooms $55-145, 6-person cottages $74-245) has adorably vintage cottages that are a short drive from the beach. The tidy grounds include a pool, a barbecue area, and a fire pit that's perfect for evenings under the stars.

Less than a mile from the shore, **Beach Acres Tent Sites & Park** (563 Post Rd., Wells, 207/646-5612, www.beachacres.com, tents $40, hookups $45-54) is spacious, if not particularly private, and its location on the trolley route makes it a good place for exploring car free. A pool, picnic tables, playgrounds, and barbecue facilities make this a popular choice for families.

Getting There and Around

Ogunquit and Wells are located on Route 1, about 50 minutes south of Portland. The Amtrak **Downeaster** (800/872-7245, www.amtrakdowneaster.com) stops in Wells on the route between Boston and Portland, and there's also a **Greyhound** (800/231-2222, www.greyhound.com, service from Portland $15, Boston $30) station in town.

During the summer season, the **Shoreline Explorer** (207/459-2932, www.shorelineexplorer.com) trolley links up the main sites and beaches, making this an appealing place to visit without a car. Taxi service is available from **Brewster's Taxi & Travel Services** (201/646-2141).

The Kennebunks

The two towns that make up southern Maine's toniest seaside destination—Kennebunk and Kennebunkport—are filled with luxurious inns that turn platoons of beach chairs toward the sea. A great, sweeping curve of beach in Kennebunk is one of the best on the southern coast, with plentiful sand and sunrise views of the bay. And the Kennebunk River, a spidering tidal waterway that divides the pretty villages, also offers places to swim and sit away from the blustering waves of the sea.

While the Kennebunks' reputation is for blue bloods and well-heeled preppies (an image bolstered by the presence of the bi-presidential Bush clan in an eye-catching compound on Ocean Avenue), it's not much more expensive than destinations up the coast. Streets are lined with old-fashioned colonial and federal homes, the whitewashed facades and bright shutters of which are classic New England. Ways to get on the water here include helming a sailboat, paddling into knee-high rollers on a surfboard, or searching for whales on the offshore banks—this is among the best places in the state for spotting them.

The Kennebunks

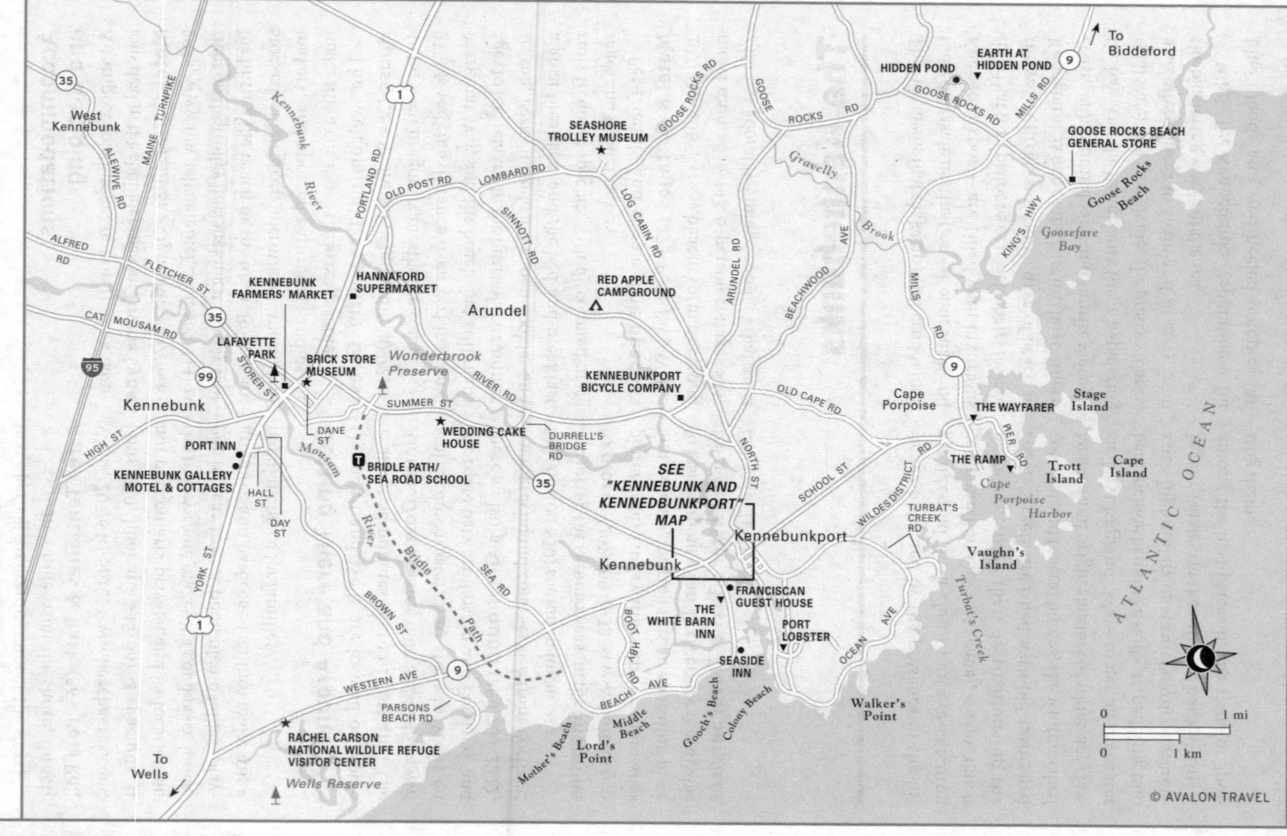

SIGHTS

You won't find the usual local historical paraphernalia at the **Brick Store Museum** (117 Main St., Kennebunk, 207/985-4802, www.brickstoremuseum.org, 10am-5pm Tues. and Thurs.-Fri., 10am-8pm Wed., 10am-4pm Sat., noon-4pm Sun., $7 adults, $6 seniors, $3 children 6-16, $20 families). Instead, the staff gets creative with frequently rotated themed displays such as The Kennebunks During the Civil War and Kennebunks A-Z. The museum also runs a walking tour of the historic district at 11am every Friday throughout the summer, and a tour of historic homes around nearby Mother's Beach at 2pm on Thursday; maps of the sites are also available if you'd prefer to explore the areas on your own (guided tours $5, maps $5).

Step back into the golden days of narrow-gauge rail at the **Seashore Trolley Museum** (195 Log Cabin Rd., Kennebunkport, 207/967-2800, www.trolleymuseum.org, 10am-5pm daily summer, Sat.-Sun. only May and Oct., closed Nov.-Apr. except during Christmas Prelude, $12 adults, $10 seniors, $9.50 children 6-15, $5 children 3-5, children under 3 free). With a collection of more than 200 trolleys (some of which you can ride through nearby woods from the museum), plus a gift shop dedicated entirely to streetcars, the museum is well suited to enthusiastic kids and train aficionados alike.

The 1825 **Wedding Cake House** (104 Summer St., Kennebunkport) has become an essential sight for many visitors, who stop along the road to peer through the fence (the house is no longer open to the public). On a street with trim and tidy colonial gems, the overwrought Carpenter Gothic exterior *is* eye-catching, though the building sinks deeper into disrepair with each passing winter.

ENTERTAINMENT AND EVENTS

Nightlife

While there's plenty of nightlife in the Kennebunks to go around, the main event is sunset, when boat drinks and microbrews flow at packed waterside bars. For a local vibe, flotsam-inspired decor, and Geary's beer on draft, the **Pilot House** (4 Western Ave., Kennebunk, 207/967-9961, 11am-1am Mon.-Sat., 11am-midnight Sun.) is right by a marina and often has live music on weekend afternoons. The cavernous **Federal Jack's** (8 Western Ave., Kennebunk, 207/967-4322, www.federaljacks.com, 11:30am-1am daily) is less atmospheric but has plenty of seating on deep balconies overlooking the water. A little farther into Kennebunk, **Old Vines Wine Bar** (173 Port Rd., Kennebunk, 207/967-2310, www.oldvineswinebar.com, 5pm-10pm daily) makes up for an inland location with a rooftop patio, gorgeously crafted cocktails, and the best wine list in town. On the other end of the spectrum, the **Arundel Wharf** (43 Ocean Ave., Kennebunkport, 207/967-3444, 11:30am-9pm daily) is more rum-and-Coke than Riesling, but you'll be served on a floating dock in the Arundel River.

Festivals and Events

Free **Concerts in the Park** (Lafayette Park, Kennebunk, 6:30pm-7:30pm Wed.) feature classic rock and jazz bands mid-June-mid-August; bring a picnic blanket to spread out on the grass. In early June, the **Kennebunk Food and Wine Festival** (www.kennebunkportfestival.com) gathers local celebrity chefs and winemakers for a series of tastings and themed dinners. Later that month, **Launch! Maritime Festival** (www.gokennebunks.com) celebrates the Kennebunks' nautical heritage with seafood cook-offs, boat parties, and the annual Blessing of the Fleet.

SPORTS AND RECREATION

Whale-Watching

Humpback, finback, and minke whales congregate and feed at offshore banks, where they luxuriate in a whale's dream buffet of tiny sea creatures. Try to catch a glimpse aboard ***Nick's Chance*** (4 Western Ave., Kennebunk, 207/967-5507, www.firstchancewhalewatch.com, 4.5-hour trip $48 adults, $28 children

3-12), an 87-foot vessel that makes daily trips mid-June-September and weekend trips in the shoulder season. The boat goes up to 20 miles offshore, so even if the weather on the beach is balmy, bring plenty of warm clothing (and your favorite seasickness remedy). No refunds are given for trips when no whales are spotted, but passengers get a free pass for a second outing. The same company also runs 1.5-hour cruises on a **lobster boat** that's a fun, inexpensive way to explore the coast and see what's on the other end of all those colorful lobster buoys ($20 adults, $15 children 3-12).

Beaches

The 1.5-mile stretch of coastline known as **Kennebunk Beach,** located where the Kennebunk River reaches the ocean and about 1.2 miles away from Dock Square, is actually a series of three beaches, scalloped curves neatly separated by small, rocky outcroppings. Farthest east and easily the most popular of the three, **Gooch's Beach** is long and easy to access (if you've already secured a parking place downtown, it's easy to reach Gooch's Beach by bicycle or on foot: Leave Dock Square heading west on Western Avenue, then turn left onto Beach Avenue), but dwindles to a thin strip of sand at high tide. Next in line is **Middle Beach,** a quieter portion where the sand gives way to smooth stones that keep away sunbathers and sandcastle builders. **Mother's Beach** is small and sandy, with a good playground that makes it a hit with young families. A $25 parking fee for Kennebunk Beach is charged mid-June-mid-September. The local Intown Trolley also makes stops at the three beaches.

On busy summer weekends, it's often worth making the trip to **Goose Rocks Beach** in Cape Porpoise. Wide and scenic, the beach is rimmed with dune grass and perfect for strolling or taking a dip into the bracingly cold water. Parking at the beach is limited, and passes are required 8am-6pm late May-early September; buy a sticker at **Goose Rocks Beach General Store** (3 Dyke Rd., Kennebunkport, 207/967-2289, 7:30am-2pm

Kennebunk Beach

Mon.-Thurs., 7:30am-7pm Fri.-Sat. May-June, 7:30am-7pm daily July-Sept., $15). A pass doesn't guarantee you'll find a spot, though, and the store advises showing up before 8:30am for the best chance at parking.

Biking

Back roads and trails around the Kennebunks invite endless exploration on two wheels. Though the way is narrow, winding, and sometimes clogged with sightseers, the eight-mile one-way ride down Ocean Avenue from Kennebunkport to **Cape Porpoise** via Wildes District Road is among the most scenic in town; the jewel-box seaside village has a few good seafood restaurants and an ice cream shop for mid-ride recovery. A gentler option is the flat, dirt **Bridle Path** that runs two miles along the Mousam River; the main access point and parking is at **Sea Road School** (29 Sea Rd., Kennebunk).

The 65-mile **Eastern Trail** (www.easterntrail.org) stretches along the coast from Kittery to South Portland, including 22 miles of smooth, off-road trail between Kennebunk and Bug Light in South Portland (parking available at Kennebunk Town Hall). Rent a hybrid, road, or mountain bike at **Kennebunkport Bicycle Company** (34 Arundel Rd., Kennebunkport, 207/385-4382, www.kennebikeport.com, 10am-5pm Mon.-Sat., 8am-3pm Sun., bikes from $20 half day, $26 full day), which also offers guided tours of local trails.

Boating

All eyes are on 55-foot schooner *Eleanor* when she cruises down the coast with gaff-rigged sails flying, and a trip with Captain Woody feels like stepping back into the grand old days of New England sailing. ***Eleanor*** (43 Ocean Ave., Kennebunkport, 207/967-8809, www.schoonereleanor.com, $50 day cruise, $60 sunset sail) makes two-hour outings daily May-September, and passengers are welcome to bring snacks and drinks aboard.

Hiking

Kennebunk Beach makes a great place to start the day with a sunrise walk. Just outside of downtown Kennebunk, **Wonder Brook Reserve** (www.kennebunklandtrust.org, parking on Plummer Ln.) has 2.5 miles of footpaths through shady upland forest and banks of rustling ferns.

Old, sandy roads-turned-walking-trails run through pine barrens and grassland at **Kennebunk Plains** (Rte. 99, www.nature.org), which The Nature Conservancy bought to protect the endangered Morefield's leather flower, threatened northern blazing star plants, and endangered grasshopper sparrows. The reserve also has a treasure trove of **wild blueberries,** and late summer brings a luxurious crop of the tiny, intensely flavored fruit (it's essential to stay on the trail when picking, however, as some of the plains' most vulnerable birds make their nests on the ground Apr.-Sept.).

Paddling

Paddle the Kennebunk River or follow the shoreline to **Goat Island Light** on a guided kayak outing with **Coastal Maine Kayak & Bike** (8 Western Ave., Kennebunk, 207/967-6065, www.coastalmainekayak.com, 3-hour tours $85, kayak rentals from $45 half day, $60 full day), which also has a fleet of stand-up paddleboards. The Arundel River winds through scenic forest as it leaves the coast and is the most popular place for independent kayak trips, but outings must be timed to the tides (some paddlers have found themselves stuck in the mud).

Surfing

Unless there's a hurricane sending giant swells to shore (and sending expert surfers to the beach), the Kennebunks' waves are relatively gentle and beginner friendly. Learn your way around the break at Gooch's Beach with one of the instructors from **Aquaholics Surf Shop** (166 Port Rd., Kennebunk, 207/967-8650, www.aquaholicsurf.com, 1.5-hour private lesson $110 for 1 person, $170 for 2, $230 for 3, rental boards from $25 half day, $35 full day), which also rents soft- and hard-top boards.

FOOD

Kennebunk

The main competition for best lobster roll in town is ★ **The Clam Shack** (2 Western Ave., 207/967-3321, www.theclamshack.net, 11am-8pm daily May-Oct., $12-25), which has gotten top scores from a who's who of food magazines and television shows. The riverside spot charges a premium for its version, but stuffs the toasted hamburger buns with a pound of lobster in large, meaty chunks bathed in your choice of mayonnaise or butter.

It's a travel truism that nothing says "tourist trap" like a giant board screaming: "Locals eat here!" The thing about the **Pilot House** (4 Western Ave., 207/967-9961, 11am-1am Mon.-Sat., 11am-midnight Sun., $8-22), though, is that locals really do spend their time on the riverside patio or bellied up to the inside bar outfitted with outboard motors and fishing gear. Geary's beer on tap, a convivial atmosphere, and a decent menu of fried grub (which many regulars like to cap off with a Jell-O shot, or three) make this a fine place to nurse a pint at the end of the day, listening to conversations about tourist foibles and fishing.

Grab a few basic foods, along with deli sandwiches and some prepared items at **H. B. Provisions** (15 Western Ave., 207/967-5762, www.hbprovisions.com, 6am-10pm daily). For a more extensive selection, a **Hannaford Supermarket** (65 Portland Rd., 207/985-9135, 7am-10pm Mon.-Sat., 7am-9pm Sun.) is on Route 1. Meet local bakers, farmers, and artisans at the **Kennebunk Farmers' Market** (3 Wells Ct., www.kennebunkfarmersmarket.org, 8am-1pm Sat. May-Nov.), rain or shine.

Kennebunkport

There's nowhere to sit at **Port Lobster** (122 Ocean Ave., 207/967-2081, www.portlobster.com, 9am-6pm daily, $9-16), but you can bring your takeout lunch across the street to the edge of the Arundel River and find park benches and views of the local fishing fleet. This seafood shop buys lobster and fish straight from the boat, and its lobster roll is simple and to the point: toasted white hot dog bun and tender meat just kissed with mayonnaise. The short menu also includes crab rolls, seafood salads, and chowder that come highly recommended.

Funky and offhandedly cool, **Bandaloop** (2 Dock Sq., 207/967-4994, www.bandaloop.biz, 5pm-10pm Tues.-Thurs., 5pm-11pm Fri.-Sat., $19-31) is an airy, energetic place to catch dinner made from organic, all-natural, and local foods served by a young, hip waitstaff. The menu changes frequently but includes creative dishes like tandoori-grilled salmon and pan-seared halibut with pepitas and pineapple chutney. Bandaloop also has beautifully prepared vegan options and is easily the best choice in town for non-meat options.

The lighthearted **Salt & Honey** (24 Ocean Ave., 207/204-0195, www.thesaltandhoney.com, breakfast and lunch 8:30am-2pm Fri.-Mon., dinner 4:30pm-9pm Wed.-Mon., breakfast $9-22, lunch $7-18, dinner $15-26) has fresh food and ambience offering a refreshing change from the seafood shack scene. Fish tacos and crab cakes are immensely popular, and you can start the day like a high roller with a lobster omelet dripping with caramelized onions and Havarti cheese.

A long-standing fine dining destination, **The White Barn Inn** (37 Beach Ave., 207/967-2321, www.whitebarninn.com, 6pm-9:30pm Mon.-Thurs., 5:30pm-close Fri.-Sun., four-course prix fixe $109, nine-course tasting menu $155, wine pairing $48-85) has won seemingly every award and honor a restaurant can earn in the United States. It has impeccable service, and the 19th-century barn setting makes a luxurious backdrop for the food, which balances classic and creative flavors.

With offbeat offerings ranging from Lemon Pink Peppercorn to Malbec & Berries, **Rococo Artisan Ice Cream** (6 Spring St., 207/251-6866, www.rococoicecream.com, 11:30am-11pm Mon.-Fri., 11am-11pm Sat.-Sun., $4-6) is the sweetest game in town. Lucky for wafflers, the shop serves ice cream in "flights" that include four small scoops of different flavors.

CAPE PORPOISE

Though it's only three miles down the road from the center of Kennebunkport, the village of Cape Porpoise is a place apart, with salt marshes and just a few places to eat in between the vacation homes lining the waterfront.

On a coast where flotsam-chic is a competitive sport—everything from clam shacks to inns are draped in fishing net, buoys, and other marine paraphernalia—**The Ramp** (77 Pier Rd., Kennebunkport, 207/967-8500, www.pier77restaurant.com, 11:30am-9pm daily, $14-25) might take the prize. Crushed shells cover the ground and rowboats stand guard over the parking lot. The menu of pub classics and seafood is solid, but it's the Portuguese-style mussels that win raves.

Out a bit farther, **Earth at Hidden Pond** (354 Goose Rocks Rd., Kennebunkport, 207/967-6550, www.earthathiddenpond.

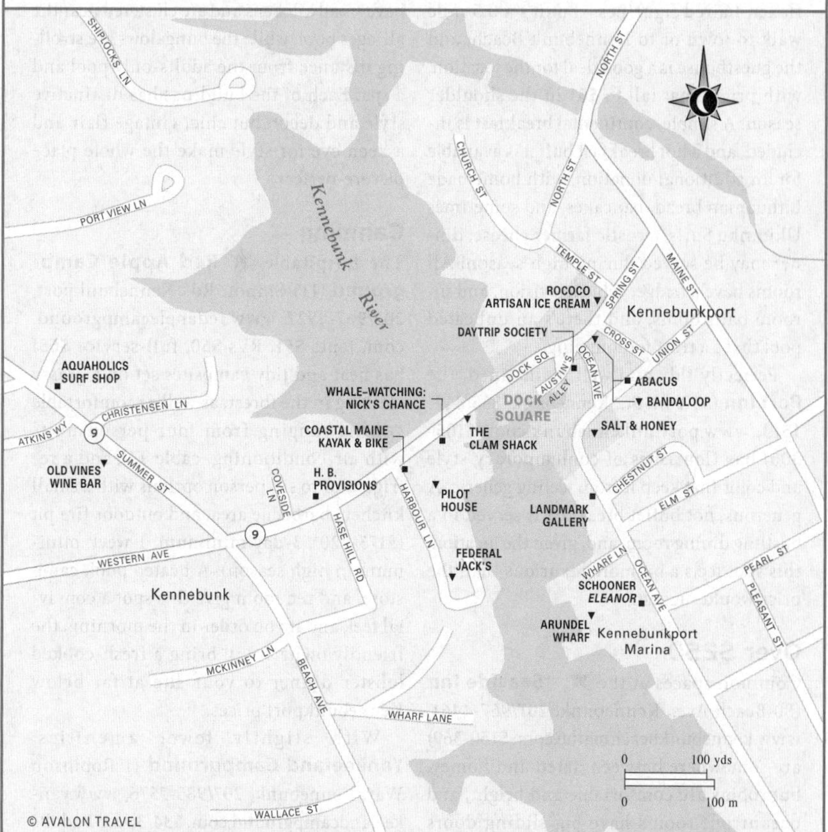

com, 5:30pm-9:30pm daily, $40-65) is a top contender for a night of splashing out with its exquisite food and modern-design-meets-rustic-chic decor. Its menu of contemporary cuisine is rooted in local products and flavors, and while any spot in the restaurant makes a lovely place to spend the evening, two private screened-in shacks (first-come, first-served) are the most stunning places to enjoy a meal.

ACCOMMODATIONS AND CAMPING

$100-150

There's nothing fancy about **Kennebunk Gallery Motel & Cottages** (65 York St., Kennebunk, 207/985-4543, www.kennebunk-cottages.com, May-Oct., $45-164), but the friendly staff and location just outside of town make it an excellent find. Larger cottages have small, simple kitchens, and a volleyball court and pool keep things cheery.

$150-250

Set on the serene grounds of a Lithuanian Franciscan monastery, the nonprofit **Franciscan Guest House** (26 Beach Ave., Kennebunk, 207/967-4865, www.francis-canguesthouse.com, $61-195) is a converted boardinghouse that hosts retreats and a regular crowd of Lithuanian summer people. The dated, very simple rooms are not for everybody—same goes for faux wood paneling and flaxen-haired figurines—but it's a 0.5 mile walk to town or to Kennebunk Beach, and the guesthouse is a good deal for the location, with prices that fall to $61 in the shoulder season. A simple, continental breakfast is included, and a hot breakfast buffet is available for an additional donation, with homemade Lithuanian bread, pancakes, and sometimes Ukininku Suris, a rustic farmer cheese; dinner may be served during high season. All rooms have a fridge, cable television, and in-room bathrooms, and there's an unheated pool that's a treat for lounging.

Perfectly tidy and well maintained, the **Port Inn** (55 York St., Kennebunk, 855/849-1513, www.portinnkennebunk.com, $105-300) has flourishes of contemporary style and color that keep it from feeling generic. A generous, hot buffet breakfast is served in a bustling dining room, and, given the location, this spot feels a bit more luxurious than the price would suggest.

Over $250

Common spaces at the ★ **Seaside Inn** (80 Beach Ave., Kennebunk, 207/967-4461, www.kennebunkbeachmaine.com, $150-369) are somewhere between dated and homey, but rooms are comfortable and bright, and oceanfront rooms have big sliding doors that let in the sound of rolling waves and the scent of the sea. For access to the beach, this spot is unmatched, with a private, sandy path that leads straight to the water. The breakfast buffet is classic, old-fashioned Maine: whole grain oatmeal, French toast with blueberries and syrup, and bowls of fresh fruit in a convivial dining room.

The closest thing in adult life to an indulgent, sleep-away summer camp may be **Hidden Pond** (354 Goose Rocks Rd., Kennebunkport, 888/967-9050, www.hiddenpondmaine.com, bungalows from $299, cottages from $499), a dreamy resort tucked into a quiet patch of woods. Guests ride cruiser bikes down the dirt roads between bungalows and gather each night to toast s'mores at a lakeside bonfire. The two-bedroom cottages have small kitchens and are clustered near the all-ages pool, while the bungalows are strolling distance from the adults-only pool and a spa. Each of the buildings has distinctive style and decor, but chic, vintage flair and a keen eye for style make the whole place picture-perfect.

Camping

The hospitable ★ **Red Apple Campground** (111 Sinnott Rd., Kennebunkport, 207/967-4927, www.redapplecampground.com, tents $51, RVs $60, full-service $65) has neat and tidy campsites set on a grassy clearing in the forest, as well as comfortable **cabins** ranging from four-person units with air-conditioning, cable TV, and a refrigerator to six-person options with a small kitchen, barbecue area, and outdoor fire pit ($175-220 , 3-day minimum, 1-week minimum in high season). A heated pool, camp store, and rec room give this spot a convivial feel, and if you order in the morning, the friendly owners will bring a fresh-cooked lobster dinner to your site at far below Kennebunkport prices.

With slightly fewer amenities, **Yankeeland Campground** (1 Robinson Way, Kennebunk, 207/985-7576, www.yankeelandcampground.com, $34/36 for 2 adults in partial/full-hookup sites, $5 extra adult, $3 extra child) is still an appealing option, especially at the lower price.

INFORMATION

All the usual pamphlets, along with maps and good advice, are available at the **chamber of commerce** (16 Water St., Kennebunk, 207/967-0857, www.gokennebunks.com, 9am-4pm Mon.-Fri.).

GETTING THERE AND AROUND

Kennebunk and Kennebunkport are on opposite sides of the Kennebunk River on Route 9, roughly 40 minutes south of Portland.

There's currently no public transportation to the Kennebunks.

Intown Trolley (207/967-3638, www.intowntrolley.com, June-Oct., $16 adults, $6 children 3-17, children under 3 free, $45 family of 2 adults and up to 4 children) follows a fixed route through town that takes in Kennebunk and Kennebunkport's main sights and beaches, with narration. Fares are good for one whole day, making this a useful option if you plan on doing a lot of sightseeing. **Shuttle-Bus** (207/282-5408, www.shuttlebus-zoom.com) operates buses around the southern coast. Fares and schedules vary.

Portland

Perched at the aft end of Casco Bay, Portland's the last bit of solidly built earth before the coastline splinters into the bays, inlets, and islands of Mid-Coast Maine. Look closer, though, and the city itself seems all shoreline: heads, breakwaters, and lighthouses wrap in on themselves, pinching Portland's peninsular center between Back Cove and the Fore River. Downtown bristles with schooner masts and wharves that give way to a rugged, working waterfront.

That blend of picturesque charm and real-world maritime culture infuses the city, and wherever you go in the Old Port and peninsula, the sea is not far away. Cobblestone streets are lined with galleries, museum, and boutiques celebrating Maine's seafaring traditions, and many of the city's chic bars and restaurants have a boat-to-table philosophy boasting chefs on a first-name basis with fishers, long-liners, and sea captains. The effect is utterly entrancing: When the weather is fine and Casco Bay sparkling, and the air smells of salt and fresh seafood, many visitors find themselves at Old Port brewpubs or on the deck of a sailing ship thinking up ways to move to Portland.

SIGHTS

To orient yourself in Portland, find its two major thoroughfares: Commercial Street runs between the Old Port and working waterfront, which anchor the heart of Portland's peninsula. The Arts District centers around Congress Street, with a collection of fine art galleries, studios, and the excellent Portland Museum of Art. Meanwhile, to the west, up-and-coming areas Munjoy Hill and West Bayside are primarily residential, with a handful of art galleries and cafés.

Lighthouses

With a craggy shoreline that's often wrapped in thick fog, it's no wonder the Portland area needs half a dozen lighthouses to keep boats off the rocks. Even with their blinking beacons, the city's seen centuries of dramatic and often tragic wrecks: the *Annie C. Maguire* ran aground right at the base of Portland Head Light on Christmas Eve 1886. Set on pretty capes and outcroppings, lighthouses are part of the Maine landscape at its most picturesque, but even on sunny days, their powerful lenses and stout architecture serve as a reminder that sailing Maine's waters has always been a dangerous undertaking.

The most iconic lighthouse in Portland is Portland Head Light, in nearby Cape Elizabeth, but there are some worthy beacons that can be spotted from the city. Watch for the squat **Bug Light** at the edge of the Portland Breakwater, **Ram Island Ledge Lighthouse** on its own tiny island, and **Spring Point Ledge Lighthouse,** which looks like a stubby, cast-iron spark plug and has excellent views of the bay.

★ Portland Museum of Art

The I. M. Pei-designed **Portland Museum of Art** (7 Congress Sq., 207/775-6148, www.portlandmuseum.org, 10am-6pm Sat.-Wed., 10am-8pm Thurs.-Fri., hours fluctuate in

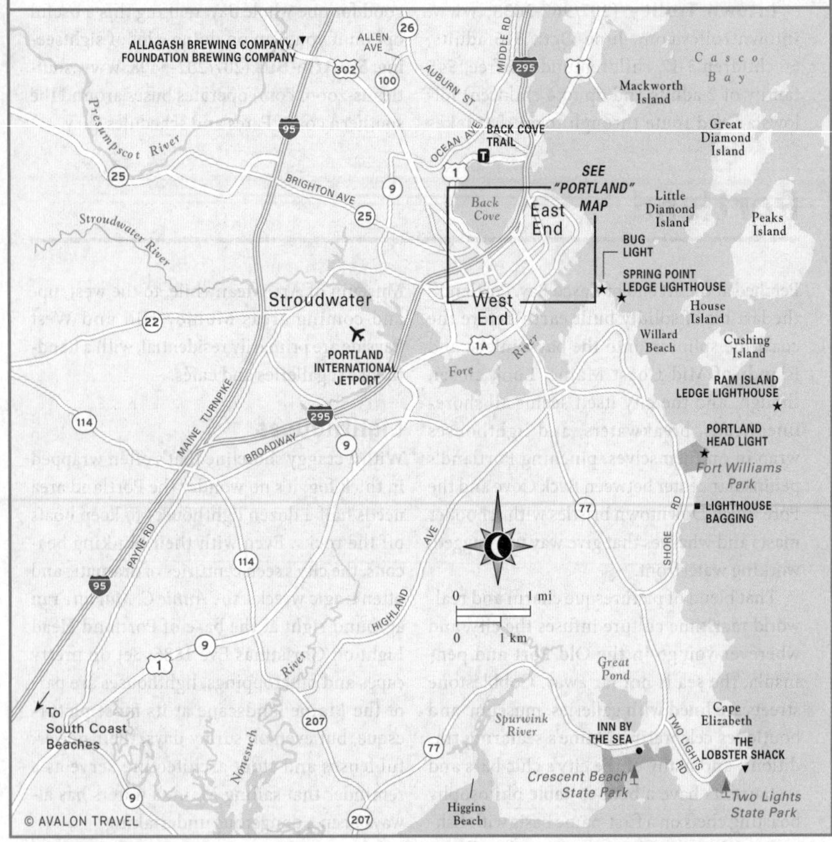

off-season, $15 adults, $13 seniors, $10 students, children under 15 free, free to all 4pm-8pm Fri.) is a world-class collection of impressionist and American work. A highlight for many visitors is work by Maine artist Winslow Homer, whose dramatic images of rescues at sea, windy shorelines, and small boats are seen as among the best American landscapes. Other noteworthy artists include Mary Cassatt, Claude Monet, Edward Hopper, and Auguste Renoir, but don't miss the dramatic engravings, lithographs, and paintings by Maine artist Rockwell Kent, many of whose mythic landscapes and woodcuts were made on the nearby island of Monhegan.

Institute of Contemporary Art at the Maine College of Art

For a more modern slice of the art scene, check out the **Institute of Contemporary Art at the Maine College of Art** (522 Congress St. or 87 Free St., 207/879-5742 or 207/669-5029, www.meca.edu, 11am-5pm Wed. & Fri.-Sun, 11am-7pm Thurs., 11am-8pm first Fri. of the month, free). The school's galleries draw cutting-edge installations from local and global artists, both established and aspiring.

Maine Historical Society

Rotating exhibitions at the **Maine Historical Society** (489 Congress St., 207/774-1822, www.mainehistory.org, 10am-5pm Mon.-Sat., noon-5pm Sun., $8 adults, $7 seniors and students, $2 children 6-17) illustrate the state's past through collections, exhibits, and lectures. Particularly riveting are the exhibits pertaining to the shelling that Portland received at the hands of the British during the Revolutionary War, when the port, then known as Falmouth, was burned to the ground in October 1775. The British captain offered mercy if the townspeople would swear allegiance to King George. No oath came, and the city was destroyed—only to be rebuilt over the next two decades.

Wadsworth-Longfellow House

Next door, the **Wadsworth-Longfellow House** (487 Congress St., 207/774-1822, www.mainehistory.org, tours noon-5pm daily May, 10am-5pm Mon.-Sat., noon-5pm Sun. June-Oct., $15 adults, $12 seniors and students, $3 children 6-17, $30 family of 2 adults and up to 3 children) was built in 1786 and achieved fame as the childhood home of poet Henry Wadsworth Longfellow. It's been restored to the time of the early 1800s, when Longfellow lived there. Tours lasting 45 minutes take in the life of the poet, as well as other members of the Longfellow family, such as Revolutionary War general Peleg Wadsworth.

Portland Observatory

Tired of waiting for boats to round Spring Point Ledge and come into view, Captain Lemuel Moody built the **Portland Observatory** (138 Congress St., 207/774-5561, www.portlandlandmarks.org, tours 10am-4:30pm daily May-Oct., sunset tours 5pm-8pm Thurs. late July-early Sept., $10 adults, $8 seniors and students, $5 children 6-16, $30 families) in 1807 so he could see harbor arrivals—and pass along the news to other shipowners for a tidy $5 annual fee. Climb the cheery red tower for Cap'n Moody's coveted lines of sight across Casco Bay and beyond, a vantage point especially sublime at sunset, when the waterfront and islands seem to glow on the sparkling water.

Victoria Mansion

Fans of Italianate architecture (or anyone who likes a pretty building) can swing by the **Victoria Mansion** (109 Danforth St., 207/772-4841, www.victoriamansion.org, tours 10am-3:45pm Mon.-Sat., 1pm-4:45pm Sun. May-Oct., 1pm-5pm Tues.-Sun. late Nov.-early Jan., $16 adults, $14 seniors, $5 students 6-17, children under 6 free, $35 families). Built by a hotel magnate between 1858 and 1860, the mansion is considered the greatest surviving example of pre-Civil War architecture in the country. Ahead of its time, it employed central heating, running water, and gas lighting in an era when such efficiencies were virtually unknown luxuries. These days the house is particularly impressive at Christmastime, when it's decorated from baseboards to ceilings with ornaments and wreaths.

ENTERTAINMENT AND EVENTS

Bars

Even if it weren't for all its breweries, Portland would have an amazing bar scene. Some of the most popular places to grab a drink are also restaurants, like **Eventide Oyster Co., Duckfat,** and **Terlingua,** but there are a few that go right to the point.

Nordic chic and Scandinavian-themed small bites prevail at the stylish **Portland Hunt & Alpine Club** (75 Market St., 207/747-4754, www.huntandalpineclub.com, 3pm-1am daily), and a happy hour lineup of four $6 cocktails is available until 6pm daily. Unless you're really looking, you'll walk right by **Novare Res Bier Cafe** (4 Canal Plaza, 207/761-2437, www.novareresbiercafe.com, 4pm-1am Mon.-Thurs., 3pm-1am Fri., noon-1am Sat.-Sun.), which is tucked down an alley between Union and Exchange Streets. Between the shady beer garden and cave-like interior, it works in any weather, and has an enormous list of beers from around the world. Drinkers who like their music on vinyl and decor eclectic will *love* **Maps** (64 Market St., 207/272-9263, 4pm-midnight Wed.-Sun.),

Portland

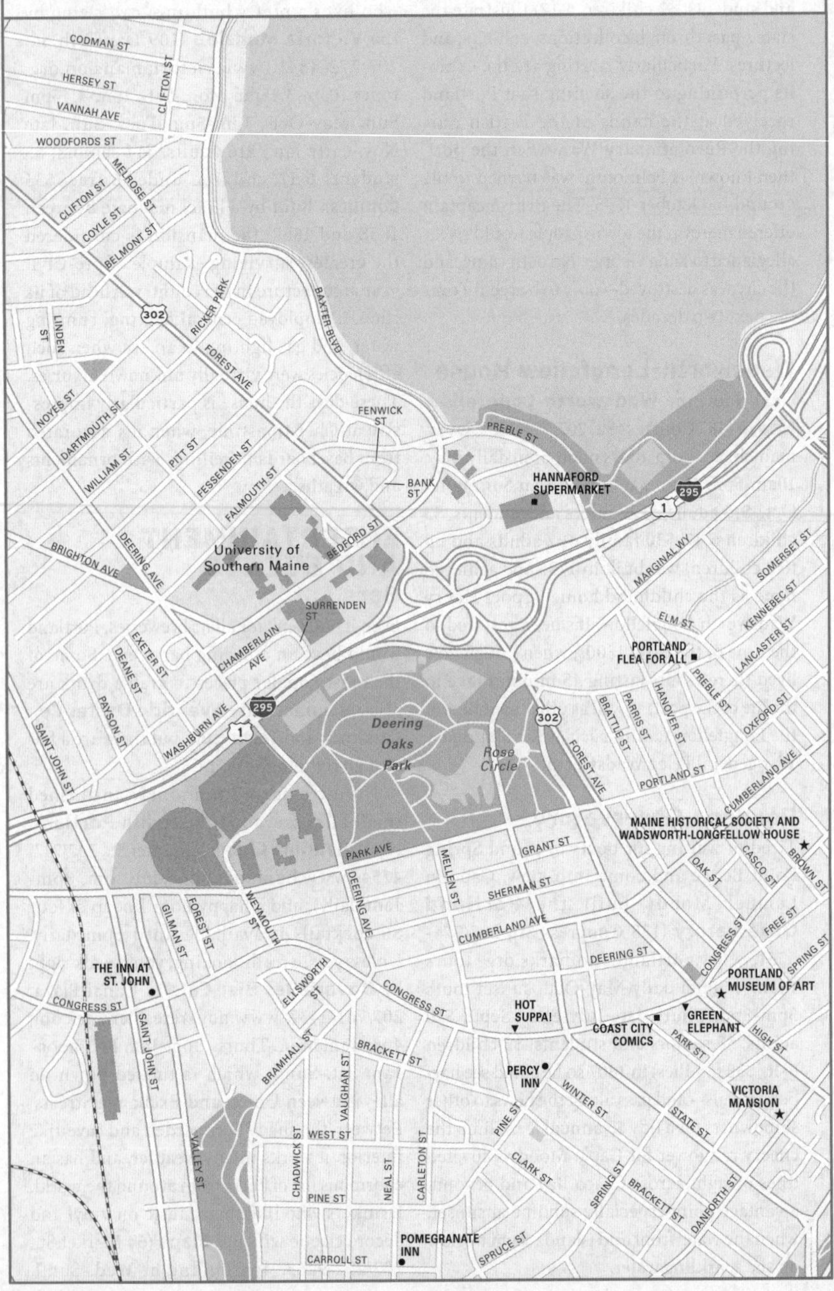
CODMAN ST
HERSEY ST
VANNAH AVE
WOODFORDS ST
CLIFTON ST
MELROSE ST
CLIFTON ST
COYLE ST
BELMONT ST
302
RICKER PARK
LINDEN ST
BAXTER BLVD
FOREST AVE
NOYES ST
DARTMOUTH ST
FENWICK ST
PREBLE ST
WILLIAM ST
PITT ST
FESSENDEN ST
BANK ST
HANNAFORD SUPERMARKET
FALMOUTH ST
295
1
BRIGHTON AVE
DEERING AVE
University of Southern Maine
BEDFORD ST
MARGINAL WY
SOMERSET ST
KENNEBEC ST
ELM ST
SURRENDEN ST
EXETER ST
DEANE ST
CHAMBERLAIN AVE
PORTLAND FLEA FOR ALL
LANCASTER ST
PREBLE ST
PAYSON ST
295
302
BRATTLE ST
PARRIS ST
HANOVER ST
OXFORD ST
WASHBURN AVE
1
Deering Oaks Park
Rose Circle
SAINT JOHN ST
FOREST AVE
PORTLAND ST
CUMBERLAND AVE
MAINE HISTORICAL SOCIETY AND WADSWORTH-LONGFELLOW HOUSE
PARK AVE
GRANT ST
MELLEN ST
OAK ST
CASCO ST
BROWN ST
GILMAN ST
FOREST ST
WEYMOUTH ST
DEERING AVE
SHERMAN ST
CUMBERLAND AVE
FREE ST
THE INN AT ST. JOHN
ELLSWORTH ST
DEERING ST
CONGRESS ST
PORTLAND MUSEUM OF ART
SPRING ST
CONGRESS ST
CONGRESS ST
HOT SUPPA!
GREEN ELEPHANT
COAST CITY COMICS
PARK ST
HIGH ST
SAINT JOHN ST
BRAMHALL ST
BRACKETT ST
PERCY INN
WINTER ST
VICTORIA MANSION
STATE ST
VAUGHAN ST
PINE ST
WEST ST
VALLEY ST
CHADWICK ST
NEAL ST
CARLETON ST
CLARK ST
SPRING ST
BRACKETT ST
DANFORTH ST
PINE ST
POMEGRANATE INN
SPRUCE ST
CARROLL ST

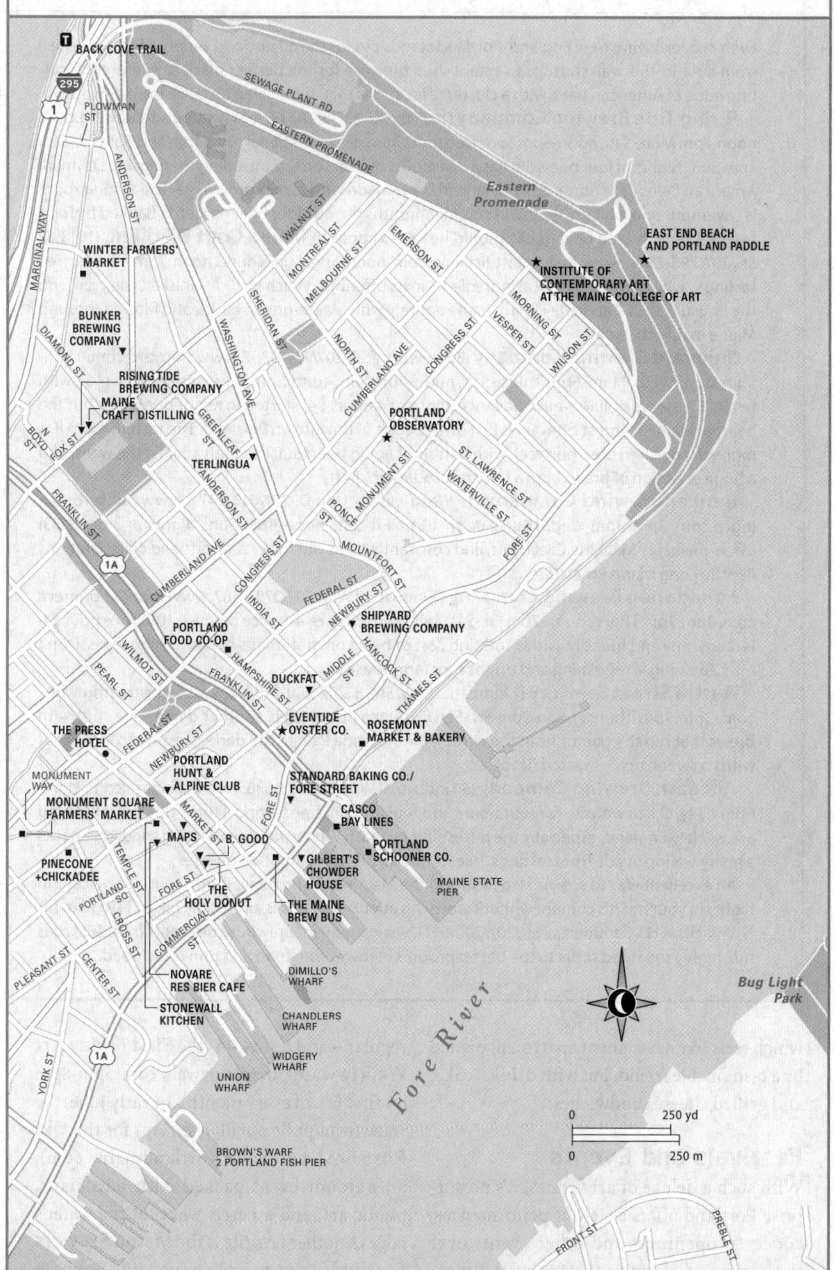
BACK COVE TRAIL
295
1
PLOWMAN ST
SEWAGE PLANT RD
EASTERN PROMENADE
Eastern Promenade
ANDERSON ST
MARGINAL WAY
WALNUT ST
MONTREAL ST
MELBOURNE ST
EMERSON ST
EAST END BEACH AND PORTLAND PADDLE
WINTER FARMERS' MARKET
INSTITUTE OF CONTEMPORARY ART AT THE MAINE COLLEGE OF ART
SHERIDAN ST
MORNING ST
BUNKER BREWING COMPANY
WASHINGTON AVE
NORTH ST
CONGRESS ST
VESPER ST
WILSON ST
DIAMOND ST
CUMBERLAND AVE
RISING TIDE BREWING COMPANY
MAINE CRAFT DISTILLING
PORTLAND OBSERVATORY
GREENLEAF ST
N BOYD ST
FOX ST
TERLINGUA
ST. LAWRENCE ST
MONUMENT ST
WATERVILLE ST
ANDERSON ST
PONCE ST
FRANKLIN ST
FORE ST
MOUNTFORT ST
1A
CUMBERLAND AVE
CONGRESS ST
FEDERAL ST
NEWBURY ST
INDIA ST
SHIPYARD BREWING COMPANY
PORTLAND FOOD CO-OP
HANCOCK ST
WILMOT ST
HAMPSHIRE ST
MIDDLE ST
DUCKFAT
PEARL ST
FRANKLIN ST
THAMES ST
EVENTIDE OYSTER CO.
THE PRESS HOTEL
FEDERAL ST
ROSEMONT MARKET & BAKERY
NEWBURY ST
PORTLAND HUNT & ALPINE CLUB
MONUMENT WAY
STANDARD BAKING CO./ FORE STREET
MONUMENT SQUARE FARMERS' MARKET
FORE ST
CASCO BAY LINES
MARKET ST
MAPS
B. GOOD
PORTLAND SCHOONER CO.
PINECONE +CHICKADEE
GILBERT'S CHOWDER HOUSE
TEMPLE ST
FORE ST
THE HOLY DONUT
MAINE STATE PIER
PORTLAND SQ
CROSS ST
COMMERCIAL ST
THE MAINE BREW BUS
PLEASANT ST
CENTER ST
NOVARE RES BIER CAFE
DIMILLO'S WHARF
STONEWALL KITCHEN
CHANDLERS WHARF
Bug Light Park
Fore River
1A
YORK ST
WIDGERY WHARF
UNION WHARF
0
250 yd
0
250 m
BROWN'S WARF
2 PORTLAND FISH PIER
FRONT ST
PREBLE ST

Portland's Best Pints

Even in beer-loving New England, Portland stands out for the quality and variety of its breweries, from hole-in-the-wall startups to established brewers. It's the perfect place to explore the cutting edge of American beer, with a cluster of locations that are walking distance from downtown.

Rising Tide Brewing Company (103 Fox St., 207/370-2337, www.risingtidebrewing.com, noon-7pm Mon.-Sat., noon-5pm Sun., free tours 3pm daily, additional tours 1pm and 5pm Fri.-Sat., 1pm Sun., flights of four beers $8) has a diverse list of beers on tap, including the flagship Daymark American Pale Ale, a gorgeously balanced brew made with locally grown rye. The tasting room is cavernous and a bit gritty, and in summer months the outdoor beer garden is flanked by food trucks. Even devoted beer geeks should head next door to **Maine Craft Distilling** (101 Fox St., 207/798-2528, www.mainecraftdistilling.com, noon-5pm Sun.-Thurs., noon-7pm Fri.-Sat., free tastings), which uses many local ingredients in its offerings, which include whiskey, rum, gin, and the unusual Black Cap Barley Spirit, made entirely with Maine-grown barley and filtered through Maine maple charcoal.

Shipyard Brewing Company (86 Newbury St., 207/761-0807, www.shipyard.com, 11am-5pm Mon.-Wed., 11am-6pm Thurs.-Sat., noon-4pm Sun., tours 5pm Tues. mid-May-Oct., $7 with tastings, reserve online well in advance, flight of 4 beers $4) started in Kennebunkport, but the heart of Maine's largest brewery is just on the edge of downtown Portland. The tasting room has more of a finished brewpub feel, with barrels of aging beers stacked high against the walls, and a huge selection of brews (and a few craft sodas) on draft.

Bunker Brewing Company (17 Westfield St., Unit D, 207/613-9471, www.bunkerbrewingco.com, 3pm-8pm Wed.-Thurs., noon-10pm Fri.-Sat., noon-6pm Sun., flights of 3 beers $3) offers mainstay Machine Czech Pilz, and constantly turns out funky one-offs and collaborations like the Long Island Potato Stout.

Foundation Brewing Company (1 Industrial Way, 207/370-8187, www.foundationbrew.com, 3pm-7pm Thurs., noon-7pm Fri.-Sat., self-guided tours, 4-ounce pour $2, 10-ounce pour $4) is teeny-tiny and friendly, with a rotating cast of beers on draft that's been winning raves. Don't miss Zuurzing, a refreshing and bright sour farmhouse ale.

Austin Street Brewery (1 Industrial Way, Ste. 8, 207/200-1994, www.austinstreetbrewery.com, 3pm-7pm Thurs., noon-7pm Fri.-Sat., 5-ounce pours $2) is another diminutive spot with brews that run the gamut from the citrusy, piney Patina Pale to the dark-as-espresso Milk Stout with its sweet, richly toasted flavor.

Allagash Brewing Company (50 Industrial Way, 207/878-5385, www.allagash.com, 11am-6pm daily, check website for tour hours and registration, free tastings) turns out beers beloved across New England, especially the refreshing Allagash White and a rich-tasting tripel that packs a malty wallop. Aside from tastings, beer is not sold for consumption on-site.

An excellent way to soak up (so to speak) the Maine brewing scene is on a tour, so you can sip flights to your heart's content without worrying about cabs, buses, or wobbly bikes. **The Maine Brew Bus** (111 Commercial St., 207/200-9111, www.themainebrewbus.com, tours from $65) runs fun, highly regarded tours to the best taprooms in town, with food and drinks included.

which feels like a basement apartment owned by a fashionable friend, but with drinks, cake, and grilled cheese sandwiches.

Festivals and Events

With such a deluge of art venues, it's no surprise Portland offers a slew of performances, concerts, openings, and other events over the course of every year. One of the most regular—and festive—is the **First Friday Art Walk** (www.firstfridayartwalk.com, 5pm-8pm on first Fri. of every month). In early June, the waterfront pulls out all the stops for the **Old Port Festival** (www.portlandmaine.com), an outdoor event packed with musicians, public art, and a Ferris wheel at the water's edge. Another favorite is the **Maine Brewers Festival** (www.mainebrewersfestival.com) in early November, which assembles the best of local beer in one place.

SHOPPING

Pretty shops line the cobblestone streets of Portland's Old Port. For the most efficient browsing, make your way along Exchange and Congress Streets. One local favorite is the sweetly hipster **Pinecone + Chickadee** (6 Free St., 207/772-9280, www.pineconeandchickadee.com, 10am-6pm daily), which stocks unique clothing, vintage finds, and doohickeys that make perfect gifts. Comic book lovers from around the East come to **Coast City Comics** (634 Congress St., 207/899-1505, www.coastcitycomics.com, 11am-8pm daily) for its collection not only of comics but also pinball and arcade games and vintage toys so fun the store could charge admission. Vintage and antiques hounds shouldn't miss the **Portland Flea-For-All** (585 Congress St., 207/370-7570, www.portlandfleaforall.com, noon-6pm Fri., 10am-6pm Sat., 10am-5pm Sun., hours can change without notice so call to confirm) for treasures covering three sprawling floors. Loved for classic jams and jellies, **Stonewall Kitchen** (182 Middle St., 207/879-2409, www.stonewallkitchen.com, 10am-8pm Mon.-Sat., 10am-6pm Sun.) is one of Maine's most recognizable brands, and the company store in Portland is a wonderland of free samples and things to buy.

SPORTS AND RECREATION

Beaches

With great sunset views and a skinny strip of sand, **East End Beach** is pleasant for walking and kayaking, and, more to the point, it's Portland's only public beach. It's set on the southern end of the **Eastern Promenade,** where monuments, cliffs, and smooth trails make for a haven from the city. If you have a day to spend on the sand, however, it's worth getting out of town to Cape Elizabeth's gorgeous **Crescent Beach.**

Boating

Take a turn hoisting the gaff-rigged sails—or let someone else do the work—on a two-hour cruise aboard the *Bagheera* or *Wendameen*, the 72- and 88-foot schooners operated by **Portland Schooner Co.** (Maine State Pier, 56 Commercial St., 207/766-2500, www.portlandschooner.com, 2-hour sailing trip $44 adults, $22 children 12 and under).

Hiking and Biking

Walking and biking paths wind through Portland's streets, and much of the scenic waterfront is pedestrian accessible. One of the finest places to walk or bike is **Back Cove Trail,** a 3.6-mile paved trail that circles a small estuary just north of downtown. Hop on (and leave your car) at Payson Park, the northern access point, or Preble Street. If you're headed from north to south, the Back Cove Trail connects to the **Eastern Promenade,** a slender waterfront park that caps Portland's East End neighborhood; 2.1 miles end-to-end, the park has walking trails, a popular swimming beach, and showstopping sunrise views. **Portland Trails** (207/775-2411, www.trails.org) maintains a website with maps and directions to many of the city's best offerings.

Paddling

Rent a kayak (or stand-up paddleboard) from **Portland Paddle** (East End Beach, Eastern Promenade, 207/370-9730, www.portlandpaddle.net, kayaks $30 for 2 hours, $40 half day, $55 full day, SUP $25 for 1 hour, $35 for 3 hours) to explore Casco Bay on your own. Paddlers with basic skills can poke along the coast and beaches, while more experienced kayakers can visit uninhabited islands, the historic Fort Gorges, and offshore communities. The company also offers guided tours: Family paddles, moonlight outings, and sunset trips are just a hair more expensive than renting the equipment alone (tours from $40 adults, $35 children 10-16).

FOOD

From old-school seafood joints to achingly hip bistros, Portland punches far above its weight in the restaurant department, and deciding where to apportion your limited meals in the city can be agonizing. Oysters and cocktails? Super-fresh salads packed with ingredients from local farms? How about a creamy bowl of chowder within earshot of the waterfront's clanging masts and foghorns?

Seafood

A refreshing throwback to Portland's pre-hipster, rough-hewn days, **Gilbert's Chowder House** (92 Commercial St., 207/871-5636, www.gilbertschowderhouse.com, 11am-10pm daily, $7-21) slings fresh corn and clam chowders in a thoroughly unpretentious space. The crisp, flaky haddock sandwiches are another treat, as is the open terrace behind the restaurant; when the restaurant is packed, order a cup of soup to go and find a spot on the nearby wharves for a very Maine picnic.

The interior of the ★ **Eventide Oyster Co.** (86 Middle St., 207/774-8538, www.eventideoysterco.com, 11am-midnight daily, $16-25) is almost too gorgeous: bright teal walls setting off a mammoth chunk of granite filled with crushed ice and sea creatures. The oysters—which mostly come from Maine, with a few out-of-state additions—are the obvious choice and centerpiece, and come with anything from "Kim Chee Ice" to classic mignonettes and cocktail sauce. Other options include small plates like duck confit salad and tuna crudo, but Eventide is famed for its lobster roll, a luscious combination of sweet lobster meat, brown butter, and chives in a soft Chinese-style steamed bun.

Bakeries

From dark chocolate with sea salt to maple bacon, the flavors of the soft, crisp-crusted treats at **The Holy Donut** (7 Exchange St., 207/775-7776, www.theholydonut.com, 7:30am-4pm Mon.-Thurs., 7:30am-8pm Fri.-Sat., 7:30am-5pm Sun., $2-5) are some of the best around—for doughnut lovers, this shop is a pilgrimage place. Arrive early to get the best selection, and avoid coming at the end of the day, as the doors close when the last doughnut sells.

A rustic, French aesthetic means great piles of croissants and fruit galettes at **Standard Baking Co.** (75 Commercial St., 207/773-2112, www.standardbakingco.com, 7am-6pm Mon.-Fri., 7am-5pm Sat.-Sun., $3-9), a beloved local institution walking distance from the Old Port. Breads and pastries are made with organic wheat flour from regional growers, and all the delightfully crusty loaves are naturally leavened.

Casual Fare

Just a few doors down, you'll find fresh fare to offset any doughnut guilt: **B. Good** (15 Exchange St., 207/747-5355, www.bgood.com, 11am-9pm Mon.-Thurs., 11am-10pm Fri.-Sat., 11am-8pm Sun., $7-12) is a chain with a couple-dozen locations across the East, but the concept of healthy food with local roots means the ingredients are sourced from Maine farmers and producers. Come for bowls of kale and quinoa, bright salads, simple burgers, and healthy smoothies, and find a seat upstairs when the place is hopping—a quiet bar and window-side tables overlook the action on Exchange Street.

Cheerful and welcoming, **Hot Suppa!** (703 Congress St., 207/871-5005, www.hotsuppa.com, 7:30am-2pm Sun.-Mon., 7am-2pm and 4pm-9:15pm Tues.-Sat., breakfast $5-11, lunch $7-12, dinner $15-24) serves an eclectic selection of comfort food with Southern flair, like pork belly with red beans and rice, catfish and grits, chicken and waffles, and some of the best corned beef hash in New England. Waits can get long, so aim to come early or late.

Named for a map-dot Texas town that hosts a yearly chili cook-off, **Terlingua** (52 Washington Ave., 207/808-8502, www.terlingua.me, 11:30am-9pm Mon.-Thurs., 11:30am-10pm Fri.-Sat., 10am-9pm Sun., $14-20) is a warm, vivid antidote to all that seafood. The barbecue fare at this laid-back restaurant is executed with a reverence for smoke and meat and Tex-Mex flair, from butternut squash empanadas to red and green chilis. Menu items like Frito pie (in the bag) lean cheeky, and regulars wash it all down with the killer house margaritas and solid beer choices.

Just down the road is another local favorite: ★ **Duckfat** (43 Middle St., 207/774-8080, www.duckfat.com, 11am-10pm daily, $8-14) serves a casual lineup of panini, salads, and golden french fries redolent of—you guessed it—duck fat. Decor is exposed brick and magnetic poetry tiles, and the poutine topped with cheese curds, gravy, and a fried egg would fortify you for a week of lighthouse bagging. If at all possible, save room for one of the shop's luxurious milkshakes, and come prepared to wait most nights.

Fine Dining

Vegetarians weary of meat-heavy Yankee fare shouldn't miss **Green Elephant** (608 Congress St., 207/347-3111, www.greenelephantmaine.com, 11:30am-2:30pm and 5pm-9:30pm Mon.-Sat., 5pm-9pm Sun., $12-15), a top-notch Asian bistro with stenciled green walls and chandeliers. The spicy ginger noodles are a favorite with regulars, as are the tofu tikka masala and crispy wontons filled with soy cheese and spinach.

Often credited with putting Portland on the international foodie map, ★ **Fore Street** (288 Fore St., 207/775-2717, www.forestreet.biz, 5:30pm-10pm Sun.-Thurs., 5:30pm-10:30pm Fri.-Sat., bar from 5pm daily, $28-40) could rest on its locally sourced, handcrafted laurels for a decade. That makes it all the more refreshing that the kitchen continues to turn out such high-quality fare. An open kitchen keeps the industrial-chic space from seeming too hushed as diners tuck in to seafood roasted in a wood-fired oven or house-made charcuterie paired with a serious wine list.

Markets

Conveniently located in the Old Port, **Rosemont Market & Bakery** (5 Commercial St., 207/699-4560, www.rosemontmarket.com, 9am-7pm Mon.-Sat., 9am-6pm Sun.) is "human sized" and stocked with regional vegetables, cheese, meat, and house-made baked goods as well as pizza and sandwiches. The **Portland Food Co-Op** (290 Congress St., 207/805-1599, www.portlandfood.coop, 8am-8pm daily) has aisles stuffed with local and organic products plus healthy, premade food. More basic options are available at **Hannaford Supermarket** (295 Forest Ave., 207/761-5965, 7am-11pm daily), at the edge of Back Cove.

Portland has three farmers markets overflowing with everything from local veggies to goat yogurt and kimchi. A carnival atmosphere commands at the downtown **Monument Square Market** (456 Congress St., 7am-1pm Wed. Apr.-Dec.), while the market at **Deering Oaks Park** (7am-1pm Sat. late Apr.-Nov.) is a bit more relaxed. The **Winter Farmers' Market** (84 Cove St., 9am-1pm Sat. Dec.-Apr.) also has live music and food trucks.

ACCOMMODATIONS

Though Portland has some wonderful top-end offerings, a lack of reasonably priced accommodations in the city makes sites like Airbnb and VBRO good options for travelers on a budget.

$100-150

Ask a local about **The Inn at St. John** (939 Congress St., 207/773-6481, www.innatstjohn.com, $75-250), and he or she will likely recall its seedy years when the West End was decidedly down-market. It's been overhauled one room at a time, however, retaining flourishes of Gilded Age glamour and gaining much-needed updates like wireless Internet, coffeemakers, and a bit of contemporary style. Continental breakfast is served in a downstairs dining room, and the rooms vary widely, from more luxurious king rooms boasting en suite baths and views of the street to somewhat garret-like singles with shared baths. The narrow, steep stairs are not for everyone.

$150-250

Set on a quiet side street in the West End, the **Percy Inn** (15 Pine St., 207/871-7638, www.percyinn.com, $89-219) is in a renovated 1830s federal-style brick house that feels like pure, old-fashioned Portland. The house has some quirks and could use a bit of updating, but the overall effect is lovely; rooms are named for famous writers, and the fire-lit library and spacious common room are welcoming.

Over $250

Somewhere between bohemian whimsy and design-chic, ★ **Pomegranate Inn** (49 Neal St., 207/772-1006, www.pomegranateinn.com, $200-359) is settled on a pretty corner in a historic neighborhood and full of visual treasures. Every room has unique hand-painted walls, and antiques are displayed alongside modern art. A 3rd-floor lounge is stocked with games, and a quiet back patio makes an ideal spot for enjoying the daily cookies, tea, and coffee. "The Pom" is now operated by Lark Hotels and serves the group's characteristic small-plate breakfast that will charm your socks off (and leave some hungry travelers looking for a bit more).

Flying typewriters and wordy art are reminders that **The Press Hotel** (119 Exchange St., 207/808-8800, www.thepresshotel.com, $225-450) was once the home of the *Portland Press Herald*, and the journo-chic theme runs throughout the property. Excellent service gives the large property a boutique feel, and the Inkwell coffee and wine bar feels like just the place to type up some hotel poetry of your own—local touches are everywhere and, all in all, Press offers some of the coolest new digs in New England.

INFORMATION

The remarkably helpful and informative **visitors bureau** (207/772-5800, www.visitportland.com) has a website full of information and links, and runs information centers on the waterfront at 14 Ocean Gateway Pier (207/772-5800, 9am-5pm Mon.-Fri., 9am-4pm Sat.-Sun., winter hours vary) and in the Jetport Terminal next to baggage claim (207/775-5809, 8am-midnight Mon. and Thurs.-Fri., 10am-midnight Sat.-Sun., winter hours vary).

GETTING THERE

Air

Maine's largest airport is **Portland International Jetport** (1001 Westbrook St., 207/774-7301, www.portlandjetport.org), with service from American, Delta, JetBlue, Southwest, and United. There you'll find national car rental agencies Alamo, Avis, Budget, Enterprise, Hertz, and National, and the **Greater Portland Transit District METRO** (207/774-0351, www.gpmetrobus.net), which has a bus from the airport to downtown Portland (Route #5, 6-15 buses daily).

Train

The Amtrak **Downeaster** (800/872-7245, www.amtrakdowneaster.com) runs from Boston to Portland five times a day, with two trains making an extended trip to Freeport and Brunswick. The Portland stop is at the **Portland Transportation Center** (100 Thompson's Point Rd.), two miles outside of downtown. Trolleys link **Wells Regional Transportation Center** with the Kennebunks, and the **Freeport station** is within walking distance of downtown shops.

Bus

Concord Coach Lines (100 Thompson's Point Rd., 800/639-3317, www.concordcoachlines.com) operates buses from Boston and New York City; long-distance routes connect to Portland, then continue to many towns along Route 1, including Brunswick (16 Station Ave.), Bath (Mail It 4 U, 10 State Rd.), Rockland (Maine State Ferry Terminal, 517A Main St.), and Camden/Rockport (Maritime Farms, 20 Commercial St./Rte. 1, Rockport).

Greyhound (950 Congress St., 207/772-6588 or 800/231-2222, www.greyhound.com)

has services to Portland from Boston and around New England.

GETTING AROUND

Portland's local bus company is **Metro** (114 Valley St., 207/774-0351, www.gpmetrobus.net, $1.50 adults, $0.75 seniors, children under 6 free, $5 all-day pass), which runs out of its downtown station to points including the airport. Compared to most capital cities, Portland has a decent amount of metered street parking, which doesn't guarantee you'll find any right away (particularly in the summer), but the odds are good. That said, the city has pay lots and garages set up every few blocks. Local taxis to call are **ABC Taxi** (207/772-8685) and **Town Taxi** (207/773-1711).

CASCO BAY ISLANDS

There are 136 islands, give or take, scattered across the broad Casco Bay—enough that they were long called the Calendar Islands, a name that evokes the dreamy possibility of spending an entire year skipping from isle to isle. The islands on Casco Bay can feel wonderfully remote, though they're just a quick ferry ride from downtown Portland, and they're well worth a day trip or overnight escape.

Peaks Island

The most accessible of the Casco Bay islands, Peaks Island is like a Portland neighborhood surrounded by water, and with many ferry departures each day, it's the easiest way to get out on the water. Most visitors leave their cars on the mainland, then rent a golf cart or bicycle for a day of exploring.

SIGHTS AND ACTIVITIES

Circle the island by bicycle on the **Peaks Island Loop,** a four-mile, mostly flat route that winds between residential neighborhoods and the waterfront. Bikes are available to rent, with helmets and maps of the island, from **Brad's Bike Rental and Repair** (115 Island Ave., 207/766-5631, 10am-6pm daily, rentals $10 per hour, $30 all day), a short walk from the ferry terminal.

Oddly wonderful and wonderfully odd, the **Umbrella Cover Museum** (62 B Island Rd., 207/766-4496, www.umbrellacovermuseum.com, 10am-1pm and 2pm-5pm Tues.-Sat., 10am-12:30pm Sun. June-early Sept.) is a deep dive into the sheaths, envelopes, and slipcovers that umbrellas come in. Tours sometimes include impromptu "umbrella songs" by the accordion-playing curator.

For the best perspective on the rugged coast, grab a paddle. Guided kayak tours are available from **Maine Island Kayak** (207/766-2373, www.maineislandkayak.com, half-day tour from $65), whose guides meet the arriving ferryboat from Portland.

FOOD

Dining options are limited on Peaks Island, but **The Cockeyed Gull Restaurant** (78 Island Ave., 207/766-2800, 11:30am-8:30pm daily, hours and days vary in winter $8-25) has seafood standards and great views of the water from its deck. Another possibility is **The Inn on Peaks Island** (33 Island Ave., 207/766-5100, www.innonpeaks.com, 11am-9pm Sun.-Thurs., 11am-10pm Fri.-Sat., $9-26), whose menu ranges from basic burgers and sandwiches to upscale entrées like lobster risotto.

GETTING THERE

Casco Bay Lines (56 Commercial St., 207/774-7871, www.cascobaylines.com, approximately 1 per hour, $7.70 adults, $3.85 children and seniors) has year-round ferry service from downtown Portland to Peaks Island.

Great Chebeague Island

Farther away from Portland both geographically and in spirit, this is a quiet place to explore by bike, or picnic on one of the island's appealing beaches. If you're looking for an overnight escape, the island's single hotel is an ideal place to get away from it all.

SIGHTS AND ACTIVITIES

For two hours on either side of low tide, the ocean exposes a slender sandbar linking Great Chebeague with **Little Chebeague Island,** an uninhabited islet that's covered in thick forest. To reach the sandbar, follow Indian Point Road to a sandy beach that looks out at Little Chebeague Island.

Close to the Chebeague Island Inn, **Hamilton Beach** is the island's best for swimming and sunbathing, with warmer water then elsewhere on Chebeague.

FOOD AND ACCOMMODATIONS

The island's main social hub is the **Slow Bell Café** (2 Walker Rd., 207/846-3078, 5pm-midnight Thurs.-Sun. Memorial Day-Labor Day, $9-20), a bar and restaurant with a laid-back, castaway feel. Seafood, salads, and sandwiches are casual and well made.

Though there's just one place to stay on the island, the lovely ★ **Chebeague Island Inn** (61 South Rd., 207/856-5155, www.chebeagueislandinn.com, $175-450) more than compensates for the lack of variety. A great, shady porch faces the water, with rocking chairs and warm blankets for morning coffee, and there are beach towels and umbrellas to borrow for a trip to the shore. Nonguests are welcome at the inn's **restaurant** (breakfast 7:30am-9:30am, lunch 11:30am-2:30pm, light fare 2:30pm-9pm, dinner 5:30pm-8pm, daily, $15-35), which serves elegant preparations using many local ingredients.

GETTING THERE AND AROUND

Casco Bay Lines (56 Commercial St., Portland, 207/774-7871, www.cascobaylines.com, 1 hr., 20 min., $11 adults, $5.50 children and seniors) has year-round ferry service from downtown Portland to Chebeague Island, with several departures each day. **Chebeague Transportation Company** (Cousins Island Wharf, Yarmouth, 207/846-3700, www.chebeaguetrans.com, 15 min., $16 adults, $4.50 children 6-11) has regular service from Yarmouth. Parking is available at the company's lot in Cumberland, with a bus shuttle to the wharf.

Getting There and Around

A network of ferries connects Portland with the islands speckling Casco Bay. **Casco Bay Lines** (56 Commercial St., 207/774-7871, www.cascobaylines.com, passenger ferry $7-12, mail boat run $16 adults, $14 seniors, $8 children) runs trips to seven islands, from a quick hop to Peaks Island to the longer trip to Chebeague. The ferry service still delivers the mail to offshore communities, and you can tag along on the **mail boat run,** which lasts 2.5-3.5 hours; while the boat doesn't linger long enough for you to explore the islands, you'll get great views, and the crew narrates the whole experience on a loudspeaker (bring your own food and drinks).

CAPE ELIZABETH

Just a short drive from the city of Portland, this seaside community offers views back across Casco Bay, and one of Maine's most recognizable lighthouses. While this is a quick day trip for most visitors, it's equally appealing as a home base for visiting the city, where you can nip into town for dinner, then return to the quiet of night by Crescent Beach.

Sights

PORTLAND HEAD LIGHT

The most iconic among Portland's lighthouses is the **Portland Head Light** (1000 Shore Rd., www.portlandheadlight.com, museum and gift shop 10am-4pm daily, park sunrise-sunset daily); its slender proportions and red-roofed keeper's house are perfectly offset by jagged outcroppings and crashing waves. It was the first lighthouse completed by the U.S. government and has been guiding ships on Casco Bay since 1791; the rocky head is rich with history, including shipwrecks and daring, stormy rescues, and some believe it's haunted by the benevolent ghost of a former lighthouse keeper. One frequent visitor was hometown poet Henry Wadsworth Longfellow, who liked to drink with the lighthouse keeper and later wrote:

Steadfast, serene, immovable, the same
Year after year, through all the silent night
Burns on forevermore that quenchless flame,
Shines on that inextinguishable light!

For the real Maine beach experience, it's worth heading out of town. Eight miles south of Portland, **Crescent Beach** (66 Two Lights Rd., 207/767-3625, www.maine.gov, 9am-sunset daily, $8 adults, $2 seniors, $1 children 5-11) is all dune grass and soft sand, a gorgeous place to watch the fishing fleet cross the horizon.

OTHER SIGHTS

A favorite spot for lighthouse bagging is **Two Lights** (Two Lights Rd.), a pretty pair of private lighthouses with a small beach and rocks perfect for hopping around and scouting for sea creatures. Confusingly, neither of the two lights is visible from Two Lights State Park, so just continue down the road until it ends in a small parking lot. Since neither lighthouse is open to the public, the views (and photo opportunities) aren't quite as good as elsewhere, but the neighboring Lobster Shack takes up the slack.

Food

Adjoining the Two Lights lighthouses, **The Lobster Shack** (225 Two Lights Rd., 207/799-1677, www.lobstershacktwolights.com, 11am-8pm daily Mar.-Oct., $12-18) has some of Maine's most beloved lobster rolls. The interior is decked out in marine bric-a-brac, and the outdoor picnic tables overlook crashing waves and the lighthouses—but be vigilant about seagulls to avoid losing bits of your meal. While the lobster roll is the main attraction here, The Lobster Shack also serves the standard lineup of market-price seafood, and a homemade strawberry rhubarb pie that gets rave reviews.

Accommodations

Set back from Crescent Beach, ★ **Inn by the Sea** (40 Bowery Beach Rd., 207/779-3134, www.innbythesea.com, $450-700) has a perfect location and gorgeous grounds. The luxurious resort has family-friendly bungalows and cottages as well as beautiful rooms in the main inn and perks like outdoor pools, a fireplace stocked with s'mores, and a spa. What sets the inn apart from other top-notch properties, though, is a remarkable focus on conservation: The on-site wetlands and meadows were overhauled to create habitat for the endangered New England cottontail rabbit, the inn runs environmental science education programs, and the chef works with local fishers to source from underutilized fish populations. It's also easy to leave the inn with an unusual memento of your stay—the staff fosters friendly dogs from the local humane society that can be adopted by guests; hundreds find new homes each year.

GETTING THERE

Cape Elizabeth is 20 minutes south of Portland on Route 77, which loops past the cape's main destinations. There's currently no public transit from Portland to the sights in Cape Elizabeth.

FREEPORT

Just 20 minutes up the coast from Portland, Freeport is a shipbuilding and fishing village turned New England-themed outlet shopping destination, a transformation that's left some interesting quirks, with boutiques, outlets, and even a McDonald's restaurant tucked into historic homes. Visitors tend to love it or hate it, but whether you're planning an all-day shopping itinerary or just want a home base for exploring Portland, it's a good place to stay, with more affordable accommodations than the city.

Sights

The undisputed headliner of Freeport's retail scene is the **L.L. Bean Flagship Store** (95 Main St., 877/755-2326, www.llbean.com), which is open 24 hours a day, 365 days a year. If the appeal of buying waterproof boots at 3am isn't enough to tempt you, the indoor trout pond or archery and clay shooting lessons might.

With some of Maine's most beloved brews, **Maine Beer Company** (525 Rte. 1, 201/221-5711, www.mainebeercompany.com, 11am-8pm Mon.-Sat., 11am-5pm Sun.) has a tasting room that keeps eight of its beers on tap—and you can watch the beer-in-progress through a big window onto the brewing facility.

Shopping

Aside from the behemoth L.L. Bean outlet, much of Freeport's big-name shopping is clustered in the **Freeport Village Station** (1 Freeport Village Station, www.onefreeport-villagestation.com, 10am-7pm Sun.-Thurs., 10am-8pm Fri.-Sat.) or along **Main Street,** including the Gap, Patagonia, Bass, and the North Face. Most stores open at 9am or 10am and remain open until 6pm or 7pm.

For a town that's made shopping its raison d'être, it only makes sense that **Black Friday**—the massive sales day following Thanksgiving—would be a kind of official carnival, with midnight trains of shoppers arriving from Boston to live music and a celebratory atmosphere.

Sports and Recreation

HIKING AND BIKING

There are five miles of walking trails at **Wolfe's Neck Woods State Park** (426 Wolfe's Neck Rd., 207/865-4465, www.maine.gov, 9am-sunset daily, $6 adults, $4 seniors), which encompasses rocky shoreline, wetlands, and fields. A pair of ospreys returns each year to nest on an island just off the shore, and the park's **White Pines Trail** offers a good vantage point over their territory from spring until they begin their long autumn trip to South America.

WINTER SPORTS

The **L.L. Bean Outdoor Discovery School** (15 Casco St., 888/552-3261, www.llbean.com/adventures) offers cross-country skiing and snowshoeing outings, and there are several parks groomed for cross-country skiing within the city limits. With views of the snowy shore and ocean, **Winslow Park** (30 Main St.) is good for both cross-country and snowshoeing, and although **Wolfe's Neck Woods State Park** is officially closed, the ungroomed access road and trails are ideal for a winter outing.

Food

Downtown Freeport is packed with national chain restaurants—like that "olde New Englande" McDonald's—but there are plenty of local spots to recover from your shopping.

One favorite is the hunting lodge-like **Broad Arrow Tavern** (162 Main St., 207/865-9377, www.harraseeketinn.com, 11:30am-10pm daily, $15-30), where Maine classics line up alongside brick-oven pizza, hearty salads, and soups.

Get a taste of Freeport's maritime past at **Harraseeket Lunch and Lobster** (36 Main St., South Freeport, 207/865-3535, www.harraseeketlunchandlobster.com, 11am-8:45pm daily Apr.-Oct. or end of season, $9-25), which leans a bit pricey for an outdoor lobster shack but has an unbeatable location at the edge of the marina.

For a quick, healthy lunch of sandwiches and salad, L.L. Bean's **1912 Café** (95 Main St., inside the store, 9am-7pm daily, $6-12) is a convenient option in the heart of the action, or head outside of town for a great bistro meal at **Conundrum** (117 Rte. 1, 207/865-0303, www.conundrumwinebistro.com, 4:30pm-10pm Tues.-Sat., $14-30), a cozy wine joint in the shadow of the "Big Indian," a beloved local landmark.

Accommodations and Camping

Clean and family-run **Casco Bay Inn** (107 Rte. 1, 207/865-4925, www.cascobayinn.com, $101-175) may not be fancy, but it's a short drive to downtown Freeport and a good value, with coffeemakers and fridges in the rooms as well as a basic continental breakfast.

Wonderfully friendly hosts and a hearty fresh breakfast make the **Nicholson Inn** (25 Main St., 207/618-9204, www.nicholsoninn.com, $130 s, $160 d) a relaxing option with a good location, period furnishings, and private baths, though young children may not be allowed. Prices drop in the off-season.

Once the home of Arctic explorer and Bowdoin grad Donald MacMillan, the **White Cedar Inn Bed and Breakfast** (178 Main St., 207/865-9099, www.whitecedarinn.com, $199-379) combines Victorian charm with modern touches like comfy beds, a guest pantry, common spaces, and a great breakfast, all within walking distance of downtown.

A shady cluster of quiet roads on 626 waterfront acres makes **Recompence Shore Campground** (134 Burnett Rd., 207/865-9307, www.freeportcamping.com, $28-52) a haven from the bustling downtown, with fun lobster bakes most Saturday nights and rustic **waterfront cabins** (from $155).

Getting There

Freeport is located off I-295 and Route 1, 18 miles north of Portland. The Amtrak **Downeaster** (800/872-7245, www.amtrakdowneaster.com) stops in Freeport on the daily, round-trip route that links Boston and Brunswick, and there's also a **Greyhound** (800/231-2222, www.greyhound.com) station in town. To reach Freeport from Portland, use the **Metro BREEZ Express Bus Service** (www.gpmetrobus.net, one-way fare $1.50-3), which has a stop by L.L. Bean.

Mid-Coast

The scattershot coast that spreads south from Route 1 is anchored by a pair of solid brick towns, and they're a study in contrasts. Brunswick is home to Bowdoin College, which rambles outward from a picturesque campus filled with elite undergraduates and grand buildings named for famous alums. Nine miles west, Bath is all union halls, shipyards, and hulking ironworks, an industrial town that once launched the world's grandest schooners.

Look closer, however, and the distinction blurs. Until it closed in 2011, the local naval air station meant that downtown pubs and cafés were likely to have as many service members as students, keeping Brunswick from feeling too precious. And while Bath's riverfront still rings with the sound of shipbuilding and workers, the pretty center is full of cafés, shops, and bookstores run by the liberal-leaning, creative community.

On a state-sized map of Maine, both towns seem to be a breath away from the sea, but it would be easy to pass through Bath and Brunswick with nothing but river views. To experience the best parts of this scenic stretch of coast, drive south, looping into the long peninsulas; the tangled coastlines are classic Maine, with fishing villages, lobster shacks, and sheltered bays that appear around every bend in the road, making for idyllic driving at a leisurely pace.

BRUNSWICK

Sights

The pretty campus of **Bowdoin College** (255 Maine St., 207/725-3000, www.bowdoin.edu) is all soaring oaks and grassy quads, and would be a worthwhile place to stroll even without the college's two fascinating museums. The tiny **Peary-MacMillan Arctic Museum** (9500 College Station, 207/725-3416, www.bowdoin.edu/arctic-museum, 10am-5pm Tues.-Sat., 2pm-5pm Sun., free) traces the Arctic adventures of two Bowdoin graduates and explorers, Donald MacMillan and Robert Peary. In addition to stuffed arctic animals and one of the original dog

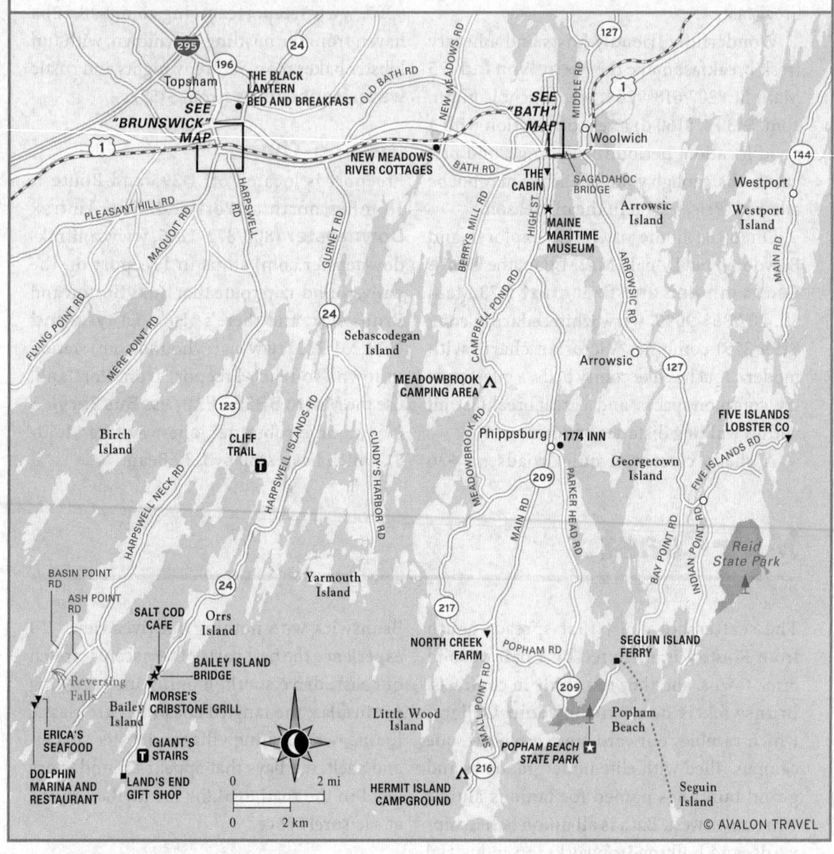

sledges from the Peary expedition, a display honors Matthew Henson, an African American explorer who was the first known person to set foot at the pole and whose contributions to exploration went unrecognized until late in his life, when he was accepted to the New York Explorers Club at age 70. The other highlight on campus is the **Bowdoin College Museum of Art** (9400 College Station, 207/725-3275, www.bowdoin.edu/art-museum, 10am-5pm Tues.-Wed. and Fri.-Sat., 10am-8:30pm Thurs., noon-5pm Sun., free), where an eclectic—and sometimes exquisite—permanent collection is on display alongside exhibits encompassing everything from Renaissance painting to edgy critiques of contemporary culture.

Food

While great views and a picturesque setting count for a great deal with most casual foodies, among devoted lobster roll hounds there's a special thrill that comes with discovering a diamond in the rough. **Libby's Market** (42 Jordan Ave., 207/729-7277, 3am-5pm Mon., 3am-7:30pm Tues.-Fri., 8am-7pm Sat., 4:30am-5pm Sun., \$6-20) is a classic example: The unprepossessing convenience store has a short-order counter and a couple of picnic tables outside, but aside from a great pile of

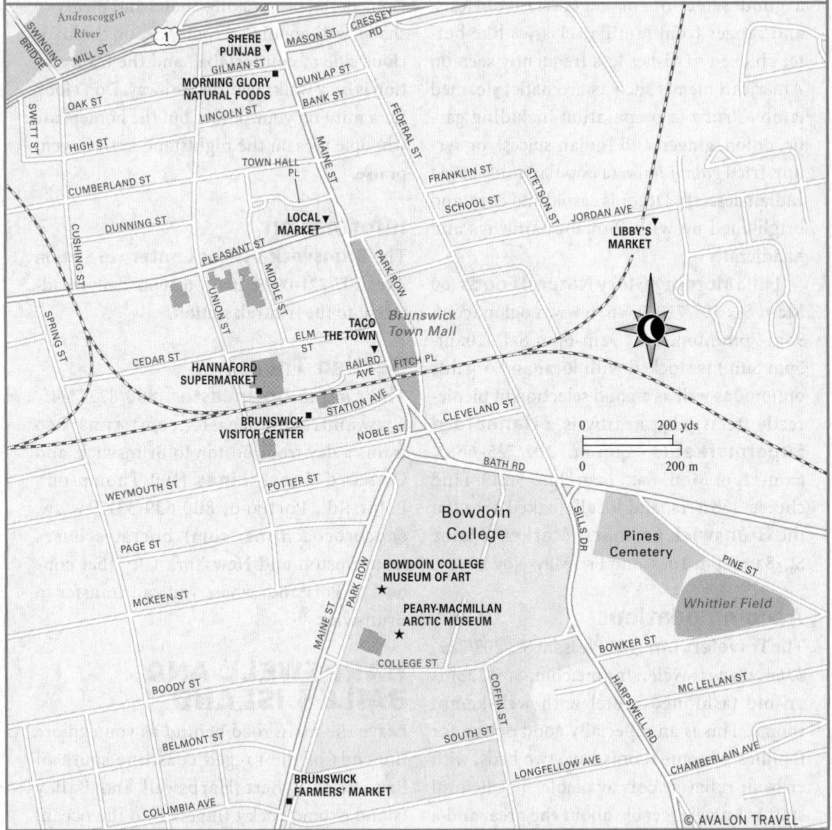

lobster traps and early, fisher-friendly hours, passersby would never guess it's a lobster roll mecca. The classic rolls come in small, medium, or large, and the meat is more finely chopped than usual, with a heavier dose of mayo. A real locals' favorite.

The best Mexican food in the Mid-Coast is served from a shiny truck just a few blocks from the Bowdoin campus. **Taco the Town** (205 Maine St., 207/632-4740, 10am-3pm Tues.-Sat., $4-9) has burritos, quesadillas, and classic tacos served with four kinds of house-made salsa. Cool off with a sweet, cinnamon-spiced *horchata* or a "cochata," a delightfully innovative coffee-*horchata* blend.

Tucked into the back of a little gourmet and kitchen store, ★ **Local Market** (148 Maine St., 207/729-1328, www.localmarket04011.com, 9:30am-6pm Mon.-Sat., 9:30am-5pm Sun., $6-12) has a pair of big communal tables and a deli counter with sandwiches, salads, and soups prepared with plenty of fresh, local, and organic ingredients. The Cobb salad gets raves, as do hearty sandwiches made with bread from Portland's Standard Baking Co.

The North Indian food at **Shere Punjab** (46 Maine St., 207/373-0422, www.sherepunjabme.com, 11am-3pm and 5pm-9pm Mon.-Thurs., 11am-9pm Fri.-Sat., noon-10pm Sun., $8-16) is full of rich flavors and spices—though the chef deftly tempers the heat for all palates. The vast menu includes a good selection of vegetarian options, and ranges from familiar classics like butter chicken to dishes less frequently seen on American menus such as aromatic, steamed lamb *dilruba* (a preparation including garlic, onion, ginger, and Indian spices), or syrupy, fried *gulabjamun* (a popular, milk-based Indian dessert). Decor is casual and cozy, and brightened up with Punjabi paintings and handicrafts.

Little **Morning Glory Natural Foods** (60 Main St., 207/729-0546, www.moglonf.com, 9am-7pm Mon.-Fri., 9am-6pm Sat., 10am-5pm Sun.) is stocked with local and organic options, as well as a good selection of picnic-ready items; also nearby is a **Hannaford Supermarket** (35 Elm St., 207/725-6683, 6am-11pm Mon.-Sat., 6am-9pm Sun.). Find cheese, lobsters, and locally baked bread at the **Brunswick Farmers' Market** (Maine St., 8am-2pm Tues. and Fri. May-Nov.).

Accommodations

The **Travelers Inn** (130 Pleasant St., 207/729-3364, www.travelersinnme.com, $65-133) is an old-fashioned motel with well-kempt rooms. This is an especially good option for families, as some rooms have two beds, with cribs or rollaway cots available. The helpful staff is knowledgeable about the area, and a basic continental breakfast of bagels, fruit, coffee, and juice is served in the lobby.

Just across the Androscoggin River from downtown Brunswick, the **Black Lantern Bed and Breakfast** (57 Elm St., Topsham, 207/725-4165, www.blacklanternbandb.com, $125-160) is walking distance from a scenic bit of riverbank, and is a gracious, welcoming place to stay. Comfortable beds, en suite baths, hearty breakfasts, and old-fashioned charm are highlights, as are Judy and Tom, the super-friendly innkeeps.

With a location in the heart of downtown, the **Brunswick Hotel & Tavern** (4 Noble St., 207/837-6565, www.thebrunswickhoteland-tavern.com, $175-350) is often filled with families visiting the nearby college, and it's a comfortable place to enjoy the town. A gracious porch has rocking chairs and plenty of shade, well-appointed rooms are on the luxurious side of comfortable, and the train station is easy walking distance away. Don't look for a mint on your pillow, but the homemade whoopie pies on the nightstand earn fervent praise.

Information

The **Brunswick Visitor Center** (16 Station Ave., 207/721-0999, 10am-6:30pm daily) is adjacent to the Amtrak station.

Getting There

The Amtrak **Downeaster** (800/872-7245, www.amtrakdowneaster.com) runs two trains a day from Boston to Brunswick, and **Concord Coach Lines** (100 Thompson's Point Rd., Portland, 800/639-3317, www.concordcoachlines.com) operates buses from Boston and New York City that connect to Portland, where you can transfer to Brunswick.

HARPSWELL AND BAILEY ISLAND

Leave the main road behind as you explore the ends of the ragged coastline south of Brunswick, where Harpswell and Bailey Island extend rocky fingers into the ocean. It's easily worth the trip for the views and a walk along the shore, but each destination has excellent seafood if you need another excuse.

Sights

Passing blocky ledges that catch crashing surf, the 0.5 mile **Giant Stairs Trail** (parking at 19 Ocean St., Bailey Island) picks its way along the coast to **Thunder Hole**—a common enough name for formations that boom in heavy waves. You'll see crystallized quartz pressed into the metamorphosed sedimentary rock, split by seams of dark basalt that have worn away from between the chunks of stone.

It would be easy to pass over **Cribstone Bridge** from Orr's Island to Bailey Island without a second glance, but the 1,150-foot span is an engineering marvel. The only bridge of its kind in the United States (or the world—accounts differ), it's built with granite "cribstones" from a quarry in Yarmouth, the heavy stones laid without mortar in a latticework that allows the powerful tides to sweep through unhindered. Some 10,000 tons of granite were used to build the 1928 bridge, which is a Historic Civil Engineering Landmark, and forever changed life in Bailey Island.

Food

A pair of seafood stops anchors each side of the cribstone bridge to Bailey Island. The **Salt Cod Cafe** (1894 Harpswell Island Rd., Orr's Island, 207/833-6210, 8am-5pm daily late May-early Oct., hours vary at beginning and end of season) has blueberry pie and quick bites that can be eaten by the shore. Across the bridge is **Morse's Cribstone Grill** (1495 Harpswell Island Rd., Bailey Island, 207/833-7775, 11:30am-8pm Mon.-Thurs., 11:30am-9pm Fri.-Sat., noon-8pm Sun., $8-30), whose deck has perfect views back toward the water. Morse's serves the usual seafood fare, plus "twin" lobster dinners for ambitious eaters.

With views to Bailey Island and beyond, **Dolphin Marina and Restaurant** (515 Basin Point Rd., Harpswell, 207/833-6000, 11:30am-8pm daily, $12-28) would be a sublime place to dine on a plate of rocks, so the nice quality of the international seafood menu is an added bonus. Many entrées come with a mystifying (but welcome) blueberry muffin on the side.

If you'd prefer your eats from a takeout window, the nearby **Erica's Seafood** (6 Malcolm Dr., Harpswell, 207/833-7354, www.ericasseafood.com, 11am-7pm daily May-Oct., $7-16) is a popular shack with haddock sandwiches, lobster rolls, and crisp, slender fries. The outdoor picnic tables are right by a working wharf, so you can watch the day's catch arrive on local fishing boats.

Getting There

Part of a network of islands and peninsulas that extend south of Brunswick, Bailey Island and Harpswell are accessed by Route 24 and Route 123, respectively. For an especially scenic drive, take Route 24 from Brunswick to Bailey Island, then backtrack to Mountain Road, which links to Route 123, where you can drive south to the end of Harpswell, or return to Brunswick.

BATH

Upstanding and brick lined, this is a city that's launched fleets around the world, from tall ships to modern-day military vessels. Bath still lives and breathes the sea, and the Kennebec River bristles with cranes, but it's the maritime past that's most enchanting for visitors, from the transporting exhibits at the Maine Maritime Museum to Maine's First Ship, a quirky project that's resurrecting a colonial-era pinnace. And beyond the city, it's worth getting sidetracked on your way to some of the Mid-Coast's best beaches and lobster rolls.

Sights

MAINE MARITIME MUSEUM

Wide, deep, and sheltered from the raging sea, the Kennebec River is the perfect place for building and launching ships; indeed, the first oceangoing ship built by English shipwrights in the Americas—the *Virginia of Sagadahoc*—was constructed here, a 30-ton pinnace measuring less than 50 feet from stem to stern. That ship was just the beginning, and in the mid-18th century, shipbuilding was a roaring industry, with a couple-dozen shipyards launching merchant, naval, and pleasure vessels connecting this clattering town in rural Maine with every corner of the globe.

One of those shipyards, Percy & Small, has been transformed into the wonderful **Maine Maritime Museum** (243 Washington St., 207/443-1316, www.mainemaritimemuseum.org, 9:30am-5pm daily, $16 adults, $14.50 seniors, $10 youth 6-12, children under 6 free),

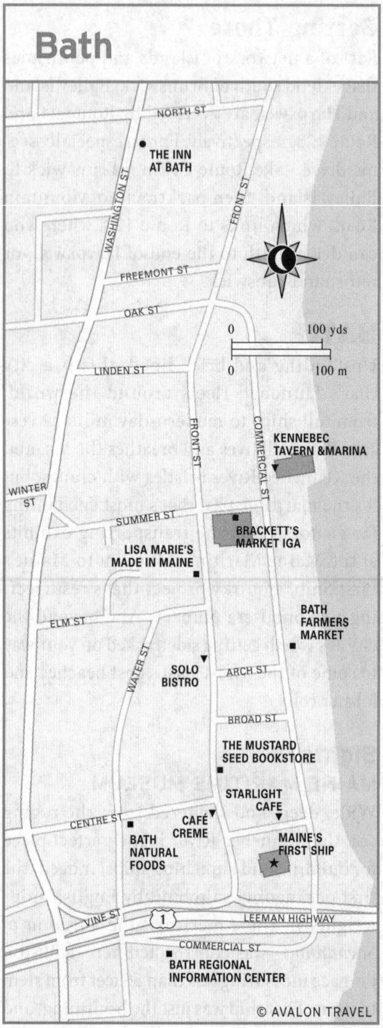

Bath

a sprawling 20-acre site with exhibits on the state's seafaring traditions.

The yard is dominated by a soaring metal skeleton that evokes the Percy & Small-built *Wyoming*, the largest schooner ever made. (Most of the sculpture's proportions are true to size, but the masts stop short of *Wyoming*'s 177 feet, as the full-sized version would require warning lights for passing aircraft.) Other highlights include reproductions of a shipyard's various workstations, in-depth explorations of lobstering on the Maine coast, and exhibits illustrating the many sides of New England's maritime traditions. Tickets are good for a second visit within a seven-day period, and admission is free if you join one of the museum's scenic cruises.

MAINE'S FIRST SHIP

In a tiny shipyard in downtown Bath, a quixotic, creative group of volunteers is reconstructing the *Virginia of Sagadahoc* based on the (very) sketchy descriptions that have survived from colonial times. In keeping with the lighthearted, ad hoc attitude of the group, some building materials are recycled, and bits of the ship's framework retain printing from former lives. But the wooden-pegged skeleton is smart as can be, and it's a treat to stop by during construction. Meet the building crew of **Maine's First Ship** (1 Front St., 207/433-4242, www.mfship.org, 11am-3pm Fri.-Sun. June-early July, 10am-3pm Tues.-Sat., 11am-3pm Sun. early July-early Sept., 11am-3pm Fri.-Sun. early Sept.-early Oct.) on open-build days, or visit any time to peek through the fence as the pinnace takes shape.

Entertainment and Events

Most of the year, **Bath Iron Works** (700 Washington St., 207/443-3311, www.gdbiw.com) is off-limits to the public. That changes during one of its infrequent but spectacular ship launchings. Then the whole town comes out for the celebration, and flags, food, and local dignitaries fill the waterfront to break champagne on the hull.

Sports and Recreation

★ POPHAM BEACH STATE PARK

With a broad swath of soft sand, **Popham Beach State Park** (10 Perkins Farm Ln., Phippsburg, 207/389-1335, $8 adults, $2 seniors, $1 children 5-11, children under 5 free), is more Miami than Mid-Coast, one of the most beloved beaches in Maine. It's hemmed in by a pair of rivers—the Kennebec and Morse Rivers reach the ocean here—and when the tide goes out, you can walk to tiny

Fox Island that's just off the beach (beware of getting stranded).

Popham's charms mean it can be jam-packed on busy days, so plan to arrive early, or head to the nearby **Reid State Park** (375 Seguinland Rd., Georgetown, 207/371-2303, 9am-sunset daily, $8 adults, $2 seniors, $1 children 5-11, children under 5 free), where you'll find two sandy beaches framed by rocky outcroppings, a headland with great views to Seguin Island lighthouse, and breaking waves for some of the best surfing in Maine.

BOATING

Get an up close look at the hulking naval ships in Bath's floating dry docks on one of Maine Maritime Museum's hour-long **Shipyards & Lighthouses Cruises** (243 Washington St., 207/443-1316, www.mainemaritimemuseum.org, noon and 2pm daily mid-June-early Sept., $34 adults, $18.50 youth 6-12, $5 children under 6, ticket prices include museum admission), which also passes by the Doubling Point Lighthouse and Kennebec Range Lights. Check the website for longer tours that go farther afield, which are available more sporadically.

Another wonderful way to explore the coastline is by hopping a boat to **Seguin Island** (207/443-4808, www.seguinisland.org), where Maine's tallest lighthouse sends beams over 20 miles to sea from a first-order Fresnel lens that's been used since 1857. Make the 30-minute trip on the passenger-only **Seguin Island Ferry** (Popham Beach, 207/841-7977, www.fishntripsmaine.com, 11am departure, 2:30pm return Sun.-Tues. and Thurs.-Fri. July-Aug., some trips available June and Sept., round-trip $30 adults, $25 children 12 and under, $40 overnights), and spend a few hours exploring beaches, trails, and the lighthouse itself.

Food

BATH

While the menu of pub classics and seafood is pretty ordinary (and reportedly inconsistent), that's not really the point at **Kennebec Tavern & Marina** (119 Commercial St., 207/442-9636, www.kennebectavern.com, 11am-9pm Sun.-Thurs., 11am-10pm Fri.-Sat., $9-30), which boasts a fabulous outdoor seating area that juts out into the current of the Kennebec River, offering great views of passing boats. On cool days, there's not much to tempt diners into the bland dining room, but summer afternoons are the perfect time to relax in the shade with a cold beer and a pile of fried scallops.

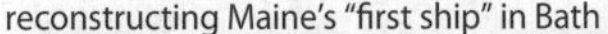

reconstructing Maine's "first ship" in Bath

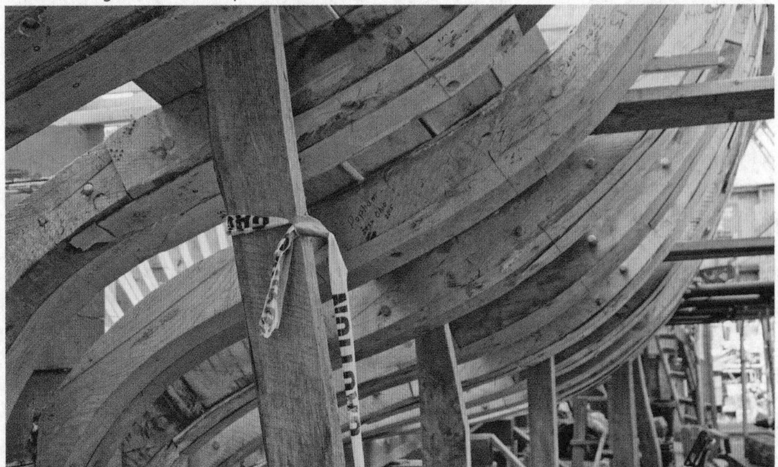

Tucked belowground on a sloping side street, **Starlight Cafe** (15 Lambard St., 207/443-3005, 7am-2pm Tues.-Fri., 8am-2pm Sat., $6-13) has a quirky dining room filled with hand-painted chairs and vintage Trivial Pursuit cards so diners can pass the time while waiting for hearty breakfasts and comforting lunch plates. Enormous raspberry pancakes, the turkey-stuffed Thanksgiving Sandwich, and haddock chowder are all favorites, and the friendly staff is pure local charm.

As the name suggests, stepping into **The Cabin** (552 Washington St., 207/443-6224, www.cabinpizza.com, 10am-10pm daily, $8-14) feels like ducking below the deck of an old ship. Nautical bric-a-brac and dark wood complete the effect, and while the pizza might not live up to its claims of "Best in Maine," it's pretty darn good all the same. Chewy crusts, generous toppings, and addictive, bready garlic knots keep this a favorite with locals and visitors. No credit cards.

With views of the action in the heart of historic Bath, **Café Crème** (56 Front St., 207/443-6454, 7:30am-5:30pm Mon.-Sat., 8:30am-5:30pm Sun., $2-8) is the place to watch the town drift by with a cup of chai or cappuccino. This little coffee shop has wireless Internet, plenty of tables, and sweet and savory treats made by a local baker.

Pick up organic produce and bulk items at **Bath Natural Market** (36 Centre St., www.bathnaturalmarket.com, 9am-6pm Mon.-Fri., 9am-5pm Sat., noon-4pm Sun.), or visit **Brackett's Market IGA** (185 Front St., 207/443-2012, 7am-8pm daily), a small, locally owned grocery store by the waterfront. Local farmers and producers operate the thriving, year-round **Bath Farmers Market** (Waterfront Park, Commercial St., 8:30am-noon Sat.May-Oct.; Bath Freight Shed, 27 Commercial St., 9am-noon Sat. Nov.-Apr., www.bathfarmersmarket.com).

SOUTH OF BATH

South of Bath in Georgetown, ★ **Five Islands Lobster Co.** (1447 Five Islands Rd., Georgetown, 207/371-2990, www.fiveislandslobster.com, check website or call for hours before visiting, $8-18) regularly makes "best of" lists for lobster rolls, steamers, and fried oysters, and it's right on the way to Reid State Park. This is a classic waterside joint with picnic tables and views of a picture-perfect bay dotted with tiny forested islands.

Cheerfully quirky and fresh as can be, **North Creek Farm** (24 Sebasco Rd., Phippsburg, 207/389-1341, www.northcreekfarm.org, 9am-6:30pm daily, café 11:30am-3:30pm Mon.-Sat., 9am-2pm Sun., $3-12) is a little bit flower nursery, a little bit country store, and a little bit café. Order a Reuben sandwich with kimchi and it comes decked in blossoms, and the homemade baked goods and fruit pies are a special treat. A Sunday morning brunch menu includes sweet and savory treats and farm eggs every way. With just a couple of small tables in the café, ordering food to-go is a good option.

Ten minutes south of downtown Bath, the **Winnegance Restaurant and Bakery** (36 High St., 207/443-3300, 6am-4pm daily, $4-11) is a popular stopover for day-trippers on their way to Popham Beach. Scones and muffins are baked fresh in the back of the old-fashioned shop, and a few small tables are available for enjoying breakfasts of pancakes or eggs and bacon, or homemade soup and sandwiches.

Accommodations and Camping

Many bed-and-breakfasts in the area are members of **Mid-Coast Maine Inns** (www.midcoastmaineinns.com), which posts a helpful spreadsheet of available rooms in the area that is usually up to date. While staying in Bath is most convenient, a few wonderful campgrounds and a historic inn are tucked down the peninsula by the water, away from the bustle of Route 1.

UNDER $100

Simple, sweet, and neat as a pin, **New Meadows River Cottages** (4 Armstrong Way, West Bath, 207/442-9299, www.newmeadowsrivercottages.com, $89-109) are nothing fancy, but the stand-alone rooms have a double bed or double and single as well as air-conditioning, coffeemakers, fridges, and little sitting areas; higher rates are for cottages with kitchenettes.

$150-200

Gardens surrounding **The Inn at Bath** (969 Washington St., Bath, 207/808-7904, www.innatbath.com, $150-190) are overflowing with blooming rhododendrons and wild mountain laurel, and the interior of the Greek Revival-style building is full of art and unfussy antiques. The quiet neighborhood is about a 15-minute walk from downtown Bath, and breakfasts are an appealing spread of fresh fruit, granola, and one hot option. All rooms have private baths and air-conditioning, but they differ widely in style and decor, and one room opens onto the kitchen.

$200-250

Historic and beautiful, the ★ **1774 Inn** (44 Parker Head Rd., Phippsburg, 207/389-1774, www.1774inn.com, $180-260) is among the most romantic places to stay along the coast, with chairs tucked around its sprawling grounds that abut the Kennebec River. Though the inn is just 7.5 miles south of Bath, the experience is serene and secluded. Many of the rooms, which vary widely in style, are exquisite, and guests rave about the thoughtful breakfasts. For an ultra-private experience, book the more rustic Woodshed Room, a self-contained suite near the river with a private veranda and stunning views.

CAMPING

Splash out for an oceanfront spot at ★ **Hermit Island Campground** (6 Hermit Island Rd., Phippsburg, 207/443-2101, www.hermitisland.com, $39-63) and you'll get prime views of sandy beaches and coastline. This is a 25-minute drive from Bath, and snagging one means planning ahead (the by-mail reservation system is byzantine), but even the "value" sites are within easy strolling distance of the shore. No credit cards.

A little bit closer to Route 1, **Meadowbrook Camping Area** (33 Meadowbrook Rd., Phippsburg, 207/443-4967, www.meadowbrookme.com, tents $31-33, hookups $35-43) has smallish sites that are a tad too closely set in woods and an open meadow, with many campers who come for the whole season, but you can sign up for daily lobster dinners and have a feast at your site or the communal outdoor seating area.

Camping is permitted on **Seguin Island**, accessible by ferry from Phippsburg's Popham Beach, mid-May-early October (207/443-4808, www.seguinisland.org, minimum $50 donation). There's no running water, but composting toilet facilities are provided. Reservations are required.

Information

The **Bath Regional Information Center** (15 Commercial St., 207/442-7291, www.visitbath.com, 9am-7pm daily mid-Apr.-Dec., 9am-7pm Mon.-Fri. Jan.-mid-Apr.) has great resources and advice for the entire Mid-Coast area, and its website is frequently updated with tours and events in town.

Getting There and Around

Bath is located on Route 1 on the banks of the Kennebec River, a 35-minute drive from Portland. South of Bath, the highway gives way to small, winding roads: follow Route 209 to Phippsburg, or Route 127 to Georgetown. Bus service to Bath is available from **Greyhound** (214/849-8966, www.greyhound.com). **Concord Coach Lines** (100 Thompson's Point Rd., Portland, 800/639-3317, www.concordcoachlines.com) operates buses from Boston and New York City that connect to Portland, where you can transfer to Brunswick.

Parking in Bath is free for up to two hours on the street or in municipal lots on Commercial, School, and Water Streets. The **town website** (www.cityofbath.com) has maps for both "Parking" and "Secret Parking." A convenient way to see Bath car-free is the **Bath Trolley** (207/443-8363, www.cityofbath.com, $1), which runs every 30 minutes on a fixed loop that connects the Winnegance General Store with the Maine Maritime Museum and downtown.

WISCASSET

Wiscasset's self-branding as the "prettiest village in Maine" might not convince passing visitors, who often remember the map-dot town more for its notorious bottleneck traffic. Get away from the backup, though, and the old-fashioned community is perfectly charming, with much of its downtown listed on the National Register of Historic Places.

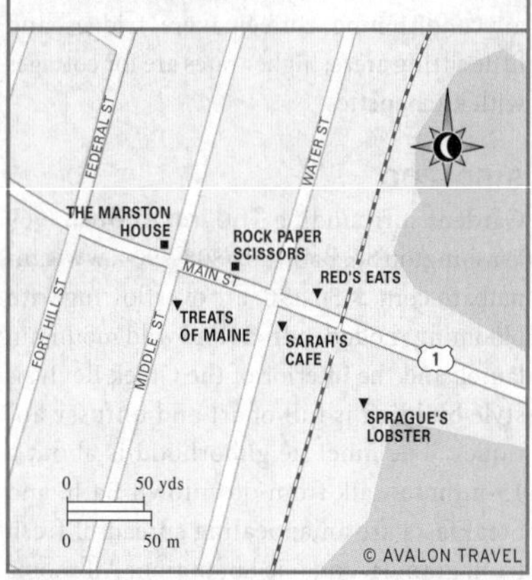

Sights

The town's **self-guided walking tour** offers a perfect ramble through old captain's homes and federal-style mansions, with informative plaques along the way. Start the tour at the large plaque adjacent to **Sarah's Café** (45 Water St.), and pick up a brochure that traces the picturesque route. Most of the stops are great for just wandering by, but it's worth popping inside **Castle Tucker** (2 Lee St., 207/882-7169, 11am-4pm Wed.-Sun. June-mid-Oct., tours every 30 minutes, $8 adults, $7 seniors, $4 students), an 1807 captain's home overlooking the river with Victorian furnishings and a stunning spiral staircase.

Shopping

Unsurprisingly, Wiscasset is a major center for antiquing, with more than two dozen shops filled with everything distressed, restored, and charmingly shabby. A sprawling collection of pieces from many dealers can be found at **Wiscasset Village Antiques** (536 Rte. 1, 207/882-4029, www.wiscassetvillageantiques.com, 9am-7pm daily); find a more curated collection of European textiles and furnishings at **The Marston House** (101 Main St., 207/882-6010, www.marstonhouse.com, noon-5pm Thurs.-Sun., or by appointment), which specializes in homespun pieces from the 18th-19th centuries. Pick up treasures with a more contemporary aesthetic at **Rock Paper Scissors** (68 Main St., 207/882-9930, 10am-5pm Mon.-Sat., noon-5pm Sun.), a pretty gift shop stocked with quirky stationery and dreamy gifts.

Food

Yet another top contender on annual "best lobster roll" lists, **Red's Eats** (41 Water St., 207/882-6128, 11:30am-10pm daily, $7-25, cash only) is a James Beard Award-winning shack that fills its buns with a pound of drawn (not chopped) meat, served with a little cup of clarified butter on the side. Picnic tables and umbrellas with views of the water are available on-site, but note two drawbacks to eating at Red's: The line can stretch upwards of an hour at busy times, and it's located right beside the idling cars stuck in Wiscasset traffic. Just across the street is **Sprague's Lobster** (22 Main St., 207/882-1236, 11am-8pm daily, $7-20); it hasn't racked up the same list of awards as Red's, but sells similar lobster rolls at a lower price (albeit with somewhat less meat).

Half country bakery, half gourmet store, **Treats of Maine** (80 Main St., 207/882-6192, www.treatsofmaine.com, 7:30am-5:30pm Mon.-Sat., 10am-4pm Sun., $3-7) serves pastries ranging from down-home to gourmet, with hefty chocolate babkas, fruit scones, muffins, and layered French confections. The long counter is a welcome place to enjoy a sweet and cup of coffee, but this place excels at takeout feasts of quiche, wine, cheese, and dessert.

A nondescript exterior hides the tasteful dining room at **Little Village Bistro** (65 Gardiner Rd., 207/687-8232, www.littlevillagebistro.com, 4:30pm-9pm Tues.-Sat., $11-20), which turns out to be a sweet haven with well-prepared, classic cuisine. Regulars love the crab cake appetizers and wild mushroom pizza, and the menu of simple pastas, braised Italian-style meats, and fresh seafood is full of flavor and thoughtful touches. Reservations are recommended.

Accommodations

Walking distance from Wiscasset's historic downtown, the **Snow Squall Inn** (5 Bradford Rd., 207/882-6892, www.snowsquallinn.com, $95-180) is all comfort and relaxation. Rooms are bright and uncluttered, with soft linens and simple furnishings, and the well-traveled, gracious owners prepare a fabulous breakfast each morning, with hot and cold options. The property includes a barn that's been converted into an airy yoga studio, and classes are offered throughout the day (www.wickedgoodyoga.com, $14).

With a convenient location on Route 1, the pet-friendly **Wiscasset Woods Lodge** (596 Rte. 1, 207/882-7137, www.wiscassetwoods.com, $90-200) runs right up against the forest, where there's a short hiking trail, a bocce court, and a fire pit for guest use (complete with s'more-making supplies). The feel is more woodsy motel than lodge, but the friendly owners serve a hearty hot breakfast that sets it apart from the other options along the highway.

Getting There

Wiscasset, and the town's famously backed-up bridge, is located on Route 1, roughly 50 minutes from Portland. Bus service to Wiscasset is available from **Greyhound** (214/849-8966, www.greyhound.com) and **Concord Coach Lines** (100 Thompson's Point Rd., Portland, 800/639-3317, www.concordcoachlines.com).

BOOTHBAY

Ask a native Mainer for directions on the Mid-Coast, and you're likely to hear the classic refrain: "You can't get there from here!" The Boothbay and Pemaquid Peninsulas, accessible from Route 1 via Wiscasset and Damariscotta, respectively, are separated by a river that opens onto jagged bays, which means the lobster shacks, gardens, and lighthouses that rim the sea are much farther apart than they appear on a map. These two peninsulas are also the primary access points for boat tours to Eastern Egg Rock, a seven-acre island whose granite shoreline offers a unique habitat for puffins, guillemots, and dozens of other nesting and migratory birds. It's the first of its kind, a restored colony, the success of which inspired dozens of imitators worldwide, as scientists work to protect the dwindling seabird population.

Boothbay is a scenic stretch of bays that culminates in the town of Boothbay Harbor, the pinnacle of Maine's fudge and T-shirt shop kitsch. It's beyond hectic during school vacation months, but with dozens of ways to get out on the water, it's easy to see why the spot is so beloved.

Sights

COASTAL MAINE BOTANICAL GARDENS

Pathways overflowing with native species, shady groves of rhododendrons, and 125 acres of carefully tended plants roll right to the water's edge at **Coastal Maine Botanical Gardens** (132 Botanical Gardens Dr., 207/633-8000, www.mainegardens.org, 9am-5pm daily mid-Apr.-Oct., $16 adults, $14 seniors, $8 children 3-18, children under 3 free), one the finest in New England. Free tours of the highlights are scheduled at 11am daily, with additional tours of native plants and rare specimens offered once a week. The garden also organizes one-hour tours up the Back River on ***The Beagle,*** a small, blessedly quiet electric boat; when bundled with garden admission, the boat tour costs approximately

Upper Mid-Coast

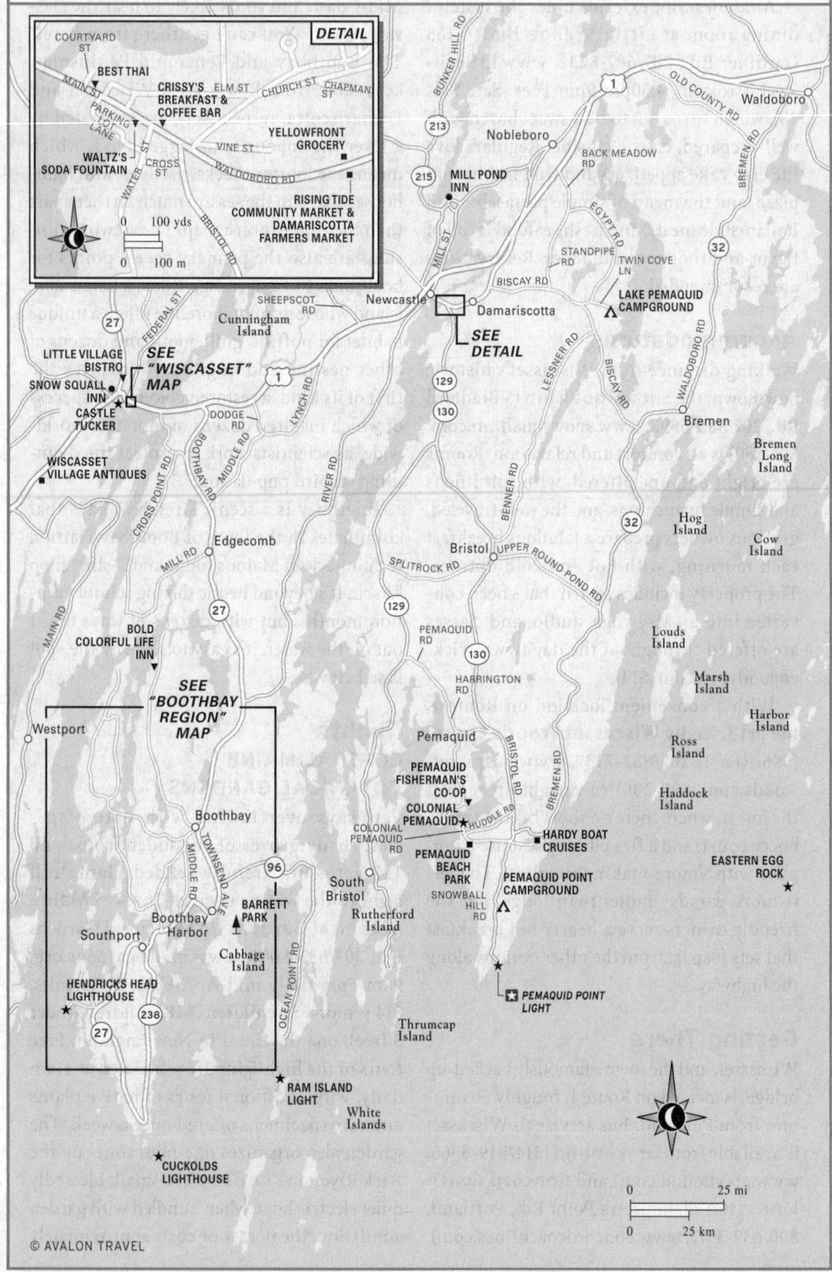
DETAIL
COURTYARD ST
MAIN ST
BEST THAI
CRISSY'S BREAKFAST & COFFEE BAR
ELM ST
CHURCH ST
CHAPMAN ST
PARKING LOT LANE
YELLOWFRONT GROCERY
VINE ST
WALTZ'S SODA FOUNTAIN
CROSS ST
WATER ST
WALDOBORO RD
RISING TIDE COMMUNITY MARKET & DAMARISCOTTA FARMERS MARKET
BRISTOL RD
0
100 yds
0
100 m
BUNKER HILL RD
1
OLD COUNTY RD
Waldoboro
213
Nobleboro
BACK MEADOW RD
BREMEN RD
215
MILL POND INN
EGYPT RD
MILL ST
STANDPIPE RD
TWIN COVE LN
32
BISCAY RD
SHEEPSCOT RD
Newcastle
Damariscotta
LAKE PEMAQUID CAMPGROUND
27
FEDERAL ST
Cunningham Island
SEE DETAIL
LITTLE VILLAGE BISTRO
SEE "WISCASSET" MAP
LESSNER RD
WALDOBORO RD
SNOW SQUALL INN
CASTLE TUCKER
LYNCH RD
129
130
BISCAY RD
DODGE RD
Bremen
BOOTHBAY RD
MIDDLE RD
Bremen Long Island
WISCASSET VILLAGE ANTIQUES
RIVER RD
BENNER RD
CROSS POINT RD
Hog Island
Cow Island
Edgecomb
Bristol
UPPER ROUND POND RD
MILL RD
SPLITROCK RD
MAIN RD
PEMAQUID RD
Louds Island
BOLD COLORFUL LIFE INN
HARRINGTON RD
Marsh Island
SEE "BOOTHBAY REGION" MAP
Harbor Island
Westport
Pemaquid
Ross Island
BRISTOL RD
PEMAQUID FISHERMAN'S CO-OP
Haddock Island
COLONIAL PEMAQUID
HUDDLE RD
BREMEN RD
Boothbay
COLONIAL PEMAQUID RD
HARDY BOAT CRUISES
TOWNSEND AVE
PEMAQUID BEACH PARK
EASTERN EGG ROCK
96
South Bristol
PEMAQUID POINT CAMPGROUND
SNOWBALL HILL RD
BARRETT PARK
Boothbay Harbor
Rutherford Island
Southport
Cabbage Island
OCEAN POINT RD
HENDRICKS HEAD LIGHTHOUSE
PEMAQUID POINT LIGHT
238
Thrumcap Island
RAM ISLAND LIGHT
White Islands
CUCKOLDS LIGHTHOUSE
0
25 mi
0
25 km
© AVALON TRAVEL

$20 per person, making it an affordable way to enjoy the coast.

BOOTHBAY RAILWAY VILLAGE

Halfway down the Boothbay Peninsula, the **Boothbay Railway Village** (586 Wiscasset Rd., 207/633-4727, www.railwayvillage.org, 10am-5pm daily late May-mid-Oct., $12 adults, $10 seniors, $6 children 3-18, children under 3 free) is a highlight for many families with children. The narrow-gauge steam train that circles the village might be the star attraction, but trains are just the beginning of this 10-acre village. Old-fashioned filling stations and homes are interspersed with displays of antique cars and firefighting equipment, blacksmithing demonstrations, baby goats, and model trains.

LIGHTHOUSES

At the tip of the Boothbay Peninsula are five **lighthouses,** of which four can be spotted by driving around Routes 96, 27, and 238. At the very tip of Route 96, the little **Ram Island Light** is visible from Ocean Point. Make a counterclockwise loop of the more westerly Southport Island to see **Hendricks Head Light** off Beach Road in West Southport; the offshore **Cuckolds Lighthouse,** visible from the tip of Town Landing Road at the southern extreme of the island; and **Burnt Island Light,** best seen from Capitol Island Road. Get a taste of what life was like on an island lighthouse station by joining a fascinating boat tour to **Burnt Island** (Pier 8, Boothbay Harbor, 207/633-2284, www.balmydayscruises.com, 1:45pm Mon. and Thurs. July-Aug., $25 adults, $15 children, children under 3 free), where actors portray the family of an early 20th-century lighthouse keeper. It's common to spot seals and porpoises during the 15-minute boat ride to the island, and the 2.5-hour island portion includes a nature walk and time to explore the scenic trails.

Entertainment and Events

Boothbay Harbor's pretty waterfront is bright with sails and flying colors as the town kicks off summer with **Windjammer Days** (www.windjammerdays.org, late June), which includes the annual Blessing of the Fleet.

Sports and Recreation

BEACHES

The Boothbay Peninsula doesn't have much sand to break up its rocky headlands, but **Barrett Park** (Lobster Cove Rd., Boothbay Harbor) is a nice place to enjoy the water views. Two rock beaches make for good tide-pooling at low tide and have shady picnic tables, swings, and bathroom facilities.

BOATING

A seven-acre sprawl of granite boulders and low-lying vegetation, **Eastern Egg Rock** doesn't look like a very cozy nesting ground, but the wildlife sanctuary was the first restored seabird colony in the world. Nesting seabird populations have been hard-hit by hunters, egg collectors, fishing practices, and pollution, and until the restoration process began, puffins hadn't shacked up here since 1885. **Puffins** are now on the island mid-June-August.

From Boothbay Harbor, book a trip with **Cap'n Fish's** (42 Commercial St., Boothbay Harbor, 207/633-3244, www.mainepuffin.com, 2.5-hour puffin tour $35 adults, $20 children 12 and under, $15 dogs; 4-hour puffin and whale tour $75 adults, $45 youth 6-14, $30 children under 6, $15 dogs), whose puffin cruises, accompanied by an Audubon naturalist, pass three lighthouses and scattered islands on the way out to Eastern Egg Rock. The company's combination puffin and whale cruises commonly spot finback and minke whales, as well as the humpback whales that arrive on the coast in July.

Food

With a mid-peninsula location just past the Boothbay botanical gardens, **Trevett Country Store** (381 W. Barter's Island Rd., Trevett, 207/633-1140, 7am-8pm daily, $5-20) might seem like a back-road convenience

Boothbay Region

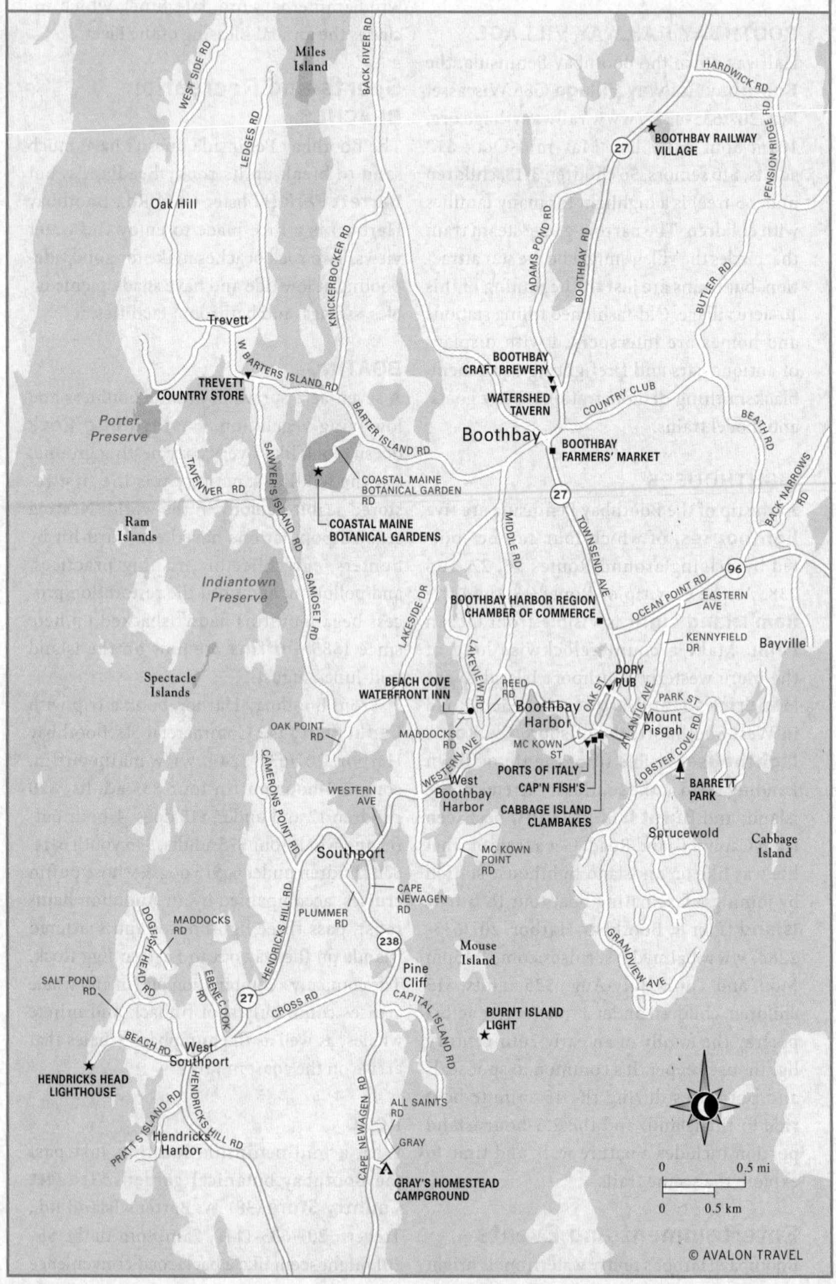

store, but it's a local favorite for sandwiches, simple breakfasts, and fresh seafood. In warm months, the outdoor sundeck is a charming place to eat, with water views and a cool breeze.

All cedar shake and dark wood, the **Watershed Tavern** (301 Adams Pond Rd., 207/633-3411, www.boothbaycraftbrewery.com, 4:30pm-8pm Wed.-Sat., $12-29) has the kind of cave-like interior best enjoyed when the weather turns blustery. The food includes a fairly standard pub lineup of burgers, salads, and pizzas, but with some meat from local farms and appealing house-made additions. This is the brewpub side of **Boothbay Craft Brewery** (207/633-3411, www.boothbaycraftbrewery.com, tours $5), which runs 30-minute tours at 3pm daily, followed by a beer tasting. Naturally, those beers are on tap at the tavern: Brews range from super-drinkable session ales to imperial stouts and red IPAs.

A destination for sophisticated, traditional food, ★ **Ports of Italy** (47 Commercial St., 207/633-1011, www.portsofitaly.com, 4:30pm-9pm daily May-Dec., $18-34) stands head and shoulders above the crowded Boothbay Harbor restaurant scene. Thoughtful service and consistently high-quality food, an excellent wine list, and pleasant seating on an outdoor patio make this a good choice for a romantic evening or celebration. Reservations are essential.

Casual cousin to the attached Thistle Inn, the **Dory Pub** (55 Oak St., Boothbay Harbor, 877/633-3541, www.thethistleinn.com, 5pm-close Tues.-Sat., $10-16) serves a simpler, solid menu in a fun space. Cozy up to the bar—made from an actual dory boat—for burgers, crab cakes, or piles of Maine mussels steamed in white wine. Great cocktails and an extensive beer and wine list make this a nice first stop of the evening for drinks and snacks.

Vendors from around the region set up stalls at **Boothbay Farmers' Market** (1 Common Dr., www.boothbayfarmersmarket.com, 9am-noon Thurs. mid-May-early Oct.).

★ LOBSTER FEAST

Like a Polynesian *imu* or Maya *p'ib*, the classic method of cooking up a New England lobster is using a pit oven lined with rocks and heated with a blazing fire. The pit is then filled with seaweed, lobsters, clams, and corn on the cob, covered with more seaweed (along with some sand or tarps), and left to cook for hours, infusing everything inside with a briny tang. Aside from swapping out the sand pit for some giant, wood-fired steamers, **Cabbage Island Clambakes** (Pier 6, Boothbay Harbor, 207/633-7200, www.cabbageislandclambakes.com, mid-June-mid-Oct., 4-hour boat tour and clambake $63) does them in classic Maine style. The family-run operation takes a slow cruise to **Cabbage Island,** where you'll sit down to two steamed lobsters, white clams, fish chowder, new potatoes, and corn, followed by blueberry cake and coffee. The experience is simply one of the finest ways to get a taste of this traditional feast in Maine.

Accommodations and Camping

$100-150

By a quiet lake between the botanical gardens and downtown Boothbay Harbor, the motel-like ★ **Beach Cove Waterfront Inn** (48 Lakeview Rd., Boothbay Harbor, 207/633-0353, www.beachcovehotel.com, $99-215) is a great budget option. All rooms have views of the water and come stocked with a fridge, microwave, and coffeemaker, and a small continental breakfast is served in the lobby. Decor is simple and a bit dated, and some visitors find the walls overly thin, but staying at the inn gets you free access to a fleet of canoes and rowboats to enjoy on the lake.

$150-250

With a great location on the quieter, southeastern side of the harbor, **Brown's Wharf Inn** (121 Atlantic Ave., Boothbay Harbor, 207/633-5440, www.brownswharfinn.com, $175-225) is a 15-minute walk to downtown shops and restaurants. Balconies in the water-facing rooms have great views across

TOP EXPERIENCE

Lobster Feasts

Dripping butter, cracking lobster shells, steaming corn on the cob...Maine's lobster may be famously sweet and tender, but enjoying the state's favorite food is about more than flavor. Settling into a lobster feast is a quintessential—and often messy—Maine experience that's been a beloved tradition for generations.

And while dining on lobster isn't cheap, the Maine lobster experience isn't haute cuisine by any stretch. In fact, the most iconic way to enjoy the crustaceans at one of the state's many venues with "lobster in the rough," where traditional dinners are served out-of-doors, often at a picnic table. This is the time to roll up your sleeves, tie on a lobster bib, and go local, using a lobster cracker and pick to extract every bit of juicy flesh.

When served "in the rough," lobster is sold by weight, so you can choose the size of your dinner—small ones are about a pound, and the biggest critters can be as large as four pounds. You may also have the option to choose a hard shell or soft shell lobster: soft shell lobsters have recently molted, or shed their shell, and tend to have slightly more tender flesh that's often preferred by Mainers. Hard shell lobsters are firmer, and cost more per pound, as there tends to be more lobster flesh packed inside the shell.

The classic accompaniments to a lobster dinner include coleslaw, corn on the cob, dinner rolls, and drawn, or clarified, butter for dunking the meat. There are lobster joints all up and down the coast, from Quoddy Head to Kittery, and while menus don't vary much, locals remain fiercely loyal to their lobster shack of choice. After rigorous sampling, here are our favorites:

- **Thurston's Lobster Pound, Acadia National Park** (9 Thurston Rd., Bernard, 207/244-7600, www.thurstonforlobster.com, daily 11am-9pm, $7-30). There are usually lines out the door of this longtime Mount Desert Island institution, but that means you'll have time to watch the fascinating seafood ballet that unfolds on the porch: servers drop net bags of clams, lobsters, and mussels into a giant steamer, setting individual timers with your order number. Meals emerge, get plated with all the fixings and a hefty chunk of blueberry cake, and are served to diners on decks that jut into lovely Bass Harbor.

- **Cabbage Island Clambakes, Boothbay Harbor** (Pier 6, Boothbay Harbor, 207/633-7200, www.cabbageislandclambakes.com, mid-June-mid-Oct., four-hr boat tour and clambake $63) serves lobster as part of their clambakes after ferrying guests to Cabbage Island. Once you arrive, sit down to two steamed lobsters, white clams, fish chowder, new potatoes and corn, followed by blueberry cake and coffee. The experience is simply one of the finest ways to get a taste of this traditional feast in Maine.

- **Chauncey Creek Lobster Pier, Kittery** (16 Chauncey Creek Rd., Kittery Point, 207/ 439-1030, www.chaunceycreek.com, 11am-8pm daily, $8-35) is an "in-the-rough" spot with bright picnic tables at the edge of a peaceful river. Make like the locals and bring your own beer, wine, and side dishes, then pick a lobster from the tank.

- **Five Islands Lobster Co., Georgetown** (1447 Five Islands Rd., Georgetown, 207/371-2990, www.fiveislandslobster.com, check website or call for hours before visiting, $8-18). A classic waterside joint with picnic tables and views of a picture-perfect-bay, this seasonal shack is worth the detour, and is also beloved for their wonderful lobster rolls. BYO beer and wine to go with lobster dinners that arrive on metal trays.

If it's hard to swallow a $30 meal served with paper napkins, get this: lobster was long considered "poverty food" in New England. Native Americans used lobsters as fishing bait and fertilizer, and early colonists dished up lobster dinners to prisoners and indentured servants. Lobster only got classy with the advent of widespread rail travel—according to lobster lore, chefs in dining cars began serving the crustaceans to inland passengers who didn't know it wasn't "fancy" food. Times, and prices, have changed.

the harbor, and while the bathrooms are a bit cramped, rooms have plenty of space to spread out.

Gorgeous lawns roll from a rambling farmhouse to the water's edge at the **Bold Colorful Life Inn** (802 Back River Rd., 207/633-6566, www.boldcolorlifeinn.com, $129-209), a laid-back estate that's halfway down the Boothbay Peninsula. Enjoy the quiet spot in a hammock, or wander the trails and gardens. Common spaces include a great room with a piano and bookshelves, and the unsurprisingly bright and colorful rooms have private baths. The inn is run by a welcoming psychotherapist and life coach.

OVER $250

Isolated and luxurious, ★ **The Inn at Cuckolds Lighthouse** (40 Town Landing Rd., Southport, 855/212-5252, www.innatcuckoldslighthouse.com, $350-600) is on a small island south of Boothbay and among the most romantic places to stay in Maine. The 1892 lighthouse has just two suites—book the whole darn island if you want a *really* private experience—and high-end amenities. Boat transportation to the island, afternoon tea and cocktails, and views of crashing waves make this a place apart, and all transportation and treats are included in the price of a night's stay.

CAMPING

Drift off to the sound of crashing waves at **Gray's Homestead Campground** (21 Homestead Rd., Southport, 207/633-4612, www.graysoceancamping.com, sites $48-53), an old-fashioned and friendly spot four miles south of Boothbay Harbor. Fire rings and a swimming beach give the campground a holiday atmosphere, and it also has laundry facilities, hot showers, and a dump station.

Information

The **Boothbay Harbor Region Chamber of Commerce** (192 Townsend Ave., Boothbay Harbor, 207/633-2353, www.boothbayharbor.com, 8am-5pm Mon.-Fri., 10am-4pm Sat.-Sun. mid-May-early Oct., 8am-5pm Mon.-Fri. early Oct.-mid-May) runs a visitors center at its office.

Getting There and Around

Boothbay Harbor is located at the southern end of the Boothbay Peninsula, accessed by Route 27, a spur that leaves Route 1 at Wiscasset (13 mi, 20 min.). There is currently no public transport to Boothbay Harbor.

The only place in this region where parking is an issue is in Boothbay Harbor, where it's worth leaving your car in one of the town's metered lots; the largest is adjacent to the **town office** (11 Harbor St., Boothbay Harbor, $1 per hour, $7 full day). That town also has the only noteworthy in-town transit, the **Rocktide Trolley,** a free sightseeing trolley that makes a limited loop through downtown starting from the **Rocktide Inn** (35 Atlantic Ave., Boothbay Harbor, 207/633-4455, www.rocktideinn.com).

PEMAQUID REGION

Across the Damariscotta River from the Boothbay Peninsula, the Pemaquid Peninsula is just as scenic, and blissfully uncrowded. The main reason travelers venture down Route 129 toward Pemaquid Point is the Pemaquid Point Light, a lonely tower that looks out at a gorgeous sweep of coastline, but it's worth lingering for a day on the beach or a wildlife-spotting trip to Eastern Egg Rock, a barren islet that's paradise for nesting puffins. At the head of the peninsula, Damariscotta is full of small-town charm and historic homes, an easy place to while away an afternoon or a weekend.

Sights

★ PEMAQUID POINT LIGHT

Crashing waves and jagged rocks are the perfect setting for **Pemaquid Point Light** (3115 Bristol Rd., New Harbor, 207/677-2492, www.visitmaine.com, 9am-5pm daily early May-late Oct., $3). Classic calendar material, it was commissioned by John Quincy Adams and is considered by many the loveliest of New England's lights—by popular vote, its image landed on the Maine state quarter. Climb a wrought-iron spiral staircase to the top of the tower for a seagull's-eye view of the craggy headland, and get an up close look at the fourth-order Fresnel lens, one of just six in the state. After exploring the tower and clambering around the rocks, it's worth stopping in to the adjoining keeper's house, where the **Fisherman's Museum** (207/677-2494, 10:30am-5pm daily mid-May-mid-Oct., free) displays mementos of the lobstering life. Also on-site is the **Pemaquid Art Gallery** (207/677-2752, 10am-5pm daily early June-late Oct.), which displays juried work from local artists.

COLONIAL PEMAQUID

Three forts were raised and destroyed at the gaping mouth of the Pemaquid River as fur traders, pirates, the English, Native Americans, the French, and early settlers scrapped for control of the strategic stronghold. **Colonial Pemaquid State Historic Site** (2 Colonial Pemaquid Dr., New Harbor, 207/677-2423, www.friendsofcolonialpemaquid.org, 9am-5pm daily late May-late Aug., $4 adults, $1 seniors, children under 12 free) offers a look at those tumultuous times, with historical reenactments, demonstrations, and nicely preserved structures. **Fort William Henry** is the centerpiece of the site (and a reconstruction of the second fort built here), where a trio of flags fly above a stone tower; the fort's permanent exhibit explores the intersection of fur trading and politics in the early years of European settlement. The sprawling grounds offer plenty to explore, including a visitors center museum, an 18th-century cemetery, and an herb garden stocked with plants that 17th-century settlers used for food and medicine, and the seaside site is a pleasant place to bring a picnic.

Entertainment and Events

During the warming days of May and early June, hundreds of thousands of **alewives** make the trip to Damariscotta Lake, traveling over a fish ladder that was first built in 1807, then restored in 2010. A few hundred years ago, these fish, a kind of herring, would have been ubiquitous in Maine's streams, but these days they're far less common. To catch the alewife run, with fish squirming between rocks as they travel upriver, head to the **Damariscotta Mills Fish Ladder** (www.damariscottamills.org); from the intersection of Route 215 and Route 1, take Route 215 north for 1.6 miles, where you'll see a small parking area on your left. In season, the website is updated with the latest whereabouts of the alewives.

Sports and Recreation

BEACHES

Just south of Colonial Pemaquid is the appealing **Pemaquid Beach Park** (Snowball Hill Rd., Bristol, 207/677-2754, 8am-5pm daily, $4 adults, children under 12 free), a 0.25 mile of pristine white sands with a concession stand, boogie board, umbrella, and beach chair rentals, and nice views along the coast.

BOATING

Just five miles from Eastern Egg Rock, **Hardy Boat Cruises** (132 Rte. 32, New Harbor, 207/677-2026, www.hardyboat.com, 1.5-hour puffin tour $32 adults, $12 children 2-11, children under 2 free) is just five miles from Eastern Egg Rock and runs early evening trips with an Audubon naturalist aboard—it's a good chance to catch the puffins rafting together in the water and lounging on the rocks. Hardy operates a somewhat smaller boat than the tours that operate from Boothbay Harbor, meaning fewer crowds and a slightly rougher ride when waves are choppy.

Food

The old-timey treats at **Waltz's Soda Fountain** (167 Main St., Damariscotta, 207/563-7632, 7am-4pm Mon.-Sat., $2-9) are right at home in Damariscotta's brick-and-window glass downtown. Twirl on the red leather stools, sip an egg cream or ice cream soda, or go all-out with a sundae under gobs of hot fudge sauce. A simple menu of sandwiches and snacks is also available, albeit overshadowed by the creamier options.

An outlier among Mid-Coast lobster shacks and bistros, **Best Thai** (74 Main St., Damariscotta, 207/5633-1440, www.bestthaimaine.com, noon-3pm and 4pm-8:30pm Tues.-Sat., lunch $8-11, dinner $12-17) really does serve the best Thai food in the region (until you hit its sister restaurant in Bath). Panang curry and noodle dishes are consistently good, and the *tom kha* (chicken soup) gets rave reviews.

Find sweet treats and the best breakfasts in town at **Crissy's Breakfast & Coffee Bar** (212 Main St., Damariscotta, 207/563-6400, www.cbandcb.com, 8am-2pm daily, $3-11). Gluten-free rice bowls are piled with meat, eggs, and veggies, while breakfast sandwiches are generous and served alongside crispy home fries. The lunch menu is also served all day, a savory mix of sandwiches, burritos, and salads.

Pemaquid's take on lobster "in the rough," the ★ **Pemaquid Fisherman's Co-Op** (32 Co-op Rd., Pemaquid, 207/677-2642, noon-7:30pm daily, $7-25) has the seafood, and you can bring the fixings. Bring beer or wine—some regulars even bring their own side salads—to go with whole lobsters swabbed in melted butter, steamers, and crabs. Outside seating offers great views of the Pemaquid River.

Find all the basics at **Yellowfront Grocery** (5 Coastal Market Dr., Damariscotta, 207/563-3507, 7am-8pm Mon.-Sat., 8am-7pm Sun.), or visit **Rising Tide Community Market** (323 Main St., Damariscotta, 207/563-5556, www.risingtide.coop, 8am-8pm daily), a cooperatively owned natural food store that also has a deli and café.

The **Damariscotta Farmers Market** (www.damariscottafarmersmarket.org) has two locations for its Monday and Friday markets. On Monday early June-late September, find the vendors at the **Rising Tide Community Market** (323 Main St., 3pm-6pm Mon.), and on Friday mid-May-late October, farmers set up at **Round Top Farm** (3 Round Top Rd., 9am-noon Fri.).

Accommodations and Camping

You'll have your own sweet little place on the beach at **Ye Olde Forte Cabins** (18 Old Fort Road, Pemaquid Beach, 207/677-2261, www.yeoldefortecabins.com, $125-260), a simple, homey resort by John's Bay. The accommodations are rustic, with a shared cookhouse and showers, and the cabins are tightly packed on the green lawn, but it's full of old-fashioned New England charm. Book well in advance, as longtime regular can fill these up in summer months.

Leave the crowds (and any hope of cell service) behind at ★ **Mill Pond Inn** (50 Main St., Nobleboro, 207/352-4044, www.millpondinn.com, $150-180), which has five guest rooms on the shore of Damariscotta Lake. Fresh flowers in each room and a wonderfully peaceful setting make this feel like a retreat from the world. The full country-style breakfast often includes blueberry pancakes or French toast, bacon, and eggs, and the friendly innkeepers have a great collection of books, games, and music to enjoy during your stay. The house was built in 1780, and retains a wonderfully historical feel.

Quiet and filled with shade trees, **Pemaquid Point Campground** (9 Pemaquid Point Campground Rd., New Harbor, 207/677-2267, www.pemaquidpointcampground.com, tent sites $27, RV sites $37, no credit cards) has hot showers, a playground, horseshoe pits, and easy access to the beach, Colonial Pemaquid, and the lighthouse, so you can beat the crowds coming from Boothbay. If you're just passing through and don't want to make the 20-minute trek down the peninsula, book a site at **Lake Pemaquid Campground** (100 Twin Cove Rd., Damariscotta, 207/563-5202, www.lakepemaquid.com, $36-48), whose 200 sites surround a pleasant, freshwater lake.

Information

Information on the area is available through the **Damariscotta Region Chamber of**

Commerce (15 Courtyard St., Damariscotta, 207/563-8340, www.damariscottaregion.com, 8:30am-4:30pm Mon.-Fri.).

Getting There

Damariscotta is located on Route 1, an hour from Portland, and the Pemaquid Peninsula extends south from town, accessed by Route 129 and Route 130. **Concord Coach Lines** (100 Thompson's Point Rd., Portland, 800/639-3317, www.concordcoachlines.com) has bus service to Damariscotta from Portland, stopping in front of **Waltz Pharmacy** (167 Main St.).

Penobscot Bay

Down East begins where the Penobscot River opens onto a scenic bay filled with low-lying rocky islands. This is classic sailing territory, though submerged shoals and the maze-like geography make navigation difficult. Lobster boat captains work hundreds of traplines passed down through generations. Much of the bay's edge is thoroughly rural, with forest broken only by the occasional village, but at the southern end is a trio of beautiful communities—Rockland, Rockport, and Camden—each with a scenic harbor and plenty to explore.

ROCKLAND

A thriving commercial fishing fleet has long been the heart of this working harbor, and at first glance the sturdy brick Main Street has a staid, old-fashioned look. It's got a deep history with the sea: The Abenaki name for the harbor is Catawamtek, "great landing place," and in the 19th century, the waterfront was alive with shipbuilding and lime production as fishing boats arrived laden with cod and lobster.

Rockland's charms have long been overshadowed by picture-perfect Camden and Rockport, but in recent years the storefronts have filled up with destination restaurants and cozy bistros, and it has begun to feel unexpectedly chic. It's a good home base for exploring Penobscot Bay, and remains fairly low-key. Even if you're making tracks for Acadia or other parts of Down East Maine, it's worth stopping to see the fabulous collection of Andrew Wyeth paintings at the Farnsworth Art Museum and walk the breakwater to the harbor lighthouse.

Sights

★ FARNSWORTH ART MUSEUM

The main draw may be the unparalleled collection of works by the artists of the Wyeth family, but the wonderful **Farnsworth Art Museum** (16 Museum St., 207/596-6457, www.farsworthmuseum.org, 10am-5pm Tues.-Sun. Nov.-Dec. and Apr.-May, 10am-5pm Wed.-Sun. Jan.-Mar., 10am-5pm daily July-Oct., $15 adults, $13 seniors, $10 students 17 and older, children under 17 free) encompasses far more. Explore beautifully curated works depicting Maine's landscape and people, including pieces by Robert Bellows, Eastman Johnson, Winslow Homer, and George Inness.

The **Wyeth Center at the Farnsworth Art Museum** highlights the very different works of Andrew Wyeth's father, N. C., and his son Jamie. Andrew Wyeth's best-known work, *Christina's World*, isn't here (it's at MoMA in New York City), but the next best thing is—the house that inspired the arresting and melancholy character study. Docents can give you directions to the museum-operated **Olson House** (Hathorn Point Rd., Cushing, $5), a half-hour drive away; it was once home to Christina Olson, disabled by illness, and her eccentric brother Alvaro. On-site guides tell the story of the painting, which was based on an actual event when Wyeth came across Christina crawling home from her parents' graves. June-September,

Penobscot Bay

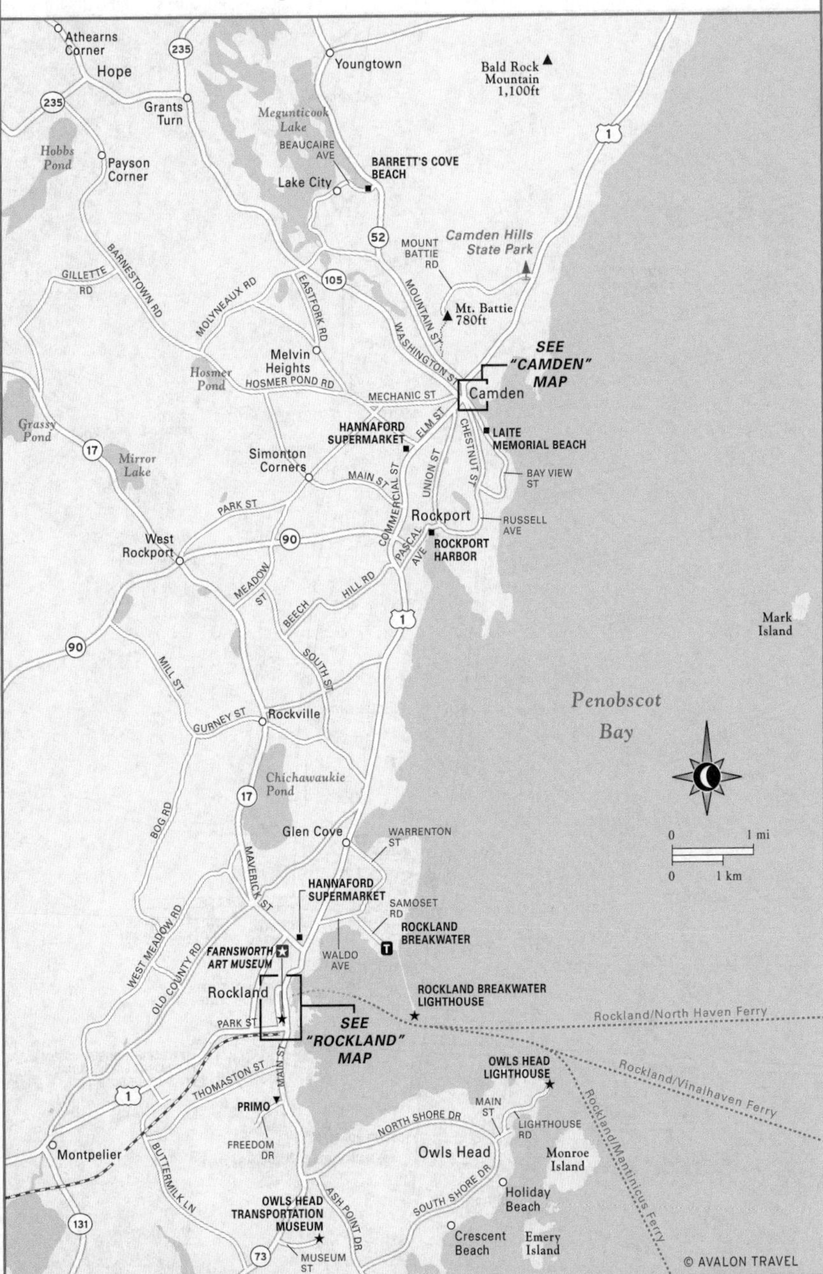

Rockland

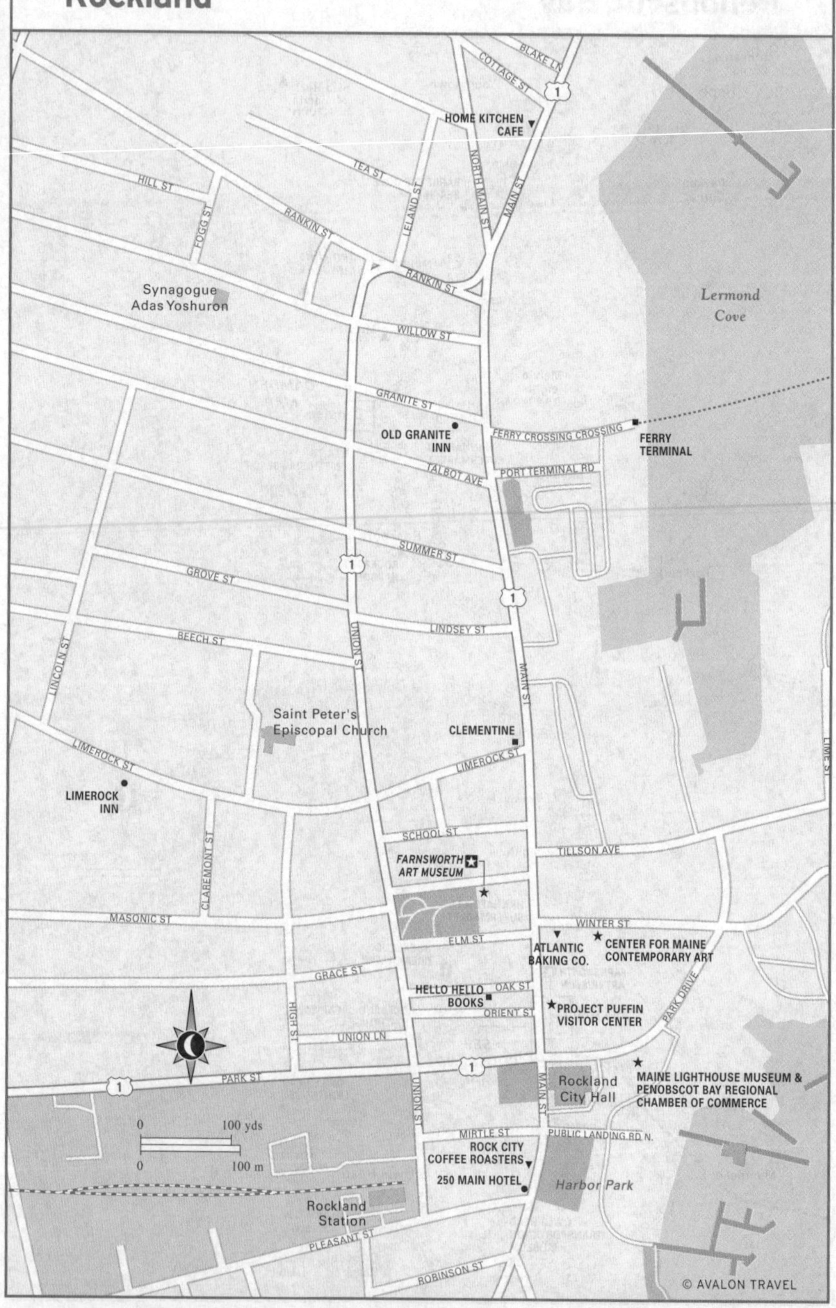
BLAKE LN
COTTAGE ST
HOME KITCHEN CAFE
TEA ST
HILL ST
NORTH MAIN ST
MAIN ST
LELAND ST
FOGG ST
RANKIN ST
Synagogue Adas Yoshuron
Lermond Cove
WILLOW ST
GRANITE ST
OLD GRANITE INN
FERRY CROSSING CROSSING
FERRY TERMINAL
TALBOT AVE
PORT TERMINAL RD
SUMMER ST
GROVE ST
LINDSEY ST
BEECH ST
UNION ST
LINCOLN ST
Saint Peter's Episcopal Church
CLEMENTINE
LIMEROCK ST
LIMEROCK INN
LIME ST
SCHOOL ST
TILLSON AVE
FARNSWORTH ART MUSEUM
CLAREMONT ST
MASONIC ST
WINTER ST
ELM ST
ATLANTIC BAKING CO.
CENTER FOR MAINE CONTEMPORARY ART
GRACE ST
PARK DRIVE
HELLO HELLO BOOKS
OAK ST
ORIENT ST
PROJECT PUFFIN VISITOR CENTER
HIGH ST
UNION LN
PARK ST
Rockland City Hall
MAINE LIGHTHOUSE MUSEUM & PENOBSCOT BAY REGIONAL CHAMBER OF COMMERCE
0
100 yds
0
100 m
MIRTLE ST
PUBLIC LANDING RD N.
ROCK CITY COFFEE ROASTERS
250 MAIN HOTEL
Harbor Park
Rockland Station
PLEASANT ST
ROBINSON ST
© AVALON TRAVEL

Life Aboard Maine's Oldest Schooner

When Captain Garth Wells and Jenny Tobin purchased the *Lewis R. French* in 2004, Wells had worked on the historic schooner for five years, long enough to know the joys—and staggering work—of sailing and maintaining a traditional ship in Maine. First launched in Christmas Cove, Maine, in 1871, the *Lewis R. French* is the oldest Maine-built schooner still afloat, and Wells and Tobin believe that she's the oldest commercial schooner that's sailing in the United States. We spoke with co-owner Jenny Tobin, who's sailed the coasts of both North and South America, and served as mate, cook, and messmate aboard the *French*.

WHAT'S A WINDJAMMER?

A windjammer is a traditionally rigged sailboat that takes passengers on overnight cruises—it's also a schooner, which is the technical term for the rig of the boat, meaning it has two or more masts, with the main mast in the back.

WHAT DO YOU LIKE ABOUT SAILING A HISTORIC VESSEL?

I like being able to keep a historic vessel alive. It has had many owners, and we want to keep her in top shape. We like being part of the history of the boat. We like that it's such a different experience for people; you can totally escape for this unplugged vacation.

HOW DO YOU KEEP THE *LEWIS R. FRENCH* IN SAILING SHAPE?

We do a lot of things. Every year we haul it out of the water in Rockland to repaint the bottom, and every 18 months the Coast Guard comes to inspect it. Two months before the sailing season, the crew arrives to sand and paint everything, and in the winter we do basic maintenance, fixing things in the rig, the blocks. And a lot of times the captains here have to make things themselves, like the booms and the gaffs, but there are a couple of traditional riggers in the country where you can still buy an old block—there's an amazing traditional sailmaker in Boothbay where we get all of our sails.

DO YOU HAVE A FAVORITE TIME OF YEAR TO SAIL IN MAINE?

I like them all! The summer is gorgeous, and the winds pick up in the fall, with really crisp, beautiful days that we get to do really great sailing. In the fall, people are amazed that they're on a historic vessel, just flying across the coast of Maine on an old boat. There are so many protected anchorages, so many islands to explore, you never run out of places to go.

admission to Farnsworth Art Museum is free 5pm-8pm on Wednesday.

OWLS HEAD TRANSPORTATION MUSEUM

The little town of Owls Head, a 10-minute drive south from Rockland, seems an unlikely place for the sprawling **Owls Head Transportation Museum** (117 Museum St., Owls Head, 207/594-4418, http://owlshead.org, 10am-5pm daily, $14 adults, $10 seniors, youth under 18 free), whose remarkable collection of pre-1940s vehicles celebrates everything that whirs, sputters, rolls, and glides. Aircraft, automobiles, and motorcycles are all fully functional, and the bicycle exhibit covers everything from an 1868 velocipede "boneshaker" to a turn-of-the-20th-century dual propulsion tricycle. Ask upon arrival about riding in a Ford Model T; if a staff member is available, he or she will take you for a turn around the grounds. Aircraft—including 19th-century gliders, a Wright flyer, biplanes, and a "Red Baron"-style triplane—get off the ground during outdoor events that take place frequently during the summer months.

OTHER SIGHTS

Almost 700,000 tons of granite were sunk off Jameson Point to create the **Rockland**

Breakwater (207/785-4609, www.rocklandharborlights.org), a 4,346-foot pile of rocks with a pretty brick lighthouse at the end. The scale of the building project, which was completed in 1900, is staggering, and the bulk of the structure is underwater—a cross section of the breakwater would be trapezoidal, with the base measuring 175 feet across. Walking the breakwater is an experience in itself, as sailboats, seabirds, and seals add to the scenery, and the **Rockland Breakwater Lighthouse** is fun to visit when open (if the flag is flying, the lighthouse is open—sharp-eyed visitors can spot the flag from Jameson Point, or check out the oddly hypnotizing live webcam feed on the breakwater website). Don't set out down the breakwater during storms, though, as heavy waves can wash over the rocks.

Short and pert, the **Owls Head Lighthouse** (Lighthouse Rd., Owl's Head, free) commands beautiful views of the rocky coastline, and is accessible via a short, gentle walk through coastal forest. Over the years, the lighthouse has collected a remarkable list of legends and ghost stories. The light is said to be haunted by two ghosts (one helpful spirit left one-way tracks in the snow when he visited to polish the brass and clean the lens), and the lighthouse has been the site of some remarkable rescues. In a December 1850 storm, a small schooner smashed up on the rocks near Owls Head, and two survivors huddled on the rocks while a third sought help. By the time a search party arrived, the two are said to have been fully encased in a block of frozen sea spray; the rescuers chipped off the ice and dunked the victims in cold water to revive them. According to legend, the two survivors later married and had four children.

While it might not thrill the casual visitor, lighthouse aficionados shouldn't miss the **Maine Lighthouse Museum** (1 Park Dr., 207/594-3301, www.mainelighthousemuseum.com, 10am-5pm Mon.-Fri., 10am-4pm Sat.-Sun., $8 adults, $6 seniors, children under 12 free), which bills itself as the country's most significant collection of lenses and artifacts. The attached chamber of commerce has brochures and maps for lighthouse hopping up the coast. If puffins are more your thing, stop by the **Project Puffin Visitor Center** (311 Main St., 207/596-5566, www.projectpuffin.audubon.org, 10am-5pm Wed.-Sun. May, 10am-5pm daily June-Oct., free), which has a small but interesting exhibit on the birds and their habitat on Eastern Egg Rock.

walking the Rockland Breakwater

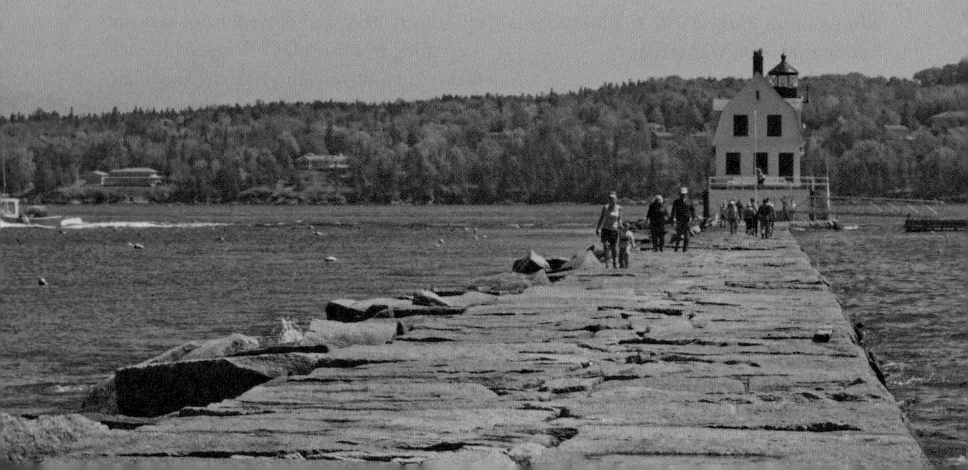

Wildlife-Watching

Lobsters might be Maine's headlining animal attraction—and the crustaceans are well worth a trip unto themselves—but the state's wildlife is far wilder than many visitors imagine. The deep inland forests are home to some 65,000 **moose,** the largest species of deer in the world: Adult males can stand almost seven feet high at the shoulder, with antlers that span six feet. It's common to see **humpback, finback,** and **minke whales** along the coast, and the luckiest sea watchers might spot a North Atlantic **right whale** on its annual migration from the Labrador Sea to warmer waters on the coastline of Georgia and Florida. An expansive coast means lots of room for birds, and Maine is home to the first restored seabird colony in the world, **Eastern Egg Rock,** where **puffins** and **terns** are making a comeback—a remarkable achievement, given that in 1901 there was just one nesting pair of Atlantic puffins in the entire United States. Here are some of the best ways to explore Maine's wild side:

puffin

Spot a whale in Kennebunk: Catch a ride on ***Nick's Chance*** (4 Western Ave., Kennebunk, 207/967-5507, www.firstchancewhalewatch.com, 4.5-hour trip $48 adults, $28 children 3-12) to the offshore banks, where whales fill their giant maws with teeny, tiny creatures of the sea.

Cuddle a crustacean at Acadia National Park: Among the best activities for kids in the state, the **Dive-In Theater Boat Cruise** (105 Eden St., Bar Harbor, 207/288-3483, www.divered.com, $42 adults, $37 seniors, $32 children 5-11, $16 children under 5) is all about getting personal with the creatures of the deep—"Diver Ed" brings everything from anemones to lobsters from the seafloor, then offers guests a chance to shake their clammy claws.

Spy on the puffins at Eastern Egg Rock: Boats depart for the rocky island from locations in Boothbay and on the Pemaquid Peninsula, both with expert naturalists aboard: **Cap'n Fish's** (42 Commercial St., Boothbay Harbor, 207/633-3244, www.mainepuffin.com, 2.5-hour puffin tour $35 adults, $20 children 12 and under, $15 dogs; 4-hour puffin and whale tour $75 adults, $45 youth 6-14, $30 children under 6, $15 dogs) has a bigger boat for a smoother ride, but **Hardy Boat Cruises** (132 Rte. 32, New Harbor, 207/677-2026, www.hardyboat.com, 1.5-hour puffin tour $32 adults, $12 children 2-11, children under 2 free) is adventurous and fun, away from the crowds of Boothbay Harbor.

Entertainment and Events

Lobster lovers arrive from all over for the five days of cook-offs and contests at the **Maine Lobster Festival** (800/596-0376, www.mainelobsterfestival.com, early Aug.), which has been held in Rockland since 1947. The event doesn't really get going until King Neptune crowns the Maine Sea Goddess on Wednesday night, and then it's a frenzy of pancake breakfasts, music, and 20,000 pounds of lobster that go straight from the boats into the world's largest lobster pot. It ends on Sunday with the International Great Crate Race, where fleet-footed contestants run across lobster crates suspended in the harbor, overseen—and sometimes fished out—by umpires in rowboats.

Sports and Recreation

Unlike more cumbersome square-rigged ships, Maine's "windjammer" schooners can sail close-hauled to the wind, making them remarkably nimble and fast for their size. Five of the nine ships that make up the **Maine Windjammer Association** (207/374-2993, www.sailmainecoast.com) are National Historic Landmarks, and they're overhauled each spring with fresh paint, polished brass, and gleaming wood. Without a steady stream of tourists, it's hard to imagine these ships staying afloat; even a small wooden sailboat is a labor of love, and a grand, historic schooner even more so.

Cruises range 3-6 days in length, poking around rocky islands, sailing into coves in search of seals, and providing evening deck views under brilliant stars. Accommodations are cramped, but increasingly the schooners are creating a more luxurious experience, with wine tastings and thoughtfully prepared food. Guests can lend a hand in hoisting sails and anchors, or just lie back and watch the show.

The ***J. & E. Riggin*** (207/594-1875, www.mainewindjammer.com, 3-day trips from $596) leaves from Rockland and is known for the best schooner food on the coast, and the 1922 ***Ladona*** (207/594-4723, www.schoonerladona.com, 3-day trips from $968) has cornered the upper end of the market after a recent overhaul, with wonderfully pristine deck chairs, luxurious beds, and elegant tiled showers.

Food

Powered by beans from the nearby Rock City Coffee Roasters, the **Rock City Cafe** (316 Main St., 207/594-4123, www.rockcitycoffee.com, 6am-7pm Mon.-Thurs., 6am-9pm Fri.-Sat., 7am-6pm Sun., $2-6) has excellent brews alongside a menu of light meals and fresh pastries.

A huge menu of hearty breakfasts and lunch plates is the draw at **Home Kitchen Café** (650 Main St., 207/596-2449, www.homekitchencafe.com, 7am-3pm Mon. and Wed.-Sat., 8am-3pm Sun., $7-13), a bright, friendly spot with a sunny rooftop patio. The recurring lobster tacos special is legendary, but the café's homemade sticky buns and corned beef hash also have passionate fans.

The busy bakers at **Atlantic Baking Co.** (351 Main St., 207/596-0505, www.atlanticbakingco.com, 7am-6pm Tues.-Sat., $3-11) turn out an impressive display of sweets, breads, and savory pastries. This centrally located spot is a favorite for quick, simple lunches of soups, salads, or sandwiches on house-made bread, and is also good for picnic supplies if you're headed out to Owls Head Lighthouse or the Rockland Breakwater.

Superb farm-to-table cuisine is beautifully presented at ★ **Primo** (2 S. Main St., 207/596-0770, www.primorestaurant.com, 5pm-10:30pm Wed.-Mon., $32-40), an Italian restaurant on a four-acre farm. James Beard Award-winning chef Melissa Kelly creates a menu that changes with the season, and plates are a heady blend of classic flavors and Maine ingredients, like seared scallops with morel mushrooms and fiddleheads, or a branzino fillet with local whelks, shrimp, and clams. Reservations are recommended: Book the downstairs dining room for a romantic, more formal feel, or dine in the upstairs lounge, full of colorful nooks, bar seating, and a convivial atmosphere. Cocktails are as garden-fresh as the food.

On the north end of town is a **Hannaford Supermarket** (75 Maverick St., 207/594-2173, 6am-11pm Mon.-Sat., 7am-9pm Sun.), and the tiny **Good Tern Natural Foods Co-Op and Café** (750 Main St., 207/594-8822, www.goodtern.com, 8am-7pm Mon.-Sat., 9am-5pm Sun.) has a good selection of organic, GMO-free foods, a deli, and a small café with a sitting area.

Accommodations

Rockland has few accommodations compared to Rockport and Camden, making Airbnb a good option here.

$150-200

Modern touches and eclectic, original art keep the ★ **Old Granite Inn** (546 Main St.,

The Lobstering Life

Leah and Leslie Ranquist got their first taste of lobstering as children when their grandfather took them out in his skiff to bait traps and band lobsters. After completing a strenuous apprentice program, the two sisters, who both prefer the traditional term "lobsterman," began carrying on the family tradition from their home on Swan's Island, where each captains a lobster boat. Following a long day of hauling some of her 600 traps, Leah shared a bit about the lobstering life:

WHAT'S A TYPICAL DAY LIKE FOR YOU?

It's pretty repetitive—at 5 or 5:30 I'll head out and haul through 180-250 traps, depending on the day, then I head back in. My sternman is there to bait the pockets and band the lobsters, and I fish singles, pairs, and triples. A triple is three traps on one buoy, so when that first trap comes up, I'll have him grab the first trap, and I'll grab the second trap.

WHAT DO YOU LIKE ABOUT LOBSTERING?

I like a lot about lobstering! I mostly like that I'm my own boss, and I can make my own schedule. It's pretty relaxed, and I like being out on the water. The beautiful days are really worth the not-so-good ones. I'll be fishing five or six days a week for six months a year, then I haul my traps out in November, and I pick away at them and fix them through the winter. I do have to work in the winter, but that's my version of taking a break.

WHAT ARE SOME CHALLENGING THINGS FACING THE MAINE LOBSTER INDUSTRY IN COMING YEARS?

We're trying to prepare for uncertainty. Lobsters have been doing very good the last few years, and not knowing if it's going to keep up, or if they'll disappear like other fisheries have, we have to plan for disaster just to keep in mind that it might not be there forever.

WHAT'S YOUR FAVORITE WAY TO EAT A LOBSTER?

Steam it in a pot, then eat it hot with hot butter! I also enjoy a lobster roll here and there.

207/594-9036, www.oldgraniteinn.com, $150-215) from feeling fusty, but the common spaces of the granite colonial house retain a historical feel. Rooms range from a compact queen with detached private bath to four-person suites that are an excellent value for families; some have electric fireplaces and whirlpool tubs, while two rooms on the 2nd floor boast views of the Rockland Harbor Lighthouse. The hearty breakfasts served in the communal dining room get raves from guests.

$200-250

The elegant Queen Anne architecture of **LimeRock Inn** (96 Limerock St., 800/546-3762, www.limerockinn.com, $169-249) is brightened up with an eye-popping coat of teal paint and garden full of blooming plants. Welcoming owners and a location that's walking distance from downtown restaurants and the Farnsworth Art Museum make this a good choice for exploring Rockland, but the gracious wraparound porch, living room, and comfortable rooms are tempting reasons to stay in as well. All rooms have a private bath and fun, varied decor that ranges from a somewhat princessly pink suite to staid Yankee plaid.

OVER $250

Luxurious and ultramodern, **250 Main Hotel** (250 Main St., 207/594-5994, www.250mainhotel.com, $279-400) offers stunning views of the harbor from many rooms, some of which feature floor-to-ceiling glass. Clever nautical touches and original art are everywhere in the hotel's 26 rooms and common spaces. Don't miss the wonderful rooftop patio.

Information

The **Penobscot Bay Regional Chamber of Commerce** (1 Park Dr., 207/596-0376, www.therealmaine.com) runs a large and well-stocked information center in a new building by the harbor.

Getting There

Rockland is located on Route 1, 1.75 hours from Portland. Daily bus service to Rockland is available from **Concord Coach Lines** (100 Thompson's Point Rd., Portland, 800/639-3317, www.concordcoachlines.com), which stops at the **Maine State Ferry Terminal** (517A Main St.). There's free, two-hour parking on Main Street, and a larger lot at **Oceanside High School** (400 Broadway, July and Aug. only).

CAMDEN AND ROCKPORT

Forested, sloping hills running straight to the water are the perfect frame for Camden's sheltered harbor and picturesque downtown; the elegant little community is one of New England's most beautiful. Schooners and sleek yachts stand at attention on mooring buoys and floating docks, and on quiet mornings you can hear spanking lines and outboard motors from all over town. There's no finer place on the coast to see Maine's windjammer fleet, breathtaking wooden vessels crowned with acres of flying sails and trim lines.

All that beauty has made Camden a tourist destination since the mid-19th century, and downtown can be a madhouse in the heat of summer. When the ice cream shop has a line out the door and there's nowhere to park within a mile of the water, it's worth taking in your harbor views from the relative quiet of Camden Hills State Park, where Mount Megunticook and Mount Battie look out on Penobscot Bay.

Just down the coast, tiny Rockport feels like Camden in dollhouse scale: Turn away at the wrong moment, and you'd totally miss the perfect little harbor and downtown. There are just a few restaurants on the little Main Street, and no sights to speak of, but the waterfront park is ideal for watching lobster boats and sailors.

Sights

Starting in the 18th century, Mainers produced lime by burning locally quarried limestone in wood- and coal-fired kilns. At the time, lime was an essential part of almost any construction project, and, at the industry's peak in 1892, millions of casks of lime left the Maine coast. Keep an eye out and you'll see traces of the lime business everywhere, including a ruined **lime kiln** by the river in the Rockport Harbor. Featuring Maine's best artists, the **Center for Maine Contemporary Art** (21 Winter St., Rockport, 207/236-2875, www.cmcanow.org, 10am-5pm Mon.-Sat., noon-5pm Sun. late May-Oct., 10am-5pm Wed.-Sat., noon-5pm Sun. Nov.-late May, $8 adults, $6 seniors, youth 18 and under and students with ID free) is worth a look for its dozens of summer art shows held in a converted firehouse.

While it's not quite as extensive as the maritime museum in Bath, the collection of nautical treasures, art, and artifacts at the **Penobscot Marine Museum** (5 Church St., Searsport, 207/548-0334, www.penobscotmarinemuseum.org, 10am-5pm Mon.-Sat., noon-5pm Sun. late May-mid-Oct., $15 adults, $12 seniors and students, $10 children 8-15, children under 8 free) is fascinating. You'll find a trove of model ships and scrimshaw here, along with practical tools and navigation equipment. The museum is about 30 minutes up the coast from Camden, in Searsport, so make a stop on the way to Acadia National Park.

Entertainment and Events

Like the other tourist towns on the coast, Camden's summer is a whirl of themed weekends and small festivals. The real

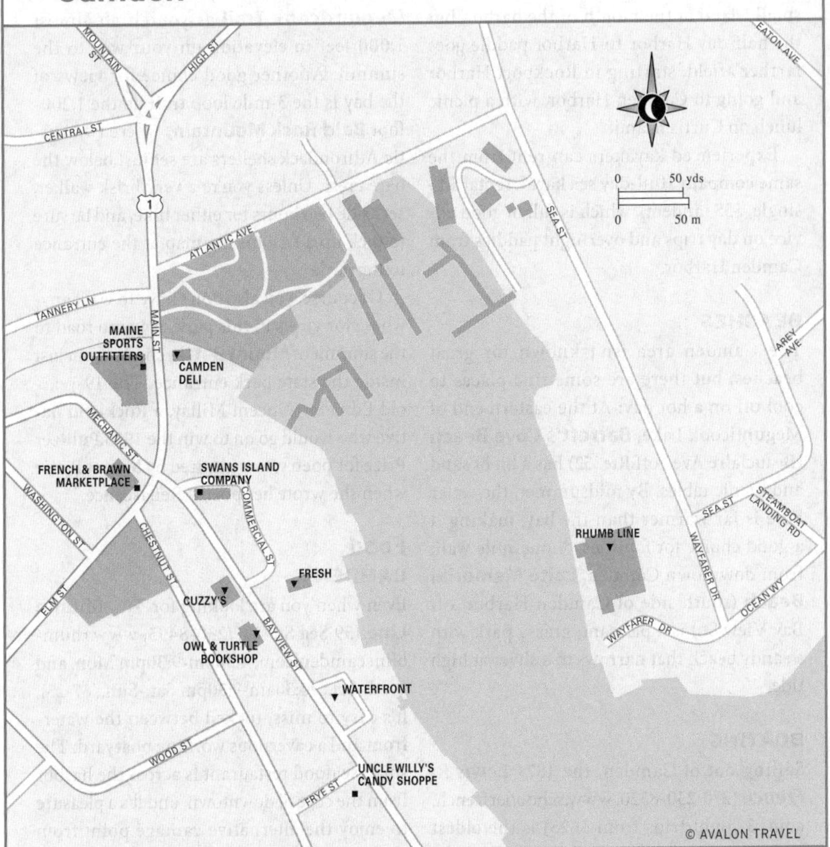

centerpiece of the season, though, is the **Camden Windjammer Festival** (207/236-4404, www.camdenwindjammerfrestival.org, early Sept.), when the harbor fills with two dozen magnificent schooners. Boat parades, fireworks, and a lobster-trap race make this a fun time to visit, but book accommodations far in advance.

Sports and Recreation

PADDLING PENOBSCOT BAY

As beautiful as Rockport and Camden are, getting out on a boat is the only way to really take in Penobscot Bay. Tiny forested isles and town-sized islands are dreamlike on sunny days, when the sparkling water lights up the coast. But the bay is a sprawl of rocky shoals and hazards, and a thick layer of fog can turn even familiar harbors into a dangerous maze. Would-be adventurers shouldn't be deterred—local captains and kayak guides are well versed in keeping people safe.

The lacy, rock edges of Penobscot Bay are perfectly suited to kayaks, which can nose in and out of coves too small for bigger boats. **Maine Sports Outfitters** (24 Main St., Camden, 207/236-8797, www.mainesport.com, kayak trips $40-125 adults, $35-75 kids 10-15) runs trips ranging from two hours to a full day. A two-hour Camden Harbor Tour is a good way to see the schooners and yachts from the water as you work your way to a small island at the mouth of the harbor, but the half-day Harbor-to-Harbor paddle goes farther afield, starting in Rockport Harbor and going to Camden Harbor, with a picnic lunch on Curtis Island.

Experienced kayakers can rent from the same company (full-day sea kayak rental $45 single, $55 tandem), which is full of good advice on day trips and overnight paddles from Camden Harbor.

BEACHES

The Camden area isn't known for great beaches, but there are some fine places to cool off on a hot day: At the eastern end of Megunticook Lake, **Barrett's Cove Beach** (Beauclaire Ave., off Rte. 52) has a bit of sand and picnic tables. By midsummer, the water here is far warmer than the bay, making it a good choice for families. A one-mile walk from downtown Camden, **Laite Memorial Beach** (south side of Camden Harbor, off Bay View St.) is a pleasant, grassy park with a sandy beach that narrows to a sliver at high tide.

BOATING

Sailing out of Camden, the 1871 ***Lewis R. French*** (270/230-8320, www.schoonerfrench.com, 3-night trips from $625) is the oldest windjammer in the United States, and still has no inboard engine; with all sails set, she flies a remarkable 3,000 square feet of canvas. Another Camden favorite is the ***Angelique*** (800/282-9989, www.sailangelique.com, 3-night trips from $595), a modern vessel that's particularly dramatic under deep-red, gaff-rigged sails.

HIKING

Aside from Mount Desert Island, **Camden Hills State Park** (280 Rte. 1, Camden, 207/236-3109, www.maine.gov, 9am-sunset daily, $6 adults, $2 seniors and children) is the only place in Maine where the mountains hew so closely to the coast, and the views of Penobscot Bay are unmatched. You'll earn your views on the steep 2.6-mile round-trip **Megunticook Trail** as you climb almost 1,000 feet in elevation on your way to the summit. Another good choice for views of the bay is the 3-mile loop trail up the 1,200-foot **Bald Rock Mountain,** where two rustic Adirondack shelters are set just below the bare crest. Unless you're a very brisk walker, set aside two hours for either hike, and be sure to pick up a free hiking map at the entrance to the park.

Of course, you also don't have to walk anywhere for views in this park. An auto road to the summit of **Mount Battie** climbs from just inside the state park entrance. The 19-year-old Edna St. Vincent Millay, a Rockland native who would go on to win the 1923 Pulitzer Prize for poetry, was inspired by Mount Battie when she wrote her poem "Renascence."

Food

CAMDEN

Even when you are looking for ★ **Rhumb Line** (59 Sea St., 207/230-8495, www.rhumblinecamden.com, 4:30pm-9:30pm Mon. and Wed.-Fri., 11:30am-9:30pm Sat.-Sun., $7-25), it's easy to miss, tucked between the waterfront and a cavernous working boatyard. The small seafood restaurant is across the harbor from the core of downtown, and it's a pleasure to enjoy the alternative vantage point from the outdoor bar and patio seating. Opened in 2016, the restaurant generated buzz with creative cocktails and fresh boat-to-table seafood. The menu includes the usual fried fare, along with offbeat sashimi and ceviche, and the rustic-chic interior is right at home on the water's edge.

Find great coffee and something to read at **Owl & Turtle Bookshop** (33 Bay View St., 207/230-7335, www.owlandturtle.com, 8am-6pm Tues.-Sat., $2-5), which also has a small selection of fresh pastries. Friendly staff and a good crowd of locals make this a nice place to linger with a crossword puzzle.

No one goes to **Cuzzy's** (21 Bay View St., 207/236-3272, www.cuzzysrestaurant.com,

Walking from Rockport to Camden

One of the area's most splendid walks is the two-mile **stroll from Rockport to Camden,** following a two-lane road past great water views and fine New England architecture. Make the first stop on the walk in Rockport, where you'll find a statue of **Andre the Seal** at the **Rockport Marine Park** (Harbor View Dr., free parking). The harbor seal, who died in 1986, was the honorary harbor master here after being raised by a local family. When he was old enough to fend for himself, Andre was released into the wild, but the seal came back to spend every summer at Rockport Harbor.

From the statue, continue across the bridge to **Russell Avenue,** which wraps through the village and into a series of fields that overflow with wildflowers in the spring. Watch for **Aldermere Farms** (70 Russell Ave., Rockport, www.aldermere.org), on the right-hand side, where Belted Galloway cows munch grass in pastures overlooking Penobscot Bay.

As you enter Camden, Russell Avenue turns into Chestnut Street and runs right into the heart of town. For a side trip to **Laite Memorial Beach** (Bay View St., Camden), turn right onto Cedar Street, which leads toward the water. There's no local bus service to loop back to Rockport, so you can make the walk a four-mile round-trip, or get a cab from **Schooner Bay Taxi** (207/594-5000, one-way trip from Camden to Rockport $9).

11am-1am daily, $5-20) for a gourmet meal, but that's somewhat beside the point. There's a huge menu of affordable pub food, very decent chowder, and all kinds of fried seafood to eat at the bar, where fishers and schooner crews come to relax in a cave-like interior or on the sunny back patio. Happy hour specials on cheap beer and pizza are available 3pm-6pm daily.

With a solid menu of seafood standards and patio seating that juts over the harbor, **Waterfront** (40 Bay View St., 207/236-3747, www.waterfrontcamden.com, 11:30am-9pm daily, $9-30) is a perennial favorite. No individual dish seems to blow anyone away, but watching the boats roll in and out of the harbor over a glass of local beer and plate of oysters is a true Camden experience. On busy nights, waits can get very long, and since the interior seating is a bit lackluster, it's often worth going elsewhere.

Reasonably priced sandwiches, soups, and salads at **Camden Deli** (37 Main St., 207/236-8343, www.camdendeli.com, 7am-9pm daily, $7-10) are a simple option right downtown. Limited seating is available inside (window seats have great views of the harbor), but this is a nice place to pick up sandwiches to take around the corner to the small park where paths and benches face the water.

In a cheerfully decorated, historic brick building, **Fresh & Co.** (1 Bay View Landing, 207/236-7005, www.freshcamden.com, 5pm-8:30pm daily, $21-28) is just that, with an eye-opening menu of international food that skews Asian. The huge, homemade lobster ravioli with wonton wrappers is a favorite here, as is the "deconstructed" lamb moussaka as well as tiger shrimp with black rice and ginger barbecue sauce. Despite the upscale food (and prices), this restaurant has a casual atmosphere, with outdoor seating and the occasional live act.

Find high-quality baked goods, meat, cheese, and drinks at **French & Brawn Marketplace** (1 Elm St., 207/236-3361, www.frenchandbrawn.com, 6am-8pm daily), which is the only market in downtown Camden. More basic goods are available from **Hannaford Supermarket** (145 Elm St., 207/236-8577, 7am-10pm Mon.-Sat., 7am-9pm Sun.), on the main road south of town. Small but vibrant, the **Camden Farmers Market** (Knox Mill between Washington and Knowlton, Sat. market 9am-1pm May-Nov., Wed. market 3:30pm-6pm mid-June-Nov.) has local breads, cheeses, vegetables, and fruit.

Rockport

Tiny Rockport doesn't have much of a dining scene, but ★ **Nina June** (24 Central St., 207/236-8880, www.ninajunerestaurant.com, 5:30pm-9:30pm Tues.-Fri., 10am-2pm and 5:30pm-9:30pm Sat., 11:30am-2pm Sun., brunch $6-18, lunch/dinner $20-30) is a noteworthy exception. A deck overlooking the Rockport Harbor makes a sublime setting for a Mediterranean menu that changes with the season. A typical fall menu might include bucatini with lamb neck ragu and grilled swordfish beside a pile of shaved cucumber and cherry tomatoes. Saturday lunch means a hearty menu of Italian specialties, while Sunday brunch ranges from traditional breakfasts like strata or pancakes to white-almond gazpacho and other savory entrées.

Accommodations and Camping

UNDER $100

The trim little cottages at ★ **Oakland Seashore Cabins** (112 Dearborn Ln., Rockport, 207/594-8104, www.oaklandseashorecabins.com, $75-150) are rustic and a bit of a tight squeeze, but they're set right on the edge of a private pebble beach between Rockland and Rockport, making them a fabulous value and wonderfully peaceful place to stay. This property also includes motel rooms at a similar price, and while they're a decent option, the cabins are the clear winner. The cabins with kitchenettes are stocked with very basic cooking equipment, and the largest sleep up to five people. No televisions, telephones, or coffeepots here (and the wireless access is hit or miss).

$100-150

A quiet, 15-minute walk from Rockport's gem of a harbor, **Schooner Bay Motor Inn** (337 Commercial St., Rockport, 888/308-8855, www.sbaymotorinn.com, $90-179) has trim furnishings and a thoughtful, local character that sets it apart from the other motels along Route 1. Light sleepers should request a room at the forested back of the property, where there's a small, shady creek. A breakfast of fresh pastries, fruit, and homemade quiche is served May-December.

If you're looking for a lower-budget place to stay in downtown Camden, **The Towne Motel** (68 Elm St., Camden, 207/236-3377, www.camdenmotel.com, $124-150) is hard to beat. The superclean, motel-style rooms are nothing fancy, but the friendly owners are gradually overhauling them; updated rooms are the same price as the older ones, but with smart, fresh colors and little artistic flourishes. All rooms have coffeemakers, cable televisions, air-conditioning, wireless Internet, and small fridges, and an appealing breakfast is served during summer months; in the off-season, the owners deliver a little breakfast packet to each room that includes their killer homemade granola.

$150-250

Find Maine country style with a few nautical touches at the **Blue Harbor House Inn** (67 Elm St., Camden, 207/236-3196, www.blueharborhouse.com, $155-199), a homey spot that's a short walk from downtown. Rooms are stocked with coffeemakers and comfortable beds, and afternoon tea and the innkeeper's two-course breakfast are served in a welcoming common room. All rooms have en suite bathrooms, and more expensive options have steam showers or claw-foot soaking tubs.

An expansive lawn rolls all the way to a private beach, a wonderful perk that makes the **High Tide Inn** (505 Rte. 1, Camden, 207/236-3724, www.hightideinn.com, $175-195, deck house $170-260) feel like a retreat just a few minutes' drive from downtown Camden. A handful of options are available on this property: the somewhat lackluster Oceanview Motel (where you can just spy a bit of blue); the sweet, compact rooms in the old-fashioned inn; a collection of oceanfront rooms a stone's throw from the water; and six little cottages, nostalgic and rustic. A homemade continental breakfast is served on a glass-enclosed porch with views to the water.

OVER $250

Find all the top-end perks at ★ **16 Bay View** (16 Bay View St., Camden, 207/706-7990, www.16bayview.com, $250-500), a 21-room boutique hotel with perfect views of the harbor from oceanside rooms and the rooftop bar. Great piles of silky pillows, gas fireplaces, spa bathrooms, and balconies are luxurious, and the hotel, which opened in early 2016, is beautifully decorated. A continental breakfast is served in the Prohibition-themed Vintage Room.

CAMPING

Set in the rolling forest along the coast, ★ **Camden Hills State Park** (280 Rte. 1, 207/236-3109, www.maine.gov, $38-49) has amazing views of Penobscot Bay, trails to explore, and level campsites that range from simple tent pads to extra-large options, with water, electric, and space for a 35-foot camper. The campground is divided into reservable sites that must be booked 48 hours in advance (though it's worth planning ahead for peak season), and a smaller number of sites set aside on a first-come, first-served basis.

Information

The **Camden-Rockport-Lincolnville Chamber of Commerce** (Public Landing, 207/236-4404 or 800/223-5459, www.visitcamden.com, 9am-4pm Mon.-Sat.) runs a helpful information center on the Camden waterfront.

Getting There and Around

Camden is located on Route 1, 1.75 hours from Portland, and two hours from Bar Harbor. Daily bus service to Rockport from Portland is available from **Concord Coach Lines** (100 Thompson's Point Rd., Portland, 800/639-3317, www.concordcoachlines.com), which stops at Maritime Farms (20 Commercial St., Rockport).

No real in-town public transit is available in any of the Penobscot Bay locales, but they're small enough to explore on foot. In Camden, free parking is available at two public lots (Washington Street, turn north when Route 1 passes the Camden Village Green).

BANGOR

The third-largest city in Maine, industrial Bangor is invigorated by students at the University of Maine, who infuse young energy into an otherwise stolid and sleepy place. If you've read anything written by resident celebrity Stephen King, however, you'll know that sleepy northern towns aren't always what they seem—a towering statue of the folk forester Paul Bunyan points to the city's past as a buzzing lumber port, and there's a remarkably good art museum on the university campus.

Stephen King Tour

Born in Portland, Stephen King came to Orono to attend college and has remained in the area ever since. The first stop on most horror-lovers' itineraries is the author's house, a **creepy Victorian** (47 W. Broadway) whose wrought-iron gate is adorned with spiders, bats, and a mythical-looking snake. For the full SK immersion, join an outing with **SK Tours of Maine** (207/947-7193, www.sk-tours.com, 3-hour tours $45 adults, children under 13 free), led by a fanatically knowledgeable guide. In addition to the author's own haunts, the tours visit places that King has woven into novels like *It* and *Pet Sematery*.

Other Sights

According to Bangor boosters, the town's **Paul Bunyan Statue** (519 Main St.) is the largest in the world—but who's counting? Built in 1959, it towers 31 feet above Main Street—and it came to life as "Giant" in the pages of Stephen King's book *It*.

A first-rate collection of contemporary work is housed at the **University of Maine Museum of Art** (Norumbega Hall, 40 Harlow St., 207/561-3350, www.umma.umaine.edu, 10am-5pm Tues.-Sat., free), which features the art of Roy Lichtenstein, Richard Estes, and David Hockney.

Food

Run by a group of Franciscan friars, the ★ **Friars' Bakehouse** (21 Central St., 207/947-3770, 8:30am-2pm Tues.-Thurs., 8:30am-1:30pm Fri., $5-20) serves a homey menu of soups and sandwiches on its house-made bread, with a pastry case full of sticky buns and oversized cookies. The lobster roll is one of the few around that's not based on store-bought white rolls, and it's stuffed with an impressive pile of meat in generous pieces.

A sign of changed times in Bangor, the stylish **Timber Kitchen & Bar** (22 Bass Park Blvd., 207/433-0844, www.timberkitchenandbar.com, 11am-11pm Mon.-Thurs., 11am-midnight Fri.-Sat., 11am-10pm Sun., $12-33) is convivial and fun, with places to gather indoors and by an outside fire. Flatbreads, burgers, and house-made pasta are the heart of the menu, but the seafood stew is outstanding. The restaurant's happy hour (4pm-6pm Mon.-Fri.) is popular, with discounted drinks and bar snacks.

With a roadhouse feel and a perpetual lineup of big-rig trucks, **Dysart's Restaurant & Truck Stop** (530 Coldbrook Rd., 207/942-4878, www.dysarts.com, 24 hours daily, $7-16) is something of a legend in these parts, the kind of place that would merit its own country song if Mainers went in for that sort of thing. Enormous sandwiches, big slices of blueberry pie, whoopie pies, cinnamon rolls the size of a (small) head, and house-made hash bring in crowds to the cavernous dining room. Breakfasts are an old-fashioned feast.

Accommodations

Aside from a cluster of chain hotels by the highway exit, Bangor's main accommodation is a clanging downtown casino, so it's often best to stick to the interstate. The best value among the roadside motels may be the **Bangor Inn & Suites** (701 Hogan Rd., 207/947-0357, www.bangorinnandsuites.com, $90-130), a basic spot with clean, if dated, rooms and an unusually good breakfast of homemade muffins, eggs cooked to order, and sides.

More spiffed up and spacious, Marriott's **TownePlace Suites Bangor** (240 Sylvan Rd., 844/631-0595, www.marriott.com, $150-300) has a reasonable self-serve breakfast in the downstairs dining area, with a gym and a pool on-site. While mostly geared toward extended stays, there are suites equipped with kitchenettes and small living rooms.

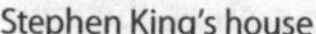
Stephen King's house

Getting There

Bangor is located on I-95, 2 hours from Portland and 1.25 hours from Bar Harbor and Acadia National Park. Daily bus service to Bangor from Portland and Boston is available from **Concord Coach Lines** (100 Thompson's Point Rd., Portland, 800/639-3317, www.concordcoachlines.com), which stops at the **Bangor Transportation Center** (1039 Union St.). **Greyhound** (214/849-8966, www.greyhound.com) also stops in town, with service around the northeast.

Blue Hill Peninsula

Another gorgeous web of bays and narrow harbors, Blue Hill Peninsula is an escape from the crowds in Bar Harbor and Camden. No one sight anchors the region's many charms, but it's an appealing place for a slow drive or lunch by the water. The far-flung seaside town of Castine has a historic center and a marine that fills with yachts and runabouts, while the community of Blue Hill remains a haven for artists and eccentrics drawn to the beauty of the coast.

SIGHTS

Castine

You can take in the heart of historic Castine on foot, and the **Castine Historical Society** (13 and 17 School St., 207/326-4118, www.castinehistoricalsociety.org) issues a free map that outlines a self-guided walking tour—the maps are available at the historical society, as well as at many shops around town.

Highlights of the walk include the astounding collection in the **Wilson Museum** (107 Perkins St., 207/326-9247, www.wilsonmuseum.org, 10am-5pm Mon.-Fri., 2pm-5pm Sat.-Sun. late May-Sept., free), which includes African prehistoric artifacts, Balinese shadow puppets, fire department memorabilia, and old maps and ships' logs.

A short and pleasant walk from downtown is **Dyce Head Lighthouse,** a 19th-century classic tapered white tower. In the summer, midshipmen conduct tours of the *State of Maine*, the 500-foot training vessel owned by the **Maine Maritime Academy** (Pleasant St., Castine, 800/464-6565, www.mainemaritime.edu). Though not available for tours, be sure to notice the academy's other beauty, the schooner *Bowdoin*, which Maine explorer Adm. Donald MacMillan took on his many expeditions to the North Pole. During the summer months, the historical society leads hour-long tours of Castine on selected Saturdays; check the website for an updated schedule.

Blue Hill

If Leonardo da Vinci had lived in Maine at the turn of the 19th century, he would have been fast friends with Jonathan Fisher, a preacher who dabbled in painting, poetry, farming, and literally dozens of other fields. Memorabilia and items made by the man himself are on view at the **Jonathan Fisher House** (44 Mines Rd., 207/374-2459, www.jonathanfisherhouse.org, hours vary, May-Sept., $5).

The gardens and hand-built home of Helen and Scott Nearing, intellectuals, writers, and farmers who helped lead the first wave of back-to-the-landers in New England, are carefully preserved at the **Good Life Center** (372 Harborside Rd., Harborside, 207/326-8211, www.goodlife.org, 1pm-4pm Thurs.-Mon. late June-early Sept., $10 suggested donation), which explores their legacy and ideals.

ENTERTAINMENT

Three dozen members strong, the **Flash! In the Pans** (207/374-2140, www.peninsulapan.org) community steel band brings a taste of the Caribbean to Maine with outdoor steel-band concerts around the peninsula all summer long. On alternate Mondays they instigate a street party in the small town of Brooksville.

FOOD

When thoughts of midday snacks start hitting, set your sights on **Markel's Bakehouse** (26 Water St., Castine, 207/326-9510, www.markelsbakehouse.com, 7am-3pm daily summer, closed Sun.-Mon. in off-season, $2-9), where the cases are filled with strawberry and cream croissants, snickerdoodle cookies, and giant honey shortbreads. The menu also includes hearty breakfasts and lunches of soups, sandwiches, and salads.

The dining room of the **Pentagöet Inn** (26 Main St., 207/326-8616, www.pentagoet.com, 8am-10pm daily mid-May-Sept., $17-26) has a refined colonial ambience that somehow strangely sympathizes with Ella Fitzgerald and Louis Armstrong crooning in the background. The menu is an impeccable mix of New England seafood and homemade pastas, highlighted by haute cuisine accents like white truffle oil, goat cheese cream, and tarragon bourride.

Easily worth a bit of a side trip from Castine or Blue Hill, ★ **Buck's Restaurant** (6 Cornfield Hill Rd., Brooksville, 207/326-8688, www.bucksrestaurant.weebly.com, 5:30pm-8pm Tues.-Sat., $19-28) serves New American dishes with lots of heart: think smoked mackerel pâté, baked pollock, and Acadian jambalaya. It's a great meal, but unfussy—you could arrive in heels or boat shoes.

ACCOMMODATIONS

A quick walk from the beach and with blissful views, the rustic **Castine Cottages** (33 Snapp's Way, Castine, 207/326-8003, www.castinecottages.com, $90-200) are two-bedroom stand-alones with full kitchens, outdoor grills, and very cute decor.

With smart New England decor and wonderfully hospitable owners, the **Blue Hill Inn** (40 Union St., Blue Hill, 207/374-2844, www.bluehillinn.com, $115-220) is beloved for blueberry pancakes and thoughtful amenities. Wine and snacks are served each evening, and some of the rooms have their own romantic little sitting areas, complete with personal fireplace.

Maine Island style gets a dose of sophistication at **The Castine Inn** (33 Main St., Castine, 207/326-4365, www.castineinn.com, $120-200). Rooms are sunny and decorated in soothing tones, queen beds, and delicate window treatments (many of which frame views of the surrounding gardens and nearby harbor). Breakfast is included and delicious—especially if the apple bread French toast is on offer.

GETTING THERE

The Blue Hill Peninsula extends south from Route 1, between Penobscot Bay and Blue Hill Bay, and is accessible on Route 175 and Route 172. No public transportation options to the area are currently available.

Acadia National Park

Look for ★ to find recommended sights, activities, dining, and lodging.

Highlights

★ **Cadillac Mountain:** The tip of this granite-topped mountain catches America's first sunrise for part of the year, and dawn gatherings on the summit are a New England rite of passage (page 461).

★ **Carriage Roads:** Bike this extraordinary network of car-free roads—or hop a horse-drawn carriage to a rocky summit (page 462).

★ **Thuya Garden and Asticou Azalea Garden:** Climb the monumental granite path to Thuya Garden, then walk paths lined with armfuls of blossoms spring-fall (page 464).

★ **Bar Island Trail:** Walk from Bar Harbor to a rocky little island on a pathway that is only exposed at low tide, watching for stranded sea creatures along the way (page 471).

★ **West Quoddy Head Light:** Make the long drive to the easternmost point in the continental United States, and you'll be rewarded with big tides and bigger views (page 475).

★ **Hiking Mount Katahdin:** The northern terminus of the 2,200-mile Appalachian Trail is one of New England's most dramatic peaks, with vertigo-inducing ridges, wild weather, and a maze of gorgeous footpaths (page 477).

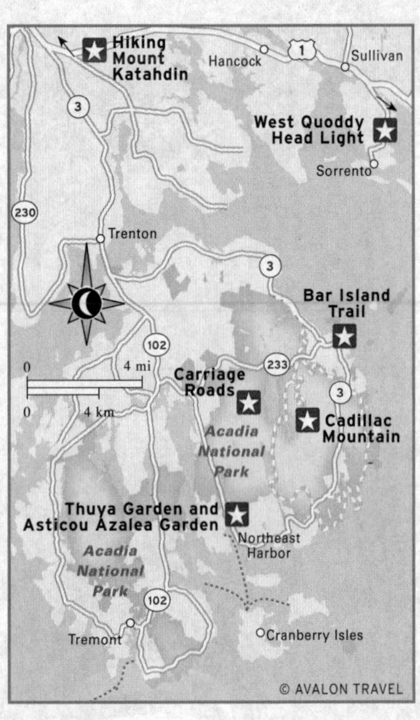

Maine's scenic drama comes to a head in Acadia National Park, a 47,000-acre preserve that spills across Mount Desert Island to the surrounding islets and shoreline.

Twenty-four mountain peaks describe the island's dramatic history in sparkling granite: 450 million years ago, mini continent Avalonia rammed into the hulking North American plate, forming a platform that would be buried under sand, silt, volcanic lava, and ash, then raked by a series of massive glaciers. Geologic clues are everywhere here, from odd-looking rocks left perched on mountaintops to ice-carved, U-shaped valleys and deep gouges in bare granite. A deep, fjord-like bay nearly splits the island in two. For ocean-view hiking, rocky trail exploration, and tide pooling, New England's only national park is incomparable.

The Wabanaki people have inhabited this stretch of coast for thousands of years, hunting and fishing in year-round settlements and trading widely with other regional groups. In 1604, French explorer Samuel de Champlain stopped by long enough to record a name—*Isles des Monts Déserts*, or Islands of Bare Peaks—and was followed by waves of Jesuit missionaries, French and British soldiers, and city people seeking simpler country pleasures.

It remains an extraordinary place, with rugged mountains, beaches, and headlands so tightly packed they can be explored in a single day. Acadia is glorious in the summer sunshine, but it's equally entrancing when thick fog creeps across the water, isolating the island into a world of its own. One vibrant town and a handful of scattered communities are interwoven with the park land, so your experience in Acadia can be as luxurious, or remote, as you choose.

Continue past Acadia National Park, and the long coast leads to the easternmost point in the continental United States, the far-flung outpost of Lubec, whose West Quoddy Head Light is a candy-striped beacon that marks the end of America.

Head far inland to Baxter State Park, where Maine's highest mountain marks the northern terminus of the 2,200-mile Appalachian Trail. It's a peak that has drawn spiritual seekers and adventurers for centuries, and

Previous: a carriage road bridge in Acadia National Park; Lubec's West Quoddy Light. **Above:** hiking on Cadillac Mountain.

to many mountain lovers, Katahdin's rocky ridges and moods outshine the more developed alpine landscape of New Hampshire's Mount Washington.

PLANNING YOUR TIME

Mount Desert Island is 108 square miles, and accounting for winding roads and slow-moving traffic, it can take quite a while to drive from one side to the other. When visiting, then, it's worth choosing one of the two sides as a home base: Opt for Bar Harbor for great access to kid-friendly activities, shops, and restaurants, or sleep on the western "quiet side" to escape the crowds. Spring-fall, the free Island Explorer shuttle makes frequent loops of the island following eight different routes; if you'd like to explore car-free (highly recommended), choose accommodations on a shuttle route. As in other destinations on coastal Maine, the true high season is during the school vacation months of July and August. Many prices drop substantially in June and September, whose mild weather and sunshine also make them some of the prettiest months on the island. The leaves begin to change color toward the end of September, reaching a brilliant peak in mid-October. While the Park Loop Road is open year-round, many restaurants and hotels close their doors between November and May.

ORIENTATION

For many people, Acadia National Park and Mount Desert Island are synonymous, but the national park is a patchwork that covers much of the island and a bit of mainland coast. The bulk of the park territory is on the eastern side of Mount Desert Island, where the Park Loop Road circles some of the most dramatic scenery and best-known hiking trails. On the other side of Somes Sound is the "quiet side," good for less frequented hikes. The remaining parkland is on the harder-to-reach Isle au Haut, and the Schoodic Peninsula, which is linked by passenger ferry to Bar Harbor.

Acadia National Park

TOP EXPERIENCE

VISITING THE PARK

Entrances

Because of the patchwork way Acadia National Park was stitched together, driving around Mount Desert Island means passing in and out of park territory, often without notice. The only real gateways to the park are the kiosks at the on-ramps to Park Loop Road, where you'll be asked to present your pass; otherwise, leave it displayed in your car (park rangers suggest that cyclists and motorcyclists carry their pass with them on hikes).

Park Passes and Fees

May-October, the entrance fee for a private vehicle seating 15 people or fewer is $25. Motorcycles with one or two passengers pay $20, cyclists and pedestrians pay $12 each, and individuals 15 years old and younger are admitted free of charge. Most passes are valid for seven days; annual passes to Acadia National Park are $50, while an Interagency Annual Pass is $80 and covers all National Park Service and Forest Service entrance fees. Active military, people with disabilities, and U.S. fourth-grade students are eligible for a free Interagency Annual Pass; a lifetime interagency pass is available to seniors for $80. Passes are sold at all park visitors centers, campgrounds, and information booths, but for trips during peak season, it's worth purchasing online to avoid lines (www.yourpassnow.com).

Visitors Centers

As Route 3 crosses the Mount Desert Narrows, the small **Thompson Island Information Center** (8:30am-5:30pm daily

Acadia National Park

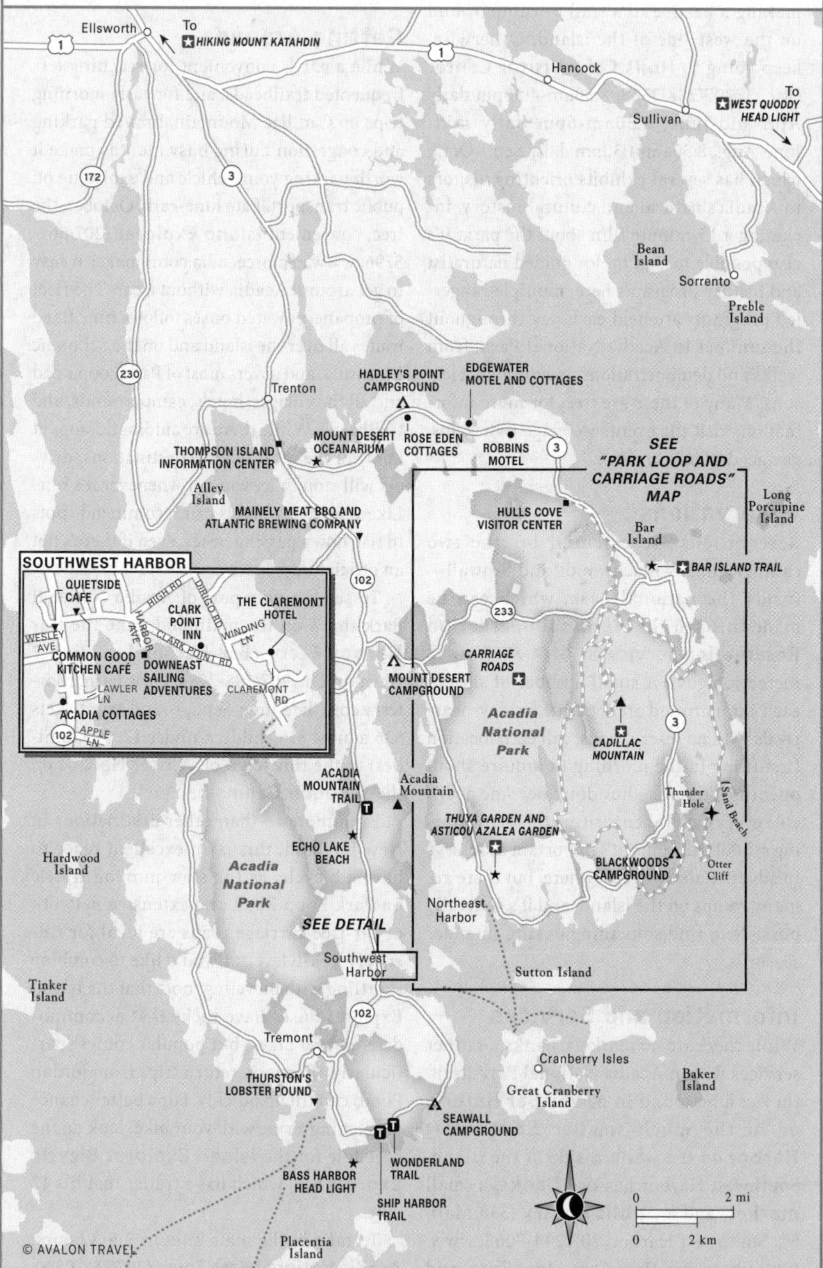
Ellsworth
To HIKING MOUNT KATAHDIN
Hancock
Sullivan
To WEST QUODDY HEAD LIGHT
Bean Island
Sorrento
Preble Island
Trenton
HADLEY'S POINT CAMPGROUND
EDGEWATER MOTEL AND COTTAGES
MOUNT DESERT OCEANARIUM
ROSE EDEN COTTAGES
ROBBINS MOTEL
THOMPSON ISLAND INFORMATION CENTER
SEE "PARK LOOP AND CARRIAGE ROADS" MAP
Alley Island
MAINELY MEAT BBQ AND ATLANTIC BREWING COMPANY
HULLS COVE VISITOR CENTER
Long Porcupine Island
Bar Island
BAR ISLAND TRAIL
SOUTHWEST HARBOR
QUIETSIDE CAFE
HIGH RD
DIRIGO RD
HARBOR AVE
CLARK POINT INN
THE CLAREMONT HOTEL
WESLEY AVE
CLARK POINT RD
WINDING LN
COMMON GOOD KITCHEN CAFÉ
DOWNEAST SAILING ADVENTURES
LAWLER LN
CLAREMONT RD
ACADIA COTTAGES
APPLE LN
CARRIAGE ROADS
MOUNT DESERT CAMPGROUND
Acadia National Park
CADILLAC MOUNTAIN
ACADIA MOUNTAIN TRAIL
Acadia Mountain
Thunder Hole
Sand Beach
THUYA GARDEN AND ASTICOU AZALEA GARDEN
ECHO LAKE BEACH
BLACKWOODS CAMPGROUND
Otter Cliff
Hardwood Island
Acadia National Park
Northeast Harbor
SEE DETAIL
Southwest Harbor
Sutton Island
Tinker Island
Tremont
Cranberry Isles
Baker Island
THURSTON'S LOBSTER POUND
Great Cranberry Island
SEAWALL CAMPGROUND
WONDERLAND TRAIL
BASS HARBOR HEAD LIGHT
SHIP HARBOR TRAIL
0
2 mi
2 km
Placentia Island
© AVALON TRAVEL
1
3
172
230
102
233

mid-May-mid-Oct.) is on the right, and it's a useful stop for passes and maps if you're making a beeline to a trail or campground on the west side of the island. Otherwise, keep going to **Hulls Cove Visitor Center** (Rte. 3, 207/288-3338, 8:30am-4:30pm daily Apr.-mid-June, 8:30am-6pm daily mid-June-Aug., 8:30am-4:30pm daily Sept.-Oct.), which has several exhibits orienting visitors to Acadia's natural and cultural history, including a 15-minute film about the park. It's also possible to sign up for guided naturalist and history programs here; multiple ranger-led programs are held each day throughout the summer in Acadia National Park, from walks and demonstrations to outdoor art lessons. Many of these are free; for more information, visit the events webpage (www.nps.gov/acad/planyourvisit).

Reservations

Reservations are essential for the two campgrounds—Blackwoods and Seawall—inside the national park, which can be made through the **National Recreation Reservation Service** (877/444-8777, www.recreation.gov). A small number of sites in each campground are set aside for day-of arrivals with no reservations; call each location first thing in the morning to inquire about openings, though sites don't become available every day. When visiting the island during school vacations, it's important to reserve in advance almost everywhere, but there are many rooms on the island, and it's generally possible to find something during shoulder seasons.

Information and Services

While there are no markets, banks, or other services within Acadia National Park itself, they can be found in nearby **Bar Harbor,** or in the much smaller **Southwest Harbor** on the western side of the island. Southwest Harbor has two **banks,** a small **market,** and a **public library** (338 Main St., Southwest Harbor, 207/244-7065, www.swhplibary.org, 9am-5pm Mon.-Tues. and Thurs.-Fri., 9am-8pm Wed., 9am-1pm Sat) with free **Internet access.**

Getting Around

While a car is convenient for reaching less frequented trailheads, and for early morning trips up Cadillac Mountain, limited parking and congestion during busy months make it worth parking your vehicle and exploring on public transport. Late June-early October, the free, convenient **Island Explorer** (207/667-5796, www.exploreacadia.com) makes it easy to get around Acadia without a car. The fleet of propane-powered buses follows nine fixed routes all over the island and on the Schoodic Peninsula, and covers most of Park Loop Road and all the villages, hotels, campgrounds, and trailheads. While there are automatic stops at many of the most notable destinations, drivers will stop to let you out whenever it's safe. Likewise, many hotels can recommend spots to flag down passing buses, even if there's not an official stop nearby.

To see the only part of Acadia National Park that's on the mainland, take the **Bar Harbor Ferry** (Bar Harbor Inn Pier, 7 Newport Dr., 207/288-2984, www.barharborferry.com, late June-Sept., round-trip tickets $26 adults, $16 children under 12, $75 families) to the tiny town of **Winter Harbor** on the **Schoodic Peninsula.**

Even more so than other destinations in New England, this is an excellent place to have a bicycle, as the slow-moving traffic on Park Loop Road and extensive network of car-free carriage roads are ideal for riders of all skill levels. If you'd like to combine shuttling with bicycling, note that the Island Explorer buses have racks that accommodate up to 6 bikes, but popular routes (particularly afternoon return trips from Jordan Pond) can fill up quickly. For a better chance of catching a ride with your bike, look up the schedule for the **Island Explorer Bicycle Express** bus, which has a trailer that fits 12 bikes.

To take in the main sites in 2.5-3 hours, **Acadia National Park Tours** (207/288-0300, www.acadiatours.com, $30 adults, $17.50 children 12 and under) runs a bus contracted with the NPS to give sightseeing tours of Park Loop Road. The 2.5-hour narrated trip includes three 15-minute stops to stretch your legs and snap photos, and tickets can be purchased from **Testa's Restaurant** (53 Main St., Bar Harbor, 207/288-3327, 8am-9pm daily).

SIGHTS

★ Cadillac Mountain

At 1,528 feet, this rounded granite mountain is the highest point on the Atlantic Seaboard. The summit is gouged with deep, north-south scratches left by retreating glaciers, and leathery, subalpine plants sprout from the rocky crevices. Even on a summer day, it's easy to imagine the icy winds that howl across the mountain in the winter, stunting spruce and pitch pine trees into gnarled miniatures. In the booming tourist years of the late 19th century, a narrow-gauge cog railway was built to the top of the mountain, much like the railway up Mount Washington, but those tracks are long gone. These days, visitors hike or drive to the summit, where there's a gentle, scenic trail and views across Penobscot Bay.

Watching the sun come up from the peak of Cadillac Mountain is an iconic part of the Acadia National Park experience. In the fall and winter months, it's the first place in the United States to see the sunrise.

The 3.5-mile **Cadillac Mountain Road,** off the Park Loop Road, winds up the mountain, which is how most visitors arrive in the early morning hours, though there are also several walking trails to the summit. The most scenic of these is the **South Ridge Trail,** a 7-mile round-trip hike that starts near Blackwoods Campground and climbs 1,350 feet at a steady, moderate pace. If you're hoping to catch the sunrise after hiking the trail, plan to bring lights and warm clothing, and allow 2-4 hours each way, depending on your hiking speed.

Although it is often crowded, it's possible—especially outside of high season—to find yourself alone on the summit as dawn breaks over Penobscot Bay, lighting up islands and deep forests. A more likely scenario involves clusters of chatting families and several sleepy hikers who started up the peak in the middle of the night. Inevitably, though, the crowd begins to thin as soon as the sky lights up, and one of the nicest times to enjoy the short 0.3-mile **Summit Loop** is when everyone else heads to Bar Harbor for breakfast.

view from Cadillac Mountain

Park Loop Road

Passing headlands, trailheads, beaches, and stunning views of Penobscot Bay, the 27-mile Park Loop Road winds through some of Acadia's finest scenery. Traffic moves one way—clockwise—from the main entrance near Hulls Cove Visitor Center to Jordan Pond, then two-way traffic completes the loop and heads all the way up to the summit of Cadillac Mountain. Alternate entrances, where passes are also checked, are at Sieur de Monts, south of Bar Harbor; Sand Beach; Stanley Brook, by Seal Harbor; and off Route 233, just north of Cadillac Mountain Road. For much of the one-way section, parking is allowed in the right-hand lane, which makes it easy to spot a view and pull over for a closer look. It also means the road is often full of unexpected parked cars, pedestrians, and cyclists (along with the occasional moose), so it's important to take the Park Loop Road at a careful pace. There are also several low bridges that may be a problem for some RVs—the lowest of these is the 10-foot, 4-inch span across the Stanley Brook Entrance.

Driving the Park Loop Road

Driving the whole road at once is a nice way to get an overview of the park, but allow plenty of time to stop for picture-taking, tide pooling, walking, and otherwise exploring. From the main entrance at Hulls Cove, the road rises steeply to **Sieur de Monts,** where the small **Wild Gardens of Acadia** re-creates typical habitats found on Mount Desert Island, from heath to coniferous forest, with over 400 species of indigenous plants.

One of the finest places to swim on the whole island is **Sand Beach,** where a parking lot and short walking trail lead to a pleasant stretch of beach and **Great Head.** Along the rocky coast that follows, be sure to stop at **Thunder Hole,** a deep inlet with a submerged cavern that can roar and send water 40 feet into the air when waves hit just right; for the best show, try to visit two hours before high tide.

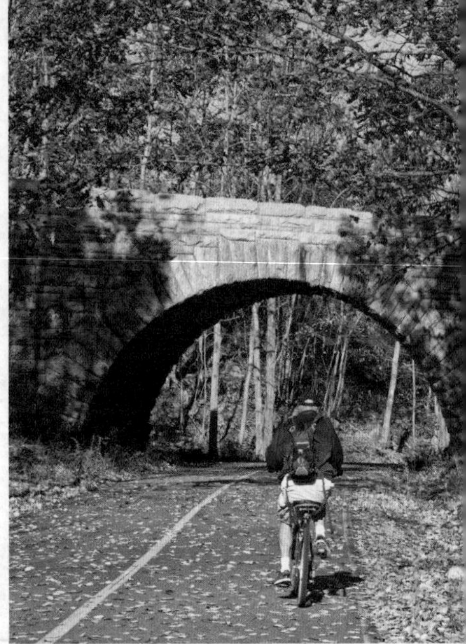

biking the carriage roads of Acadia National Park

The horizon opens back up at **Otter Cliff,** a 110-foot granite wall that's one of the tallest coastal headlands this side of Rio de Janeiro. After the turn back inland, the **Jordan Pond House** is a traditional stopping-off point for afternoon tea and hot popovers, with a view of a glacial tarn and distant mountains. Finally, a side road rises through a series of switchbacks to the park's grand attraction, the road to the top of **Cadillac Mountain.**

★ Carriage Roads

Concerned that Mount Desert Island would be destroyed with the introduction of automobiles, John D. Rockefeller Jr. started building a vast network of roads in 1913, determined they would remain closed to motorized traffic. Today, the 47 miles of crushed-stone roads are perfect for walking and biking as well as a favorite destination of cross-country skiers in the winter. The roads curve gently through a forest of birch, beech, and maple trees, over beautifully crafted

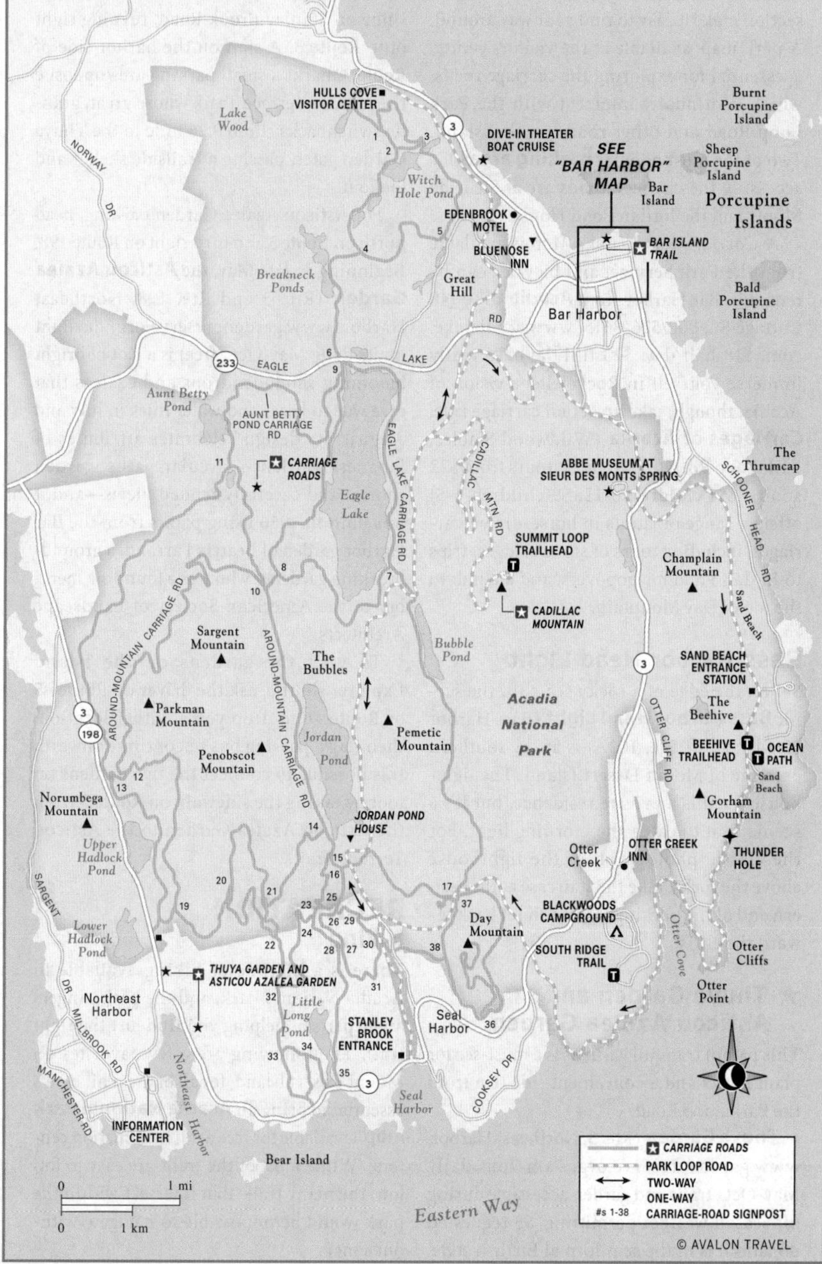
Park Loop and Carriage Roads
HULLS COVE VISITOR CENTER
Lake Wood
NORWAY DR
DIVE-IN THEATER BOAT CRUISE
SEE "BAR HARBOR" MAP
Burnt Porcupine Island
Sheep Porcupine Island
Bar Island
Porcupine Islands
Witch Hole Pond
EDENBROOK MOTEL
BLUENOSE INN
BAR ISLAND TRAIL
Breakneck Ponds
Great Hill
Bar Harbor
Bald Porcupine Island
EAGLE LAKE RD
Aunt Betty Pond
AUNT BETTY POND CARRIAGE RD
CARRIAGE ROADS
Eagle Lake
EAGLE LAKE CARRIAGE RD
CADILLAC MTN RD
ABBE MUSEUM AT SIEUR DES MONTS SPRING
The Thrumcap
SCHOONER HEAD RD
SUMMIT LOOP TRAILHEAD
Champlain Mountain
CADILLAC MOUNTAIN
Sand Beach
AROUND-MOUNTAIN CARRIAGE RD
Sargent Mountain
The Bubbles
Bubble Pond
SAND BEACH ENTRANCE STATION
Parkman Mountain
Acadia National Park
OTTER CLIFF RD
The Beehive
Jordan Pond
Pemetic Mountain
Penobscot Mountain
BEEHIVE TRAILHEAD
OCEAN PATH
Sand Beach
Norumbega Mountain
JORDAN POND HOUSE
Gorham Mountain
Upper Hadlock Pond
Otter Creek
OTTER CREEK INN
THUNDER HOLE
SARGENT DR
Lower Hadlock Pond
Day Mountain
BLACKWOODS CAMPGROUND
SOUTH RIDGE TRAIL
Otter Cove
Otter Cliffs
Otter Point
THUYA GARDEN AND ASTICOU AZALEA GARDEN
Northeast Harbor
MILLBROOK RD
Little Long Pond
STANLEY BROOK ENTRANCE
Seal Harbor
COOKSEY DR
MANCHESTER RD
Northeast Harbor
INFORMATION CENTER
Seal Harbor
Bear Island
Eastern Way
0 1 mi
0 1 km
CARRIAGE ROADS
PARK LOOP ROAD
TWO-WAY
ONE-WAY
#s 1-38 CARRIAGE-ROAD SIGNPOST
© AVALON TRAVEL

granite bridges, and through tunnels and arches, perfect for exploration by bicycle. Numbered wooden signposts at each intersection make it easy to find your way around. A park map, available at the visitors center, is essential for exploring the carriage roads, which continually intersect with the Park Loop Road and other roads on the island. Two of the most popular **parking areas** for accessing the carriage roads are at Sieur de Monts and the Jordan Pond House.

A *Carriage Road User's Map* is available from the Park Service, and bicycles can be rented in Bar Harbor from **Acadia Bike** (48 Cottage St., 800/526-8615, www.acadiabike.com, $18 half day, $23 full day). To really immerse yourself in Rockefeller's vision of Acadia, though, take an actual carriage ride. **Carriages of Acadia** (Wildwood Stables, Park Loop Rd., 207/276-3622, tours from $22 adults, $14 children 6-12, $9 children 4-5) offers a range of jaunts in horse-drawn carriages, including tours of stone bridges, trips to Jordan Pond for popovers, and a climb to the top of Day Mountain.

Bass Harbor Head Light

Set on the edge of a rocky sea cliff, the scenic **Bass Harbor Head Light** (Bass Harbor Head Rd., off Rte. 102A) is at the southern extreme of Mount Desert Island. The lighthouse itself is a private residence, but it's a scenic spot to catch the morning light. For the classic photograph of the lighthouse above the rocks, take the staircase at the eastern end of the parking lot and shoot back toward the cliffs.

★ Thuya Garden and Asticou Azalea Garden

This pair of tranquil gardens is a must-see for plant lovers and a convenient side trip from the Park Loop Road.

Thuya Garden (Rte. 3, Northeast Harbor, www.gardenpreserve.org, 7am-7pm daily May-Oct., trails and garden accessible during off-season weather permitting, $5 requested donation) is in the semiformal English style, with butterfly gardens, pavilions, and a pretty reflecting pool. To approach the gardens from Park Loop Road, head southwest and continue on Stanley Brook Road, turning right onto Route 3. A sign on the harbor side of Route 3 marks a small parking area opposite the Asticou Terrace Trail, whose great, granite switchbacks climb 0.25 mile to the Thuya Garden gates, passing a trailside shelter and lookout.

For Asticou Azalea Garden parking, head north on Route 3 and turn right on Route 198. Beginning in late May, the **Asticou Azalea Garden** (Rte. 3 and Rte. 198, Northeast Harbor, www.gardenpreserve.org, daylight hours daily May-Oct., free) is a riot of bright blooming rhododendrons and azaleas that give way to irises and water lilies in July and August. Its design celebrates attributes of Japanese gardens—circular paths, garden rooms, and carefully tended views—and it was built in 1956 using plants from the Bar Harbor garden of Beatrix Farrand, a groundbreaking gardener who was a founding member of the American Society of Landscape Architects.

To visit the gardens on the Island Explorer shuttle, ask the driver on Route #5 or Route #6 to drop you at either location, then flag a passing bus to continue onward. It is possible to connect the two gardens on foot by taking the sidewalk on Route 3 from the Asticou Azalea Garden to the Asticou Terrace Trail.

RECREATION

Hiking

There is a lifetime of hiking available in Acadia National Park, and the park rangers are experts at helping you find just the right trail. The following are a few favorites on Mount Desert Island; for all of these hikes, it's essential to bring an **Acadia National Park map** (available for free at all information centers). While most of the trails are easy to follow, the many trails that intersect within the park would be impossible to navigate without a map.

CADILLAC MOUNTAIN SOUTH RIDGE TRAIL

This strenuous, 3.5-mile hike to the summit of Cadillac Mountain departs from the Park Loop Road near Blackwoods Campground, passing through thick forest, then emerging onto pink granite with gorgeous views of the surrounding mountains. Hike the **South Ridge Trail** as an out-an-back, or continue down the other side, following the 2.2-mile **North Ridge Trail** to a trailhead on the one-way section of the Park Loop Road, where you can flag down an Island Explorer shuttle.

ACADIA MOUNTAIN

For fabulous views to Somes Sound and the ocean, the 1.8-mile round-trip walk up **Acadia Mountain** is a favorite; with 500 feet of elevation gain, it's an easier peak to hike than Cadillac Mountain. The clearly marked parking lot for the Acadia Mountain Trail is on Route 102, 3.1 miles north of Southwest Harbor.

WONDERLAND TRAIL AND SHIP HARBOR TRAIL

The "quiet side" of Mount Desert Island has plenty of hikes as well, and these are often less busy than the eastern trails. On the southern edge of the island, the 1.3-mile round-trip **Ship Harbor Trail** is a good place to walk through scenic coastal forest offering views along a deep inlet, and the 1.5-mile round-trip **Wonderland Trail** is just up the road, with great tide pools on a rocky beach, and a jumble of granite boulders. For the trailheads, drive south from Southwest Harbor and turn left onto Route 102A to follow the coast. The clearly marked Wonderland Trailhead is 4.1 miles past the turnoff onto Route 102A, and the Ship Harbor Trailhead is a short distance farther. Both have parking lots.

BEEHIVE TRAIL

Sure-footed hikers can head up one of the island's "iron rung" trails, where the paths are supplemented by metal bars set directly in the granite. The strenuous **Beehive Trail** is one of these, with exposed, stony sections along the south face of the 520-foot Beehive peak that make the hike seem longer than its 1.6 miles round-trip. To reach the trailhead, leave your car in the Sand Beach parking lot (which is also a stop on the Island Explorer shuttle bus) and cross the Park Loop Road.

Tidepools

Fluctuating water levels strand sea creatures in rocky pools all along the Mount Desert Island coast, but finding them involves careful planning. Pick up a copy of the *Acadia Weekly* or stop by any of the ranger stations for information on the tides, which range between 10 and 15 feet around the island. The best time to spot wildlife is 1.5 hours before and after extreme low tide.

When searching for tidepools, bring a pair of shoes with good traction that you don't mind getting wet and sandy, and pay close attention to water levels, as some rocky outcroppings can be stranded by rising water.

One favorite way to explore is by walking to **Bar Island** from downtown Bar Harbor (follow Bridge St.); for 1.5 hours before and after low tide, a 0.8-mile gravel bar that leads from the end of Bridge Street is exposed. There are walking trails on the tiny island, and the outgoing tide usually leaves some sea stars and crabs in sandy tidepools along the bar.

On the southwest side of the island, **Ship Harbor** and **Wonderland Trails** are also good choices, with plenty of nooks and crannies to trap interesting things in the intertidal zone. **Ranger-led tidepool programs** (www.nps.gov/acad/planyourvisit/calendar.htm) are held at Ship Harbor and Sand Beach in July and August. Drive south from Southwest Harbor and turn left onto Route 102A to find the well-marked Wonderland Trailhead 4.1 miles past the turnoff onto Route 102A, and the Ship Harbor Trailhead a short distance farther. Both have parking lots.

Paddling

Get a harbor seal's view of the island's rugged coast by touring in a sea kayak. A handful of well-regarded operators lead trips open to paddlers of all skill levels. Visit the remoter western side of the island with **National Park Sea Kayak Tours** (39 Cottage St., Bar Harbor, 800/347-0940, www.acadiakayak.com, $48-52), which plans its trips through Western Bay and Blue Hill Bay so you head downwind. Tours last 2.5-3 hours. **Acadia Park Kayak Tours** (Bar Harbor, 207/266-1689, www.acadiaparkkayak.com, $45-60) launches right in downtown Bar Harbor and schedules exciting nighttime stargazing tours. Tours run 3.5-4 hours.

Swimming

There are two beaches in Acadia with summer lifeguards. The water at **Sand Beach,** just off the Park Loop Road, stays in the high 50s throughout the summer, but that's warm enough for plenty of visitors; come here for saltwater, views, and a beach vacation atmosphere. Find (somewhat) warmer water at **Echo Lake Beach,** on the west side of Route 102 between Somesville and Southwest Harbor. The lake floor drops gradually from the shoreline, making this a good choice for families with children.

Boating

If Maine's lobstermen had a celebrity spokesperson, it would have to be Captain John Nicolai of ***Lulu* Lobster Boat Ride** (55 West St., Bar Harbor, 207/963-2341, www.lululobsterboat.com, 2-hour tour $35 adults, $32 seniors and U.S. military, $20 children 6-12), who keeps up a great running patter about the lobstering life (and the life of a lobster). Come April-early June to spot adorable baby seals lolling around near Egg Rock Lighthouse.

By far one of the best things to do on the island with nature-loving kids is head out on a **Dive-In Theater Boat Cruise** (105 Eden St., Bar Harbor, 207/288-3483, www.divered.com, $42 adults, $37 seniors, $32 children 5-11, $16 children under 5) with "Diver Ed." Ed (and his sidekick "mini Ed") suit up in scuba gear equipped with underwater microphones and cameras. The crowd on decks can follow along, then Ed reappears with underwater creatures that kids can touch before sending them back to the ocean floor. The boat departs from the College of the Atlantic, where you can park for free in the North Lot.

A classic style of sailboat along the East Coast is the Friendship sloop, a graceful, gaff-rigged boat that originated in Friendship, Maine, in the late 19th century. Friendship sloop *Surprise*, operated by **Downeast Sailing Adventures** (Cranberry Island Dock, Southwest Harbor, 207/288-2216, www.downeastsail.com, 2-hour sail $50 pp, private sail $125 per hour for up to 6 people), has been sailing the Maine coast since 1964 and offers an intimate, beautiful way to experience it.

FOOD

The Jordan Pond House is the only restaurant in the park proper, but there are places to eat scattered around the island, and some make great destinations unto themselves.

Enjoying popovers and tea on the lawn at ★ **Jordan Pond House** (2928 Park Loop Rd., Seal Harbor, 207/276-3316, www.acadiajordanpondhouse.com, 11am-9pm daily, $7-25) is a classic Acadia experience: The warm, oversized pastries are perfect with melting butter and house-made strawberry jam, and the restaurant has stunning views of the glacial tarn with the granite "bubbles" in the background. The restaurant itself was rebuilt in 1979 and the interior is fairly charmless, but the afternoon tea experience is delightful and should not be missed.

Jordan Pond House doesn't completely own the popover world on Mount Desert Island. While it has no views to speak of, everyone agrees ★ **Common Good Kitchen Café** (19 Clark Point Rd., Southwest Harbor, 207/266-2733, www.commongoodsoupkitchen.org, 7:30am-11am daily May-Oct., by donation) would win hands down in a popover-to-popover showdown. A simple menu of oatmeal, coffee, and popovers is served by volunteers on a sunny patio, with all proceeds going to a meal delivery service for disadvantaged islanders during the winter months.

With a location between Route 102 and Route 3, **Mainely Meat BBQ** (15 Knox Rd., Bar Harbor, 207/288-9200, www.atlanticbrewing.com, 11:30am-8pm daily May-Oct., $11-19) is the convenient and casual on-site restaurant of **Atlantic Brewing Company** (10am-6pm daily May.-Oct., free tastings). Large portions of barbecue basics come with coleslaw, potato salad, and baked beans; ribs are a favorite for many visitors. Tours of the brewery are at 2pm, 3pm, and 4pm daily during peak season, and are capped at 25 people.

A menu of sandwiches, seafood, and pizza served in a family-run diner setting makes the **Quietside Café** (360 Main St., Southwest Harbor, 207/244-9444, 11am-10pm Mon.-Sat., 11am-9pm Sun., hours vary in off-season, $6-12) a mainstay for laid-back lunches, dinners, and ice cream. The butter lobster stew is a favorite, and the blueberry pie à la mode also gets rave reviews.

If this lobster-loving author had to choose just one of the many lobster places to eat in Maine, it would be ★ **Thurston's Lobster Pound** (9 Thurston Rd., Bernard, 207/244-7600, www.thurstonforlobster.com, 11am-9pm daily, $7-30), just outside the park off Route 102 in Bernard. Consider arriving early or late to avoid the line, which can stretch far out the door, but it's worth making an evening trip to the "quiet side" for a traditional lobster dinner or an overstuffed lobster roll (perhaps followed by sunset at the Bass Harbor Head Light). The restaurant has two sides: Line up on the right to order a whole lobster dinner or sit in the main dining area, or head to the left to sit in the bar, where the rest of the menu is available. You can also sit in the bar with a lobster dinner—it just needs to be ordered in that long line. It's not an unpleasant wait, though, as it's fascinating to watch the servers run in and out with great bags of clams and lobsters to drop in the industrial-sized boiler outside. A casual atmosphere, local beers on tap, and views of the pretty harbor make this a true gem.

ACCOMMODATIONS AND CAMPING

A couple of campgrounds are within Acadia National Park's boundaries, but there are no hotels or inns within the park itself; lodging listings here cover places to stay on the "quiet side" that are still convenient to park activities and sights.

$100-150

Completely surrounded by national park land, the **Otter Creek Inn** (47 Otter Creek Dr., 207/288-5151, www.ottercreekmaine.com, May-Oct., $115-180) is a perfect place (almost) for non-campers to stay in Acadia. The rooms and cabins are simple but sufficient, and a continental breakfast is served in the attached market. Some guests have noted the rooms' thin walls, but the price, which drops below $100 outside of peak season, is hard to beat.

$150-250

The self-contained units at ★ **Acadia Cottages** (410 Main St., Southwest Harbor, 207/244-5388, www.acadia-cottages.com, $140-170) are simple and old-fashioned, but well-appointed kitchens, outdoor fire pits, and comfortable mattresses are a cut above other cabins on the island. Wooded grounds make these feel relatively private, and the cottages are walking distance from Southwest Harbor.

Views of Southwest Harbor and a friendly, hospitable atmosphere are the draws at **Clark Point Inn** (109 Clark Point Rd., Southwest Harbor, 207/244-9828, www.clarkpointinn.com, $169-239), which has five guest rooms cheerfully decorated in country style. Three-course breakfasts, afternoon cookies and snacks, and welcoming common spaces make this a favorite with adults-only guests.

Over $250

Perched on the end of Somes Sound, **The Claremont Hotel** (22 Claremont Rd., Southwest Harbor, 207/244-5036, www.theclaremonthotel.com, inn $220-342, cottages $318-444) is an 1884 grande dame that rambles across a six-acre, waterfront property. The 24 rooms in the main house have been recently renovated, but are full of historical charm, their old-fashioned quirks left intact (which is not necessarily to everyone's taste). This feels like a glimpse of old Maine, and for afternoons on the porch, games of croquet on the perfectly trimmed lawn, and sunset drinks at a dockside bar, it remains a wonderful destination.

Camping

Only two of the campgrounds on Mount Desert Island are inside the park proper, set on the southernmost part of Mount Desert Island on opposite sides of Somes Sound. It's worth reserving either of these far in advance for busy times, but each sets aside a small number of non-reservable sites. Call first thing in the morning to check availability. **Blackwoods Campground** is right on Park Loop Road (Rte. 3, 207/288-3274, www.nps.gov/acad, May-Oct. $30, Apr. and Nov. $15, free primitive sites available Dec.-Mar.), adjacent to an Island Explorer shuttle stop and convenient to Bar Harbor and Cadillac Mountain. The 306 forested sites often fill up; the campground can feel busy and noisy during peak season. There's no hookups or showers, but free firewood is provided, and a spot just outside the entrance offers hot, coin-operated showers. Or set up your tent on the "quiet side" at **Seawall Campground** (Rte. 102A, 207/244-3600, www.nps.gov/acad, late May-early Sept., $22-30), 18 miles from Bar Harbor, and a prime location for beautiful sunsets on the shore as well as access to less trafficked hikes and Bass Harbor Head Light. Like Blackwoods, Seawall has no hookups or showers, but it offers coin-operated showers and a general store five minutes away. Many cell phones get no reception on this side of the island.

The privately owned ★ **Mount Desert Campground** (516 Sound Dr., off Rte. 2, 207/244-3710, www.mountdesertcampground.com, late May-early Oct., $39-69) splits the difference, with a superb location at the head of Somes Sound that's the perfect jumping-off point for exploring all of the island. Tent sites roll right up to the water (pricing varies depending on the season and proximity of the site to the water), hookups are available, and the campground rents all kinds of boards and boats for getting in the sound, as well as a launching ramp for private boats. Bathhouses have free hot showers, and the small, convivial "gathering place" offers wireless Internet, snacks, coffee, and ice cream.

There's a summer camp atmosphere at **Hadley's Point Campground** (33 Hadley Point Rd., off Rte. 3, 207/288-4808, www.hadleyspoint.com, mid-May-mid-Oct., tents $27-30, hookups $37-48, cabins $60-80), making it a good choice for families, though tent sites are set close together and don't provide much privacy. A heated swimming pool, coin-operated showers, laundry facilities, a playground, and wireless Internet are available. The campground is on the Island Explorer shuttle bus route for easy access to Bar Harbor, and there's a public beach within easy walking distance. The rustic, tidy cabins have private bathrooms, three beds, and a fire pit (bring your own linens).

SCHOODIC PENINSULA

Facing the eastern side of Mount Desert Island, on the mainland Schoodic Peninsula, this quiet section of Acadia National Park is perfect for exploring when the main site starts getting overcrowded. You can reach the Schoodic Peninsula from the mainland, or hop a ferry from Bar Harbor, then get around by car, bike, or on the Island Explorer.

Schoodic Loop Road

This scenic, 6-mile loop road passes through some of the most spectacular scenery on the Schoodic Peninsula, with a turnout to **Schoodic Point,** the jutting tip of the peninsula, which commands great views of the Atlantic Ocean and Mount Desert Island.

Much of the road is one-way, traveling from Winter Harbor, then looping counter-clockwise toward Birch Harbor, with a series of picnic spots and pullouts, often with short walking trails. RVs are not allowed past Schoodic Woods Campground.

Sports and Recreation

Far less trafficked than the Mount Desert Island section of the park, the **Schoodic Peninsula** is great for **bicycles.** The highlight is the Schoodic Loop Road, but it's possible to explore all day by linking the paved road to the 8.3 miles of **off-road bike trails** that loop through the interior of the peninsula. For a complete circuit, start riding the Schoodic Loop Road at the Schoodic Woods Campground, then return to the starting point on the trails, cutting back west just before the one-way section of the road ends at Bunker Harbor.

Camping

The newest campground in the Acadia National Park network, **Schoodic Woods Campground** (54 Far View Dr., Winter Harbor, 207/288-3338, www.recreation.gov, tents $22-30, RVs $30) has 93 sites, including a section of walk-in-only spots that's great for a secluded night in the woods. There are campfire rings and a dump station, but no showers, and the closest supplies are two miles away in Winter Harbor. The campground is located on the Schoodic Peninsula Island Express loop.

Information

Maps and information are available at the Schoodic Woods Campground **nature center** (54 Far View Dr., Winter Harbor, 207/288-3338, www.recreation.gov, 8am-10pm daily, off-season hours may vary), which is a good first stop for maps and information.

Getting There and Around

The Schoodic Peninsula is south of Route 1, linked to the highway by Route 186, which passes through the community of Winter Harbor.

To reach the Schoodic Peninsula from Mount Desert Island, take the **Bar Harbor Ferry** (Bar Harbor Inn Pier, 7 Newport Dr., 207/288-2984, www.barharborferry.com, late June-Sept., round-trip tickets $26 adults, $16 children under 12, $75 families) to the tiny town of **Winter Harbor** on the **Schoodic Peninsula.**

It's possible to reach all the key sites on the Schoodic Peninsula on the #8 loop of the **Island Explorer** (207/667-5796, www.exploreacadia.com), which connects with the ferry terminal in Winter Harbor.

Bar Harbor

Times have changed since the first 19th-century "rusticators" came to Bar Harbor for society parties with wilderness views. The stunning landscape of forested islands is still there, but the town itself can feel overstuffed and kitschy, an ice cream-fueled frenzy of T-shirt shops and lobster souvenirs. Still, Bar Harbor is the "town" for Mount Desert Island, with restaurants, museums, services, and loads of places to stay. This is the jumping-off point for many boat cruises and activities, and a perfect foil to the quiet trails and mountaintops inside Acadia National Park.

SIGHTS

Step into the world of Mount Desert Island's earliest locals at the **Abbe Museum,** which has two campuses focusing on modern-day and bygone Wabanaki lives. Visit the **Abbe Museum downtown location** (26 Mount Desert St., 207/388-2519, www.abbemuseum.org, 10am-5pm daily May-Oct., call for off-season hours, $8 adults, $4 children 11-17, children under 11 and Native Americans free) for a stronger focus on today's Wabanaki, along with stories from the past and a few artifacts. Located inside Acadia National Park, the **Abbe Museum**

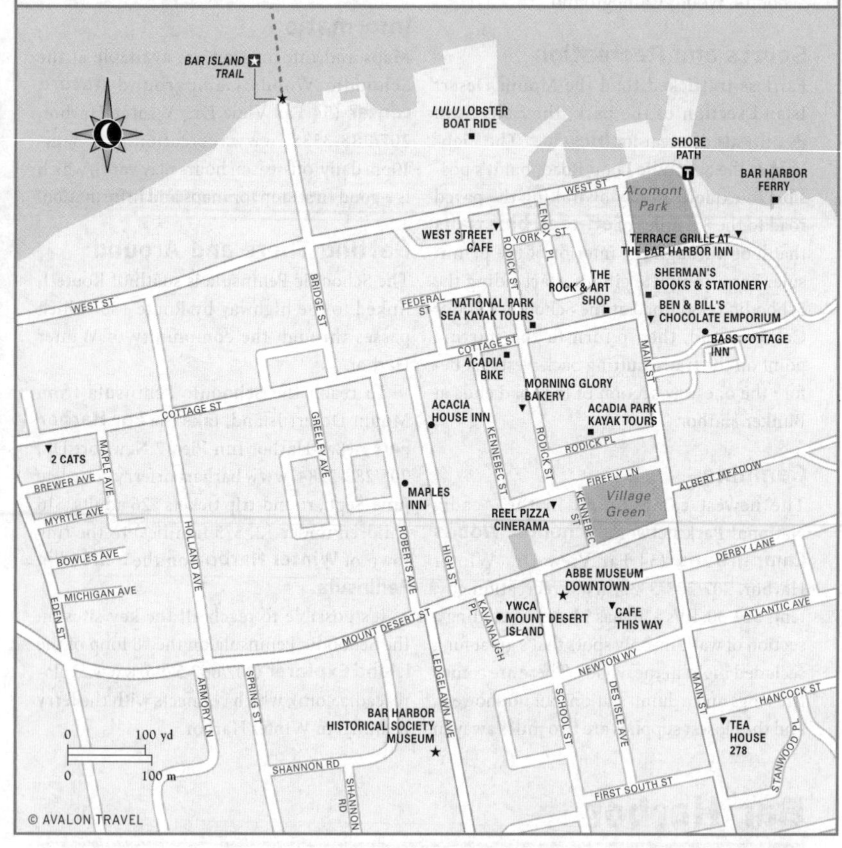

at Sieur de Monts Spring (Sieur de Monts, Park Loop Rd. and Rte. 3, 10am-5pm daily late May-mid-Oct., $3 adults, $1 children 11-17, children under 11 and Native Americans free) is much smaller, but has fascinating artifacts and depictions of archaeological digs in the area. A ticket to Abbe Downtown also includes admission to the Sieur de Monts Spring venue, and the cost of the Abbe Museum at Sieur de Monts Spring ticket is deducted from the admission price if you visit the downtown location as well.

Small but interesting, the **Bar Harbor Historical Society Museum** (33 Ledgelawn Ave., 207/288-3807, www.barharborhistorical.org, 1pm-4pm Mon.-Fri. June-Oct., by appointment in winter, free) has a remarkable collection of images from the town's Gilded Age heyday—think lots of full-length tennis skirts and boating parties. The 1916 building in which it's housed is as intriguing as the contents. It was built by Colonel and Louise Drexel Morell (who appear in stained-glass windows on the 2nd floor). Louise was sister to Saint Katherine Drexel, who gave up her share of the family's considerable fortune to become a missionary in the American Southwest. She was a strong advocate for Native American and African American rights and was canonized in 2000.

Follow the life of a lobster from itsy-bitsy hatchling to full-grown, claw-snapping adult at **Mount Desert Oceanarium** (1351 Rte. 3, 207/288-5005, www.theoceanarium.com, 9am-5pm Mon.-Sat. mid-May-late Oct., $15 adults, $10 children), a bayside nature center with a lobster hatchery, live seals, and marsh trails. The museum tour, a series of three 30-minute presentations, is a bit long and stationary for active kids, but Audrey and David Mills have been talking lobsters for years and are a great source of info about Maine's marine ecology.

★ Bar Island Trail

There's a 0.8-mile gravel bar leading from downtown to **Bar Island,** a path that's only exposed for 1.5 hours before and after low tide. To reach the **Bar Island Trail,** follow Bridge Street to the end, then keep walking across the sand, watching for the many tide pools that are exposed by the retreating tide. Once you're at the island, a small footpath winds through the trees, to an overlook with great views back toward Bar Harbor.

Or you can catch the ships come in and out of the harbor from Bar Harbor's gentle **Shore Path,** a paved walking trail that stretches 0.75 mile from the town pier to Wayman Lane. It's especially nice as a morning walk, when the harbor begins to flood with early sunshine.

ENTERTAINMENT AND EVENTS

After a day of hiking peaks and ocean swimming, **Reel Pizza Cinerama** (33 Kennebec Pl., 207/288-3811, www.reelpizza.net, pizzas $14-23) beckons; the single-screen theater is stocked with comfy, mismatched couches and counter seats for settling in with pizza and beer. End of June-mid-August, the **Bar Harbor Town Band** (www.barharborband.org) plays hour-long concerts on the Village Green; shows are at 8pm on Monday and Thursday. Another summer tradition is heading to the **Great Room** lounge at the **Bluenose Inn** (90 Eden St., 800/445-4077, www.barharborhotel.com), where pianist Bill Trowell plays laid-back favorites every night at 7pm late May-October.

SHOPPING

Many of the shops in Bar Harbor sell variations on a theme—lobster and moose stuffed animals, T-shirts, Christmas ornaments. Find these along Main Street. Before you go on a wildlife expedition, stop by **Sherman's Books & Stationery** (56 Main

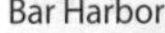

Bar Harbor

St., 207/288-3161, www.shermans.com, 9am-10:30pm daily), which carries an exceptional selection of bird-watching and wildlife guides and trail maps in addition to a full stock of books and cards. Another fun stop is **The Rock & Art Shop** (13 Cottage St., 207/288-4800, www.therockandartshop.com, 9am-8pm daily, hours vary seasonally), which does have both rocks and art, but also stuffed fish, skulls, and other fascinating, odd treasures.

FOOD

In a bright, rambling home on the edge of downtown, ★ **2 Cats** (130 Cottage St., 207/288-2808, www.twocatsbarharbor.com, 7am-1pm daily, $4-9) is a funky gem and the best place for breakfast on the island. Simple breakfast classics like eggs Benedict and blueberry pancakes are done nicely, and the café's fresh, flaky biscuits come with a dreamy side of homemade strawberry butter. Come early to snag a spot on the deep wraparound porch.

For fresh pastries, espresso, and sandwiches on bagels and house-made bread, **Morning Glory Bakery** (39 Rodick St., 207/288-3041, 7am-5pm Mon.-Fri., 8am-5pm Sat.-Sun., $3-12) is a longtime favorite. You'll find a few tables inside (and wireless Internet) at this casual, counter-service spot, but don't miss the back patio on sunny days, where comfy Adirondack chairs and a little garden await.

A menu of classic seafood options, salads, and pasta is surprisingly reasonable at this waterside spot, given that the ★ **Terrace Grille at the Bar Harbor Inn** (7 Newport Dr., 207/288-3351, www.barharborhinn.com, 11:30am-dark daily, $12-30) has the best outdoor seating in town. Tables on the lawn and patio overlook the harbor and Bar Island, making this a great place to catch a sunset over a bowl of chowder or lobster stew. At $39, the lobster bake—a boiled lobster with chowder, clams, mussels, sides, and blueberry pie—is an excellent deal for downtown Bar Harbor.

A quiet atmosphere, simple decor, and a pretty garden make **Tea House 278** (278 Main St., 207/288-2781, www.teahouse278.com, 11am-7pm Wed.-Sat., 11am-5pm Sun. mid-May-early Oct., $3-13) a respite from bustling Bar Harbor, and servers are trained in the traditional preparation of Chinese teas. A small menu of snack food includes tea eggs, sweets, nuts, and egg rolls.

Simple, sunny, and laid-back, **West Street Cafe** (76 West St., 207/288-5242, www.weststreetcafe.com, 11am-9pm daily, $14-30) has a big menu of beef and chicken dinners, pastas, and seafood. The lunch menu of "Earlybird Specials" is served until 6pm, and is an excellent value for an early dinner, especially the $20 lobster plate and $25 lobster dinner with chowder and blueberry pie.

It would be easy to miss **Cafe This Way** (14 Mt. Desert St., 207/288-4483, www.cafethisway.com, 7am-11:30am and 5:30pm-9pm Tues.-Sat., 8am-1pm and 5:30pm-9pm Sun., breakfast $6-12, dinner $19-28), a restaurant with art nouveau flair that's tucked down an alley between School and Main Streets. Breakfast omelets, burritos, and blueberry pancakes get raves, and a menu of grilled seafood and salads is full of fresh flavors. While most Bar Harbor kids' menus are identical lists of fried food and cheesy pasta, Cafe This Way stands out with small plates of grilled meat and seafood served with mashed potatoes and corn on the cob.

Farmers and artisans from around Penobscot Bay attend the **Eden Farmers Market** (YMCA, 21 Park St., 9am-noon Sun. mid-May-Oct.), which is a great place to find farm-fresh Maine blueberries in season.

There are two ice cream greats in downtown Bar Harbor: The granddaddy is **Ben & Bill's Chocolate Emporium** (66 Main St., 207/288-3281, www.benandbills.com, 8:30am-10pm Mon.-Sat., 10am-10pm Sun., $3-7), a candy store with a zillion flavors (including Maine lobster), big servings, and a landmark lobster sculpture out front that's a classic Bar Harbor selfie spot. The scoop-wielding young Turks of the waffle cone scene are at **Mount Desert Ice Cream** (7 Firefly Ln., 207/801-4001, www.mdiic.com, 11am-11:30pm daily June-early Sept., hours vary during shoulder season, $3-7), where flavors range from Maine Sea Salt Caramel to Blueberry Sour Cream and Chocolate Wasabi. Not all the flavors are quite so offbeat—President Barack Obama ordered a scoop of plain ol' coconut while visiting with his family in 2010.

ACCOMMODATIONS

Under $100

Seriously no frills, **Robbins Motel** (Rte. 3, 207/288-4659, www.robbinsmotel.com, May-mid-Oct., $39-69) features the rates of yesteryear and rooms to match. Amenities include cable TV, a pool, and wireless Internet, but the overall experience is pretty bare bones.

Right in the heart of Bar Harbor, the **YWCA Mount Desert Island** (3 Mt. Desert St., 207/288-5008, www.ywcamdi.org, $44, discounts for longer stays) has dorm-like housing for women only, with a large communal kitchen and shared baths. It's generally important to book well in advance to stay here, but worth asking about last-minute availability.

$100-150

The smallest cottages at **Rose Eden Cottages** (864 Rte. 3, 207/288-3038, www.roseeden.com, $55-178) are like nautical dollhouses, with just enough room for a double bed, coffeemaker, and compact bathroom. Each of the 11 cottages is different, some with kitchenettes, second bedrooms, and sitting areas; the largest has a full kitchen. A location on the main road 7.5 miles outside of Bar Harbor means that the sounds of traffic are an issue for some guests, but the owners provide white noise machines, and some units are set farther back on the grassy property, which has a gas grill and laundry facilities for guests. The friendly owners also prepare good-value lobster dinners to go.

One of the best values among the generic digs that line Route 3 is **Edenbrook Motel** (96 Rte. 3, 800/323-7819, www.edenbrookmotelbh.com, $85-130), which is adjacent to the College of the Atlantic and 1.5 miles outside of Bar Harbor. The simple, superclean rooms have air-conditioning, television and coffeemakers, and the Island Explorer shuttle stops right in front, making it a breeze to head into town or the park.

Smart, whitewashed cottages and tidy motel-style rooms look out on Frenchman's Bay at ★ **Edgewater Motel and Cottages** (137 Old Bar Harbor Rd., 207/288-3941, www.edgewaterbarharbor.com, cottages $82-170, motel $86-145), where a broad lawn dotted with Adirondack chairs gives a resort feel to this five-acre property that's 6.5 miles from Bar Harbor. The cottage kitchens are stocked with cooking equipment and coffeemakers, and you can spot harbor seals and porpoises from the outdoor decks.

$150-250

With a location right in downtown Bar Harbor, the ★ **Acacia House Inn** (6 High St., 800/551-5399, www.acaciahouseinn.com, $80-195) is a wonderful value, with sweet, simple decor and great breakfasts cooked with lots of local and organic ingredients, including eggs from the friendly innkeepers' own chickens. All rooms have private bathrooms, organic cotton sheets, and cable TV. The quiet side street the inn sits on lends a surprisingly laid-back atmosphere given the downtown location.

Another downtown gem is the **Maples Inn** (16 Roberts Ave., 207/618-6823, www.maplesinn.com, $119-219), a charming Victorian bed-and-breakfast with seven well-appointed rooms (one has a detached private bath, while others have private in-room baths). One of the owners is a professional chef who prepares personalized menus and afternoon cookies for guests, and the rocking chairs on the shady front porch are an idyllic place to relax after a day of exploring.

Over $250

Stylish and luxurious, the **Bass Cottage Inn** (14 The Field, 207/288-1234, www.basscottage.com, $260-400) strikes a balance between the personal experience of a bed-and-breakfast and the thoughtful service of a top-end hotel. The inn is tucked down a private lane a few minutes' walk from the waterfront, so it feels like a retreat in downtown Bar Harbor. The 1885 building has been carefully restored with a clean, airy design and comfortable common spaces. Breakfast is prepared to order, and evening wine and snacks create a convivial atmosphere.

INFORMATION AND SERVICES

The **city's informative website** (www.barharborinfo.com) has useful walking maps of the town, and there's a **visitors center** (19 Firefly Ln., 207/288-3338, 8am-5pm daily June-Oct.) on the Bar Harbor Green. There are several **banks** and **ATMs** located along Main Street and Cottage Street in downtown, and free wireless Internet is available at **Jesup Public Library** (34 Mt. Desert St., 207/288-4245, www.jesuplibrary.org, 10am-8pm Wed.-Thurs., 10am-5pm Fri.-Sat. and Tues.).

GETTING THERE

Air

It's relatively easy to reach Bar Harbor without wheels of your own. **Cape Air** (a JetBlue affiliate) and **Pen Air** offer direct flights from Boston to **Bar Harbor-Hancock County Airport** (www.bhbairport.com); during its months of operation between June and mid-October, the **Island Explorer** (207/667-5796, www.exploreacadia.com) shuttle has free service from the airport to Bar Harbor. Hertz and Enterprise both offer car rentals at the airport.

Train

The Amtrak **Downeaster** (800/872-7245, www.amtrakdowneaster.com) runs from Boston along the coast as far as Brunswick, where it's possible to rent a car or connect with a twice-daily bus service to Bangor on **Concord Coach Lines** (800/639-3317, www.concordcoachlines.com).

Bus

Greyhound (800/231-2222, www.greyhound.com) offers bus service to Bangor from Brunswick and Portland, as does **Concord Coach Lines** (800/639-3317, www.concordcoachlines.com). From Bangor, **Downeast Transportation** (207/667-5796, www.downeasttrans.org) operates an afternoon bus to Bar Harbor on Monday and Friday from the Concord Coach station. You can also take the **Bar Harbor-Bangor Shuttle** van service (207/479-5911, www.barharborshuttle.com, $45, advance reservation required).

GETTING AROUND

As in the national park, the **Island Explorer** (207/667-5796, www.exploreacadia.com) is the best way to get around Bar Harbor. The **Eden Street route** connects major hotels along Route 3 with the Bar Harbor Green. For the most part, though, the town is easy to walk on foot. Metered parking is available throughout downtown, but the only RV parking is on Main Street south of Park Street on the way out of town.

Down East Maine

A remote stretch of coast with a head-scratcher of a name, "Down East" is the northernmost part of the shore, stretching off toward the wilds of New Brunswick and Nova Scotia. While driving toward the Canadian border might look like "up" to the average landlubber, sailors have a downwind run as they catch the prevailing winds that blow toward Lubec, the easternmost point in the mainland United States—hence the name.

Once you get past Mount Desert Island, the crowds will disappear in your rearview mirror, giving way to long stretches of thick forest and the occasional gas station stocked with hunting and fishing gear. What's the draw? Big tides, big trees, and big country, mostly, or the charm of following Route

1 (U.S. Highway 1), which begins in Key West, Florida, all the way to the edge of the country, and to catch a sunrise from Lubec's candy-striped lighthouse.

LUBEC

★ West Quoddy Head Light

Poking into the Quoddy Narrows that divides Maine and Campobello Island, **Quoddy Head State Park** (973 S. Lubec Rd., 207/733-0911, www.maine.gov/quoddyhead, 9am-sunset daily, visitors center 10am-4pm daily mid-May-mid-Oct., $4 adults, $1 seniors) is the easternmost point of the mainland United States.

Right at the end is one of the most distinctive lighthouses in Maine, **West Quoddy Head Light,** a tower whose bold stripes grace just about every Maine lighthouse calendar that goes to print. In point of fact, the 49-foot-high tower is one of only two in the country painted with red and white stripes—a common practice in Canada as it helps them stand out against the snow. While the tower is not open to the public, the keeper's house has a small museum, and the cliffs are prime viewing for seals, bald eagles, and sometimes even whales.

Setting out from West Quoddy Head Light, **The Coastal Trail** (4-mile round-trip), wraps around the coast, passing **Gulliver's Hole,** a dramatic vertical chasm that drops away through the volcanic rock, and ending at **Carrying Place Cove,** which is ringed by an attractive sandy beach.

Another great walk is the **Bog Trail,** a 0.5-mile spur that passes through swampy terrain that's ideal for pitcher plants, Labrador tea, and baked appleberry, common in the wetlands of northern Canada, but a rarity south of the border.

Other Sights

Smoked fish and salted fish used to be big business on this isolated coast, but when Lubec's local herring processor closed its doors in 1991, it was the last one in the state. Now, the **McCurdy Smokehouse Museum** (50 S. Water St., 207/733-2197, www.lubeclandmarks.org, 10am-4pm daily, free) preserves that fishy history with displays that show how deeply the lives of Mainers has been entwined with the health of fisheries and global fish markets.

Food

The sign at **Frank's Dockside Restaurant** (24 Water St., 207/733-4484, www.franksdockside.net, 11am-7pm Thurs.-Tues., $11-25)

West Quoddy Head Light

announces that all are welcome, including "suits, clam boots, whackies, khakis, squid snaggers, carpet baggers, deadheads & dreads," and that's about the size of it. Just about everyone in town ends up at Frank's, where classic Maine seafood shares a menu with steaks, burgers, and sandwiches. Prepare to wait, but as the sign suggests, there's some appealing people-watching to do while you're there.

Find locally brewed craft beer and better-than-average pub food at **Lubec Brewing Company** (41 S. Water St., 207/733-4555, 2pm-8:30pm Thurs.-Sun., kitchen opens at 5pm, $7-13), which serves darn-good flatbreads topped with local ingredients like fiddleheads, the crisp green tips of ostrich ferns. On nights with live music, or when the open mic night is happening, this is *the* place to be in Lubec.

Accommodations and Camping

Once a sardine factory, the fishy tang is long gone from ★ **The Inn on the Wharf** (69 Johnson St., 207/733-4400, www.theinnonthewharf.com, $90-180), a motel-style property with tidy apartments and suites. Decks jut out toward the ocean, and there are kitchen and laundry facilities on-site—shared for the suites, with private versions in the apartments. There's an attached restaurant that's an appealing option for fresh seafood.

Full of old-fashioned charm, **Peacock House Bed & Breakfast** (27 Sumer St., 207/733-2403, www.peacockhouse.com, $115-165) is beautifully cared for and welcoming, with plenty of common spaces to relax with a book after a day of exploring. The owners keep the dining room stocked with fresh coffee and homemade cookies, and the breakfasts are outstanding.

With a mix of tent sites and spots for rigs, the main attraction at **Sunset Point RV Park** (37 Sunset Rd., 207/733-2272, www.sunsetpointrvpark.com, $30-40) is the view across Johnson Bay. As the name suggests, sunsets are a specialty, but it's worth rising early to catch the morning sun. If you want to pick up some lobsters or crabs for a boil, the owners have a propane cooker and pots for guest use, and the campground has a small beach for launching kayaks or canoes. The open layout offers little privacy.

Information

A small kiosk on Washington Street is stocked with maps and brochures, and other information is available from Lubec's **Town Hall Office** (40 School St., 207/733-2341, www.townoflubec.com).

Getting There

Lubec is a four-hour drive from Portland, and that's if you take the interstate, following I-95 and I-295 through the interior forest. Opt for the coastal road, and it's closer to five hours, not including (the inevitable) traffic. There is currently no bus or train service to Lubec.

Inland Maine

BAXTER STATE PARK

Mount Katahdin, the 5,267-foot peak at the heart of this thickly forested park, is more than Maine's tallest mountain. It's the northern terminus of the epic, 2,200-mile Appalachian Trail, a summit whose bare, rocky ridges have long inspired adventurers and dreamers alike. In the Abenaki language of the Penobscot people, Katahdin means "The Greatest Mountain," and it looms large in Maine history. After trying (unsuccessfully) to reach the summit in 1846, Henry David Thoreau wrote about Katahdin's terrible beauty, which generations since have often compared to New Hampshire's Mount Washington. While the New Hampshire peak cranes more than 1,000 feet above Katahdin, this is the wilder of the two—no trains or roads to the summit, just a winding, rocky footpath that makes every visitor earn their views.

Visiting the Park

Day-trippers fill up the lots in Baxter State Park, and while it's a wonderful outing, spending a night within the park's boundaries is the best way to experience the silence and scale of the Maine woods. Above all, it's worth planning ahead, as the park is extremely popular. Some forethought means you can book your parking spot in advance and sleep in one of the sought-after campsites with views to the peak. There is no cell phone service in the park.

ENTRANCES AND VISITORS CENTER

There are two entrances to Baxter State Park. If you're traveling from Millinocket, you'll follow Baxter Park Road to the **Togue Pond Gate,** which is by far the most visited, while the northernmost traffic is funneled through **Matagamon Gate** on Grand Lake Road. While information and maps are available at both gates, the only **visitors center** is on the road to Togue Pond Gate—a full 42-mile drive from the other entrance. Hours vary, call the **reservation line** for details (207/723-5140). Admission to the park is $15.

RESERVATIONS

Unless you're feeling lucky, camping reservations are essential, though last-minute arrivals can sometimes be accommodated at the gate. In addition to the **reservation line** (207/723-5140), it's also possible to reserve parking spots in the day-use lot online, ensuring you won't be turned away upon arrival (www.baxterstatepark.org).

Hiking

While Mount Katahdin is the heart of the park, there are 200 miles of trail to explore, including day hikes that are far easier than the strenuous trek to the summit. One favorite is the **Daicey Pond Nature Trail,** beginning at the Daicey Pond Campground. The 1.4-mile loop circles the pond and coincides with the Appalachian Trail. For catching a moose in its favorite hangout, head to **Sandy Stream Pond,** a 0.5 mile hike from **Roaring Brook Campground.** To give the moose the space and quiet they need, access to the pond is limited: Arrive early at Togue Pond Gate for one of the first come, first served **"moose passes"** that are dispensed to hikers.

★ MOUNT KATAHDIN

If you're planning to take on **Mount Katahdin,** it's essential to be prepared—hikers have died on the peak, and many more have been rescued in operations that endanger park staff. The mountain can be summited as a super-strenuous 10.4-mile round-trip day hike from the **Katahdin Stream Campground,** climbing the Hunt Trail to great views of **Katahdin Stream Falls,** across a series of open ledges, and up a final stretch to the summit, which you might share with some celebrating thru-hikers who've just arrived after months on the trail. Plan between 8 and 12 hours for the round-trip hike.

There are a handful of ways on and off the mountain, and one great option is to make an overnight trip by hiking in to the backcountry **Chimney Pond Campground,** spending the night, then rising early for the summit trek. For experienced, strong hikers who don't mind some exposure and scrambling, walking the spectacular **Knife Edge** is surely New England's most dramatic stretch of "trail." The rocky ridge loops southeast from the summit of Katahdin, then curves back north toward Chimney Pond. It's impassible in bad weather, as it's just a walk across the bare rocks, and the tiring descent to Chimney Pond means climbing from one mammoth boulder to the next.

Food

There are no services or restaurants within the park. Approaching from the south, the last services are at the **North Woods Trading Post** (1605 Baxter State Park Rd., Millinocket, 207/723-4326, www.nwoodstradingpost.com, hours vary, call first), which sells gas, camping fuel, and basic groceries. All other restaurants are located in Millinocket, a 30-minute drive from the southern park entrance.

Perfect for a big breakfast before heading into the woods (or a hearty, post-trail lunch), the **Appalachian Trail Café** (210 Penobscot Ave., Millinocket, 207/723-6720, 5am-4pm daily, $4-12) is a favorite for hefty servings and a friendly, small-town atmosphere. This is the land of eggs and fresh hash, juicy burgers, and enormous mounds of fries, but the luxurious bread pudding wins raves.

Blessed with a great location on Millinocket Lake, **River Drivers Restaurant & Pub** (New England Outdoor Center, 30 Twin Pines Rd., Millinocket, 207/723-4528, www.neoc.com, 11am-9pm Mon.-Fri., 7am-9pm Sat.-Sun., $12-34) serves a more grown-up version of post-trail food, from haddock roulade to ribeye steak. Breakfasts are hearty burritos and egg sandwiches, and the Friday fish fry dinner special is a blast (and an excellent deal).

With pizza, beer, and the occasional bonfire out back, **Boatman's Bar & Grill** (10 Medway Rd., Millinocket, 207/723-3200, www.threeriversfun.com, 4pm-11pm daily, reduced hours in spring and fall, call first, $7-18) is run by a local river guiding operation, and if you can catch them while they're serving food, it's a rowdy way to ease back into civilization.

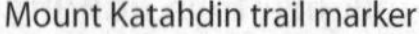

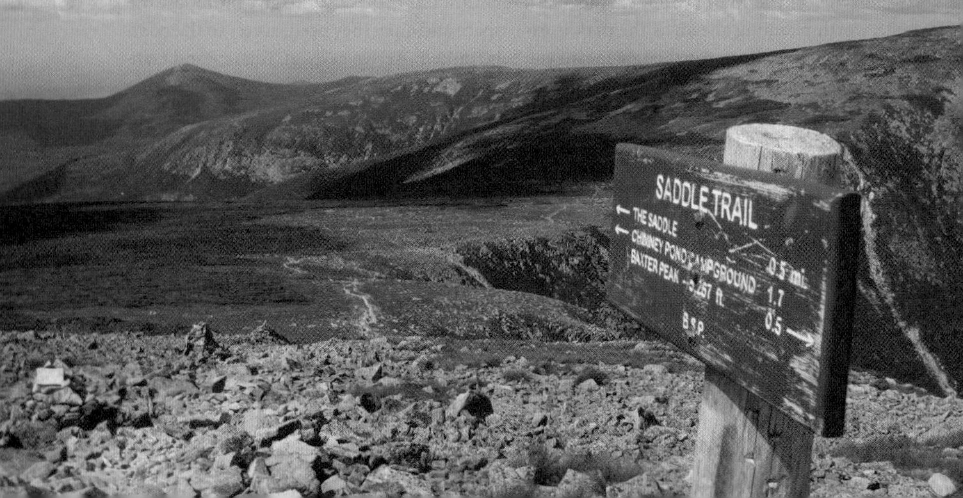

Mount Katahdin trail marker

Accommodations and Camping

Anyone not ready to set up camp can find digs in the town of Millinocket, 30 minutes south of the park's Togue Pond Gate entrance.

With rustic, basic rooms and a friendly, summer camp-like atmosphere, the **Appalachian Trail Lodge** (33 Penobscot Ave., Millinocket, 207/723-4321, www.appalachiantraillodge.com, bunks $25, shared-bath private rooms $35-55, en suite $95-105) is the place to rub shoulders with the thru-hiker set. If you just want to clean up on your way out of the park, the lodge offers showers for $5 a pop, including towels and soap.

In an old-fashioned house downtown, the **Young House Bed and Breakfast** (193 Central St., Millinocket, 207/723-5452, www.theyounghousebnb.com, $115-135) is cozy and friendly, and the big front porch is great for relaxing after a day of exploring. The hosts serve a big and hearty breakfast, and they're able to pack lighter breakfasts to go if you're rising early for a hike.

CAMPING

There are 11 campgrounds within the park, both front-country and backcountry versions. None of the campgrounds has treated water, so visitors must bring their own, or come prepared to treat the natural sources. Toilets are outhouses, and there are no showers. Visitors with a camping reservation must check in at the gate before 8:30pm. To book campgrounds, call the park's **reservation line** (207/723-5140). Campground tent sites are $32, backcountry spots are $21, and rustic cabins are available from $57 (bring your own bedding).

On the northern end of the park, **South Branch Pond Campground** is among the prettiest, with some lean-tos right at the edge of the water. The pond is excellent for swimming, and the campground lends out canoes and kayaks for a nominal $1 fee.

Earn an excellent night's sleep on your way to **Chimney Pond Campground,** a 3.2-mile walk from the Roaring Brook trailhead. Campers have wonderful views across the pond to the Katahdin summit, and it's perfectly placed for hiking the peak.

Information and Services

The **Baxter State Park** website (www.baxterstatepark.com) covers all the basics, with maps and reservation information, but hard copies of maps are available to purchase at the park entrances. There are several banks with ATMs on the main drag in Millinocket, as well as a handful of grocery stores, including **Hannaford Supermarket** (843 Central St., 207/723-8047, 7am-9pm Mon.-Sat., 8am-8pm Sun.).

Getting There

Baxter State Park is accessed by Baxter State Park Road, and the closest town is Millinocket; the park is 1.5 hours from Bangor. There is no public transit to the park.

Background

The Landscape

Covering just over 70,000 square miles, the six states that make up New England could be squeezed into North Dakota. Within that area, however, the region contains a multitude of landforms and habitats. The coastline runs from the sandy beaches of Connecticut and Rhode Island to Cape Cod's barrier beaches, then hardens into the granite headlands that splinter the coasts of New Hampshire and Maine. In between, the land rolls through fertile farms, deep pine forests, and mountains covered with old-growth oaks and maples, but the human geography is just as varied, from the densely populated urban corridor that surrounds Boston to Maine and Vermont, among the most rural states in America.

GEOLOGY

New England's weather can seem defined by extremes—steamy summers, freezing winters—but modern-day temperatures have nothing on the fire and ice that first shaped the region. Fire came first, in the form of molten lava that bubbled up violently from the earth's core starting some half a billion years ago. At that time, most of what would become New England was underwater, just off the leading edge of a proto-continent known as Laurentia. As the tectonic plate that held Laurentia moved slowly eastward, it folded under its neighbor and melted, causing an upwelling of magma beneath the surface of the ocean. That upwelling formed a chain of island peaks off the coast of the continent. Eventually, the land mass of Laurentia crashed into these islands during the Ordovician era around 440 million years ago, pushing them up into what is now the Taconic Mountains of far western Massachusetts and southwestern Vermont.

About 100 million years later, in the Devonian era, Laurentia crashed into a subcontinent called Avalonia to the south, rolling over the smaller landmass to create more upwelling of magma. At the same time, the continent collided with its neighboring continent Baltica—the precursor to Europe—causing the ocean floor between them to buckle and fold back over the continent. The combination created the Berkshire Hills, which have backbones of volcanic rock topped with older "basement rock" of gneiss and quartz that once sat on the floor of the sea. The ocean, meanwhile, was squeezed out over Avalonia to create a vast delta of sedimentary rock that now forms the bulk of eastern Connecticut, Rhode Island, and eastern Massachusetts. A bit later, during the Triassic period, a great fault opened up in the middle of the region, creating a 100-mile-long rift valley that would later become the Connecticut River.

At this time, all of the world's continents briefly joined together in a giant landmass called Pangaea. The commingling didn't last long, however. By the Jurassic era, 200 million years ago, the continents were again on the move, and North America and Europe split up to create the Atlantic Ocean. Around the same time, a field of volcanoes opened up in the area of New Hampshire, spewing hot magma in plutons and ring dikes to form the massive granite peaks of the White Mountains. The Whites are the youngest mountains in the region, and the last evidence of volcanic activity, which ended about 130 million years ago. New England's fiery birth was followed by a long period of erosion and settling before fire handed off its job to ice, and the last great ice age began.

Previous: visiting Acadia National Park at Bar Harbor; replica of the *Mayflower* at Plimouth Plantation in Massachusetts.

Temperatures began to cool gradually about a million years ago. By the Pleistocene era, some 80,000 years ago (a mere hiccup in geological time), a massive ice sheet began to build up over Canada, more than a mile thick in places. As it did, the sheer weight of the ice caused it to flow southward in a huge glacier, leveling the earth, gouging out valleys, and breaking off mountaintops as it flowed. The farthest glacier reached all the way down to New York City, depositing millions of tons of rocks in a terminal moraine that today forms Long Island, Block Island, Martha's Vineyard, and Nantucket. (Since so much of the earth's water was tied up in ice, sea levels were lower, and all of those islands were once mountains.) A more intense, but less far-reaching, glacier left a second terminal moraine around 20,000 years ago to form the northern spur of Long Island, along with Cape Cod and the Elizabeth Islands.

While the terminal moraines are the most visible result of the glaciers, all of New England was definitively shaped by the ice, which rolled and ebbed across the region for thousands of years. Mountains were pushed over and broken, so that even today in the Whites, the northern slopes offer more gradual ascents for hikers, while the steep southern faces present grueling challenges for rock climbers. Mountaintops and boulders, meanwhile, were picked up by the advancing ice sheet and often deposited miles away from their origins. In some places, these huge glacial boulders, also known as erratics, have become local landmarks, such as the 5,000-ton Madison Boulder in New Hampshire's lake region, the largest erratic in New England.

The glaciers changed the land in other ways as well. As it advanced, the ice sheet pushed away the softer substrate, exposing the harder, immovable granite. In many places, lone mountains called "monadnocks" remain to lord over the surrounding plains. The most famous of these is Mount Monadnock in southern New Hampshire, whose views as far as Boston on a clear day make it an irresistible magnet for hikers. In Rhode Island, the advancing ice gouged away the softer substrate in Narragansett Bay to expose granite islands, including the island on which Newport is located and from which the state gets its name.

The last of the glaciers retreated by 15,000 years ago. In their wake, however, the Connecticut River Valley was closed off and filled with meltwater to create a huge inland lake named Lake Hitchcock. For more than 2,000 years, the lake stretched 200 miles from Connecticut to Vermont's Northeast Kingdom. (It was probably quite a sight, colored the striking azure blue of the glacial lakes that now grace Canada and Patagonia.) The layers of silt deposited by the drying lake helped create the rich, loamy soil of Massachusetts's Pioneer Valley—which stands in marked contrast to the rocky, glacial till of the rest of New England. Another glacial lake, Lake Vermont, formed to the west of New England, and drained into modern-day Lake Champlain.

Other land features marked by glaciers include long, straight grooves in the earth known as glacial scarring; teardrop-shaped hills called drumlins, which are especially common in Rhode Island and southeastern Massachusetts; and round depressions known as kettle holes, which were caused by standing water from glacial melt drilling down into the earth—now beloved as excellent swimming holes.

CLIMATE

A location on the dividing line between the cold polar air mass to the north and the warm tropical air currents from the south brings dramatic temperature changes and some climatic surprises. Add a constant supply of moisture from the ocean, and you are guaranteed an unpredictable mix. Despite the regular precipitation, however, New England sees more than its fair share of clear days, when the sky is blue and you can see for miles from the peak of Mount Washington. Moreover, the moderating effect of the warm Gulf Stream ocean currents ensures that New England doesn't see the same extremes of temperature that affect the middle part of the country. Both summers and winters are comparatively mild—though it might not seem that way in the middle of a frigid January cold snap or the sweltering dog days of August.

The coldest part of the year is in January, when the region's temperature averages 21 degrees Fahrenheit, but it can easily sink to 20 below zero for days at a time. That snap of extreme cold is often followed by a period of milder weather known as the January thaw, which sets the stage for February, when the region sees the bulk of its snowfall. The number and severity of winter storms vary with the wind. The hardest hitters come when a zone of low pressure sits off to the east, bringing cold, wet air counterclockwise down from the Maritimes to form a classic nor'easter. Spend much time in the region, and you are bound to hear about the famous Blizzard of '78, a nor'easter that buried areas in up to five feet of snow and caused rises in tides of up to 15 feet.

When winter begins to taper off, the frozen ground melts into a soggy mess, what folks in New Hampshire, Vermont, and western Massachusetts call "mud season." Not that early spring is entirely charmless—this is the time to visit if you want to taste maple syrup fresh from the evaporating pan. The cycle of cold nights and warming days might make for hazardous back road driving, but it's what drives the pump-like action of maple trees, drawing sap into the trunk where it's collected in buckets or tubes.

Following mud season, the world breaks into bloom, with wildflowers poking up from the barren forest floor and lilacs scenting the air. Before you know it, though, summer arrives in all its sweltering glory. Average temperatures only reach 70 degrees, though, so the hottest stretches of 90-degree weather rarely last longer than a few weeks at a time.

Finally, after Labor Day comes many New Englanders' favorite season—fall. The days are crisp but not yet cold, and the air is often dry and pleasantly breezy. As the green chlorophyll leeches out of the tree leaves, it leaves the spectacular reds, oranges, and yellows of New England's star attraction—its famed fall foliage. Not that this season is without its perils, however. While hurricanes aren't as common here as in southern states, every few years in August or September a humdinger speeds over the Gulf Stream and crashes into the Connecticut or Rhode Island coast.

Of course, the foregoing describes a typical year in central New England. Keep in mind that the region stretches 400 miles from the Canadian border to Long Island Sound—the same distance roughly between New York City and Columbia, South Carolina. Correspondingly, temperatures can vary as much as 20 degrees or more from north to south. Boston, for example, averages a high of 36 for January and a high of 82 for July. Compare that to Caribou in far northern Maine, which averages a high of just 19 in January and just 76 in July. Adventurer Ranulph Fiennes once noted that "there's no bad weather, only inappropriate clothing"—and that's certainly true in New England.

Plants and Animals

PLANTS

Accustomed to the denuded European landscape, early settlers to New England were bowled over by the deep forests full of timber and game as far as the eye could see. Soaring pines, stretching oaks, and stately chestnuts filled the new land, prompting superlatives in many a Puritan's travel journal. While centuries of lumbering have taken their toll on the woods of the region, much of New England is still appealingly forested. In recent decades, abandoned farms have been reclaimed by the trees, creating even more wooded landscape. And unlike clear-cut land out West, the North Woods of Maine have for centuries been home to sustainable logging practices that have kept the wilderness wild.

Trees

Traditionally, the forests of the region have been divided into three zones: an oak-chestnut forest in Connecticut, Rhode Island, and far eastern Massachusetts; a hemlock-white pine-transition hardwood forest in central and western Massachusetts, southern New Hampshire, Vermont, and Maine; and a spruce-northern hardwood forest in northern New Hampshire, Vermont, and Maine. Of course, this greatly simplifies a landscape in which 50 different species of trees each has its own range and habitat—but it does provide a good working framework for understanding local fauna.

Chestnuts roasting on an open fire may have been part of the holidays for early New Englanders, but those days are sadly gone. After surviving in New England for millions of years, the mighty chestnut was wiped out by a blight imported from Japan in the early part of the 20th century. The forests of southern and eastern New England, however, are still abundant with red oak, scarlet oak, hickory, maple, birch, and beech. In the wetlands of Rhode Island and southeastern Massachusetts, the landscape is dominated by red maple and Atlantic white cedar, which thrives in swampy ground. Along the coast, larger trees give way to hardy pitch pine and scrub oak more suited to salty air and sandy soils.

Central New England has a good mix of broadleaf trees and evergreens. The forest here is dominated by oak and maple—including the famous sugar maple that yields the region's annual crop of maple syrup every spring. The most common tree is the white oak, named for the color of its bark and prized both for its straight timber and wide-spreading canopy. Arguably, this is the best region for leaf-peeping, since maples produce some of the brightest colors, while oaks are slower to turn, extending the season and providing a range of colors at any one time. White pine becomes more common as you travel north, where it can frequently be found growing on reclaimed agricultural land. That tree has smoother bark than its cousin, the red or Norway pine; to tell them apart, count the needles: White pines grow in clusters of five (W-H-I-T-E), while red grow in clusters of three (R-E-D). Other trees growing in this region include hemlock and ash.

In the Great North Woods of northern New England, the deciduous trees eventually give way to endless tracts of boreal forest, consisting of spruce and fir. Unlike pines, whose needles grow in clusters, spruce and fir needles are directly attached to the stem. These coniferous trees are better suited to the short growing season and nutrient-poor soil of Maine, and they've provided an endless source of timber for shipbuilding and fuel. Mixed in with the evergreens is an understory of hardy broadleaf trees, including aspen, beech, and birch. Few New England scenes are more iconic than a stand of white-and-black-striped birch trees in winter, or festooned with canary yellow leaves in fall.

Flowers

The jewel of the New England woodlands is the delicate lady slipper, a member of the orchid family that grows in wetland areas and gets its name from down-curving flowers that resemble women's shoes. The translucent flower, found in pink, white, and yellow varieties, is notoriously difficult to transplant or grow, since it relies on companionable fungi in the soil for its nutrients. If you are lucky enough to see one in the wild, take care not to disturb it, since some species are endangered, and some are even illegal to pick in Massachusetts.

Much more common, if no less beloved by naturalists, is trillium, so called because of its distinctive three-petal flowers. The flower grows in many colors throughout the New England woods, including bright white, deep red, and the particularly beautiful painted trillium, which sports a magenta center tapering off to white edges. One of the first flowers to bloom in April is the bloodroot, which carpets the ground with clusters of white flowers. As the season progresses, other wildflowers visible in the fields and meadows include the fuchsia-colored, anemone-like New England aster; orange clusters of wood poppy; wild bleeding heart; bright-red wild columbine with its distinctive tubelike flowers; and the ghostly sharp-lobed hepatica, which grows in deep woods and swamps and features eight blue-purple petals arranged around an explosion of fine white stamens.

ANIMALS

The best opportunities for seeing wildlife in New England occur along the water. Many animal tours offer chances to see seals and seabirds off the New England coast. Even inland, you are much more apt to stumble upon a moose or black bear from the vantage of a kayak than hiking along a trail. Most of New England's fauna is harmless—the charismatic megafauna of the western states has been mostly hunted to extinction, despite dubious reports of mountain lion sightings that crop up periodically. Even so, use caution when approaching a moose or black bear—especially if its young are in the area. You don't want to get on the receiving end of antlers or claws.

Land Mammals

Up to 6 feet tall, 9 feet long, and with an antler span of 5.5 feet, a bull moose often startles those unprepared for just how *big* it is. It has the air of a gentle giant, but moose can certainly be dangerous, and it's worth giving them a very wide berth, whether you're on foot or in a vehicle. Signs all over New Hampshire and Maine warn drivers about "moose crossings," since countless times each season a car is totaled after hitting one of the 1,500-pound beasts. Take care when driving in those regions at dawn and dusk, especially during the spring and summer months, when the giant animals range widely in search of food. In the autumn, moose retreat to the deep forest, where they are much harder to encounter.

Not quite as imposing are the white-tailed deer that are common in the backwoods of all six states. In some places, such as the island of Nantucket, deer are so plentiful that they have even become a nuisance. The last documented specimen of mountain lion—also called catamount—was taken in Maine in 1938, and the giant cat is generally accepted to be extinct from the region. Every year, however, there are some 100 supposed mountain lion sightings; among the most credible was one in 2009 by a Fish and Game employee outside Concord, New Hampshire. None of the sightings to date, however, have yielded any tracks, fur, or scat that would definitely confirm that mountain lions are back in the region, leaving their fabled existence on par with UFOs or Sasquatch. The smaller bobcat, however, is quite commonly sighted, often mistaken for a small dog. And in far northern New Hampshire and Maine, hikers even occasionally spot the slightly bigger lynx, identifiable by the pointed tufts on its ears.

Not to be confused with the more aggressive grizzlies of western states, the timid black bear is a reclusive tree-inhabiting animal that can sometimes be seen exploring garbage dumps of northern New England at night. Red foxes inhabit both open fields and mixed forest, while the larger gray fox prefers the deep woods of southern New England. Coyotes are more apt to be heard than seen. And gray wolves make only rare visits to northern Maine from their habitat in Canada. No breeding populations currently exist in the region.

The most common mammals, by far, are rodents, which exist in multitudes throughout the six-state area. Gray and red squirrels, chipmunks, and raccoons are familiar sights in both suburban and rural areas. Wilderness locales are home to skunk, marten, mink, ermine, seven types of shrew, three types of mole, mouse, rabbit (including cottontail, jackrabbit, and snowshoe hare), flying squirrel, beaver, vole, otter, and porcupine. One of the lesser-known rodents is the fisher, a large mink-like animal known for its vicious temperament that has become more common in past years. In addition to smaller rodents, it's been known to prey on raccoons, porcupines, and even small deer. Finally, New England is home to nine different species of bat, which roost in abandoned barns and trees, and can often be heard screeching at night in search of insects to eat.

Reptiles and Amphibians

The streams and ponds of New England thrive with frogs, toads, turtles, and other amphibians. Anyone who has camped near standing water in New England is familiar with the deep-throated sound of the bullfrog, which can seem like competing bullhorns at night as the eight-inch-long males puff up their resonant throat sacks in competition for mates. An even more cherished sound in parts of New England is the high-pitched chirping of the spring peeper frogs, which heralds the beginning of warm weather. A dozen different types of turtle inhabit the area; most common is the painted turtle, which sports colorful mosaics of yellow stripes on its neck and shell. More rare is the common snapping turtle, which can live up to its name if provoked. Wetland areas and swamps are also home to many species of salamander, which outdo each other with arresting shades of red, blue, and yellow spots and stripes. The most striking of all is the Day-Glo orange body of the red-spotted newt.

The most typically encountered snake is the common garter snake, a black-and-green-striped snake that is ubiquitous throughout the region, even on offshore islands. Aquatic habitats are inhabited by ribbon snakes and the large northern water snake, which is harmless despite its aggressive demeanor. Woodland habitats are home to the eastern hognose, ringneck, and milk snake, among other species. Only two types of snake in New England are venomous. The northern copperhead is a yellow color with brown diamond-shaped markings on its back; it is extremely rare, located only in the lower Connecticut River Valley and coastal region of Connecticut, with another small population around Plymouth, Massachusetts. The timber rattler is even more rare, existing only in remote, isolated pockets in New Hampshire, Vermont, Massachusetts, and Connecticut. Thankfully, rattlers tend to shun areas inhabited by humans—and hibernate a full eight months out of the year, from September to April. If hiking in the backcountry of the Berkshires or Taconics, however, be wary of their distinctive dry rattling sound.

Insects and Arachnids

Ask any New Englander about native insects, and he's apt to immediately identify two: the mosquito and the blackfly. The former find ample breeding ground in the wetlands of the region and feast annually on the blood of hikers and beachgoers. The blackfly is, if anything, even more vicious. Thankfully it is more limited in both range and time period, thriving only in the late spring and early summer in northern New England. The other regional scourge is the gypsy moth, which every 10 years or so appears in the form of thousands of tiny caterpillars that decimate the foliage. Many attempts have been made to curtail the menace, including introduction of a parasitic fly that eats gypsy moth larvae. Unfortunately, the fly also eats larvae of the luna moth, a delicate greenish moth with a wingspan of up to five inches that is New England's most beautiful insect. In recent years, the luna moth has made a comeback, and it is a more common nighttime visitor in the region.

Due to all the variations in habitat, New England is a rich breeding ground for creepy-crawlies, most of which are absolutely harmless. There are more spiders in New York and New England than there are bird species in all of North America. The only poisonous variety, however, is the black widow, which is recognizable by its jet-black body with a broken red hourglass on its abdomen. These spiders are extremely rare, and while their venom is a neurotoxin, only about 1 percent of bites end in death.

Sealife

Cape Cod didn't get its name for nothing; early settlers to New England were overwhelmed by its rich fishing stocks, thanks to the shallow-water glacial deposits of Stellwagen Bank north of Cape Cod and Georges Bank south of Nantucket. Both are rich breeding grounds for cod, stripers, bluefish, and other species. They are also popular stopovers for migratory whale species, including humpback, fin, mike, and North American right whales. Other visitors to New England's oceans include white-sided and bottlenose dolphins, harbor porpoises, leatherback sea turtles, and grey seals, which are especially prevalent on Cape Cod in summer. Despite the filming of *Jaws* on Martha's Vineyard, great white sharks are rare; boaters and divers are more apt to see a harmless basking shark, which likes to feed on surface plankton.

Closer to shore, the most popular animal is the New England clam, of which there are two varieties: the soft-shelled clam or steamer, and the hard-shelled clam or quahog, which is also known as littleneck or cherrystone depending on its size, and is generally found in deeper waters. Tidepoolers are apt to encounter both rock crabs and hermit crabs, along with sea stars, urchins, and periwinkle snails. New England's most famous sea dweller, the lobster, inhabits deep, rocky underwater coves all over the eastern United States. Ninety percent of lobsters, however, are found in Massachusetts, Rhode Island, and Maine. Contrary to popular belief, they are usually brown, blue, or green in color, and only turn red upon cooking. The biggest lobster ever caught was over two feet long and weighed almost 40 pounds.

Birds

New England's location on the Atlantic Flyway from Canada makes the region prime bird-watching country. The region is home to some 200 species of birds that breed, winter, or live year-round in the region. Some common species like the black-and-white chickadee, blue jay, and cardinal are spotted commonly in both rural and urban areas. Others, like the elusive wood thrush, inhabit only the deep forest, where its liquid warblings reward hikers with a mellifluous serenade. Likewise, the ghostly "laughing" of the common loon is a regular sound on lakes in Maine, where the bird also graces the state license plate. Several decades ago, bald eagles were introduced into the cliffs around the Quabbin Reservoir in central Massachusetts; now there are some 40 of the birds in the area, making them a relatively common sight for hikers and boaters.

Likewise, efforts have been made to preserve the coastal breeding grounds of 30 species of shorebirds, including plovers, sandpipers, and oystercatchers. Seabirds that are commonly seen near land include sea ducks, gulls, terns, and cormorants, while farther out to sea, boaters can spy petrels, puffins, jaegers, and auks. Many of the area's wildlife refuges have active communities of bird-watchers who track recurring species on both land and water.

ENVIRONMENTAL ISSUES

The biggest issue in southern New England is urban sprawl, caused by the region's increasing population coupled with a lack of developable space. The home-rule governments in much of New England routinely squelch any larger regional planning initiatives, along with so-called smart growth plans that would cluster population around town centers and public transit. As a result, much of the area around Boston is hampered by a lack of affordable housing and an encroachment on open space that has caused tensions between developers and conservationists. (That may slowly change, however, as Massachusetts has finally pushed through the first major reforms to its zoning laws in 30 years, requiring every town to have a master plan to manage growth.)

At the same time, species that were once seen only in the deep woods have been increasingly spotted in the suburbs, where foxes, coyotes, fishers and other animals have posed a threat to family pets. In northern New England, it is not urban sprawl but tourist development that has threatened the wide tracts of open space. With the decline of the timber industry, which generally had a good relationship with outdoorsmen and environmentalists, residents of Maine and New Hampshire have looked for new sources of income from the tourist trade, and struck uneasy bargains to preserve some tracts of land while developing others for roads and resorts.

New England's regulatory economy has ensured that much of the area enjoys clean air and water, even as efforts have been made to clean up the pollution of the mills and factories that boosted the economy in the 20th century. Isolated chemical factories and power plants continue to cause problems in some specific areas. One of the country's first nuclear power plants was commissioned at Seabrook in coastal New Hampshire, which became the site of a protest in the late 1970s that sparked the national movement against nuclear power. Despite that protest and periodic rumblings by environmentalists, Seabrook is still an operating power plant and a tourist destination to boot.

One of the most contentious ongoing issues in the region is the controversy over how to effectively manage the coastal stock of fish and shellfish. Rampant overfishing had decimated the stock of cod, flounder, and other groundfish species by the mid-1980s. At that point, the federal government seized the entire region's fisheries and began a desperate bid to restore populations using quotas and periodic bans. While the effort has been successful at restoring some species, such as haddock and bluefish, others still languish at severely reduced levels—with cod even less plentiful than in the 1980s. And along with the fish stocks, many fishermen have languished as well. Tensions between fishermen and regulators have led to angry protests and outright flouting of quotas, as well as disputes over the numbers used by scientists and environmentalists to justify them. At this point, the two sides are cooperating in an uneasy peace. And while New England's fishing community is nowhere near as vibrant as it once was, it has nevertheless managed to survive.

History

EARLY HISTORY

Native Inhabitants

Hard on the heels of the last glaciers retreating northward, humans began to move into the area now known as New England about 10,000 years ago. By the time European settlers began to poke around the coasts, there were already anywhere from 25,000 to 100,000 Native Americans inhabiting the region. Unlike the Iroquois Confederacy in upstate New York or the mighty Algonquain tribes of Quebec, however, most New England tribes were small and unaffiliated with larger governments, making them both extremely mobile and vulnerable to manipulation and extermination by European settlers.

In southern New England, tribes such as Wampanoags, Narragansetts, and Pequots grew corn, beans, squash, tobacco, and other crops to supplement hunting and fishing. Most extraordinary is the way the groups cultivated the forest itself, burning wide swaths to get rid of the undergrowth and allow park-like land that was ideal for hunting game and harvesting berries—it was said that in the colonial era, it was possible to ride a horse through the forest at a full gallop, as the trees were widely spaced and free of brush. Anyone who's tried to thwack their way up a trail-less mountain knows that times have changed.

North of the Saco River in Maine, tribes such as the Micmacs, Abenakis, Penobscots, and Passamaquoddys were more nomadic by nature, subsisting entirely on hunting, fishing, and gathering. In the spring, they made use of fishing grounds on the coast for shellfish and birds; in the summer, they moved inland to ply the rivers with birch-bark canoes in search of larger game like elk and moose.

Early Visitors

Viking long ships might have sailed the rivers of New England as early as the 11th century; if they did, however, they left no traces to definitively prove it. Instead, legends of Norse visitors from Iceland and Greenland remain just that—legends—supplemented only by highly dubious reports of "discoveries" of Viking rune stones in areas of the Maine and Massachusetts coast. As late as the 1950s, however, historians also doubted that Vikings had colonized Newfoundland—until a settlement was unearthed there in 1960. This settlement was thought by many to be Vinland, a land mentioned in the Viking sagas as founded by Erik the Red west of Greenland. Others, however, have noted that grapes don't grow that far north and instead surmise that the actual location of Vinland is farther south in New England, perhaps on Cape Cod or in the area of Popham Beach, Maine.

The first documented European mariner to spy the New England coast was Giovanni da Verrazano, who sailed up from New York in 1524 and explored Block Island and Narragansett Bay, and rounded Cape Cod to Maine before returning to France. The first settlements in the region, however, didn't come until a half century later, when Bartholomew Gosnold formed a small outpost southeast of Cape Cod (which he named) on what is now Cuttyhunk Island in 1602. That settlement was abandoned, however, when the explorers returned home in the winter.

To the north, French captain Samuel de Champlain sailed along the coast of Maine and New Hampshire, gave his name to Lake Champlain in 1609, and founded several small fur-trading settlements north of New England along the St. Lawrence River in Quebec. Other settlements followed down the coast, mostly small French and English fishing villages on the islands and peninsulas of the Maine coast, which were also abandoned when holds were filled with enough salt cod or beaver pelts to make a profitable crossing back to Europe.

Feeling Blue?

There's a reason we call them Puritans. The early inhabitants of New England had one of the strictest codes of laws known to man. And just a glance through their annals could leave one with the impression that they were originators of modern sadomasochism as well. Punishments regularly doled out included whipping, dunking, hanging, and forcing lawbreakers to stand for hours in the stocks—not necessarily in that order. The first few laws listed in their 1647 law book are nothing if not consistent. Having false gods: death. Witchcraft: death. Conspiracy: death. Murder: death. Poisoning, kidnapping, sodomy, bestiality: death. Talking back to your parents after you turn 16: death (a fun fact to share with your kids during vacation). In 1692, laws were passed against "unnecessary and unseasonable" walking in the streets on Sundays, being French, and using witchcraft to "entertain, employ, feed, or reward any evil and wicked spirit." Just in case anyone was still having fun, the civic fathers in 1711 made it illegal to sing, dance, fiddle, pipe, or use a musical instrument at night. In 1787, a law was passed to jail pipers, fiddlers, runaways, and "stubborn children." The part about stubborn children wasn't deleted until 1973. While most of these colonial prohibitions have long since disappeared, some have survived in the form of so-called **blue laws** that still put the damper on fun. Connecticut, for example, still has laws against buying or selling alcohol on Sunday. In Massachusetts, "happy hour" drink specials are forbidden. And then there are the early bar closing times (by 1 or 2am in Boston) that have rankled generations of New England college students. They should just be happy they weren't born in 1650!

Pilgrims and Puritans

In the end, it was spiritual rather than commercial desires that established a European foothold in New England. After years of fighting between Catholics and Protestants in England, Queen Elizabeth I passed the Act of Uniformity in 1559, making it illegal not to attend official Church of England services. Throughout the next few decades, an increasingly persecuted minority of separatists advocated a break with the official church. After several of their leaders were executed, the separatists fled to Holland in 1608. But the Netherlands alliance with England against Spain meant that persecutions continued there, and the separatists eventually hatched a plan to journey beyond the reach of the Queen by founding a colony in the New World. They received backing from the Virginia Company to set sail aboard the *Mayflower* in 1620.

The Pilgrims, as they would later be called, originally intended to set sail for the nascent colony of Jamestown in Virginia. Blown off course, however, they landed in what is now Plymouth, Massachusetts, outside of the jurisdiction of their backers. Before disembarking, they drafted the Mayflower Compact, a hastily arranged document that established the government of their new Plymouth Bay Colony. The primary author of the document, Rev. William Bradford, became governor. Of the 102 passengers aboard ship, almost half of them were not Pilgrims at all, but adventurers who hitched a ride to the New World, including the capable Captain Myles Standish, hired to be military commander for the colony. His skills were not initially needed, since Wampanoag people under their chief, Massasoit, were friendly to the new colonists, helping them plant corn and hunt. The cold and scarcity of resources took a harsh toll on the colonists, however, causing more than half to die in the first year. By the time Bradford called for celebration of the first Thanksgiving in the fall of 1621, he was thanking God not only for the bountiful harvest, but also for the colony's very survival.

The real settlement of New England didn't begin until the arrival a decade later of another band of religious seekers, the Puritans. Unlike the Pilgrims, the Puritans did not advocate a complete break from the Church of England. Rather, they believed the church could be reformed from within by returning to a stricter interpretation of the Bible and dispensing with many of the trappings and rituals that the Church of England had picked up from Catholicism. An increasingly dictatorial King Charles I, however, abolished parliament and began cracking down on any religion that didn't subscribe to the official tenets of the Church of England. In 1629, settlers under minister and orator John Winthrop decided to leave England altogether to found a new "shining city on a hill" that would serve as a paragon of morality to the rest of the world.

The following year, 1630, a full complement of eleven ships carrying more than 1,000 passengers landed on the tip of Cape Cod near Provincetown. Finding scarce resources, they moved on to land on another small peninsula that the Native Americans called Shawmut, or "Land of Living Waters," due to the teeming schools of fish in its harbor. There they resolved to found their city, which they named Boston, after the city in East Anglia where many of them had originated.

Boston wasn't exactly uninhabited—the first English settler of the peninsula was Rev. William Blackstone, a hermit who came there alone around 1623 and built a house by a freshwater spring beneath three hills he called the "trimountain." But he was happy to sell the land to the new arrivals, and Winthrop and his crew declared Boston the new capital of the Massachusetts Bay Colony in 1632. Immediately, they proceeded to enforce a strict moral code that imposed death as punishment for crimes ranging from taking the Lord's name in vain to talking back to your parents. From that center, colonists quickly spread out north and west to form dozens of new cities and towns, fueled by waves of thousands of new immigrants over the next decade. The settlement of New England had officially begun.

More Settlers Arrive

At the same time that the Pilgrims and Puritans were settling Massachusetts, a hardier band of hunters and woodsmen finally established beachheads in northern New England. English aristocrat Sir Ferdinando Gorges established the Council of New England in 1621 and began making land grants and sending groups to hunt and fish the area. An early grant called the Laconia Company spanned the Merrimack and Kennebec Rivers north of Massachusetts Bay. While the company was disbanded a few years later, many of the settlers remained, forming a loose confederation of parishes in what would later become New Hampshire and Maine. In 1624, they sent the first shipment of white pine to England, starting what would later become a rich trade in lumber for ships' masts.

Meanwhile, as the persecuted Puritans became themselves persecutors, religious "heretics" left Massachusetts Bay in search of new colonies where they could themselves worship in peace. A Salem minister named Roger Williams, an early proponent of the separation of church and state, was found guilty of heresy and banished in 1636. Traveling southwest, Williams and a few followers settled on Narragansett Bay and founded the city of Providence. A few years later, the English crown dispensed an official charter for the Colony of Rhode Island. From the beginning, this colony proved infinitely more tolerant than others in New England, recognizing freedom of religion, freedom of speech, and other rights we recognize today. Williams also enjoyed friendly relations with the Narragansett people, who were proving more hostile to the Puritans.

Soon after Williams founded Providence, another group led by Anne Hutchinson, a teacher who believed that inspiration came directly from God without need of a church, came to Rhode Island to found the city of Portsmouth in 1638. Some of these settlers later moved farther south to found the city of Newport. At the same time, Hutchinson's fellow iconoclast, Rev. John Wheelwright, took his congregation north to settle in what would later become New Hampshire. Originally founding the town of Strawbery Banke (which would later become Portsmouth), Wheelwright was kept moving by the expanding boundaries of Massachusetts Bay Colony, founding the towns of Exeter, New Hampshire, and eventually Wells, Maine.

Finally, several factions within the Puritan sect split off to form their own colonies. Discouraged with the strictures on government participation in Boston, Rev. Thomas Hooker set out to found Hartford along the Connecticut River in 1636, and set up a more inclusive form of government in which every male member of the church could vote. Farther south, a pair of English merchants formed the colony of New Haven in 1638. The two colonies merged to form the colony of Connecticut in 1662.

King Philip's War

Unlike in Rhode Island, however, the new inhabitants of Connecticut didn't enjoy friendly relations with the native inhabitants. Soon after Europeans made incursions into the area, a pair of British merchants were found killed by Pequots on the Connecticut River. That incident set off an escalation that led to raids and reprisals on both sides and eventually a plan by the settlers to wipe out their native enemies. The Pequot War of 1637 was in reality a quick business, in which 130 settlers together with Narragansett and Monhegan allies wiped out the entire Pequot tribe.

That war was only a skirmish in the upcoming Indian Wars that would completely alter the colonies in the next few decades. After the deaths of Plymouth Colony's Governor Bradford and his Native American ally Massasoit, tensions between settlers and the Wampanoag people along the Massachusetts-Rhode Island border began to simmer. They eventually boiled over in 1675 in what would become known as King Philip's War. The conflict began when colonists arrested Massasoit's son Alexander on spurious charges. During the march he was forced to make to Plymouth, he sickened and died. Seeing the writing on the wall, Massasoit's younger son Metacomet (whom the colonists called Philip) launched a preemptive raid on the Massachusetts town of Swansea. The colonists counterattacked by invading the Wampanoag camp at Mount Hope in Bristol, forcing 1,500 of the Wampanoag to escape by floating rafts across the river.

The war that followed drew together many of the Native American tribes in New England in a last-gasp attempt to push back English expansion. Despite burning Providence and many other towns in the yearlong campaign, the Native Americans were defeated by their lack of supplies and treachery among warring tribes as much by the English force of arms. By the time peace was signed in 1676, Philip and more than 5,000 Native Americans had been killed, with many more sold into slavery; on the English side, 500 colonists had been killed. After the war, many area tribes were permanently relocated to Rhode Island's South County, near the town of Charlestown, effectively spelling an end to autonomous Native American presence in southern New England in all but the far western frontier of Massachusetts.

The Colonial Period

Following King Philip's War, the residents of New England continued to expand and prosper. At the same time, England's Puritan-friendly regent, Oliver Cromwell, was replaced by the restoration of the monarchy under James II, who saw an opportunity to bring greater control over the bustling colonies. The ill-fated Dominion of New England, as the new government was called, only lasted two years—in some sense, however, it began the conflict between England and its colonies that would end in war a century later. In 1685, James named Sir Edmund Andros as viceroy over Massachusetts, Plymouth, Rhode Island, Connecticut, New Hampshire, and New York. After he levied taxes on the colonists, however, there were widespread protests against the arrangement. When William and Mary overthrew James in England's "Glorious Revolution," New Englanders also overthrew Andros, returning the colonies to direct rule by governors (including a united

Massachusetts colony when Massachusetts Bay and Plymouth merged in 1691).

For the next century, New England's seemingly limitless supply of natural resources ensured that the region soon became a major player in the world's economy. In Massachusetts, religious zealotry gave way to a new dominion—not of God, but of cod. The "almighty codfish" was full of meat, could be salted and dried for long voyages by sea, and filled the waters around Massachusetts Bay by the schoolful. Based on the rich trade in the fish, along with lumber, furs, and rum, Boston became the third-busiest port in the entire British Empire by the early 1700s (after London and Bristol). By mid-century, Boston and other New England ports, including Portsmouth, Salem, Newport, and New Haven bustled with ships bringing in coffee, tea, textiles, and luxury goods imported from England.

Along with the benefits of being a colony, however, New Englanders had to shoulder the responsibilities. In 1754, when the mother country became embroiled in a dispute with France over trading rights in the Ohio Valley, they were drawn into the fray. The resulting conflict, known as the French and Indian Wars, was fought in New York, Pennsylvania, and Quebec and eventually spelled the end of French claims to North America when it was resolved by the Treaty of Paris in 1763. However, many New Englanders fought in the conflict, and its aftermath was strongly felt in the region. The war directly benefited traders in Maine, New Hampshire, and the burgeoning territory of Vermont by eliminating competition from the French in the fur and lumber trade. Because the Native Americans allied with the French, the war also caused the defeat of the Algonquain and Mohawk tribes who badgered inhabitants in western and northern New England with periodic raids. The most important effect of the war, however, was economic. Saddled with debt from its mammoth military undertakings, England decided to levy taxes on the colonies to pay for the war. After all, the Crown reasoned, hadn't the colonies been the ones who benefited the most from the defeat of the French and Native American tribes? Unfortunately for England, the colonists saw things differently.

WAR AND REVOLUTION

Early Rumblings

A decade before the outbreak of the Revolutionary War, few American colonists even considered independence from the Crown. Relations with England, while sometimes tense, were mutually beneficial for both parties, giving the colonies protection and a ready market for their goods, and giving England a source of raw materials and income. Millions of words have been spilled over what caused the quick snowball to war, but it essentially comes down to one: taxes. Even before the French and Indian Wars, the colonies had been curtailed by the Navigation Acts, which prohibited the colonies from trading directly with countries other than England (smugglers carrying molasses from the West Indies, of course, had no trouble circumventing these laws). Another provision that reserved any tree over 24 inches in diameter for use of the Royal Navy rankled northern woodsmen. But it wasn't until after the war that the British crown levied a tax directly on the colonies in the form of a stamp required for licenses and legal services. The protests against the Stamp Act of 1765 were surprising to the Crown in their vehemence—throughout the colonies, citizens fumed about taxation without representation in parliament and took to the streets to show their displeasure. The furor was so great that the law was repealed a year later.

In its place, however, Parliament enacted a series of laws that were even more damaging to the maritime trade of New England—the Townshend Acts of 1767. Named for the British Chancellor of the Exchequer, these acts levied a series of taxes on imports, including paint, lead, paper, and, most outrageous to the colonists, tea. Merchants in Boston immediately responded with boycotts of British products, convincing their colleagues in New York and Philadelphia to follow suit. In 1770,

Bostonians even sent thousands of pounds of British goods back to England on a ship owned by rich merchant John Hancock. Eventually Parliament capitulated and repealed all of the taxes except one—the tax on tea.

In this atmosphere of heightened animosity, a simple argument about the payment of a barber's bill by a British soldier led to a confrontation with an angry mob that left five colonists dead. An early instance of the use of propaganda, the act was dubbed the Boston Massacre by Whig politician Samuel Adams and used to stir up resentment against British troops quartered in the city. Adams was a member of the Sons of Liberty, a radical underground group of activists who sought greater autonomy from the British Empire. After the incident, he scored a victory when British troops were removed from Boston. However, the incident did little to advance the cause of independence. The troops were defended by Adams's cousin, John Adams, and acquitted of murder at trial.

Elsewhere in New England, incidents displayed the growing sentiment of the colonists against the British. In Connecticut, the local branch of the Sons of Liberty succeeded in deposing the colonial governor and installing one of their own members, Jonathan Trumbull, in his place. In 1772, a group of patriots in Providence, Rhode Island, raided and set fire to the Royal Navy ship *Gaspee*. But the road to revolution was by no means sure until the night of December 16, 1773. That year, Parliament passed an even more stringent law on the importation of tea. Colonists fought back by dressing up as Native Americans and stealing aboard three British ships at night. There they dumped 90,000 pounds of tea into the harbor in an act provocatively dubbed the Boston Tea Party.

British retribution was swift. Upon receiving word of the act, Parliament passed the so-called Intolerable Acts, which set up a blockade of Boston Harbor and consolidated more power over the colonies in the hands of the Crown. Sympathetic governments in Rhode Island and Connecticut delivered aid to the residents of Boston during the blockade. The following September, delegates from all of the 13 colonies met in Philadelphia in the first Continental Congress and escalated the tension, declaring their opposition to *any* British law enacted without representation from the colonies. The stage was set for war.

From Lexington to Bunker Hill

After the Boston Tea Party, Sam Adams, John Hancock, and the rest of the Sons of Liberty moved quickly to prepare for the eventuality of armed conflict. With Hancock's money and Adams's fiery rhetoric, they were able to prepare colonists around the region both physically and emotionally for battle. They also began caching arms and ammunition in various storehouses close to Boston, and helped to organize militia companies that could join battle at a moment's notice—calling them "minutemen." For their part, the British army commanders knew that they were severely outnumbered by the colonists if war should break out, and realized that their best hope lay in seizing the caches of arms before the general populace could be whipped up to a war frenzy.

When British troops finally marched out from Boston to capture the ammunition stores in Concord in April 1775, setting alight the Revolutionary War, it wasn't the first time they had tried. A few months earlier, British general Thomas Gage had ordered a scouting party north of Boston in Marblehead to search for munitions stored in Salem. Despite a tense standoff with local minutemen, that day ended without bloodshed. In response, the Sons of Liberty set up an elaborate warning system to alert the populace should the troops try again. Two months later, on April 16, riders including Paul Revere had already raised the alarm ahead of the 700 soldiers that marched out of the city en route to Concord. At the time, Adams and Hancock were staying with a friend in the nearby town of Lexington. They hastily organized a show of resistance before themselves escaping back to Boston. By the time an advance party of 300 men under

Major John Pitcairn marched into town, they found several-dozen minutemen and veterans of the French and Indian Wars ranged on the town common warily clutching their muskets. Someone fired a shot, and by the time the smoke cleared eight colonists were dead. The first battle of the American Revolution took only a few moments, but it was only the beginning of a day of increasing bloodshed.

The Battle of Lexington was followed by another battle a few hours later in Concord. There several hundred minutemen had assembled from neighboring towns on the hill overlooking the North Bridge. Seeing smoke rising in the distance, some feared that the British had set fire to the town, and began to march toward the bridge. A British platoon opened fire, killing two of the colonists. As word spread of the casualties to their comrades, minutemen by the thousands began taking up positions behind houses, trees, and stone walls between Concord and Boston. After destroying what they could of the colonial munitions (most had been hidden before British arrival), the tired British began marching back to Boston through a deathtrap. In the long march back, 73 British soldiers were killed, with another 200 wounded or missing. On the rebels' side, only 49 were dead, with 44 wounded or missing. The implications of the battles, however, went far beyond the actual results. By proving that they could stand up to the most fearsome army in the world and win, the patriots recruited many other colonists to their cause.

Their next test occurred two months later at the Battle of Bunker Hill. The battles at Concord and Lexington were mere skirmishes compared to the bloody confrontation that occurred in Charlestown on June 17, 1775. A few days before, the newly formed Continental Army took up a position in Charlestown, just across the harbor from the British forces in Boston. For General Gage that was too close, and he decided it was time to knock out the colonials once and for all. Due to a last-minute change in plans, the so-called Battle of Bunker Hill actually occurred on Breed's Hill. Before the battle began, the colonists' commanding officer, Colonel William Prescott, noting that his troops were low on powder, supposedly made the famous statement: "Don't fire until you see the whites of their eyes." The ensuing battle succeeded in dislodging the colonists, forcing them to retreat back to Cambridge. But like Concord and Lexington, the battle showed the force of the inexperienced Americans over the superior fighting power of the British. In three assaults up the hill, the British lost more than 1,000 men, while the colonists only lost half that. Perhaps wishing to even the score, the British commander Howe later said that the death of popular American general Joseph Warren was equal to the death of 500 patriots. Nevertheless, the Battle of Bunker Hill showed the world that the American Revolution was definitely *on*.

The Siege of Boston

After Lexington, Concord, and Bunker Hill, the British Army found itself in a precarious position, holed up in Boston surrounded on all sides by countryside teeming with hostile colonists. Schooled by the French and Indian War, many of the colonists were skilled fighters and military strategists. One of them, George Washington, now assumed command of the Continental Army in Cambridge, Massachusetts, in June 1775, and began a tense standoff with British general William Howe, who had replaced Gage as commander. Not eager to risk another bloody battle like the one at Breed's Hill, Washington commissioned Boston bookseller Henry Knox to drag 59 cannons to Boston from Fort Ticonderoga in upstate New York, which had been captured the previous month by a force of Massachusetts and Connecticut soldiers under the command of Benedict Arnold, and Ethan Allen's Green Mountain Boys of Vermont. Knox arrived at the fort in December 1775, and took more than two months to complete the journey across more than 200 miles of snow and ice. On the night of March 14, 1776, Washington's forces quietly dragged the cannons to the top of Dorchester Heights, where they commanded a deadly vantage over the city. A few days later, on March 17, 1776, Gage evacuated the city by ship to Nova Scotia without firing a shot—leaving much of New England free from British forces on land.

Battles Across New England

After the early successes in Massachusetts, the most important engagements of the war continued in the southern and mid-Atlantic states. However, over the next seven years of fighting, each of the New England states except New Hampshire would see blood spilled on its soil. Before he famously turned traitor, Benedict Arnold took his troops through the woods of northern Maine in an ill-fated attempt to attack Quebec City on December 31, 1776. Undone by hunger and smallpox, Arnold was defeated in his attacks on the city. Most of the fighting that did occur in Maine itself happened off its coast. Even before Dorchester Heights, ships of the fledgling Maine navy captured the loyalist sloop *Margaretta* off the coast of Machias in what is regarded as the first naval battle of the war. In response, the British sent a fleet of six ships to bombard Falmouth, Maine (outside Portland), nearly burning the entire town to the ground. Later in the war, in 1779, Maine saw one of the conflict's largest naval battles, when more than 20 colonial ships attacked a fleet of British warships stationed in Castine in Penobscot Bay. The campaign ended in disaster, however, in part due to the foolhardy actions of one Paul Revere, who was captaining a ship at the end of the Continental line and broke ranks, foiling the fighting formation. In one of the ironies of history, the commanding officer of the British fleet was General Peleg Wadsworth, the grandfather of Henry Wadsworth Longfellow, who years later would immortalize Revere in his poem "The Midnight Ride of Paul Revere."

Amazingly, even after the Battle of Bunker Hill, colonists were still split on the virtues of declaring full independence from Great Britain. First among the colonies, Rhode Island bit the bullet to declare itself a sovereign nation on May 4, 1776, two months before the Declaration of Independence. The state did not fare well in the ensuing war, however. In December 1776, after a sea battle off the coast of Point Judith, the British fleet blockaded Narragansett Bay, trapping much of the Continental Navy in Providence. For the next few years, they occupied Newport, terrorizing the populace and bringing shipping to a standstill. In 1778, Washington attempted to liberate the port by sending Massachusetts general John Sullivan and 8,000 men to attack. However, a fierce storm prevented allied French ships from landing with reinforcements, and Sullivan was unable to take the city. The British remained in Newport until 1779, when they voluntarily withdrew to aid fighting farther south.

Of all the New England states, the hardest hit during the war was Connecticut, which was an enticing target due to its rich industrial base and its proximity to British strongholds in New York. In April 1777, 2,000 British troops sacked Danbury, defeating 200 militiamen (again led by Arnold) and destroying vast amounts of tents, food, and other stores that would have come in handy for Washington when he was freezing in Valley Forge that winter. To help the troops survive, Connecticut governor Jonathan Trumbull helped round up cattle and drive them down to Pennsylvania for Washington's troops. Over the next few years, Connecticut was pillaged several more times, at Greenwich, New Haven, Fairfield, and Norwalk. The most devastating attack took place in September 1781, toward the end of the war, in Groton and New London. There Benedict Arnold—now fighting on the British side—took 2,000 troops and decimated the forts in both cities, burning much of New London to the ground.

The Battle of Bennington

When the war broke out, Vermont wasn't even yet an independent colony. Much of what would become Vermont was occupied by settlers in land grants from the governor of New Hampshire, who fought competing claims against encroachers from New York. In January 1777, an assembly declared Vermont an independent republic, initially called New Connecticut. (Even so, neither Vermont nor Maine were among the original 13 states. Vermont wasn't admitted into the union until 1791. Maine remained part of Massachusetts until 1820.) The fledgling republic gained new legitimacy a few months later during the Battle of Bennington, which proved to be the first battle in which the colonials beat the British in combat. The crucial victory led to the turning point of the war a few months later at Saratoga, and helped convince France and Spain to intervene on the side of the Americans.

The battle took place in two parts in August 1777, when, fresh from victory at Fort Ticonderoga, British general John "Gentleman Johnnie" Burgoyne was marching down the Hudson River Valley to meet up with British troops from New York. The plan was to cut off New England from receiving supplies and reinforcements from the rest of the colonies, thereby setting it up for easy capture. Feeling the pinch of lack of supplies himself, however, the general made a fatal mistake when he decided along the way to capture a large storehouse of food and munitions in the small town of Bennington, Vermont.

Under command of German colonel Friedrich Baum, Burgoyne sent some 500 troops—including several hundred of the dread Hessian mercenaries—to raid the town. Unbeknownst to him, however, American colonel John Stark had previously set off from New Hampshire with 1,500 troops of his own. On August 16, Stark took the battle to the enemy, swarming up a ridge along the Wolloomsac River to attack Baum's position. In a short but bloody battle, his militiamen killed Baum and captured many of his men. Certain of victory, the excited Americans began pursuing the enemy, when they were surprised by a relief column of another 600 Hessian soldiers under Lieutenant Colonel Heinrich von Breymann. Stark was pushed to retreat back toward Bennington. The tide of the battle turned once more, however, with the arrival of Colonel Seth Warner and 300 of his Green Mountain Boys, who had marched from Manchester, Vermont. In the second engagement, the Germans were routed and fled to the Hudson, while the Americans claimed victory.

The battle was an embarrassing defeat for Burgoyne, whose army suffered some 900 casualties to Stark's 70. At a time in the war when American morale was low, the battle also proved once again that backcountry farmers and militiamen could defeat the most disciplined troops of Europe. Just two months later, with his forces depleted and short on provisions, Gentleman Johnnie was forced to surrender at Saratoga.

War's Aftermath

As any history book will tell you, the Revolutionary War was won not by the Americans, but by the French and Spanish, who entered the war after the victory at Saratoga and blockaded American ports against the British, swinging the tide of battle in favor of the newly independent republic. In 1783, a full decade after the Boston Tea Party, British general Charles Cornwallis surrendered at Yorktown, leaving 13 newly independent states. Like most of the rest of the country, New England was in rough shape by war's end, hamstrung by debt from the massive amounts of money needed for the war effort. Because of its unique position, however, it was able to bounce back more quickly than other areas. Since most of the fighting had occurred farther south, New England ended up with its infrastructure intact—in fact, once its blockades were lifted, it even benefited from the lack of competition from New York and Philadelphia, which were still embroiled in fighting. Initially the region felt the loss of the Tory upper class, which fled once fighting started. In their place, however, rose a new American merchant class who had made fortunes in previous decades smuggling molasses and financing privateers against the British. They quickly assumed control of New

The Forgotten Patriot

Amid the graves in Boston's Granary Burying Ground is the final resting place of the man who has been called the Father of the Revolution, but who is virtually forgotten today. Born in 1725, **James Otis** was the most gifted speaker of the colonial era. More than a decade before the shots were fired at Lexington, he made a five-hour speech in court arguing against the Writs of Assistance (which allowed the Crown to search for smuggled goods on colonial vessels) and stated for the first time that "taxation without representation is tyranny." No less a figure than John Adams pinpointed the moment as the start of resistance against England. Otis later led the charge against the Stamp Act and the Townshend Acts with Samuel Adams. During a tavern brawl in 1769, however, he was hit on the head by a British soldier and literally lost his senses. For the rest of his life, he ran around the streets of Boston half-clothed, half-drunk, shooting off his musket at odd hours, and generally becoming an embarrassment to his fellow Sons of Liberty. He did at least get one final wish. Before his madness, he had written to his sister that he hoped when God decided to "take me out of time into eternity, that it will be by a flash of lightning." In May 1783, just a month after Congress officially declared victory in the Revolution, Otis was struck by lightning in Andover, Massachusetts, and died, virtually forgotten and disowned by the country he helped start. Not even his gravestone in Boston makes mention of the role he played in the beginnings of America.

England and set about doing what Yankees did best—making money.

19TH CENTURY

The Federal Period

No longer hampered by British strictures on trade, this new class of bourgeoisie was soon sending ships to the far ports of the world in search of trading goods. For a time, the city of Salem was the richest in the world from its cornering of the trade in pepper with the East Indies. Whaling ships from Nantucket and New Bedford sailed the South Seas in search of whales, growing rich themselves off the trade in spermaceti oil and whalebone corsets, which were all the rage on the Continent. Boston, meanwhile, remained the largest port in the United States, vying for supremacy with Philadelphia and New York in the years after the Revolution. All over the region, signs of the new wealth appeared in the form of stunning brick mansions and elm-lined streets.

Politically, New England also vied with the other colonial powerhouses—Pennsylvania, New York, and Virginia—to determine the path of the new country. Many prominent Bostonians, including John Hancock, Samuel Adams, and John Adams, were part of the founding fathers at the Constitutional Convention in 1789, where they pushed for a stronger federal government to raise armies, tax the populace, and set trade policies. The Federalists, as they came to be known, had their strongholds in New England and New York, and reached their apogee when John Adams was elected president in 1796. A national backlash, however, soon found the southern agrarians in power under Virginian Thomas Jefferson, and the influence of the Federalists waned. Many New England states opposed the War of 1812 with Britain and abstained from sending troops (thankfully, a push to secede and form the New England Confederacy around this time failed). Over the ensuing decades, the Federalists competed with the more agrarian southern states to push policies that would benefit the manufacturers that became the underpinning of the northern economy.

Industrialization

The "dark satanic mills" (as English Romantic poet William Blake called them) sprouted throughout England in the 18th century, transforming Europe into an industrialized economy. North America was slow to follow suit until after the war. In 1790, a British engineer named Samuel Slater was called in to rebuild the machinery at Moses Brown's textile mill in Pawtucket, Rhode Island. The innovations he put in place transformed the factory and began a trend that would blanket New England with mills at a record pace over the next few decades. In many ways the region was ideally suited for manufacturing, with many fast-running rivers to generate power, a steady supply of raw materials thanks to the shipping trade, and poor soil for the competing industry of farming. In short order, cities were transformed into mill towns with sturdy brick factories and blocks of rowhouses for low-wage workers who toiled endlessly spinning and weaving textiles. Along with the textile mills, other cities in the region won fame for production of consumer goods, including shoes, paper, and clocks. A Scottish visitor to New England in the 1830s declared Niagara Falls and the mill town of Lowell, Massachusetts, the two greatest wonders of America.

As the New England factories churned out the goods, a new class of aristocrats emerged on Beacon Hill and in the seaport and manufacturing towns. Called Brahmins, they were known as much for their wealth as for their enlightened sense of noblesse oblige. Many were educated at universities such as Harvard, Yale, and Brown, which became national centers of learning and spawned scholars and researchers in natural science. Espousing Yankee values of thrift and modesty, many of the Brahmins eschewed more garish forms of wealth for the prestige of philanthropy and the arts. After all, many of their fortunes were one generation removed from rum running and opium trading. Many Brahmins never forgot how they came by their wealth and took measures to redeem themselves, founding the first public library in Boston and museums such as the Museum of Fine Arts.

Abolitionists and Transcendentalists

When Oliver Wendell Holmes Jr. declared in 1858 that Boston was the "hub of the solar system," he was referring not only to its wealth and financial influence, but also its intellectual influence. Over the two centuries since the Puritans arrived, Bostonians had gradually shed their strict morals and small-minded prejudices to develop a new, more all-embracing religious philosophy. The austerity of Puritanism—which taught that people were either elected to be saved or they were destined to be damned—may have commanded fear and respect in the days of the colonies, but post-Revolutionary New England was a prosperous, urbane culture, proud of its status as a national center of ideas.

Called Unitarianism, the new religion taught that God's salvation was available to anyone, not just those chosen few who were predestined for heaven. One by one, the New England Congregational churches "went Unitarian" and embraced this new philosophy, which emphasized an intellectual approach to the divine. And along with it came a new national conscience. Although early Unitarians were socially conservative, on political issues they were emphatically liberal. Congregants such as suffragist Susan B. Anthony were instrumental in organizing the women's movement. And prodded by ministers like William Ellery Channing and firebrand Theodore Parker, Boston stood at the forefront of the abolitionist movement—despite a long tradition of slavery in New England, which was a prominent part of the "triangle trade" linking the United States, Britain, and the Caribbean Islands in a brutal trading cycle of human lives, molasses, and rum.

At the same time that Unitarianism was spreading across the country, it spawned a rebellion against itself in the form of a new philosophy, transcendentalism. In many ways, transcendentalism took the fundamental tenet of Unitarianism, that anyone could be saved, and took it a step further, declaring that churches themselves were unnecessary since people could experience a direct connection to the divine. Transcendentalists found this in a mystical communion with the natural world. Buoyed by a mystical communion with nature, its adherents called for a radical individualism that would break free from the tired conventions of Europe. From their home base in Concord, its two chief adherents, Ralph Waldo Emerson and Henry David Thoreau, laid down its philosophy and formed a nucleus of writers, including Bronson Alcott (and his daughter Louisa May) and Nathaniel Hawthorne, who would begin the flowering in American literature.

New England in the Civil War

No amount of philosophizing, however, could prevent the inevitable political clash of the Civil War. While none of the actual fighting of the war took place in New England, it could be argued that it was a New Englander who fired the first shot. Outraged by the passage of the Fugitive Slave Act, which demanded that captured slaves be returned to southern masters, Brunswick, Maine, resident Harriet Beecher Stowe wrote the novel *Uncle Tom's Cabin,* which galvanized public support in favor of the war. Tens of thousands of New Englanders enlisted in the fight, forming regiments from all six New England states. Among the most acclaimed was the Massachusetts 54th, the nation's first all-black regiment, which was led by Bostonian Colonel Robert Gould Shaw, and suffered tremendous casualties in the heroic but tragic assault on Fort Wagner in July 1863. That same month, another New Englander, Joshua Chamberlain, won renown for his role in the Battle of Gettysburg. A professor at Bowdoin College, also in Brunswick, Maine, Chamberlain led the heroic defense of Little Round Top, saving the Union line through a dramatic flanking maneuver that caught the enemy by surprise. Two years later, in 1865, he received the flag of truce from the Confederate Army. Thus it's said in Maine that Brunswick both started and ended the war.

MODERN TIMES

The Immigrants Arrive

After the Civil War, the Golden Age of Sail gave way to the Age of Steam, as the railroad emerged to transport goods long distances. Increasingly isolated in the corner of a vast and growing country, New England gradually gave up its advantages in trade and manufacturing. New York surpassed Boston as the nation's largest port, and the opening up of the West and California decreased New England's dominance in the China trade. Even so, New England's Brahmin class continued to preside over vast amounts of wealth from their factories, and they began to show it in more and more elaborate ways. In addition to travel to other parts of the country, the railroad opened up many parts of New England to tourism, and grand Victorian "summer cottages" (read: mansions) and hotels were built along the coasts of Rhode Island and Maine, in the mountains of New Hampshire, and in the valleys of the Berkshires.

By the turn of the century, however, changes were occurring in the population. The first waves of immigrants from Ireland began in the early 1800s, but they intensified during the Great Hunger of 1850, during which two million people emigrated from the country. Many of them found their way to Boston, the closest major American city, and from there dispersed throughout the region. Poor but hardworking, many of them were welcomed in the mills. As their numbers swelled, however, a violent anti-Irish backlash began to coalesce among traditional Yankees anxious to hold on to their power and influence. In the mid-1850s, political groups called Know-Nothings burned Catholic churches and terrorized Irish communities.

The Irish won out by sheer numbers. By 1850, they comprised one-third of the city of Boston, with other cities boasting similar percentages. The new immigrants also organized themselves politically, forming a network of patronage politics in urban wards. Within just a few generations, they completely changed the political makeup of the region, as represented in Boston by the colorful politician James Michael Curley. Curley spent almost as much time in prison as in political office in his early years—but eventually worked his way up to get elected to the U.S. House of Representatives in 1911. After failing to get reelected, he returned to Boston, where he presided over the city as mayor or governor for 30 years. A hugely popular and hugely corrupt politician, he was eventually convicted of mail fraud and pardoned by President Harry Truman in 1947.

Waves of other immigrants followed the Irish, including Italians and French Canadians, who also found work in the factories of the region. Not as complacent as the mill girls of a century earlier, the new immigrants helped push for improvements in working conditions. A 21-year-old Irish woman led her fellow female immigrants of more than two dozen different nationalities in walking out of a mill in Lawrence, Massachusetts, to perpetrate the Bread and Roses strike, one of the most significant watersheds in the labor movement. On the darker side, two Italian anarchists, Nicola Sacco and Bartolomeo Vanzetti, were unfairly accused of robbery and murder in 1920. Their case became a national cause célèbre, stirring up strong sentiments and prejudices about communists, immigrants, the labor movement, and the death penalty. Despite shoddy evidence and the intervention of prominent intellectuals such as Upton Sinclair and H. L. Mencken, however, they were found guilty and executed in 1927. Exactly 50 years later, Massachusetts governor Michael Dukakis issued a proclamation exonerating them.

Decline and Rebirth

By the time of World War II, New England was in a period of slow decline. Many of the mills and factories that generated New England's wealth had become obsolete, and companies left the region in search of cheaper labor in other states and countries. At the same time, the urban centers that thrived in the previous century were abandoned by the middle class, who settled in streetcar suburbs on their outskirts. Despite various schemes to resurrect their cores, "urban renewal" was mostly a disaster, further hollowing out cities by bulldozing neighborhoods and erecting lifeless skyscrapers in their wakes. The sole bright spot in the postwar era was the election of one of New England's native sons, the charismatic war hero John Fitzgerald Kennedy, as president in 1960. Even that hope was dimmed, however, when Kennedy was killed by an assassin's bullet three years later. After struggling with the rest of the nation through the 1960s and 1970s, however, the region rebounded in the 1980s by playing to one of its strengths: knowledge.

New England was one of the first regions of the country to realize the potential of the computer to transform American society. Led by a wealth of well-educated engineers from Massachusetts Institute of Technology (MIT) and other area colleges, small technology firms grew into huge computer companies within a decade. The so-called Massachusetts Miracle revitalized the region and began a reversal of fortunes that injected wealth and self-confidence back into the cities. Since then, New England has been at the forefront of other technological revolutions, including the Internet and biotechnology, which has further bolstered its population and industrial base and left it well poised for the 21st century.

Government and Economy

GOVERNMENT AND POLITICS

It's been said that democracy was founded in Greece and perfected in New England, though it was likely a self-congratulating local that said it. But for many living in small towns, there's the opportunity to participate in "town hall meetings" that are far more participatory than in other regions of the country, and there's a deep focus on the local. In cities, meanwhile, Democratic politics hold enormous sway. There is more political diversity to the region than immediately meets the eye, however, from the Republican strongholds of southern Connecticut to the liberal values of Vermont, as well as the more libertarian voters in New Hampshire. Even in liberal Massachusetts, the majority of voters are registered Independents, not Democrats, highlighting the individualism that has run through the political fiber of the region since the Revolution.

ECONOMY

Four industries dominate the modern New England economy: technology, academia, medicine, and finance—with tourism a close fifth. The area is second only to Silicon Valley in its concentration of technology firms, which tends to make booms bigger and recessions deeper than in other parts of the country. The great number of colleges and universities in the area has spawned a cottage industry of professors and researchers, who have also contributed to the region's status as a hub of medical innovation.

In addition to these urban pursuits, the area still has substantial concentrations of farming (particularly dairy), fruit cultivation (cranberries, apples, and blueberries), and fishing (whitefish and lobster). All these industries, however, struggle to compete with cheaper imports from other countries or overfishing of fragile stocks. Where there is hope for local farms, it lies in the burgeoning sectors of organic foods and community-supported agriculture, which has strong local support.

People and Culture

Imagine a New Englander—are you thinking of a flinty, white, English-speaking Yankee? There are certainly plenty of those, but the region's always been far more diverse than the stereotype implies. Dozens of tribal groups came first, and early immigration added English, French, and African people to the mix—the first enslaved African arrived in 1619, and many more followed.

Drive through Massachusetts and Rhode Island and you'll pick up Portuguese-speaking radio stations, or you can head to northern Vermont to catch the last strains of French Canadian accents. Dozens of languages are spoken in some schools, especially urban ones, with accents that range from Sudanese to Salvadoreño.

Which isn't to say that there's no such thing as a "New England" character. Locals see themselves as hardily self-sufficient, shaped by the cold winters and history of independent thought. It's not quite as gregarious as the openly friendly South and West, but wind someone up about the weather, fishing, politics, weather, beer, or weather, and you'll get an earful.

STATISTICS

New England is home to some 14.4 million people, with the majority of New England's population centered in the southern part of the region. Massachusetts is most populated, with 6.8 million people, followed by Connecticut, with 3.6 million. Maine and New Hampshire each has 1.3 million each—staggering considering the vast size difference between the two—while little Rhode Island has a little over 1 million. Meanwhile, Vermont tops out with just 600,000 people, fewer than the population of Boston proper.

ETHNICITY AND CULTURE

The most recent census figures reveal that New England averages slightly higher than the rest of the country in its numbers of white and Hispanic residents: just above 83 percent, compared to the nation's 77 percent. The second-largest group of inhabitants are black, at roughly 7 percent, followed by 1 percent Chinese Americans.

Two major strands of culture typify the region: the thriving rural culture that keeps alive farming, fishing, and livestock traditions, and the educated, intellectual culture that flows from the colleges and universities. The most typical New England towns contain evidence of both: county fairs that still generate excitement in the populace, and cultural institutions such as museums, theaters, and art galleries that can be found in even the most remote corners of the region.

RELIGION

The region's earliest settlers may have been strict English Protestants, but due to waves of immigrants from French Canada, Italy, Ireland—and most recently, from Latin and South America—Catholics are now far and away New England's largest religious group.

The most popular branches of Protestantism (members of which make up roughly one-third of the area's population) are Episcopalian, Congregational, Baptist, Methodist, and Pentecostal. Meanwhile, one of the world's most sizable concentrations of practicing Jews calls Massachusetts home, and groups of the liberal-minded Unitarian Universalist church can also be spotted throughout New England. Sizable Muslim and Hindu populations can be found in many of the region's cities.

LANGUAGE

English is by far the most widely spoken tongue in each of New England's states, with pockets of other languages, which include both the Native American languages that predate European arrival, and many languages spoken by more recent immigrants.

Should outsiders give their best shot at a New England accent, odds are good that they'd imitate something from Boston, or perhaps Maine. The classic characteristics, including dropping word-final r's, and what linguists call the "cot-caught merger"—while some English speakers pronounce the words "cot" and "caught" (or "nod" and "gnawed") as distinct, New Englanders often produce them as identical sounds.

In many places, the most distinctive accents are harder and harder to come by, much to the chagrin of residents with an ear for appreciating quirky dialect. Language and accent change is complex, but it's worth noting that there's not an inexorable shift toward standardization, as many observers assume. In fact, New England was the site of a famous linguistic experiment that showed just the opposite. In the decades following World War II, when there was greatly increased mobility and tourism, the linguist William Labov found that some characteristics of the Martha's Vineyard accent were getting even stronger, theorizing that the shift was a reaction against some of the social changes that were then transforming island life.

THE ARTS

A love of music and the arts has dominated New England's cultural scene for centuries, and thanks to the legacy of the Boston Brahmins (those blue-blooded families who ruled the city's society and industry in the 19th century) there are plenty of places to appreciate all of them—from large institutions like the Peabody Essex Museum and Boston Symphony Orchestra in Massachusetts, and the Portland Museum of Art in Maine, to the small theaters of North Conway, New Hampshire, and the independent art galleries of Burlington, Vermont.

Literature is also a big part of New England's abundant arts community—historically and in the present day. Writers Nathaniel Hawthorne, Edith Wharton, and Henry David Thoreau helped define the American character as they saw it from New England, and scribes such as Arthur Miller and John Updike have continued the tradition.

But much of the culture found in this area of the country is just as easily found in its streets, pubs, and parks. In and around Boston, Providence, and Portland, a thriving rock and folk music scene dominates the nightclubs and bars. (Boston in particular is the birthplace of bands ranging from The Pixies to Aerosmith.) Farther afield, in rural areas, you'll find plenty of folk-inspired performances—perhaps most notably distinct are the Acadian and Quebecois dance and folk music in northern areas of Maine.

HOLIDAYS AND FESTIVALS

Year-round festivals celebrate everything from maple syrup to jazz, and there's hardly a tourist destination that doesn't claim at least one.

In March, Boston is the place to be to toast St. Patrick's Day—both in the city's myriad Irish pubs and by watching its famed parade. June's highlights include the Arts & Ideas Festival in New Haven, Connecticut, and Boston's Harborfest, full of maritime history of the area along with fireworks, concerts, and historical reenactments.

The Newport Folk Festival takes over the Rhode Island seaside in July, followed by August's Newport Jazz Festival, which pulls in some of the world's biggest names in jazz. That same month, the Camden Windjammer Festival in Maine celebrates the state's fleet of sailing ships.

Autumn brings changing leaves and the harvest: check out Wellfleet's Oyster Festival in October, the Sea Harvest at Mystic Seaport, and the Stowe Foliage Arts Festival in northern Vermont.

The holidays gear up early in New England, with an impressive Christmas Craft Market in Rockport, Maine, stocked with locally made crafts from more than 70 vendors and artists. Then, come December, the quaint streets of Portsmouth, New Hampshire, take a Rockwellian turn during the Candlelight Stroll at Strawbery Banke, as festively decorated period homes open their doors to tours, cider is passed around, and 1,000 candles are lit throughout the town.

Essentials

Getting There

New England is easily accessible by road, rail, and air (and even sea if you are coming by ferry from New York or Canada). While Logan Airport, in Boston, is the most obvious entrance, several of the region's smaller airports may offer cheaper flights from some cities. Amtrak's rail network isn't very extensive, but it does connect to most major New England cities, a good car-free option for exploring. If you want to get beyond urban areas, however, having your own transportation is essential.

AIR

With up to 1.5 million passengers passing through its gates each month, **Boston-Logan International Airport** (One Harborside Dr., East Boston, 617/428-2800, www.massport.com/logan-airport/) is the largest and busiest transportation hub in the region. The airport serves nearly 50 airlines, of which 13 are international, including Aer Lingus, Air Canada, Air France, Alitalia, British Airways, Iberia, Icelandair, Lufthansa, SATA (Azores Express), Swiss, and Virgin Atlantic Airways. International flights arrive in Terminal E. From the airport, a variety of options take passengers to downtown Boston, which is only a mile away.

Several of the area's smaller regional airports are a good option for travelers looking to save a few bucks or get to other New England states without having to pass through Boston first. Rhode Island's **Providence/T. F. Green Airport** (2000 Post Rd., Warwick, 401/737-8222, www.pvdairport.com) is served by all the major domestic carriers, and has an increasing variety of flights linking the airport with international destinations. The airport is a 15-minute drive to Providence, and regular bus service is available.

Another option for southern New England is **Bradley International Airport** (Schoephoester Rd., Windsor Locks, CT, 860/292-2000, www.bradleyairport.com), located halfway between Springfield, Massachusetts, and Hartford, Connecticut; it's about a 45-minute drive from either city. In New Hampshire, **Manchester Airport** (1 Airport Rd., Manchester, 603/624-6556, www.flymanchester.com) has competed aggressively with Logan in the areas of price and convenience. It's located about a 1.5 hour drive from the White Mountains, and a 30-minute drive from Portsmouth, New Hampshire, and carries a half-dozen domestic airlines as well as Air Canada.

While not usually cheaper, several other regional airports offer easy access to northern New England. **Burlington International Airport** (1200 Airport Dr., S. Burlington, VT, 802/863-1889, www.btv.aero) is located right in downtown Burlington, and offers limited flights from cities including Atlanta, Cleveland, Detroit, New York, and Washington DC. **Portland International Jetport** (207/774-7301, www.portlandjetport.com) also offers several domestic routes from cities in the eastern United States to those looking for easy access to south and Mid-Coast Maine. Both Burlington and Portland are served by discount flights from New York on JetBlue airlines. Lastly, far northern Maine is home to **Bangor International Airport** (207/992-4600, www.flybangor.com), which offers flights from a handful of cities including Atlanta, New York, Philadelphia, Cincinnati, Detroit, and Minneapolis. The airport is also served by shuttles from Boston

Previous: a tractor on a farm road in Vermont; Boston harbor pier.

via American and Delta. Despite their names, none of the three northern New England airports offers commercial international flights.

TRAIN

Amtrak (800/872-7245, www.amtrak.com) runs frequent trains along the Northeast corridor to Boston, including the **Acela Express,** the first U.S. high-speed service, from New York (3.5 hours) and Washington DC (6 hours). But unless you are in a rush, it can often make more sense to save $50 and take the **Regional** service, which also runs to Boston from New York (4.5 hours) and Washington (7 hours), stopping along the way in New Haven, New London, Providence, and several smaller cities on the Connecticut and Rhode Island coasts.

For travelers heading to northern New England, Amtrak offers the aptly named **Vermonter** route, which runs to St. Albans from New York (10 hours) and Washington DC (14 hours). Along the way, it passes through a number of cities in the Connecticut River Valley, including New Haven, Hartford, Amherst, Brattleboro, Waterbury, and Burlington—though the "Burlington" station is in Essex Junction, eight miles from downtown. Also, Amtrak's **Ethan Allen** route offers once-a-day service to Rutland, Vermont, from New York City (10 hours) by way of Albany.

From the west, Amtrak's **Lake Shore Limited** route offers service to Boston from Buffalo (12 hours), and Cleveland (15 hours), stopping along the way in Springfield and Worcester. Connecting to that route, Amtrak's **Adirondack** route offers service to Boston from Montreal, Quebec (12 hours), with a change of train in Albany.

BUS

New England is accessible from many domestic and Canadian locations via **Greyhound Bus Lines** (800/231-2222, www.greyhound.com). Nearby major cities offering service to Boston include New York (4.5 hours), Philadelphia (7.5 hours), Montreal (7.5 hours), Washington (10.5 hours), Buffalo (10.5 hours), Toronto (14 hours), and Cleveland (16 hours).

In recent years, the budget carrier **Megabus** (www.us.megabus.com) has expanded service in New England, linking Boston with Burlington (4 hours), Hartford (2 hours), New Haven (3 hours), Portland (2 hours), and New York (2 hours), often at lower prices.

CAR

The major auto route into New England is I-95, which enters the southeast corner of Connecticut and snakes up the coast to Boston. The drive takes about three hours from the New York border without stops—four hours from New York or eight hours from Washington DC. This direct route, however, can often get clogged with truck traffic, especially through areas of eastern Connecticut and Rhode Island, where it drops to two lanes each way. Many travelers prefer to take a detour at New Haven north on I-91, then west on I-84 and I-90 to Boston; while slightly longer, this route is often quicker.

From the west, the main route into New England is I-90, also known as the Massachusetts Turnpike (or Mass Pike for short). I-90 is a toll road, and it takes a little over two hours to drive its length, from the border of western Massachusetts to Boston. From Canada, there are two border crossings into Vermont; one is at I-89, which offers quick access to Burlington and central Massachusetts and Connecticut by way of connection to I-91. The other crossing, at the far northern end of I-91, offers quicker access to New Hampshire and Boston via connection to I-93. Several smaller highways offer border crossings into the wilderness of northern Maine. Some of New England's highways have tolls, and it's worth traveling with cash and small change to be prepared.

SEA

Travelers coming from Atlantic Canada can take the express route from Yarmouth, Nova Scotia, to Portland, Maine (6.5 hours) aboard

The CAT (877/359-3760, www.catferry.com), a high-speed car ferry that makes round-trips on each route daily. Two year-round car ferries also make the trip to Connecticut from New York's Long Island. **Cross Sound Ferry Services** (860/443-5281, www.longislandferry.com) offers several daily trips from Orient Point to New London (1.5 hours). The **Bridgeport & Port Jefferson Steamboat Company** (631/473-0286, www.bpjferry.com) offers trips between those two cities (1.25 hours) every hour.

Getting Around

While it's possible to explore New England using public transportation, that means planning your trip around the most convenient networks—opting to see just the towns on bus and train lines would make a great vacation, but good luck getting to a small Maine or Vermont town without a car.

Once you're there, however, many places are wonderfully pleasant to see on foot or by bicycle, without the hassle of paying for parking or negotiating urban traffic.

AIR

Puddle-jumpers between Boston and many of the area's regional airports offer a quick and easy way to shoot around the region. Be forewarned, however, that relying on air travel for inter-city travel isn't cheap. In most cases, you'll save money by flying direct from your home to a regional airport, rather than stopping in Boston first. Better yet, it's often more economical to rent a car or travel by bus between cities.

The exceptions to the rule are flights to the islands, where high demand keeps costs in check, and the added expense can more than make up for the hassle of driving to the ferry and spending time at sea (to say nothing of the exorbitant rates ferries charge for automobile transit). Contact **Cape Air** (800/352-0714, www.capeair.com) for flights to Nantucket or Martha's Vineyard, or **New England Airlines** (800/243-2460, www.block-island.com/nea) for Block Island.

TRAIN

In addition to the routes coming in from outside New England, **Amtrak** (800/872-7245, www.amtrak.com) offers the regional **Downeaster** service from Boston to Portland (2.5 hours). The train stops in several smaller towns along the way, including Dover, New Hampshire; and Wells and Old Orchard Beach, Maine. Note, however, that it's not possible to buy a one-ticket ride from New York to Portland, since the southern train runs to South Station, and the Downeaster embarks from North Station. Travelers from the South Shore to Maine must take a short subway trip between the two Boston stations to continue their trip. The other main rail line is the **Vermonter** service, which links Washington DC and New York with the Connecticut coast, central Massachusetts, and a series of stops in Vermont.

The **Massachusetts Bay Transportation Authority** (617/222-5000, www.mbta.com) runs commuter rail service around Boston, with trains venturing to Worcester, Providence, and throughout the North and South Shores. The regional railways and commuter rails that once crisscrossed all six New England states, however, have all but disappeared. Despite attempts by some state governments and private companies to revive them for transportation, the fragments that remain (such as the scenic railway in Conway, New Hampshire, and the narrow-gauge railroad in Portland, Maine) are more tourist attractions than actual options for transportation.

Car Rental Companies

The following companies have branches at major cities and airports:

- **Alamo:** 800/462-5266, www.alamo.com
- **Avis:** 800/331-1212, www.avis.com
- **Budget:** 800/527-0700, www.budget.com
- **Dollar:** 800/800-4000, www.dollar.com
- **Enterprise:** 800/261-7331, www.enterprise.com
- **Hertz:** 800/654-3131, www.hertz.com
- **National:** 800/227-7368, www.nationalcar.com
- **Thrifty:** 800/367-2277, www.thrifty.com

BUS

It may not be the fastest way to tour New England, but **Greyhound** (800/231-2222, www.greyhound.com) maintains a comprehensive web of routes that touches most cities, colleges, and tourist attractions in the region. Until recently, the Springfield-based **Peter Pan Bus Lines** (800/343-9999, www.peterpanbus.com) was an independent company that competed with the national behemoth. Now the two companies share routes and schedules, however, making travel on either interchangeable. Peter Pan also runs **Bonanza Bus Lines** (800/556-3815, www.bonanzabus.com), which serves Connecticut, Rhode Island, and Cape Cod. Other smaller, regional carriers serve out-of-the-way parts of northern New England—the largest being **Concord Coach Lines** (603/228-3300 or 800/639-3317, www.concordcoachlines.com). Other carriers have slowly been disappearing in recent years, snatched up by Greyhound—often at a loss of regional routes with low ridership. (See the appropriate destination chapters for more details.)

CAR

Highways are efficient and in general well maintained, and traffic moves briskly aside from rush hour around major cities. The region is bisected north-south by I-91, which runs along the Connecticut River Valley along the border of New Hampshire and Vermont and down through central Massachusetts and Connecticut. In Vermont it connects with I-89 and in New Hampshire with I-93, which runs all the way to Boston. An alternative to I-93 is U.S. 3, which parallels the interstate in New Hampshire and then runs through Boston along the South Shore to Cape Cod. Skirting around the city, I-95 is the main coastal thoroughfare from the Connecticut-New York border all the way to northeast Maine. For inland Maine, travelers are relegated to slower undivided highways, including U.S. 201 to the Moosehead Lake region, and Route 11 to the Allagash.

East to west, the region is bisected by I-90, otherwise known as the Massachusetts Turnpike or Mass Pike, which runs the length of Massachusetts. To the south, the Pike connects near Worcester to I-84, which then runs east-west through Connecticut. North of the Pike, the highway is paralleled by Route 2, which is slower but can be a more efficient way to get to the northern Berkshires and southern Vermont. Traveling east or west in northern New England, meanwhile, can be a frustrating exercise, since all major roads lead north-south to Boston. Several federal highways, including U.S. 2 and U.S. 4, aid to accomplish the task, but if you use them, be sure to leave more time for small-town stoplights and mountain switchbacks.

BICYCLE

The rural parts of New England—especially Vermont—are justifiably popular with bike tourists. Because the landscape is relatively gentle compared with the western United States, small roads wander throughout the countryside. Traffic can be an issue in some places, as those small roads serve as daily commutes for rural residents, but drivers are generally aware of and friendly to cyclists.

Some of the cities are quite bike friendly, as well. Burlington tops the list, but Portland and Portsmouth are easy to navigate on two wheels. The ultimate New England bike vacation might be Acadia National Park, where a network of carriage roads winds all over the island.

SEA

Ferries run from the mainland to many offshore islands, including Block Island, Nantucket, Martha's Vineyard, Monhegan, and various islands in Penobscot Bay. Additionally, other ferries run from Boston to the South Shore, Marblehead, and Provincetown. (See destination chapters for details.)

Sports and Recreation

The abundance of mountains, lakes, beaches, parks, and ocean all over New England means lots of outdoor fun. In winter, skiers flock to snowy peaks in New Hampshire, Maine, and Vermont. Summer brings mountain biking and hiking, and waterways fill with craft of all kinds.

Serious sea lovers head to the coasts and islands of Maine, Rhode Island, and Massachusetts—areas with a longstanding and venerable history of fishing and boating, and plenty of resources to show for it. Meanwhile, the widely varied parks and preservation lands throughout New England are excellent grounds for bird-watching of all kinds, year-round.

HIKING AND CAMPING

New Englanders love camping, and prove it year after year by filling their region's campsites in droves—on holiday weekends, finding one with available sites can be a challenge. On such popular dates, it pays to make a reservation. Also, not all campgrounds offer sites for both RVs and tents; call ahead to be sure.

BIKING

Bikers in rural New England are blessed with countless terrain options: Much of Cape Cod and its islands have bike paths and lanes carved out on picturesque bays; the entire region's small country towns sport wide and pretty roads meandering through historic villages. In many areas, old rail beds have been transformed into bicycle trails that are easy, mostly flat ways to cruise around.

ROCK CLIMBING

Northern New England is a veritable playground for mountaineers, who flock in all seasons to the area's challenging rock-climbing faces. Popular climbing areas are found in Acadia National Park and in New Hampshire's White Mountains, including Franconia Notch, Cathedral Ledge, Ragged Mountain, and Cannon Cliff.

KAYAKING AND CANOEING

Wherever there's a coast in New England, there are usually plenty of places to put in a kayak and head out to sea for a salty run. The most pristine rivers in the region are in northern Maine, where the St. John and Allagash Rivers offer more than 100 miles of interconnected lakes and rivers, most of which are a gentle Class I or II in difficulty. The same can't be said of the Penobscot and Kennebec Rivers slightly farther south, near Baxter State Park. This is where *serious* kayakers and rafters go to get wet, with rapids rising to Class IV, and one stretch of Class V on the Penobscot that will test even the most experienced paddlers. The longest canoe trail in the Northeast, the **Northern Forest Canoe Trail** (www.northernforestcanoetrail.org) spans 740 miles for rivers and waterways on the way from Old Forge, New York, to Port Kent, Maine.

SAILING

Coastal New England is quite literally awash in sailing culture—from preppy spectators to lifelong, bona fide seadogs. With New England winters as harsh as they are, sailing communities tend to come alive in the late spring, summer, and fall. For the largest concentrations of charters and docks (public and private), sailing schools and outfitters, head in the direction of those towns with a long tradition of seafaring. Newport, Rhode Island; Nantucket, Massachusetts; and Portland, Maine, are examples of such well-known spots, but even the smaller and less touristy communities up and down the coast often offer excellent waters and perfectly accommodating berths.

HUNTING, FISHING, AND BIRD-WATCHING

Every season, without fail, droves of dedicated sportsmen and sportswomen descend upon the backwoods and seas of New England, seeking to watch, catch, or take home some of its bounty. Local regulations and licensing requirements can be strict; certain animals (marine mammals, for example) are protected in certain districts, and specific rules apply to most species for trapping, baiting, shooting, and catching. So be certain to check with the local fish and game offices of your area of interest before planning your trip.

Hunting areas are well regulated and plentiful, particularly in northern New England, where animals from woodcock and deer to turkey and moose roam.

Deep-sea fishing is one fruitful option in the summer and fall. Fish such as cod, striped bass, tuna, and lobster are popular catches—though many forms of fishing (particularly lobstering) are largely chartered activities. Moving-water fishing, meanwhile, takes place mostly in summer and early fall. Serious trout and bass anglers gravitate toward the Rapid and Kennebec Rivers in Maine; the Androscoggin, Saco, and Mohawk Rivers in New Hampshire; and the Missisquoi, Batten Kill, and Connecticut Rivers in Vermont. In winter, ice fishing is popular in many small, northern towns—particularly in the area around Lake Champlain, Vermont. The sport requires hardy enthusiasts to cut holes in the ice above ponds and lakes, and catch fish as they cruise beneath the hole.

Any time of year, bird-watchers can feast their eyes in any number of wildlife refuges. Some of the best include Maine's Moosehorn and Petit Manan refuges; the Pleasant Valley Sanctuary in Massachusetts's Berkshires; Rhode Island's wildlife sanctuaries; and Vermont's Missisquoi and Silvio O Conte refuges.

SKIING AND WINTER SPORTS

Skiing and snowboarding in New England keep entire small-town economies revved up December-March (and for true addicts, April), and every year pulls many an urbanite out from their city bubble and into face-to-face, downhill encounters with nature.

New England slopes vary greatly in difficulty and the crowds they draw. As would be expected, the more southern resorts and better-known, big-name spots tend to get packed with day-trippers from Boston, whereas the out-of-the way and independently owned and operated resorts often have small, dedicated followings of skiers. Every New England state (except Rhode Island) boasts its share of good slopes, though some are undeniably better than others. In Connecticut, Mohawk Mountain, Woodbury, and Powder Ridge are small but respectable runs. Favorites in Maine include

Sugarloaf, Sunday River, Big Squaw, and Saddleback. New Hampshire's mountains are plentiful, offering a wealth of downhill options. The best are Bretton Woods, Attitash, Loon Mountain, Waterville Valley, and Wildcat. Skiing in Massachusetts revolves mostly around the bigger resorts at Wachusett and Nashoba Valley, which tend to get crowded. Vermont, meanwhile, draws some of the region's most serious skiers—to top mountains like Stowe, Stratton, Okemo, Killington, Jay Peak, and Mad River Glen.

Ice-skating, too, is a popular winter activity—done in town and city parks, and at recreation rinks. Most are open to the public, usually charge a small fee, and are listed with local town halls. Local parks are also full of sledding opportunities.

Food and Accommodations

Throughout the text, food listings include the range of prices for dinner entrées, including sandwiches but not salads. Lunch is often significantly cheaper. Accommodations listings include the range of rates for a standard double room in high season (roughly May-October). Depending on location, prices can be much higher during peak times (e.g., foliage or ski season) and steeply discounted in winter and spring.

NEW ENGLAND CUISINE

Traditional New England fare revolves around the seafood of the area's coast, but pays homage to the cooking methods of its British origins—the likes of boiled lobsters, baked stuffed shrimp, fried cod, and steamed clams. Other foodstuffs native to the region also play a big part in the regional cuisine—cranberry sauce, maple syrup, corn bread, and baked beans, for starters.

These days, the culinary options in New England are as diverse as the population; you're as apt to find Thai-inspired bouillabaisse and tapas-style Punjabi specialties as you are classic clam chowder. But if you're up for trying the region's specialties at their source, don't miss these traditional New England dishes:

The clambake: A great pile of seafood that includes steamed lobster, mussels, and clams is served with traditional sides, usually corn on the cob and potatoes. Traditionally these are steamed together in a hole dug on a beach, but restaurant versions are certainly available.

Lobster: Steamed or broiled, this native crustacean is a messy but glorious affair. The meat lies inside a tough shell, which is cracked by the diner using metal crackers and a small fork, and dipped in melted butter before eating.

Clams: Generally divided into types—hard shell or soft shell—clams are a true New England delicacy. Soft shells, or steamers, are usually eaten either steamed or fried. (If steamed, diners pull them from the shell, remove and discard the neck casing, and dip them in broth and drawn butter before eating.)

Hard shell clams are served differently: The smallest ones, known as littlenecks and cherrystones, are most frequently served raw with horseradish and cocktail sauce, while the largest hard shells are chopped up and used in chowders and stuffings.

Clam chowder: Dating back to the 18th century, New England clam chowder is by far the most popular of the region's creamy fish stews. Most restaurants have their own recipes, using a bit more potatoes here, a different ratio of bacon to cream there (but not tomatoes—that is what distinguishes Manhattan clam chowder and is therefore heresy in New England). Sampling and finding your favorite is the real fun.

Boston Baked Beans: Not for nothing is Boston nicknamed Beantown. This

How to Eat a Lobster

For some, it's an intimidating and off-putting exercise in utter messiness. For others, it's a deliciously visceral process with a delightful end: some of the sweetest crustacean meat on the planet. However you view the process of eating a lobster, experts agree that the best way to tackle the creature is from the outside in, and working from small to big. Note that while plenty of creative preparations of the delicacy do exist, purists swear by a simple boiled specimen—its precious meat dressed only in a squeeze of lemon and dipped in drawn butter.

- Start by breaking off the legs, holding the lobster by its back and pulling/twisting off the legs individually. Snap each in half at its joint and chew out the meat.
- Next, take off the claws, tearing them at the joint closest to the body (twisting if necessary), then again at the joint closest to the claw itself. Use your fork to push out all the meat (many say the knuckle meat is the most delicious). Next use your crackers to crush the large claw, extracting all the meat, ideally in one large piece.
- Grasp the tail with one hand and the back with the other hand, then twist and gently pull to separate the two sections. Some people also choose to eat the green tomalley (the digestive gland) and, in a female lobster, the roe (the unfertilized eggs). Whether you follow suit depends on your personal palate.
- Hold the tail with both hands, your thumbs placed just on the inside, on the white cartilage, your index fingers wrapped around the red shell on the tail's back. Pressing in with your index fingers and out with your thumbs, split the tail down the middle, revealing the whole of the tail. Pull out with a fork or your fingers and devour.

dish—made of dried beans baked slowly with salt pork and molasses—was a staple in colonial times, and remains a favorite today.

ACCOMMODATIONS

Many tourist destinations celebrate their peak seasons in the summer, when the weather is the nicest; not so in New England. Peak travel here is in the fall, particularly in late September and October when the foliage is at its most dramatic and students are pouring into area colleges. Many hotels jack up their prices by a factor of two or even three during this brief crowded season. The same can be said, on a smaller scale, for ski season, especially around February vacation, when rates in some locations in northern New England can reach a peak higher than their nearby ski mountains.

If leaf-peeping and skiing aren't your thing, you can save a lot of money by traveling in late August or early September when the summer humidity has dissipated, but hotel prices haven't yet skyrocketed. Of course, the opposite holds true for beach destinations. New Englanders make the most of their brief period of heat between Memorial Day and Labor Day. Do yourself a favor and schedule your beach vacation on either side of these magical dates, when you'll beat both the crowds and high prices—and the weather is often just as nice (of course, you are gambling that New England's mercurial climate will cooperate).

Along with the rest of the country, New England has seen a steady rise in the price of accommodations at all levels, making it difficult to find any bargains among the major-name hotels. Bed-and-breakfasts, especially in more rural areas, can be an attractive alternative; often run by couples or families, they can offer dirt-cheap prices without sacrificing amenities or hominess. Those who prefer the anonymity of a motel will find more bargains (though less consistency) in independent operations.

Travel Tips

HEALTH AND SAFETY

People travel to New England from all over the globe simply to receive care from the area's doctors and hospitals, which are widely regarded as among the best there is. So rest assured, should you need any medical attention while here, you'll be in good hands. That said, certain precautions will help you stay as safe as possible.

Compared with the rest of the nation, New England is relatively low in crime. Even in capitals like Boston, Portland, Providence, and Hartford, if you follow the basic rules of common sense (take precautions in watching your belongings, avoid walking alone late at night, and be aware of your surroundings), odds are safety won't be a problem.

In the New England countryside, one of the biggest threats to visitors' safety can be the natural world they seek. When hiking the White Mountains or canoeing the endless rivers, it is essential to know about the dangers of exposure to the elements. Visit the local tourism offices for specific tips on preparing for an outing, and if you are at all unsure of your outdoors skills, consider hiring a guide to take you on your excursion.

STUDENT TRAVELERS

You'll be hard-pressed to find an area of the country more welcoming to students; with such a hefty roster of colleges and universities, New England teems with—and oftentimes caters to—young people. Youth hostels can be found in Boston, Cape Cod, Providence, Burlington, Maine, and New Hampshire.

SENIOR TRAVELERS

If you are over 60 years of age, ask about potential discounts. Nearly all attractions, amusement parks, theaters, and museums offer discount benefits to seniors. Be sure to have some form of valid identification such as a driver's license or passport.

Ticks and Lyme Disease

Forget snakes, bears, and moose—ask a New Englander what wildlife they're scared of, and they'll say **ticks.** The eight-legged creatures are tiny—from the size of a poppyseed to just under three millimeters—and easy to miss. Some are carriers of **Lyme disease,** a dangerous bacterial infection. Not all ticks can carry Lyme disease, but the deer tick sometimes does, and it's the most common species in the Northeast. Taking the following precautions will help protect against Lyme:

- Wear long pants tucked into your socks when walking through high grass and bushy areas.
- Use insect repellent that contains DEET, which is effective against ticks.
- Shower within a few hours of coming inside, and check carefully for ticks. If you find a tick, use tweezers to grasp it near to your skin, and firmly remove without twisting. Don't worry if the mouthparts remain in the skin; once the tick is separated from the body, it can no longer transmit the bacteria that cause Lyme.

Carefully checking for ticks once a day is a good practice. Don't panic if you find a tick, as it takes around 36 hours for the bacteria to spread. The first symptoms of Lyme disease are often flu-like, and occur 3-30 days after infection. They're often accompanied by a rash or bull's-eye redness around the bite. If you experience these symptoms, it's smart to visit a doctor. Prompt treatment of Lyme disease is generally effective, but the disease can be fatal if untreated.

GAY AND LESBIAN TRAVELERS

Few regions in the country are friendlier to LGBT visitors than New England. Same-sex marriage is legal in every state, and cities like Boston, Portland, and Providence have significant and thriving gay and lesbian communities. Meanwhile, resort towns such as Provincetown, Massachusetts, and Ogunquit, Maine, are major destinations for LGBT visitors from around the world.

ACCESS FOR TRAVELERS WITH DISABILITIES

Public transportation in the vast majority of New England is wheelchair-accessible, as are most major hotels, museums, and public buildings. Even many beaches and campgrounds in Massachusetts are accessible, though the remoter the destination, the greater the possibility that it will not be.

The greatest challenge for travelers in wheelchairs in New England may be accessing historic neighborhoods and inns that have not been retrofitted with wider doorways and elevators. Some inns have converted one or more rooms with roll-in showers, while others are completely inaccessible.

Those with permanent disabilities, including the visually impaired, should inquire about a free **Access Pass** (888/275-8747, ext. 3) from the National Park Service. It is offered as part of the America the Beautiful—National Park and Federal Recreational Lands Pass Series. You can obtain an Access Pass in person at any federal recreation site or by submitting a completed application (www.nps.gov/findapark/passes.htm, $10 processing fee may apply) by mail. The pass does not provide benefits for special recreation permits or concessionaire fees.

TRAVELING WITH CHILDREN

Travel all over New England is extremely family friendly. Most hotels offer cribs in the room upon request, and public transportation and attractions offer discounted fares for children. The majority of restaurants are happy to offer high chairs, and many have kids' menus.

Some inns and bed-and-breakfasts, however, are not open to children—generally drawing the line at 12 or so.

INFORMATION AND SERVICES

Internet and Cellular Access

Wireless Internet is available in most cafés, as well as many other businesses. Local libraries are a good place to find computers with Internet access free of charge, as most make these services available to visitors. Most hotels and bed-and-breakfasts offer free wireless Internet, though some smaller, rural inns may not.

While all New England cities have full cell coverage, many rural areas do not, so it's worth having access to a paper map when traveling through the countryside.

Business Hours

Business hours vary widely between cities and towns, but most stores and offices in state capital cities follow a schedule of 9am-5pm -6pm Monday-Friday, 10am-6pm Saturday, and noon-5pm Sunday. In smaller cities and towns, particularly those in rural areas, expect more erratic weekend hours—or the possibility that they may simply stay closed until Monday.

Tipping

A 15-20 percent tip is expected in New England restaurants, and 15 percent is customary in bars, hair salons, and spas if you are satisfied with the level of your service. At hotels, $1 per bag for porters is the norm, doormen usually receive $1 for hailing a taxi, maids usually receive $1-2 per night, and concierges are given anywhere from a few dollars to $20, depending on the services they have provided. In taxis, 10-15 percent is customary.

Magazines

Several regional magazines provide useful information for travelers, including *New England Travel*, an annual but comprehensive magazine exploring all of the region's attractions, and *Yankee Magazine*, for events, festivals, landmarks, restaurants, and tours all over New England. Several states and cities and even subregions produce their own magazines as well, including *Boston*, *Cape Cod Magazine*, *Rhode Island Monthly*, *Vermont Life*, and *Down East*, the monthly periodical dedicated to all things Maine.

Visas and Officialdom

PASSPORTS AND VISAS

Visitors from other countries must have a **valid passport** and **visa.** Visitors with current passports from one of the following countries qualify for **visa waivers:** Andorra, Australia, Austria, Belgium, Brunei, Chile, Czech Republic, Denmark, Estonia, Finland, France, Germany, Greece, Hungary, Iceland, Ireland, Italy, Japan, Latvia, Liechtenstein, Lithuania, Luxembourg, Malta, Monaco, the Netherlands, New Zealand, Norway, Portugal, San Marino, Singapore, Slovakia, Slovenia, South Korea, Spain, Sweden, Switzerland, Taiwan, and the United Kingdom. They must apply online with the Electronic System for Travel Authorization at www.cbp.gov and hold a **return plane ticket** to their home countries less than 90 days from their time of entry. Holders of **Canadian passports** don't need visas or waivers. In most countries, the local U.S. embassy can provide a **tourist visa.** Plan for at least two weeks for visa processing, longer during the busy summer season (June-Aug.). More information is available online at http://travel.state.gov.

EMBASSIES AND CONSULATES

New York City and Boston are home to consulates from around the world. Travelers in legal trouble or those who have lost their passports should contact the consulate of their home country immediately. The **U.S. State Department** (www.state.gov) has contact info for all foreign embassies and consulates. The **British Consulate** (www.gov.uk) has offices in the **Boston** area (1 Broadway, Cambridge, 617/245-4500) and **New York City** (845 3rd Ave., 212/745-0200). The **Australian Consulate** has an office in **New York City** (150 E. 42nd St., 34th Fl., 212/351-6600), and the **Canadian Consulate-General** is in **Boston** (3 Copley Pl. #400, 617/247-5100) and **New York City** (1251 Avenue of the Americas, 212/596-1628).

CUSTOMS

Foreigners and U.S. citizens age 21 or older may import (free of duty) the following: one liter of alcohol, 200 cigarettes (one carton), 50 cigars (non-Cuban), and $100 worth of gifts. International travelers must declare amounts that exceed $10,000 in cash (U.S. or foreign), traveler's checks, or money orders. Meat products, fruits, and vegetables are prohibited due to health and safety regulations.

Resources

Suggested Reading

REFERENCE

Feintuch, Bert, ed. *The Encyclopedia of New England.* New Haven, CT: Yale University Press, 2005. A good book to read *before* you go, this 1,600-page, eight-pound tome will tell you everything you want to know about New England and then some, including entries on Walden Pond, fried clams, Ben & Jerry's, and the Red Sox. Instead of a disjointed alphabetical arrangement, the book cogently organizes contents by subject matter.

HISTORY

Cronon, William. *Changes in the Land: Indians, Colonists, and the Ecology of New England.* New York: Hill and Wang, 1983. The classic study of early New England history debunks myths and shatters preconceptions about Pilgrims and Native Americans and how each interacted with the landscape.

Fairbrother, Trevor. *Painting Summer in New England.* New Haven, CT: Yale University Press, 2006. From a recent exhibition of the same name at the Peabody Essex Museum, this beautiful art book includes dozens of paintings by American impressionists, along with stories about the artists.

Howard, Brett. *Boston: A Social History.* New York: Hawthorn, 1976. Detailing the impact of the city's leaders and most prominent families over the centuries, Howard shows the impact Boston Brahmins have had on local politics and the cultural landscape.

McCullough, David. *1776.* New York: Simon & Schuster, 2005. Rather than writing a start-to-finish account of the Revolution, McCullough drills down to the pivotal year in which the fortunes of George Washington turned, from the tense standoff of the siege of Boston to the ultimate victories at Trenton and Princeton.

Paine, Lincoln P. *Down East: A Maritime History of Maine.* Gardiner, ME: Tilbury House Publishers, 2000. A look back at more than four centuries of pirates, privateers, lobstermen, and windjammers from a maritime historian and native Downeaster.

Rappeleye, Charles. *Sons of Providence: The Brown Brothers, the Slave Trade, and the American Revolution.* New York: Simon & Schuster, 2006. A fascinating journey into the heart of colonial America, told through the history of the most enlightened city in the New World—which nevertheless founded its fortune on the slave trade.

Vowell, Sarah. *The Wordy Shipmates.* New York: Riverhead, 2007. The popular essayist and National Public Radio contributor not only writes one of the most irreverent and entertaining histories of the early days of Puritan and Pilgrim New England, but makes those ancient times surprisingly relevant to our own United States.

Woodard, Colin. *The Lobster Coast: Rebels, Rusticators, and the Struggle for a Forgotten*

Frontier. New York: Viking, 2004. From early Scotch-Irish woodchoppers to 20th-century oil painters, this clearly written account populates the map of Maine with colorful historical characters.

NATURAL HISTORY AND ECOLOGY

Albers, Jan. *Hands on the Land: A Natural History of the Vermont Landscape.* Boston: MIT Press, 2002. In a gorgeous oversized book, Albers details the various factors—geological, ecological, and economic—that have transformed the Green Mountain State.

Kessler, Brad. *Goat Song: A Seasonal Life, A Short History of Herding, and the Art of Making Cheese.* New York: Scribner, 2009. In this lovely and earnest little book, long-time writer Brad Kessler sets out to live the dream that tugs at many of us: leaving the city to live a simpler life on the farm. What he finds in two years of raising goats is nothing short of connection to our most mythic religious archetypes.

Kurlansky, Mark. *Cod: A Biography of the Fish That Changed the World.* New York: Penguin, 1998. The settlement and economic rise of New England is inseparable from the plentiful groundfish that once populated its waters in astounding numbers.

National Audubon Society. *National Audubon Society Regional Guide to New England.* New York: Knopf, 1998. The amateur naturalist would do well to pick up this guide, which details many local species of trees, wildflowers, reptiles, and mammals, with 1,500 full-color illustrations.

Wessels, Tom. *Reading the Forested Landscape: A Natural History of New England.* Woodstock, VT: Countryman Press, 2005. A good read before heading off into the hills, this book helps put features of the landscape into their proper context.

LITERATURE

Douglass, Frederick. *Narrative of the Life of Frederick Douglass, An American Slave: Written by Himself.* 1845, Signet Classics, 2005. The quintessential slave narrative includes details of Douglass's life as an abolitionist in Boston.

Frost, Robert. *The Poetry of Robert Frost: The Collected Poems, Complete and Unabridged.* Henry Holt and Co., 1979. The New England landscape infuses Frost's poetry, much of which was written in Vermont and New Hampshire.

Hawthorne, Nathaniel. *The House of Seven Gables.* 1851, Signet Classics, 2001. The tragic story of several interlocking families is set in a house that still exists in Salem.

James, Henry. *The Bostonians.* 1886, Modern Library Classics, 2003. Beacon Hill comes alive in this evocation of 19th-century Boston.

Jewett, Sarah Orne. *The Country of the Pointed Firs.* 1896, Dover, 2011. Maine's customs, dialect, and traditions come to life in this often-overlooked masterpiece.

Melville, Herman. *Moby-Dick.* 1851, Penguin Classics, 2002. From the opening scene in New Bedford, Massachusetts, this classic tale brings New England's grand, tragic whaling history to the page; written from Melville's country home in the Berkshires.

Stegner, Wallace. *Crossing to Safety.* 1987, Random House, 2002. A quintessential Western author tells a finely woven story of love and loss against the backdrop of northern Vermont.

Thoreau, Henry David. *Walden.* 1854, Modern Library Classics, 2000. The classic account of Thoreau's two years living a hermit's life on Walden Pond is a philosophical treatise, a timeless glimpse into

19th-century rural New England, and inspiration for the modern-day environmental movement. Look for an edition that includes *The Maine Woods* and *Cape Cod*, travelogues that blend the author's sharp eye and wry sense of humor.

Wharton, Edith. *The Age of Innocence*. 1920, CreateSpace, 2015. A stormy romance brings the Gilded Age New York and Newport society to life.

CONTEMPORARY FICTION AND MEMOIR

Bergman, Megan Mayhew. *Birds of a Lesser Paradise*. Simon & Schuster, 2012. Writing from a farm in Vermont, Bergman draws New England's cows, chickens, and exotic birds into her intimate short stories.

Beston, Henry. *The Outermost House: A Year of Life on the Great Beach of Cape Cod*. New York: Owl Books, 1928. Beston's attempt to "go Thoreau" by living for a year in a small house in the dunes remains the most joyous evocation of Cape Cod's unique ecology.

Elder, John. *Reading the Mountains of Home*. Cambridge, MA: Harvard University Press, 1999. With the company of Robert Frost's poetry, a Vermont writer watches a year unfold in the Green Mountains.

Greenlaw, Linda. *The Lobster Chronicles: Life on a Very Small Island*. New York: Hyperion, 2003. The sword boat captain featured in Sebastian Junger's nonfiction book *The Perfect Storm* returns with a fascinating memoir of her return to her family's home on Isle Au Haut in Maine to try her hand at the lobstering business.

Irving, John. Many of the most popular books of this cult American novelist are set in New England. For example, *The Cider House Rules* (New York: William Morrow, 1995) is centered around an orphanage in Maine, *The World According to Garp* (New York: Ballantine, 1990) takes place in part at a New England boarding school, and *A Prayer for Owen Meany* (New York: William Morrow, 1989) concerns several generations of a troubled New England family.

MacDonald, Michael Patrick. *All Souls: A Family Story from Southie*. New York: Ballantine, 2000. In writing his moving memoir of Irish American life, MacDonald does for South Boston what Frank McCourt did for Dublin.

GUIDEBOOKS

Appalachian Mountain Club Books (www.outdoors.org/publications) publishes dozens of guides considered gospel by outdoors enthusiasts in the region. They are jam-packed with no-nonsense directions for hiking and canoeing every inch of the New England wilderness. Among them are the *White Mountain Guide* and *Maine Mountain Guide*, as well as several guides for canoeing and kayaking.

Corbett, William. *Literary New England: A History and Guide*. New York: Faber and Faber, 1993. An excellent guide to sights associated with poets and writers who called New England home, it includes detailed directions to hard-to-find graves, historic sites, and houses.

Hartnett, Robert. *Maine Lighthouses Map & Guide*. Howes Cave, NY: Hartnett House Map Publishing, 2000. A foldout map that provides detailed directions to every lighthouse along the rocky fingers of the Maine coast. Hartnett also publishes a map to lighthouses in Massachusetts and New Hampshire (yes, there are two).

Kershner, Bruce, and Robert Leverett. *The Sierra Club Guide to the Ancient Forests of the Northeast*. San Francisco: Sierra Club Books, 2004. Despite centuries of human habitation and exploitation, a surprising number of old-growth stands still exist in

New England. This guide takes you inside their mossy interiors, and explains what makes old-growth forests so unique.

PODCASTS

Crimetown, Gimlet Media (www.crimetownshow.com). Unrolling the seamy mob history of Providence, Rhode Island, Crimetown also tells the story of Buddy Cianci, an ex-felon and the city's former mayor.

Rumble Strip (www.rumblestripvermont.com). Host Erica Heilman shares fresh and unexpected stories from Vermont's farmers, criminals, waitresses, and musicians.

Freedom Trail Podcasts (www.thefreedomtrail.org). A series of four podcasts on Boston's Revolutionary history features the Freedom Trail Players and local historians.

NEXT, New England Public Radio (www.nepr.net). Weekly shows hosted by Connecticut-based John Dankosky showcase the most interesting reporting from public radio stations around New England.

Internet Resources

The websites maintained by state tourism agencies can be surprisingly useful, with tips on finding scenic byways, events, and on-call staff.

NEW ENGLAND

Discover New England
www.discovernewengland.org
This site highlights seasonal events and current happenings in every corner of New England, and suggests driving tours and weather information, plus gives a brief primer on each state.

NewEngland.com
www.newengland.com
Run by *Yankee* magazine, this site is packed with local landmarks, recommended itineraries, foliage reports, event listings, and vacation planners.

FALL FOLIAGE REPORTS

Get in-depth and up-to-date foliage reports on each state, starting in early September and throughout autumn, from the following websites: **Vermont** (www.vermont.com/foliage.cfm), **New Hampshire** (www.visitnh.gov/foliage-tracker), **Maine** (www.mainefoliage.com), and **Massachusetts** (www.massvacation.com).

DESTINATION WEBSITES

Expect to find basic background information about the destination, plus essentials such as hours, locations, entrance fees, driving directions, and special deals or packages currently offered.

Massachusetts

Greater Boston Convention & Visitors Bureau
www.bostonusa.com
The site provides a full list of events throughout the year and visitor information on lodging, restaurants, sights, shopping, and transportation.

The Freedom Trail Foundation
www.thefreedomtrail.org
Find tourist info, historical background notes, and the latest news on tours and events for the 16 historical sites that make up Boston's Freedom Trail.

The Berkshires
www.berkshires.org
This site offers lots of advice on dining and lodging in the area, plus other diversions such as spas, concerts, family outings, and outdoor excursions, plus a list of current getaway deals.

Cape Cod Chamber of Commerce
www.capecodchamber.org
Find full business listings, information on where to stay and eat, background on the 15 towns that make up Cape Cod, help on getting around the area, plus information on golfing, baseball, football, and other sporting opportunities in the area.

Nantucket Island
www.nantucket.net
Plan your island vacation with this easy site's listings of local restaurants, hotels and inns, beaches, and museums. There's also plenty of information on where and how to go boating, fishing, golfing, and biking, plus a section on where to take kids around the island.

Martha's Vineyard Island
www.mvy.com
From diving and sailing to horseback riding and beach-going, this site details all there is to do on and around Martha's Vineyard. It also lists accommodations and restaurants, posts a calendar of events and festivals, and provides information on car rentals and ferries, as well as vacation rentals. The last-minute lodging feature is particularly useful.

Maine

Maine Tourism
www.visitmaine.com
This site offers information on everything to see and do in Maine, including fall foliage, outdoor recreation, family-friendly outings, restaurants, shopping, events, and accommodations.

Portland, ME
www.visitportland.com
With coverage that stretches across southern Maine, this site is an excellent resource for trip planning.

Acadia National Park, ME
www.nps.gov/acad
Maps, campground information and booking services, and online passes are available on this site.

New Hampshire

New Hampshire Tourism
www.visitnh.gov
Find all kinds of visitors' information on the state, including local foliage reports, travel itineraries, online photo galleries, deals on seasonal travel packages, and lodging and restaurant listings.

Mt. Washington Valley, NH
www.mtwashingtonvalley.org
Just about anything happening in the valley shows up on this site: local events throughout the year, dogsledding and cross-country skiing—plus how to find the best local crafters and artists, as well as shopping, restaurant, and hotel listings.

Vermont

Vermont Tourism
www.vermontvacation.com
Here you'll find information on nightlife and dining, shopping, accommodations, ski resorts, local churches, and businesses, plus help on getting around the area by public transportation and finding local festivals.

Rhode Island

Providence Chamber of Commerce
www.goprovidence.com
This site offers information not just on visiting Providence, but on moving there as well.

Newport, RI
www.discovernewport.org
Find full listings of local businesses on the site, along with useful visitor information on events, historic sites, and nightlife by area and neighborhood.

The Preservation Society of Newport County
www.newportmansions.org
The Preservation Society operates the majority of mansions open to the public in Newport.

Find out more about the history and character of each one on this in-depth site—plus essentials such as events, hours, and online ticketing.

Connecticut

Connecticut Tourism
www.ctvisit.com
Built primarily for visitors to the state, this site lists weekend getaway itineraries and events happening throughout the year. It also offers help on getting to and around the different counties, and special deals on hotels.

Mystic, CT
www.mystic.org
The town's official site lists everything currently happening there, from the aquarium's exhibits to the Seaport's presentations. Also find restaurant, hotel, and shopping listings.

Index

C

INDEX

D

E

F

G

H

INDEX

I

J

K

L

M

N

INDEX

QR

S

T

UV

W

XYZ

INDEX

List of Maps

Front Map

Discover New England

Boston

Cape Cod and the Islands

The Berkshires

Connecticut

Rhode Island

Vermont

New Hampshire Seacoast and Lakes Region

New Hampshire's White Mountains

Coastal Maine

Acadia National Park

Photo Credits

Title page photo: © Jen Rose Smith; page 4 © Jiawangkun | Dreamstime.com; page 5 © Jen Rose Smith; page 6 (top left) © Jen Rose Smith, (top right) © MOTT/Kindra Clineff, (top) © Blackstone Valley Tourism Council; page 7 (top) © Jen Rose Smith, (bottom left) © Jo Ann Snover | Dreamstime.com, (bottom right) © Connecticut Office of Tourism; page 8 © Michael Ver Sprill | Dreamstime; page 10 (top) © Demerzel21 | Dreamstime, (middle) © Snehitdesign | Dreamstime, (bottom) © Lunamarina | Dreamstime; page 11 (top) © Demerzel21 | Dreamstime, (bottom) © Brett Pelletier | Dreamstime; page 12 (top) © James Kirkikis | Dreamstime, (middle) © F11photo | Dreamstime, (bottom) © Jerry Coli | Dreamstime; page 13 © Donland | Dreamstime; page 14 © Jen Rose Smith; page 18 © Schooner Lewis R. French; page 20 (top left) © Jen Rose Smith, (top right) © Jen Rose Smith; page 22 © Jen Rose Smith; page 23 © Jen Rose Smith; page 26 © Jen Rose Smith; page 28 (top left) © Yale University/Michael Marsland, (top right) © Jen Rose Smith; page 30 (top left) © Jen Rose Smith, (top right) © South County Tourism Council; page 31 (top) © Sierra Machado, (bottom) © Fgcanada | Dreamstime.com; page 33 © MOTT/Justin Knight; page 35 © Sierra Machado; page 41 © Sierra Machado; page 44 © Sepavo | Dreamstime.com; page 63 © Jen Rose Smith; page 77 © MOTT; page 79 © MOTT; page 83 © MOTT; page 85 (top) © Lunamarina | Dreamstime.com, (bottom) © Alwoodphoto | Dreamstime.com; page 87 © Jen Rose Smith; page 101 © MOTT; page 105 © Daniel Logan | Dreamstime; page 110 © Jon Bilous | Dreamstime; page 125 © Captblack76 | Dreamstime; page 143 © Jen Rose Smith; page 154 (top) © MOTT/David Dashiell, (bottom) © Whitefringetree | Dreamstime.com; page 155 © MOTT; page 162 © MOTT; page 166 © MOTT; page 171 © MOTT; page 182 © MOTT; page 185 (top) © Yale University/Michael Marsland, (bottom) © Connecticut Office of Tourism; page 187 © Connecticut Office of Tourism; page 196 © Connecticut Office of Tourism; page 197 © Connecticut Office of Tourism; page 199 © Yale University/Michael Marsland; page 202 © Connecticut Office of Tourism; page 205 © Yale University/Michael Marsland; page 209 © Connecticut Office of Tourism; page 222 © Connecticut Office of Tourism; page 227 © Michael Melford/Connecticut Office of Tourism; page 229 (top) © Block Island Tourism Council, (bottom) © South County Tourism Council; page 231 © Jen Rose Smith; page 238 © GoProvidence; page 243 © Blackstone Valley Tourism Council; page 248 © Chee-onn Leong | Dreamstime; page 256 © Americanspirit | Dreamstime; page 265 © South County Tourism Council; page 271 © Block Island Tourism Council; page 274 (top) © Jeb Wallace-Brodeur/Mad River Glen, (bottom) © Sierra Machado; page 275 © Peanutroaster | Dreamstime.com; page 278 © Jen Rose Smith; page 289 © Reinhardt | Dreamstime.com; page 297 © Chandler Burgess/Killington Resort; page 303 © Jeb Wallace-Brodeur/Mad River Glen; page 311 © Anikasalsera | Dreamstime.com; page 314 © Howardliuphoto | Dreamstime.com; page 320 © Ronibenish | Dreamstime.com; page 326 © Alwoodphoto | Dreamstime.com; page 330 © Marshall Webb; page 334 (top) © George Disario/NH Division of Travel & Tourism, (bottom) © George Disario/NH Division of Travel & Tourism; page 335 © The Chamber Collaborative of Greater Portsmouth/Rick Dumont Images; page 338 © The Chamber Collaborative of Greater Portsmouth/Rick Dumont Images; page 346 © David J Murray/Portsmouth Chamber of Commerce; page 357 © Squam Lakes Natural Science Center; page 360 (top) © Sierra Machado, (bottom) © Sierra Machado; page 361 © Rob Karosis/NH Division of Travel & Tourism; page 370 © NH Division of Travel & Tourism; page 372 © Jen Rose Smith; page 374 © NH Division of Travel & Tourism; page 382 © Rob Karosis/NH Division of Travel & Tourism; page 387 (top) © Appalachianviews | Dreamstime.com, (bottom) © Nick Cote/Maine Office of Tourism; page 389 © Pinkcandy | Dreamstime.com; page 395 © Nick Cote/Maine Office of Tourism; page 400 © Iainhamer | Dreamstime.com; page 425 © Jen Rose Smith; page 442 © Jen Rose Smith; page 443 © Alwoodphoto | Dreamstime; page 452 © Maine Office of Tourism; page 455 (top) © R51coffey | Dreamstime.com, (bottom) © Phil Savignano Photography/Maine Office of Tourism; page 457 © Kittycat | Dreamstime.com; page 461 © Ryan Flynn | Dreamstime; page 462 © Karenfoleyphotography | Dreamstime.com; page 471 © Jen Rose Smith; page 475 © Maine Office of Tourism; page 478 © Jen Rose Smith; page 480 (top) © Luckydoor | Dreamstime.com, (bottom) © Cllhnstev | Dreamstime.com; page 505 (top) © Americanspirit | Dreamstime.com, (bottom) © Chengusf | Dreamstime.com

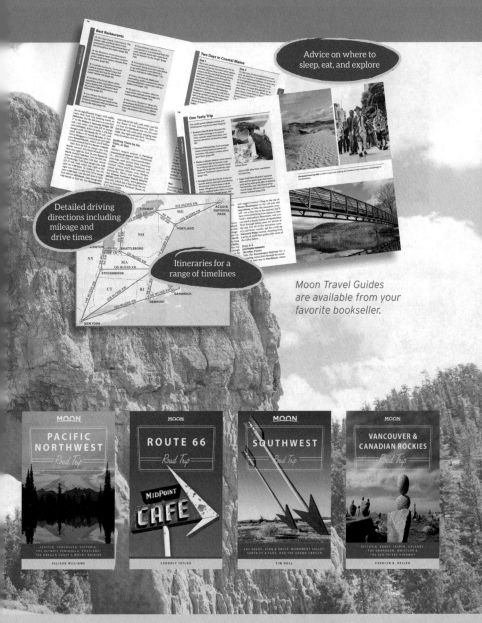

MAP SYMBOLS

Expressway	City/Town	Airport	Golf Course
Primary Road	State Capital	Airfield	Parking Area
Secondary Road	National Capital	Mountain	Archaeological Site
Unpaved Road	Point of Interest	Unique Natural Feature	Church
Feature Trail	Accommodation	Waterfall	Gas Station
Other Trail	Restaurant/Bar	Park	Glacier
Ferry	Other Location	Trailhead	Mangrove
Pedestrian Walkway	Campground	Skiing Area	Reef
Stairs			Swamp

CONVERSION TABLES

°C = (°F − 32) / 1.8
°F = (°C x 1.8) + 32
1 inch = 2.54 centimeters (cm)
1 foot = 0.304 meters (m)
1 yard = 0.914 meters
1 mile = 1.6093 kilometers (km)
1 km = 0.6214 miles
1 fathom = 1.8288 m
1 chain = 20.1168 m
1 furlong = 201.168 m
1 acre = 0.4047 hectares
1 sq km = 100 hectares
1 sq mile = 2.59 square km
1 ounce = 28.35 grams
1 pound = 0.4536 kilograms
1 short ton = 0.90718 metric ton
1 short ton = 2,000 pounds
1 long ton = 1.016 metric tons
1 long ton = 2,240 pounds
1 metric ton = 1,000 kilograms
1 quart = 0.94635 liters
1 US gallon = 3.7854 liters
1 Imperial gallon = 4.5459 liters
1 nautical mile = 1.852 km

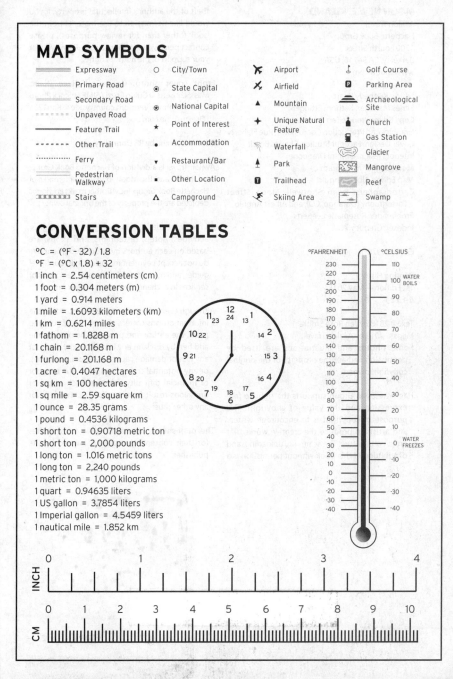

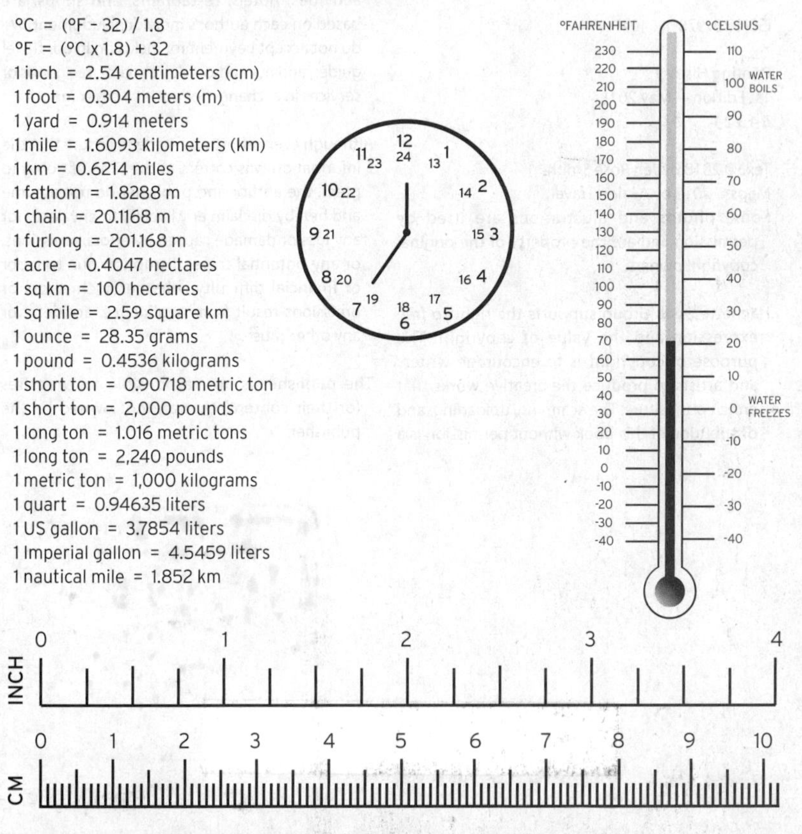

MOON NEW ENGLAND
Avalon Travel
Hachette Book Group
1700 Fourth Street
Berkeley, CA 94710, USA
www.moon.com

Editor: Kimberly Ehart
Series Manager: Kathryn Ettinger
Copy Editor: Ann Seifert
Graphics and Production Coordinator: Rue Flaherty
Cover Design: Faceout Studios, Charles Brock
Interior Design: Domini Dragoone
Moon Logo: Tim McGrath
Map Editor: Albert Angulo
Cartographers: Brian Shotwell, Moon Street Cartography (Durango, CO), and Albert Angulo
Proofreader: Rosemarie Leenerts
Indexer: Greg Jewett

ISBN-13: 978-1-64049-174-8

Printing History
1st Edition —May 2018
5 4 3 2 1

Front cover photo: Cape Cod, Race Point, Massachusetts © Guido Cozzi / SIME / eStock Photo
Back cover photo: Vermont countryside © Kan1234 | Dreamstime.com

Printed in China by RR Donnelley